THE FIELDSTON ETHICS READER

Edited by

Mark Weinstein
Beatrice Banu

UNIVERSITY
PRESS OF
AMERICA

Copyright © 1988 by

The Ethical Culture Schools

4720 Boston Way
Lanham, MD 20706

All rights reserved

Printed in the United States of America

Co-published by arrangement with
The Ethical Culture Schools

Library of Congress Cataloging-in-Publication Data

The Fieldston ethics reader / edited by Mark Weinstein and Beatrice
Banu.
p. cm.
1. Ethics. 2. Social ethics. I. Weinstein, Mark, 1940–
II. Banu, Beatrice.
BJ1025.F28   1988
170–dc 19   88–1080 CIP
ISBN 0–8191–6897–1 (alk. paper)
ISBN 0–8191–6898–X (pbk. : alk. paper)

All University Press of America books are produced on acid-free
paper which exceeds the minimum standards set by the National
Historical Publications and Records Commission.

DEDICATION

To the students of the Fieldston School, for their vitality, their intelligence and their moral insights. The *READER* came from you; it is returned to you with admiration, and with respect.

ACKNOWLEDGMENTS

"Abortion Decision: One Year Later," an editorial from *AMERICA*, 1/19/74. Reprinted with permission of America Press, Inc., 106 West 56 Street, New York, NY 10019. (c) 1974 All Rights Reserved.

"The Mind's I," from *THE MIND'S I* by Douglas R. Hofstadter and Daniel C. Dennett, Copyright (c) 1981 by Basic Books, Inc., Publishers. Reprinted by Permission of Basic Books, Inc.

"The Overcoat," by Sally Benson from *THE AMERICAN DREAM* by Sally Benson. With acknowledgment to the Estate of Sally Benson.

"I Thought About This Girl," "My Father Sits in the Dark," by Jerome Weidman from *MY FATHER SITS IN THE DARK AND OTHER STORIES*. Copyright, 1934 by Jerome Weidmen, Copyright renewed (c) by Jerome Weidman. Reprinted by permission of Brandt and Brandt Literary Agents, Inc.

"Slipping Beauty," by Jerome Weidmen from *THE HORSE THAT COULD WHISTLE DIXIE AND OTHER STORIES*. Copyright, 1934 by Jerome Weidman. Copyright Renewed (c) 1961 by Jerome Weidman. Reprinted by permission of Brandt & Brandt Literary Agents, Inc.

"A Song in the Front Yard," by Gwendolyn Brooks from *THE WORLD OF GWENDOLYN BROOKS*. Reprinted by permission of the author.

"The Sacredness of Life," from *THE SACREDNESS OF LIFE*. Reprinted by permission of Catholic Information Service, Nights of Columbus.

"Is Abortion Murder," by Dale Crowley from *CAPITAL VOICE* 7/19/73. With acknowledgment to the author.

"Where Are You Going, Where Have You Been?" by Joyce Carol Oates. Reprinted by permission of the author and her agent, Blanche C. Gregory, Inc. Copyright (c) 1966 by Joyce Carol Oates.

"Miss Temptation," Adam," excerpted from the book *WELCOME TO THE MONKEY HOUSE* by Kurt Vonnegut Jr. "Miss Temptation," copyright (c) 1954 by Kurt Vonnegut Jr. Originally published in *SATURDAY EVENING POST.* "Adam," copyright (c) 1954 by Kurt Vonnegut Jr. Originally published in *COSMOPOLITAN.* Reprinted by permission of DELACORTE PRESS/ SEYMOUR LAWRENCE

"I Stand Here Ironing," excerpted from the book *TELL ME A RIDDLE* by Tillie Olsen. Copyright (c) 1956 by Tillie Olsen. Reprinted by permission of DELACORTE PRESS/SEYMOUR LAWRENCE

"The Ant and the Grasshopper," copyright 1924 by W. Somerset Maughan, from *COSMOPOLITANS*. Reprinted by permission of Doubleday Publishing

"My Papa's Waltz by Theodore Roethke copyright 1924 by Hearst Magazines, Inc. from *THE COLLECTED POEMS OF THEODORE ROETHKE*. Reprinted by permission of Doubleday Publishing.

TABLE OF CONTENTS

PART II: WHAT CONTROLS ME?
SECTION 1: CHILDREN AND FAMILY

The Value of Education

SECTION 5: SOCIAL CONTROL—WORK

The Social Context

The Person Responds

Striking Back

Personal Goals

The System

Success and Consequences

Success and Choices

Autonomy

SECTION 6: CONCEPTS THAT CONTROL: SEXISM

Sex Roles

Tradition

Beauty

Discrimination

Stereotypes and Change

Social Policy

Another Perspective

Society and Relativism

PART III: WHERE AM I GOING?

SECTION 1: LOVE AND SEX

PREFACE

Now in their second century, The Ethical Culture/Fieldston Schools bring to their 1500 students in two elementary schools (Fieldston Lower and Midtown) and a high school (Fieldston) the strengths of a tradition of educational achievement in academic studies, in moral education, and in community service. Nurtured by the idealism of 19th century reform and the insights of progressivism, the Schools have responded distinctively to the question: what is good education? We answer that good education is of necessity ethical education. The study and practice of ethical values is woven in and through the practice of teaching and learning.

Our humanism continues to insist on a three-fold purpose to education: cultural knowledge and skills, social responsibility and criticism, usefulness. That is why humanistic studies are central to the Schools' curriculum. That is why the Schools maintain diversity in their student body with an extensive financial aid program. That is why community service is required of all students.

Ethics classes were introduced with the founding of the Schools and remain today a distinctive part of the elementary and high school curriculum. One outcome is *THE FIELDSTON ETHICS READER*. While based on the ideas and experiences of many teachers and students at The Fieldston School, it is the effort of Mark Weinstein assisted by Beatrice Banu that has brought this project to completion. We trust that the *READER* will be useful to others as we have found it to be while testing it in the classroom. Above all, we hope that the integration of ethics and education will be furthered by the work we have done.

Howard B. Radest
Director
The Ethical Culture/Fieldston Schools

INTRODUCTION

The purpose of the *FIELDSTON ETHICS READER* is to give you the opportunity to think and talk about some of the most important issues that confront human beings. This book may be different from the text books you are used to. There are few facts; nothing to memorize; no black and white solutions. The issues raised are as ordinary as ordinary life and, at the same time, are among the most profound questions discussed in philosophical and religious writings for over two thousand years.

To show how these issues relate to you and your life the *READER* is organized around the concept of the *Self*. It is divided into three parts, each of which is focused on a fundamental and perplexing question. The questions are: Who am I? What controls me? Where am I going?

Each Part is composed of integrated sections consisting of several short pieces: stories, poems, excerpts from philosophical writings, and contemporary non-fiction. The exercises and discussion plans included after each selection are designed to focus discussion on important issues. We have, however, intentionally selected readings that are rich in ideas so that you may pick issues that stimulate your interest. The *READER* permits and, indeed, encourages you to be creative in your thinking about the ethical problems presented.

Important ethical questions have a way of cropping up again and again. An issue that is discussed early in the text is not over and done with. Expect to see it as it appears in totally different contexts. Each new context should provide new insights, allow you to make new connections and generate new ideas.

Don't be frustrated if the problems are too interesting and complex for you to come up with easy solutions. The point of the *READER* is not to resolve issues, but to help raise and clarify them. By the time you have finished this book, you may expect to have a growing understanding of ethical concepts and problems. Most important, you will have built a framework that you will be able to use to organize your thinking about ethics in the future.

The *READER* includes many provocative issues. We hope that you will be provoked.

PART I: WHO AM I?

Philosophy, Ethics and Value

Ethics is a part of life. When we worry about what is right and wrong or who is good and bad, we are thinking about ethical problems. Ethics is also a part of philosophy. It is that part of philosophy that focuses on the study of value as related to human beings: their actions, their relationships and their beliefs. In this book we will be asking you to think about the philosophical issues that surround ethical problems.

Philosophical ethics concerns itself with the source of value, those aspects of individual and societies that determine how a person or a group is to have its actions evaluated. Our actions are judged on the basis of what we intend, the rules we follow and the consequences they produce. The first philosophical question we have to ask is: what is value? Issues of value turn up when we start making judgments.

We all make judgments that place people and things into categories. When I identify a passing car as a Ford, I have made a judgment about the make of the car, but I have not made a value judgment. I can also say, "That's a great looking car." This second statement is a value judgment. What is the difference between these two statements? Many judgments are descriptive, "John is about 6 feet tall," "The tomatoes are still green." You judge John's height against a firmly established standard of inches and feet. You judge the tomatoes against a standard of color and ripeness of fruit that you remember from past experiences. To make any judgment you must measure some thing, action, person, or event against some standard or model that you think applies in a particular case. The same applies to value judgments. Value judgments are just like any other judgments in that they require standards. But in other ways value judgments seem quite different.

Is saying that Mary has the highest grades in the class the same as saying that Mary is smart? Is saying that Gandhi led the Indian masses to challenge

1

the British authorities the same as saying that Gandhi was a good leader? Is it the same as saying that Gandhi is a good man? Is calling the nuclear arms race dangerous the same as calling it evil? Upon what basis do we make value judgments and how do they differ from other judgments? How do they differ from judgments of fact and how do they differ from other judgments of opinion? Thinking about these questions will give you some insight into the complex issues that surround the study of values.

Ethics and the Self

Earlier we said that ethics studies values in relation to human beings: their actions, relationships and beliefs. The most obvious philosophical question, after "what is value?", is: what is the connection between human beings and value?

"Human being" is a classification within ordinary life and within biology; it characterizes us as different from other living things on the basis of important properties that we have that other living things do not. Throughout history we have marked ourselves as a special species, not just because we stand upright and use tools, but because we have minds, culture and the ability to make choices. What all of these factors have in common is that they have the force of placing responsibility on human beings for what they do. This burden of responsibility is said to give us the dubious privilege of deciding what values we want to use. Let us take a closer look at the connection between responsibility and value.

What is the difference between sneezing and spitting at someone? Between your car going out of control and causing an accident or driving while drunk and causing an accident? Is getting cancer the same, from an ethical point of view, as getting VD? Is taking LSD the same as getting food poisoning? In the last case getting food poisoning is bad in the descriptive sense but not in the ethical sense. Things seem quite different with taking LSD and we mark the difference by saying that taking LSD is something you are responsible for. You choose to do it and you could do otherwise. Consciousness of what you are doing combined with free choice seems crucial in making the value of your actions ethical. The ability to choose and the right to choose is a mixed blessing. Rights generate responsibilities. There is no one to blame but yourself if the choice was yours. But is the choice really yours?

In making ethical decisions not only must you choose what to do but you are also responsible for choosing the right values. How do individuals such as yourself choose values? To begin to understand how to go about answering this very important question, we must consider what kinds of values are available to choose from. There are two kinds of values: relative and absolute. Let's consider relative values first.

Values that depend on what country we or our parents come from, what race we belong to, what religion we believe in or when we were born are called relative values. The values are relative in the sense that they express the beliefs of a particular society or culture, class or ethnic group. Each group might have its own standard. When there are many standards for right and wrong, there can be a lot of confusion. Think about some of these problems. Was pre-marital sex wrong 30 years ago and all right now? Is the free expression of political dissent good in the USA and not in the USSR? Is abortion wrong for Catholics but right for non-Catholics? Members of these different groups would use very different ethical standards to decide the issue. Are ethical values all relative to time and place? If you were sent back in time to ancient Rome, should you discard your modern values and adopt those of the Romans, perhaps enthusiastically throwing a few Christians to the lions? If you moved to Japan where people think very differently about themselves and their neighbors, should you hold on to your American values or adopt Japanese ones? These are just some of the troublesome questions you might ask yourself.

There is also another sense in which values are considered relative. We generally take the circumstances surrounding an action or event into consideration in either deciding what to do, explaining what we have done or attributing innocence or guilt. When the value of a belief or action is determined by circumstances, it is relative. Consider for a moment: is a drunk driver who totals his car as culpable as one who kills a child? Is cheating on a spelling test in third grade as serious as cheating on an exam in medical school? Is lying to prevent someone from being killed the same as lying to get your parents to give you $50.00 for tickets to a rock concert? Can we always find circumstances to justify our actions? Should we rely on circumstances to get us off the hook? Is there a bottom line beneath which circumstances cannot save us?

Some people will argue that there are real values that do not depend on who, what, where or when. These real values are called absolute. They never vary from person to person, place to place, time to time. If a person living in the 20th century is going to be a morally good person, she must use the same set of values as a person living in the 4th century. In some sense having a standard of absolute values would make life much easier. At least you would always know what the standards are. You wouldn't have to worry about standards changing. It would give you a nice sense of security. All you would have to worry about is doing the right thing, applying the standard correctly. But many people feel uneasy with the idea of absolute standards of value because there are three fundamental problems with absolutes. First, do they really exist? Second, if they do exist, how can we get to know about them? Third, who or what is their source? If you think about it for awhile, you'll find that those who believe in relative values are not too much better off. The only question they do not have to answer is the first. Relative values do exist. That is obvious. But there is another question we could ask: are any relative values better than others and how can we tell without some standard which is not relative?

Ethics and Metaphysics

Whether it be absolute or relative, we all search for real value, attempting to discover those persons, objects, events and actions that are truly desirable (that is, worthy of our desiring them) as opposed to merely being desired. But how can we decide which is which? And is anything truly desirable? The search for value like the search for anything else requires that we have some idea of the things we are searching for. Here we face a paradox, the paradox of knowledge. We do not know what value is and we want to find out. But if we don't know what we are looking for, how will we ever find it? Our only chance is to ask ourselves some hard questions about what we might already know about the nature of value. The kinds of questions that must be asked are called "metaphysical." Metaphysical questions are directed at finding out what the true nature of things is, what is real.

Many of the most fundamental questions of ethics and value are metaphysical questions about the source and object of value. Most philosophers put the person at the center of ethical inquiry. It is the person that is the object of value; that is, value is determined in terms of how actions affect persons. And persons are the source of value; that is, the actions, intentions and beliefs of persons are the basis for value. This raises a fundamental metaphysical question: what is a person?

Generally, persons are thought to be organisms, called human beings, who have physical and mental properties: a body and a mind. (In religious contexts sometimes the mind is called the soul.) The source of value is often connected with the assertion that persons have minds or consciousness. We define minds, in turn, by pointing to certain properties, mental properties, that human beings have. Talking and acting as if you know what you are doing is taken as a sign that you have these mental properties that are your thoughts and feelings, and thoughts and feelings are nearly always taken as a sign that the being which has them must have a mind.

Mental properties are strangely different from physical properties. They are not visible, tangible or audible like physical properties. How much does love weigh? Where is anger and what does it look like? Can you touch memory? What color is your belief in God? All these questions seem peculiar to ask about thoughts and feelings although they would be quite unexceptional if asked about physical objects. We have ideas, but not in the same way we have long hair and blue eyes or even blood pressure and gastric juices.

Ideas are not objectively measurable like the head and the brain with which they are often associated. In fact, the mental is usually identified with the subjective, the personal, the private aspect of us that is most truly ourselves.

Now we have run up against another tough philosophical problem. The source of ethical value is connected to our being responsible for our actions and personal responsibility is traceable to our mental capacities. Mental properties are what make us persons; but mental properties are invisible. All we actually see are physical signs of them. When I am angry, I shout. Shouting is a sign that I am feeling angry. But I can shout and not feel angry. I can shout in order to make you think that I am angry. How can you tell the difference between my shouting when I am angry and my shouting in order to make you think I am angry? Do I ever really know if you are truly sorry for having done something nasty to me? How will either one of us ever know the true value of our actions?

The invisibility and intangibility of the mind open up many difficult questions. Some of these questions focus on the relationship of the mind to the self. The self, unlike the mind, seems to have some physical characteristics. My self is somehow connected with a particular body, my body. But the self also seems to have an intimate connection to the mind. My character is part of my self and my character is how I think and feel. What is the self? How much responsibility do I have for my self? Can any one really know my self, besides me? Can I know my self? Do we need to know the "real you" in order to judge your actions?

Ethics and Epistemology

If we are going to place the right value on something, it seems necessary to know what it really is. Diamonds are more valuable than cut glass. We need to know what we are dealing with. We have many ways of finding out what objects really are, e.g. chemical analysis, close and thorough inspection, etc. But what are the ways in which we find out about persons? Ethics requires that we know about objects and persons.

Questions about how we know are called epistemological questions in philosophy. *Episteme* is the ancient Greek word for the highest and best kind of knowledge. Philosophers have disagreed about how we come to know and understand. Some dismiss the whole problem by saying that we can never know the truth. In their opinion we must always remain skeptical about everything. Perhaps we ought to remain skeptical about what they tell us too. Other philosophers maintain that we can know the truth by looking inside ourselves for ideas that, they claim, have always been in our minds. We were born with these ideas but for some reason we have forgotten them. These innate ideas are very important. They are not ideas about particular things, events or people. They are ideas of values such as beauty, truth, goodness and justice. If these ideas do exist in us, we would have a very good chance of finding an absolute standard by which we could determine values. This kind of knowledge is called intuitive. The ancient Greek philosophers that said "Know thyself" were talking about this kind of knowledge. They believed that, if you could understand the nature of your mind (the true self), you could discover the nature of the universe because the mind and the universe were presumed to work on the same principle. This view of knowledge has been passed down to us in one form or another. In ethics people often mean an intuitive kind of knowledge about right and wrong when they speak about conscience.

On the other hand, there are some philosophers who refuse to believe that there is any such thing as intuitive or innate knowledge. They believe that we are born knowing nothing and that gradually through experience we fill up our minds with thoughts and feelings, e.g. the color of our mother's hair, the sensation of being picked up and cuddled, the pain of being pricked by a pin, the fear of being left alone, etc. Our senses start working and, according to these philosophers, we start knowing about our bodies and the world around us. This kind of knowledge is called empirical, from experience. Add all our experiences up and we have the self. The self is a bundle or collection of our thoughts, sensations and feelings.

These two different kinds of philosophers have radically different views about the nature of the self. Are we born with a self and gradually discover what it really is? Or are we born without any self, with just a body and a brain, the tools by which the self is assembled from bits and pieces of experience? Both kinds of philosophers locate the source of value in the self. Philosophers who believe in intuitive knowledge tend to think that values are absolute whereas philosophers who accept only empirical knowledge generally believe that values are all relative. Who is right? What is the self? And what, consequently, is the nature of value?

The Philosophical Point of View

To enter into philosophical thought is to first admit that things might not be as obvious as they seem. Also it is to have a sense of the value of the thoughtful as opposed to the thoughtless life. From its earliest history philosophers have epitomized the view, expressed by Socrates, "the unexamined life is not worth living." We can think of no better way to introduce students to philosophical thought than through Plato's classic image of the search for truth and reality.

Plato, "The Allegory of the Cave" from *The Republic*

A dialogue between Socrates and Glaucon. Socrates speaks first.

Next, said I, here is a parable to illustrate the degrees in which our nature may be enlightened or unenlightened. Imagine the condition of men living in a sort of cavernous chamber underground, with an entrance open to the light and a long passage all down the cave. Here they have been from childhood, chained by the leg and also by the neck, so that they cannot move and can see only what is in front of them, because the chains will not let them turn their heads. At some distance higher up is the light of a fire burning behind them; and between the prisoners and the fire is a track with a parapet built along it, like the screen at a puppet-show, which hides the performers while they show their puppets over the top.

I see, said he.

Now behind this parapet imagine persons carrying along various artificial objects, including figures of men and animals in wood or stone or other materials, which project above the parapet. Naturally, some of these persons will be talking, others silent.

It is a strange picture, he said, and a strange sort of prisoners.

Like ourselves, I replied; for in the first place prisoners so confined would have seen nothing of themselves or of one another except the shadows thrown by the fire-light on the wall of the Cave facing them, would they?

Not if all their lives they had been prevented from moving their heads.

And they would have seen as little of the objects carried past.

Of course.

Now, if they could talk to one another, would they not suppose that their words referred only to those passing shadows which they saw?

Necessarily.

And suppose their prison had an echo from the wall facing them? When one of the people crossing behind them spoke, they could only suppose that the sound came from the shadow passing before their eyes.

No doubt.

In every way, then, such prisoners would recognize as reality nothing but the shadows of those artificial objects.

Inevitably.

Now consider what would happen if their release from the chains and the healing of their unwisdom should come about in this way. Suppose one of them set free and forced suddenly to stand up, turn his head, and walk with eyes lifted to the light, all these movements would be painful, and he would be too dazzled to make out the objects whose shadows he had been used to see. What do you think he would say, if someone told him that what he had formerly seen was meaningless illusion, but now, being somewhat nearer to reality and turned towards more real objects, he was getting a true view? Suppose further that he were shown the various objects being carried by and were made to say, in reply to questions, what each of them was. Would he not be perplexed and believe the objects now shown him to be not so real as what he formerly saw?

Yes, not nearly so real.

And if he were forced to look at the fire-light itself, would not his eyes ache, so that he would try to escape and turn back to the things which he could see distinctly, convinced that they really were clearer than these other objects now being shown to him?

Yes.

And suppose someone were to drag him away forcibly up the steep and rugged ascent and not let him go until he had hauled him out into he sunlight, would he not suffer pain and vexation at such treatment, and when he had come out into the light, find his eyes so full of its radiance that he could not see a single one of the things that he was told were real?

Certainly he would not see them all at once.

He would need, then, to grow accustomed before he could see things in that upper world. At first it would be easiest to make out shadows, and then the images of men and things reflected in water, and later on the things themselves. After that, it would be easier to watch the heavenly bodies and the sky itself by night, looking at the light of the moon and stars rather than the Sun and the Sun's light in the daytime.

Yes, surely.

Last of all, he would be able to look at the Sun and contemplate its nature, not as it appears when reflected in water or any alien medium, but as it is in itself in its own domain.

No doubt.

And now he would begin to draw the conclusion that it is the Sun that produces the seasons and the course of the year and controls everything in the visible world, and moreover is in a way the cause of all that he and his companions used to see.

Clearly he would come at last to that conclusion.

Then if he called to mind his fellow prisoners and what passed for wisdom in his former dwelling-place, he would surely think himself happy in the change and be sorry for them. They may have had a practice of honouring and commending one another, with prizes for the man who had the keenest eye for the passing shadows and the best memory for the order in which they followed or accompanied one another, so that he could make a good guess as to which was going to come next. Would our released prisoner be likely to cover those prizes or to envy the men so exalted to honour and power in the Cave? Would he not feel like Homer's Achilles, that he would far sooner be on earth as a hired servant in the house of a landless man or endure anything rather than go back to his old beliefs and live in the old way?

Yes, he would prefer any fate to such a life.

Now imagine what would happen if he went down again to take his former seat in the Cave. Coming suddenly out of the sunlight, his eyes would be filled with darkness. He might be required once more to deliver his opinion on those shadows, in competition with the prisoners who had never been released, while his eyesight was still dim and unsteady; and it might take some time to become used to the darkness. They would laugh at him and say that he had gone up only to come back with his sight ruined; it was worth no one's while even to attempt the ascent. If they could lay hands on the man who was trying to set them free and lead them up, they would kill him.

Yes, they would.

Every feature in this parable, my dear Glaucon is meant to fit our earlier analysis. The prison dwelling corresponds to the region revealed to us through the sense of sight, and the fire-light within it to the power of the Sun. The ascent to see the things in the upper world you may take as standing for the upward journey of the soul into the region of the intelligible; then you will be in possession of what I surmise, since that is what you wish to be told. Heaven knows whether it is true; but this, at any rate, is how it appears to me. In the world of knowledge, the last thing to be perceived and only with great difficulty is the essential Form of Goodness. Once it is perceived, the conclusion must follow that, for all things, this is the cause of whatever is right and good; in the visible world it gives birth to light and to the lord of light, while it is itself sovereign in the intelligible world and the parent of intelligence and truth. Without having had a vision of this Form no one can act with wisdom, either in his own life or in matters of state.

Discussion Plan:

1) Go over the selection and carefully explain each of the elements in the allegory. What does each one mean? What makes the choice of metaphor an effective vehicle to present the idea it represents?
2) What large points are made by the allegory?
3) Does the allegory offer insights into the problem it attempts to describe?
4) Do you agree with Plato's point of view?
5) Construct realistic analogues to the points Plato makes?
6) Present realistic analogues that support your point of view if it is different from Plato's.

Exercise:

How is the world "true (truth)" used in the following sentences:
1) Tell me the truth.
2) She's a true friend.
3) It's not true that Columbus discovered America.
4) Is it true there's a bear in the cave?
5) Merchants must give you true weight.
6) What the Bible says is true.
7) Be true to yourself.
8) "I swear to tell the whole truth and nothing but the truth."

Are the following sentences all true in the same way?
1) A straight line is the shortest distance between two points.
2) You are fifteen years old.
3) January comes before February.
4) $4 + 4 = 8$
5) You are your parents' child.
6) Molecules are made of atoms.
7) The universe will end in a black hole.
8) Humans have evolved from lower primates.
9) George Washington is the father of our country.
10) Moses led the Jews out of Egypt.
11) Romeo loved Juliette.

SECTION 1:
DISCOVERING THE SELF

Mark Weinstein
56 North Oxford Walk
Brooklyn, New York
U.S.A.
North America
The Earth
The Solar System
The Galaxy
The Universe

Does that look familiar to you? When I was in the third grade that was the standard label on my books. Did you do something similar? Let's take a look at it for a moment. It has my name, my street address and then a number of designations: a country, a planet and some vague astronomical labels. Perhaps kids would be more sophisticated now—naming the galaxy, or including more elaborate political categories. The idea, however, is the same: to locate oneself, to define the person you are by generating a context. I used a vocabulary composed of geo-political and astronomical labels—using space itself. But there are other ways, different 'spaces' so to speak. We can locate ourselves within a family tree of our ancestors, or we can furnish pigeonholes through a set of organized social roles. We can use relationships with others or chemical elements. We can pick the most striking events in our life history or describe an astrological chart. We can trace our ethnic heritage or our family's occupations. But how does that locate the person? And more importantly who is the person so located?

The question is, for each of us: Who am I? Am I the sum of all my experiences? Am I everything I would be willing to say about myself? Do some things define me better than others? What can I leave out of the picture? What language should I use to describe myself? In what space am I to be located? And who gets to say? Do I get to define myself? Do my parents? The government? Society in some general way?

In this first part of the *Fieldston Ethics Reader* we will begin to sort out some of these questions, offering tentative answers. We will be defining categories and building systems of classification.

Let's start with a short exercise and then our first story.

Exercise:

1. Make a short, but ordered list, using between ten and twenty items that define you within some space (social, personal, autobiographical etc.) The list should be composed of factors that you think help define who you are. Try to order the list according to some principle; my list used spatial location going from small to large.
2. What sort of list did you make? What are the concepts you used in defining yourself? What principle did you use in ordering the concepts?
3. How does your list tell you, or anyone else, what sort of person you are?
4. Is your list a 'true' list? Is any other list truer?
5. Make up an imaginary list. Try to write one that presents you as the best sort of person you can be.
6. How did you construct this list; what concepts and principles did you use here?
7. Make up one more list. Construct it to make yourself as undesirable as possible.

Seeming and Being

A great deal of what we are is based on how we see ourselves. No matter how much we may seem to be controlled by other people or by the events that make up our life history, we seem to have a crucial role in determining who we are—what our life is to be. We are the ones who make choices for ourselves. Our decisions are made within a framework that is defined by our desires, our purposes and beliefs. We are to some degree responsible for the world we think is real and independent of our whims and wishes. We make that world conform to our standards. Sometimes we are aware of what we are doing and, what is worse, sometimes we are not.

Fritz Leiber, Mariana

Mariana had been living in the big villa and hating the tall pine trees around it for what seemed like an eternity when she found the secret panel in the master control panel of the house.

The secret panel was simply a narrow blank of aluminum—she'd thought of it as room for more switches if they ever needed any, perish the thought!— between the air-conditioning controls and the gravity controls. Above the switches for the three-dimensional TV but below those for the robot butler and maids.

Jonathan had told her not to fool with the master control panel while he was in the city because she would wreck anything electrical, so when the secret panel came loose under her aimlessly questing fingers and fell to the solid rock floor of the patio with a musical 'twing' her first reaction was fear.

Then she saw it was only a small blank oblong of sheet aluminum that had fallen and that in the space it had covered was a column of six little switches. Only the top one was identified. Tiny glowing letters beside it spelled TREES and it was on.

When Jonathan got home from the city that evening she gathered her courage and told him about it. He was neither particularly angry nor impressed.

"Of course there's a switch for the trees," he informed her deflatingly, motioning the robot butler to cut his steak. "Didn't you know they were radio trees? I didn't want to wait twenty-five years for them and they couldn't grow on this rock anyway. A station in the city broadcasts a master pine tree and sets like ours pick it up and project it around homes. It's vulgar but convenient."

After a bit she asked timidly, "Jonathan, are the radio pine trees ghostly as you drive through them?"

"Of course not! They're solid as this house and the rock under it—to the eye and to the touch too. A person could even climb them. If you ever stirred outside you'd know these things. The city station transmits pulses of alternating matter at sixty cycles a second. The science of it is over your head."

She ventured one more question: "Why did they have the tree switch covered up?"

"So you wouldn't monkey with it—same as the fine controls on the TV. And so you wouldn't get ideas and start changing the trees. It would unsettle me, let me tell you, to come home to oaks one day and birches the next. I like consistency and I like pines." He looked at them out of the dining-room picture window and grunted with satisfaction.

She had been meaning to tell him about hating the pines, but that discouraged her and she dropped the topic.

About noon the next day, however, she went to the secret panel and switched off the pine trees and quickly turned around to watch them.

At first nothing happened and she was beginning to think that Jonathan was wrong again, as he so often was though would never admit, but then they began to waver and specks of pale green light churned across them and then they faded and were gone, leaving behind only an intolerably bright single point of light—just as when the TV is switched off. The star hovered motionless for what seemed a long time, then backed away and raced off toward the horizon.

Now that the pine trees were out of the way Mariana could see the real landscape. It was flat gray rock, endless miles of it, exactly the same as the rock on which the house was set and which formed the floor of the patio. It was the same in every direction. One black two-lane road drove straight across it—nothing more.

She disliked the view almost at once—it was dreadfully lonely and depressing. She switched the gravity to moon-normal and danced about dreamily, floating over the middle-of-the-room bookshelves and the grand piano and even having the robot maids dance with her, but it did not cheer her. About two o'clock she went to switch on the pine trees again, as she had intended to do in any case before Jonathan came home and was furious.

However, she found there had been changes in the column of six little switches. The TREES switch no longer had its glowing name. She remembered that it had been the top one, but the top one would not turn on again. She tried to force it from "off" to "on" but it would not move.

All of the rest of the afternoon she sat on the steps outside the front door watching the black two-lane road. Never a car or a person came into view until Jonathan's tan roadster appeared, seeming at first to hang motionless in the distance and then to move only like a microscopic snail although she knew he always drove at top speed—it was one of the reasons she would never get in the car with him.

Jonathan was not as furious as she had feared. "Your own damn fault for meddling with it," he said curtly. "Now we'll have to get a man out here. Dammit, I hate to eat supper looking at nothing but those rocks! Bad enough driving through them twice a day."

She asked him haltingly about the barrenness of the landscape and the absence of neighbors.

"Well, you wanted to live way out," he told her. "You wouldn't ever have known about it if you hadn't turned off the trees."

"There's one other thing I've got to bother you with Jonathan," she said. "Now the second switch—the one next below—has got a name that glows. It just says HOUSE. It's turned on—I haven't touched it! Do you suppose..."

"I want to look at this," he said, bounding up from the couch and slamming his martini-on-the-rocks tumbler down on the tray of the robot maid so that she rattled. "I bought this house as solid, but there are swindles. Ordinarily I'd spot a broadcast style in a flash, but they just might have slipped me a job relayed from some other planet or solar system. Fine thing if me and fifty other multi-megabuck men were spotted around in identical houses, each thinking his was unique."

"But if the house is based on rock like it is ...":

"That would just make it easier for them to pull the trick, you dumb bunny!"

They reached the master control panel. "There it is," she said helpfully, jabbing out a finger... and hit the HOUSE switch.

For a moment nothing happened, then a white churning ran across the ceiling, the walls and furniture started to swell and bubble like cold lava, and then they were alone on a rock table big as three tennis courts. Even the master control panel was gone. The only thing that was left was a slender rod coming out of the gray stone at their feet and bearing at the top, like some mechanistic fruit, a small block with the six switches—that and an intolerably bright star hanging in the air where the master bedroom had been.

Mariana pushed frantically at the HOUSE switch, but it was unlabeled now and locked in the "off" position, although she threw her weight at it stiff-armed.

The upstairs star sped off like an incendiary bullet, but its last flashbulb glare showed her Jonathan's face set in lines of fury. He lifted his hands like talons.

"You little idiot!" he screamed, coming at her.

"No, Jonathan, no!" she wailed, backing off, but he kept coming.

She realized that the block of switches had broken off in her hands. The third switch had a glowing name now: JONATHAN. She flipped it.

As his fingers dug into her bare shoulders they seemed to turn to foam rubber, then to air. His face and gray flannel suit seethed iridescently, like a leprous ghost's, then melted and ran. His star, smaller than that of the house but much closer, seared her eyes. When she opened them again there was nothing at all left of the star or Jonathan but a dancing dark afterimage like a black tennis ball.

She was alone on an infinite flat rock plain under the cloudless star-specked sky.

The fourth switch had its glowing name now: STARS.

It was almost dawn by her radium-dialed wristwatch and she was thoroughly chilled when she finally decided to switch off the stars. She did not want to do it—in their slow wheeling across the sky they were the last sign of orderly reality—but it seemed the only move she could make.

She wondered what the fifth switch would say. ROCKS? AIR? Or even ...?

She switched off the stars.

The Milky Way, arching in all its unalterable glory, began to churn, its component stars darting about like midgets. Soon only one remained, brighter even than Sirius or Venus—until it jerked back, fading and darted to infinity.

The fifth swith said DOCTOR and it was not on but off.

An inexplicable terror welled up in Mariana. She did not even want to touch the fifth switch. She set the block of switches down on the rock and backed away from it.

But she dared not go far in the starless dark. She huddled down and waited for dawn. From time to time she looked at her watch dial and at the night-light glow of the switch label a dozen yards away.

It seemed to be growing much colder.

She read her watch dial. It was two hours past sunrise. She remembered they had taught her in third grade that the sun was just one more star.

She went back and sat down beside the block of switches and picked it up with a shudder and flipped the fifth switch.

The rock grew soft and crisply fragrant under her and lapped up over her legs and then slowly turned white.

She was sitting in a hospital bed in a small blue room with a white pinstripe.

A sweet mechanical voice came out of the wall, saying, "You have interrupted the wish-fulfillment therapy by your own decision. If you now recognize your sick depression and are willing to accept help, the doctor will come to you. If not, you are at liberty to return to the wish-fulfillment therapy and pursue it to its ultimate conclusion."

Mariana looked down. She still had the block of switches in her hands and the fifth switch still read DOCTOR.

The wall said, "I assume from your silence that you will accept treatment. The doctor will be with you immediately."

The inexplicable terror returned to Mariana with compulsive intensity.

She switched off the doctor.

She was back in the starless dark. The rocks had grown very much colder. She could feel icy feathers falling on her face—snow.

She lifted the block of switches and saw, to her unutterable relief, that the sixth and last switch now read, in tiny glowing letters: MARIANA.

Discussion Plan:

1. In what way was Mariana mistaken about her environment?
2. Was she mistaken about particular matters of fact or was she confused about some very general things?
3. What do you think 'wish-fulfillment' therapy has to do with the story?
4. What is the relationship between Mariana's inner wishes and the choices that were offered to her?
5. Why is Mariana in a hospital?
6. What do you think will happen if she presses the button labeled "MARIANA"?

Knowing

People come up with the most outrageous ideas. How do they do it? Where do these ideas come from? These questions get to the heart of a fundamental philosophical problem: the origin of our ideas. In the following selection David Hume, an 18th century Scottish philosopher, explains a theory called empiricism: everything we know or imagine can be traced back to our direct impressions of the world. No experience, no ideas!

David Hume, An Inquiry Concerning Human Understanding

... Nothing, at first view, may seem more unbounded than the thought of man, which not only escapes all human power and authority, but is not even restrained within the limits of nature and reality. To form monsters and join incongruous shapes and appearances costs the imagination no more trouble than to conceive the most natural and familiar objects. And while the body is confined to one planet, along which it creeps with pain and difficulty, the thought can in an instant transport us into the most distant regions of the universe, or even beyond the universe into the unbounded chaos where nature is supposed to lie in total confusion. What never was seen or heard of, may yet be conceived, nor is anything beyond the power of thought except what implies an absolute contradiction.

But though our thought seems to posses this unbounded liberty, we shall find upon a nearer examination that it is really confined within very narrow limits, and that all this creative power of the mind amounts to no more than the faculty of compounding, transposing, augmenting, or diminishing the materials afforded us by the senses and experience. When we think of a golden mountain, we only join two consistent ideas, "gold" and "mountain," with which we were formerly acquainted. A virtuous horse we can conceive, because from our own feeling, we can conceive virtue; and this we may unite to the figure and shape of a horse, which is an animal familiar to us. In short, all the materials of thinking are derived either from our outward or inward sentiment; the mixture and composition of these belongs alone to the mind and will, or, to express myself in philosophical language, all our ideas or more feeble perceptions are copies of our impressions or more lively ones ...

Exercise:

Mariana, like us all, seems to know the world by the awareness that she has of her own inner states—her mind with its feelings, memories and perceptions. This awareness is called direct or immediate awareness. Our direct awareness of our inner worlds is taken as an indicator of what the world around us is like. But how reliable an indicator is it? As Hume says in the short section above, all of our thoughts are "derived" from our experiences. But how reliable is that "derivation"? How can you be sure that your thoughts are a good reflection of what is around you? Think of fun house mirrors. What if all your thoughts, perceptions and impressions were like the images in fun house mirrors? How could you ever know what was true? The following questions will help you to begin to explore the issue of illusion and the senses.

1. Is an object the size it seems to be?
2. What is the real color of an object? In what light? Against what background?
3. If something looks pretty, is it really pretty?
4. If something looks solid, is it really solid?
5. If something feels solid, is it really solid?
6. Are surfaces the way they appear to the naked eye?
7. Are things really the way they appear under a magnifying glass?
8. If we had the sense organs of, say, bats, would the world appear the same?
9. How can we tell if we are seeing illusions?

Reality

At the end of *Mariana* there is the suggestion that Mariana herself might be an illusion. This strikes us as peculiar since if she, as the central character, is reporting on her thoughts and feelings, isn't she, of necessity real? That is, no matter how mistaken a person may be, the mere fact that they are mistaken implies that they are real, at least in some sense.

The argument just presented is based on a similar argument by French philosopher Rene Descartes. Descartes came to the conclusion that thinking proves that whatever is thinking has to exist—at least while it is thinking. He arrived at his conclusion by trying an experiment. He decided to doubt everything that could be doubted and see if he had anything left that he couldn't doubt. He did! "I am, I exist," he thought. He was sure of that.

He also decided, based on this experiment, that all truth had to be based on abstract thinking processes (called reason) and not on his experiences. His experiences might always be doubted, but thinking clearly led to the truth. This view is called rationalism and it is the opposite of empiricism.

Rene Descartes, Meditations On First Philosophy

... Everything which I have thus far accepted as entirely true and assured has been acquired from the senses or by means of the senses. But I have learned by experience that these senses sometimes mislead me, and it is prudent never to trust wholly those things which have once deceived us.

But it is possible that, even though the senses occasionally deceive us about things which are barely perceptible and very far away, there are many other things which we cannot reasonably doubt, even though we know them through the senses—as, for example, that I am here, seated by the fire, wearing a winter dressing gown, holding this paper in my hands, and other things of this nature. And how could I deny that these hands and this body are mine, unless I am to compare myself with certain lunatics whose brain is so troubled and befogged by the black vapors of the bile that they continually affirm that they are kings while they are paupers, that they are clothed in gold and purple while they are naked; or imagine that their head is made of clay, or that they are gourds, or that their body is glass? But this is ridiculous; such men are fools and I would be no less insane than they if I followed their example.

Nevertheless, I must remember that I am a man, and that consequently I am accustomed to sleep and in my dreams to imagine the same things that lunatics imagine when awake, or sometimes things which are even less plausible. How many times has it occurred that the quiet of the night made me dream of my usual habits: that I was here, clothed in a dressing gown, and sitting by the fire, although I was in fact lying undressed in bed! It seems apparent to me now, that I am not looking at this paper with my eyes closed, that this head that I shake is not drugged with sleep, that it is with design and deliberate intent that I stretch out this hand and perceive it. What happens in sleep seems not at all as clear and as distinct as all this. But I am speaking as though I never recall having been misled, while asleep, by similar illusions! When I consider these matters carefully, I realize so clearly that there are no conclusive indications by which waking life can be distinguished from sleep that I am quite astonished, and my bewilderment is such that it is almost able to convince me that I am sleeping...

Nevertheless, I have long held the belief that there is a God who can do anything, by whom I have been created and made what I am. But how can I be sure that he has brought it to pass that there is no earth, no sky, no extended bodies, no shape, no size, no place, and that nevertheless I have the impressions of all these things and cannot imagine that things might be other than as I now see them? And furthermore, just as I sometimes judge that others are mistaken about those things which they think they know best, how can I be sure that God has brought it about that I am always mistaken when I add two and three or count the sides of a square, or when I judge of something else even easier, if I can imagine anything easier than that?...

I will therefore suppose that, not a true God, who is very good and who is the supreme source of truth, but a certain evil spirit, not less clever and deceitful than powerful, has bent all his efforts to deceiving me. I will suppose that the sky, the air, the earth, colors, shapes, sounds, and all other objective things that we see are nothing but illusions and dreams that he has used to trick my credulity. I will consider myself as having no hands, no eyes, no flesh, no blood, nor any senses, yet falsely believing that I have all these things...

I suppose, accordingly, that everything that I see is false, I convince myself that nothing has ever existed of all that my deceitful memory recalls to me. I think that I have no senses; and I believe that body, shape, extension, motion, and location are merely inventions of my mind. What then could still be thought true? Perhaps nothing else, unless it is that there is nothing certain in the world.

But how do I know that there is not some entity, of a different nature from what I have just judged uncertain, of which there cannot be the last doubt? Is there not some God or some other power who gives me these thoughts? But I need not think this to be true, for possibly I am able to produce them myself. Then, at the very least, am I not an entity myself? But I have already denied that I had any senses or body. However, at this point I hesitate, for what follows from that? Am I so dependent upon the body and the senses that I could not exist without them? I have just convinced myself that nothing whatsoever existed in the world, that there was no sky, no earth, no minds, and no bodies; have I not thereby convinced myself that I did not exist? Not at all; without doubt I existed if I was convinced or even if I thought anything. Even though there may be a deceiver of some sort, very powerful and very tricky, who bends all his efforts to keep me perpetually deceived, there can be no slightest doubt that I exist, since he deceives me; and let him deceive me as much as he will, he can never make me be nothing as long as I think that I am something. Thus, after having thought well on this matter, and after examining all things with care, I must finally conclude and maintain that this proposition: *I am, I exist,* is necessarily true every time that I pronounce it or conceive it in my mind ...

Exercise:

Reconstructing the argument:

1. What is the main issue dealt with by Descartes?
2. What conclusion do you think he reaches?
3. Write a list composed of about ten sentences, each one of which represents what you think is a key step in the argument.
4. Order the sentences in the list so that they lend support to each other, building a coherent argument. Draw arrows in between sentences that you think make important connections.
5. Are all of the sentences in your list true?
6. Are some of the sentences in the list more plausible than others? Try to rank them on a scale of '1' to '5', with the least plausible being given '1', the most plausible being given '5'; assign intermediate values to the rest, according as they seem more or less plausible.
7. Are some of the sentences on your list important to the argument although they are neither true nor plausible?
8. What could the function of implausible or untrue sentences be in an argument?

Exercise:

What is real?

Real is often contrasted with unreal, but unreal comes in a variety of forms, for example:
  a) non-existent
  b) imaginary
  c) artificial
  d) imitation
  e) insincere
Complete the following sentences using the word that is most appropriate.
1. Are those real pearls or are they
2. Dinosaurs aren't real; they are
3. Does he really love you or is he being
4. Santa Claus isn't real; he is
5. Since I hate watering plants, I prefer plants that are
6. When you say ghosts aren't real, you mean they are
7. Is that a genuine Picasso or is it
8. The fruit in the basket looks real, but it is
9. The doctor said that she wasn't sick: her pains were

Discussion Plan:

How can we tell what is real? What sorts of evidence would help you decide? Discuss how you could tell if the following are real using:
  a) your senses
  b) reasoning
  c) documentary evidence
  d) workability
1. I thought I saw a mouse under the couch, but is it real?
2. I can't really believe in Superman: no one who could fly could be real.
3. How could the Germans have done such horrible things: those stories can't be real.
4. I think I love her, but are my feelings real?
5. John says that if I study I'll pass math; I wonder if that will really happen.
6. Someone told me that I could earn hundreds of thousands of dollars in my lifetime. That seems unreal to me.
7. My brother says that his real dream is to be an astronaut, but I think he is just fooling himself.
8. When I read about the Middle Ages it seems so unreal to me; I wonder what it was really like.

9. I wonder if atoms are real.

10. My girlfriend said I'm not a real man; I wonder what she means by that.

11. I wonder if therapy is the real answer to my problems.

12. John promised me $10;
    I wonder if he'll really come through.

13. Is Marge a real friend, let's see, how can I tell?

14. I'll bet the solution is really ammonia, let's see.

15. I'll bet the solution is really 2,456, let's see.

16. I'll bet the solution is to study harder, let's see.

17. I'll bet the solution is, 'the butler did it', let's see.

Discussion Plan:

Something to think about:

The label for a name brand of chocolate syrup reads:
VITAMIN FORTIFIED
BOSCO
REAL CHOCOLATE
FLAVORED
SYRUP
with natural and
artificial flavors
Is *Bosco* real chocolate syrup? Is it real chocolate flavored syrup? Is there a difference between the two?
The ingredients on the back label are: *sugar, water, corn syrup, dextrose, cocoa, malt extract, artificial color, caramel color, salt, xanthan gum (for body), potassium sorbate (a preservative) with vitamin A , niacin and riboflavin and iron (ferrous sulfate) added.*
Does the list of ingredients help us to decide whether *Bosco* is real?
Is *Bosco* real *Bosco*? What would unreal *Bosco* be?
How could we go about answering these questions?

Identity and Memory

Wherever our knowledge comes from, it seems clear that a crucial source of our sense of self is the ability to relate present thoughts and experiences to the past. We feel that our lives are continuous over time and that gives us a sense of identity. We "feel" this, but on what is this feeling based. Memory does not guarantee that our lives form a continuous whole because we do not remember an uninterrupted sequence of events. Rather our memories are composed of specific incidents separated by extended periods of time that we cannot, or do not, actively recollect. Why do we remember certain things and not others? By comparing the things that we actually recall to the history of our lives, we can learn something significant about the sense we have of our selves. What we forget is often not accidental.

Ben Hecht, The Lost Soul

It would be dawn soon.

The man in the cell was unable to sleep. He had dressed himself. He stood looking out of a small barred window at the waning night and the winter stars going away.

Two heavy-set men with tired puffy unshaven faces were also in this cell. They stared at the cell walls with a remarkable ox-like persistency.

Then, as if overcome by a secret curiosity, they turned their eyes on the man at the barred window and looked shyly over his shoulder at the first colours of dawn.

Yet a fourth man appeared.

The two heavy-set men greeting him with unexpected dignity in their voices.

"Hello, Doc," said one.

"What time is it?" said the other.

The cell door was unlocked. The doctor came in. He took a small silver pencil out of his vest pocket and began rolling it back and forth between his thumb and fingers. Then he cocked his eye at the unshaded electric light burning high up in the cell. He was very nervous.

"Hello," he said.

The one at the window turned. He was smiling.

"How do you feel?" the doctor asked, continuing with the silver pencil.

The one at the window shook his head with a rather queer good-humoured politeness.

"I didn't sleep well," he answered. "I suppose it doesn't help any to worry. But ... well ... I was just talking to these two men here who have been good enough to keep me company. You see, I'm in a very awkward predicament … I don't know who I am."

The doctor blinked. Then he turned and stared at the two heavy-set men. They looked remarkably inscrutable—even for oxen. The doctor put the silver pencil away and removed a black leather case from his coat pocket. He opened it and took out a stethoscope.

"Just a normality," he muttered. "Open your shirt, please."

He put the instrument on the man's chest and listened.

"Very remarkable," he spoke after a long pause of listening. "Normal. Absolutely normal heart action."

The two heavy-set men nodded mechanically but correctly. There is a certain etiquette of nodding and staring which the laity proudly observe in their relation with the professions.

"I don't know who I am," the man at the window resumed in a slightly high-pitched tone, rebuttoning his shirt. "I feel all right, doctor. But I haven't the faintest idea"—the queer good-natured smile played apologetically behind his words—"I haven't the slightest idea what my name is. I presume the officials are working hard and doing all they can … to determine. But it's getting a little on my nerves. It's lucky I have a sense of humour. Otherwise. Well. Imagine finding yourself in jail. And just not knowing who the deuce you are or where you come from. I suppose I was picked up roaming around. Nevertheless it doesn't seem right to me to put a man in jail. They might have been decent enough to think of a hospital. Or a hotel. I unquestionably have a family who are worrying. You know, I've been trying to figure out what sort of man I am. It's very interesting. For instance, I'm obviously educated and unused to jails."

The doctor turned to the two heavy-set men. They shrugged their shoulders. The doctor looked at his wrist-watch hurriedly.

"What time is it?" one of the heavy-set men asked in a shy voice.

The one at the window sighed and went on talking as the doctor, with a secretive gesture, held his wrist-watch for the two heavy-set men to look at. They looked and nodded.

"I've searched through my pockets," he was saying from the window, "and not a shred of identification. No pocket-book or handkerchief or any marks. Of course—my hands. Not those of a working man, I should say. And—a—"

He stopped and began rubbing the back of his head.

"Don't you remember coming here?" the doctor asked, looking intently at the man.

"No, I can't say I do," he answered. "I feel quite aware of everything in the present. But the past. Well! the past—"

He closed his eyes and frowned. A slightly bewildered and contemptuous chuckle started his words again.

"Of course, efficiency is more than one has a right to expect from the police. Or they would have had me photographed. As I was telling these two men. And my picture put in the newspapers so that my family would see it and sort of claim me. Obviously"—he stared at the doctor with some anger— "obviously I'm somebody of importance."

The doctor drew a deep breath.

"Don't you remember," he began.

"Nothing," the man at the window interrupted irritably. "Pardon me. I don't mean to get angry. But it's damned awkward. You know, I might be somebody very important—with all sorts of people dependent and worried. There's some medical term for this condition, isn't there, doctor? I forget at the moment. The sensation is decidedly queer. And amusing."

He was staring at the beginning of morning light beyond the barred window.

"I don't know why I should feel amused," he chuckled. "In reality what it amounts to, I suppose, is that I have lost my soul. Or, that is, misplaced it for the time being. A most serious matter, it seems to me. But, damn it, I must be a humorist or something. Because the situation makes me want to laugh. I'm sure most men would be wailing and tearing their hair if they suddenly lost their soul. But really, I—"

His face spread in a grin and he began laughing softly.

"By God, what a beautiful morning," he murmured, his eyes again on the world outside. "Doctor,"—he crossed to where the doctor stood regarding him, the silver pencil again working between his thumb and fingers. "Doctor, if I could only get hold of my name," he whispered, "who am I... who..."

The doctor cleared his throat.

"Your name is," he began, "is—"

He stopped. There were footsteps in the corridor. People were coming.

A group of six men came walking toward the cell. The two heavy-set men stood up and shook their legs. The doctor grew excited. He stepped into the group and began talking hurriedly and in a lowered voice.

"Don't read it," he repeated, "it'll just give us a lot of trouble, sheriff. He's amnesic. It'd just be borrowing trouble to wake him up. Let him go this way."

"Well, he'll find out pretty soon," said the sheriff.

"I doubt it," the doctor whispered. " Anyway, by the time he does you'll have him strapped and—"

"All right"—the sheriff thrust a sheet of typewritten paper in his pocket— "let's go."

"Come on." The doctor returned to the cell.

The man at the window nodded good-naturedly. The doctor took his arm and led him into the group.

They fell into place around him—two on each side, two in front, the two heavy-set men behind and the doctor still holding his arm and watching his face.

"You see," the man in the center began talking at once, eagerly, quickly, as if a dizziness swayed the edges of his words, "I haven't the least idea who I am, gentlemen. But if you'll be patient with me, I'm sure my family or some other clue ... I dislike being such a bother. Is that a clergyman? Where, by the way, are you taking me? Good God!"

Silently, without answer to this amazing question, the marchers escorting James Hartley to the gallows continued on their way.

And in the tall, gloomy death chamber a hundred or more spectators sat waiting for the hanging of the creature known as the Axe Fiend who a few months ago had murdered his wife and two children in their sleep.

The group of marchers stepped through an opened door on to the gallows platform.

A confusion ensued. Figures moved about on the platform. Then, out of the bustle on the high platform, an amazed face looked down on the spectators. The mouth of this face was opened as if it were about to scream. Its eyes moved wildly as if they had become uncentered. Gasps came from it.

A shiny yellow-rope was being tightened around its neck.

A man was adjusting a voluminous white wrapper about the figure under the rope.

Another man was stepping forward with a white hood in his hands. Suddenly the face screamed.

Three words filled the smoke-laden air—three words uttered in a sob so pitiful, so agonized, so startled that the sheriff paused with the white hood.

"This ain't me!" screamed the face. "This ain't ME!"

The spectators held their breaths, and stared.

A white bundle was swaying and twisting on the end of a long thin yellow rope.

Discussion Plan:

1. Why do you think the prisoner in the story forgot who he was?
2. Do you think his forgetfulness is genuine?
3. Why did James Hartley, the prisoner, scream "This ain't ME!" at the last minute of his life? Who did he think it was? Contrast this with Descartes' absolute certainty that saying or thinking "This is me!" proves it.
4. Suppose James Hartley was really guilty of murdering his wife and children and suppose he has also completely forgotten everything. Should he have been executed?

Discussion Plan:

Responsibility:

The question of James Hartley's responsibility raises the general question of a person's responsibility for his actions. The most usual answer is that a person is responsible for what he does when either he does it intentionally, understanding what the consequences will be, or he does it carelessly without considering what he was doing and he should have known better. Often the degree of responsibility is determined in response to the seriousness of an action. Killing someone, even accidentally, carries a greater weight of responsibility than breaking a window, even intentionally.

In the following situations describe whether the circumstances would tend to increase or decrease the responsibility of the person performing the act.

1. John knocks over the lamp while dancing.
2. Mary rolls over and breaks the glass while sleeping.
3. Jane vomits on the sofa while drunk.
4. Tom crashes the car into a lamppost while drunk.
5. Sue uses obscenities at her mother during an argument.
6. John hits his younger brother who is annoying him while he is studying for an important test. The brother is seriously injured.
7. A three year old child sets the house on fire while playing with matches.
8. A sixteen year old sets the house on fire while smoking in bed.
9. Your mother cleans your room and throws out a prized possession.
10. Your father tells your boyfriend that you had a great time at the party last night, but you hadn't gone with your boyfriend.

Exercise:

Should you still be blamed?

1. In tenth grade they discover that you had cheated on a ninth grade regents.
2. You are in graduate school and they discover that you shouldn't have been permitted to graduate from college because you hadn't satisfied a phys. ed. requirement.
3. You participated in a gang rape at sixteen; you are now thirty-four and happily married.
4. Your boss discovered that you had served time in prison and decides to fire you from the job that you have been successfully performing for the last five years.

5. You are a politician running for office and they discover that you were a member of the KKK as a youth.

6. A high school principal now, they find out that you performed in a classic porn film while in college.

7. Your present wife discovers that you had been arrested and treated for child abuse in a former marriage.

8. Your present husband discovers that you had been a prostitute before you married him.

Discussion Plan:

Memories are things that happen in our minds and things that we use as indicators of events that happened earlier in time. This raises important issues as to the reliability of memory as a source of knowledge.

1. If you think you remember do you have a memory?
2. Are only true memories real memories?
3. If no one remembers an event did it happen?
4. How can we tell whether what we think happened, happened?
5. Would at least some memories have to be true if memories are to be useful as a guide to the past?
6. Could memories be useful if they were only occasionally correct?
7. How do written documents and other artifacts interact with memories?
8. How does causal knowledge, knowledge of how the world works, interact with memories?
9. Are memories of events or do we also have to remember how to do things?
10. Do the words 'memories' and 'remembering' mean the same as used in question 9?

Identity and Others

We live in a world full of others, each person reflecting and being reflected by the people around him. How others treat us is often determined more by how they see us than what we really are. We are characterized in terms of the appearances we give as well as by our past history—and in most cases all we have to go by are the appearances.

Kurt Vonnegut, Miss Temptation

Puritanism had fallen into such disrepair that not even the oldest spinster thought of putting Susanna in a ducking stool; not even the oldest farmer suspected that Susanna's diabolical beauty had made his cow run dry.

Susanna was a bit-part actress in the summer theater near the village, and she rented a room over the firehouse. She was a part of village life all summer, but the villagers never got used to her. She was forever as startling and desirable as a piece of big-city fire apparatus.

Susanna's feathery hair and saucer eyes were as black as midnight. Her skin was the color of cream. Her hips were like a lyre, and her bosom made men dream of peace and plenty for ever and ever. She wore barbaric golden hoops on her shell-pink ears, and around her ankles were chains with little bells on them.

She went barefoot and slept until noon every day. And as noon drew near, the villagers on the main street would grow as restless as beagles with a thunderstorm on the way.

At noon, Susanna would appear on the porch outside her room. She would stretch languidly, pour a bowl of milk for her black cat, kiss the cat, fluff her hair, put on her earrings, lock her door, and hide the key in her bosom.

And then, barefoot, she would begin her stately, undulating, titillating, tinkling walk-down the outside stairway, past the liquor store, the insurance agency, the real-estate office, the diner, the American Legion post, and the church, to the crowded drugstore. There she would get the New York papers.

She seemed to nod to all the world in a dim, queenly way. But the only person she spoke to during her daily walk was Bearse Hinkley, the seventy-two-year-old pharmacist.

The old man always had her papers ready for her.

"Thank you, Mr. Hinkley. You're an angel," she would say, opening a paper at random. "Now, let's see what's going on back in civilization."

While the old man would watch, fuddled by her perfume, Susanna would laugh or gasp or frown at items in the paper—items she never explained.

Then she would take the papers, and return to her nest over the firehouse. She would pause on the porch outside her room, dip her hand into her bosom, bring out the key, unlock the door, pick up the black cat, kiss it again, and disappear inside.

The one-girl pageant had a ritual sameness until one day toward the end of summer, when the air of the drugstore was cut by a cruel, sustained screech from a dry bearing in a revolving soda-fountain stool.

The screech cut right through Susanna's speech about Mr. Hinkley's being an angel. The screech made scalps tingle and teeth ache. Susanna looked indulgently in the direction of the screech, forgiving the screecher. She found that the screecher wasn't a person to be indulged.

The screech had been made by the stool of Cpl. Norman Fuller, who had come home the night before from eighteen bleak months in Korea. They had been eighteen months without war—but eighteen months without cheer, all the same. Fuller had turned on the stool slowly, to look at Susanna with indignation. When the screech died, the drugstore was deathly still.

Fuller had broken the enchantment of summer by the seaside—had reminded all in the drugstore of the black, mysterious passions that were so often the mainsprings of life.

He might have been a brother, come to rescue his idiot sister from the tenderloin; or an irate husband, come to a saloon to horsewhip his wife back to where she belonged, with the baby. The truth was that Corporal Fuller had never seen Susanna before.

He hadn't consciously meant to make a scene. He hadn't meant to underplay his indignation, to make it a small detail in the background of Susanna'a pageant—a detail noticed by only one or two connoisseurs of the human comedy.

But the screech had made his indignation the center of the solar system for all in the drugstore—particularly for Susanna. Time had stopped, and it could not proceed until Fuller had explained the expression on his granite Yankee face.

Fuller felt his skin glowing like hot brass. He was comprehending destiny. Destiny had suddenly given him an audience, and a situation about which he had a bitter lot to say.

Fuller felt his lips move, heard the words come out, "Who do you think you are?" he said to Susanna.

"I beg your pardon?" said Susanna. She drew her newspapers about herself protectively.

I saw you come down the street like you were a circus parade and I just wondered who you thought you were," said Fuller.

Susanna blushed gloriously. "I—I'm an actress," she said.

"You can say that again," said Fuller. "Greatest actresses in the world American women."

"You're very nice to say so," said Susanna uneasily.

Fuller's skin glowed brighter and hotter. His mind had become a fountain of apt, intricate phrases. "I'm not talking about theaters with seats in 'em. I'm talking about the stage of life. American women act and dress like they're gonna give you the world. Then, when you stick out your hand, they put an ice cube in it."

"They do?" said Susanna emptily.

"They do, " said Fuller, "and it's about time somebody said so." He looked challengingly from spectator to spectator, and found what he took to be dazed encouragement. "It isn't fair," he said.

"What isn't?" said Susanna, lost.

"You come in here with bells on your ankles, so's I'll have to look at your ankles and your pretty pink feet," said Fuller. "You kiss the cat, so's I'll have to think about how it'd be to be that cat," said Fuller. "You call an old man an angel, so's I'll have to think about what it'd be like to be called an angel by you," said Fuller. "You hide your key in front of everybody, so's I'll have to think about where that key is," said Fuller.

He stood. "Miss," he said, his voice full of pain, "you do everything you can to give lonely, ordinary people like me indigestion and the heeby-jeebies, and you wouldn't even hold hands with me to keep me from falling off a cliff."

He strode to the door. All eyes were on him. Hardly anyone noticed that his indictment had reduced Susanna to ashes of what she'd been moments before. Susanna now looked like what she really was—a muddle-headed nineteen-year-old clinging to a tiny corner of sophistication.

"It isn't fair," said Fuller. "There ought to be a law against girls acting and dressing like you do. It makes more people unhappy than it does happy. You know what I say to you, for going around making everybody want to kiss you?"

"No," piped Susanna, every fuse in her nervous system blown.

"I say to you what you'd say to me, if I was to try and kiss you," said I Fuller grandly. He swung his arms in an umpire's gesture for "out." "The hell with you," he said. He left, slamming the screen door.

He didn't look back when the door slammed again a moment later, when the patter of running bare feet and the wild tinkling of little bells faded away in the direction of the firehouse.

That evening, Corporal Fuller's widowed mother put a candle on the table, and fed him sirloin steak and strawberry shortcake in honor of his homecoming. Fuller ate the meal as though it were wet blotting paper, and he answered his mother's cheery questions in a voice that was dead.

" Aren't you glad to be home?" said his mother, when they'd finished their coffee.

"Sure," said Fuller.

"What did you do today?" she said.

"Walked," he said.

"Seeing all your old friends?" she said.

"Haven't got any friends," said Fuller.

His mother threw up her hands. "No friends?" she said. "You?"

"Times change, ma," said Fuller heavily. "Eighteen months is a long time. People leave town, people get married—"

"Marriage doesn't kill people, does it?" she said.

Fuller didn't smile. "Maybe not," he said. "But it makes it awful hard for 'em to find any place to fit old friends in."

"Dougie isn't married, is he?"

"He's out west, ma—with the Strategic Air Command," said Fuller. The little dining room became as lonely as a bomber in the thin, cold stratosphere.

"Oh," said his mother. "There must be somebody left."

"None," said Fuller. "I spent the whole morning on the phone, ma. I might as well have been back in Korea. Nobody home."

"I can't believe it," she said. " Why, you couldn't walk down Main Street without being almost trampled by friends."

"Ma," said Fuller hollowly, "after I ran out of numbers to call, you know what I did? I went down to the drugstore, ma, and just sat there by the soda fountain, waiting for somebody to walk in—somebody I knew maybe just even a little. Ma," he said in anguish, "all I knew was poor old Bearse Hinkley. I'm not kidding you one bit." He stood, crumpling his napkin into a ball. "Ma, will you please excuse me?"

"Yes. Of course," she said. " Where are you going now?" She beamed. "Out to call on some nice girl, I hope?"

Fuller threw the napkin down. "I'm going to get a cigar!" he said. "I don't know any girls. They're all married too."

His mother paled. "I—I see," she said. "I—I didn't even know you smoked."

"Ma," said Fuller tautly, "can't you get it through your head? I been away for eighteen months, ma—eighteen months!"

"It is a long time, isn't it?" said his mother, humbled by his passion. "Well, you go get your cigar." She touched his arm. "And please don't feel so lonesome. You just wait. Your life will be so full of people again, you won't know which one to turn to. And, before you know it, you'll meet some pretty young girl, and you'll be married too."

"I don't intend to get married for some time, mother," said Fuller stuffily. "Not until I get through divinity school."

"Divinity school!" said his mother. "When did you decide that?"

"This noon," said Fuller.

"What happened this noon?"

"I had a kind of religious experience, ma," he said. "Something just made me speak out."

In Fuller's buzzing head there whirled a rhapsody of Susanna. He saw again all the professional temptresses who had tormented him in Korea, who had beckoned from makeshift bed-sheet movie screens, from curling pin-ups on damp tent walls, from ragged magazines in sand-bagged pits. The Susannas had made fortunes, beckoning to lonely Corporal Fullers everywhere—beckoning with stunning beauty, beckoning the Fullers to come nowhere for nothing.

The wraith of a Puritan ancestor, stiff-necked, dressed in black, took possession of Fuller's tongue. Fuller spoke with a voice that came across centuries, the voice of a witch hanger, a voice redolent with frustration, self-righteousness and doom.

"What did I speak out against?" he said. "Temp-ta-tion."

Fuller's cigar in the night was a beacon warning carefree, frivolous people away. It was plainly a cigar smoked in anger. Even the moths had sense enough to stay away. Like a restless, searching red eye, it went up and down every street in the village, coming to rest at last, a wet, dead butt, before the firehouse.

Bearse Hinkley, the old pharmacist, sat at the wheel of the pumper, his eyes glazed with nostalgia—nostalgia for the days when he had been young enough to drive. And on his face, for all to see, was a dream of one more catastrophe, with all the young men away, when an old man or nobody would drive the pumper to glory one more time. He spent warm evenings there, behind the wheel—and had for years.

"Want a light for that thing?" he said to Corporal Fuller, seeing the dead cigar between Fuller's lips.

"No, thanks, Mr. Hinkley," he said. " All the pleasure's out of it."

"Beats me how anybody finds any pleasure in cigars in the first place," said the old man.

"Matter of taste," said Fuller. "No accounting for tastes."

"One man's meat's another man's poison," said Hinkley. "Live and let live, I always say." He glanced at the ceiling. Above it was the fragrant nest of Susanna and her black cat. "Me? All my pleasures are looking at what used to be pleasures."

Fuller looked at the ceiling, too, meeting the unmentioned issue squarely. "If you were young," he said, "you'd know why I said what I said to her. Beautiful, stuck-up girls give me a big pain."

"Oh, I remember that," said Hinkley. "I'm not so old I don't remember the big pain."

"If I have a daughter, I hope she isn't beautiful," said Fuller. "The beautiful girls at high school—by God, if they didn't think they were something extra-special."

"By God, If I don't think so, too," said Hinkley.

"They wouldn't even look at you if you didn't have a car and an allowance of twenty bucks a week to spend on 'em," said Fuller.

"Why should they?" said the old man cheerfully. "If I was a beautiful girl, I wouldn't." He nodded to himself.

"Well, anyway, I guess you came home from the war and settled that score. I guess you told her."

"Ah-h-h," said Fuller. "You can't make any impression on them."

"I dunno," said Hinkley. "There's a fine old tradition in the theater: The show must go on. You know, even if you got pneumonia or your baby's dying, you still put on the show."

"I'm all right," said Fuller. "Who's complaining? I feel fine."

The old man's white eyebrows went up. "Who's talking about you?" he said. "I'm talking about her."

Fuller reddened, mousetrapped by egoism. "She'll be all right," he said.

"She will?" said Hinkley. "Maybe she will. All I know is, the show's started at the theater. She's supposed to be in it and she's still upstairs."

"She is?" said Fuller, amazed.

"Has been," said Hinkley, "ever since you paddled her and sent her home."

Fuller tried to grin ironically. "Now, isn't that too bad?" he said. His grin felt queasy and weak. "Well, good-night, Mr. Hinkley."

"Good-night, soldier boy," said Hinkley. "Good-night."

As noon drew near on the next day, the villagers along the main street seemed to grow stupid. Yankee shopkeepers made change lackadaisically, as though money didn't matter any more. All thoughts were of the great cuckoo clock the firehouse had become. The question was: Had Corporal Fuller broken it or, at noon would the little door on top fly open, would Susanna appear?

In the drugstore, old Bearse Hinkley fussed with Susanna's New York papers, rumpling them in his anxiety to make them attractive. They were bait for Susanna.

Moments before noon, Corporal Fuller—the vandal himself—came into the drugstore. On his face was a strange mixture of guilt and soreheadedness. He had spent the better part of the night awake, reviewing his grievances against beautiful women. All they think about is how beautiful they are, he'd said to himself at dawn. They wouldn't even give you the time of day.

He walked along the row of soda-fountain stools and gave each empty stool a seemingly idle twist. He found the stool that had screeched so loudly the day before. He sat down on it, a monument of righteousness. No one spoke to him.

The fire siren gave its perfunctory wheeze for noon. And then, hearselike, a truck from the express company drove up to the firehouse. Two men got out and climbed the stairs. Susanna's hungry black cat jumped to the porch railing and arched its back as the expressmen disappeared into Susanna's room. The cat spat when they staggered out with Susanna's trunk.

Fuller was shocked. He glanced at Bearse Hinkley, and he saw that the old man's look of anxiety had become the look of double pneumonia—dizzy, blind, drowning.

"Satisfied, corporal?" said the old man.

"I didn't tell her to leave," said Fuller.

"You didn't leave her much choice," said Hinkley.

"What does she care what I think?" said Fuller. "I didn't know she was such a tender blossom."

The old man touched Fuller's arm lightly. "We all are, corporal—we all are," he said. "I thought that was one of the few good things about sending a boy off to the army. I thought that was where he could find out for sure he wasn't the only tender blossom on earth. Didn't you find that out?"

"I never thought I was a tender blossom," said Fuller. "I'm sorry it turned out this way, but she asked for it." His head was down. His ears were hot crimson.

"She really scared you stiff, didn't she?" said Hinkley.

Smiles bloomed on the faces of the small audience that had drawn near on one pretext or another. Fuller appraised the smiles, and found that the old man had left him only one weapon—utterly humorless good citizenship.

"Who's afraid?" he said stuffily. "I'm not afraid. I just think its a problem somebody ought to bring up and discuss."

"It's sure the one subject nobody gets tired of, " said Hinkley.

Fuller's gaze, which had become a very shifty thing, passed over the magazine rack. There was tier upon tier of Susannas, a thousand square feet of wet-lipped smiles and sooty eyes and skin like cream. He ransacked his mind for a ringing phrase that would give dignity to his cause.

"I'm thinking about juvenile delinquency!" he said. He pointed to the magazines. "No wonder kids go crazy."

"I know I did," said the old man quietly. "I was as scared as you are."

"I told you, I'm not afraid of her," said Fuller.

"Good!" said Hinkley. "Then you're just the man to take her papers to her. They're paid for." He dumped the papers in Fuller's lap.

Fuller opened his mouth to reply. But he closed it again. His throat had tightened, and he knew that, if he tried to speak, he would quack like a duck.

"If you're really not afraid, corporal," said the old man, "that would be a very nice thing to do—a Christian thing to do."

As he mounted the stairway to Susanna's nest, Fuller was almost spastic in his efforts to seem casual.

Susanna's door was unlatched. When Fuller knocked on it, it swung open. In Fuller's imagination, her nest had been dark and still, reeking of incense, a labyrinth of heavy hangings and mirrors, with somewhere a Turkish corner, with somewhere a billowy bed in the form of a swan.

He saw Susanna and her room in truth now. The truth was the cheerless truth of a dirt-cheap Yankee summer rental—bare wood walls, tree coat hooks, a linoleum rug. Two gas burners, an iron cot, an icebox. A tiny sink with naked pipes, a plastic drinking glass, two plates, a murky mirror. A frying pan, a saucepan, a can of soap powder.

The only harem touch was a white circle of talcum powder before the murky mirror. In the center of the circle were the prints of two bare feet. The marks of the toes were no bigger than pearls.

Fuller looked from the pearls to the truth of Susanna. Her back was to him. She was packing the last of her things into a suitcase.

She was now dressed for travel—dressed as properly as a missionary's wife.

"Papers," croaked Fuller. "Mr. Hinkley sent 'em."

"How very nice of Mr. Hinkley," said Susanna. She turned. "Tell him—" No more words came. She recognized him. She pursed her lips and her small nose reddened.

"Papers," said Fuller emptily. "From Mr. Hinkley."

"I heard you," she said. "You just said that. Is that all you've got to say?"

Fuller flapped his hands limply at his sides. "I'm—-I—I didn't mean to make you leave," he said. "I didn't mean that."

"You suggest I stay?" said Susanna wretchedly. "After I've been denounced in public as a scarlet woman? A tart? A wench?"

"Holy smokes, I never called you those things!" said Fuller.

"Did you ever stop to think what it's like to be me?" she said. She patted her bosom. "There's somebody living inside here, too, you know."

"I know," said Fuller. He hadn't known, up to then.

"I have a soul," she said.

"Sure you do," said Fuller, trembling. He trembled because the room was filled with a profound intimacy. Susanna, the golden girl of a thousand tortured day-dreams, was now discussing her soul, passionately, with Fuller the lonely. Fuller the homely. Fuller the bleak.

"I didn't sleep a wink last night because of you," said Susanna.

"Me?" He wished she'd get out of his life again. He wished she were in black and white, a thousandth of an inch thick on a magazine page. He wished he could turn the page and read about baseball or foreign affairs.

"What did you expect?": said Susanna. "I talked to you all night. You know what I said to you?"

"No," said Fuller, backing away. She followed, and seemed to throw off heat like a big iron radiator. She was appallingly human.

"I'm not Yellowstone Park!" she said. "I'm not supported by taxes! I don't belong to everybody! You don't have any right to say anything about the way I look!"

"Good gravy!" said Fuller.

"I'm so tired of dumb toots like you!" said Susanna. She stamped her foot and suddenly looked haggard. "I can't help it if you want to kiss me! Whose fault is that?"

Fuller could now glimpse his side of the question only dimly, like a diver glimpsing the sun from the ocean floor.

"All I was trying to say was, you could be a little more conservative," he said.

Susanna opened her arms. "Am I conservative enough now?" she said. "Is this all right with you?"

The appeal of the lovely girl made the marrow of Fuller's bones ache. In his chest was a sigh like the lost chord. "Yes," he said. And then he murmured, "Forget about me."

Susanna tossed her head. "Forget about being run over by a truck," she sad. "What makes you so mean?"

"I just say what I think," said Fuller.

"You think such mean things," said Susanna, bewildered. Her eyes widened. "All through high school, people like you would look at me as if they wished I'd drop dead. They'd never dance with me, they'd never talk to me, they'd never even smile back." She shuddered. "They'd just go slinking around like small-town cops. They'd look at me the way you did—like I'd just done something terrible."

The truth of the indictment made Fuller itch all over. "Probably thinking about something else," he said.

"I don't think so," said Susanna. "You sure weren't. All of a sudden, you started yelling at me in the drugstore, and I'd never even seen you before." She burst into tears. "What is the matter with you?"

Fuller looked down at the floor. "Never had a chance with a girl like you—that's all," he said. "That hurts."

Susanna looked at him wonderingly. "You don't know what a chance is," she said.

"A chance is a late model convertible, a new suit, and twenty bucks," said Fuller.

Susanna turned her back to him and closed her suitcase. "A chance is a girl," she said. "You smile at her, you be friendly, you be glad she's a girl." She turned and opened her arms again. "I'm a girl. Girls are shaped this way," she said. "If men are nice to me and make me happy, I kiss them sometimes. Is that all right with you?"

"Yes, " said Fuller humbly. She had rubbed his nose in the sweet reason that governed the universe. He shrugged. "I better be going. Good-by."

"Wait!" she said. "You can't do that—just walk out, leaving me feeling so wicked." She shook her head. "I don't deserve to feel wicked."

"What can I do?" said Fuller helplessly.

"You can take me for a walk down the main street, as though you were proud of me," said Susanna. "You can welcome me back to the human race." She nodded to herself. "You owe that to me."

Cpl. Norman Fuller, who had come home two nights before from eighteen bleak months in Korea, waited on the porch outside Susanna's nest, with all the village watching.

Susanna had ordered him out while she changed, while she changed for her return to the human race. She had also called the express company and told them to bring her trunk back.

Fuller passed the time by stroking Susanna's cat. "Hello, kitty, kitty, kitty, kitty," he said, over and over again. Saying, "Kitty, kitty, kitty, kitty," numbed him like a merciful drug.

He was saying it when Susanna came out of her nest. He couldn't stop saying it, and she had to take the cat away from him, firmly, before she could get him to look at her, to offer his arm.

"So long, kitty, kitty, kitty, kitty, kitty, kitty," said Fuller.

Susanna was barefoot, and she wore barbaric hoop earrings, and ankle bells. Holding Fuller's arm lightly, she led him down the stairs, and began her stately, undulating, titillating, tinkling walk past the liquor store, the insurance agency, the real-estate office, the diner, the American Legion post, and the church, to the crowded drugstore.

"Now, smile and be nice," said Susanna. "Show you're not ashamed of me."

"Mind if I smoke?" said Fuller.

"That's very considerate of you to ask," said Susanna. "No, I don't mind at all."

By steadying his right hand with his left, Corporal Fuller managed to light a cigar.

Discussion Plan:

1. What values did Susanna appear to represent? From Fuller's perspective? From Mr. Hinkley's?
2. How do you think she wanted to be seen?
3. What is the basis of Fuller's judgment of Susanna?
4. What of Mr. Hinkley'd judgment of Fuller?
5. What is the basis for the reconciliation of Susanna and Fuller?
6. Do you think their eventual understanding of each other is truer than their initial impression? In what respect?
7. Do you think that their feelings will enable them to have a clear perception of each other, if they become close friends?

Exercise:

For the following descriptions write a list of at least five assumptions that you might make about the people described based on their appearances. Then assign to each assumption a number from '1' to '5'. '1' is given to those assumptions that seem least warranted; '5' to the most warranted assumptions.

1. A student is wearing a jacket that says Bronx High School of Science.
2. A girl is wearing a football team jacket.
3. A large boy is wearing a football team jacket.
4. Someone has a "No Nukes" button on their jacket.
5. A girl is dressed very fashionably.
6. A boy has an extreme 'punk' haircut.
7. A group of boys is acting very loud and boisterous on a bus.
8. A group of students is passing what seems to be a cigarette around in a circle.
9. A couple comes into the party from the backyard.
10. Two students have very similar term papers.
11. A couple have been going steady all through high school.

Go over your list. Next to each of your assumptions mark a second number from '1' to '5'. Give '5' to the assumption that seems to give the most information relevant to deciding how to act towards the person(s) described; '1' to the one that gives the least. Can you generalize about the value of safe and risky assumptions? What, if anything, does this tell you about knowing other people on the basis of their appearance?

Personal Identity

For most of us the problems of Descartes and Mariana are easily solved with a strong common sense realism. The world is very much the way it seems to be and we are what we are—a particular body with a life history beginning sometime around our birth and extending uninterruptedly, whether remembered or not, until the present time. There does not seem to be room for a great deal of perplexity here; or is there?

Douglas Hofstadter and Daniel Dennett, The Mind's I

You see the moon rise in the east. You see the moon rise in the west. You watch two moons moving toward each other across the cold black sky, one soon to pass behind the other as they continue on their way. You are on Mars, millions of miles from home, protected from the killing, frostless cold of the red Martian desert by fragile membranes of terrestrial technology. Protected but stranded, for your spaceship has broken down beyond repair. You will never ever return to Earth; to the friends and family a places you left behind.

But perhaps there is hope. In the communication compartment of the disabled craft you find a Teleclone Mark IV teleporter and instructions for its use. If you turn the teleporter on, tune its beam to the Teleclone receiver on Earth, and then step into the sending chamber, the teleporter will swiftly and painlessly dismantle your body, producing a molecule-by-molecule blueprint to be beamed to Earth, where the receiver, its reservoirs well stocked with the requisite atoms, will almost instantaneously produce, from the beamed instructions—you! Whisked back to Earth at the speed of light, into the arms of your loved ones, who will soon be listening with rapt attention to your tales of adventures on Mars.

One last survey of the damaged spaceship convinces you that the Teleclone is your only hope. With nothing to lose, you set the transmitter up, flip the right switches, and step into the chamber. 5, 4, 3, 2, 1, FLASH! You open the door in front of you and step out of the Teleclone receiver chamber into the sunny, familiar atmosphere of Earth. You've come home, none the worse for wear after your long-distance Teleclone fall from Mars. Your narrow escape from a terrible fate on the red planet calls for a celebration, and as your family and friends gather around, you notice how everyone has changed since last you saw them. It has been almost three years, after all, and you've all grown older. Look at Sarah, your daughter, who must now be eight and a half. You find yourself thinking, "Can this be the little girl who used to sit on my lap?" Of course it is, you reflect, even though you must admit that you do not so much recognize her as extrapolate from memory and deduce her identity. She is so much taller, looks so much older, and knows so much more. In fact, most of the cells now in her body were not there when last you cast eyes on her. But in spite of growth and change, in spite of replacement of cells, she's the same little person you kissed good-bye three years ago.

Then it hits you: "Am I, really, the same person who kissed this little girl good-bye three years ago? Am I this eight-year-old child's mother or am I actually a brand-new human being, only several hours old, in spite of my memories—or apparent memories—of days and years before that? Did this child's mother recently die on Mars, dismantled and destroyed in the chamber of a Teleclone Mark IV?

"Did I die on Mars? No, certainly I did not die on Mars, since I am alive on Earth. Perhaps, though, someone died on Mars—Sarah's mother. Then I am not Sarah's mother. But I must be! The whole point of getting into the Teleclone was to return home to my family! But I keep forgetting; maybe I never got into that Teleclone on Mars. Maybe that was someone else—if it ever happened at all. Is that infernal machine a teleporter—a mode of trans-portation—or, as the brand name suggests, a sort of murdering twinmaker? Did Sarah's mother survive the experience with the Teleclone or not? She thought she was going to. She entered the chamber with hope and anticipa-tion, not suicidal resignation. Her act was altruistic, to be sure—she was taking steps to provide Sarah with a loved one to protect her—but also selfish—she was getting herself out of a jam into something pleasant. Or so it seemed. How do I know that's how it seemed? Because I was there; I was Sarah's mother thinking those thoughts; I am Sarah's mother. Or so it seems."...

Discussion Plan:

Criteria for identity.

1. Why does the question of Sarah's mother's identity arise?
2. What is the problem of identifying Sarah?
3. What is the relation of Sarah's mother's thoughts and feeling to her identity?

Exercise:

When are two thing the same?
1. Are two copies of the same magazine the same?
2. Are two Big Macs the same?
3. When have you written the same answer as your friend on a math test?
4. Does Christmas fall on the same day every year?
5. Is New York the same city as it was fifty years ago?
6. If you repot a cutting from a plant, is it the same as the original plant?

7. If you follow your mother's recipe exactly, have you made the same pie that she does?
8. Is a reprint of the first issue of Superman comics the same as the original?
9. If you see a movie with your friend, do you both see the same movie?

Discuss the following: I have an old heirloom watch that has been passed down in my family for hundreds of years. Each generation, however, has had to replace some of the parts. We are very careful to replace the parts using the finest craftsmen who duplicate the part replaced as carefully as possible. I have reason to suppose that many if not all of the parts of the watch have been replaced at some time or another. Do I have the same watch as the other members of my family had?

Exercise:

Using criteria.

In discussing the last selection and thinking about the discussion questions you made use of standards by which you argued that something was or was not the same. When you use standards in order to make decisions, you are using criteria. *Criteria* are standards or considerations that enable us to make decisive judgments: that is, they are considerations that count. We can use different criteria from someone to whom we are talking and that leads to confusion. For example if I am thinking about mice, I might think that a rat is large; if you are using horses as your criteria, you would think that a rat is small. Here our disagreement is not about the size of the rat, but rather about the standard or criterion that we are employing in making our decision.

Go back over the answers you gave and try to enumerate the criteria by which you decided that the things were or were not the same.

Now go back and systematically change your answers. Describe what criteria you are now using.

Permanence and Change

We are governed by two powerful intuitions about our identity. We are always changing and yet, we are always the same—in some important sense. What remains the same is at the core of our identity. It unifies experience and makes it our own. But what is it? Could our sense of self be an illusion, a construct built up out of changing experiences? If so, who is having these experiences?

William Shakespeare, As You Like It

All the world's a stage,
And all the men and women merely players,
They have their exits and their entrances,
And one man in his time plays many parts,
His acts being seven ages. At first, the infant,
Mewling and puking in the nurse's arms.
Then the whining schoolboy, with his satchel
And shining morning face, creeping like snail
Unwillingly to school. And then the lover,
Sighing like furnace, with a woeful ballad
Made to his mistress' eyebrow. Then a soldier,
Full of strange oaths and bearded like the bard,
Jealous in honor, sudden and quick in quarrel,
Seeking the bubble reputation
Even in the cannon's mouth. And then the justice,
In fair round belly with good capon lined,
With eyes severe and beard of formal cut,
Full of wise saws and modern instances;
And so he plays his part. The sixth age shifts
Into the lean and slippered pantaloon,
With spectacles on nose and pouch on side;
His youthful hose, well saved, a world too wide
For his shrunk shank, and his big manly voice,
Turning again toward childish trebel, pipes
And whistles in his sound. Last scene of all,
That ends this strange eventful history,
Is second childishness and mere oblivion,
Sans teeth, sans eyes, sans taste, sans everything.

Hugh Prather, Notes to Myself

... Just when I think I have learned the way
to live, life changes and I am left the
same as I began. The more things change
the more I am the same. It appears that
my life is a constant irony of maturity
and regression, but my sense of progress
is based on the illusion that things out
there are going to remain the same and
that, at last, I have gained a little control.
But there will never be means to ends,
only means. And I am means. I am
what I started with, and when it is all
over I will be all that is left of me ...

Discussion Plan:

What makes you, you?

1. Would you be the same person if you had another name?
2. Would you be the same person if you spoke another language?
3. If you gained fifty pounds, would you still be you?
4. If you had plastic surgery and looked like a beautiful movie star, would you be the same person?
5. If you suffered an accident and lost the use of your limbs?
6. If you had a sex-change operation?
7. If you suffered a traumatic experience, for example, being unjustly jailed for years?
8. If you lived through a war fought in your immediate vicinity?
9. Are you the same as you were yesterday?
10. Are you the same person as you were when you were two years old?
11. Are you the same as you will be when you are sixty years old?
12. Does the career you choose change who you are?
13. If you were more happy (or more sad), would that change who you are?
14. If you changed most of your tastes, would it still be you?
15. If you could be transported into another time or culture, would you still be you?
16. If you had different parents, would you still be you?
17. If your personality was altered, would you still be the same?
18. If you lost all of your memories, would you still be you?
19. If you thought differently, would it still be you?
20. If you had radically different values and made totally different choices, would you still be you?

David Hume, Treatise of Human Nature

There are some philosophers who imagine we are every moment intimately conscious of what we call our *self*; that we feel its existence and its continuance in existence; and are certain, beyond the evidence of a demonstration, both of its perfect identity and simplicity. The strongest sensation, the most violent passion, say they, instead of distracting us from this view, only fix it the more intensely, and make us consider their influence on *self* either by their pain or pleasure…

…For my part, when I enter most intimately into what I call *myself*, I always stumble on some particular perception or other, of heat or cold, light or shade, love or hatred, pain or pleasure. I never can catch *myself* at any time without a perception, and never can observe anything but the perception. When my perceptions are removed for any time, as by sound sleep, so long am I insensible of *myself*, and may truly be said not to exist. And were all my perceptions removed by death, and could I neither think, nor feel, nor see, nor love, nor hate, after the dissolution of my body, I should be entirely annihilated, nor do I conceive what is further requisite to make me a perfect nonentity. If any one, upon serious and unprejudiced reflection, thinks he has a different notion of *himself*, I must confess I can reason no longer with him…

…I may venture to affirm of mankind, that they are nothing but a bundle or collection of different perceptions, which succeed each other with an inconceivable rapidity, and are in a perpetual flux and movement. Our eyes cannot turn in their sockets without varying our perceptions. Our thought is still more variable than our sight; and all our other senses and faculties contribute to this change; nor is there any single power of the soul, which remains unalterably the same, perhaps for one moment. The mind is a kind of theatre, where several perceptions successively make their appearance; pass, repass, glide away, and mingle in an infinite variety of postures and situations. There is properly no *simplicity* in it at one time, nor *identity* in different, whatever natural propension we may have to imagine that simplicity and identity. The comparison of the theatre must not mislead us. They are the successive perceptions only, that constitute the mind; nor have we the most distant notion of the place where these scenes are represented, or of the materials of which it is composed …

Exercise:

Hume offers an argument that seems to undermine our deep conviction that we know immediately and certainly who we are. Write a one or two page response to Hume, either supporting his position or arguing for an alternative. Use whatever insights you have gained from earlier readings and discussions.

SECTION 2:
THE SELF IN CONTEXT—
CULTURE AND TRADITION

For the most part our identity is established in fairly ordinary ways by using the simple criteria of physical resemblance and historical continuity. We are who we are because we are the sole continuously existent creature whose physical processes have lead from birth to the present moment. In other words our physical history constitutes our identity in the eyes of the world. But we have already seen how it is possible to doubt that our bodies are the same throughout time or that they exist at all or that they have anything to do with the identity of the real self. In the next section we will encounter problems that multiply these problems by the number of people we meet in our lifetimes. Here we are faced with determining who we are within the context of our culture. In a society like ours where cultural diversity is the norm, it is sometimes a real question what our cultural identity is.

The Core of the Self

We all make choices—what to wear, how to present ourselves, how to deal with reality. But no matter how many choices we are given, there are many things we cannot choose. Obviously we cannot choose the era into which we are born any more than we can choose the genes that we have inherited. But there are more subtle constraints on our choices. Pervasive forces so deeply limit our lives that they are hardly noticed. Like the proverbial fish in the water, we never notice that we are wet.

Anton Chekhov, The Darling

Olenka Plemyannikova, the daughter of a retired collegiate assessor, was sitting on her porch, which gave on the courtyard, deep in thought. It was hot, the flies were persistent and annoying, and it was pleasant to think that it would soon be evening. Dark rainclouds were gathering in the east and there was a breath of moisture in the wind that occasionally blew from that direction.

Kukin, a theater manager who ran a summer garden known as The Tivoli and lodged in the wing of the house, was standing in the middle of the courtyard, staring at the sky.

"Again!" he was saying in despair. "It's going to rain again! Rain every day, every day, as if to spite me! It will be the death of me! It's ruin! Such a frightful loss every day!"

He struck his hands together and continued, turning to Olenka:

"There, Olga Semyonovna, that's our life. It's enough to make you weep! You work, you try your utmost, you wear yourself out, you lie awake nights, you rack your brains trying to make a better thing of it, and what's the upshot? In the first place, the public is ignorant, barbarous, I give them the very best operatta, an elaborate spectacle, first-rate vaudeville artists. But do you think they want that? It's all above their heads. All they want is slapstick! Give them trash! And then look at the weather! Rain almost every evening. It started raining on the tenth of May, and it has kept it up all May and June. It's simply terrible. The public doesn't come, but don't I have to pay the rent? Don't I have to pay the artists?"

The next day toward evening the sky would again be overcast and Kukin would say, laughing hysterically:

"Well, go on, rain? Flood the garden, drown me! Bad luck to me in this world and the next! Let the artists sue me! Let them send me to prison—to Siberia—to the scaffold! Ha, ha, ha!"

The next day it was the same thing all over again.

Olenka listened to Kukin silently, gravely, and sometimes tears would come to her eyes. In the end his misfortunes moved her and she fell in love with him. He was a short, thin man with a sallow face, and wore his hair combed down over his temples. He had a thin tenor voice and when he spoke, his mouth twisted, and his face perpetually wore an expression of despair. Nevertheless he aroused a genuine, deep feeling in her. She was always enamored of someone and could not live otherwise. At first it had been her papa, who was now ill and sat in an armchair in a darkened room, breathing with difficulty. Then she had devoted her affections to her aunt, who used to come from Bryansk every other year. Still earlier, when she went to school, she had been in love with her French teacher. She was a quiet, kind, soft hearted girl, with meek, gentle eyes, and she enjoyed very good health. At the sight of her full pink cheeks, her soft white neck with a dark birthmark on it, and the kind artless smile that came into her face when she listened to anything pleasant, men said to themselves, "Yes, not half bad," and smiled too, while the ladies present could not refrain from suddenly seizing her hand in the middle of the conversation and exclaiming delightedly, "You darling!"

The house in which she lived all her life and which was to be hers by her father's will, was situated on the outskirts of the city on what was known as Gypsy Road, not far from the Tivoli. In the evening and at night she could hear the band play and the skyrockets go off, and it seemed to her that it was Kukin fighting his fate and assaulting his chief enemy, the apathetic public. Her heart contracted sweetly, she had not desire to sleep, and when he returned home at dawn, she would tap softly at her bedroom window, and, showing him only her face and one shoulder through the curtain, give him a friendly smile.

He proposed to her, and they were married. And when he had a good look at her neck and her plump firm shoulders, he struck his hands together and exclaimed, "Darling!"

He was happy but as it rained on their wedding day and the night that followed, the expression of despair did not leave his face.

As a married couple, they got on well together. She presided over the box office, looked after things in the summer garden, kept accounts and paid salaries; and her rosy cheeks, the radiance of her sweet artless smile showed now in the box office window, now in the wings of the theater, now at the buffet. And she was already telling her friends that the theater was the most remarkable, the most important, and the most essential thing in the world, and that it was only the theater that could give true pleasure and make you a cultivated and humane person.

"But do you suppose the public understands that?" she would ask. "What it wants is slapstick! Yesterday we gave 'Faust Inside Out,' and almost all the boxes were empty, and if Vanichka and I had put on something vulgar, I assure you the theater would have been packed. Tomorrow Vanichka and I are giving 'Orpheus in Hell.' Do come."

And what Kukin said about artists and the theater she would repeat. Like him she despised the public for its ignorance and indifference to art; she took a hand in the rehearsals, correcting the actors, kept an eye on the musicians, and when there was an unfavorable notice in the local paper, she wept and went to see the editor about it.

The actors were fond of her and called her "the darling," and "Vanichka-and-I." She was sorry for them and would lend them small sums, and if they cheated her, she cried in private but did not complain to her husband.

The pair got on just as well together when winter came. They leased the municipal theater for the season and sublet it for short periods to a Ukrainian troupe, a magician, or a local dramatic club. Olenka was gaining weight and beamed with happiness, but Kukin was getting thinner and more sallow and complained of terrible losses, although business was fairly good during the winter. He coughed at night, and she would make him an infusion of raspberries and linden blossoms, rub him with eau de Cologne and wrap him in her soft shawls.

"What a sweet thing you are!" she would say quite sincerely, smoothing his hair. "My handsome sweet!"

At Lent he left for Moscow to engage a company of actors for the summer season, and she could not sleep with him away. She sat at the window and watched the stars. It occurred to her that she had something in common with the hens: they too stayed awake all night and were disturbed when the cock was absent from the hen house. Kukin was detained in Moscow, and wrote that he would return by Easter, and in his letters he sent instructions about The Tivoli. But on the Monday of Passion Week, late in the evening, there was a sudden ominous knock at the gate: someone was banging at the wicket as though it were a barrel—boom, boom, boom! The sleepy cook, her bare feet splashing through the puddles, ran to open the gate.

"Open, please!" someone on the other side of the gate was saying in a deep voice. "There's a telegram for you."

Olenka had received telegrams from her husband before, but this time for some reason she was numb with fright. With trembling hands she opened the telegram and read the following:

Ivan Petrovich died suddenly today awaiting prot instructions tuneral Tuesday."

That is exactly how the telegram had it: "tuneral," and there was also the incomprehensible word "prot"; the signature was that of the director of the comic opera company.

"My precious!" Olenka sobbed. "Vanichka, my precious, my sweet! Why did we ever meet! Why did I get to know you and to love you! To whom can your poor unhappy Olenka turn?"

Kukin was buried on Tuesday in the Vagankovo Cemetery in Moscow. Olenka returned home on Wednesday, and no sooner did she enter her room than she sank onto the bed and sobbed so loudly that she could be heard in the street and in the neighboring courtyards.

"The darling!" said the neighbors, crossing themselves. "Darling Olga Semyonovna! How the poor soul takes on!"

Three months later Olenka was returning from Mass one day in deep mourning and very sad. It happened that one of her neighbors, Vasily Andreich Pustovalov, the manager of Babakayev's lumberyard, who was also returning from church, was walking beside her. He was wearing a straw hat and white waistcoat, with a gold watch-chain, and he looked more like a landowner than a businessman.

"There is order in all things, Olga Semyonovna," he was saying sedately, with a note of sympathy in his voice; "and if one of our dear ones passes on, then it means that this was the will of God, and in that case we must keep ourselves in hand and bear it submissively."

Having seen Olenka to her gate, he took leave of her and went further. All the rest of the day she heard his sedate voice, and as soon as she closed her eyes she had a vision of his dark beard. She liked him very much. And apparently she too had made an impression on him, because a little later a certain elderly lady, whom she scarcely knew, called to have coffee with her, and no sooner was she seated at table than the visitor began to talk about Pustovalov, saying that he was a fine, substantial man, and that any mar-riageable woman would be glad to go to the altar with him. Three days later Pustovalov himself paid her a visit. He did not stay more than ten minutes and he said little, but Olenka fell in love with him, so deeply that she stayed awake all night burning as with fever, and in the morning she sent for the elderly lady. The match was soon arranged and then came the wedding.

As a married couple Pustovalov and Olenka got on very well together. As a rule he was in the lumberyard till dinnertime, then he went out on business and was replaced by Olenka, who stayed in the office till evening, making out bills and seeing that orders were shipped.

"We pay twenty per cent more for lumber every year," she would say to customers and acquaintances. "Why, we used to deal in local timber, and now Vasichka has to travel to the province of Mogiley for timber regularly. And the freight rates!" she would exclaim, putting her hands to her cheeks in horror. "The freight rates!"

It seemed to her that she had been in the lumber business for ages, that lumber was the most important, the most essential thing in the world, and she found something intimate and touching in the very sound of such words as beam, log, batten, plank, box board, lath, scantling, slab...

At night she would dream of whole mountains of boards and planks, of endless caravans of carts hauling lumber out of town to distant points. She would dream that a regiment of beams, 28 feet by 8 inches, standing on end, was marching in the lumberyard, that beams, logs, and slabs were crashing against each other with the hollow sound of dry wood, that they kept tumbling down and rising again, piling themselves on each other. Olenka would scream in her sleep and Pustovalov would say to her tenderly: "Olenka, what's the matter, darling? Cross yourself!"

Whatever ideas her husband had, she adopted as her own. If he thought that the room was hot or that business was slow, she thought so too. Her husband did not care for entertainments and on holidays stayed home—

"You are always at home or in the office," her friends would say. "You ought to go to the theater, darling, or to the circus."

"Vasichka and I have no time for the theater," she would answer sedately. "We are working people, we're not interested in such foolishness. What good are these theaters?"

On Saturdays the two of them would go to evening service, on holidays they attended early Mass, and returning from the church they walked side by side, their faces wearing a softened expression. There was an agreeable aroma about them, and her silk dress rustled pleasantly. At home they had tea with shortbread, and various kinds of jam, and afterwards they ate pie. Every day at noon, in the yard and on the street just outside the gate, there was a delicious smell of borshch and roast lamb or duck, and on fast days there was the odor of fish, and one could not pass the Pustovalov gate without one's mouth watering.

In the office the samovar was always boiling and the customers were treated to tea with doughnuts. Once a week the pair went to the baths and returned side by side, both with red faces.

"Yes, everything goes well with us, thank God," Olenka would say to her friends. "I wish everyone were as happy as Vasichka and I."

When Pustovalov went off to the provinces of Mogilev for timber, she missed him badly and lay awake nights, crying. Sometimes, in the evening, a young army veterinary, by the name of Smirnin, who rented the wing of their house, would call on her. He chatted or played cards with her and that diverted her. What interested her most was what he told her about his domestic life. He had been married and had a son, but was separated from his wife because she had been unfaithful to him, and now he hated her; he sent her forty rubles a month for the maintenance of the child. And listening to him, Olenka would sigh and shake her head: she was sorry for him.

"Well, God keep you," she would say to him as she took leave of him, going to the stairs with him, candle in hand. "Thank you for relieving my boredom, and may the Queen of Heaven give you health!"

She always expressed herself in this sedate and reasonable manner, in imitation of her husband. Just as the veterinary would be closing the door behind him, she would recall him and say:

"You know, Vladimir Platonych, you had better make up with your wife. You ought to forgive her, at least for you son's sake! I am sure the little boy understands everything."

And when Pustovalov came back, she would tell him in low tones about the veterinary and his unhappy domestic life, and both of them would sigh and shake their heads and speak of the boy, who was probably missing his father. Then by a strange association of ideas they would both turn to the icons, bow down to the ground before them and pray that the Lord would grant them children.

Thus the Pustovalovs lived in peace and quiet, in love and harmony for Andreich went out without this cap to see about shipping some lumber, caught a chill and was taken sick. He was treated by the best doctors, but the illness had its own way with him, and he died after four months. Olenka was a widow again.

"To whom can I turn now, my darling?" she sobbed when she had buried her husband. "How can I live without you, wretched and unhappy as I am? Pity me, good people, left all alone in the world—"

She wore a black dress with white cuffs and gave up wearing a hat and gloves for good. She hardly ever left the house except to go to church or to visit her husband's grave, and at home she lived like a nun. Only at the end of six months did she take off her widow's weeds and open the shutters. Sometimes in the morning she was seen with her cook going to market for provisions, but how she lived now and what went on in her house could only be guessed. People based their guesses on such facts as that they saw her having tea with the veterinary in her little garden, he reading the newspaper aloud to her, and that, meeting an acquaintance at the post office, she would say:

"There is no proper veterinary inspection in our town, and that's why there is so much illness around. So often you hear of people getting ill from the milk or catching infections from horses and cows. When you come down to it. the health of domestic animals must be as well cared for as the health of human beings."

She now repeated the veterinary's words and held the same opinions about everything that he did. It was plain that she could not live even for one year without an attachment and that she had found new happiness in the wing of her house. Another woman would have been condemned for this, but of Olenka no one could think ill: everything about her was so unequivocal. Neither she nor the veterinary mentioned to anyone the change that had occurred in their relations; indeed, they tried to conceal it, but they didn't succeed, because Olenka could not keep a secret. When he had visitors, his regimental colleagues, she, pouring the tea or serving the supper, would begin to talk of the cattle plague, of the pearl disease, of the municipal slaughterhouses. He would be terribly embarrassed and when the guests had gone, he would grasp her by the arms and hiss angrily:

"I've asked you before not to talk about things that you don't understand! When veterinaries speak among themselves, please don't butt in! It's really annoying!"

She would look at him amazed and alarmed and ask, "But Volodickha what shall I talk about?"

And with tears in the eyes she would hug him and get him not to be angry, and both of them were happy.

Yet this happiness did not last long. The veterinary left, left forever, with his regiment, which was moved to some remote place, it may have been Siberia. And Olenka remained alone.

Now she was quite alone. Her father had died long ago, and his armchair stood in the attic, covered with dust and minus one leg. She got thinner and lost her looks, and passers-by in the street did not glance at her and smile as they used to. Obviously her best years were over, were behind her, and now a new kind of life was beginning for her, an unfamiliar kind that did not bear thinking of. In the evening Olenka sat on her porch, and heard the band play at The Tivoli and the rockets go off, but this no longer suggested anything to her mind. She looked apathetically at the empty courtyard, thought of nothing, and later, when night came she would go to bed and dream of the empty courtyard. She ate and drank as though involuntarily.

Above all, and worst of all, she no longer had any opinions whatever. She saw objects about her and understood what was going on, but she could not form an opinion about anything and did not know what to talk about. And how terrible it is not to have any opinions! You see, for instance, a bottle, or the rain, or a peasant driving in a cart, but what is the bottle for, or the rain, or the peasant, what is the meaning of them, you can't tell, and you couldn't, even if they paid you a thousand rubles. When Kukin was about, or Pustova-lov, or, later the veterinary, Olenka could explain it all and give her opinions about anything you like, but now there was the same emptiness in her head and in her heart as in the courtyard. It was weird, and she felt as bitter as if she had been eating wormwood.

Little by little the town was extending in all directions. Gypsy Road was now a regular street, and where The Tivoli had been and the lumberyards, houses had sprung up and lanes had multiplied. How swiftly time passes! Olenka's house had taken on a shabby look, the roof was rusty, the shed sloped, and the whole yard was invaded by burdock and stinging nettles. Olenka herself had aged and grown homely. In the summer she sat on the porch, feeling empty and dreary and bitter, as before; in the winter she sat by the window and stared at the snow. Sometimes at the first breath of spring or when the wind brought her the chime of church bells, memories of the past would overwhelm her, her heart would contract sweetly and her eyes would brim over with tears. But this only lasted a moment, and then there was again emptiness and once more she was possessed by a sense of the futility of life; Trot, the black kitten, rubbed against her and purred softly, but Olenka was not affected by these feline caresses. Is that what she needed? She needed an affection that would take possession of her whole being, her soul, her mind, that would give her ideas, a purpose in life, that would warm her aging blood. And she would shake the kitten off her lap, and say irritably: "Scat! Scat! Don't stick to me!"

And so it went, day after day, year after year, and no joy, no opinion! Whatever Mavra the cook would say, was well enough.

One hot July day, toward evening, when the cattle were being driven home and the yard was filled with clouds of dust, suddenly someone knocked at the gate. Olenka herself went to open it and was dumbfounded at what she saw: at the gate stood Smirnin, the veterinary, already gray and wearing civilian clothes. She suddenly recalled everything and, unable to control herself, burst into tears, silently letting her head drop on his breast. She was so agitated that she scarcely noticed how the two of them entered the house and sat down to tea.

"My dear," she murmured, trembling with joy. "Vladimir Platonych, how-ever did you get here?"

"I have come here for good," he explained. "I have retired from the army and want to see what it's like to be on my own and live a settled life. And besides, my son is ready for high school. I have made up with my wife, you know."

"Where is she?"

"She's at the hotel with the boy, and I'm out looking for lodgings."

"Goodness, Vladimir Platonych, take my house! You don't need to look further! Good Lord, and you can have it free," exclaimed Olenka, all in a flutter and beginning to cry again. "You live here in the house, and the wing will do for me. Heavens, I'm so glad!"

The next day they began painting the roof and whitewashing the walls, and Olenka, her arms akimbo, walked about the yard, giving orders. The old smile had come back to her face, and she was lively and spry, as though she had waked from a long sleep. Presently the veterinary's wife arrived, a thin, homely lady with bobbed hair who looked as if she were given to caprices. With her was the little boy, Sasha, small for his age (he was going on ten), chubby, with clear blue eyes and dimples in his cheeks.

No sooner did he walk into the yard than he began chasing the cat, and immediately his eager, joyous laughter rang out.

"Auntie, is that your cat?" he asked Olenka. "When she has little ones, please give us a kitten. Mama is terribly afraid of mice."

Olenka chatted with him, then gave him tea, and her heart suddenly grew warm and contracted sweetly, as if this little boy were her own son. And in the evening, as he sat in the dining-room doing his homework, she looked at him with pity and tenderness and whispered:

"My darling, my pretty one, my little one! How blond you are, and so clever!"

"An island," he was reciting from the book, "is a body of land entirely surrounded by water."

"An island is a body of land ..." she repeated and this was the first opinion she expressed with conviction after so many years of silence and mental vacuity.

She now had opinions of her own, and at supper she had a conversation with Sasha's parents, saying that studying in high school was hard on the children, but that nevertheless the classical course was better than the scientific one because a classical education opened all careers to you: you could be either a doctor or an engineer.

Sasha started going to high school. His mother went off to Kharkov to visit her sister and did not come back; every day his father left town to inspect herds and sometimes he stayed away for three days together, and it seemed to Olenka that Sasha was wholly abandoned, that he was unwanted, that he was being starved, and she moved him into the wing with her and settled him in a little room there.

For six months now Sasha has been living in his wing. Every morning Olenka comes into his room; he is fast asleep, his hand under his cheek, breathing quietly. She is sorry to wake him.

"Sashenka," she says sadly, "get up, my sweet! It's time to go to school."

He gets up, dresses, says his prayers, and sits down to his breakfast: he drinks three glasses of tea and eats two large doughnuts, and half a buttered French roll. He is hardly awake and consequently cross.

"You haven't learned the fable, Sashenka," says Olenka, looking at him as though she were seeing him off on a long journey. "You worry me. You must do your best, darling, study. And pay attention to your teachers."

"Please leave me alone!" says Sasha.

Then he walks down the street to school, a small boy in a big cap, with his books in a rucksack. Olenka follows him noiselessly.

"Sashenka!" she calls after him. He turns around and she thrusts a date or a caramel into his hand. When they turn into the school lane, he feels ashamed at being followed by a tall stout woman; he looks round and says: "You'd better go home, auntie; I can go alone now."

She stands still and stares after him until he disappears at the school entrance. How she loves him! Not one of her former attachments was so deep; never had her soul surrendered itself so unreservedly, so disinterestedly and with such joy as now when her maternal instinct was increasingly asserting itself. For this little boy who was not her own, for the dimples in his cheeks, for his very cap, she would have laid down her life, would have laid it down with joy, with tears of tenderness. Why? But who knows why?

Having seen Sasha off to school, she goes quietly home, content, fed, tranquil, brimming over with love; her face, grown younger in the last six months, beams with happiness; people meeting her look at her with pleasure and say:

"Good morning, Olga Semyonovna, darling! How are you, darling?"

"They make the children work so hard at high school nowadays," she says, as she does her marketing. "Think of it: yesterday in the first form they had a fable to learn by heart, a Latin translation and a problem for homework. That's entirely too much for a little fellow."

And she talks about the teachers, the lessons, the textbooks—saying just what Sasha says about them.

At three o'clock they have dinner together, in the evening they do the homework together, and cry. When she puts him to bed, she takes a long time making the sign of the cross over him and whispering prayers. Then she goes to bed and thinks of the future, distant and misty, when Sasha, having finished his studies, will become a doctor or an engineer, will have a large house of his own, horses, a carriage, will marry and become a father. She falls asleep and her dreams are of the same thing, and tears flow down her cheeks from her closed eyes. The black kitten lies beside her purring: Purr-purrr-purrr.

Suddenly there is a loud knock at the gate. Olenka wakes up, breathless with fear, her heart palpitating. Half a minute passes, and there is another knock.

"That's a telegram from Kharkov," she thinks, beginning to tremble from head to foot. "Sasha's mother is sending for him from Kharkov—O Lord!"

She is in despair. Her head, her hands, her feet grow chill and it seems to her that she is the most unhappy woman in the world. But another minutes passes, voices are head: it's the veterinary returning from the club.

"Well, thank God!" she thinks.

Little by little the load rolls off her heart and she is again at ease; she goes back to bed and thinks of Sasha who is fast sleep in the next room and sometimes shouts in his sleep:

"I'll give it to you! Scram! No fighting!"

Discussion Plan:

It is a natural response to feel sympathy for Olenka. She seems trapped into a role that severely limits her choices; whatever changes happen in her life, her responses reflect a pattern that she seems almost fated to repeat. Could this be true of many of us? Would an outsider to our culture see mindless repetitions where we see spontaneity and choice. For each of the social roles described below, explore some aspects of that role that might condition responses—resulting in lack of real freedom.

1. a high school teacher
2. a corporate vice president
3. a concert violinist
4. a football player
5. a young mother
6. a high school student
7. a world traveling hippie
8. a millionaire by inheritance
9. a world famous rock star
10. a Nobel prize winning scientist

Social Role

We do not live out our lives as solitary individuals. We inhabit stations in life and play social roles that define the range of our possibilities and the meaning of our experience. These roles differ from society to society and from social group to social group. In a society like ours, in which there is a great deal of personal mobility, values are not rigidly tied to social role or to group membership. In many other societies status defines the very essence of self and consequently the values applied to the person.

Aldous Huxley, Fard

They had been quarreling now for nearly three-quarters of an hour. Muted and inarticulate, the voices floated down the corridor, from the other end of the flat. Stooping over her sewing, Sophie wondered, without much curiosity, what it was all about this time. It was Madame's voice that she heard most often. Shrill with anger and indignant with tears, it burst out in gusts, in gushes. Monsieur was more self-controlled, and his deeper voice was too softly pitched to penetrate easily the closed doors and to carry along the passage. To Sophie, in her cold little room, the quarrel sounded, most of the time, like a series of monologues by Madame, interrupted by strange and ominous silences. But every now and then Monsieur seemed to lose his temper outright, and then there was no silence between the gusts, but a harsh, deep, angry shout. Madame kept up her loud shrillness continuously and without flagging; her voice had, even in anger, a curious, level monotony. But Monsieur spoke now loudly, now softly, with emphases and modulations and sudden outbursts, so that his contributions to the squabble, when they were audible, sounded like a series of separate explosions. Bow, wow, wow-wow-wow, wow-a dog barking rather slowly.

After a time Sophie paid no more heed to the noise of quarrelling. She was mending one of Madame's camisoles, and the work required all her attention. She felt very tired; her body ached all over. It had been a hard day; so had yesterday, so had the day before. Every day was a hard day, and she wasn't so young as she had been. Two years more and she'd be fifty. Every day had been a hard day since she could remember. She thought of the sacks of potatoes she used to carry when she was a little girl in the country. Slowly, slowly she was walking along the dusty road with the sack over her shoulder. Ten steps more; she could manage that. Only it never was the end; one always had to begin again.

She looked up from her sewing, moved her head from side to side, blinked. She had begun to see lights and spots of color dancing before her eyes; it often happened to her now. A sort of yellowish bright worm was wriggling up towards the right-hand corner of her field of vision; and though it was always moving upwards, upwards, it was always there in the same place. And there were starts of red and green that snapped and brightened and faded all round the worm. They moved between her and her sewing; they were there when she shut her eyes. After a moment she went on with her work; Madame wanted her camisole most particularly tomorrow morning. But it was difficult to see round the worm.

There was suddenly a great increase of noise form the other end of the corridor. A door had opened; words articulated themselves.

"... *bien tort, mon ami, si tu crois que je suis ton esclave. Je ferai ce que je voudrai."*

"Moi aussi." Monsieur uttered a harsh, dangerous laugh. There was the sound of heavy footsteps in the passage a rattling in the umbrella stand; then the front door banged.

Sophie looked down again at her work. Oh, the worm, the coloured stars, the aching fatigue in all her limbs! If one could only spend a whole day in bed—in a huge bed, feathery, warm and soft, all the day long....

The ringing of the bell startled her. It always made her jump, that furious wasplike buzzer. She got up, put her work down on the table, smoothed her apron, set straight her cap, and stepped out into the corridor. Once more the bell buzzed furiously. Madame was impatient.

"At last, Sophie. I thought you were never coming." Sophie said nothing; there was nothing to say. Madame was standing in front of the open wardrobe. A bundle of dresses hung over her arm, and there were more of them lying in a heap on the bed.

"Une beaute a la Rubens," her husband used to call her when he was in an amorous mood. He liked these massive, splendid, great women. None of your flexible drainpipes for him. "Helene Fourmont" was his pet name for her.

"Some day," Madame used to tell her friends, "some day I really must go to the Louvre and see my portrait. By Rubens, you know. It's extraordinary that one should have lived all one's life in Paris and never have seen the Louvre. Don't you think so?"

She was superb tonight. Her cheeks were flushed; her blue eyes shone with an unusual brilliance between their long lashes; her short, red-brown hair had broken wildly loose.

"Tomorrow, Sophie," she said dramatically, "we start for Rome. Tomorrow morning." She unhooked another dress from the wardrobe as she spoke, and threw it on to the bed. With the movement her dressing-gown flew open, and there was a vision of ornate underclothing and white exuberant flesh. "We must pack at once."

"For how long, Madame?"

"A fortnight, three months—how should I know?"

"It makes a difference, Madame."

"The important thing is to get away. I shall not return to this house, after what has been said to me tonight, till I am humbly asked to."

"We had better take the large trunk, then, Madame; I will go and fetch it."

The air in the backroom was sickly with the smell of dust and leather. The big trunk was jammed in a far corner. She had to bend and strain at it in order to pull it out. The worm and the coloured stars flickered before her eyes; she felt dizzy when she straightened herself. "I'll help you pack, Sophie," said Madame, when the servant returned, dragging the heavy trunk after her. What a death's-head the old woman looked nowadays! She hated having old, ugly people near her. But Sophie was so efficient; it would be madness to get rid of her.

"Madame need not trouble." There would be no end to it, Sophie knew, if Madame started opening drawers and throwing things about. "Madame had much better go to bed. It's late."

No, no. She wouldn't be able to sleep. She was to such a degree enervated. These men ...What an *embeastment*! One was not their slave. One would not be treated in this way.

Sophie was packing. A whole day in bed, in a huge, soft bed, like Madame's. One would doze, one would wake up for a moment, one would doze again.

"His latest game," Madame was saying indignantly, "is to tell me he hasn't got any money. I'm not to buy any clothes, he says. Too grotesque. I can't go about naked, can I?" She threw out her hands. "And as for saying he can't afford it, that's simply nonsense. He can, perfectly well. Only he's mean, mean, horribly mean. And if he'd only do a little honest work, for a change, instead of writing silly verses and publishing them at his own expense, he'd have plenty and to spare." She walked up and down the room. "Besides," she went on, "there's his old father. What's he for, I should like to know? 'You must be proud of having a poet for a husband,' he says." She made her voice quaver like an old man's. "It's all I can do not to laugh in his face. 'And what beautiful verses Hegesippe writes about you! What passion, what fire!'" Thinking of the old man, she grimaced, wobbled her head, shook her finger, doddered on her legs. "And when one reflects that poor Hegesippe is bald and dyes the few hairs he has left." She laughed. "As for the passion he talks so much about in his beastly verses," she laughed—"that's all pure invention. But, my good Sophie, what are you thinking of? Why are you packing that hideous old green dress?"

Sophie pulled out the dress without saying anything. Why did the woman choose this night to look so terribly ill? She had a yellow face and blue teeth. Madame shuddered; it was too horrible. She ought to send her to bed. But, after all, the work had to be done. What could one do about it? She felt more than ever aggrieved.

"Life is terrible." Sighing, she sat down heavily on the edge of the bed. The buoyant springs rocked her gently once or twice before they settled to rest.

"To be married to a man like this. I shall soon be getting old and fat. And never once unfaithful. But look how he treats me." She got up again and began to wander aimlessly about the room. "I won't stand it though," she burst out. She had halted in front of the long mirror, and was admiring her own splendid tragic figure. No one would believe, to look at her, that she was over thirty. Behind the beautiful tragedian she could see in the glass a thin, miserable, old creature, with a yellow face and blue teeth, crouching over the trunk. Really, it was too disagreeable. Sophie looked like one of those beggar women one sees on a cold morning, standing in the gutter. Does one hurry past, trying not to look at them? Or does one stop, open one's purse, and give them one's copper and nickel—even as much as a two-franc note, if one has no change? But whatever one did, one always felt uncomfortable, one always felt apologetic for one's furs. That was what came of walking. If one had a car—but that was another of Hegesippe's meannesses—one wouldn't, rolling along behind closed windows, have to be conscious of them at all. She turned away from the glass.

"I won't stand it," she said, trying not to think of the beggar woman, of blue teeth in a yellow face; "I won't stand it." She dropped into a chair.

But think of a lover with a yellow face and blue uneven teeth! She closed her eyes shuddered at the thought. It would be enough to make one sick. She felt impelled to take another look: Sophie's eyes were the color of greenish lead, quite without life. What was one to do about it? The woman's face was a reproach, an accusation. And besides, the sight of it was making her feel positively ill. She had never been so profoundly enervated.

Sophie rose slowly and with difficulty from her knees; an expression of pain crossed her face. Slowly she walked to the chest of drawers, slowly counted out six pairs of silk stockings. She turned back towards the trunk. The woman was a walking corpse.

"Life is terrible," Madame repeated with conviction. "Terrible, terrible, terrible."

She ought to send the woman to bed. But she would never be able to get packing done by herself. And it was so important to get off tomorrow morning. She had told Hegesippe she would go, and he had simply laughed; he hadn't believed it. She must give him a lesson this time. In Rome she would see Luigino. Such a charming boy, and a marquis, too. Perhaps ... But she could think of nothing but Sophie's face; the leaden eyes, the bluish teeth, the yellow, wrinkled skin.

"Sophie," she said suddenly, it was with difficulty that she could prevent herself screaming, "look on my dressing table. You'll see a box of rough, the Dorin number twenty-four. Put a little on your cheeks. And there's a stick of lip save in the right-hand drawer."

She kept her eyes resolutely shut while Sophie got up—with what a horrible creaking of the joints!—walked over to the dressing table, and stood there, rustling faintly through what seemed an eternity. What a life, my God what a life! Slow footsteps trailed back again. She opened her eyes. Oh, that was far better, far better.

"Thank you, Sophie. You look much less tired now." She got up briskly. "And now we must hurry." Full of energy she ran to the wardrobe. "Goodness me," she exclaimed, throwing up her hands,, "You've forgotten to put in my blue evening dress. How could you be so stupid, Sophie?"

Discussion Plan:

1. Despite her wealth and authority how is Madame a product of her culture?
2. How is Sophie shown to be a product of her culture?
3. What personal values does Madame represent?
4. How does Sophie represent the dilemma of the formation of self within culture?
5. How are social roles given? Are they assigned? Are they chosen?
6. What is the relationship between the personality of an individual and the social role? Which role is Madame most suited for? Sophie?
7. What is the relationship of the changing cultural context to the problem of social roles?
8. What values does the author assume in his telling of the story?
9. What values do you, as reader, bring to the story?

Exercise:

How do social roles define the self?

Below is a list of social roles; for each of those list ways that people who fill these roles see themselves. Choose either personality traits or characteristic forms of behavior.

1. teacher	6. punk rock fan
2. father	7. hippie
3. policeman	8. campus queen
4. athlete	9. computer wiz
5. nurse	10. student

Go through the list of traits and actions that you have compiled. Show how each one contributes, if it does, to the fulfillment of the role.

Could the roles be fulfilled in the absence of some of the traits?

Are any of the traits destructive to other aspects of personality or behavior?

Professional Role

We are, among other things, what we do. But we do many things, many of them generating conflicting views of the self. And some of the time we pretend to be things that are incompatible with what we feel we are really. Some of the time we lose track.

Time Magazine, Lost Identity

Last November at Bacon's, a department store outside Louisville, the store detective nabbed a man she thought was about to steal $157 worth of clothing. He said his name was Pat Salamone and produced a driver's license as identification. Louisville police booked Salamone and discovered that he was actually Patrick Livingston, a local FBI agent.

As part of an FBI sting operation from 1977 until 1980, Livingston used the alias "Pat Salamone" while masquerading as a Miami pornography distributor. He hobnobbed with gangsters, buying their smut, counterfeit Hollywood films and even 50 submachine guns. The sting ended in 54 arrests, but for Livingston the charade had become muddled with reality. He kept bank accounts in his pseudonym and introduced himself regularly as Pat Salamone. According to Fred Schwartz, the Assistant U.S. Attorney prosecuting the sting defendants, Livingston has "psychiatric problems that make it difficult for him to distinguish between his real identity and his undercover identity."

Livingston, 37, realized during the undercover operation that he had submerged himself into the fantasy, and went to a psychiatrist. His friendships dissolved; he separated from his wife.

An FBI agent for twelve years, Livingston was especially adept at undercover work, frequently risking death. Says William Brown, his attorney and an old friend: "Anyone who lives the extremely stressful five years that Pat has lived will manifest the stress in some manner. The FBI has had no program to prepare agents for living a schizophrenic life."

Ten of the sting's targets have been convicted so far. Some of the other defendants cite Livingston's seeming mental problems in their defense. The shoplifting charges against Livingston were dropped, and he is now posted to the FBI office in Chicago. He returns periodically to Miami to testify against his dupes.

Exercise:

Rate the following situations from 'I' to '5' as to their potential for generating a level of involvement that would alter your personality.

1. You are normally very shy; you go away for the summer and have a summer romance.
2. You spend a summer with a cousin that is into motorcycles.
3. You have the opportunity to tour for a summer with a rock band.
4. You have a secret affair with an older person.
5. You do psychodelics regularly at summer camp.
6. You take a summer internship with a TV producer.
7. You work as a sweeper in a factory over Christmas vacation.
8. You join a martial arts class.
9. You start to hang around with a street gang.
10. You become a part of a school project to visit the elderly.
11. You get the lead in the musical comedy and play a prostitute.
12. You play Hitler in a play that has twenty performances.
13. You write a term paper on racism.
14. You are elected student chairman of the school senate.
15. You become a counselor for a group of retarded children.

Race

In our society, as in most others, being racially or culturally different creates severe problems for the development of self. The tremendous diversity of the people in our society increases the tension. The tendency to judge people of different ethnic groups harshly exists side by side with the need to find some accommodation between the various groups that are thrown together in the 'melting pot'. For the individual trying to come to terms with racial or ethnic prejudice the job of finding one's self often includes coping with racism inherited and encountered.

Jesus Colon, Little Things Are Big

It was very late at night on the eve of Memorial Day. She came into the subway at the 34th Street Pennsylvania Station. I am still trying to remember how she managed to push herself in with a baby on her right arm, a valise in her left hand and two children, a boy and gal about three and five years old, trailing after her. She was a nice looking white lady in her early twenties.

At Nevins Street, Brooklyn, we saw her preparing to get off at the next station—Atlantic Avenue—which happened to be the place where I too had to get off. Just as it was a problem for her to get on, it was going to a problem for her to get off the subway with two small children to be taken care of a baby on her right arm and a medium sized valise in her left hand.

And there I was, also preparing to get off at Atlantic Avenue, with no bundles to take care of—not even the customary book under my arm without which I feel that I am not completely dressed.

As the train was entering the Atlantic Avenue station, some white man stood up from his seat and helped her out, placing the children on the long, deserted platform. There were only two adult persons on the long platform some time after midnight on the eve of last Memorial Day.

I could perceive the steep, long concrete stairs going down to the Long Island Railroad or into the street. Should I offer my help as the American white man did at the subway door placing the two children outside the subway car? Should I take care of the girl and the boy, take them by their hands until they reached the end of the steep long concrete stairs of the Atlantic Avenue station?

Courtesy is a characteristic of the Puerto Rican. And here I was—a Puerto Rican—hours past midnight, a valise, two white children and a white lady with a baby on her arm palpably needing somebody to help her at least until she descended the long concrete stairs.

But how could I, a Negro and a Puerto Rican, approach this white lady who very likely might have preconceived prejudices against Negroes and everybody with foreign accents, in a deserted subway station very late at night?

What would she say? What would be the first reaction of this white American woman, perhaps coming from a small town, with a valise, two children and a baby on her right arm? Would she say: Yes, of course you may help me. Or would she think that I was just trying to get too familiar? Or would she think worse than that perhaps? What would I do if she let out a scream as I went toward her to offer my help?

Was I misjudging her? So many slanders are written every day in the daily press against the Negroes and Puerto Ricans. I hesitated for a long, long minute. The ancestral manners that the most illiterate Puerto Rican passes on from father to son were struggling inside me. Here was I, way past midnight, face to face with a situation that could very well explode into an outburst of prejudices and chauvinistic conditioning of the "divide and rule" policy of present day society.

It was a long minute. I passed on by her as if I saw nothing. As if I was insensitive to her need. Like a rude animal walking on two legs, I just moved on half running by the long subway platform leaving the children and the valise and her with the baby on her arm. I took the steps of the long concrete stairs in twos until I reached the street above and the cold air slapped my warm face.

This is what racism and prejudice and chauvinism and official artificial divisions can do to people and to a nation!

Perhaps the lady was not prejudiced after all. Or not prejudiced enough to scream at the coming of a Negro toward her at a solitary subway station a few hours past midnight.

If you were not that prejudiced, I failed you, dear lady. I know that there is a chance in a million that you will read these lines. I am willing to take that millionth chance. If you were not that prejudiced, I failed you, lady. I failed you, children. I failed myself to myself.

I buried my courtesy early on Memorial Day morning. But here is a promise that I make to myself here and now; if I am ever faced with an occasion like that again, I am going to offer my help regardless of how the offer is going to be received.

Then I will have my courtesy with me again.

Discussion Plan:

1. Can a person rise above the prejudice that he encounters?
2. Do other people's attitudes towards you justify your actions towards them?
3. Is a person justified in fearing people on the basis of common beliefs?
4. Should people be suspicious when they are responsible for the well being of others?
5. Should an individual try to change his own attitudes or wait until the society justifies such a change?

Exercise:

Rising above the circumstances:

In the following decide whether you ought to help.
1. Someone is drowning and you can't swim. Should you try to save him?
2. A beggar asks you for some money, but you have only your carfare and $1.
3. A friend asks you for an old term paper for a course.
4. A friend asks whether he can use your parents' house when they are away and you know your parents would disapprove.
5. A person asks you to be a witness to a car accident.
6. A friend asks you to store drugs in your house.
7. A girlfriend asks you to let her stay at your house after an abortion so that her parents won't find out.
8. You are asked to chip in for a present for a teacher you dislike.
9. You are questioned about a fight in school by the principal and the truth is that your best friend started it.
10. You are terrified of heights but all your friends want to go rock climbing—either you pay your share or they can't go.

RELIGION

People are categorized within many kinds of frameworks, social role, race and religion are among the most pervasive. What is most interesting about such modes of classification is that we frequently give them more credence than we give our own estimation of the individual's worth. We refer to the labels rather than to the particular circumstances within which the judgment is to be made. We appeal to the category although we know that the individual differences between the people in the category are significant and important, frequently outweighing the similarities on the basis of which they are categorized.

Jerome Weidman,
I Thought About This Girl

I thought about this girl quite a lot. We all did—my mother, my father, my brothers, all of us. It seemed silly to let ourselves be upset by a girl who worked for us, but we couldn't help it. She worried us. All we knew was that for a long time she was happy with us, and then suddenly she wasn't.

She said nothing, of course, right up to the end. She was too considerate and friendly and kind to say anything, but we could tell. We could tell by the way she stood behind the counter in our little bakery, by the way she served a customer. She used to laugh all the time and keep the whole store bright with her energy and her smile and her pleasant voice. People spoke about it. It was such a pleasure to be served by her, they said.

"The smartest thing I ever did," my father would say with a smile as he watched her. "Hiring that girl was the smartest thing I ever did."

It wasn't that way very long, though. Not that we had any fault to find. She still came in early. She still worked hard. She still was polite and friendly and quick, but it wasn't the same. She didn't laugh any more. She stood very quietly when it wasn't busy and looked out of the window. She was worried about something.

At first we thought it would pass away, but it didn't. It got worse and worse. We did the obvious thing, of course. We asked her what was wrong.

"Nothing," she said at once, smiling quickly. "Nothing is wrong."

We asked her many times, but we still got the same answer, and knew it wasn't true.

It annoyed my mother.

"Why should we be bothered like this?" she asked sharply. "We've treated her like a daughter. Why should she be unhappy? Anyway, we didn't need her to start with."

And, of course, we didn't. We had always managed pretty well in the store. We were seldom overworked, because it is only a small bakeshop, though business is brisk and profitable. It happened very simply. A woman, a very good customer of ours, came in one day and told us about her—a poor girl from Poland, whose parents were still on the other side and who had no one here to take care of her except an old aunt, herself far from wealthy. Wouldn't it be wonderful, this customer said to my mother, if it were possible to find some sort of job for the girl, something to help her support herself and make her less of a burden to her aunt? My mother was sympathetic and interested at once—she is always like that—and the woman went on to wonder casually if we mightn't be able to find a place for this girl in our own shop. Poor Mother was too far gone in compassion to realize that she had been trapped, and said quickly that we certainly could; she would talk to my father.

At first, of course, we laughed. There was scarcely enough work in the shop to keep all of us busy. It seemed ridiculous to hire anybody else.

"We'll be waiting on each other," my father said.

In the end, honever, Mother brought us around. We can afford it, she said, and think how nice it would be to have a young girl's face in the store, how nice for the customers. Her arguments weren't very impressive, but Father seldom denies Mother anything she wants, so he said all right, let's take a look at her. And then, of course, as soon as we saw her, we were lost. She was so fresh and cheerful and bright, with her round face and her ready smile and her yellow hair.

"My God," my father said, "she looks like she was made for a bakery."

He pinched his chin between his thumb and forefinger and said well, maybe now he'd be able to have a little time for himself. There was a book on elementary chemistry that he'd been nibbling at cautiously for almost thirty years, ever since he came to America. Now, he said, he might get a chance to read it. There were also a lot of things my mother had always wanted to do. There were dishes she had yearned to make but had never dared try. Now she'd have time to experiment a little.

"You'll be able to cook," my father roared. "After thirty years you'll finally be able to cook."

It was a boisterous and happy occasion. The girl had done that for us.

After she had been with us a short while, however, we began to notice that my father hadn't made much progress with his chemistry and that there were no startling innovations at my mother's table. We knew the reason, of course. The habits of thirty years are not easily broken, and they were spending as much time as ever in the shop. But nobody seemed to mind. It was pleasant just to watch this girl with her bouncing energy and her happy laugh. Often my father would cock his head admiringly and repeat, "Smartest thing I ever did, hiring that girl."

Then suddenly he didn't say it any more. He still thought the world of her. We all did, but he was just as worried as the rest of us. What was wrong? Why was she no longer happy?

Before we could find an answer, and before our vague irritation could turn to anger, however, she came to us. She said she was leaving.

It was typical of her to wait until we were all together before she told us. She could have told my father or my mother or any one of us, but she knew how we all felt about her. It was hard for her to say it to all of us at the same time. She picked the harder way, because it seemed to her to be the right way.

"Leaving?" we asked, startled.

"Yes," she said quietly, dropping her eyes from ours. "I must leave."

Apparently it was something she had been wanting to tell us for a long time, something she had been afraid to tell us.

"But why?" we asked. "Why are you leaving?"

She didn't answer. She just shook her head and bit her lip.

"Aren't you happy here?" we asked.

"I am very happy here," she said.

"Don't we pay you enough?" we asked. "Do you want more?"

She shook her head quickly.

"No," she said. "You pay me enough."

We didn't want to make her cry, but somehow we couldn't stop asking questions.

"You have another job, maybe? A better one?"

She shook her head again.

"No, I have no other job."

"But you need a job, don't you?"

"Yes," she said. "I need a job."

"Then why?"

She didn't want to tell us, but we liked her too well not to insist on knowing.

"You can tell us, Mary," my mother said kindly. "We are your friends. You can tell us."

She looked up at us. She seemed confused and beaten, but she saw she would have to tell us.

"My mother,' she began almost inaudibly, "my mother wrote me a letter from Poland—"

She stopped to blink away the tears, and then began again.

"My mother wrote me it isn't right," she said softly, brokenly. "She says it isn't right to—it isn't right to work for Jews."

She kept her puzzled, tearful glance upon us for another moment. Then she turned and walked away, her shoulders shaking with her sobs.

Exercise:

Characteristics that count:

Below are a list of characteristics that are frequently used to make judgments about others. They are criteria on the basis of which we make decisions about a person's social rights and obligations. For the following; what are some judgments that these criteria are justifiably used to make?

1. being eighteen
2. having a high school diploma
3. being Catholic
4. completing medical school
5. getting at least 65% on an exam
6. being white
7. being male
8. being married
9. passing a job interview
10. being the best candidate for a position
11. getting the most votes

Go back over the list. This time find judgments that might be made on the basis of these criteria that you would not feel are justified.

Sexual Identity

Among our most deeply seated prejudices are those associated with appearance and with sex. We are frequently harsh in our judgment of people who deviate from social norms for acceptable appearance. Until very recently we were extraordinarily intolerant of those that did not comply with the social restrictions placed on sexual behavior, most especially those whose sexual practices did not correspond to the demands of gender, i.e. homosexuals of whatever sort. Our intolerance is deeply rooted in a number of social practices that define separate and non-overlapping roles for males and females, requiring distinctive patterns of appearance, attitude and behavior.

Frederick Pohl, Day Million

Dora—we will call her that; her "name" was omicron-Dibase seven-group totter-ootS Doradus 5314, the last part of which is a colour specification corresponding to a shade of green—Dora, I say, was feminine, charming and cute. I admit she doesn't sound that way. She was, as you might put it, a dancer. Her art involved qualities of intellection and expertise of a very high order, requiring both tremendous natural capacities and endless practice; it was performed in null-gravity and I can best describe it by saying that it was something like the performance of a contortionist and something like classical ballet, maybe resembling Danilova's dying swan. It was also pretty damned sexy. In a symbolic way, to be sure, but face it, most of the things we call "sexy" are symbolic, you know, except perhaps an exhibitionist's open clothing. On Day Million when Dora danced, the people who saw her panted, and you would too.

About this business of her being a boy. It didn't matter to her audiences that genetically she was male. It wouldn't matter to you, if you were among them, because you wouldn't know it—not unless you took a biopsy cutting of her flesh and put it under an electron-microscope to find the XY chromosome—and it didn't matter to them because they didn't care. Through techniques which are not only complex but haven't yet been discovered, these people were able to determine a great deal about the aptitudes and casements of babies quite a long time before they were born—at about the second horizon of cell-division, to be exact, when the segmenting egg is becoming a free blastocyst—and then they naturally helped those aptitudes along. Wouldn't we? If we find a child with an aptitude for music we give him a scholarship to Juilliard. If they found a child whose aptitudes were for being a woman, they made him one. As sex had long been dissociated from reproduction this was relatively easy to do and caused no trouble and no, at least very little, comment.

How much is "very little"? Oh, about as much as would be caused by our own tampering with Divine Will by filling a tooth. Less than would be caused by wearing a hearing aid. Does it sound awful? Then look closely at the next busty baby you meet and reflect that she may be a Dora, for adults who are genetically male but somatically female are far from unknown even in our own time. An accident of environment in the womb overwhelms the blueprints of heredity. The difference is that with us it happens only by accident and we don't know about it except rarely, after close study; whereas the people of Day Milllion did it often, on purpose, because they wanted to.

Well, that's enough to tell you about Dora. It would only confuse you to add that she was seven feet tall and smelled of peanut butter. Let us begin our story.

On Day Million, Dora swam out of her house, entered a tranportation tube, was sucked briskly to the surface in its flow of water and ejected in its plume of spray to an elastic platform in front of her—ah—call it her rehearsal hall.

"Oh, hell!" she cried in pretty confusion, reaching out to catch her balance and finding herself tumbled against a total stranger, whom we will call Don.

They met cute. Don was on his way to have his legs renewed. Love was the furthest thing from his mind. But when, absentmindedly taking a shortcut across the landing platform for submarites and finding himself drenched, he discovered his arms full of he loveliest girl he had ever seen, he knew at once they were meant for each other. "Will you marry me?" he asked. She said softly, "Wednesday," and the promise was like a caress.

Don was tall, muscular, bronze and exciting. His name was no more Don than Dora's was Dora, but the personal part of it was Adonis in tribute to his vibrant maleness, and so we will call him Don for short. His personality colour-code, in Angstrom units, was 5,290, or only a few degrees bluer than Dora's 5,314—a measure of what they had intuitively discovered at first sight; that they possessed many affinities of taste and interest.

I despair of telling you exactly what it was that Don did for a living—I don't mean for the sake of making money, I mean for the sake of giving purpose and meaning to his life, to keep him from going off his nuts with boredom—except to say that it involved a lot of travelling in interstellar spaceships. In order to make a spaceship go really fast, about thirty-one male and seven genetically female human beings had to do certain things, and Don was one of the thirty-one. Actually, he contemplated options. This involved a lot of exposure to radiation flux—not so much from his own station in the propulsive system as in the spillover form the next stage, where a genetic female preferred selections, and the sub-nuclear particles making the selections she preferred demolished themselves in a shower of quanta. Well, you don't give a rat's ass for that, but it meant that Don had to be clad at all times in a skin of light, resilient, extremely strong copper-coloured metal. I have already mentioned this, but you probably thought I meant he was sunburned.

More than that, he was a cybernetic man. Most of his ruder parts had long since replaced with mechanisms of vastly more permanence and use. A cadmium centrifuge, not a heart, pumped his blood. His lungs moved only when he wanted to speak out loud, for a cascade of osmotic filters rebreathed oxygen out of his own wastes. In a way, he probably would have looked peculiar to a man from the 20th century, with his glowing eyes and seven-fingered hands. But to himself, and of course to Dora, he looked mighty manly and grand. In the course of his voyages Don had circled Proxima Centauri, Procyon and the puzzling worlds of Mira Ceti; he had carried agricultural templates to the planets of Canopus and brought back warm, witty pets from the pale companion of Aldebaran. Blue-hot or red-cool, he had seen a thousand stars and their ten thousand planets. He had, in fact, been travelling the starlanes, with only brief leaves on Earth, for pushing two centuries. But you don't care about that, either. It is people who make stories, not the circumstances they find themselves in, and you want to hear about these two people. Well, they made it. The great thing they had for each other grew and flowered and burst into fruition on Wednesday, just as Dora had promised. They met at the encoding room, with a couple of well-wishing friends apiece to cheer them on, and while their identities were being taped and stored they smiled and whispered to each other and bore the jokes of their friends with blushing repartee. Then they exchanged their mathematical analogues and went away, Dora to her dwelling beneath the surface of the sea and Don to his ship.

It was an idyll, really. They lived happily ever after—or anyway, until they decided not to bother any more and died.

Of course, they never set eyes on each other again.

* * * * * * * *

Oh, I can see you now, you eaters of charcoal-broiled steak, scratching an incipient bunion with one hand and holding this story with the other, while the stereo plays d'Indy or Monk. You don't believe a word of it, do you? Not for one minute. People wouldn't live like that, you say with a grunt as you get up to put fresh ice in a drink.

And yet there's Dora, hurrying back through the flushing commuter pipes toward her underwater home (she prefers it there; has had herself somatically altered to breathe the stuff). If I tell you with what sweet fulfillment she fits the recorded analogue of Don into the symbol manipulator, hooks herself in and turns herself on ... if I try to tell you any of that you will simply stare. Or glare; and grumble, what the hell kind of love-making is this? And yet I assure you, friend, I really do assure you that Dora's ecstasies are as creamy and passionate as any of James Bond's lady spies', and one hell of a lot more so than anything you are going to find in "real life." Go ahead, glare and grumble. Dora doesn't care. If she thinks of you at all, her thirty-times-great-great-grandfather, she thinks you're a pretty primordial sort of brute.

You are. Why, Dora is farther removed from you than you are from the australopithecines of five thousand centuries ago. You could not swim a second in the strong currents of her life. You don't think progress goes in a straight line, do you? Do you recognize that it is an ascending, accelerating, maybe even exponential curve? It takes hell's own time to get started, but when it goes it goes like a bomb. And you, you Scotch-drinking steak-eater in your relaxacizing chair, you've just barely lighted the primacord of the fuse. What is it now, the six or seven hundred thousandth day after Christ? Dora lives in Day Million, the millionth day of the Christian Era. Ten thousand years from now. Her body fats are polyunsaturated, like Crisco. Her wastes are haemodialysed out of her bloodstream while she sleeps—that means she doesn't have to go to the bathroom. On whim, to pass a slow half-hour, she can command more energy than the entire nation of Portugal can spend today, and use it to launch a weekend satellite or remould a crater on the Moon. She loves Don very much. She keeps his every gesture, mannerism, nuance, touch of hand, thrill of intercourse, passion of kiss stored in symbolic mathematical form. And when she wants him, all she has to do is turn the machine on and she has him.

And Don, of course, has Dora. Adrift on a sponson city a few hundred yards over her head, or orbiting Areturus fifty light years away, Don has only to command his own symbol-manipulator to rescue Dora from the ferrite files and bring her to life for him, and there she is; and rapturously, tirelessly they love all night. Not in the flesh, of course, but then his flesh has been extensively altered and it wouldn't really be much fun. He doesn't need the flesh for pleasure. Genital organs feel nothing. Neither do hands, nor breasts, nor lips; they are only receptors, accepting and transmitting impulses. It is the brain that feels; it is the interpretation of those impulses that makes agony or orgasm, and Don's symbol manipulator gives him the analogue of cuddling, the analogue of kissing, the analogue of wild, ardent hours with the eternal, exquisite and incorruptible analogue of Dora. Or Diane. Or sweet Rose, or laughing Alicia; for to be sure, they have each of them exchanged analogues before, and will again.

Rats, you say, it looks crazy to me. And you—with your aftershave lotion and your little red car, pushing papers across a desk all day and chasing tail all night—tell me, just how the hell do you think you would look to Tiglath-Pileser, say or Attila the Hun?

Discussion Plan:

Tolerance:

The author tries to justify the behavior of the characters by, eventually, showing us how different they are from us. First, list all the behaviors that you think the author expects you to be disturbed by. Then list the characteristics that the author presents as compensations.

1. Are the behaviors described repulsive in ordinary people?
2. Which of the characteristics of the characters compensate for the repugnant behaviors?
3. Do you think that the behavior described would be inappropriate in a society of people like ourselves?
4. Are there any characteristics of ordinary people that would justify the behavior that you identify in question 3?
5. What characteristics does the author attribute to the reader that you find repugnant?
6. Do you think they were repugnant to people when the story was first published?.

The Givens

Our bodies and the feelings that go with them are among the things that we identify with most closely. But they do not always meet with our expectations or our ideals. Such disappointment with ourselves breeds other feelings, negative feelings of self-censure and self-doubt. This frequently results in hostility turned outward as well as inward. Which of all of these are we responsible for? How can we stop the vicious circle of negativity feeding into more negativity?

Hugh Prather, Notes to Myself

...Both my body and my emotions were
given to me and it is as futile for me
to condemn myself for feeling scared,
insecure, selfish or revengeful as it is for
me to get mad at myself for the size of
my feet. I am not responsible for my
feelings, but for what I do with them.
It is equally as useless for me to be
disgruntled about having had the thought I
just had as it is for me to criticize myself
for something I did last year. Okay, that
is what I just thought—now this is what
I'm thinking....

Exercise:

Rate the following on a scale of '1' to '5'. '1' are the things you are least responsible for; '5', the things you are most responsible for.

1. your weight
2. your race
3. your parents' economic status
4. your appearance
5. getting angry
6. crying in public
7. being prejudiced against other ethnic groups
8. cheating on exams
9. failing exams
10. having the I. Q. you do
11. not loving your boyfriend any more
12. getting disgusted at your father's table manners
13. wanting to quit school
14. being afraid of the water
15. hating mathematics

Obligations

We frequently judged in terms of how well we fulfill our obligations. To be a good person is often defined in terms of being a good student or a good daughter, a good friend or a good worker. But these obligations imposed upon us by the outside world, are often felt to be external to the center of our personality. The things that are expected of us are frequently seen by us as foreign to what we truly strive to be. Even though they start as external pressure, obligations can become so important to our sense of self that we cannot conceive of ourselves apart from them.

Leo Tolstoy, Alyosha the Pot

Alyosha was a younger brother. He was nicknamed 'the Pot,' because once, when his mother sent him with a pot of milk for the deacon's wife, he stumbled and broke it. His mother thrashed him soundly, and the children in the village began to tease him, calling him 'the Pot.' Alyosha the Pot: and this is how he got his nickname.

Alyosha was a skinny little fellow, lop-eared—his ears stuck out like wings —and with a large nose. The children always teased him about this, too, saying 'Alyosha has a nose like a gourd on a pole!'

There was a school in the village where Alyosha lived, but reading and writing and such did not come easy for him, and besides there was no time to learn. His older brother lived with a merchant in town, and Alyosha had begun helping his father when still a child. When he was only six years old, he was already watching over his family's cow and sheep with his younger sister in the common pasture. And long before he was grown, he had started taking care of their horses day and night. From his twelfth year he plowed and carted. He hardly had the strength for all these chores, but he did have a certain manner—he was always cheerful. When the children laughed at him, he fell silent or laughed himself. If his father cursed him, he stood quietly and listened. And when they finished and ignored him again, he smiled and went back to whatever task was before him.

When Alyosha was nineteen years old, his brother was taken into the army, and his father arranged for Alyosha to take his brother's place as a servant in the merchant's household. He was given his brother's old boots and his father's cap and coat and was taken into town. Alyosha was very pleased with his new clothes, but the merchant was quite dissatisfied with his appearance.

'I thought you would bring me a young man just like Semyon,' said the merchant, looking Alyosha over carefully. 'But you've brought me such a sniveller. What's he good for?'

'Ah, he can do anything—harness and drive anywhere you like. And he's a glutton for work. Only looks like a stick. He's really very wiry.'

'That much is plain. Well, we shall see.'

'And above all he's a meek one. Loves to work.'

'Well, what can I do? Leave him.'

And so Alyosha began to live with the merchant.

The merchant's family was not large. There were his wife, his old mother and three children. His older married son, who had only completed grammar school, was in business with his father. His other son, a studious sort, had been graduated from the high school and was for a time at the university, though he had been expelled and now lived at home. And there was a daughter, too, a young girl in the high school.

At first they did not like Alyosha. He was too much the peasant and was poorly dressed. He had no manners and addressed everyone familiarly as in the country. But soon they grew used to him. He was a better servant than his brother and was always very responsive. Whatever they set him to do he did willingly and quickly, moving from one task to another without stopping. And at the merchant's, just as at home, all the work was given to Alyosha. The more he did, the more everyone heaped upon him. The mistress of the household and her old mother-in-law, and the daughter, and the younger son, even the merchant's clerk and the cook—all sent him here and sent him there and ordered him to do everything that they could think of. The only thing that Alyosha ever heard was 'Run do this, fellow,' or 'Alyosha, fix this up now,' or 'Did you forget, Alyosha? Look here, fellow don't you forget!' And Alyosha ran, and fixed, and looked, and did not forget, and managed to do everything and smiled all the while.

Alyosha soon wore out his brother's boots, and the merchant scolded him for walking about in tatters with his bare feet sticking out and ordered him to buy new boots in the market. These boots were truly new, and Alyosa was very happy with them, but his feet remained old all the same, and by evening they ached so from running that he got mad at them. Alyosha was afraid that when his father came to collect his wages, he would be very annoyed that the master had deducted the cost of the new boots from his pay.

In winter Alyosha got up before dawn, chopped firewood, swept out the courtyard, fed grain to the cow and the horses and watered them. Afterwards, he lit the stoves, cleaned the boots and coats of all the household, got out the samovars and polished them. Then, either the clerk called him into the shop to take out the wares or the cook ordered him to knead the dough and to wash the pans. And later he would be sent into town with a message, or to the school for the daughter, or to fetch lamp oil or something else for the master's old mother. 'Where have you been loafing, you worthless thing?' one would say to him, and then another. Or among themselves they would say 'Why go yourself? Alyosha will run for you. Alyosha, Alyosha!' And Alyosha would run.

Alyosha always ate breakfast on the run and was seldom in time for dinner. The cook was always chiding him, because he never took meals with the others, but for all that she did feel sorry for him and always left him something hot for dinner and for supper.

Before and during holidays there was a lot more work for Alyosha, though he was happier during holidays, because then everyone gave him tips, not much, only about sixty kopeks usually; but it was his own money, which he could spend as he chose. He never laid eyes on his wages, for his father always came into town and took from the merchant Alyosha's pay, giving him only the rough edge of his tongue for wearing out his brother's boots too quickly. When he had saved two rubles altogether from tips, Alyosha bought on the cook's advice a red knitted sweater. When he put it on for the first time and looked down at himself, he was so surprised and delighted that he just stood in the kitchen gaping and gulping.

Alyosha said very little, and when he did speak, it was always to say something necessary abruptly and briefly. And when he was told to do something or other or was asked if he could do it, he always answered without the slightest hesitation, 'I can do it.' And he would immediately throw himself into the job and do it.

Alyosha did not know how to pray at all. His mother had once taught him the words, but he forgot even as she spoke. Nonetheless, he did pray, morning and evening, but simply, just with his hands, crossing himself.

Thus Alyosha lived for a year and a half, and then, during the second half of the second year, the most unusual experience of his life occurred. This experience was his sudden discovery, to his complete amazement, that besides those relationships between people that arise from the need that one may have for another, there also exist other relationships that are completely different: not a relationship that a person has with another because that other is needed to clean boots, to run errands, or to harness horses; but a relationship that a person has with another who is in no way necessary to him, simply because that other one wants to serve him and to be loving to him. And he discovered, too, that he, Alyosha, was just such a person. He realized all this through the cook Ustinja. Ustinja was an orphan, a young girl yet, and as hard a worker as Alyosha. She began to feel sorry for Alyosha, and Alyosha for the first time in his life felt that he himself, not his services, but he himself was needed by another person. When his mother had been kind to him or had felt sorry for him, he took no notice of it, because it seemed to him so natural a thing, just the same as if he felt sorry for himself. But suddenly he realized that Ustinja, though completely a stranger, felt sorry for him, too. She always left him a pot of kasha with butter, and when he ate, she sat with him, watching him with her chin propped upon her fist. And when he looked up at her and she smiled, he, too, smiled.

It was all so new and so strange that at first Alyosha was frightened. He felt that it disturbed his work, his serving, but he was nonetheless very happy. And when he happened to look down and notice his trousers, which Ustinja had mended for him, he would shake his head and smile. Often while he was working or running an errand, he would think of Ustinja and mutter warmly, 'Ah, that Ustinja!' Ustinja helped him as best she could, and he helped her. She told him all about her life, how she had been orphaned when very young, how an old aunt had taken her in, how this aunt later sent her into town to work, how the merchant's son had tried stupidly to seduce her, and how she put him in his place. She loved to talk, and he found listening to her very pleasant. Among other things he heard that in town it often happened that peasant boys who came to serve in households would marry the cooks. And once she asked him if his parents would marry him off soon. He replied that he didn't know and that there was no one in his village whom he wanted.

'What, then, have you picked out someone else?' she asked.

'Yes. I'd take you. Will you?'

'O Pot, my Pot, how cunningly you put it to me!' she said, cuffing him playfully on the back with her ladle.

At Shrovetide Alyosha's old father came into town again to collect his son's wages. The merchant's wife had found out that Alyosha planned to marry Ustinja, and she was not at all pleased. 'She will just get pregnant, and then what good will she be!' she complained to her husband.

The merchant counted out Alyosha's money to his father. 'Well, is my boy doing all right by you?' asked the old man. 'I told you he was a meek one, would do anything you say.'

'Meek or no, he's done something stupid. He has got it into his head to marry the cook. And I will not keep married servants. It doesn't suit us.'

'Eh, that little fool! What a fool! How can he think to do such a stupid thing! But don't worry over it. I'll make him forget all that nonsense.'

The old man walked straight into the kitchen and sat down at the table to wait for his son. Alyosha was, as always, running an errand, but he soon came in all out of breath.

'Well, I thought you were a sensible fellow, but what nonsense you've thought up!' Alyosha's father greeted him.

'I've done nothing.'

'What'd you mean nothing! You've decided to marry. I'll marry you when the time comes, and I'll marry you to whoever I want, not to some town slut.'

The old man said a great deal more of the same sort. Alyosha stood quietly and sighed. When his father finished, he smiled.

'So, I'll forget about it,' he said.

'See that you do right now,' the old man said curtly as he left.

When his father had gone and Alyosha remained alone with Ustinja, who had been standing behind the kitchen door listening while his father was talking, he said to her: 'Our plan won't work out. Did you hear? He was furious, won't let us.'

Ustinja began to cry quietly into her apron. Alyosha clucked his tongue and said, 'How could I not obey him? Look, we must forget all about it.'

In the evening, when the merchant's wife called him to close the shutters, she said to him, 'Are you going to obey your father and forget all this nonsense about marrying?'

'Yes, of course. I've forgot it.' Alyosha said quickly, then smiled and immediately began weeping.

From that time Alyosha did not speak again to Ustinja about marriage and lived as he had before.

One morning during Lent the clerk sent Alyosha to clear the snow off the roof. He drawled up onto the roof, shovelled it clean and began to break up the frozen snow near the gutters when his feet slipped out from under him and he fell headlong with his shovel. As ill luck would have it, he fell not into the snow, but onto an entry-way with an iron railing. Ustinja ran up to him, followed by the merchant's daughter.

'Are you hurt, Alyosha?'

'Yes. But it's nothing. Nothing.'

He wanted to get up, but he could not and just smiled. Others came and carried him down into the yard-keeper's lodge. An orderly from the hospital arrived, examined him and asked where he hurt. 'It hurts all over,' he replied. 'But it's nothing. Nothing. Only the master will be annoyed. Must send word to Papa.'

Alyosha lay abed for two full days, and then, on the third day, they sent for a priest.

'You're not going to die, are you?' asked Ustinja.

"Well, we don't all live forever. It must be some time,' he answered quickly, as always. "Thank you, dear Ustinja, for feeling sorry for me. See, it's better they didn't let us marry, for nothing would have come of it. And now all is fine.'

He prayed with the priest, but only with his hands and with his heart. And in his heart he felt that if he was good here, if he obeyed and did not offend, then there all would be well.

He said little. He only asked for something to drink and smiled wonderingly. Then he seemed surprised at something, and stretched out and died.

Discussion Plan:

1. How would you describe Alyosha's personality?
2. In what sense was he a 'good servant'?
3. What was the significance of his smiling?
4. How would you explain his motivation?
5. Is it possible to justify Alyosha's father's keeping his wages?
6. Do you think Alyosha's actions satisfy any of his needs?
7. Do you think Alyosha's actions are based on his choice?
8. What is the difference between someone needing you and someone needing your services?
9. Why doesn't Alyosha marry the cook?
10. Do you think that Alyosha is fulfilling his own needs?
11. Do you think that Alyosha is happy?

Discussion Plan:

Does a person have duties that take precedence over desires? Comment on the following situations. Build your discussion by speculating on the background conditions that might make a difference.

1. You are expected to clean your room, but if you don't leave right now, you'll miss the movie.
2. You have promised your kid brother a day at the movies, but the only movie is one that you believe to be a waste of time.
3. You have the money saved to go to a concert, but it is Father's Day and you have to buy your father a present.
4. You are deeply in love with a person of another race, but you see that the relationship is having a serious negative effect on your mother.
5. You are ready to start college and you are offered a job as a roadie with a name rock and roll band.
6. You are the only person in the family who can take over the family business, but you dream of a career as a ballet dancer.
7. Your dog has bitten your landlord's child and your landlord is insisting that either you destroy your dog or you move.
8. Your girlfriend, whom you dearly love, has become pregnant with your child; you would willingly have the child, but you are scheduled to start college in the fall.
9. Your country is at war and you think of volunteering for military service.

Writing Assignment:

Write a modern version of Alyosha. Make it plausible given the relationships between parents and children in modern America.

SECTION 3:
THE SELF IN CONFLICT

Life pulls us in different directions. There are times when these directions are in completely opposite to each other. On the one hand, we have a growing sense of self, of independence and of individuality. On the other hand, we have duties and responsibilities, the demands placed on us by our interactions with others and by social conventions. Our roles and our desires, the outer and inner selves, are in a tug-of-war. What results is tension, pain and sometimes change in the developing individual.

Dividing the Self

Our sense of self grows in response to the demands that our experiences place upon us. New situations place new stresses on the person. And, frequently, the resolution of conflict requires the separating of the self into different personalities. This can become especially perplexing for the growing child, for the response to the split is often to question which is self and which is other.

Shirley Jackson, Charles

The day my son Laurie started kindergarten he renounced corduroy overalls with bibs and began wearing blue jeans with a belt. I watched him go off the first morning with the older girl next door, seeing clearly that an era of my life was ended, my sweet-voiced nursery-school tot replaced by a long-trousered, swaggering character who forgot to stop at the corner and wave good-bye to me.

He came home the same way, the front door slamming open, his hat on the floor, and the voice suddenly become raucous shouting, "Isn't anybody *here?*"

At lunch he spoke insolently to his father, spilled his baby sister's milk, and remarked that his teacher said we were not to take the name of the Lord in vain.

"How *was* school today?" I asked, elaborately casual.

"All right," he said.

"Did you learn anything?" his father asked.

Laurie regarded his father coldly. "I didn't learn nothing," he said.

"Anything," I said. "Didn't learn anything."

"The teacher spanked a boy, though," Laurie said, addressing his bread and butter. "For being fresh," he added, with his mouth full.

"What did he do?" I asked. "Who was it?"

Laurie thought. "It was Charles," he said. "He was fresh. The teacher spanked him and made him stand in a corner. He was awfully fresh."

"What did he do?" I asked again, but Laurie slid off his chair, took a cookie, and left, while his father was still saying, "See here, young man."

The next day Laurie remarked at lunch, as soon as he sat down, "Well, Charles was bad again today." He grinned enormously and said, "Today Charles hit the teacher."

"Good heaven," I said, mindful of the Lord's name. "I suppose he got spanked again?"

"He sure did," Laurie said. "Look up," he said to his father.

"What?" his father said, looking up.

"Look down," Laurie said. "Look at my thumb. Gee, you're dumb." He began to laugh insanely.

"Why did Charles hit the teacher?" I asked quickly.

"Because she tried to make him color with red crayons," Laurie said. "Charles wanted to color with green crayons so he hit the teacher and she spanked him and said nobody play with Charles but everybody did."

The third day—it was Wednesday of the first week—Charles bounced a see-saw on the head of a little girl and made her bleed, and the teacher made him stay inside all during recess. Thursday Charles had to stand in a corner during story-time because he kept pounding his feet on the floor. Friday Charles was deprived of blackboard privileges because he threw chalk.

On Saturday I remarked to my husband, "Do you think kindergarten is too unsettling for Laurie? All this toughness and bad grammar, and this Charles boy sounds like such a bad influence."

"It'll be all right," my husband said reassuringly. "Bound to be people like Charles in the world. Might as well meet them now as later."

On Monday Laurie came home late, full of news. "Charles," he shouted as he came up the hill; I was waiting anxiously on the front steps. "Charles," Laurie yelled all the way up the hill. "Charles was bad again."

"Come right in," I said, as soon as he came close enough. "Lunch is waiting."

"You know what Charles did?" he demanded, following me through the door. "Charles yelled so in school they sent a boy in from first grade to tell the teacher she had to make Charles keep quiet, and so Charles had to stay after school. And so all the children stayed to watch him."

"What did he do?" I asked.

"He just sat there," Laurie said, climbing into his chair at the table. "Hi, Pop, y'old dust mop."

"Charles had to stay after school today," I told my husband. "Everyone stayed with him."

"What does this Charles look like?" my husband asked Laurie. "What's his other name?"

"He's bigger than me," Laurie said. "And he doesn't have any rubbers and he doesn't ever wear a jacket."

Monday night was the first Parent-Teachers meeting, and only the fact that the baby had a cold kept me from going; I wanted passionately to meet Charles' mother. On Tuesday Laurie remarked suddenly, "Our teacher had a friend come to see her in school today."

"Charles' mother?" my husband and I asked simultaneously.

"Naaah," Laurie said scornfully. "It was a man who came and made us do exercises, and we had to touch our toes. Look." He climbed down from his chair and squatted down and touched his toes. "Like this," he said. He got solemnly back into his chair and said, picking up his fork, "Charles didn't even do exercises."

"That's fine," I said heartily. "Didn't Charles want to do the exercises?"

"Naaah," Laurie said. "Charles was so fresh to the teacher's friend he wasn't *let* to do exercises."

"Fresh again," I said.

"He kicked the teacher's friend," Laurie said. "The teacher's friend told Charles to touch his toes like I just did and Charles kicked him."

"What are they going to do about Charles, do you suppose?" Laurie's father asked him.

Laurie shrugged elaborately. "Throw him out of school, I guess," he said.

Wednesday and Thursday were routine; Charles yelled during story hour and hit a boy in the stomach and made him cry. On Friday Charles stayed after school again and so did all the other children.

With the third week of kindergarten Charles was an institution in our family; the baby was being a Charles when he filled his wagon full of mud and pulled it through the kitchen; even my husband, when he caught his elbow in the telephone cord and pulled telephone, ashtray, and a bowl of flowers off the table, said, after the first minute, "Looks like Charles."

During the third and fourth weeks it looked like a reformation in Charles; Laurie reported grimly at lunch on Thursday of the third week, "Charles was so good today the teacher gave him an apple."

"What?" I said, and my husband added warily, "You mean Charles?"

"Charles," Laurie said. "He gave the crayons around and he picked up the books afterward and the teacher said he was her helper."

"What happened?" I asked incredulously.

"He was her helper, that's all," Laurie said, and shrugged.

"Can this be true, about Charles?" I asked my husband that night. "Can something like this happen?"

"Wait and see," my husband said cynically. "When you've got a Charles to deal with, this may mean he's only plotting."

He seemed to be wrong. For over a week Charles was the teacher's helper; each day he handed things out and he picked things up; no one had to stay after school.

"The PTA meeting's next week again," I told my husband one evening. "I'm going to find Charles's mother there."

"Ask her what happened to Charles," my husband said. "I'd like to know."

"I'd like to know myself," I said.

On Friday of that week things were back to normal. "You know what Charles did today?" Laurie demanded at the lunch table, in a voice slightly awed. "He told a little girl to say a word and she said it and the teacher washed her mouth out with soap and Charles laughed."

"What word?" his father asked unwisely, and Laurie said, "I'll have to whisper it to you, it's so bad." He got down off his chair and went around to his father. His father bent his head down and Laurie whispered joyfully. His father's eyes widened.

"Did Charles tell the little girl to say *that*?" he asked respectfully.

"She said it *twice*," Laurie said. "Charles told her to say it *twice*."

"What happened to Charles?" my husband asked.

"Nothing," Laurie said. "He was passing out the crayons."

Monday morning Charles abandoned the little girl and said the evil word himself three or four times, getting his mouth washed out with soap each time. He also threw chalk.

My husband came to the door with me that evening as I set out for the PTA meeting. "Invite her over for a cup of tea after the meeting," he said. "I want to get a look at her."

"If only she's there," I said prayerfully.

"She'll be there," my husband said. "I don't see how they could hold a PTA meeting without Charles' mother."

At the meeting I sat restlessly, scanning each comfortable matronly face, trying to determine which one hid the secret of Charles. None of them looked to me haggard enough. No one stood up in the meeting and apologized for the way her son had been acting. No one mentioned Charles.

After the meeting I identified and sought out Laurie's kindergarten teacher. She had a plate with a cup of tea and a piece of chocolate cake, I had a plate with a cup of tea and a piece of marshmallow cake. We maneuvered up to one another cautiously, and smiled.

"I've been so anxious to meet you," I said. "I'm Laurie's mother."

"We're all so interested in Laurie," she said.

"Well, he certainly likes kindergarten," I said. "He talks about it all the time."

"We had a little trouble adjusting, the first week or so," she said primly, "but now he's a fine little helper. With occasional lapses, of course."

"Laurie usually adjusts very quickly," I said. "I suppose this time it's Charles' influence."

"Charles?"

"Yes," I said, laughing, "you must have your hands full in that kindergarten, with Charles."

"Charles?" she said. "We don't have any Charles in the kindergarten."

Discussion Plan:

1. Why does Laurie's behavior change when he starts going to school?
   Did you have difficulty when you first started school?
2. Who is Charles?
3. Does Laurie like Charles? Does he admire Charles? Does he need Charles? Why?
4. Does Laurie do the things he says Charles does or does he wish he could do them?
5. Which represents this little kid's real self, Laurie or Charles or both or neither?
6. Do you think Laurie knows why he is having trouble: why his behavior has changed?
7. If he does know, should he be blamed (held responsible) for his actions and for telling stories about Charles? If he doesn't know, should he be held responsible? Why?

Exercise:

Doing and admitting wrong:

1. In the list of socially unacceptable actions are ones that we might admit to
   and ones that we might not—classify them according to whether you
   would or would not admit to them.
   a. smoke pot
   b. cheat on a test
   c. gossip about a friend
   d. lie to a parent
   e. have sex before the legal age of consent
   f. take money from your parents' dresser
   g. take barbituates regularly
   h. break a promise to a friend
   i. date someone fifteen years older than you
   j. torture a stray animal
2. Is there anyone that you would admit these actions to?
3. What kind of a person could you admit these actions to? Be specific about
   which actions and be as specific as you can about the person and his traits.
4. Are there any of these that you might pretend to do even if you didn't?
5. To whom would you pretend? Be specific as in 3. above.

Goodself, Badself

Social forces and personal standards generate self evaluation. Conscience as well as the society around us offer norms for behavior that provide the basis for judgments of self worth. The person, in response to moral requirements, frequently distinguishes those tendencies that support acceptable behavior and feelings from those that tend toward non-compliance with accepted norms and standards. The self is, thus, divided into the 'good self' and the 'bad self'.

F. H. Bradley, Ethical Studies

...The existence of two selves in a man, a better self which takes pleasure in the good, and a worse self which makes for the bad, is a fact which is too plain to be denied. In the field of religion we hear of an inward man delighting in God's law, which would have me do what I do not do, and of another self which takes pleasure in what I abhor; but in morals we have nothing to do with these. We can not consider either the good or bad self in its relation to the divine will, because that would be to pass at once beyond mere morality. But, apart from religion, the good and bad selves no doubt exist, and every one knows what they mean. I feel at times identified with the good, as though all my self were in it; there are certain good habits and pursuits and companies which are natural to me, and in which I feel at home. And then again there are certain bad habits and pursuits and companies in which perhaps I feel no less at home, in which also I feel myself to be myself; and I feel that, when I am good and when I am bad, I am not the same man but quite different, and the world to the one self seems quite another thing to what it does to the other. Nor is it only at different times that I feel so different, but also at one and the same time: I feel in myself impulses to good in collision with impulses to bad, and I feel myself in each of them, and, whichever way I go, I satisfy myself and yet fail to do so. If I yield to the bad self, the good self is dissatisfied; and if I yield to the good self, the bad self is discontented; and I am driven to believe that two souls, two opposing principles, are at war in me, and make me at war with myself; each of which loves what the other hates, and hates what the other loves. In this strife I know that the good is the true self, it is certainly more myself than the other; and yet I can not say that the other is not myself, and when I enter the lists again it, it is at my own breast that I lay my lance in rest....

Writing Assignment:

The analysis of "goodself" and "badself" is easy to apply to Laurie and "Charles." It may be more difficult to apply to your own experience.

Write a paragraph about a personal experience in which your good self and your bad self were in conflict. Explain how it felt to fight with yourself. How was the dispute resolved? Were you satisfied with the results?

Exercise:

The word 'good' has many meanings. Among the more prominent are:
a) morally right
b) satisfactory in quality
c) right or proper
d) well behaved
e) functional

Which of the senses of 'good' seems most appropriate in the following cases?

1. Is the screwdriver good for this job?
2. It is important to look good when you go tonight.
3. John was good during recess today.
4. That pie sure looks good.
5. Being good is more important than being successful.
6. Good girls don't neck on the first date.
7. That was a good movie.
8. Was the performance any good?
9. We should strive for the Good, the True and the Beautiful.
10. Smoking cigarettes isn't good for you.
11. For goodness sake!
12. The good life is the best life.
13. What good does it do to do well in school?
14. That's a good fit.

Are there senses of 'good' not listed above that seem to fit the examples better?

Define 'bad'; list a sense for 'bad' that corresponds to each sense of 'good' used in a) through e) above.

Make a similar list of statements to reflect the various uses of 'bad'.

Fantasy

When our expectations don't match our achievements, we can retreat in disappointment or forge ahead with a renewed motive for change. But sometimes change seems to cease and routine takes over; life can go too smoothly. When the self does not encounter challenges in the outer world, it turns inward, imagining a world in which it can be successful and glamorous—or anything it wants to be.

James Thurber, The Secret Life of Walter Mitty

"We're going through!" The Commander's voice was like thin ice breaking. He wore his full-dress uniform, with the heavily braided white cap pulled down rakishly over one cold gray eye. "We can't make it, sir. It's spoiling for a hurricane, if you ask me." "I'm not asking you, Lieutenant Berg," said the Commander. "Throw on the power lights! Rev her up to 8,500! We're going through!" The pounding of the cylinders increased; ta-pocketa-pocketa-pocketa-*pocketa-pocketa*. The Commander stared at the ice forming on the pilot window. He walked over and twisted a row of complicated dials. "Switch on No. 8 auxiliary!" he shouted. "Switch on No. 8 auxiliary!" repeated Lieutenant Berg. "Full strength in No. 3 turret!" shouted the Commander. "Full strength in No. 3 turret!" The crew, bending to their various tasks in the huge, hurtling eight-engined Navy hydroplane, looked at each other and grinned. "The Old Man'll get us through," they said to one another. "The Old Man ain't afraid of Hell!"…

"Not so fast! You're driving too fast!" said Mrs. Mitty. "What are you driving so fast for?"

"Hmm?" said Walter Mitty. He looked at his wife, in the seat beside him, with shocked astonishment. She seemed grossly unfamiliar, like a strange woman who had yelled at him in a crowd. "You were up to fifty-five," she said. "You know I don't like to go more than forty. You were up to fifty-five." Walter Mitty drove on toward Waterbury in silence, the roaring of the SN 202 through the worst storm in twenty years of Navy flying fading in the remote, intimate airways of his mind. "You're tensed up again," said Mrs. Mitty. "It's one of your days. I wish you'd let Dr. Renshaw look you over."

Walter Mitty stopped the car in front of the building where his wife went to have her hair done. "Remember to get those overshoes while I'm having my hair done," she said. "I don't need overshoes," said Mitty. She put her mirror back into her bag. "We've been all through that," she said, getting out of the car. "You're not a young man any longer." He raced the engine a little. "Why don't you wear your gloves? Have you lost your gloves?" Walter Mitty reached in a pocket and brought out the gloves. He put them on, but after she had turned and gone into the building and he had driven on to a red light, he took them off again. "Pick it up, brother!" snapped a cop as the light changed, and Mitty hastily pulled on his gloves and lurched ahead. He drove around the streets aimlessly for a time, and then he drove past the hospital on his way to the parking lot.

..."It's the millionaire banker, Wellington McMillan," said the pretty nurse. "Yes?" said Walter Mitty, removing his gloves slowly. "Who has the case?" "Dr. Renshaw and Dr. Benbow, but there are two specialists here, Dr. Remington from New York and Dr. Pritchard-Mitford from London. He flew over." A door opened down a long, cool corridor and Dr. Renshaw came out. He looked distraught and haggard. "Hello, Mitty," he said. "We're having the devil's own time with McMillan, the millionaire banker and close personal friend of Roosevelt. Obstreosis of the ductal tract. Tertiary. Wish you'd take a look at him." "Glad to," said Mitty.

In the operating room there were whispered introductions: "Dr. Remington, Dr. Mitty. Dr. Pritchard-Mitford, Dr. Mitty." "I've read your book on streptothricosis," said Pritchard-Mitford, shaking hands. "A brilliant performance, sir." "Thank you," said Walter Mitty. "Didn't know you were in the States, Mitty," grumbled Remington. "Coals to Newcastle, bringing Mitford and me up here for a tertiary." "You are very kind," said Mitty. A huge, complicated machine, connected to the operating table, with many tubes and wires, began at this moment to go pocketa-pocketa-pocketa. "The new anaesthetizer is giving away!" shouted an intern. "There is no one in the East who knows how to fix it!" "Quiet, man!" said Mitty, in a low, cool voice. He sprang to the machine, which was now going pocketa-pocketa-queep-pocketa-queep. He began fingering delicately a row of glistening dials. "Give me a fountain pen!" he snapped. Someone handed him a fountain pen. He pulled a faulty piston out of the machine and inserted the pen in its place. "That will hold for ten minutes," he said. "Get on with the operation." A nurse hurried over and whispered to Renshaw, and Mitty saw the man turn pale. "Coreopsis has set in," said Renshaw nervously. "If you would take over, Mitty?" Mitty looked at him and at the craven figure of Benbow, who drank, and at the grave, uncertain faces of the two great specialists. "If you wish," he said. They slipped a white gown on him; he adjusted a mask and drew on thin gloves; nurses handed him shining ...

"Back it up, Mac! Look out for that Buick!" Walter Mitty jammed on the brakes. "Wrong lane, Mac," said the parking-lot attendant, looking at Mitty closely. "Gee. Yeh," muttered Mitty. He began cautiously to back out of the lane marked "Exit Only." "Leave her sit there," said the attendant. "I'll put her away." Mitty got out of the car. "Hey, better leave the key." "Oh," said Mitty, handing the man the ignition key. The attendant vaulted into the car, backed it up with insolent skill, and put it where it belonged.

They're so damn cocky, thought Walter Mitty, walking along Main Street; they think they know everything. Once he had tried to take his chains off, outside New Milford, and he got them wound around the axles. A man had had to come out in a wrecking car and unwind them, a young, grinning garage man. Since then Mrs. Mitty always made him drive to a garage to have the chains taken off. The next time, he thought, I'll wear my right arm in a sling; they won't grin at me then. I'll have my right arm in a sling and they'll see I couldn't possibly take the chains off myself. He kicked at the slush on the sidewalk. "Overshoes," he said to himself, and he began looking for a shoe store.

When he came out into the street again, with the overshoes in a box under his arm, Walter Mitty began to wonder what the other thing was his wife had told him to get. She had told him, twice before they set out from their house for Waterbury. In a way he hated these weekly trips to town—he was always getting something wrong. Kleenex, he thought, Squibb's, razor blades? No. Toothpaste, toothbrush, bicarbonate, carborundum, initiative and referendum? He gave it up. But she would remember it. "Where's the what's-its-name?" she would ask. "Don't tell me you forgot the what's-its-name." A newsboy went by shouting something about the Waterbury trial.

…"Perhaps this will refresh your memory." The District Attorney suddenly thrust a heavy automatic at the quiet figure on the witness stand. "Have you ever seen this before?" Walter Mitty took the gun and examined it expertly. "This is my Webley-Vickers 50.80," he said calmly. An excited buzz ran around the courtroom. The judge rapped for order. "You are a crack shot with any sort of firearms, I believe?" said the District Attorney, insinuatingly. "Objection!" shouted Mitty's attorney. "We have shown that the defendant could not have fired the shot. We have shown that he wore his right arm in a sling on the night of the fourteenth of July." Walter Mitty raised his hand briefly and the bickering attorneys were stilled. "With any known make of gun," he said evenly, "I could have killed Gregory Fitzhurst at three hundred feet *with my left hand.*" Pandemonium broke loose in the courtroom. A woman's scream rose above the bedlam and suddenly a lovely, dark-haired girl was in Walter Mitty's arms. The District Attorney struck at her savagely. Without rising from his chair, Mitty let the man have it on the point of the chin. "You miserable cur!"…

"Puppy biscuit," said Walter Mitty. He stopped walking and the buildings of Waterbury rose up out of the misty courtroom and surrounded him again. A woman who was passing laughed. "He said 'Puppy biscuit'," she said to her companion. "That man said 'Puppy biscuit' to himself." Walter Mitty hurried on. He went into an A.& P., not the first one he came to but a smaller one farther up the street. "I want some biscuit for small, young dogs," he said to the clerk. "Any special brand, sir?" The greatest pistol shot in the world thought a moment. "It says 'Puppies Bark for It' on the box," said Walter Mitty.

His wife would be through at the hairdresser's in fifteen minutes, Mitty saw in looking at his watch, unless they had trouble drying it; sometimes they had trouble drying it. She didn't like to get to the hotel first; she would want him to be there waiting for her as usual. He found a big leather chair in the lobby, facing a window, and he put the overshoes and the puppy biscuit on the floor beside it. He picked up an old copy of Liberty and sank down into the chair. "Can Germany Conquer the World through the Air?" Walter Mitty looked at the pictures of bombing planes and of ruined streets.

...."The cannonading has got the wind up in young Raleigh, sir," said the sergeant. Captain Mitty looked up at him through tousled hair. "Get him to bed," he said wearily, "with the others. I'll fly alone." "But you can't, sir, " said the sergeant anxiously. "It takes two men to handle that bomber and the Archies are pounding hell out of the air. Von Richtman's circus is between here and Saulier." "Somebody's got to get that ammunition dump," said Mitty. "I'm going over. Spot of brandy?" He poured a drink for the sergeant and one for himself. War thundered and whined around the dugout and battered at the door. There was a rending of wood and splinters flew through the room. "A bit of a near thing," said Captain Mitty carelessly. "The box barrage is closing in," said the sergeant. "We only live once, sergeant," said Mitty, with his faint, fleeting smile. "Or do we?" He poured another brandy and tossed it off. "I never see a man could hold his brandy like you, sir," said the sergeant. "Begging your pardon, sir." Captain Mitty stood up and strapped on his huge Webley-Vickers automatic. "It's forty kilometers through hell, sir," said the sergeant. Mitty finished one last brandy. "After all," he said softly, "what isn't?" The pounding of the cannon increased; there was the rat-tat-tatting of machine guns, and from somewhere came the menacing pocketa-pocketa-pocketa of the new flame-throwers. Walter Mitty walked to the door of the dugout humming "Au pres de Ma Blonde." He turned and waved to the sergeant. "Cheerio!" he said ...

Something struck his shoulder. "I've been looking all over this hotel for you," said Mrs. Mitty. "Why do you have to hide in this old chair? How did you expect me to find you?" "Things close in," said Walter Mitty vaguely. "What?" Mrs. Mitty said. "Did you get the what's-its-name? The puppy biscuit? What's in that box?" "Overshoes," said Mitty. "Couldn't you have put them on in the store?" "I was thinking," said Walter Mitty. "Does it ever occur to you that I am sometimes thinking?" She looked at him. "I'm going to take your temperature when I get you home," she said.

They went out through the revolving doors that made a faintly derisive whistle sound when you pushed them. It was two blocks to the parking lot. At the drugstore on the corner she said, "Wait here for me. I forgot something. I won't be a minute." She was more than a minute. Walter Mitty lighted a cigarette. It began to rain, rain with sleet in it. He stood up against the wall of the drugstore, smoking.... He put his shoulders back and his heels together. "To hell with the handkerchief," said Walter Mitty scornfully. He took one last drag on his cigarette and snapped it away. Then, with that faint, fleeting smile playing about his lips, he faced the firing squad; erect and motionless, proud and disdainful, Walter Mitty the Undefeated, inscrutable to the last.

Discussion Plan:

Fantasy can be a goad for self development or it can be an escape from responsibility. For the following fantasies describe ways that they could result in behavior that seems positive in terms of personal growth. Then describe ways that the same fantasy could result in negative consequences.

1. You pretend that you are more beautiful than you are.
2. You dream of becoming an astronaut.
3. You think of revenging yourself on a friend who has hurt you.
4. You construct an imaginary family, a spouse and children.
5. You become deeply involved in the details of the life of a sports hero and hope to emulate her.
6. You read about ancient Greece and become convinced that their way of life is the best model for human beings to emulate.

Enumerate the standards that you used in distinguishing positive from negative consequences. Think of any principles that would justify your choice of standards?

Function

A human being plays various roles in life, each of these requiring different skills, attitudes and behavior. Is it reasonable to expect that the sense of self remains unified in the face of divergent demands? Perhaps the unitary self is a myth, imposed on us by the way we speak and the physical continuity of the body. Perhaps each of us is an ensemble, composed of discrete and autonomous selves, a community of different individuals working together for some common goals.

Lewis Thomas, The Selves

There are psychiatric patients who are said to be incapacitated by having more than one self. One of these, an attractive intelligent young woman in distress, turned up on a television talk show a while back, sponsored to reveal her selves and their disputes. She possessed, she said, or was possessed by, no fewer than eight other separate women, all different, with different names, arguing and elbowing their way into control of the enterprise, causing unending confusion and embarrassment. She (they) wished to be rid of all of them (her), except of course herself (themselves).

People like this are called hysterics by the professionals, or maybe schizophrenics, and there is, I am told, nothing much that can be done. Having more than one self is supposed to be deeply pathological; I hope not. Eight strikes me personally as a reasonably small and easily manageable number. It is the simultaneity of their appearance that is the real problem, and I should think psychiatry would do better by simply persuading them to queue up and wait their turns, as happens in the normal rest of us. Couldn't they be conditioned some way, by offering rewards or holding out gently threatening sanctions? "How do you do, I'm absolutely delighted to see you here and I have exactly fifty-five minutes, after which I very much regret to say someone else will be dropping in, but could I see you again tomorrow at this same time, do have a chocolate mint and let's just talk, just the two of us." That sort of thing might help at least to get them lined up in some kind of order.

Actually, it would embarrass me to be told that more than a single self is a kind of disease. I've had, in my time, more than I could possibly count or keep track of. The great difference, which keeps me feeling normal, is that mine (ours) have turned up one after the other, on an orderly schedule. Five years ago I was another person, juvenile, doing and saying things I couldn't possibly agree with now. Ten years ago I was a stranger. Twenty-four years ago.... I've forgotten. The only thing close to what you might call illness, in my experience, was in the gaps in the queue when one had finished and left the place before the next one was ready to start, and there was nobody around at all. Luckily, that has happened only three or four times that I can recall, once when I'd become a very old child and my adolescent hadn't appeared, and a couple of times later on when there seemed to be some confusion about who was next up. The rest of the time they have waited turns and emerged on cue ready to take over, sometimes breathless and needing last-minute briefing but nonetheless steady enough to go on. The surprising thing has always been how little background information they seemed to need, considering how the times changed. I cannot remember who it was five years ago. He was reading linguistics and had just discovered philosophy, as I recall, but he left before getting anything much done.

To be truthful there have been a few times when they were all there at once, like those girls on television, clamoring for attention, whole committees of them, a House Committee, a Budget Committee, a Grievance Committee, even a Committee on Membership, although I don't know how any of them ever got in. No chairman, ever, certainly not me. At the most I'm a sort of administrative assistant. There's never an agenda. At the end I bring in the refreshments.

What do we meet about? It is hard to say. The door bangs open and in they come, calling for the meeting to start, and then they all talk at once. Odd to say, it is not just a jumble of talk; they tend to space what they're saying so that words and phrases from one will fit into short spaces left in silence by the others. At good times it has the feel of an intensely complicated conversation, but at others the sounds are more like something overheard in a crowded station. At worse times the silences get out of synchrony, interrupting each other; it is as though all the papers had suddenly blown off the table.

We never get anything settled. In recent years I've sensed an increase in their impatience with me, whoever they think I am, and with the fix they're in. They don't come right out and say so, but what they are beginning to want more than anything else is a chairman.

The worst times of all have been when I've wanted to be just one. Try walking out on the ocean beach at night, looking at stars, thinking. Be one, be one. Doesn't work, ever. Just when you feel ascension, turning, wheeling, and that whirring sound like a mantel clock getting ready to strike, the other selves begin talking. Whatever you're thinking, they say, it's not like that at all.

The only way to quiet them down, get them to stop, is to play music. That does it. Bach stops them every time, in their tracks, almost as though that's what they've been waiting for.

Discussion Plan:

Within modern biology the human body is frequently looked at as a collection of discrete and semi-independent organisms. Thomas, who is a biologist, has applied the same concept to the personality.

Discuss the following as a debate: The human being, when working at her best, functions, not as a unified individual, but as a society, a coordinated number of distinct personalities working together.

Function

There is a long history within philosophy of looking.at the personality as composed of distinct and mutually antagonistic components. One of the earliest and most influential of these views is found in The Republic *of Plato.*

Plato, "The Three Parts of the Soul," from *The Republic*

A dialogue between Socrates and Glaucon. Socrates speaks first.

... It is clear that the same thing cannot act in two opposite ways or be in two opposite states at the same time, with respect to the same part of itself, and in relation to the same object. So if we find such contradictory actions or states among the elements concerned, we shall know that more than one must have been involved.

Very well.

Consider this proposition of mine, then. Can the same thing, at the same time and with respect to the same part of itself, be at rest and in motion?

Certainly not.

We had better state this principle in still more precise terms, to guard against misunderstanding later on. Suppose a man is standing still, but moving his head and arms. We should not allow anyone to say that the same man was both at rest and in motion at the same time, but only that part of him was at rest, part in motion. Isn't that so?

Yes....

Now, would you class such things as assent and dissent, striving after something and refusing it, attraction and repulsion, as pairs of opposite actions or states of mind—no matter which?

Yes, they are opposites.

And would you not class all appetites such as hunger and thirst, and again willing and wishing, with the affirmative members of those pairs I have just mentioned? For instance, you would say that the soul of a man who desires something is striving after it, or trying to draw to itself the thing it wishes to possess, or again, in so far as it is willing to have its wants satisfied, it is giving its assent to its own longing, as if to an inward question.

Yes.

And, on the other hand, disinclination, unwillingness, and dislike, we should class on the negative side with acts of rejection or repulsion.

Of course.

That being so, shall we say that appetites form one class, the most conspicuous being those we call thirst and hunger?

Yes.

Thirst being desire for drink, hunger for food?

Yes.

Now, is thirst, just in so far as it is thirst, a desire in the soul for nothing more than simply drink? Is it, for instance, thirst for hot drink or for cold, for much drink or for little, or in a word for drink of any particular kind? It is not rather true that you will have a desire for cold drink only if you are feeling hot as well as thirsty, and for hot drink only if you are feeling cold; and if you want much drink or little, that will be because your thirst is a great thirst or a little one? But, just in itself, thirst or hunger is a desire for nothing more than its natural object, drink or food, pure and simple....

... And if the drink desired is of a certain kind, the thirst will be correspondingly qualified. But thirst which is just simply thirst is not for drink of any particular sort—much or little, good or bad—but for drink pure and simple.

Quite so.

We conclude, then, that the soul of a thirsty man, just in so far as he is thirsty, has no other wish than to drink. That is the object of its craving, and towards that it is impelled.

That is clear.

Now if there is ever something which at the same time pulls it the opposite way, that something must be an element in the soul other than the one which is thirsting and driving it like a beast to drink; in accordance with our principle that the same thing cannot behave in two opposite ways at the same time and towards the same object with the same part of itself. It is like an archer drawing the bow: it is not accurate to say that his hands are at the same time both pushing and pulling it. One hand does the pushing, the other the pulling.

Exactly.

Now, it is sometimes true that people are thirsty and yet unwilling to drink?

Yes, often.

What, then, can one say of them, if not that their soul contains something which urges them to drink and something which holds them back, and that this latter is a distinct thing and overpowers the other?

I agree.

And is it not true that the intervention of this inhibiting principle in such cases always has its origin in reflection; whereas the impulses driving and dragging the soul are engendered by external influences and abnormal conditions?

Evidently.

We shall have good reason, then, to assert that they are two distinct principles. We may call that part of the soul whereby it reflects, rational; and the other, with which it feels hunger and thirst and is distracted by sexual passion and all the other desires, we will call irrational appetite, associated with pleasure in the replenishment of certain wants.

Yes, there is good ground for that view.

Let us take it, then, that we have now distinguished two elements in the soul. What of that passionate element which makes us feel angry and indignant? Is that a third, or identical in nature with one of those two?

It might perhaps be identified with appetite.

I am more inclined to put my faith in a story I once heard about Leontius, son of Aglaion. On his way up from the Piraeus outside the north wall, he noticed the bodies of some criminals lying on the ground, with the executioner standing by them. He wanted to go and look at them, but at the same time he was disgusted and tried to turn away. He struggled for some time and covered his eyes, but at last the desire was too much for him. Opening his eyes wide, he ran up to the bodies and cried, 'There you are, curse you; feast yourselves on this lovely sight!'

Yes, I have heard that story too.

The point of it surely is that anger is sometimes in conflict with appetite, as if they were two distinct principles. Do we not often find a man whose desires would force him to go against his reason, reviling himself and indignant with this part of his nature which is trying to put constraint on him? It is like a struggle between two factions, in which indignation takes the side of reason. But I believe you have never observed, in yourself or anyone else, indignation make common cause with appetite in behaviour which reason decides to be wrong.

No, I am sure I have not.

Again, take a man who feels he is in the wrong. The more generous his nature, the less can he be indignant at any suffering, such as hunger and cold, inflicted by the man he has injured. He recognizes such treatment as just, and, as I say, his spirit refuses to be roused against it.

That is true.

But now contrast one who thinks it is he that is being wronged. His spirit boils with resentment and sides with the right as he conceives it. Persevering all the more for the hunger and cold and other pains he suffers, it triumphs and will not give in until its gallant struggle has ended in success or death; or until the restraining voice of reason, like a shepherd calling off his dog, makes it relent.

An apt comparison, he said; and in fact it fits the relation of our Auxiliaries to the Rulers: they were to be like watch-dogs obeying the shepherds of the commonwealth.

Yes, you understand very well what I have in mind. But do you see how we have changed our view? A moment ago we were supposing this spirited element to be something of the nature of appetite; but now it appears that, when the soul is divided into factions, it is far more ready to be up in arms on the side of reason.

Quite true.

Is it, then, distinct from the rational element or only a particular form of it, so that the soul will contain no more than two elements, reason and appetite? Or is the soul like the state, which had three orders to hold it together, traders, Auxiliaries, and counsellors? Does the spirited element make a third, the natural auxiliary of reason, when not corrupted by bad upbringing?

It must be a third.

Yes, I said, provided it can be shown to be distinct from reason, as we saw it was from appetite.

That is easily proved. You can see that much in children, they are full of passionate feelings from their very birth; but some, I should say, never become rational, and most of them only late in life....

Exercise:

1. Outline Plato's argument that the soul is divided into three parts.
2. What principles does Plato assume in his argument?
3. How does Plato's argument compare to the argument that you presented in your debate in the preceding selection?

Feelings

In extraordinary cases people respond to stress by creating a totally unrealistic image of themselves. The image provides a protective screen behind which the stressful forces cannot penetrate. What is remarkable is that the self is transformed by the image; it becomes the image. In the story which follows the image chosen is of a machine. A human child becomes inhuman to protect himself.

Bruno Bettelheim, Joey: A 'Mechanical Boy'

Joey, when we began our work with him, was a mechanical boy. He functioned as if by remote control, run by machines of his own powerfully creative fantasy. Not only did he himself believe that he was a machine but, more remarkably, he created this impression in others. Even while he performed actions that are intrinsically human, they never appeared to be other than machine-started and executed. On the other hand, when the machine was not working we had to concentrate on recollecting his presence, for he seemed not to exist. A human body that functions as if it were a machine and a machine that duplicates human functions are equally fascinating and frightening. Perhaps they are so uncanny because they remind us that the human body can operate without a human spirit, that body can exist without soul. And Joey was a child who had been robbed of his humanity.

Not every child who possesses a fantasy world is possessed by it. Normal children may retreat into realism of imaginary glory or magic powers, but they are easily recalled from these excursions. Disturbed children are not always able to make the return trip; they remain withdrawn, prisoners of the inner world of delusion and fantasy. In many ways Joey presented a classic example of this state of infantile autism....

At the Sonia Shankman Orthogenic School of the University of Chicago it is our function to provide a therapeutic environment in which such children may start life over again. I have previously described the rehabilitation of another of our patients. ("Schizophrenic Art: A Case Study": [*i*] Scientific American [*r*] April, 1952.) This time I shall concentrate upon the illness, rather than the treatment. In any age, which the individual has escaped into a delusional world, he has usually fashioned it from bits and pieces of the world at hand. Joey, in his time and world, chose the machine and froze himself in its image. His story has a general relevance to the understanding of emotional development in a machine age.

Joey's delusion is not uncommon among schizophrenic children today. He wanted to be rid of his unbearable humanity, to become completely automatic. He so nearly succeeded in attaining this goal that he could almost convince others, as well as himself, of his mechanical character. The descriptions of autistic children in the literature take for their point of departure and comparison the normal or abnormal human being. To do justice to Joey I would have to compare him simultaneously to a most inept infant and a highly complex piece of machinery. Often we had to force ourselves by a conscious act of will to realize that Joey was a child. Again and again his acting-out of his delusions froze our own ability to respond as human beings.

During Joey's first weeks with us we would watch absorbedly as this at once fragile-looking and imperious nine-year-old went about his mechanical existence. Entering the dining room, for example, he would string an imaginary wire from his "energy source"—an imaginary electric outlet—to the table. There he "insulated" himself with paper napkins and finally plugged himself in. Only then could Joey eat, for he firmly believed that the "current" ran his ingestive apparatus. So skillful was the pantomine that one had to look twice to be sure there was neither wire nor outlet nor plug. Children and members of our staff spontaneously avoided stepping on the "wires" for fear of interrupting what seemed the source of his very life.

For long periods of time, when his "machinery" was idle, he would sit so quietly that he would disappear from the focus of the most conscientious observation. Yet in the next moment he might be "working" and the center of our captivated attention. Many times a day he would turn himself on and shift noisily through a sequence of higher and higher gears until he "exploded," screaming "Crash, crash!" and hurling items from his ever present apparatus—radio tubes, light bulbs, even motors or, lacking these, any handy breakable object. (Joey had an astonishing knack for snatching bulbs and tubes unobserved.) As soon as the object thrown had shattered, he would cease his screaming and wild jumping and retire to mute, motionless nonexistence.

Our maids, inured to difficult children, were exceptionally attentive to Joey; they were apparently moved by his extreme infantile fragility, so strangely coupled with megalomaniacal superiority. Occasionally some of the apparatus he fixed to his bed to "live him" during his sleep would fall down in disarray. This machinery he contrived from masking tape, cardboard, wire and other paraphernalia. Usually the maids would pick up such things and leave them on a table for the children to find, or disregard them entirely. But Joey's machine they carefully restored: "Joey must have the carburetor so he can breathe." Similarly they were on the alert to pick up and preserve the motors that ran him during the day and the exhaust pipes through which he exhaled.

How had Joey become a human machine? From intensive interviews with his parents we learned that the process had begun even before birth. Schizo-

phrenia often results from parental rejection, sometimes combined ambiva-
lently with love. Joey, on the other hand, had been completely ignored.

"I never knew I was pregnant," his mother said, meaning that she had
already excluded Joey from her consciousness. His birth, she said, "did not
make any difference." Joey's father, a rootless draftee in the wartime civilian
army, was equally unready for parenthood. So, of course, are many young
couples. Fortunately most such parent close their indifference upon the
baby's birth. But not Joey's parents. "I did not want to see or nurse him," his
mother declared. I had no feeling of actual dislike—I simply didn't want to
take care of him." For the first three months of his life Joey "cried most of the
time." A colicky baby, he was kept on a rigid four-hour feeding schedule, was
not touched unless necessary and was never cuddled or played with. The
mother, preoccupied with herself, usually left Joey alone in the crib or
playpen during the day. The father discharged his frustrations by punishing
Joey when the child cried at night.

Soon the father left for overseas duty, and the mother took Joey, now a year
and a half old, to live with her at her parents' home. On his arrival the
grandparents noticed that ominous changes had occurred in the child.
Strong and healthy at birth, he had become frail and irritable; a responsive
baby, he had become remote and inaccessible. When he began to master
speech, he talked only to himself. At an early date he became preoccupied
with machinery, including an old electric fan which he could take apart and
put together again with surprising deftness.

Joey's mother impressed us with a fey quality that expressed her insecu-
rity, her detachment from the world and her low physical vitality. We were
struck especially by her total indifference as she talked about Joey. This
seemed much more remarkable than the actual mistakes she made in handling him. Certainly he was left to cry for hours when hungry, because she
fed him on a rigid schedule; he was toilet-trained with great rigidity so that
he would give no trouble. These things happen to many children. But Joey's
existence never registered with his mother. In her recollections he was fused
at one moment with one event or person; at another, with something or
somebody else. When she told us about his birth and infancy, it was as if she
were talking about some vague acquaintance, and soon her thoughts would
wander off to another person or to herself.

When Joey was not yet four, his nursery school suggested that he enter a
special school for disturbed children. At the new school his autism was
immediately recognized. During his three years there he experienced a slow
improvement. Unfortunately a subsequent two years in a parochial school
destroyed this progress. He began to develop compulsive defenses, which he
called his "preventions." He could not drink, for example, except through
elaborate piping systems built of straws. Liquids had to be "pumped" into

him, in his fantasy, or he could not suck. Eventually his behavior became so upsetting that he could not be kept in the parochial school. At home things did not improve. Three months before entering the Orthogenic School he made a serious attempt at suicide.

To us Joey's pathological behavior seemed the external expression of an overwhelming effort to remain almost nonexistent as a person. For weeks Joey's only reply when addressed was "Bam." Unless he thus neutralized whatever we said, there would be an explosion, for Joey plainly wished to close off every form of contact not mediated by machinery. Even when he was bathed he rocked back and forth with mute engine-like regularity, flooding the bathroom. If he stopped rocking, he did this like a machine too; suddenly he went completely rigid. Only once, after months of being lifted from his bath and carried to bed, did a small expression of puzzled pleasure appear on his face as he said very softly: "They even carry you to your bed here."

For a long time after he began to talk he would never refer to anyone by name, but only as "that person" or "the little person" or "the big person." He was unable to designate by its true name anything except through neologisms or word contaminations. For a long time he spoke about "master paintings" and "a master painting room" (i.e., masturbating and masturbating room). One of his machines, the "criticizer," prevented him from "saying words which have unpleasant feelings." Yet he gave personal names to the tubes and motors in his collection of machinery. Moreover, these dead things had feelings; the tubes bled when hurt and sometimes got sick. He consistently maintained this reversal between animate and inanimate objects.

In Joey's machine world everything, on pain of instant destruction, obeyed inhibitory laws much more stringent than those of physics. When we came to know him better, it was plain that in his moments of silent withdrawal, with his machine switched off, Joey was absorbed in pondering the compulsive laws of his private universe.

His preoccupation with machinery made it difficult to establish even practical contacts with him. If he wanted to do something with a counselor, such as play with a toy that had caught his vague attention, he could not do so: "I'd like this very much, but first I have to turn off the machine." But by the time he had fulfilled all the requirements of his preventions, he had lost interest. When a toy was offered to him, he could not touch it because his motors and his tubes did not leave him a hand free. Even certain colors were dangerous and had to be strictly avoided in toys and clothing, because "some colors turn off the current, and I can't touch them because I can't live without the current."

Joey was convinced that machines were better than people. Once when he bumped into one of the pipes on our jungle gym he kicked it so violently that his teacher had to restrain him to keep him from injuring himself. When she explained that the pipe was much harder than his foot, Joey replied: "That proves it. Machines are better than the body. They don't break; they're much harder and stronger." If he lost or forgot something, it merely proved that his brain ought to be thrown away and replaced by machinery. If he spilled something, his arm should be broken and twisted off because it did not work properly. When his head or arm failed to work as it should, he tried to punish it by hitting it. Even Joey's feelings were mechanical. Much later in his therapy, when he had formed a timid attachment to another child and had been rebuffed, Joey cried: "He broke my feelings."

Gradually we began to understand what had seemed to be contradictory in Joey's behavior—why he held on to the motors and tubes, then suddenly destroyed them in a fury, then set out immediately and urgently to equip himself with new and larger tubes. Joey had created these machines to run his body and mind because it was too painful to be human. But again and again he became dissatisfied with their failure to meet his need and rebellious at the way they frustrated his will. In a recurrent frenzy he "exploded" his light bulbs and tubes, and for a moment became a human being—for one crowning instant he came alive. But as soon as he had asserted his dominance through the self-created explosion, he felt his life ebbing away. To keep on existing he had immediately to restore his machines and replenish the electricity that supplied his life energy.

What deep-seated fears and needs underlay Joey's delusional system? We were long in finding out, for Joey's prevention effectively concealed the secret of his autistic behavior. In the meantime we dealt with his peripheral problems one by one.

During his first year with us Joey's most trying problem was toilet behavior. This surprised us, for Joey's personality was not "anal" in the Freudian sense; his original personality damage had antedated the period of his toilet-training. Rigid and early toilet-training, however, had certainly contributed to his anxieties. It was our effort to help Joey with this problem that led to his first recognition of us a human beings.

Going to the toilet, like everything else in Joey's life, was surrounded by elaborate preventions. We had to accompany him; he had to take off all his clothes; he could only squat, not sit, on the toilet seat; he had to touch the wall with one hand, in which he also clutched frantically the vacuum tubes that powered his elimination. He was terrified lest his whole body be sucked down.

To counteract this fear we gave him a metal wastebasket in lieu of a toilet. Eventually, when eliminating into the wastebasket, he no longer needed to take off all his clothes, nor to hold on to the wall. He still needed the tubes and motors which, he believed, moved his bowels for him. But here again the all-important machinery was itself a source of new terrors. In Joey's world the gadgets had to move their bowels too. He was terribly concerned that they should, but since they were so much more powerful than men, he was also terrified that if his tubes moved their bowels, their feces would fill all of space and leave him no room to live. He was thus always caught in some fearful contradiction.

Our readiness to accept his toilet habits, which obviously entailed some hardship for his counselors, gave Joey the confidence to express his obsessions in drawings. Drawing these fantasies was a first step toward letting us in, however, distantly, to what concerned him most deeply. It was the first step in a year-long process of externalizing his anal preoccupations. As a result he began seeing feces everywhere; the whole world became to him a mire of excrement. At the same time he began to eliminate freely wherever he happened to be. But with this release from his infantile imprisonment in compulsive rules, the toilet and the whole process of elimination became less dangerous. Thus far it had been beyond Joey's comprehension that anybody could possibly move his bowels without mechanical aid. Now Joey took a further step forward; defecation became the first physiological process he could perform without the help of vacuum tubes. It must not be thought that he was proud of his ability. Taking pride in an achievemenb presupposes that one accomplishes it of one's own free will. He still did not feel himself an autonomous person who could do things on his own. To Joey defecation still seemed enslaved to some incomprehensible but utterly binding cosmic law, perhaps the law his parents had imposed on him when he was being toilet-trained.

It was not simply that his parents had subjected him to rigid, early training. Many children are so trained. But in most cases the parents have a deep emotional investment in the child's performance. The child's response in turn makes training an occasion for interaction between them and for the building of genuine relationships. Joey's parents had no emotional investment in him. His obedience gave them no satisfaction and won him no affection or approval. As a toilet-trained child he saved his mother labor, just as household machines saved her labor. As a machine he was not loved for his performance, nor could he love himself.

So it had been with all other aspects of Joey's existence with his parents. Their reactions to his eating or noneating, sleeping or wakening, urinating, or defecating, being dressed or undressed, washed or bathed did not flow from any unitary interest in him, deeply embedded in their personalities. By treating him mechanically his parents made him a machine. The various functions of life—even the parts of his body—bore no integrating relationship to one another or to any sense of self that was acknowledged and confirmed by others. Though he had acquired mastery over some functions, such as toilet-training and speech, he had acquired them separately and kept them isolated from each other. Toilet-training had thus not gained him a pleasant feeling of body mastery; speech had not led to communication of thought of feeling. On the contrary, each achievement only steered him away from self-mastery and integration. Toilet-training had enslaved him. Speech left him talking in neologisms that obstructed his and our ability to relate to each other. In Joey's development the normal process of growth had been made to run backward. Whatever he had learned put him not at the end of his infantile development toward integration but, on the contrary, farther behind than he was at its very beginning. Had we understood this sooner, his first years with us would have been less baffling.

It is unlikely that Joey's calamity could befall a child in any time and culture but our own. He suffered no physical deprivation; he starved for human contact. Just to be taken care of is not enough for relating. It is a necessary but not a sufficient condition. At the extreme where utter scarcity reigns, the forming of relationships is certainly hampered. But our society of mechanized plenty often makes for equal difficulties in a child's learning to relate. Where parents can provide the simple creature-comforts for their children only at the cost of significant effort, it is likely that they will feel pleasure in being able to provide for them; it is this, the parents' pleasure, that gives children a sense of personal worth and sets the process of relating in motion. But if comfort is so readily available that the parents feel no particular pleasure in winning it for their children, then the children cannot develop the feeling of being worthwhile around the satisfaction of their basic needs. Of course parents and children can and do develop relationships around other situations. But matters are then no longer so simple and direct. The child must be on the receiving end of care and concern given with pleasure and without the exaction of return if he is to feel loved and worthy of respect and consideration. This feeling gives him the ability to trust; he can entrust his well-being to persons to whom he is so important. Out of such trust the child learns to form close and stable relationships.

For Joey relationship with his parents was empty of pleasure in comfort-giving as in all other situations. His was an extreme instance of a plight that sends many schizophrenic children to our clinics and hospitals. Many months passed before he could relate to us; his despair that anybody could like him made contact impossible.

When Joey could finally trust us enough to let himself become more infantile, he began to play at being a papoose. There was a corresponding change in his fantasies. He drew endless pictures of himself as an electrical papoose. Totally enclosed, suspended in empty space, he is run by un-known, unseen powers through wireless electricity.

As we eventually came to understand, the heart of Joey's delusional sys-tem was the artificial, mechanical womb he had created and into which he had locked himself. In his papoose fantasies lay the wish to be entirely reborn in a womb. His new experiences in the school suggested that life, after all, might be worth living. Now he was searching for a way to be reborn in a better way. Since machines were better than men, what was more natural than to try rebirth through them? This was the deeper meaning of his electrical papoose.

As Joey made progress, his pictures of himself became more dominant in his drawings. Though still machine-operated, he has grown in self-importance. Now he has acquired hands that do something, and he has had the courage to make a picture of the machine that runs him. Later still the papoose became a person, rather than a robot encased in glass.

Eventually Joey began to create an imaginary family at the school: the "Carr" family. Why the Carr family" In the car he was enclosed as he had been in his papoose, but at least the car was not stationary; it could move. More important, in a car one was not only driven but also could drive. The Carr family was Joey's way of exploring the possibility of leaving the school, of living with a good family in a safe, protecting car.

Joey at last broke through his prison. In this brief account it has not been possible to trace the painfully slow process of his first true relations with other human beings. Suffice it to say that he ceased to be a mechanical boy and became a human child. This newborn child was, however, nearly 12 years old. To recover the lost time is a tremendous task. That work has occupied Joey and us ever since. Sometimes he sets to it with a will; at other times the difficulty of real life makes him regret that he ever came out of his shell. But he has never wanted to return to his mechanical life.

One last detail and this fragment of Joey's story has been told. When Joey was 12, he made a float for our Memorial Day parade. It carried the slogan: "Feelings are more important than anything under the sun." Feelings, Joey had learned, are what make for humanity; their absence, for a mechanical existence. With this knowledge, Joey entered the human condition.

Discussion Plan:

1. If Joey were really a machine, could he have been a person too? How would we treat a machine that looked like a person? What do machines lack that persons are supposed to have?
2. When Joey was pretending to be a machine, he really believed that he was a machine. Was he also a person, but didn't know it? Can you be a person and not know it?
3. Why do you think that Joey decided to "become a machine?" What are the reasons that the therapist writing the story suggests?
4. How important were Joey's parents in influencing him to become a machine? Are parents always important in helping a child build a self-image?
5. Why wouldn't Joey refer to anyone by name? What's so important about names?

6. Joey thinks initially that machines are better than people. List the advantages of being a machine and the disadvantages. Is Joey right?

7. At the end of his therapy, Joey writes that " Feelings are more important than anything under the sun." Has he contradicted what he thought in the beginning (see question 6)? Is he right?

Exercise:

Are people machines?

Below is a list of human behaviors. Rank them on a scale of 1 to 5.
The most machine-like behaviors are to be ranked '1'; the least machine-like, '5'.

1. eating
2. studying
3. defecating
4. 'making out'
5. playing sports
6. practicing a musical instrument
7. doing math
8. writing poetry
9. breathing
10. riding a bike
11. ballroom dancing
12. disco dancing
13. punk rock dancing
14. memorizing a poem
15. fighting
16. having a discussion on the civilian casualties in Nicaragua.
17. You discover that your mother is working on newer more powerful intercontinental missile.

Identify the criteria you used in making your evaluations. Make a list of machine-like characteristics.

Feelings

Joey sees having feelings as the difference between people and machines. In a sense we can agree. Machines can do a great deal that humans can do, but there is no evidence that machines feel. What kind of advantage is the ability to have feelings? Some people would agree with Joey's earlier statement "Machines are better than people," because feelings are troublesome, creating unacceptable behavior and confusing the issue. If we are to value ourselves as feeling creatures, it seems that some reconciliation between the demands of feeling and the consequences of feeling must be made.

Hugh Prather, Notes to Myself

... At first I thought that to "be myself" meant simply to act the way I feel. I would ask myself a question such as, "What do I want to say to this person?" and very often the answer was surprisingly negative. It seemed that when I looked inside, the negative feelings were the ones I noticed first. Possibly I noticed them because of their social unusualness; possibly they stood out because acting negatively was what I feared. But I soon found that behind most negative feelings were deeper, more positive feelings—if I held still long enough to look. The more I attempted to "be me" the more "me's" I found there were. I now see that "being me" means acknowledging all that I feel at the moment, and then taking responsibility for my actions by consciously choosing which level of my feelings I am going to respond to.

When I first began trying to be myself, I at times felt trapped by my feelings. I thought that I was stuck with the feelings I had, that I couldn't change them, and shouldn't try to even if I could. I saw many negative feelings inside me that I didn't want, and yet I felt that I must express them if I were going to be myself.

Since then I have realized that my feelings do change and that I can have a hand in changing them. They change simply by my becoming aware of them. When I acknowledge my feelings they become more positive. And they change when I express them. For example, if I tell a man I don't like him, I usually like him better.

The second thing I have realized is that my not wanting to express a negative feeling is a feeling in itself, a part of me, and if I want *not* to express the negative feeling more than I *do*, then I will be acting more like myself by not expressing it. ...

Discussion Plan:

1. Prather describes a number of strategies for dealing with negative feelings. What are they?
2. What criteria does he offer for identifying negative feelings?
3. Do you agree with his "level" theory of feelings?
4. Do you agree that positive feelings often underlie negative ones?
5. Give five examples of negative feelings that have some positive feeling beneath them.
6. Can we choose which feelings to respond to?

In the following situations describe the positive and negative feelings that you believe might be generated. Which feelings do you think we ought to respond to in similar situations?

1. A coach tells you that you haven't made the team.
2. You win a science award, but your best friend, who worked as hard, didn't.
3. Your best friend's girlfriend "comes on to you."
4. Your best friend breaks a date with you to go out with a boy.
5. You are sexually harrassed by a boss who fires you when you object.
6. During a heated discussion an acquaintance blurts out a racial slur.
7. You are, unfairly, penalized for cheating on a test.
8. Your best friend submits an old term paper of yours and gets a better grade than you do.
9. Your parent becomes seriously ill.
10. Your parent loses a job and you have to get a job instead of going away on vacation.
11. Your parents cannot afford to send you to college.
12. You and your lover discover that you are having a baby.

Prather claims that expressing and being aware of feelings changes them from negative to positive. In the following situations decide whether it would make things better or worse if you became aware of the feelings. Would expressing them openly tend to convert them into more positive feelings as Prather suggests?

1. You slop soup on your clothes at a dinner with the school principal.
2. You make anti-semitic remarks to a person who you discover is Jewish.
3. You get turned on by your sister's boyfriend.
4. You think that your English teacher is a moron.
5. You think that your father looks ridiculous in the outfit he has chosen to go to a party in.
6. You think that your mother's dress is too sexually revealing.
7. You feel that your audition was much better than your friend's, but your friend got the part.
8. You think that your mother's paintings are stupid and ugly.
9. You discover that you have a serious disease.
10. Your closest friend gets leukemia.
11. A popular boy in school gets hit by a drunk driver and dies.
12. You see a graphic movie of the Holocaust.
13. You are required to register for the draft.
14. You read an article on the civilian casualties in Nicaragua.
15. You discover that your mother is working on a new powerfull intercontinental ballistics missile.

Values

Who we are is an outgrowth of many factors. A great deal depends on our native endowments—our bodies and our talents. A great deal depends on our environment—the opportunities we are given and the opportunities that we take. How we value ourselves is not only based on our actual achievements, but is also a reflection of the standards that we apply to ourselves. And these standards are often the result of comparing ourselves to others.

Carson McCullers, Wunderkind

She came into the living room, her music satchel plopping against her winter-stockinged legs and her other arm weighted down with school books, and stood for a moment listening to the sounds from the studio. A soft procession of piano chords and the tuning of a violin. Then Mister Bilderbach, called out to her in his chunky, guttural tone:

"That you, Bienchen?"

As she jerked off her mittens she saw that her fingers were twitching to the motions of the fugue she had practiced that morning. "Yes," she answered. "It's me."

"I," the voice corrected. "Just a moment."

She could hear Mister Lafkowitz talking—his words spun out in a silky, unintelligible hum. A voice almost like a woman's, she thought, compared to Mister Bilderbach's. Restlessness scattered her attention. She fumbled with her geometry book and *Le Voyage de Monsieur Perrichon* before putting them on the table. She sat down on the sofa and began to take her music from the satchel. Again she saw her hands—the quivering tendons that stretched down from her knuckles, the sore finger tip capped with curled, dingy tape. The sight sharpened the fear that had begun to torment her for the past few months.

Noiselessly she mumbled a few phrases of encouragement to herself. A good lesson—a good lesson—like it used to be—Her lips closed as she heard the stolid sound of Mister Bilderbach's footsteps across the floor of the studio and the creaking of the door as it slid open.

For a moment she had the peculiar feeling that during most of the fifteen years of her life she had been looking at the face and shoulders that jutted from behind the door, in a silence disturbed only by the muted, blank plucking of a violin string. Mister Bilderbach. Her teacher, Mister Bilderbach. The quick eyes behind the horn-rimmed glasses; the light, thin hair and narrow face beneath; the lips full and loose shut and the lower one pink and shining from the bites of his teeth; the forked veins in his temples throbbing plainly enough to be observed across the room.

"Aren't you a little early?" he asked, glancing at the clock on the mantel piece that had pointed to five minutes of twelve for a month. "Josel's in here. We're running over a little sonatina by someone he knows."

"Good," she said, trying to smile. "I'll listen." She could see her fingers sinking powerless into a blur of piano keys. She felt tired—felt that if he looked at her much longer her hands might tremble.

He stood uncertain, halfway in the room. Sharply his teeth pushed down on his bright, swollen lip. "Hungry, Bienchen?" he asked. "There's some apple cake Anna made, and milk."

"I'll wait till afterward," she said. "Thanks."

"After you finish with a very fine lesson—eh?" His smile seemed to crumble at the corners.

There was a sound from behind him in the studio and Mister Lafkowitz pushed at the other panel of the door and stood beside him.

"Frances?" he said, smiling. "And how is the work coming now?"

Without meaning to, Mister Lafkowitz always made her feel clumsy and overgrown. He was such a small man himself, with a weary look when he was not holding his violin. His eyebrows curved high above his sallow Jewish face as though asking a question, but the lids of his eyes drowsed languorous and indifferent. Today he seemed distracted. She watched him come into the room for no apparent purpose, holding his pearl-tipped bow in his still fingers, slowly gliding the white horse-hair through a chalky piece of resin. His eyes were sharp bright slits today and the linen handkerchief that flowed down from his collar darkened the shadows beneath them.

"I gather you're doing a lot now," smiled Mister Lafkowitz, although she had not yet answered the question.

She looked at Mister Bilderbach. He turned away. His heavy shoulders pushed the door open wide so that the later afternoon sun came through the window of the studio and shafted yellow over the dusty living room. Behind her teacher she could see the squat long piano, the window, and the bust of Brahms.

"No," she said to Mister Lafkowitz, "I'm doing terribly." Her thin fingers flipped at the pages of her music. "I don't know what's the matter," she said, looking at Mister Bilderbach's stooped muscular back that stood tense and listening.

Mister Lafkowitz smiled. "There are times, I suppose, when one—"

A harsh chord sounded from the piano. "Don't you think we'd better get on with this?" asked Mister Bilderbach.

"Immediately," said Mister Lafkowitz, giving the bow one more scrape before starting toward the door. She could see him pick up his violin from the top of the piano. He caught her eye and lowered the instrument. "You've seen the picture of Heime?"

Her fingers curled tight over the sharp corner of the satchel. "What picture?"

"One of Heime in the *Musical Courier* there on the table. Inside the top cover."

The sonatina began. Discordant yet somehow simple. Empty but with a sharp-cut style of its own. She reached for the magazine and opened it.

There Heime was—in the left-hand corner. Holding his violin with his fingers hooked down over the strings for a pizzicato. With his dark serge knickers strapped neatly beneath his knees, a sweater and rolled collar. It was a bad picture. Although it was snapped in profile his eyes were cut around toward the photographer and his finger looked as though it would pluck the wrong string. He seemed suffering to turn around toward the picture-taking apparatus. He was thinner—his stomach did not poke out now—but he hadn't changed much in six months.

Heime Israelsky, talented young violinist, snapped while at work in his teacher's studio on Riverside Drive. Younger Master Israelsky, who will soon celebrate his fifteenth birthday, has been invited to play the Beethoven Concerta with—

That morning, after she had practiced from six until eight, her dad had made her sit down at the table with the family for breakfast. She hated breakfast; it gave her a sick feeling afterward. She would rather wait and get four chocolate bars with her twenty cents lunch money and munch them during school—bringing up little morsels from her pocket under cover of her handkerchief, stopping dead when the silver paper rattled. But this morning her dad had put a fried egg on her plate and she had known that if it burst—so that the slimy yellow oozed over the white—she would cry. And that had happened. The same feeling was upon her now. Gingerly she laid the magazine back on the table and closed her eyes.

The music in the studio seemed to be urging violently and clumsily for something that was not to be had. After a moment her thoughts drew back from Heime and the concerta and the picture—and hovered around the lesson once more. She slid over on the sofa until she could see plainly into the studio—the two of them playing, peering at the notations on the piano, lustfully drawing out all that was there.

She could not forget the memory of Mister Bilderbach's face as he stared at her a moment ago. Her hands, still twitching unconsciously to the motions of the fugue, closed over her bony knees. Tired, she was. And with a circling, sinking away feeling like the one that often came to her just before she dropped off to sleep on the nights when she had over-practiced. Like those weary half-dreams that buzzed and carried her out into their own whirling space.

A *Wunderkind—*a *Wunderkind—*a *Wunderkind.* The syllables would come out rolling in the deep German way, roar against her ears and then fall to a murmur. Along with the faces circling, swelling out in a distortion, diminishing to pale blobs—Mister Bilderbach, Mrs. Bilderbach, Heime, Mister Lafkowitz. Around and around in a circle revolving to the guttural *Wunderkind.* Mister Bilderbach looming large in the middle of the circle, his face urging—with the others around him.

Phrases of music seesawing crazily. Notes she had been practicing falling over each other like a handful of marbles dropped downstairs. Bach, Debussy, Prokofieff, Brahms—timed grotesquely to the far-off throb of her tired body and the buzzing circle.

Sometimes—when she had not worked more than three hours or had stayed out from high school—the dreams were not so confused. The music soared clearly in her mind and quick, precise little memories would come back—clear as the sissy "Age of Innocence" picture Heime had given her after their joint concert was over.

A *Wunderkind—*a *Wunderkind.* That was what Mister Bilderbach had called her when, at twelve, she first came to him. Older pupils had repeated the word.

Not that he had ever said the word to her. "Bienchen—" (She had a plain American name but he never used it except when her mistakes were enormous.) "Bienchen," he would say, "I know it must be terrible. Carrying around all the time a head that thick. Poor Bienchen—"

Mister Bilderbach's father had been a Dutch violinist. His mother was from Prague. He had been born in this country and had spent his youth in Germany. So many times she wished she had not been born and brought up in just Cincinnati. How do you say "cheese" in German? Mister Bilderbach, what is Dutch for "I don't understand you"?

The first day she came to the studio. After she played the whole Second Hungarian Rhapsody from memory. The room graying with twilight. His face as he leaned over the piano.

"Now we begin all over," he said that first day. "It—playing music—is more than cleverness. If a twelve-year-old girl's fingers cover so many keys to a second—that means nothing."

He tapped his broad chest and his forehead with his stubby hand. "Here and here. You are old enough to understand that." He lighted a cigarette and gently blew the first exhalation above her head. "And work—work—work. We will start now with these Bach Inventions and these little Schumann pieces." His hands moved again—this time to jerk the cord of the lamp behind her and point to the music. "I will show you how I wish this practiced. Listen carefully now."

She had been at the piano for almost three hours and was very tired. His deep voice sounded as though it had been straying inside her for a long time.

She wanted to reach out and touch his muscle-flexed finger that pointed out the phrases, wanted to feel the gleaming gold band ring and the strong hairy back of his hand.

She had lessons Tuesday after school and on Saturday afternoons. Often she stayed, when the Saturday lesson was finished, for dinner, and then spent the night and took the streetcar home the next morning. Mrs. Bilderbach liked her in her calm, almost dumb way. She was much different from her husband. She was quiet and fat and slow. When she wasn't in the kitchen, cooking the rich dishes that both of them loved, she seemed to spend all her time in their bed upstairs, reading magazines or just looking with a half-smile at nothing. When they had married in Germany she had been a *lieder* singer. She didn't sing any more (she said it was her throat). When he would call her in from the kitchen to listen to a pupil she would always smile and say that it was *gut*, very *gut*.

When Frances was thirteen it came to her one day that the Bilderbachs had no children. It seemed strange. Once she had been back in the kitchen with Mrs. Bilderbach when he had come striding in from the studio, tense with anger at some pupil who had annoyed him. His wife stood stirring the thick soup until his hand groped out and rested on her shoulder. Then she turned—stood placid—while he folded his arms about her and buried his sharp face in the white, nerveless flesh of her neck. They stood that way without moving. And then his face jerked back suddenly, the anger diminished to a quiet inexpressiveness, and he had returned to the studio.

After she had started with Mister Bilderbach and didn't have time to see anything of the people at high school, Heime had been the only friend of her own age. He was Mister Lafkowitz's pupil and would come with him to Mister Bilderbach's on evenings when she would be there. They would listen to their teachers' playing. And often they themselves went over chamber music together—Mozart sonatas or Bloch.

A *Wunderkind*—a *Wunderkind.*

Heime was a *Wunderkind.* He and she, then.

Heime had been playing the violin since he was four. He didn't have to go to school; Mister Lafkowitz's brother, who was crippled, used to teach him geometry and European history and French verbs in the afternoon. When he was thirteen he had as fine a technique as any violinist in Cincinnati—everyone said so. But playing the violin must be easier than the piano. She knew it must be.

Heime always seemed to smell of corduroy pants and the food he had eaten and rosin. Half the time, too, his hands were dirty around the knuckles and the cuffs of his shirts peeped out dingily from the sleeves of his sweater. She always watched his hands when he played— thin only at the joints with the hard little blobs of flesh bulging over the short-cut nails and the babyish-looking crease that showed so plainly in his bowing wrist.

In the dreams, as when she was awake, she could remember the concert only in a blur. She had not known it was unsuccessful for her until months after. True, the papers had praised Heime more than her. But he was much shorter than she. When they stood together on the stage he came only to her shoulders. And that made a difference with people, she knew. Also, there was the matter of the sonata they played together. The Bloch.

"No, no—I don't think that would be appropriate," Mister Bilderbach had said when the Bloch was suggested to end the programme. "Now that John Powell thing—the Sonate Virginianesque."

She hadn't understood then; she wanted it to be the Bloch as much as Mister Lafkowitz and Heime.

Mister Bilderbach had given in. Later, after the reviews had said she lacked the temperament for that type of music, after they called her playing thin and lacking in feeling, she felt cheated.

"That oie oie stuff," said Mister Bilderbach, crackling the newspapers at her. "Not for you, Bienchen. Leave all that to the Heimes and vitses and skys."

A *Wunderkind*. No matter what the papers said, that was what he had called her.

Why was it Heime had done so much better at the concert than she? At school sometimes, when she was supposed to be watching someone do a geometry problem on the blackboard, the question would twist knife-like inside her. She would worry about it in bed, and even sometimes when she was supposed to be concentrating at the piano. It wasn't just the Bloch and her not being Jewish—not entirely. It wasn't that Heime didn't have to go to school and had begun his training early, either. It was—?

Once she thought she knew.

"Play the Fantasia and Fugue," Mister Bilderbach had demanded one evening a year ago—after he and Mister Lafkowitz had finished reading some music together.

The Bach, as she played, seemed to her well done. From the tail of her eye she could see the calm, pleased expression on Mister Bilderbach's face, see his hands rise climactically from the chair arms and then sink down loose and satisfied when the high points of the phrases had been passed successfully. She stood up from the piano when it was over, swallowing to loosen the bands that the music seemed to have drawn around her throat and chest. But—

"Frances—" Mister Lafkowitz had said then, suddenly, looking at her with his thin mouth curved and his eyes almost covered by their delicate lids. "Do you know how many children Bach had?"

She turned to him, puzzled. "A good many. Twenty some odd."

"Well then—" The corners of his smile etched themselves gently in his pale face. "He could not have been so cold—then."

Mister Bilderbach was not pleased; his guttural effulgence of German words had *Kind* in it somewhere. Mister Lafkowitz raised his eyebrows. She had caught the point easily enough, but she felt no deception in keeping her face blank and immature because that was the way Mister Bilderbach wanted her to look.

Yet, such things had nothing to do with it. Nothing very much, at least, for she would grow older. Mister Bilderbach understood that, and even Mister Lafkowitz had not meant just what he said.

In the dreams Mister Bilderbach's face loomed out and contracted in the center of the whirling circle. The lip surging softly, the veins in his temples insisting.

But sometimes, before she slept, there were such clear memories; as when she pulled a hole in the heel of her stocking down, so that her shoe would hide it. "Bienchen, Bienchen!" And bringing Mrs. Bilderbach's workbasket in and showing her how it should be darned and not gathered together in a lumpy heap.

And the time she graduated from Junior High.

"What you wear?" asked Mrs. Bilderbach the Sunday morning at breakfast when she told them about how they had practiced to march into the auditorium.

"An evening dress my cousin had last year."

"Ah—Bienchen!" he said, circling his warm coffee cup with his heavy hands, looking up at her with wrinkles around his laughing eyes. "I bet I know what Bienchen wants—"

He insisted. He would not believe her when she explained that she honestly didn't care at all.

"Like this, Anna," he said, pushing his napkin across the table and mincing to the other side of the room, swishing his hips, rolling up his eyes behind his horn-rimmed glasses.

The next Saturday afternoon, after her lessons, he took her to the department stores downtown. His thick fingers smoothed over the filmy nets and crackling taffetas that the saleswomen unwound from their bolts. He held colors to her face, cocking his head to one side, and selected pink. Shoes, he remembered too. He liked best some white kid pumps. They seemed a little like old ladies' shoes to her and the Red Cross label in the instep had a charity look. But it really didn't matter at all. When Mrs. Bilderbach began to cut out the dress and fit it to her with pins, he interrupted his lessons to stand by and suggest ruffles around the hips and neck and a fancy rosette on the shoulder. The music was coming along nicely then. Dresses and commencement and such made no difference.

Nothing mattered much except playing the music as it must be played, bringing out the thing that must be in her, practicing, practicing, playing so that Mister Bilderbach's face lost some of its urging look. Putting the thing into her music that Myra Hess had, and Yehudi Menuhin—even Heime!

What had begun to happen to her four months ago? The notes began springing out with a glib, dead intonation. Adolescence, she thought. Some kids played with promise—and worked and worked until, like her, the least little thing would start them crying, and worn out with trying to get the thing across—the longing thing they felt—something queer began to happen—But not she! She was like Heime. She had to be. She—

Once it was there for sure. And you didn't lose things like that. A *Wunderkind. A Wunderkind....*

Of her he said it, rolling the words in the sure, deep German way. And in the dreams even deeper, more certain than ever. With his face looming out at her, and the longing phrases of music mixed in with the zooming, circling round, round, round—a *Wunderkind. A Wunderkind....*

This afternoon Mister Bilderbach did not show Mister Lafkowitz to the front door, as he usually did. He stayed at the piano, softly pressing a solitary note. Listening, Frances watched the violinist wind his scarf about his pale throat.

"A good picture of Heime," she said, picking up her music. "I got a letter from him a couple of months ago—telling about hearing Schnabel and Huberman and about Carnegie Hall and things to eat at the Russian Tea Room."

To put off going into the studio a moment longer she waited until Mister Lafkowitz was ready to leave and then stood behind him as he opened the door. The frosty cold outside cut into the room. It was growing late and the air was seeped with the pale yellow of winter twilight. When the door swung to on its hinges, the house seemed darker and more silent than ever before she had known it to be.

As she went into the studio Mister Bilderbach got up from the piano and silently watched her settle herself at the keyboard.

"Well, Bienchen," he said, "This afternoon we are going to begin all over. Start from scratch. Forget the last few months."

He looked as though he were trying to act a part in a movie. His solid body swayed from toe to heel, he rubbed his hands together, and even smiled in a satisfied, movie way. Then suddenly he thrust this manner brusquely aside. His heavy shoulders slouched and he began to run through the stack of music she had brought in. "The Bach—no, not yet," he murmured. "The Beethoven? Yes. The Variation Sonata. Opus 26."

The keys of the piano hemmed her in—stiff and white and dead-seeming.

"Wait a minute," he said. He stood in the curve of the piano, elbows propped, and looked at her. "Today I expect something from you. Now this sonata—it's the first Beethoven sonata you ever worked on. Every note is under control—technically—you have nothing to cope with but the music. Only music now. That's all you think about."

He rustled through the pages of her volume until he found the place. Then he pulled his teaching chair halfway across the room, turned it around and seated himself, straddling the back with his legs.

For some reason, she knew, this position of his usually had a good effect on her performance. But today she felt that she would notice him from the corner of her eye and be disturbed. His back was stiffly tilted, his legs looked tense. The heavy volume before him seemed to balance dangerously on the chair back. "Now we begin," he said with a peremptory dart of his eyes in her direction.

Her hands rounded over the keys and then sank down. The first notes were too loud, the other phrases followed dryly.

Arrestingly his hand rose from the score. "Wait! Think a minute what you're playing. How is this beginning marked?"

"An *andante*."

"All right. Don't drag it into an *adagio* then. And play deeply into the keys. Don't snatch it off shallowly that way. A graceful, deep-toned *andante*—'"

She tried again. Her hands seemed separate from the music that was in her.

"Listen," he interrupted. "Which of these variations dominates the whole?"

"The dirge," she answered.

"Then prepare for that. This is an *andante*—but it's not salon stuff as you just played it. Start out softly, *piano*, and make it swell out just before the arpeggio. Make it warm and dramatic. And down here—where it's marked *dolce* make the counter melody sing out. You know all that. We've gone over all that side of it before. Now play it. Feel it as Beethoven wrote it down. Feel that tragedy and restraint."

She could not stop looking at his hands. They seemed to rest tentatively on the music, ready to fly up as a stop signal as soon as she would begin, the gleaming flash of his ring calling her to halt. "Mister Bilderbach—maybe if I—if you let me play on through the first variation without stopping I could do better."

"I won't interrupt."

Her pale face leaned over too close to the keys. She played through the first part, and, obeying a nod from him, began the second. There were no flaws that jarred on her, but the phrases shaped from her fingers before she had put into them the meaning that she felt.

When she had finished he looked up from the music and began to speak with dull bluntness: "I hardly heard those harmonic fillings in the right hand. And incidentally, this part was supposed to take on intensity, develop the fore-shadowings that were supposed to be inherent in the first part. Go on with the next one, though."

She wanted to start it with subdued viciousness and progress to a feeling of deep, swollen sorrow. Her mind told her that. But her hands seemed to gum in the keys like limp macaroni and she could not imagine the music as it should be.

When the last note had stopped vibrating, he closed the book and deliberately got up from the chair. He was moving his lower jaw from side to side—and between his open lips she could glimpse the pink healthy lane to his throat and his strong, smoke-yellowed teeth. He laid the Beethoven gingerly on top of the rest of her music and propped his elbows on the smooth, black piano top once more. "No," he said simply, looking at her.

Her mouth began to quiver. "I can't help it. I—"

Suddenly he strained his lips into a smile. "Listen, Bienchen," he began in a new, forced voice. "You still play the Harmonious Blacksmith, don't you? I told you not to drop it from your repertoire."

"Yes," she said, "I practice it now and then."

His voice was the one he used for children. "It was among the first things we worked on together—remember. So strongly you used to play it—like a real blacksmith's daughter. You see, Bienchen, I know you so well—as if you were my own girl. I know what you have—I've heard you play so many things beautifully. You used to—"

He stopped in confusion and inhaled from his pulpy stub of cigarette. The smoke drowsed out from his pink lips and clung in a gray mist around her lank hair and childish forehead.

"Make it happy and simple," he said, switching on the lamp behind her and stepping back from the piano.

For a moment he stood just inside the bright circle the light made. Then impulsively he squatted down to the floor. "Vigorous," he said.

She could not stop looking at him, sitting on one heel with the other foot resting squarely before him for balance, the muscles of his strong thighs straining under the cloth of his trousers, his back straight, his elbows staunchly propped on his knees. "Simply now," he repeated with a gesture of his fleshy hands. "Think of the blacksmith—working out in the sunshine all day. Working easily and undisturbed."

She could not look down at the piano. The light brightened the hairs on the backs of his outspread hands, made the lenses of his glasses glitter.

"All of it," he urged. "Now!"

She felt that the marrows of her bones were hollow and there was no blood left in her. Her heart that had been springing against her chest all afternoon felt suddenly dead. She saw it gray and limp and shriveled at the edges like an oyster.

His face seemed to throb out in space before her, come closer with the lurching motion in the veins of his temples. In retreat, she looked down at the piano. Her lips shook like jelly and a surge of noiseless tears made the white keys blur in a watery line. "I can't," she whispered. "I don't know why, but I just can't—can't any more."

His tense body slackened and, holding his hand to his side, he pulled himself up. She clutched her music and hurried past him.

Her coat. The mittens and galoshes. The schoolbooks and the satchel he had given her on her birthday. All from the silent room that was hers. Quickly—before he would have to speak.

As she passed through the vestibule she could not help but see his hands— held out from his body that leaned against the studio door, relaxed and purposeless. The door shut to firmly. Dragging her books and satchel she stumbled down the stone steps, turned in the wrong direction, and hurried down the street that had become confused with noise and bicycles and the games of other children.

Discussion Plan:

The self and standards:

1. Frances seems to fail when judged against the standards of music. What evidence in the text is given of the standards that are applied to her?
2. Distinguish the various sources of the standards applied to Frances.
3. Are any of the standards applied to Frances standards she herself accepts?
4. How is her sense of self related to the standards applied to Heime?
5. Are the standards applied to Frances objective?
6. Are the standards applied to Frances relative? And, if so, relative to what?

Exercise:

Standards are said to be *objective* when they are based on considerations that apply equally to all people judged and when the judgment is based on some operation that anyone who understands them can perform. Standards are said to be *relative* when they are based on some particular set of principles that are not universally shared. Standards are said to be *subjective* when they are applied by a particular person in some unique way. In the following decide whether the practices involved are judged by standards that are objective, relative or subjective. A question that you may ask as you work is: Are the three categories of standards mutually exclusive?

1. grading math papers
2. correcting papers for grammar
3. correcting essays for ideas
4. judging a beauty contest

5. deciding on the winner of a race

6. deciding whether to go steady with someone

7. choosing a career

8. picking the class valedictorian

9. fixing the price of a car

10. discovering the gross national product

11. deciding if a car is safe

12. deciding on a strategy for nuclear peace

13. picking a religion

14. accepting the scientific world view

15. deciding whether Homer existed

Standards are frequently thought to be fair or unfair. In the following rank the application of standards on a scale of 1 to 5; '1' most unfair, '5' most fair.

1. Choosing your friends because of race

2. Choosing your boyfriend because of good looks

3. Choosing the class president by a vote

4. Picking the lead in a school play through audition

5. Admitting only the top 5% of high school graduates to college

6. Compensating women for past unfair treatment by preferential hiring

7. Condemning a person to death for a murder that he committed

8. Using animals for medical experiments

9. Permitting drug companies to market dangerous drugs freely in third world countries

10. Prohibiting Americans from buying cheap goods from abroad.

Go over your answers. Elicit the standards that you thought applied to the practices. Are they objective, subjective or relative? Does this tend to make them more or less fair?

Values

Most of us aspire to be successful; and success is most often defined in social terms. A very few of us, because of natural abilities, hard work and sound counsel, can reach pinnacles of success that make us perfect examples of the fulfillment of the social ideals. People in this category are frequently found in the arts, especially the popular arts, where success means acceptance, having a great deal of money and a great deal of fun. On the one hand, we envy such people and fantasize about having similar achievements. On the other hand, we frequently ask: But are they really happy?

Tom Wolfe, The Girl of the Year

Bangs manes bouffants beehives Beale caps butter faces brush-on lashes decal eyes puffy sweaters French thrust bras flailing leather blue jeans stretch pants stretch jeans honeydew bottoms eclair shanks elf boots ballerina Knight slippers, hundreds of them, these flaming little buds, bobbing and screaming, rocketing around inside the Academy of Music Theater underneath that vast old mouldering cherub dome up there—aren't they super-marvelous!

"Aren't they super-marvelous!" says Baby Jane, and then: "Hi, Isabel! Isabel! You want to sit backstage—with the Stones!"

The show hasn't even started yet, the Rolling Stones aren't even on the stage, the place is full of great shabby mouldering dimness, and these flaming little buds.

Girls are reeling this way and that way in the aisle and through their huge black decal eyes, sagging with Tiger Tongue Lick Me brush-on eyelashes and black appliques, sagging like display window Christmas trees, they keep staring at—her—Baby Jane—on the aisle. What the hell is this? She is gorgeous in the most outrageous way. Her hair rises up from her head in a huge hairy corona, a huge tan mane around a narrow face and two eyes opened—swock!—like umbrellas, with all that hair flowing down over a coat made of zebra! Those motherless stripes! Oh, damn! Here she is with her friends, looking like some kind of queen bee for all flaming little buds everywhere. She twists around to shout to one of her friends and that incredible mane swings around on her shoulders, over the zebra coat.

"Isabel!" says Baby Jane, "Isabel, hi! I just saw the Stones! They look super-divine!"

That girl on the aisle, Baby Jane, is a fabulous girl. She comprehends what the Rolling Stones *mean*. Any columnist in New York could tell them who she is ... a celebrity of New York's new era of Wog Hip....

Baby Jane Holzer. Jane Holzer in *Vogue*, Jane Holzer in *Life*, Jane Holzer in Andy Warhol's underground movies, Jane Holzer in the world of High

Camp, Jane Holzer at the rock and roll, Jane Holzer is—well, how can one put it into words? Jane Holzer is This Year's Girl, at least, the New Celebrity, none of your old ideas of sexpots, prima donnas, romantic tragediennes, she is the girl who knows ...The Stones, East End vitality...

Then the show begins. An electronic blast begins, electric guitars, electric bass, enormous speakers up there on a vast yellow-gray stage. Murray the K, the D.J. and M.C., O.K.?, comes out from the wings, doing a kind of twist soft shoe, wiggling around, a stocky chap, thirty-eight years old, wearing Italian pants and a Sun Valley snow lodge sweater and a Stingy Brim straw hat. Murray the K! Girls throw balls of paper at him, and as they are onto the stage, the stage lights explode off them and they look like falling balls of flame.

And, finally, the Stones, now—how can one express it? The Stones come on stage—

"Oh, God, Andy, aren't they *divine!*"

—and spread out over the stage, the five Rolling Stones, from England, who are modeled after the Beatles, only more lower-class-deformed. One, Brian Jones, has an enormous blonde Beatle bouffant ...

"eeeeeeeeeeeeeeeeyes!" says Diana Vreeland, the editor of *Vogue.* "Jane Holzer is the most contemporary girl I know."

Jane Holzer at the rock and roll—

Jane Holzer in the underground movies—in Andy's studio, Andy Warhol, the famous Pop artist, experiencing the rare world of Jonas and Adolph Mekas, truth and culture in a new holy medium, underground movie-making on the lower East Side. And Jane is wearing a Jax shirt, strung like a Christmas tree with Diamonds, and they are making *Dracula,* or *Thirteen Beautiful Women* or *Soap Opera* or *Kiss*—in which Jane's lips ... but how can one describe an underground movie? It is ... avant-garde. "Andy calls everything super," says Jane. "I'm a super star, he's a super-director, we make super epics—and I mean, it's a completely new and natural way of acting. You can't imagine what really beautiful things can happen!"

Jane Holzer—with The New Artists, photographers like Jerry Schatzberg, David Bailey and Brian Duffy, and Nicky Haslam, the art director of *Show.* Bailey, Duffy and Haslam are English. Schatzberg says the photographers are the modern-day equivalents of the Impressionists in Paris around 1910, the men with a sense of New Art, the excitement of the artistic style of life, while all the painters, the old artists, have moved uptown to West End Avenue and live in apartment buildings with Kwik-Fiks parquet floors and run around the corner to get a new cover for the ironing board before the stores close.

Jane in the world of High Camp—a world of thin young men in an environment, a decor, an atmosphere so—how can one say it?—so indefinably Yellow Book. Jane in the world of Teen Savage—Jane modeling here and there—wearing Jean Harlow dresses for *Life* and Italian fashions for *Vogue* and doing the most fabulous cover for Nicky at *Show*, David took the photograph, showing Jane barebacked wearing a little yacht cap and a pair of "World's Fair" sunglasses and holding an American flag in her teeth, so—so Beyond Pop Art, if you comprehend.

Jane Holzer at the LBJ Discotheque—where they were handing out aprons with a target design on them, and Jane Holzer put it on backwards so that the target was behind and *then* did The Swim, a new dance ...

Jane has on a "Poor" sweater, clinging to the ribs, a new fashion, with short sleeves. Her hair is up in rollers. She is wearing tight slacks. Her hips are very small. She has a boyish body. She has thin arms and long, long fingers. She sits twisted about on a couch, up in her apartment on Park Avenue, talking on the telephone.

"Oh, I know what you mean," she says, "but I mean, couldn't you wait just two weeks? I'm expecting something to jell, it's a movie, and then you'd have a real story. You know what I mean? I mean you would have something to write about and not just Baby Jane sitting up in her Park Avenue apartment with her gotrocks. You know what I mean?...well, all right, but I think you'll have more of a story...well, all right ... bye, pussycat."

Then she hangs up and swings around and says, "That makes me mad. That was——. He wants to do a story about me and do you know what he told me? 'We want to do a story about you,' he told me, 'because you're very big this year. Do you know what that made me feel like? That made me feel like, All right, Baby Jane, we'll let you play this year, so get out there and dance, but next year, well, it's all over for you next year, Baby Jane, I mean—! You know? I mean, I felt like telling him, 'Well, pussycat, you're the Editor of the Minute, and you know what? Your minute's up!"

The thought leaves Jane looking excited but worried. Usually she looks excited about things but open, happy, her eyes wide open and taking it all in. Now she looks worried, as if the world could be such a simple and exhilarating place if there weren't so many old and arteriosclerotic people around to muck it up. There are two dogs on the floor at her feet, a toy poodle and a Yorkshire terrier, who rise up from time to time in some kind of secret needle-toothed fury, barking coloratura.

"Oh,————," says Jane, and then, "You know, if you have anything at all, there are so many bitchy people just waiting to carve you up. I mean, I went to the opening of the Met and I wore a white mink coat, and do you know what a woman did? A woman called up a columnist and said, 'Ha, ha, Baby Jane rented that coat she went to the Met in. Baby Jane rents her clothes.' That's how bitchy they are. Well, that coat happens to be a coat my mother gave me two years ago when I was married. I mean, I don't care if somebody thinks I rent clothes. O.K.————-! Who cares?"

Inez, the maid, brings in lunch on a tray, one rare hamburger, one cheeseburger, and a glass of tomato juice. Jane tastes the tomato juice.

"Oh,————!" she says. "It's diet."

The Girl of the Year. It is as though nobody wants to give anyone credit for anything. They're only a *phenomenon*. Well, Jane Holzer did a great deal of modeling before she got married and still models, for that matter, and now some very wonderful things may be about to happen in the movies. Some of it, well, she cannot go into it exactly, because it is at that precarious stage— you know? But she has one of the best managers, a woman who manages the McGuire Sisters. And there has been talk about Baby Jane for Who's Afraid of Virginia Woolf, the movie, and Candy—

"Well, I haven't heard anything about it—but I'd love to play Candy."

And this afternoon, later on, she is going over to see Sam Spiegel, the producer.

"He's wonderful. He's, you know, sort of advising me on things at this point."…

"Bailey is fantastic," says Jane. "Bailey created four girls that summer. He created Jean Shrimpton, he created me, he created Angela Howard and Susan Murray. There's no photographer like that in America. Avedon hasn't done that for a girl, Penn hasn't, and Bailey created four girls in one summer. He did some pictures of me for the English Vogue, and that was all it took."

But how does one really explain about the Stones, about Bailey, Shrimp and Mick—well, it's not so much what they do, that's such an old idea, what people do—it's what they are, it's a revolution, and it's the kids from the East End, Cockneys, if you want, who are making it …

"I mean, we don't lie to ourselves. Our mothers taught us to be pure and you'll fall in love and get married and stay in love with one man all your life. O.K. But we know it doesn't happen that way and we don't lie to ourselves about it. Maybe you won't ever find anybody you love. Or maybe you find somebody you love for four minutes, maybe ten minutes. But I mean, why lie to yourself? We know we're not going to love one man all of lives. Maybe it's the Bomb—we know it could all be over tomorrow, so why try to fool yourself today. Shrimp was talking about that last night. She's here now, she'll be at the party tonight—"… Ooooooooooooooooooosh! Baby Jane blows out all the candles. It is her twenty-fourth birthday. She and everybody, Shrimp, Nicky, Jerry, everybody but Bailey, who is off in Egypt or something, they are all up in Jerry Schatzberg's … *pad* … his lavish apartment at 333 Park Avenue South, up above his studio. There is a skylight. The cook brings out the cake and Jane blows out the candles. Twenty-four! Jerry and Nicky are giving a huge party, a dance, in honor of the Stones, and already the people are coming into the studio downstairs. But it is also Jane's birthday. She is wearing a black velvet jump suit by Luis Estevez, the designer. It has huge bell bottom pants. She puts her legs together… it looks like an evening dress. But she can also spread them apart, like so, and strike very Jane-like poses. This is like the Upper Room or something. Downstairs, they're all coming in for the party, all those people one sees at parties, everybody who goes to parties in New York, but up here is is like a tableau, like a tableau of …Us. Shrimp is sitting there with her glorious pout and her textured white stockings, Barbara Steele, who was so terrific in *8 1/2* with thin black lips and wrought-iron eyelashes. Nicky Haslam is there with his Byron shirt and his tiger skin vest and blue jeans and boots. Jerry is there with his hair flowing back in curls. Lennie, Jane's husband, is there in a British suit and a dark blue shirt he bought on 42nd Street for this party, because this is a party for the Rolling Stones. The Stones are not here yet, but here in the upper room are Goldie and the Gingerbreads, four girls in gold lamé tights who will play rock and roll for the party. Nicky discovered them at the Wagon Wheel. Gold lamé, can you imagine? Goldie, the leader, is a young girl with a husky voice and nice kind of slightly thick—you know—glorious kind of *East End* features, only she is from New York—ah, the delicacy of minor grossness, unabashed. The Stones' music is playing over the hi-fi.

Finally the Stones come in, in blue jeans, sweat shirts, the usual, and people get up and Mick Jagger comes in with his mouth open and his eyes down, faintly weary with success, and everybody goes downstairs to the studio, where people are now piling in, hundreds of them. Goldie and the Gngerbreads are on a stand at one end of the studio, all electric, electric guitars, electric bass, drums, loud speakers, and a couple of spotlights exploding off the gold lamé. *Baby baby baby where did your love go.* The music suddenly fills up the room like a big egg slicer. Sally Kirkland, Jr. a young actress, is out on the studio floor in a leopard print dress with her vast mane flying, doing the frug with Jerry Schatzberg. And then the other Girl of the Year, Caterine Milinaire, is out there in a black dress, and then Baby Jane is out there with her incredible mane and her Luis Estevez jump suit, frugging ...until 5 a.m.—gleeang—Goldie pulls all the electric cords out and the studio is suddenly just a dim ochre studio with broken glass all over the floor, crushed underfoot, and the sweet smell of brown whiskey rising from the floor.

Monday's papers will record it as the Mod and Rockers Ball, as the Party of the Year, but that is Monday, a long way off. So they all decide they should go to the Brasserie. It is the only place in town where anybody would still be around. So they all get into cabs and go up to the Brasserie, up on 53rd Street between Park and Lexington. The Brasserie has a great entrance, elevated with tables like a fashion show almost. There are, what? 36 people in the Brasserie. They all look up, and as the first salmon light of dawn comes through the front window, here come...four teen-age girls in gold lamé tights, and a chap in a tiger skin vest and blue jeans and a gentleman in an English suit who seems to be wearing a 42nd street hood shirt and a fellow in a sweater who has flowing curly hair... and then, a girl with an incredible mane, a vast tawny corona, wearing a black velvet jump suit. One never knows who is in the Brasserie at this hour—but are there any so dead in here that they do not get the point? Girl of the Year? Listen, they will *never* forget.

134

Discussion Plan:

1. What makes Baby Jane the "Girl of the Year?" What are her qualifications? Did she have to do anything to earn the title?
2. Is there anything that Jane can do to remain "Girl of the Year" indefinitely?
3. Jane says that a photographer named Bailey "created four girls" one summer. What does she mean? Would you want to be "created"?
4. How does the author show us that Baby Jane "has style"? What is style?
5. What are the advantages and disadvantages of having style?
6. Who is in control of style? Are you?

Exercise:

Baby Jane is presented as a success within the culture that she represents. What does her success have to do with the person she is?

1. Make a list of the factors that are indicators of Baby Jane's success. Distinguish between those items on the list that you think are the result of her achievements and those that reflect the achievements of others.
2. Go back over the list. Distinguissh between those things that are indicative of aspects of Baby Jane's life that are objectively desirable, things that are culturally desirable relative to contemporary society, and things that you feel are, even if subjectively desireable, unworthy of approval from within your value position.

Exercise:

Self worth:

Using a scale from '1' to '5', rate the following in terms of the feelings of self worth that they promote.

1. Being voted the most beautiful girl in the class.
2. Winning a merit scholarship.
3. Losing weight.
4. Helping to score a winning run.
5. Getting a summer job.
6. Helping a younger sibling with a difficult personal problem.
7. Doing volunteer work with the needy elderly.
8. Being asked out by the most popular girl in the class.
9. Being taken to Europe by your grandparents.
10. Going cross-country by bus with a friend.

Specify criteria by which your judgments of self worth can be defended.
Are your criteria, objective, relative or subjective.

PART II: WHAT CONTROLS ME?

From the time we are conceived, there are forces in our environment working on us, making us what we are and will be. There are physical factors which shape us. Our genetic heritage sets the stage: Are you big for your age, do you have musical talent? Then there is the food you eat, the disease organisms you are exposed to, the accidents you suffer. All of these place restrictions on how your natural capabilities develop.

There are social factors. We are born into a society and an historical epoch, a context that defines roles into which we will fit. An astronaut today might have been a knight in the Middle Ages. Born rich we get used to people serving us, born on a farm we think nothing of getting up at 5:00 A.M. to feed the animals.

Other people are major influences that help shape us: parents, siblings, teachers, friends. We are judged by the company we keep and the family we come from—in part because we mirror those who surround us. Without that junior high school you might have never studied medicine, without your sister to talk to....

Not least of all we exist within a culture: traditions and attitudes, ideas that inform what we see, telling us what to look for. Become a housewife or a surgeon, look to money for personal rewards or dedicate your life to helping others, these are messages we get from the culture within which we are nurtured.

We can view these factors in different ways. We can react negatively, seeing the world in which we exist as alien to ourselves: a callous fate that limits our possibilities, mindless traditions forcing us to conform, empty authority imposing standards through force. The network of causes that influence can be seen as limiting the self, restrictions that curtail personal freedom. Rejecting the values of parents and teachers is a symptom of a negative view of the causes that surround us. But causes may also be seen as positive forces, giving us the opportunity to achieve. Your genes make it possible for you to excel in ballet, your teachers give you the opportunity be a research chemist, or an architect.

In Part I of the *Reader,* we explored the issue: *Who Am I?* We saw that defining the self is not always as easy as it seems. The distinction between who we are and what made us what we are is not always clear. It is often said, "you are what you eat," the food we eat gets digested and forms the substance of our body. What our parents teach us when we are very young becomes what we think, believe and feel. We never even realize we can question it: What originates with us and what comes from others?

The same is true of social influences. People look at us and judge us. They say we are smart or stupid, pretty or ugly. If enough people, or very crucial people say it, we begin to believe it and act accordingly. Were we stupid to begin with? Have we become stupid? What is really going on here?

Fortunately for the growing individual the environment usually gives more than one message. Our culture is rich in messages and these messages frequently conflict, and so the individual is faced with choices. We are not salmon swimming upstream. We are aware of many different directions that our lives might take. But this richness of possibilities creates problems, especially for the growing individual. For choices bring us into conflict with those that would make those choices for us. And choices bring responsibility.

SECTION 1: CHILDREN AND FAMILY

It is within the context of our families that we first learn to use such phrases as "good girl," "don't or you'll get in trouble" and "you're not supposed to." Associated with such phrases are other ideas, "Daddy said not to," "Mommy won't like it" and "I'm allowed to."

Our development as moral individuals begins with simple prohibitions based on the authority and attitudes of significant adults. Later, as our circle of acquaintances grows to include other adults and children we are confronted with conflicting rules and alternative systems of judgment. This forces our perceptions of morality to move beyond the limits defined by the adults in our immediate vicinity. We begin to learn phrases like, "How would you like it if he did it to you," "Be fair," and "That's wrong." For some of us such statements are reinforced with ideas like, "It's a sin," for some of us emphasis is put on "Respect the right of others" or "Can't you see what will happen if you do that."

Each of the phrases in the preceding paragraphs is a characteristic expression of moral concern; and each of them is part of a rich tradition of human practice and human thought, a practice consolidated over many generations by families and societies, by individual behavior and by systems of rules and laws. The resulting structures of moral thought and action have been codified into bodies of law and have been elaborated and discussed by thoughtful men and women, religious thinkers and philosophers, social critics and careful thinkers of all sorts.

These moral ideas are found in all of our lives, in our speech and in our action, and they are reflected in the literature that represents our lives for us, the imaginative constructions of fiction and poetry and the descriptions based on fact and current problems found in contemporary non-fiction.

In the following selections we continue the task of becoming aware of the moral framework within which we all live. We start with the experience of childhood to try to bring to our conscious thought those encounters and beliefs that initiate the structuring of our moral life.

138

The Classic Image

Most children want their parents to be perfect, to be just what parents are supposed to be. Similarly, most parents try as hard as they can to live up to the standard of mothering and fathering that they have learned. Sometimes these standards grow out of the life experiences of the people involved. As often these standards reflect the ideals of parenting that are part of the culture and tradition of a society. We look at three poems that express deeply rooted images of what parenting, in particular fathering, is supposed to be. We leave it to you to explore the reasonableness of these almost mythic presentations. We then ask you to construct your own images of what mothering is all about.

Norman H. Russell, "my father's hands held mine"

my fathers hands held mine
the first flint
now my hands alone
cut our arrows
the deer that dies from them
falls from both our hands
wife of my heart your mothers hands
help you sew my moccasins
my father speaks to me in many ways
i feel his hands on me
he is always with me
i will always touch my sons

Theodore Roethke, My Papa's Waltz

The whiskey on your breath
Could make a small boy dizzy;
But I hung on like death:
Such waltzing was not easy.
We romped until the pans
Slid from the kitchen shelf;
My mother's countenance
Could not unfrown itself.
The hand that held my wrist
Was battered on one knuckle;
At every step you missed

My right ear scraped a buckle.
You beat time on my head
With a palm caked hard by dirt,
Then waltzed me off to bed
Still clinging to your shirt.

Henry Wadsworth Longfellow, The Children's Hour

Between the dark and the daylight,
    When the night is beginning to lower,
Comes a pause in the day's occupations,
    That is known as the Children's Hour.
I hear in the chamber above me
    The patter of little feet,
The sound of a door that is opened,
    And voices soft and sweet.
From my study I see in the lamplight,
    Descending the broad hall stair,
Grave Alice, and laughing Allegra,
    And Edith with golden hair.
A whisper, and then a silence:
    Yet I know by their merry eyes
They are plotting and planning together
    To take me by surprise.
A sudden rush from the stairway,
    A sudden raid from the hall!
By three doors left unguarded
    They enter my castle wall!
They climb up into my turret
    O'er the arms and back of my chair;
If I try to escape, they surround me;
    They seem to be everywhere.
They almost devour me with kisses,
    Their arms about me entwine,
Till I think of the Bishop of Bingen
    In his Mouse Tower on the Rhine!
Do you think, O blue-eyed banditti,
    Because you have scaled the wall,
Such an old mustache as I am
    Is not a match for you all!
I have you fast in my fortress,

And will not let you depart,
But put you down into the dungeon
In the round tower of my heart.
And there I will keep you forever,
Yes, forever and a day,
Till the walls shall crumble to ruin,
And molder in dust away.

Exercise:

The three selections we have just looked at involved male parents. Do you think they would have been different had the focus been on mothers instead of fathers?

Express, by writing short poems, a perception that characterizes what you believe to be the central images in mothering.

Discussion Plan:

It is frequently said that the basis for parent-child relationships is the love that they feel for each other.
1. Is physical affection, hugging and kissing, a sign of love between parents and children?
2. Is being willing to experience discomfort?
3. Is being willing to spend time together?
4. Is having interests in common?
5. How about parents sacrificing for their children?
6. Is spending money on children a sign of love?
Using the questions as a guide, write a list of things people do that are concrete expressions of love between parents and children. Think of motives other than love, for the behavior and activities you have included in your lists.

Natural and Unnatural

Becoming a parent is a natural thing to do. Both common sense and psychology agree that feeling love for the child is as natural as the biology of reproduction. But what is natural? Is natural what always occurs? What usually occurs? What would occur if the surroundings were normal? In this selection we explore some very unnatural seeming behavior within a context that gives us reason to wonder both about what is natural and also about how the natural and the morally acceptable are related.

Sharon Begley, The Baby Killers

A baby bird breaks out of its shell and immediately encounters a hostile sibling; within three days the newborn has been pecked to death by its nest mate. A male baboon snatches a baby from its mother's arms and, scampering off into the bushes, bites, mauls and partially cannibalizes it. A female chimp chases and catches another female with a newborn infant; she forces the mother to move away, then bites through the baby's skull and kills it instantly.

Infanticide is not a subject that scientists like to discuss—and until recently, they didn't. The killing of infants was always regarded as an aberration unworthy of serious study. Now, however, biologists no longer ask if infanticide occurs but why. The answers range from the expected—because it controls population—to the startling—because evolution selects for it. Infanticide has become a central issue of biology and that, perhaps combined with its grissly provocation, has attracted dozens of researchers to a field that didn't even exist 10 years ago.

Programmed Behavior: Infanticide occurs throughout the animal kingdom. Many pet owners have stories to tell about hamsters that devoured their own young. In humans, too, it is a long if ignoble tradition. From Abraham's readiness to sacrifice Isaac, to today's mother who throws her infant out the tenement window, child killing has been so common that some anthropologists call it the most widespread means of "birth" control in history. Two weeks ago three dozen scientists gathered at Cornell University for the first major symposium on infanticide. Their research provided an intriguing test for the young field of sociobiology, which claims that many forms of behavior—like altruism, sexism and infanticide—are not learned but are programmed into the genes. Although most of the papers reported on animal infanticide, the scientists hope that learning why animals abuse and kill their young might explain similar behavior in humans. "You can't prevent infanticide in humans until you understand what influences it," said

Frank Mallory of Wilfrid Laurier University in Ontario, Canada, "and that's one way to rationalize this nasty business we're in."

Scientists first began to question their belief that infanticide was deviant behavior in 1974. At that time Harvard primatologist Sarah Blaffer Hardy reported on baby killing in the langurs she was studying in India. She suggested that the practice might be a male reproductive scheme. Langurs— a type of monkey—live in troops consisting of several adult females and one adult male, who mates with any or all of them. In addition, she said, bands of all-male langurs roam the jungle, occasionally trying to take over the troop and its mating privileges. A male who usurps leadership might kill infants for several reasons, she argued. First it reduces the number of competitors his own offspring will face. Most important, it lets him mate with the mothers sooner: a lactating female cannot conceive, but an infanticidal male can bring her into heat and sire a new generation almost immediately after killing her young. Even the female might benefit from this arrangement. But letting her offspring die, she can mate with a dominant male who might confer higher status and better genes on her young.

Estrus: Just such a scenario was played out in Jodhpur, India, this summer. The reigning male in a langur troop was toppled from power. The new male attacked all three infants in the troop that were under four months old; one disappeared and one was found dead. Within two weeks the mothers went into estrus and mated with the new male.

If infanticide is a beneficial reproductive strategy in primates, it should be advantageous in animals with similar social structures, too. Lions, like langurs, live in prides of many females and one male; roving groups of three or so males occasionally try to take over and mate with the females. Craig Packer and Anne Pusey of the University of Chicago reported that in 17 of 19 takeovers observed on Tanzania's Serengeti Plain, females lost their entire litters. Cubs that disappeared were under four months old (older ones were evicted, not killed). This pattern supports the theory that new males have the most to gain by killing the youngest infants to bring their mothers into heat; mothers of almost-weaned cubs will be ready for mating soon, anyway.

Despite similar evidence from many diverse species, not all scientists agree that infanticide is an evolutionary adaptation. Some argue that it is simply a result of the violence that accompanies troop takeovers; infants, the smallest and most vulnerable members, are the most likely to get hurt. Others maintain that killing infants is just another means of population control. Much of the criticism boils down to one question: infanticide is so advantageous for males, why don't all males practice it?

Glenn Hausfater of Cornell offered one answer: infanticide, however useful, might not be the best strategy for all males all of the time. What if the infanticidal male rules only briefly and is replaced by an equally murderous rival? Chances are that the first male's offspring will be born just when the new killer arrives on the scene; they would die. But if the first male had not committed infanticide, and had instead waited a few months to mate, his children would be safe in their mother's womb when the killer arrived on scene. A male who does not kill infants, therefore, "can sometimes time his mating to sneak his offspring through the window of vulnerability," Hausfater explains.

Since theories of infanticide are so common, scientists like to test them under controlled conditions in the lab. That presents the ethical problem of how to justify letting animals eat each other. Some scientists, like Robert Elwood of Queens University in Belfast, don't allow it: he snatches gerbil pups from the jaws of cannibals just before they're about to be eaten. Elwood's studies show that female gerbils that have never been pregnant invariably try to cannibalize pups placed in their nests. They seem to be following their instinct for feeding. But when the females become pregnant they develop a new outlook on life. Those in the last quarter of pregnancy usually don't harm the pups. This suggests that pregnancy shuts off murderous tendencies so that a female will not eat her own brood. Pregnancy also seems to make her more aggressive toward males, something that seems to shift their hormonal balance as well. Virgin males housed with a pregnant female are less likely to kill unrelated pups placed in the cage. Such males living with females that are not pregnant, on the other hand, devour the pups two-third of the time.

Gory Scene: Birds, at first glance seem different from other animals that commit infanticide because the killers are usually related to the victims. This is hardly a good way to perpetuate their genes, but Douglas Mock of the University of Oklahoma says the practice is rampant: of those chicks that die young, about 75 percent are killed by their siblings. The gory scene is set when parents hatch chicks at different times and allow the older and stronger to peck the younger to death. Mock believes this lets the older bird "launch a pre-emptive strike against impending competition." But then why do parents virtually never try to stop the killing? Mock suggests that in an environment often too poor to support two chicks, it is better to concentrate on feeding only one.

Infanticide is a rare case where humans behave more like birds than like primates; human infanticide is usually committed by relatives, too. Although the practice is less common now than it was before the Industrial Revolution, it has by no means disappeared. In one survey of 112 preindustrial cultures, 36 percent were found to practice infanticide "commonly" and 13 percent did so "occasionally." Yet it received little attention until recently. "Anthropologists served as defenders of the 'noble savage' idea" says Mildred Dickermann of Sonoma State University. "To claim that the way of life in primitive cultures was valid we had to shove a lot of unpleasant stuff under the rug—including infanticide."

High Caste: Girls tend to be killed more often than boys because, traditionally, they are less useful to their families economically and politically. And sometimes special social customs breed infanticide. If women usually marry above their class, as they do in northern India, female infanticide is the rule. Since members of low castes outnumber those of higher castes, there are fewer possible grooms than brides. The cost of rearing daughters then outweighs the possible gain, and extra females in a family are often killed. Sometimes the numbers can be ghastly. In the last century, the British counted only 63 females living in Kathiawar, an area of more than 4,000.

Is there a biological basis for human infanticide, or for child abuse? Most scientists believe not. It is more likely that economic or psychological stress pushes parents to abuse their children. That, however, does not explain why men mistreat their stepchildren more than their own. Hausfater speculates that some atavism of evolution just might be at work: the men believe, perhaps unconsciously, that children who don't share their genes aren't worth caring for. It is hardly a comforting thought, but then, neither is the realization that infanticide can no longer be called "abnormal." It is, instead, as "normal" as parenting instincts, sex drives and self-defense—and every other behavior that lets an animal save a little piece of itself from death by passing its genes into the next generation.

Discussion Plan:

Are the following natural actions (emotions or beliefs)?
1. Mary is peeling onions and begins to cry.
2. John, when informed that his dog has died, goes into the other room to cry.
3. Sarah wants to be a baseball player.
4. James likes to wear his sister's silk scarves.
5. Ralph wants to be a priest.
6. Mary's goal is to be a corporate vice president.
7. James thinks only a male could be a father.
8. Otto believes that his parents act in his best interest.
9. Nancy is sure that she will love her children.
10. Ann cooks breakfast for her family.
11. Ralph helps his mother with her dress making business.
12. Jim has a crush on Marilyn Monroe.
13. Roberta is in love with her math teacher.
14. Sam feels that he will never be in love.

Natural is frequently distinguished from *cultural*, i.e., behavior that is the result of social customs or traditions. Are the following natural or cultural?

1. Eating breakfast.
2. Being loyal to your family
3. Men wearing trousers.
4. Women (as opposed to men) wearing brassieres.
5. Covering our sex organs in public.
6. Wanting to make money.
7. Wanting security.
8. Leaving your parents when you reach adulthood.
9. Wanting children.
10. Being jealous of the person you love.
11. Being competitive.
12. Being seductive.

Infanticide and the Severely Deformed

What appears natural in the animal world does not necessarily seem natural when translated into human terms. This is even more apparent when we trace out the relation between natural and moral. The grossly immoral is frequently referred to as "unnatural." But is what is natural, moral?

Our society's perception of infanticide is clear. Killing an infant is a sign of a deep psychological problem; it is an unnatural act. Further it is an immoral act—except, perhaps, in very special cases. An examination of these special cases reveals our thinking on the issues of the natural and the moral. We meet this issue head-on by exploring the opinions expressed and implied in letters and news reports involving the death of severely deformed infants.

News Report: Judge Plays God

The parents of a deformed baby whose 15 days of life sparked a legal and moral controversy have criticized the court for playing God. David Patrick Houle, the infant son of Air Force Sgt. and Mrs. Robert B.T. Houle of Westbrook, died Sunday in the Main Medical Center here after being in poor condition since the previous Tuesday. The baby had undergone court-ordered surgery after the hospital sued the parents when they reportedly refused permission for an operation.

The Houles said in a statement released by their lawyer, Navy Ltd. James Freyer, that they were "most disturbed by the actions of the court in divesting them of the right to make an intimate parental decision that they believe was rightfully theirs." The statement added, "Since nature determined that this infant was not a viable life, it was the court and not the parents that played God in deciding that the infant should be kept alive contrary to the laws of nature. Mercifully, as between nature and the Superior Court, nature was the court of last resort."

The baby's physician had told the court that corrective surgery would probably not be of any benefit to the infant.

Superior Court Justice David G. Roberts ordered the operation, saying the parents had no right to withhold the treatment because the baby had a "right to life."

Surgery was performed to place a food tube in the baby's stomach. A second operation to connect the esophagus to the stomach was to be performed next. The child was born with no left eye or ear canal and other deformities.

"If the infant had lived the life of suffering which might well have resulted from the court's decision, the parents could not have escaped the feeling of responsibility that would come from knowing that they were the ones who brought it into the world, yet they were deprived of any and all say as to its future," the Houles' statement said.

Letter: 'Murdered' Infants

.... I would like to know why these so-called doctors and parents haven't been locked up?

The taking of a human life is murder, no matter how much you try to justify it. It was always my understanding that the duty of a doctor was to prolong life, not to stifle it by withholding treatment.

How can the parents of a deformed baby say that it is too expensive to keep the baby alive? If the baby were healthy, the parents wouldn't hesitate to spend $15,000 or more for its education.

A deformed baby is a human life, and who are doctors—or parents, for that matter—to decide whether that life should exist or not? A baby of any kind is a gift from God, and only God has the right to take it away.

News report: The Hardest Choice

In Baltimore three years ago, the parents of a newborn Mongoloid baby refused to allow an operation to correct a fatal defect in the infant's digestive tract. Despite pressure from doctors and hospital personnel, they refused to change their minds, and the child slowly starved to death.

In Portland, Me., last month, when parents made a similar decision about their severely deformed infant, hospital officials asked a court to decide. A judge, holding that the baby had a right to live, issued an order that allowed doctors to operate on the child. Despite the surgery, the infant died 15 days after birth.

These cases illustrate a vexing dilemma now confronting modern medicine. Should lives of retarded infants or those with multiple birth defects be prolonged—at great cost in manpower, money and anguish—especially if the life that is preserved will almost certainly be one of pain or merely vegetable-like existence?

Few, if any, doctors are willing to establish guidelines for determining which babies should receive lifesaving surgery or treatment and which should not. But many recognize that there are cases, particularly those involving multiple anomalies, when a hands-off attitude is probably for the best. Says Dr. Joan Hodgman, professor of pediatrics at the University of Southern California School of Medicine: "If we have a baby that I know is malformed beyond hope, I make no attempt to preserve life."

Time of Need. Other doctors, too, are speaking out on the subject. Drs. Raymond Duff and A.G.M. Campbell reported in the *New England Journal of Medicine* on a study of 299 deaths among 2,171 children treated in the special-care nursery at Yale-New Haven Hospital over a 2 1/2 year period. They found that 43 of the infants died after parents and doctors decided jointly to discontinue treatment. The other 256,
who received the best treatment modern medicine could provide, fared no better; few lived longer than the infants who received no special care. Furthermore, their short existence in many cases bore little relation to human life. One infant, who could not breathe on his own, was kept alive for five months as a virtual extension of a mechanical respirator.

Duff and Campbell believe that in such cases doctors must at least consider whether or not their efforts are in the infant's best interests. "Pretending there is no decision to be made is an arbitrary and potentially devastating decision by default," they write. "It may constitute a victimizing abandonment of patients and their families in times of greatest need."

Not all doctors agree. Some feel that they are bound by the Hippocratic oath to do all they can to preserve life. Others, aware that an incurable condition today may be a manageable one tomorrow, fear making the wrong decision. "No matter how expert we are, we can't predict outcome," says Dr. Judah Folkman, surgeon in chief at Children's Hospital Medical Center in Boston.

Letter: Life-and-Death Decisions

I'll wager any entire root system and as much fertilizer as it would take to fill Yale University that you have never received a letter from a vegetable before this one, but, much as I resent the term, I must confess that I fit the description of a "vegetable"....

Due to severe brain damage incurred at birth, I am unable to dress myself, toilet myself, or write; my secretary is typing this letter. Many thousands of dollars had to be spent on my rehabilitation and education in order for me to reach my present professional status as a counseling psychologist. My parents were also told, 35 years ago, that there was "little or no hope of achieving meaningful 'humanhood'" for their daughter. Have I reached "humanhood"? Compared with Drs. Duff and Campbell, I believe I have surpassed it!

Instead of changing the law to make it legal to weed out us "vegetables, let us change the laws so that we may receive quality medical care, education and freedom to live as full and productive lives as our potentials allow.

Exercise:

The death of the infants is an extremely emotional issue, and the pieces that we have read present opinions using vivid and compelling language. Within the pieces are also arguments, attempts to rationally justify a course of action.

First: Go through each of the pieces and pick out the major point the author is trying to make.

Second: Find the reasons given for the conclusion reached.

Third: Make a chart of the argument, using arrows to show how the ideas are connected.

Fourth: Evaluate the arguments in terms of the plausibility of the reasons and the connections between premise and conclusion.

Now write an argument of your own. Picking a side, but taking into account the arguments that you explored and evaluated.

Expectations

The birth of a new baby means different things to different parents—but it is usually very important, a focus for aspirations, for concern and for commitment. What we hope and fear for the new baby determines, to a large extent, how we see our obligations and our privileges as parents.

Kurt Vonnegut, Adam

It was midnight in a Chicago lying-in hospital.

"Mr. Sousa," said the nurse, "your wife had a girl. You can see the baby in about twenty minutes."

"I know, I know, I know," said Mr. Sousa, a sullen gorilla, plainly impatient with having a tiresome and familiar routine explained to him. He snapped his fingers. "Girl! Seven, now. Seven girls I got now. A houseful of women. I can beat the stuffings out of ten men my own size. But, what do I get? Girls."

"Mr. Knechtmann," said the nurse to the other man in the room. She pronounced the name, as almost all Americans did, a coloress Netman. "I'm sorry. Still no word on your wife. She is keeping us waiting, isn't she?" She grinned glassily and left.

Sousa turned on Knechtmann. "Some little son of a gun like you, Netman, you want a boy, bing! You got one. Want a football team, bing, bing, bing, eleven, you got it." He stomped out of the room.

The man he left behind, all alone now, was Heinz Knechtmann, a presser in a dry-cleaning plant, a small man with thin wrists and a bad spine that kept him slightly hunched, as though forever weary. His face was long and big-nosed and thin-lipped, but was so overcast with good-humored humility as to be beautiful. His eyes were large and brown, and deep-set and long-lashed. He was only twenty-two, but seemed and felt much older. He had died a little as each member of his family had been led away and kiled by the Nazis, until only in him, at the age of ten, had life and the name of Knechtmann shared a soul. He and his wife, Avchen, had grown up behind barbed wire.

He had been staring at the walls of the waiting room for twelve hours now, since noon, when his wife's labor pains had become regular, the surges of slow rollers coming in from the sea a mile apart, from far, far away. This would be his second child. The last time he had waited, he had waited on a straw tick in a displaced-persons camp in Germany. The child, Karl Knechtmann, named after Heinz's father, had died, and with it, once more, had died the name of one of the finest cellists ever to have lived.

When the numbness of weary wishing lifted momentarily during this second vigil, Heinz's mind was a medley of proud family names, gone, all gone, that could be brought to life again in this new being—if it lived. Peter Knechtmann, the surgeon; Kroll Knechtmann, the botanist; Friederich Knechtmann, the playwright. Dimly recalled uncles. Or if it was a girl, and if it lived, it would be Helga Knechtmann, Heinz's mother, and she would learn to play the harp as Heinz's mother had, and for all Heinz's ugliness, she would be beautiful. The Knechtmann men were all ugly, the Knechtmann women were all lovely as angels, though not all angels. It had always been so—for hundreds and hundreds of years.

"Mr. Netman," said the nurse, "it's a boy, and your wife is fine. She's resting now. You can see her in the morning. You can see the baby in twenty minutes."

Heinz looked up dumbly.

"It weighs five pounds nine ounces." She was gone again, with the same prim smile and officious, squeaking footsteps.

"Knechtmann," murmured Heinz, standing and bowing slightly to the wall. "The name is Knechtmann." He bowed again and gave a smile that was courtly and triumphant. He spoke the name with an exaggerated Old World pronunciation, like a foppish footman announcing the arrival of nobility, a guttural drum roll, unsoftened for American ears. "Khhhhhhhhhhhh-NECHT!mannnnnnnnnnn."

"Mr. Netman?" A very young doctor with a pink face and closecropped red hair stood in the waiting-room door. There were circles under his eyes, and he spoke through a yawn.

"Dr. Powers!" cried Heinz, clasping the man's right hand between both of his. "Thank God, thank God, thank God, and thank you."

"Um," said Dr. Powers, and he managed to smile wanly.

"There isn't anything wrong, is there?"

"Wrong?" said Powers. "No, no. Everything's fine. If I look down in the mouth, it's because I've been up for thirty-six hours straight." He closed his eyes, and leaned against the doorframe. "No, no trouble with your wife," he said in a faraway voice. "She's made for having babies. Regular pop-up toaster. Like rolling off a log. Schnip-schnap."

"She is?" said Heinz incredulously.

Dr. Powers shook his head, bringing himself back to consciousness. "My mind—conked out completely. Sousa—I got your wife confused with Mrs. Sousa. They finished in a dead heat. Netman, you're Netman. Sorry. Your wife's the one with pelvis trouble."

"Malnutrition as a child," said Heinz.

"Yeah. Well, the baby came normally, but, if you're going to have another one, it'd better be a Caesarean. Just to be on the safe side."

"I can't thank you enough," said Heinz passionately.

Dr. Powers licked his lips, and fought to keep his eyes open. "Uh huh. 'S O.K.," he said thickly. "'Night. Luck." He shambled out into the corridor.

The nurse stuck her head into the waiting room. "You can see your baby, Mr. Netman."

"Doctor—" said Heinz, hurrying out into the corridor, wanting to shake Powers' hand again so that Powers would know what a magnificent thing he'd done. "It's the most wonderful thing that ever happened." The elevator doors slithered shut between them before Dr. Powers could show a glimmer of response.

"This way," said the nurse. "Turn left at the end of the hall, and you'll find the nursery window there. Write your name on a piece of paper and hold it against the glass."

Heinz made the trip by himself, without seeing another human being until he reached the end. There, on the other side of a large glass panel, he saw a hundred of them cupped in shallow canvas buckets and arranged in a square block of straight ranks and files.

Heinz wrote his name on the back of a laundry slip and pressed it to the window. A fat and placid nurse looked at the paper, not at Heinz's face, and missed seeing his wide smile, missed an urgent invitation to share for a moment his ecstasy.

She grasped one of the buckets and wheeled it before the window. She turned away again, once more missing the smile.

"Hello, hello, hello, little Knechtmann," said Heinz to the red prune on the other side of the glass. His voice echoed down the hard, bare corridor, and came back to him with embarrassing loudness. He blushed and lowered his voice. "Little Peter, little Kroll," he said softly, "little Friederich—and there's Helga in you, too. Little spark of Knechtmann, you little treasure house. Everything is saved in you."

"I'm afraid you'll have to be more quiet," said a nurse, sticking her head out from one of the rooms.

"Sorry," said Heinz. "I'm very sorry." He fell silent, and contented himself with tapping lightly on the window with a fingernail, trying to get the child to look at him. Young Knechtmann would not look, wouldn't share the moment, and after a few minutes the nurse took him away again.

Heinz beamed as he rode on the elevator and as he crossed the hospital lobby, but no one gave him more than a cursory glance. He passed a row of telephone booths and there, in one of the booths with the door open, he saw a soldier with whom he'd shared the waiting room an hour before.

"Yeah, Ma—seven pounds six ounces. Got hair like Buffalo Bill. No, we haven't had time to make up a name for her yet. . . That you, Pa? Yup, mother and daughter doin' fine, just fine. Seven pounds six ounces. Nope, no name . . . That you, Sis? Pretty late for you to be up, ain't it? Doesn't look like anybody yet. Let me talk to Ma again . . . That you, Ma? Well, I guess that's all the news from Chicago. Now, Mom, Mom take it easy—don't worry. It's a well-looking baby, Mom. Just the hair looks like Buffalo Bill, and I said it as a joke, Mom. That's right, seven pounds six ounces...."

There were five other booths, all empty, all open for calls to anyplace on earth. Heinz longed to hurry into one of them breathlessly, and tell the marvelous news. But there was no one to call, no one waiting for the news.

But Heinz still beamed, and he strode across the street and into a quiet tavern there. In the dank twilight there were only two men, tete-a-tete, the bartender and Mr. Sousa.

"Yes sir, what'll it be?"

"I'd like to buy you and Mr. Sousa a drink," said Heinz with a heartiness strange to him. "I'd like the best brandy you've got. My wife just had a baby!"

"That so? said the bartender. "What do you know."

"Netman," said Sousa, "wha'dja get?"

"Boy," said Heinz proudly.

"Never knew it to fail," said Sousa bitterly. "It's the little guys, all the time the little guys."

" Boy, girl," said Heinz, "it's all the same, just as long as it lives. Over there in the hospital, they're too close to it to see the wonder of it. A miracle over and over again—the world made new."

"Wait'll you've racked up seven, Netman." said Sousa. "Then, you come back and tell me about the miracle."

"You got seven?" said the bartender. "I'm one up on you. I got eight." He poured three drinks.

"Far as I'm concerned," said Sousa, "you can have the championship."

Heinz lifted his glass. "Here's long life and great skill and much happiness to—to Peter Karl Knechtmann." He breathed quickly, excited by the decision.

"There's a handle to take ahold of," said Sousa. "You'd think the kid weighed two hundred pounds."

"Peter is the name of a famous surgeon," said Heinz, "the boy's great-uncle, dead now. Karl was my father's name."

"Here's to Pete K. Netman," said Sousa, with a cursory salute.

"Pete," said the bartender, drinking.

"And here's to your little girl—the new one," said Heinz.

Sousa sighed and smiled wearily. "Here's to her. God bless her."

"And now, I'll propose a toast," said the bartender, hammering on the bar with his fist. "On your feet, gentlemen. Up, up everybody up."

Heinz stood and held his glass high, ready for the next step in camaraderie, a toast to the whole human race, of which the Knechtmanns were still a part.

"Here's to the White Sox!" roared the bartender.

"Minoso, Fox, Mele," said Sousa.

"Fain, Lollar, Rivera!" said the bartender. He turned to Heinz. "Drink up, boy! The White Sox! Don't tell me you're a Cub fan."

"No," said Heinz, disappointed. "No—I don't follow baseball, I'm afraid." The other two men seemed to be sinking away from him. "I haven't been able to think about much but the baby."

The bartender at once turned his full attention to Sousa. "Look," he said intensely, "they take Fain off of first, and put him at third, and give Pierce first. Then move Minoso in from left field to shortstop. See what I'm doing?"

"Yep, yep," said Sousa eagerly.

"And then we take that no-good Carrasquel and . . ."

Heinz was all alone again, with twenty feet of bar between him and the other two men. It might as well have been a continent.

He finished his drink without pleasure, and left quietly.

At the railroad station, where he waited for a local train to take him home to the South Side, Heinz's glow returned again as he saw a co-worker at the dry-cleaning plant walk in with a girl. They were laughing and had their arms around each other's waist.

"Harry," said Heinz, hurrying toward them. "Guess what, Harry. Guess what just happened." He grinned broadly.

Harry, a tall, dapper, snub-nosed young man, looked down at Heinz with mild surprise. "Oh—hello, Heinz. What's up, boy?"

The girl looked on in perplexity, as though asking why they should be accosted at such an odd hour by such an odd person. Heinz avoided her slightly derisive eyes.

"A baby, Harry. My wife just had a boy."

"Oh," said Harry. He extended his hand. "Well, congratulations." The hand was limp. "I think that's swell, Heinz, perfectly swell." He withdrew his hand and waited for Heinz to say something else.

"Yes, yes—just about an hour ago," said Heinz. "Five pounds nine ounces. I've never been happier in my life."

"Well, I think it's perfectly swell, Heinz. You should be happy."

"Yes, indeed," said the girl.

There was a long silence, with all three shifting from one foot to the other.

"Really good news," said Harry at last.

"Yes, well," said Heinz quickly, "well, that's all I had to tell you."

"Thanks," said Harry. "Glad to hear about it."

There was another uneasy silence.

"See you at work," said Heinz, and strode jauntily back to his bench, but with his reddened neck betraying how foolish he felt.

The girl giggled.

Back home in his small apartment, at two in the morning, Heinz talked to himself, to the empty bassinet, and to the bed. He talked in German, a language he had sworn never to use again.

"They don't care," said Heinz. "They're all too busy, busy, busy to notice life, to feel anything about it. A baby is born." He shrugged. "What could be duller? Who would be so stupid as to talk about it, to think there was anything important or interesting about it?"

He opened a window on the summer night, and looked out at the moonlit canyon of gray wooden porches and garbage cans. "There are too many of us, and we are all too far apart," said Heinz. "Another Knechtmann is born, another O'Leary, another Sousa. Who cares? Why should anyone care? What difference does it make? None."

He lay down in his clothes on the unmade bed, and, with a rattling sigh, went to sleep.

He awoke at six, as always. He drank a cup of coffee, and with a wry sense of anonymity, he jostled and was jostled aboard the downtown train. His face showed no emotion. It was like all the other faces, seemingly incapable of surprise or wonder, joy or anger.

He walked across town to the hospital with the same detachment, a gray, uninteresting man, a part of the city.

In the hospital, he was as purposeful and calm as the doctors and nurses bustling about him. When he was led into the ward where Avchen slept behind white screens, he felt only what he had always felt in her presence— love and aching awe and gratitude for her.

"You go ahead and wake her gently, Mr. Netman," said the nurse.

"Avchen—" He touched her on her white-gowned shoulder. "Avchen. Are you all right, Avchen?"

"Mmmmmmmmmm?" murmured Avchen. Her eyes opened to narrow slits. "Heinz. Hello, Heinz."

"Sweetheart, are you all right?"

"Yes, yes," she whispered. "I'm fine. How is the baby, Heinz?"

"Perfect. Perfect, Avchen."

"They couldn't kill us, could they, Heinz?"

"No."

"And here we are, alive as we can be."

"Yes."

"The baby, Heinz—" She opened her dark eyes wide. "It's the most wonderful thing that ever happened, isn't it?"

"Yes," said Heinz.

Discussion Plan:

Do the following expectations tend to be reasonable as opposed to unreasonable?
1. You expect that your child will be a girl.
2. You expect that your son will be more handsome than his father.
3. Your child will make more money than you will.
4. Your child will be healthy.
5. Your child will be emotionally stable.
6. Your child will live long enough to use the things that you have bought him.
7. Your child will be physically healthy.
8. Your child will be heterosexual.
9. Your child will accept your faith.

Go back over your answers and systematically change them to their opposite.

Do your changed expectations alter the way in which would you treat your child? The way you should treat your child?

Control

Examining extreme cases can be useful for finding the moral foundation that underlies our judgments. But most of us are concerned with more ordinary cases. The central issue, however, is still the same: What is the right course of action? As children we are not given the right to determine what is best for ourselves. Parents control our behavior in the name of our "best interests." But the limits placed on us by our parents' perception of what is required frequently come in conflict with our growing sense of ourselves.

William Carlos Williams, The Use of Force

They were new patients to me, all I had was the name, Olson. Please come down as soon as you can, my daughter is very sick.

When I arrived I was met by the mother, a big startled looking woman, very clean and apologetic who merely said, Is this the doctor? and let me in. In the back, she added. You must excuse us, doctor, we have her in the kitchen where it is warm. It is very damp here sometimes.

The child was fully dressed and sitting on her father's lap near the kitchen table. He tried to get up, but I motioned for him not to bother, took off my overcoat and started to look things over. I could see that they were all very nervous, eyeing me up and down distrustfully. As often, in such cases, they weren't telling me more than they had to, it was up to me to tell them; that's why they were spending three dollars on me.

The child was fairly eating me up with her cold, steady eyes, and no expression to her face whatever. She did not move and seemed, inwardly, quiet; an unusually attractive little thing, and as strong as a heifer in appearance. But her face was flushed, she was breathing rapidly, and I realized that she had a high fever. She had magnificent blonde hair, in profusion. One of those picture children often reproduced in advertising leaflets and the photogravure sections of the Sunday papers.

She's had a fever for three days, began the father and we don't know what it comes from. My wife has given her things, you know, like people do, but it don't do no good. And there's been a lot of sickness around. So we tho't you'd better look her over and tell us what is the matter.

As doctors often do I took a trial shot at it as a point of departure. Has she had a sore throat?

Both parents answered me together, No.... No, she says her throat don't hurt her.

Does your throat hurt you? added the mother to the child. But the little girl's expression didn't change nor did she move her eyes from my face.

Have you looked?

I tried to, said the mother, but I couldn't see.

As it happens we had been having a number of cases of diphtheria in the school to which this child went during that month and we were all, quite apparently, thinking of that, though no one had as yet spoken of the thing.

Well, I said, suppose we take a look at the throat first. I smiled in my best professional manner and asking for the child's first name I said, come on, Mathilda, open your mouth and let's take a look at your throat.

Nothing doing.

Aw, come on, I coaxed, just open your mouth wide and let me take a look. Look, I said opening both hands wide, I haven't anything in my hands. Just open up and let me see.

Such a nice man, put in the mother. Look how kind he is to you. Come on, do what he tells you to. He won't hurt you.

At that I ground my teeth in disgust. If only they wouldn't use the word 'hurt' I might be able to get somewhere. But I did not allow myself to be hurried or disturbed but speaking quietly and slowly I approached the child again.

As I moved my chair a little nearer suddenly with one cat-like movement both her hands clawed instinctively for my eyes and she almost reached them too. In fact she knocked my glasses flying and they fell, though unbroken, several feet away from me on the kitchen floor.

Both the mother and father almost turned themselves inside out in embarrassment and apology. You bad girl, said the mother, taking her and shaking her by one arm. Look what you've done. The nice man....

For heaven's sake, I broke in. Don't call me a nice man to her. I'm here to look at her throat on the chance that she might have diphtheria and possibly die of it. But that's nothing to her. Look here, I said to the child, we're going to look at your throat. You're old enough to understand what I'm saying. Will you open it now by yourself or shall we have to open it for you?

Not a move. Even her expression hadn't changed. Her breaths however were coming faster and faster. Then the battle began. I had to do it. I had to have a throat culture for her own protection. But first I told the parents that it was entirely up to them. I explained the danger but said that I would not insist on a throat examination so long as they would take the responsibility.

If you don't do what the doctor says you'll have to go to the hospital, the mother admonished her severely.

Oh yeah? I had to smile to myself. After all, I had already fallen in love with the savage brat, the parents were contemptible to me. In the ensuing struggle they grew more and more abject, crushed, exhausted while she surely rose to magnificent heights of insane fury of effort bred of her terror of me.

Now truly she was furious. She had been on the defensive before but now she attacked. Tried to get off her father's lap and fly at me while tears of defeat blinded her eyes.

Discussion Plan:

What gives parents the right to make decisions for their children?

Do you think the following are good reasons?
Your parents say, "You should do what we say because:
1. we love you."
2. we have more experience in the world than you do."
3. we support you."
4. you are still legally a minor."
5. we are responsible for your well being."
6. we have considered all sides thoughtfully."
7. you are living under our roof so we make the rules."
8. you agreed to it yourself."
9. your grandfather would have never let me do it."
10. none of your friends have permission to do it either."
11. you will be severely punished unless you agree."
12. it is a school rule."
13. it is illegal to do otherwise."
14. we will be humiliated if you don't."
15. it will be unfair to your brothers and sisters."

Go over your answers, invent scenarios to support your position. Now change your answers, invent scenarios to support the changed answers.

Justifying Actions

Throughout the *Reader* we are asking you to make decisions as to the rightness or wrongness of acts and attitudes. But so far we have not explored, at all, what makes an action right. In the following, Bentham presents his classic position: What makes an act right or wrong is the pleasure or pain that results from it.

Jeremy Bentham, Of the Principle of Utility

Nature has placed mankind under the governance of two sovereign masters, pain and pleasure. It is for them alone to point out what we ought to do, as well as to determine what we shall do. On the one hand the standard of right and wrong, on the other the chain of causes and effects, are fastened to their throne. They govern us in all we do, in all we say, in all we think.

By utility is meant that property in any object, whereby it tends to produce benefit, advantage, pleasure, good, or happiness (all this in the present case comes to the same thing) or (what comes again to the same thing) to prevent the happening of mischief, pain, evil, or unhappiness to the party whose interest is considered: if that party be the community in general, then the happiness of the community: if a particular individual, then the happiness of that individual.

Value of a Lot of Pleasure or Pain. How to Be Measured

Pleasures then, and the avoidance of pains, are the ends which the legislator has in view: it behooves him therefore to understand their value. Pleasures and pains are the instruments he has to work with: it behooves him therefore to understand their force, which is again, in other words, their value.

To a person considered by himself, the value of a pleasure or pain considered by itself, will be greater or less, according to the four following circumstances.

1. Its intensity.
2. Its duration.
3. Its certainty or uncertainty.
4. Its propinquity or remoteness.

These are the circumstances which are to be considered in estimating a pleasure or a pain considered each of them by itself. But when the value of any pleasure or pain is considered for the purpose of estimating the tendency of any act by which it is produced, there are two other circumstances to be taken into account; these are,

5. Its fecundity, or the chance it has of being followed by sensations of the same kind: that is, pleasures, if it be a pleasure: pains, if it be a pain.

6. Its purity, or the chance it has of not being followed by sensations of the opposite kind: that is, pains if it be a pleasure: pleasures if it be a pain.

These two last, however, are in strictness scarcely to be deemed properties of the pleasures or the pain itself; they are not, therefore, in strictness to be taken into account of the value of that pleasure or that pain. They are in strictness to be deemed properties only of the act, or other event, by which such pleasure or pain has been produced; and accordingly are only to be taken into the account of the tendency of such an act or such event.

To a number of persons, with reference to each of whom the value of a pleasure or pain is considered, it will be greater or less, according to seven circumstances: to wit, the six preceding ones; viz.

1. Its intensity.
2. Its duration.
3. Its certainty or uncertainty.
4. Its propinquity or remoteness.
5. Its fecundity.
6. Its purity.

And one other, to wit:

7. Its extent; that is, the number of persons to whom it extends; or (in other words) who are affected by it.

To take an exact account then of the general tendency of any act, by which the interests of a community are affected, proceed as follows. Begin with any one person of those whose interests seem most immediately to be affected by it: and take an account.

1. Of the value of each distinguishable pleasure which appears to be produced by it in the first instance.

2. Of the value of each pain which appears to be produced by it in the first instance.

3. Of the value of each pleasure which appears to be produced by it after the first. This constitutes the fecundity of the first pleasure and the impurity of the first pain.

4. Of the value of each pain which appears to be produced by it after the first. This constitutes the fecundity of the first pain, and the impurity of the first pleasure.

5. Sum up all the values of all the pleasures on the one side, and those of all the pains on the other. The balance, if it be on the side of pleasure, will give the good tendency of the act upon the whole, with respect to the interest of that individual person; if on the side of pain, the bad tendency of it upon the whole.

6. Take an account of the number of persons whose interests appear to be concerned; and repeat the above process with respect to each. Sum up the numbers expressive of the degrees of good tendency, which the act has, with respect to each individual, in regard to whom the tendency of it is good upon the whole: do this again with respect to each individual, in regard to whom the tendency of it is bad upon the whole. Take the balance; which, if on the side of pleasure, will give the general good tendency of the act, with respect to the total number of community of individuals concerned; if on the side of pain, the general evil tendency with respect to the same community.

Exercise:

Using Bentham's methods of measuring pleasure and pain, comment on the rightness or wrongness of the following acts.
1. Eating a hot fudge sundae.
2. Going on a strict weight loss diet.
3. Getting drunk at a party.
4. Smoking a joint after school
5. Smoking a joint on the way to school.
6. Making out on the first date.
7. Petting in the living room while your parents are asleep.
8. Having intercourse.

Comment on the following social policies.
1. Giving heroin to terminal cancer patients.
2. Compulsory income tax.
3. Drafting people into the armed forces.

SECTION 2:
ADOLESCENCE AND AUTONOMY

When the child is small, parental control goes, for the most part, unchallenged; but there comes a time when the original relationship between parent and child must be redefined. In our culture that time is usually adolescence. Adolescence brings with it obvious changes in physical and emotional maturity. But more important from the point of view of the ethical issues involved, adolescence involves radical changes in the self concept of the adolescent. The new adolescent self frequently looks to redefine her relationships with others. Self-control as opposed to control by others becomes an issue that permeates the adolescent response to those with whom the development of the child was entrusted. In the next few selections we explore the issue of the relationship between the adolescent and his parents. We offer a number of points of view that express different attitudes towards the problem of adolescent autonomy and control. We present these points of view through selections drawn from the popular media. In reading them try to look at both the message and the way in which the message is presented.

Personal Perspective

The adolescent frequently sees herself as the person best suited to make the judgments that relate to her own personal life. Parents are frequently seen by the adolescent as both powerful and out of touch with the contemporary personal and social reality. Since parents seldom relinquish their power easily, especially in areas that they perceive as crucial to the safety and well-being of their children, adolescents often resort to manipulation. Manipulation preserves the appearance of parental control while giving the adolescent the opportunity to take some control of her own life.

Francine Pascal,
My First Love and Other Disasters

It happens exactly like I said only a little different. First thing my fathers says is "No, and I don't want to hear about it anymore."

Of course this is a very bad start, but I push on. I give them the business about how I'm fifteen and they still treat me like a baby. That's an old argument so they know how to answer that easily. Even I know how to answer that. All you say is, "When you can't take no for an answer, that's acting like a baby so we treat you like one."

Then I give them the business about how every other girl in the entire high school is going to be a mother's helper this summer and before they can say anything, I rattle off six names ending with Laura Wolfe, the only one I absolutely know is going to.

Up to now the toad has been gorging on fettucine. Now suddenly she zeroes in to destroy my life. "Uh, uh," says Nina, "Laura Wolfe is going on a camping trip with her parents."

"She is not, smarty, she's going to be a mother's helper for the Kramers out in East Hampton, so there." I could kill her, I swear it.

"Uh, uh." She shakes her dumb head, and the strings of the fettucine hanging out of her mouth swing back and forth.

"She is so!"

"Nope."

"Is so, creep!"

"Ma!"

"Jerk."

"That's enough!" hissed my father. "I don't care what Laura Wolfe or anyone else is doing with her summer."

"But she is, Daddy." I insist. "I know because she said."

"Well, she isn't anymore because her sister, Linda is in my class, and she said...."

"Did you hear your father?" Now my mother's in it. And suddenly the couples at the next table are all dying to hear about Laura Wolfe. "And, Nina, for God's sake, swallow that food. How many times do I have to tell you not to eat spaghetti with half of it hanging down to your chin!"

"I can't help it," she whines, "it just slips out."

"Roll it on the spoon the way I showed you," my father tells her.

"I did."

"If you did it properly it wouldn't fall out of your mouth like that. Do it like this." And my mother starts rolling up a spoonful of spaghetti on her spoon and then pops it into her mouth perfectly. "You see? It's simple. Now let me see you do it."

"I don't have a spoon," says Nina.

"Why are you telling me you rolled it when you don't even have a spoon?"

"I did but it dropped."

Naturally everybody at the surrounding three tables starts hunting for Nina's spoon.

"Ask the waiter for another one," my mother says, embarrassed and completely out of patience.

"I know Laura Wolfe is definitely going." I have to get them back on the track.

"Laura who?" my father says, as if he never heard the name before.

"The girl who's going to be a mother's helper."

"Uh, uh," says my gross sister, and she's got a new batch of spaghetti dripping out of her mouth.

"Shut up!" I tell her.

"How many times do I have to tell you not to say shut up to your sister!" my mother snaps.

"Then make her mind her own business," I say.

"Why do we always have to have these arguments over dinner?" my mother says. "I look forward to a pleasant meal with my family and this is what it turns into."

"Girls," says my father, "enough, you're ruining your mother's dinner. I don't want to hear anything more about Laura Wolfe or what she's doing for the summer. Do you understand?

"And you," he says to Nina. "Don't order spaghetti anymore if you don't know how to eat it."

"But I don't like anything else."

"Then stay home," I tell her.

"Mind your own business, Victoria, I'm talking to Nina," my father says.

"She's always minding my business, and besides just because of her I didn't even get to ask a very important question. It's not fair!"

"Okay, Nina, be quiet," my father says. "Now what's your question, Victoria?"

"Can I?"

"Can you what?" He turns to my mother in exasperation. "Can she what?"

"Can she be a mother's helper," my mother says.

"Well, I don't know." Good sign that my father didn't say absolutely no. "Maybe she's a little young. Maybe next year. What do you think, Felicia?"

Super. He's sticking her with it. Now she can't say, "Your father doesn't want you to," or something like that. It's very bad when you get in the middle of one of those things and then each one keeps blaming the other and you never get the right answer.

"I don't know, Phil, you may be right."

She throws it right back to him.

"If that's what you think, dear."

He grabs it and shoots it back to her. I've got to get it away or they'll just keep passing it back and forth forever.

"Liz started when she was fifteen," I volunteer. Liz is my cousin from Philadelphia, and she really did start last year.

"That's true," says my father, like it's maybe not such a bad idea to do, especially since his favorite sister, Liz's mother, let her do it. "It worked out okay, didn't it."

"I think so," says my mother.

"It was perfect," I pipe up. "Liz said she really learned a whole lot that summer." You bet she did. But I'm not crazy enough to say what she learned.

"Except, now that I think about it," my mother says, "there was some problem about the people leaving her alone for a weekend. I think they went away or something like that. I know Dinah"—my aunt—"was very upset about that. Fifteen-year old girls shouldn't be left alone with small children overnight."

I swear to them that Cynthia Landry—wonderful, mature, responsible Cynthia—would never go any place and leave me alone with the kids overnight. I tell them how she really needs me because now that she's working she has to have someone with the kids.

"Will she be going into an office every day?" my mother wants to know.

I tell her no, mostly she works from home. But she'll probably be going in to the city maybe about three times a week. And then I make a big thing about how Cynthia and the kids really want me, especially because I've been baby-sitting for them for almost three years and the kids are crazy about me. I can see that they're considering the matter seriously and that it's looking good. Even Nina is minding her own business. Maybe she ate some octopus. I keep my fingers crossed.

They kick it around awhile, and then they ask me a million questions. Practically Cynthia's whole family history and where on Fire Island and what kind of a house and on and on, and then right in the middle of dessert they decide. Of course, they want to talk to Cynthia and drive out and see the house and all that, but so far the answer is yes.

I practically freak out, I'm so excited. I jump up and hug and kiss both of them. Now the other people and even the waiters are all smiling. Everyone wanted me to go. I almost expect applause, they're all so pleased.

"But...."

I knew it! The big "but." Probably my mother will have to come along too, or maybe Nina, or maybe they'll hire a mother's helper for me or something grotesque like that, I just know it.

"But," says my mother, "we must be absolutely certain that Mrs. Landry knows that we don't want you to be left alone overnight with the children."

"That's very important, Victoria," my father says. "Mrs. Landry must understand our feelings on that. It's far too big a responsibility for a young girl to have."

"I'll tell her you said so," I say.

"We'll bring it up when we have our talk with her," my father says.

"Please, Daddy, let me tell her."

"I think it's better if we do it ourselves."

"Please, I want to try to handle everything myself. I want her to see that you think I'm responsible enough to make my own arrangements. Then she'll feel better about trusting me."

"That's a good point, honey." Sometimes my dad's absolutely perfect. "She's right, Felicia," he tells my mom. "Let her make her own arrangements. She knows what has to be done."

This was even better than I expected, and I grin like a fool—right at Nina.

Actually talking to Cynthia myself may be a little tricky, because you know, I don't want to sound like I'm telling her what to do. I can't say to her, "Hey, you can't stay out overnight," like I'm her mother or something. Still, I don't really think she would do it, so it probably won't even come up. If it does—well, I'll just have to figure a way to handle it when it happens. Anyway, it's nothing to worry about now. The main thing is that I'm going. I can't believe it. I'm really going to be on Fire Island with Jim for an entire summer. Wow! Fifteen is going to be a great year!

Discussion Plan:

What are the limits of parental control?

1. John who has asthma is kept out of gym by his parents.
2. Sharon, at fourteen, is prohibited from wearing make-up.
3. Rachel is forced to wear braces at age twelve.
4. Sam's father makes him join Little League.
5. Roberta has taken ballet lessons from age five till age thirteen, she wants to quit but her parents won't let her.
6. Mary, age fifteen needs corrective back surgery, she must be in a full body cast for six months—otherwise her back will continue to be deformed. She wants to make the decision for herself.
7. Ralph's father insists that he learn self defense.
8. Mary's best friend, age seventeen, thinks she is gay, Mary's mother finds out and demands that Mary break off the friendship.
9. If Jane doesn't agree to go to college her parents will withhold her inheritance; they have the legal right to.
10. Sam is prohibited from dating girls of other religions.
11. Jim's parents insist that he go to an all boy high school.
12. Martha is forced to go to a religiously affiliated high school.
13. Michele's parents belong to a religious group which forbids them to have any kind of surgery. Michele has heart problems and will die without open-heart surgery. Michele's parents refuse to allow surgery.

A Traditional View

Adolescence is a time for personal change; the maturing individual strives for autonomy, attempting to take more and more control of her life. To insure that change is for the best, tradition states that a parent or adult guardian must supervise and guide the individual's choices. This view argues that adolescents both need and desire limits. Parents, it is claimed, should see what the adolescent needs and that the real message of his behavior is: "restrict my control to areas that I can safely handle; launch the ship but keep a firm hand on the tiller."

Francine Klagsbrun,
Hooray for Jewish Mothers!

Have you heard the latest light-bulb joke? How many Jewish mothers does it take to change a light bulb? None—"Don't bother, I'll sit in the dark."

I've been treated to this barb at least three times in the past month, each time prefaced by a good-natured "you'll really enjoy this one." If you're Jewish and a mother, as I am, you are subjected to every new Jewish-mother quip that makes the rounds. Worse, you're never quite certain the jokes aren't aimed directly at you. If you're not Jewish, but a mother, you still find yourself vulnerable, for the Jewish-mother stereotype has long since cut across religious and racial boundaries. You can be Chinese, Black, Puerto Rican or Italian. All you need to do to be labeled a Jewish mother is to demonstrate one or more of the maligned characteristics of the species—that is, to be over-protective, demanding, self-sacrificing or guilt-inducing.

The Jewish-mother caricature first burst upon us in the early 1960s, when Jewish writers and comedians (all of them male, few of them fathers) discovered in their immigrant mothers useful targets for both their humor and their anger. Since then, the Jewish mother has come to be viewed as the embodiment of a parent's worst impulses. As a result, all mothers have learned to be self-conscious and cautious in their child-rearing practices. Do you want to remind your daughter to wear a scarf and gloves on a cold winter day? Stop it. Don't be one of those overprotective Jewish mothers who swaddles her children in snowsuits and galoshes. Do you think your son should work harder to improve his school grades? Boy, you really are a pushy Jewish mother!

Insights: I believe the time has come for us to take a new look at the Jewish-mother stereotype. God knows, we don't seem to have improved much as parents since we began renouncing the Jewish-mother way. Our adolescent suicide rate has doubled in the last two decades, teen-age pregnancies rise year after year, drug abuse continues to plague many families and cults lure the innocent and insecure. Perhaps we can find some insights we overlooked within those very qualities we have ridiculed and rejected for the last 20 years.

Take, for example, overprotection. The proverbial Jewish mother is nothing if not overprotective, drowning her children in chicken soup at the slightest sign of a sniffle (Did you know that chicken soup has been found to be a medicinally sound remedy for a cold?) She doesn't know, as we do, that overprotection stifles independence. Or does it? I would submit, in our revisionist view, that overprotection builds a firm base of security in a child. Children who are carefully protected know that they are loved and important and because they are important to their parents they become important to themselves. Fortified with their self-esteem, they can become strong and independent adults. Moreover, studies have shown that overprotected children are far less susceptible to peer pressure than children turned loose on their environment at a young age. True, some Jewish mothers have been known to slip from overprotection to smothering, but often kids are able to carve out their own identities because of the very need to push away from their parents. In pushing hard against encircling arms, they strengthen their own muscles, shape their own space, develop their own centers.

Oh, but the demands—what of those demands and expectations Jewish-mother types have placed on their children? Sure, when parental demands exceed the abilities of a child, they can be dangerous and destructive. But we've also seen the dangers of leaning over backward not to pressure kids, not to burden them with expectations. The results are young people who feel confused, lacking in self-discipline, reluctant to put themselves on the line. Intelligent "pushiness" often pushes children to stretch as far as they can.

And self-sacrifice? Portnoy complained that his mother was "vying with twenty other Jewish women to be the patron saint of self-sacrifice." I don't deny that a little sigh of martyrdom may occasionally have escaped the lips of Jewish mothers. Still, if I had to choose between excessive self-sacrifice and excessive self-fulfillment as parental goals, I would stick with self-sacrifice. Jewish mothers have known how to give of themselves. In doing so, they provided not only love and support, but models for their children of what commitment and caring are all about.

Virtues of Guilt: Ah, you may say, but what about guilt, the Jewish mother's ultimate weapon? There's guilt and there's guilt. If a mother threatens to put her head in the stove at the slightest sign of disobedience, that's a bad use of guilt. But parents have to set standards. If you forbid your 15-year old son to drink beer at a party and he drinks anyway, his feeling guilty may prevent his drinking next time or the time after that. This is guilt well used. Jewish mothers of old knew this. They stood firm for what they believed to be right and wrong, and minced no words in conveying those beliefs. Many of us today have lost either our convictions or our ability to transmit them, or both. And many "guilt free" kids are the worse for it.

We've all known extremist Jewish mothers—just as we've known extremist mothers of the remote, "Ordinary People" school—and extremists deserve to be laughed at. The negative stereotypes, however, have gone much further, undermining the many good values of Jewish motherhood. It has been said that the stereotypes will disappear soon because the Jewish mother herself is becoming extinct, now that so many women work outside their homes. Possibly, I prefer to believe that there are still plenty of Jewish mothers in our midst, working or not. They have simply gone underground in the past two decades, practicing their art clandestinely for fear of becoming the butt of yet one more round of jokes.

To those closet Jewish mothers of all races and religions, I say: come out. We need you now. We want to observe you. We want to learn from you. And we want to celebrate you with the traditional toast of our people: l'chaim, may you live and be well, and go on mothering for 120 years!

Exercise:

1. List ten areas in which your parents have influenced you the most.
2. List ten things that would be different if your parents were of a very different social class.
3. List many things that would be different if you did (or didn't) have both parents living with you throughout your childhood.
4. If you were (or were not) the favorite child in your family, how would things be different?
5. If you did (or did not) live near your aunts and uncles how would things be different?
6. How would your life change if your parents become (or didn't become) divorced?
7. What are the five major areas in your life that your grandparents affect?
8. If you rank the ten most important people in your life, where do your parents and siblings rank?

Here are some more questions about parents and you.

1. What are five areas of your life that would improve if your parents were much stricter with you than they are?
2. What are ten areas that would suffer under the same conditions?
3. Do you feel guilty if you do poorly in school?
4. Do you hide your school problems from your parents?
5. Do you hide your personal problems from your parents?
6. Do you dress to please your parents?
7. Do you pick friends that your parents will like?
8. Would you marry someone that your family would strongly disapprove of?

Let's explore things the other way around.

1. Do you feel responsible if your parents fight?
2. If they don't succeed in business?
3. Do you interfere with their social life?
4. Do your parents owe you a middle class upbringing?
5. Do your parents owe you a happy home environment?
6. Do your parents owe you a college education?

One more set of questions.

1. If you marry a person of another religion, do you think you should convert?
2. Would you be willing to have children of another race even if your parents disapproved?
3. Do you think you will be much richer than your parents?
4. Would you be willing to be much poorer than your parents if you could succeed in some very important accomplishments?
5. Do you feel you should have children so your parents can have grandchildren?
6. Do you owe it to your parents to be better educated than they are?
7. Do you owe it to your parents to succeed?
8. Do you think it fair to your parents to join a cult?
9. Would you engage in a profession your parents disapprove of?
10. Do you care if your parents think that you are a success?

The Social Perspective

In a society where individuality is prized, privacy is seen as a protection against interference and unfair influence. The need for privacy is deeply felt by teenagers who are just beginning to assert the rights that comes with young adulthood. Privacy is most crucial in areas of sexuality and feeling, areas that teenagers perceive as crucial to their own sense of identity. These are frequently the very ones that parents are most worried about.

Christopher T. Cory,
Parent-Teenager Space Wars

A 15-year old boy brings his girlfriend home for dinner and then takes her into his bedroom. Should his parents make them leave the door open?

Against her parents' wishes, a 14-year-old girl wants to get birth-control information from the family doctor. Should her parents forbid the doctor to see her?

Even progressive parents these days have trouble deciding how much to meddle in the lives of their teenage children. Sophisticated young people may well be capable of handling more responsibility than their parents' generation, but how much is never certain.

In a recent study, 1,002 residents of Los Angeles were asked whether they would back the parents or the child in 42 hypothetical family situations, such as the two above. The majority strongly supported firm parental guidance of teenagers' sex lives. However, respondents were more inclined to grant teenagers autonomy in matters relating to religion, educational choices, and personal grooming.

The cross-section of Angelinos in the survey ranged in age from 17 to 94; 42 percent of them were parents. Eighty-four percent of the group supported parents who insist that a 15-year-old boy leave the door open when in his bedroom with his girl-friend. Ninety percent supported the mother who is "refusing to discuss the matter" when a 15-year-old girl who has had two dates with a college boy announces that she is going to spend the weekend with him. And 86 percent said that parents should insist that a 14-year-old boy tell the principal that a male teacher has made sexual advances to him, even though the boy says that making the report would be "too embarrassing with his classmates."

Seventy-one percent backed parents who refuse to let a 14-year-old girl go to school if she joins the "latest fashion" and does not wear a bra. (Changing times, however, seem to have clipped debates about the length of boys' hair; only 42 percent backed parents who insist a 12-year-old boy cut his hair to a length they favor.) Adult sympathy for censoring teen-agers' books and movies emerged in the 71 percent backing parents who refuse to let a 12-year-old boy read best sellers because the books have "sexual references," or go to a movie that contains nude scenes.

In medical areas involving sex, 60 percent of the respondents supported a father who asks a pharmacist not to sell his 14-year-old son more condoms after the pharmacist (obviously in a small town) telephones to report that the son has bought some. The adults were almost evenly split on whether a father should insist on going along to the doctor with a 14-year-old boy who thinks that he has contracted VD. The overall sympathy for parental restrictions on teenage sex makes all the more striking the 70 percent who said they would side with a 14-year-old girl whose parents find out that she has asked the family doctor for advice on birth control and forbid the doctor to see her. (The survey did not investigate the issue now being heard in various state courts—whether parents should be notified before their adolescent daughters can obtain abortions.)

Responding to the only question explicitly dealing with mental health, 72 percent backed a mother who sets up an appointment with a psychiatrist for a 10-year-old son who "has nightmares once in a while," even though the son objects.

The adults sympathized with some, but not all, parental fears about children's religious choices. Seventy-eight percent favored parents who will not let a 14-year-old girl accept a full scholarship to attend a private school run by a group that believes in "an oriental religion"; 71 percent supported parents who insist that their 10-year-old son go with them to church even though he precociously says he does not believe in the existence of "a god." Still, 64 percent would support a 14-year-old Protestant boy who wants to convert to Catholicism, and 65 percent would permit a 10-year-old Jewish girl who is "uninterested" in her own faith to attend the services of a variety of other religions.

Likewise, a total of 52 percent supported a 12-year-old boy who agrees to return a stolen bike but balks at his parents' insistence on "taking him to the police to confess." Fifty-four percent of the adults sided with a 16-year-old girl whose parents object to her leaving high school to accept a scholarship studying singing and dancing full-time at a drama school; adult support rose to 69 percent for a 12-year-old girl who wants to drop her after-school music lessons in order to join the basketball team.

The strongest support for teenagers came on less momentous issues, like hair length, or the case of a 13-year-old boy who keeps love poems he has written his girlfriend in a locked drawer while he waits for the right time to give them to her. Even then the respondents were not unanimous. Eighty-three percent said the boy's parents should not demand to know where the key to the drawer is kept.

Discussion Plan:

Discuss the attitudes reported in the selection in light of your answers to the following questions:

1. Do you believe that people will tell surveyors what they really think?
2. What is the relationship between the questions asked in a survey and the kind of answers you get?
3. Do you think that the social attitudes as reflected in surveys affects you?
4. What does the popularity of a view have to do with whether you or others should accept it?

Group Project:

Make up a questionnaire on the issues of parental control of adolescent behavior. Give the questionnaire to three different groups: your class, a class that has not used the *Reader* and parents. Tabulate the results and write a report describing what the survey has shown.

The Law

Law is one of the forces that shape society, promoting or retarding social change. The law amplifies tendencies in society by making the will of some the rule over all. This is especially critical when a law seems to disregard the rights of some individuals. Even if the law is the will of the majority there may be an unwilling minority that is forced to act in accordance with the dictates of the law. How is this conflict to be resolved; can the rights of individuals be legislated out of existence?

Newsweek, A New 'Squeal Rule'

"If I had sex, I wouldn't want my mom to find out unless I was the one to tell her," says Julia N., a high-school student in Silver Lake, Calif. And, Julia adds, if someone started telling parents that their sexually active teen-agers were trying to get prescriptions for contraceptives, there would be "more chance of kids getting pregnant."

Such sentiments, echoed by thousands of teen-agers across the country—and many of their parents as well—has not prevented the Reagan administration from endorsing what critics have come to call the "squeal rule." Last week the Department of Health and Human Services published the final version of one of its most controversial initiatives: starting Feb. 25, all federally funded family-planning clinics will be required to notify the parents of "unemancipated" teen-agers under 18 within 10 days when they are given prescriptions for contraceptives. The main exception is when the notification might cause the adolescent to suffer physical abuse at home.

The controversy began more than a year ago, after congressional conservatives failed in an effort to cut off federal funds to clinics that provide family-planning services. Instead, Congress passed an amendment to the Public Health Service Act: "To the extent practical, entities which receive grants or contracts under this (law) shall encourage family participation in projects assisted under this (law)." The Reagan administration seized upon this language as a way to weaken what it saw as government interference in family business. "The government should not construct a Berlin wall between parents and children," argued HHS Secretary Richard Schweiker. And as one of his last acts before leaving office for the private sector, he released the rules that were promulgated last week.

Infant Mortality: Critics, ranging from teen-agers themselves to civil-liberties and medical groups, are furious. "This is just an ugly example of the way the ideology of this administration gets in the way of looking at something on the merits," says one government official who argued strenuously against the proposal. Health professionals, including the American Public

Health Association, point out that pregnancy and childbirth are five times riskier for teen-age girls than taking the pill, that the maternal death rate among women under the age of 15 is more than twice that for women aged 20 to 24, and that abortion and infant-mortality rates are likely to rise if the regulations go into effect.

No sooner had the rules been promulgated than opponents rushed into court to challenge them on both constitutional and statutory grounds. The constitutional argument is that parental notification violates a teen-ager's right to privacy, and that the regulations discriminate against girls, since boys do not need prescriptions for contraceptives. The statutory challenge insists that HHS's rules go far beyond Congress's intent as stated in the amendment. "The statutory argument is extremely strong," says Suzanne Lynn, an attorney for the American Civil Liberties Union. "This thing is a political gesture by the administration. They feel they have to give this to the New Right."

Ironically, Schweiker's replacement at Health and Human Services may not support the new rule. Former Congresswoman Margaret Heckler twice signed letters to the president—along with 32 other members of the Congressional Women's Caucus—that strongly opposed the new regulation. But since her nomination as HHS secretary last month, Heckler has remained silent on the subject of teen-age contraception—and has refrained from talking publicly about her position on the "squeal rule" itself.

Discussion Plan:

What do you think of the following:

A. Does the child control its body?
1. Johnny, a ten year old, wants to quit school and go to work.
2. Peter, at fourteen, wants to start pumping iron.
3. Mary at thirteen wants to cut her hair very short.
4. Susan, a sixteen year old, wants to tatoo a large butterfly on her buttock.

B. Do the parents control the child's body?
1. Mary's parents are willing to let Mary, a thirteen year old, be a full time baby sitter for a wealthy family.
2. Jon is expected to work in the family store from 3:00 p.m. to 8:00 p.m. every day.
3. Racquel is expected to marry her thirty five year old second cousin, Racquel is fourteen.
4. Jack is forced to learn Hebrew and to be confirmed in his faith.
5. Samantha, at 165 pounds, age thirteen, is forced to go to weight loss camp.

6. Sam is expected to play baseball with his father every weekend, at what age can Sam say no?
7. When can Mary decide to go steady?

C. Does the state control our bodies?
1. The drinking age is raised from eighteen to nineteen due to the large number of teenagers involved in drunk-driving accidents.
2. Boys are required to register for the draft at eighteen.
3. No one can work after school before fourteen years old.
4. Children are forced to go to school until they are sixteen.
5. No child under eighteen can participate in a nude show.

Responsibility

The idea that people are ultimately responsible for their choices has been part of the philosophy behind punishing criminals. But even if we consider humans in general responsible for what they do, there have always been limitations. Insane people are generally held not criminally liable for what they do because they can not tell "right from wrong." Being under age is also used as an extenuating circumstance, freeing the youthful offender from the more severe punishment reserved for adults.

Time, The Age of Accountability

When do juveniles become adults?

Authorities in Milpitas, Calif., had never seen such a case of bleak amorality and callousness. Last month, they report, Anthony Jacques Broussard bragged to friends about strangling his former girlfriend and then invited them out to see the body. One onlooker tossed a stone at the corpse; another helped to hide it; for two days no one notified the authorities. These were not hardened ex-convicts or members of a motorcycle gang. They were teen-age students at Milpitas High School. Anthony Broussard was 16, and the dead girl, Marcy Renee Conrad, was just 14. Even while they try to understand the nature of such a horror, California juvenile officials are now considering a confounding legal question: Should the alleged killer be tried as a juvenile or as an adult?

It is a question that is increasingly posed by a society that has become terrified of its young. When is a juvenile no longer a juvenile? To a growing number of lawyers, politicans and citizens, the answer is that youthful offenders who commit "grownup" crimes should no longer be treated as children. Says Harvard Law Professor Arthur Miller: "The pendulum is swinging in favor of making juveniles accountable as adults, for adult crimes, at an earlier age." Sometimes a single crime is enough to change the rules. In Vermont last spring, two boys, ages 15 and 16, allegedly raped, stabbed and beat two twelve-year-old girls, killing one; an outraged legislature swiftly lowered the "magic line" at which a person charged with a serious offense may be tried and sentenced as an adult. Vermont's new age limit: ten.

Nine states have no limit at all. "Theoretically, it is possible to condemn a seven-year-old kid to death in six of these states," says Hunter Hurst, director of the National Center for Juvenile Justice. In most states, though, a serious juvenile offender between the ages of 14 and 16 is eligible to be tried as an adult. The actual treatment of each child is usually left to the discretion of the juvenile judge. Among the criteria that judges use in making their decisions: the seriousness of the charge, the history of the child and the availability of effective facilities for the rehabilitation of the minor.

But most such detention centers are nearly as noxious as adult prisons. "They are nothing more than crime factories and sodomy schools," says Andrew Vachss, director of the Juvenile Justice Planning Project. Yet the court system itself still reflects a traditional, perhaps outdated, belief in the fundamental innocence of children. The handling of juveniles, says Professor Miller, "is based on broad assumptions about 14- and 15-year-old naivete which in turn is based on 19th century conceptions about youth."

Whatever the failings of today's youth courts and lockups, the problem that most stirs public anger is the length of time violent young criminals serve. Last July in Texas, David Keeler shot to death his mother and father, who was president of ARCO Oil & Gas Co.; David will no longer be under the control of juvenile officials when he reaches 18. Authorities typically lose jurisdiction when juveniles are no longer minors, and the offenders often go free.

Punishment can be far more severe in an adult court. Last March in California, two boys of 17 who raped and attempted to murder a young woman were each sentenced to 72 years to life in prison by an adult court. Neither will be eligible for parole until he is 65.

Until now the U.S. Supreme Court has not set maximum limits on the punishment of youthful criminals. But the court is currently considering a juvenile death penalty case. In 1977 Monty Lee Eddings, then 16, murdered an Oklahoma highway patrolman with a sawed-off shotgun; he was condemned to death by an adult court. His lawyers have asked the Justices to rule that death is a disproportionate penalty for so young an offender. However the court rules, though, the public mood apparently holds that anyone old enough to commit the crime is old enough to pay the price.

Discussion Plan:

The list below includes many of the responsibilities and rights that are limited by virtue of the age of the person to whom they are assigned. Discuss whether age is an appropriate factor in determining the limits of these rights and responsibilities. If you think age is relevant, discuss how the age is to be decided.

1. Driving at 17.
2. Compulsory education until 16.
3. Registering for the draft at 18.
4. Inheriting wealth, usually 21 but sometimes older.
5. Marriage without parental permission, 21 for boys, 18 for girls.
6. Sign yourself into a hospital, 18 or older.
7. Drinking at 19.

8. Posing for commercial nude pictures at 18.

9. A person cannot legally agree to have sex before 17 (statutory rape).

Freedom and Determinism

We have looked at the issue of control by exploring the relationships between young people and the people who seem to influence them the most. Is this influence so strong that the child is forever destined to act out the patterns established before he was able to make real choices? Philosophers, who look at issues in the most fundamental ways, have seen the issue of control centered on the problem of "freedom and determinism." Some philosophers maintain that freedom of choice is an illusion and that whatever we do, we cannot have done otherwise. The debate between adherents of free choice and the supporters of determinism boils down to the issue of the reality of freedom.

In this selection Clarence Darrow, one of the foremost attorneys in American history, argues that Leopold and Loeb, two young men who viciously murdered 14 year old Bobby Franks, should not be held responsible for a crime that they could not help but commit. The jury decided otherwise, Leopold and Loeb were convicted of their crimes. But matters are not so simple, for although legally responsible, the question for us is: Are they morally responsible? It is usually held that a person is only morally responsible for actions that could have been otherwise, for actions where the person was free either to do or not to do. If Darrow is right about Leopold and Loeb, wouldn't the same argument hold for anyone else? and if so is anyone morally responsible for anything?

Clarence Darrow, The Crime of Compulsion

I have tried to study the lives of these two most unfortunate boys. Three months ago, if their friends and the friends of the family had been asked to pick out the most promising lads of their acquaintance, they probably would have picked these two boys. With every opportunity, with plenty of wealth, they would have said that those two would succeed.

In a day, by an act of madness, all this is destroyed, until the best they can hope for now is a life of silence and pain, continuing to the end of their years.

How did it happen?

Let us take Dickie Loeb first.

I do not claim to know how it happened; I have sought to find out. I know that something, or some combination of things, is responsible for this mad act. I know that there are no accidents in nature. I know that effect follows cause. I know that, if I were wise enough, and knew enough about this case, I could lay my finger on the cause. I will do the best I can, but it is largely speculation.

The child, of course, is born without knowledge.

Impressions are made upon its mind as it goes along. Dickie Loeb was a child of wealth and opportunity. Over and over in this court Your Honor has been asked, and other courts have been asked, to consider boys who have no chance; they have been asked to consider the poor, whose home had been the street, with no education and no opportunity in life, and they have done it, and done it rightfully.

But, Your Honor, it is just as often a great misfortune to be the child of the rich as it is to be the child of the poor. Wealth has its misfortunes, and I am asking Your Honor to consider the rich as well as the poor (nothing else). Can I find something wrong? I think I can, here is a boy at a tender age, placed in the hands of a governess, intellectual, vigorous, devoted, with a strong ambition for the welfare of the boy. He was pushed in his studies as plants are forced in hothouses. He had no pleasures, such as a boy would have, except as they were gained by lying and cheating.

...He, scheming, and planning as healthy boys would do, to get out from under her restraint; she putting before him the best books, which children generally do not want; and he, when she was not looking, reading detective stories, which he devoured, story after story, in his young life. Of all of this there can be no question.

What is the result? Every story he read was a story of crime. We have a statute in this state, passed only last year, if I recall it, which forbids minors reading stories of crime. Why? There is only one reason. Because the legislature in its wisdom felt that it would produce criminal tendencies in the boys who read them. The legislature of this state has given its opinion, and forbidden boys to read these books. He read them day after day. He never stopped. While he was passing through college at Ann Arbor he was still reading them. When he was a senior he read them, and almost nothing else.

...The boy early in his life conceived the idea that there could be a perfect crime, one that nobody could ever detect; that there could be one where the detective did not land his game—a perfect crime. He had been interested in the story of Charley Ross, who was kidnaped. He was interested in these things all his life. He believed in his childish way that a crime could be so carefully planned that there would be no detection, and his idea was to plan and accomplish a perfect crime. It would involve kidnaping and involve murder.

...The whole life of childhood is a dream and an illusion, and whether they take one shape or another shape depends not upon the dreamy boy but on what surrounds him. As well might I have dreamed of burglars and wished to be one as to dream of policemen and wished to be one. Perhaps I was lucky, too, that I had no money. We have grown to think that the misfortune is in not having it. The great misfortune in this terrible case is the money. That has destroyed their lives. That has fostered these illusions. That has promoted this mad act. And, if Your Honor shall doom them to die, it will be because they are the sons of the rich....

I know where my life has been molded by books, amongst other things. We all know where our lives have been influenced by books. The nurse, strict and jealous and watchful, gave him one kind of book; by night he would steal off and read the other.

Which, think you, shaped the life of Dickie Loeb? Is there any kind of question about it? A child. Was it pure maliciousness? Was a boy of five or six or seven to blame for it? Where did he get it? He got it where we all get our ideas, and these books became a part of his dreams and a part of his life, and as he grew up his visions grew to hallucinations.

... Suppose, Your Honor. that instead of this boy being here in this court, under the plea of the State that Your Honor shall pronounce a sentence to hang him by the neck until dead, he had been taken to a pathological hospital to be analyzed, and the physicians had inquired into his case. What would they have said? There is only one thing that they could possibly have said. They would have traced everything back to the gradual growth of the child.

...Where is the man who has not been guilty of delinquencies in youth? Let us be honest with ourselves. Let us look into our own hearts. How many men are there today—lawyers and congressmen and judges, and even state's attorneys—who have not been guilty of some mad act in youth? And if they did not get caught, or the consequences were trivial, it was their good fortune.

... But, Your Honor, that is not all there is to boyhood. Nature is strong and she is pitiless. She works in her own mysterious way, and we are her victims. We have not much to do with it ourselves. Nature takes this job in hand, and we play our parts. In the words of old Omar Khayyam, we are only:

But helpless pieces in the game He plays
Upon this checkerboard of nights and days;
Hither and thither moves, and checks, and slays,
And one by one back in the closet lays.

What had this boy to do with it? He was not his own father; he was not his own mother; he was not his own grandparents. All of this was handed to him. He did not surround himself with governesses and wealth. He did not make himself. And yet he is to be compelled to pay.

There was a time in England, running down as late as the beginning of the last century, when judges used to convene court and call juries to try a horse, a dog, a pig, for crime. I have in my library a story of a judge and jury and lawyers trying and convicting an old sow for lying down on her ten pigs and killing them.

What does it mean? Animals were tried. Do you mean to tell me that Dickie Loeb had any more to do with his making than any other product of heredity that is born upon the earth?

...From the age of fifteen to the age of twenty or twenty-one, the child has the burden of adolescence, or puberty and sex thrust upon him. Girls are kept at home and carefully watched. Boys without instruction are left to work the period out for themselves. It may lead to excess. It may lead to disgrace. It may lead to perversion. Who is to blame? Who did it? Did Dickie Loeb do it?

Your Honor, I am almost ashamed to talk about it. I can hardly imagine that we are in the twentieth century. And yet there are men who seriously say that for what nature has done, for what life has done, for what training has done, you should hang these boys.

Now, there is no mystery about this case. Your Honor, I seem to be criticizing their parents. They had parents who were kind and good and wise in their way. But I say to you seriously that the parents are more responsible than these boys. And yet few boys had better parents.

...To believe that any boy is responsible for himself or his early training is an absurdity that no lawyer or judge should be guilty of today. Somewhere this came to the boy. If his failing came from his heredity, I do not know where or how. None of us are bred perfect and pure; and the color of our hair, the color of our eyes, our stature, the weight and fineness of our brain, and everything about us could, with full knowledge, be traced with absolute certainty to somewhere. If we had the pedigree it could be traced just the same in a boy as it could in a dog, a horse or a cow.

...All I know is that it is true, and there is not a biologist in the world who will not say that I am right.

...Every effort to protect society is an effort toward training the youth to keep the path. Every bit of training in the world proves it, and it likewise proves that it sometimes fails. I know that if this boy had been understood and properly trained—properly for him—and the training that he got might have been the very best for someone; but if it had been the proper training for him he would not be in this courtroom today with the noose above his head. If there is responsibility anywhere, it is back of him; somewhere in the infinite number of his ancestors, or in his surroundings, or in both. And I submit, Your Honor, that under every principle of conscience, of right, and of law, he should not be made responsible for the acts of someone else...

Exercise:

1. Outline Darrow's arguments. What are the main conclusions he argues for? What are the main points he offers in support for them?
2. Using your reconstruction of the arguments offer counterarguments in places that you think Darrow's argument is weak.
3. If you were on the jury would you convict the two murderers? Give a justification in terms of the argument you have outlined.
4. Darrow seems to be blaming others for the crimes of Leopold and Loeb. Is this the same as holding others morally responsible? Why or why not?
5. If we accept Darrow's argument is anyone morally responsible for anything? If not, what are we to do with people who commit serious crimes?

SECTION 3: SIGNIFICANT OTHERS

The most important people in a child's early life are those that are closest to her, parents, grandparents, sisters and brothers. These people create the environment within which the growing child matures. This environment is physical, social and psychological, a life space within which the child's inner and outer realities interact, shaping attitudes and beliefs. As the child grows the circle of individuals that influence her grows with her. More and more people become important to her—more people and different kinds of people. The child's life space grows, expanding like the ripples on a pond, bending and distorting as the expanding circle of the child's experience meets the unexpected. The individuals that alter the child's lifespace are "significant others," persons whose presence alters what the developing individual feels about herself and others. Significant others range from friends to culture heroes, real people as well as fantasies created by history books and the media. In this section we explore some of the issues arising as the center of value for the maturing individual shifts from the family to the world outside.

Friends

As a child's friendships extend beyond the immediate home environment, the background of values and expectations that form the family's shared experience is sometimes challenged. The child, moving into the larger world extends his perceptions by coming to terms with issues that redefine the way the family looks at things. Such experiences begin the process of distinguishing one generation from another—developing the set of values and expectations that the new generation will see as its own.

Shirley Jackson,
After You, My Dear Alphonse

Mrs. Wilson was just taking the gingerbread out of the oven when she heard Johnny outside talking to someone.

"Johnny," she called, "you're late. Come in and get your lunch."

"Just a minute, Mother," Johnny said. "after you, my dear Alphonse."

"After you, my dear Alphonse," another voice said.

"No, after you, my dear Alphonse," Johnny said.

Mrs. Wilson opened the door. "Johnny," she said, "you come in this minute and get your lunch. You can play after you've eaten."

Johnny came in after her, slowly. "Mother," he said, "I brought Boyd home for lunch with me."

"Boyd?" Mrs. Wilson thought for a moment. "I don't believe I've met Boyd. Bring him in, dear, since you've invited him. Lunch is ready."

"Boyd!" Johnny yelled. "Hey, Boyd, come on in!"

"I'm coming. Just got to unload this stuff."

"Well, hurry, or my mother'll be sore."

"Johnny, that's not very polite to either your friend or your mother," Mrs. Wilson said. "Come sit down, Boyd."

As she turned to show Boyd where to sit, she saw he was a Negro boy, smaller than Johnny but about the same age. His arms were loaded with split kindling wood. "Where'll I put this stuff, Johnny?" he asked.

Mrs. Wilson turned to Johnny. "Johnny," she said, "what did you make Boyd do? What is this wood?"

"Dead Japanese," Johnny said mildly. "We stand them in the ground and run over them with tanks."

"How do you do, Mrs. Wilson?" Boyd said.

"How do you do, Boyd? You shouldn't let Johnny make you carry all that wood. Sit down now and eat lunch, both of you."

"Why shouldn't he carry the wood, Mother? It's his wood. We got it at his place."

"Johnny," Mrs. Wilson said, "go on and eat your lunch."

"Sure," Johnny said. He held out the dish of scrambled eggs to Boyd. "After you, my dear Alphonse."

"After you, my dear Alphonse," Boyd said.

"After you, my dear Alphonse," Johnny said. They began to giggle.

"Are you hungry, Boyd?" Mrs. Wilson asked.

"Yes, Mrs. Wilson."

"Well, don't you let Johnny stop you. He always fusses about eating, so you just see that you get a good lunch. There's plenty of food here for you to have all you want."

"Thank you, Mrs. Wilson."

"Come on, Alphonse," Johnny said. He pushed half the scrambled eggs on to Boyd's plate. Boyd watched while Mrs. Wilson put a dish of stewed tomatoes beside his plate.

"Boyd don't eat tomatoes, do you, Boyd?" Johnny said.

"Doesn't eat tomatoes, Johnny. And just because you don't like them, don't say that about Boyd. Boyd will eat anything."

"Bet he won't," Johnny said, attacking his scrambled eggs.

"Boyd wants to grow up and be a big strong man so he can work hard," Mrs. Wilson said. "I'll bet Boyd's father eats stewed tomatoes."

"My father eats anything he wants to," Boyd said.

"So does mine," Johnny said. "Sometimes he doesn't eat hardly anything. He's a little guy, though. Wouldn't hurt a flea."

"Mine's a little guy, too," Boyd said.

"I'll bet he's strong, though," Mrs. Wilson said. She hesitated. "Does he ...work?"

"Sure," Johnny said. "Boyd's father works in a factory."

"There, you see?" Mrs. Wilson said. "And he certainly has to be strong to do that—all that lifting and carrying at a factory."

"Boyd's father doesn't have to," Johnny said. "He's a foreman."

Mrs. Wilson felt defeated. "What does your mother do, Boyd?"

"My mother?" Boyd was surprised. "She takes care of us kids."

"Oh. She doesn't work, then?"

"Why should she?" Johnny said through a mouthful of eggs. "You don't work."

"You really don't want any stewed tomatoes, Boyd?"

"No, thank you, Mrs. Wilson," Boyd said.

"No, thank you, Mrs. Wilson, no, thank you, Mrs. Wilson, no, thank you, Mrs. Wilson," Johnny said. " Boyd's sister's going to work, though. She's going to be a teacher."

"That's a very fine attitude for her to have, Boyd." Mrs. Wilson restrained an impulse to pat Boyd on the head. "I imagine you're all very proud of her?"

"I guess so," Boyd said.

"What about all your other brothers and sisters? I guess all of you want to make just as much of yourselves as you can."

"There's only me and Jean." Boyd said. "I don't know yet what I want to be when I grow up."

"We're going to be tank drivers, Boyd and me," Johnny said. "Zoom." Mrs. Wilson caught Boyd's glass of milk as Johnny's napkin ring, suddenly transformed into a tank, plowed heavily across the table.

"Look, Johnny," Boyd said. "Here's a foxhole. I'm shooting at you."

Mrs. Wilson, with the speed born of long experience, took the gingerbread off the shelf and placed it carefully between the tank and the foxhole.

"Now eat as much as you want to, Boyd," she said. "I want to see you get filled up."

"Boyd eats a lot, but not as much as I do," Johnny said. "I'm bigger than he is."

"You're not much bigger," Boyd said. "I can beat you running."

Mrs. Wilson took a deep breath. "Boyd," she said. Both boys turned to her. "Boyd, Johnny has some suits that are a little too small for him, and a winter coat. It's not new, of course, but there's lots of wear in it still. And I have a few dresses that your mother or sister could probably use. Your mother can make them over into lots of things for all of you, and I'd be very happy to give them to you. Suppose before you leave I make up a big bundle and then you and

Johnny can take it over to your mother right away. . ." Her voice trailed off as she saw Boyd's puzzled expression.

"But I have plenty of clothes, thank you," he said. "And I don't think my mother knows how to sew very well, and anyway I guess we buy about everything we need. Thank you very much, though."

"We don't have time to carry that old stuff around, Mother," Johnny said. "We got to play tanks with the kids today."

Mrs. Wilson lifted the plate of gingerbread off the table as Boyd was about to take another piece. "There are many little boys like you, Boyd, who would be very grateful for the clothes someone was kind enough to give them."

"Boyd will take them if you want him to, Mother," Johnny said.

"I didn't mean to make you mad, Mrs. Wilson," Boyd said.

"Don't think I'm angry, Boyd. I'm just disappointed in you, that's all. Now let's not say anything more about it."

She began clearing the plates off the table, and Johnny took Boyd's hand and pulled him to the door. "Bye, Mother," Johnny said. Boyd stood for a minute, staring at Mrs. Wilson's back.

"After you, my dear Alphonse," Johnny said, holding the door open.

"Is your mother still mad?" Mrs. Wilson heard Boyd ask in a low voice.

"I don't know," Johnny said. "She's screwy sometimes."

"So's mine," Boyd said. He hesitated. "After you, my dear Alphonse."

Exercise:

Johnny's mother makes assumptions about Boyd that Johnny obviously does not share.

Write a series of short paragraphs outlining relationships with friends that have influenced you to change attitudes that you once shared with your family. Give both the situation and a brief analysis of how the relationship caused you to change your views.

The Group

The new value system that emerges from adolescent experience is seen by the adolescent as an improvement over the one he had before. Sometimes it is and sometimes it isn't. New perspectives and outlooks can form the basis for a more enlightened attitude towards others, but the lifespace the new values generate may not be so positive. The new value system is frequently based upon peer pressure: conformity to group standards reinforced by threat and ridicule. Such challenges to status frequently force action that is both alien to social standards and dangerous to the adolescent himself.

Jim Carroll, The Basketball Diaries

Every crowd of young guys has its little games to prove if you're punk or not. My cousin in Newark plays "chickie," which is two cars heading towards each other at about 80 mph. The first driver to swerve out of the way is, of course, the chicken. On the Lower East Side they'd make you press a lit cigarette onto your arm and have it burn all the way up to the filter without the slightest flinch. Here in upper Manhattan, guys jump off cliffs into the Harlem River, where the water is literally shitty because right nearby are the giant sewer deposits where about half a million toilets empty their goods daily. You had to time each jump, in fact, with the "shit lines" as they flowed by. That is, there were these lines of water crammed with shit along the surface about five feet long that would come by once every forty seconds. So you had to time your jump in between the lines just like those jitterbugs down in Acapulco got to time their jumps so they hit the water just as the wave is beginning to break.

It was also a big thrill and a standard joke whenever a really giant scumbag floated by. Man, did we see some whoppers: the people in this sewer district sure have big dicks. One time we even saw a dead pig float by (the animal, that is). He must have come off the Hudson from upstate, freed himself from a livestock barge and drowned maybe. It was scary white and jelly-like, bloated to double its normal size. I remember the sight of it cruising by and (really) no one swam for about three days.

So today we met in the park near the basketball courts, Johnny, Danny, and I, played a few quick games, downed a couple of beers, and headed up the street....Well, we walked our way up to the 225th Street bridge, cross over into the Bronx, shimmy to get down to the railroad tracks to get down to the cut (which is the name of a huge rock you jump off). Meanwhile, on the way, we're chased by the huge watchdog, a ferocious German Shepherd, and we had to run our balls off and climb over another fence to avoid it. So we made it for a change because sometimes we're not so lucky with that mutt and it will tear the leg of your pants off in one chomp, perhaps a good part of your ass with it. One day we were with Sam McGiggle and he couldn't make it to the fence in time so we told him to freeze perfectly still and the dog wouldn't bother him. So he statued himself in some insane position and the mutt came up to him, sort of sniffed at him for a second or two, and just as old Sam felt relieved, it bit him, accordingly right square in the bum-bum.

Well, we made it to the cut and poked around the bushes at the base to find our hidden swim suits and jocks (since there were no lockers this was the next best thing). Then we buried our money in the safest spot, and began to change. Just down to our scivvies, we hear giggles shooting up from behind the bushes and wheel around to find three chicks there trying to dig on the show. No other solution, we saw, but to attack, so we whip off our underwear and charge after them, totally naked and slinging jocks around in our hands. Their true purity exposed, they were off in the breeze, giggling and peeking back now and then at our free swinging tools. On go our suits and we begin to ascend the cut. The cut is actually only about twelve feet wide, with the Harlem River on one side, and the Hudson-Harlem train line tracks in the rear. It has a series of minor cliffs to jump off, and they gradually get higher until you reach the top, about eighty-five feet. Every plateau you jump has its own separate name like Suicide and Hell's Gate, Angel's Toe and the top, the elite goal that all this bullshit is about, Hell's Angel.

That's where we were, the very top, flat solid rock which is cracked in parts so that small clover-like plants grow out of the crevices. We sat tense, waiting for the sightseeing boat, The Circle Line, to make the turn around the bend down near the bridge and head toward us. That was what really made the jump worthwhile, with all the lame couples like old tourists from Ohio, and nuns, and Japanese executives, and other odd N.Y.C. visitors who got fished into paying five beans to sail around the island, watching us go down into the stinking water. Well, Danny was the first, Johnny and I peering over the edge as he made it clear over the first and only obstacle, a small tree that shot out of the rock about five feet below, then straight ahead, hands close at sides, body stiff, and feet locked tightly, hitting the surface missile-like. From up there it seemed like 5008 feet to the bottom. But Danny had jumped Hell's Angel before, so it was old hat to him, but now it was John's turn, and he, like me, was a rookie at the top. Scared shit and mouth wide, he peeped one more time onto the river, waved at the waiting sightseers, took one step back, five hundred deep breaths, muttered, "Fuck it," then yelled out the same thing, clutched his balls with both hands and jumped. Down he was going, legs spread far apart, and jitterbugging like he was doing the Popeye or some-thing, still firmly clutching his crotch. "Bad form," I sighed, as he hit the water, and what a fucking understatement that was. It was pitiful, he hit the water like a fucking octopus, limbs flying everywhere, and the splash con-tained a smacking sound that hurt all the way up to me at the top of the cliff.

192

When he came up to the surface he swam to the shore with one hand paddling and holding his sore, sore ass with the other, so that he was slow enough to get attacked by a fair sized shit line, the whole fucking scene having Danny in stitches over on the shore near the tracks. My turn now, the boat almost past, all the people at attention yelling for me to do it, the sadistic bastards.

I didn't really think, I didn't even take my sneakers off, I just jumped into this jerky dream that lasted all the way down until I hit bottom. The falling isn't movement anyway, but rather being suspended in front of the sheer cliff, mid-air, with the waters rising up sharp and fast at you. I hit water hard, but I didn't go too deep, coming up to see all the sightseers applauding. Then I swam to shore to meet the others and we turned, pulled down our shorts, and flashed our moons to the old sightseeing buggers as the boat pulled away and headed for the Hudson. We got dressed and went back.... I got back to the neighborhood and decided to go home to eat and write and sleep; I know I can always wait till tomorrow to go around and brag and let everyone know what a big shit I am and all that.

Exercise:

Describe factors that would make an adolescent perform the following acts, even if they seem to lead to social or parental disapproval.
1. Get a radical hairstyle.
2. Cut classes.
3. Smoke cigarettes.
4. Have sex.
5. Drive drunk.
6. Shoplift.
7. Experiment with drugs.
8. Have an illicit romance with an older person.
9. Have a baby out of wedlock.
10. Drop out of school.

Special Persons

New friends and new attitudes are the classic components of coming of age. But the new often conflicts with the old, as individuals or circumstances play a decisive role in presenting new perspectives. How can the individual decide between the various points of view he encounters in his life? How can we reconcile the demands of the groups we belong to and the people we cherish. And how can we use these critical life experiences to come to decisions, to form new values?

Mark Twain, Huckleberry Finn

We slept most all day, and started out at night, a little ways behind a monstrous long raft that was as long going by as a procession. She had four long sweeps at each end, so we judged she carried as many as thirty men, likely. She had five big wigwams aboard, wide apart, and an open campfire in the middle, and a tall flag-pole at each end. There was a power of style about her. It amounted to something being a raftsman on such a craft as that.

We went drifting down into a big bend, and the night clouded up and got hot. The river was very wide, and was walled with solid timber on both sides; you couldn't see a break in it hardly ever, or a light. We talked about Cairo, and wondered whether we would know it when we got to it. I said likely we wouldn't, because I had heard say there warn't but about a dozen houses there, and if they didn't happen to have them lit up, how was we going to know we was passing a town. Jim said if the two big rivers joined together there, that would show. But I said maybe we might think we was passing the foot of an island and coming into the same old river again. That disturbed Jim—and me too. So the question was, what to do? I said, paddle ashore the first time a light showed, and tell them pap was behind, coming along with a trading-scow, and was a green hand at the business, and wanted to know how far it was to Cairo. Jim thought it was a good idea, so we took a smoke on it and waited.

There warn't nothing to do now but to look out sharp for the town, and not pass it without seeing it. He said he'd be mighty sure to see it, because he'd be a free man the minute he seen it, but if he missed it he'd be in a slave country again and no more show for freedom. Every little while he jumps up and says:

"Dah she is?"

But it wasn't. It was Jack-o'lanterns, or lightning-bugs, so he set down again, and went to watching, same as before. Jim said it made him all over trembly and feverish to be so close to freedom. Well, I can tell you it made me all over trembly and feverish, too, to hear him, because I begun to get it through my head that he was most free—and who was to blame for it? Why, me, I couldn't get that out of my conscience, no how nor no way. It got to troubling me so I couldn't rest; I couldn't stay still in one place. It hadn't ever come home to me before, what this thing was that I was doing. But now it did; and it stayed with me, and scorched me more and more. I tried to make out to myself that I warn't to blame, because I didn't run Jim off from his rightful owner; but it warn't no use, conscience up and says, every time, "But you knowed he was running for his freedom, and you could 'a' paddled ashore and told somebody." That was so—I couldn't get around that no way. That was where it pinched. Conscience says to me, "What had poor Miss Watson done to you that you could see her nigger go off right under your eyes and never say one single word? What did that poor old woman do to you that you could treat her so mean? Why, she tried to learn you your book, she tried to learn you your manners, she tried to be good to you every way she knowed how. That's what she done."

I got to feeling so mean and so miserable I most wished I was dead. I fidgeted up and down the raft, abusing myself to myself, and Jim was fidgeting up and down past me. We neither of us could keep still. Every time he danced around and says, "Dah's Cairo!" it went through me like a shot, and I thought if it was Cairo I reckoned I would die of miserableness.

Jim talked out loud all the time while I was talking to myself. He was saying how the first thing he would do when he got to a free state he would go to saving up money and never spend a single cent, and when he got enough he would buy his wife, which was owned on a farm close to where Miss Watson lived; and then they would both work to buy the two children, and if their master wouldn't sell them, they'd get an Abolitionist to go and steal them.

It most froze me to hear such talk. He wouldn't ever dared to talk such talk in his life before. Just see what a difference it made in him the minute he judged he was about free. It was according to the old saying, "Give a nigger an inch and he'll take an ell." Thinks I, this is what comes of my not thinking. Here was this nigger, which I had as good as helped to run away, coming right out flat-footed and saying he would steal his children—children that belonged to a man I didn't even know; a man that hadn't ever done me no harm.

I was sorry to hear Jim say that, it was such a lowering of him. My conscience got to stirring me up hotter than ever, until at last I says to it, "Let up on me—it ain't too late yet—I'll paddle ashore at the first light and tell." I felt easy and happy and light as a feather right off. All my troubles was gone. I went to looking out sharp for a light, and sort of singing to myself. By and by one showed. Jim sings out.

"We's safe, Huck, we's safe! Jump up and crack yo' heels! Dat's de good ole Cairo at las', I jis knows it!"

I says:

"I'll take the canoe and go and see, Jim. It mightn't be, you know."

He jumped and got the canoe ready, and put his old coat in the bottom for me to set on, and give me the paddle; and as I shoved off, he says:

"Pooty soon I'll be a-shout'n' for joy, en I'll say, it's all on accounts o'Huck. I's a free man, en I couldn't ever ben free ef it hadn'ben for Huck. Huck done it. Jim won't ever forgit you, Huck; you's de bes' fren' Jim's ever had; en you's de only fren' ole Jim's got now."

I was paddling off, all in a sweat to tell on him; but when he says this, it seemed to kind of take the tuck all out of me. I went along slow then, and I warn't right down certain whether I was glad I started or whether I warn't. When I was fifty yards off, Jim says:

"Dah you goes, de ole true Huck; de on'y white genlman dat ever kep' his promise to ole Jim."

Well, I just felt sick. But I says, I got to do it—I can't get out of it. Right then along comes a skiff with two men in it with guns, and they stopped and I stopped. One of them says:

"What's that yonder?"

"A piece of a raft," I says.

"Do you belong on it?"

"Yes, sir."

"Any men on it?"

"Only one, sir."

"Well, there's five niggers run off to-night up yonder, above the head of the bend. Is your man white or black?"

I didn't answer up prompt. I tried to, but the words wouldn't come. I tried for a second or two to brace up and out with it, but I warn't man enough—hadn't the spunk of a rabbit. I see I was weakening; so I just give up trying, and up and says:

"He's white."

"I reckon we'll go and see for ourselves."

"I wish you would," says I, "because it's pap that's there, and maybe you'd help me tow the raft ashore where the light is. He's sick—and so is mam and Mary Ann."

"Oh, the devil! we're in a hurry, boy. But I s'pose we've got to. Come, buckle to your paddle, and let's get along."

I buckled to my paddle and they laid to their oars. When we had made a stroke or two, I says:

"Pap'll be mighty much obleeged to you, I can tell you. Everybody goes away when I want them to help me tow the raft ashore, and I can't do it by myself."

"Well, that's infernal mean. Odd, too. Say, boy, what's the matter with your father?"

"It's the—a—the—well, it ain't anything much."

They stopped pulling. It warn't but a mighty little ways to the raft now. One says:

"Boy, that's a lie. What is the matter with you pap? Answer up square now, and it'll be better for you."

"I will, sir, I will, honest—but don't leave us, please. It's the—the-Gentlemen, if you'll only pull ahead, and let me heave you the headline, you won't have to come-a-near the raft—please do."

"Set her back, John, set her back!" says one. They backed water. "Keep away, boy—keep to looard. Confound it, I just expect the wind has blowed it to us. Your pap's got the smallpox, and you know it precious well. Why didn't you come out and say so? Do you want to spread it all over?"

"Well," says I, a-blubbering, "I've told everybody before, and they just went away and left us."

"Poor devil, there's something in that. We are right down sorry for you, but we—well, hang it, we don't want the smallpox, you see. Look here, I'll tell you what to do. Don't you try to land by yourself, or you'll smash, everything to pieces. You float along down about twenty miles, and you'll come to a town on the left-hand side of the river. It will be long after sun-up then, and when you ask for help you tell them your folks are all down with chills and fever. Don't be a fool again, and let people guess what is the matter. Now we're trying to do you a kindness; so you just put twenty miles between us, that's a good boy. It wouldn't do any good to land yonder where the light is—it's only a wood-yard. Say, I reckon your father's poor, and I'm bound to say he's in pretty hard luck. Here, I'll put a twenty-dollar gold piece on this board, and you get it when it floats by. I feel mighty mean to leave you; but my kingdom! it won't do to fool with smallpox, don't you see?"

"Hold on, Parker," says the man, "here's twenty to put on the board for me. Good-by, boy; you do as Mr. Parker told you, and you'll be all right."

"That's so, my boy—good-by, good-by. If you see any runaway niggers you get help and nab them, and you can make some money by it."

"Good-by, sir," says I, "I won't let no runaway niggers get by me if I can help it."

They went off and I got aboard the raft, feeling bad and low, because I knowed very well I had done wrong, and I see it warn't no use for me to try to learn to do right; a body that don't get started right when he's little ain't got no show—when the pinch comes there ain't nothing to back him up and keep him to his work, and so he get beat. Then I thought a minute, and says to myself, hold on; s'pose you'd a'done right and give Jim up, would you felt better than what you do now? No, says I, I'd feel bad—I'd feel just the same way I do now. Well, then, says I, what's the use you learning to do right when it's troublesome to do right and ain't no trouble to do wrong, and the wages is just the same? I was stuck. I couldn't answer that. So I reckoned I wouldn't bother no more about it, but after this always do whichever comes handiest at the time.

I went into the wigwam; Jim warn't there. I looked all around; he warn't anywhere. I says:

"Jim!"

"Here I is, Huck. Is dey out o'sight yit? Don't talk loud."

He was in the river under the stern oar, with just his nose out. I told him they were out of sight, so he come aboard. He says:

"I was a-listening' to all de talk, en I slips into de river en was gwyne to shove for sho' if dey come aboard. Den I was gwyne to swim to de raf' again when dey was gone. But lawsy, how you did fool 'em, Huck! Dat wuz de smartes' dodge! I tell you, chile, I 'spec it save' ole Jim—ole Jim ain't going to forgit you for dat, honey."

Then we talked about the money. It was a pretty good raise—twenty dollars apiece. Jim said we could take deck passage on a steamboat now, and the money would last us as far as we wanted to go in the free states. He said twenty mile more warn't far for the raft to go, but he wished we was already there.

Towards daybreak we tied up, and Jim was mighty particular about hiding the raft good. Then he worked all day fixing things in bundles, and getting all ready to quit rafting.

That night about ten we hove in sight of the lights of a town away down in a left-hand bend.

I went off in the canoe to ask about it. Pretty soon I found a man out in the river with a skiff, setting trot-line. I ranged and says:

"Mister, is that town Cairo?"

"Cairo? no. You must be a blame' fool."

"What town is it, mister?"

"If you want to know, go and find out. If you stay here botherin' around me for about a half a minute longer you'll get something you won't want."

I paddled to the raft. Jim was awful disappointed, but I said never mind, Cairo would be the next place, I reckoned.

We passed another town before daylight, and I was going out again; but it was high ground, so I didn't go. No high ground about Cairo, Jim said. I had forgot it. We laid up for the day on a towhead tolerable close to the left-hand bank. I begun to suspicion something. So did Jim. I says:

"Maybe we went by Cairo in the fog that night."

He says:

"Doan' le's talk about it, Huck. Po' niggers can't have no luck...."

Exercise:

Huck Finn is faced with a conflict of values.

1. List the main values that are involved in the various decisions Huck makes in the story.
2. Make a short list next to each main value, of other values that Huck thinks are in conflict with it.
3. In each case construct arguments that show why Huck should or should not have resolved the conflict in the way he resolves them in the story.

Discussion Plan:

The value conflict that Huck Finn had to deal with was based on the special status that Jim had. As a black. Jim was not given the full rights accorded to other people. He was not a full person according to the law and to the social ethic. The concept of person is a tricky one. It defines an individual who has full protection of the law and full legal privileges and obligations. Some human individuals are denied these rights, for example, children, the insane, criminals. This raises the issue of where we ought to draw the line. Who should be considered a person?

1. Is being a person a natural fact about people?
2. Are all people persons?
3. Does a child become a person at 21, at 18?
4. Does the age of personhood vary in different societies?
5. Are intelligent people more persons than dull people?
6. Are self-supporting people more persons than people who rely on others?
7. Does gender have anything to do with being a person?

Friendship

After looking a three kinds of friendship we might agree with Aristotle when he says, "Not a few things about friendship are matters of debate." Most fundamentally: What makes for friendship? Aristotle distinguishes between the friendships that characterize different personalities and motives. The different reasons for friendship are frequently crucial to determining how seriously the friendship should be taken, especially since the values growing out of the friendship frequently create conflicts.

Aristotle, Nicomachean Ethics

... Not a few things about friendship are matters of debate. Some define it as a kind of likeness and say like people are friends, whence come the sayings 'like to like', 'birds of a feather flock together', and so on; others on the contrary say 'two of a trade never agree'...

...The kinds of friendship may perhaps be cleared up if we first come to know the object of love. For not everything seems to be loved but only the lovable, and this is good, pleasant, or useful; but it would seem to be that by which some good or pleasure is produced that is useful, so that it is the good and the useful that are lovable as ends. Do men love, then, the good, or what is good for them? These sometimes clash. So too with regard to the pleasant. Now it is thought that each loves what is good for himself, and that the good is without qualification lovable, and what is good for each man is lovable for him; but each man loves not what is good for him but what seems good. This however will make no difference; we shall have to say that this is 'that which seems lovable'. Now there are three grounds on which people love; of the love of lifeless objects we do not use the word 'friendship'; for it is not mutual love, nor is there a wishing of good to the other (for it would surely be ridiculous to wish wine well; if one wishes anything for it, it is that it may keep, so that one may have it oneself); but to a friend we say we ought to wish what is good for his sake. But to those who thus wish good we ascribe only goodwill, if the wish is not reciprocated; goodwill when it is reciprocal being friendship...

There are therefore three kinds of friendship, equal in number to the things that are lovable; for with respect to each there is a mutual and recognized love, and those who love each other wish well to each other in that respect in which they love one another. Now those who love each other for their utility do not love each other for themselves but in virtue of some good which they get from each other. So too with those who love for the sake of pleasure; it is not for their character that men love ready-witted people, but because they find them pleasant. Therefore those who love for the sake of utility love for the sake of what is good for themselves, and those who love for the sake of pleasure do so for the sake of what is pleasant to themselves, and not in so far as the other is the person loved but in so far as he is useful or pleasant. And thus these friendships are only incidental; for it is not as being the man he is that the loved person is loved, but as providing some good or pleasure. Such friendships, then, are easily dissolved, if the parties do not remain like themselves; for if the one party is no longer pleasant or useful the other ceases to love him.

Now the useful is not permanent but is always changing. Thus when the motive of the friendship is done away, the friendship is dissolved, inasmuch as it existed only for the ends in question. This kind of friendship seems to exist chiefly between old people (for at that age people pursue not the pleasant but the useful) and, of those who are in their prime or young, between those who pursue utility. And such people do not live much with each other either; for sometimes they do not even find each other pleasant; therefore they do not need such companionship unless they are useful to each other; for they are pleasant to each other only in so far as they rouse in each other hopes of something good to come. Among such friendships people also class the friendship of host and guest. On the other hand the friendship of young people seems to aim at pleasure; for they live under the guidance of emotion, and pursue above all what is pleasant to themselves and what is immediately before them; but with increasing age their pleasures become different. This is why they quickly become friends and quickly cease to be so; their friendship changes with the object that is found pleasant, and such pleasure alters quickly. Young people are amorous too; for the greater part of the friendship of love depends on emotion and aims at pleasure; this is why they fall in love and quickly fall out of love, changing often within a single day. But these people do wish to spend their days and lives together; for it is thus that they attain the purpose of their friendship.

Perfect friendship is the friendship of men who are good, and alike in virtue; for these wish well alike to each other *qua* good, and they are good in themselves. Now those who wish well to their friends for their sake are most truly friends; for they do this by reason of their own nature and not incidentally; therefore their friendship lasts as long as they are good—and goodness is an enduring thing ...

... But those who exchange not pleasure but utility in their amour are both less truly friends and less constant. Those who are friends for the sake of utility part when the advantage is at an end; for they were lovers not of each other but of profit.

For the sake of pleasure or utility, then, even bad men may be friends of each other, or good men of bad, or one who is neither good nor bad may be a friend to any sort of person, but for their own sake clearly only good men can be friends; for bad men do not delight in each other unless some advantage come of the relation ...

Friendship being divided into these kinds, bad men will be friends for the sake of pleasure or of utility, being in this respect like each other, but good men will be friends for their own sake, i.e., in virtue of their goodness. These, then, are friends without qualification; the others are friends incidentally and through a resemblance to these.

Discussion Plan:

Using Aristotle's analysis, what sort of friendship relationships, if any, could the following pairs of individuals have?

1. tennis partners
2. parent and child
3. teacher and student
4. members of a band
5. boyfriend and girlfriend
6. grocer and customer
7. prostitute and customer
8. dope dealer and customer
9. soldiers in the field
10. criminal conspirators

Culture Heroes

We all seem to need role models, persons who we look up to and pattern our behavior after. These role models can be people we know, but often they are people "in the news," people who have achieved something that we admire. Looking carefully at the culture heros or heroines of a group tells us a lot about the values and aspirations of members of that group.

Ralph Schoenstein, The Modern Mount Rushmore

My daughter Lori, who is eight, told me last night that she wants to grow up to sing like either Judy Garland or Michael Jackson. "Try for Judy Garland," I said. "A girl needs a great soprano to be Michael Jackson."

These two singers have become Lori's first hero and heroine. They are hardly figures for commemorative stamps, but many children have no heroes or heroines anymore, no noble achievers they yearn to emulate. They emulate their parents, most of whom look up to no one but trapeze acts. Recently when asked to name the women who were her mentors, Jane Fonda replied that she had none. In love with her leotard, Jane is at the center of the Age of Self-Involvement, where heroines like Marie Curie, Joan of Arc and Victoria Regina have been replaced by Marie Osmond, Joan Collins and Victoria Principal.

Champions: When my sister and I were children, our heroes and heroines did no endorsements for vaginal sprays, and no one ever cartwheeled out of the Olympics and into a women's hygiene ad. My sister loved medicine, so she idolized Clara Barton, who had founded the American Red Cross, and Florence Nightingale, the great British nurse in the Crimean War, and Sister Elizabeth Kenny, the Australian nurse who developed a treatment for polio. I, who dreamed of glory in sports, idolized the two classiest champions America has ever known, Joe Louis and Joe DiMaggio, and my third god was Franklin D. Roosevelt, who needed no media consultant to make millions of Americans want to be brave just for him.

A few years later, Joe DiMaggio was promoting a coffee maker and President Roosevelt's affair with Lucy Mercer was being dramatized on television. America—especially its children—had clearly lost something precious. The glory had given way to gossip and the idolatry to "Eyewitness News." Most of our heroes and heroines now had not only feet of clay but heads of Silly Putty too. People lowered their eyes from Mount Rushmore to see if the scandal sheets could tell:

Was Betsy Ross a lesbian?

Did Abraham Lincoln cross-dress?

Was Florence Nightingale's bedside manner better inside the bed?

By the 1970s Americans were so busy splattering their heroes with mud that two other giants of my youth, Mohandas Gandhi and Albert Einstein, were revealed as having been cool to their wives. Not Thomas Jefferson, however, who was portrayed by the Broadway musical "1776" as a man less concerned with acts of Congress than with acts of sex.

A few months ago I started rooting for the San Diego Padres because they gave sanctuary to escapees from that bedlam in the Bronx; but then the daily sports scandal section revealed that three of the Padres belong to the John Birch Society and feel that democracy is overrated. Now that I know that the Padres have fielders who can go to their right like no others in baseball, rooting for this team has become like rooting for Italy in the '36 Olympics.

Watching my three daughters group up in this land of rampant detraction, where Indiana Jones is not a hero but a satire of one, I nervously waited for the revelation that Mister Rogers owned slums in his neighborhood. Even John F. Kennedy, who had inspired my generation, was pulled off his pedestal and dropped into bed. When my eldest daughter was 10, she came to me one day and said, "Dad, do presidents always have their girlfriends in the White House?"

"Of course not," I replied. "Some of them meet outside."

It is now nearly impossible for a public official to be a hero to anyone. Heroism, in fact, may actually have been a burden to presidential candidate John Glenn, for Americans today find less appeal in the right stuff than in the right fluff. Moreover, in a book that became the top best seller, the mayor of New York presents most of the public officials he has known as weaklings, frauds or fools, and seems to enjoy making them squirm. Like most of us, he is looking down, which is not the view I had when I made heroes of Winston Churchill, Teddy Roosevelt and Oliver Wendell Holmes after reading the stories of their lives. Could Edward Koch be the hero of any child today? Only one in a rotten mood.

Where has all this exposing and debunking left our kids? One day last spring I stood before 20 children of eight and nine in Lori's third-grade class to see if any heroes or heroines were inspiring them. I asked each child to give me the names of the three greatest people he had ever heard about.

"Michael Jackson, Brooke Shields and Boy George," said a small blond girl, giving me one from all three sexes.

"Michael Jackson, Spider-Man and God," a boy then said, naming a new holy trinity.

Immortal: When the other children recited, Michael Jackson's name was spoken again and again, but Andrew Jackson, never, nor Washington, Lincoln or any other presidential immortal. Just Ronald Reagan, who made it twice, once behind Batman and once behind Mr. T, a hero who likes to move people by saying, "Sucker, I'll break your face." When my wife was eight,

Eleanor Roosevelt was the greatest woman in the world to her, but no child gave a modern equivalent of Eleanor Roosevelt. And I heard no modern equivalent of Charles A. Lindbergh, America's beloved "Lone Eagle," even though with Armstrong and Aldrin, the Eagle had landed on the moon.

What were Lori's classmates' dreams? To make the "Who's Hot" edition of _US_ magazine. What were they yearning to be? To be wildly famous, androgynous and good at climbing walls.

In answer to my request for heroes, I had expected to hear such names as Michael Jackson, Mr. T, Brooke Shields and Spider-Man from the kids, but I had not expected the replies of the eight who answered "Me." Their heroes were themselves. The children of Jane Fonda had spoken.

It is sad enough to see the faces on Mount Rushmore replaced by rock stars, brawlers and cartoons, but it is sadder still to see Mount Rushmore replaced by a mirror.

Exercise:

Whether or not we agree or disagree with a point of view depends on many things. Writers frequently try to persuade by drawing subtle, or not so subtle, conclusions through their use of language. A position is presented in a way that slants the information. This is often done by using culturally loaded images—descriptions that have strong emotive and evaluative connotations.

Analyze the Schoenstein piece looking for the hidden values that his use of language and choice of examples implies.

What values do the culture heroes he chooses imply?

Can you give an argument based on values for the culture heroes picked by the young people he speaks about?

Can you offer non-value reasons for the young peoples choices?

Research Project

Each generation is reflected in the culture heroes it selects. That choice is often an enigma to other.

Do a study of one or more of the culture heroes of your parents' generation. Write an explanation of the personal and social values that you think explain the culture heroes of that time.

Breaking Away

The following selection allows us to closely examine the deep underlying structures that determine an individual's choice. Connie lives in a world that is becoming devalued for her. We follow her to a moment of crisis.

Joyce Carol Oates,
Where Are You Going?
Where Have You Been?

FOR BOB DYLAN

Her name was Connie. She was fifteen and she had a quick, nervous giggling habit of craning her neck to glance into mirrors or checking other people's faces to make sure her own was all right. Her mother, who noticed everything and knew everything and who hadn't much reason any longer to look at her own face, always scolded Connie about it. "Stop gawking at yourself. Who are you? You think you're so pretty?" she would say. Connie would raise her eyebrows at these familiar old complaints and look right through her mother, into a shadowy vision of herself as she was right at that moment: she knew she was pretty and that was everything. Her mother had been pretty once too, if you could believe those old snapshots in the album, but now her looks were gone and that was why she was always after Connie.

"Why don't you keep your room clean like your sister? How've you got your hair fixed—what the hell stinks? Hair spray? You don't see your sister using that junk."

Her sister June was twenty-four and still lived at home. She was a secretary in the high school Connie attended, and if that wasn't bad enough—with her in the same building—she was so plain and chunky and steady that Connie had to hear her praised all the time by her mother and her mother's sisters. June did this, June did that, she saved money and helped clean the house and cooked and Connie couldn't do a thing, her mind was all filled with trashy daydreams. Their father was away at work most of the time and when he came home he wanted supper and he read the newspaper at supper and after supper he went to bed. He didn't bother talking much to them, but around his bent head Connie's mother kept picking at her until Connie wished her mother was dead and she herself was dead and it was all over. "She makes me want to throw up sometimes," she complained to her friends. She had a high, breathless, amused voice that made everything she said sound a little forced, whether it was sincere or not.

There was one good thing: June went places with girl friends of hers, girls who were just as plain and steady as she, and so when Connie wanted to do that her mother had no objections. The father of Connie's best girl friend drove the girls the three miles to town and left them at a shopping plaza so they could walk through the stores or go to a movie, and when he came to pick them up again at eleven he never bothered to ask what they had done.

They must have been familiar sights, walking around the shopping plaza in their shorts and flat ballerina slippers that always scuffed on the sidewalk, with charm bracelets jingling on their thin wrists; they would lean together to whisper and laugh secretly if someone passed who amused or interested them. Connie had long dark blond hair that drew anyone's eye to it, and she wore part of it pulled up on her head and puffed out and the rest of it she let fall down her back. She wore a pull-over jersey blouse that looked one way when she was at home and another way when she was away from home. Everything about her had two sides to it, one for home and one for anywhere that was not home: her walk, which could be child-like and bobbing, or languid enough to make anyone think she was hearing music in her head; her mouth, which was pale and smirking most of the time, but bright and pink on these evenings out; her laugh, which was cynical and drawing at home—"Ha, ha, very funny,"—but high-pitched and nervous anywhere else, like the jingling of the charms on her bracelet.

Sometimes they did go shopping or to a movie; but sometimes they went across the highway, ducking fast across the busy road, to a drive-in restaurant where older kids hung out. The restaurant was shaped like a big bottle, though squatter than a real bottle, and on its cap was a revolving figure of a grinning boy holding a hamburger aloft. One night in midsummer they ran across, breathless with daring, and right away someone leaned out a car window and invited them over, but it was just a boy from high school they didn't like. It made them feel good to be able to ignore him. They went up through the maze of parked and cruising cars to the bright-lit, fly-infested restaurant, their faces pleased and expectant as if they were entering a sacred building that loomed up out of the night to give them what haven and blessing they yearned for. They sat at a counter and crossed their legs at the ankles, their thin shoulders rigid with excitement and listened to the music that made everything so good; the music was always in the background, like music at a church service; it was something to depend upon.

A boy named Eddie came in to talk with them. He sat backwards on his stool, turning himself jerkily around in semicircles and then stopping and turning back again, and after a while he asked Connie if she would like something to eat. She said she would so she tapped her friend's arm on her way out—her friend pulled her face up into a brave, droll look—and Connie said she would meet her at eleven across the way. "I just hate to leave her like that," Connie said earnestly, but the boy said that she wouldn't be alone for long. So they went out to his car, and on the way Connie couldn't help but let her eyes wander over the windshields and faces all around her, her face gleaming with a joy that had nothing to do with Eddie or even this place; it might have been the music. She drew her shoulders up and sucked in her breath with the pure pleasure of being alive, and just at that moment she happened to glance at a face just a few feet away from hers. It was a boy with shaggy black hair, in a convertible jalopy painted gold. He stared at her and then his lips widened into a grin. Connie slit her eyes at him and turned away, but she couldn't help glancing back and there he was, still watching her. He wagged a finger and laughed and said, "Gonna get you, baby," and Connie turned away again without Eddie noticing anything.

She spent three hours with him, at the restaurant where they ate hamburgers and drank Cokes in wax cups that were always sweating, and then down an alley a mile or so away, and when he left her off at five to eleven only the movie house was still open at the plaza. Her girl friend was there, talking with a boy. When Connie came up, the two girls smiled at each other and Connie said, "How was the movie?" and the girl said, "You should know." They rode off with the girl's father, sleepy and pleased, and Connie couldn't help but look back at the darkened shopping plaza with its big empty parking lot and its signs that were faded and ghostly now, and over at the drive-in restaurant where cars were still circling tirelessly. She couldn't hear the music at this distance.

Next morning June asked her how the movie was and Connie said, "So-so."

She and that girl and occasionally another girl went out several times a week, and the rest of the time Connie spent around the house—it was summer vacation—getting in her mother's way and thinking, dreaming about the boys she met. But all the boys fell back and dissolved into a single face that was not even a face but an idea, a feeling, mixed up with the urgent insistent pounding of the music and the humid night air of July. Connie's mother kept dragging her back to the daylight by finding things for her to do or saying suddenly, "What's this about the Pettinger girl?"

And Connie would say nervously, "Oh, her. That dope." She always drew thick clear lines between herself and such girls, and her mother was simple and kind enough to believe it. Her mother was so simple, Connie thought, that it was maybe cruel to fool her so much. Her mother went scuffling around the house in old bedroom slippers and complained over the telephone to one sister about the other, then the other called up and the two of them complained about the third one. If June's name was mentioned her mother's tone was approving, and if Connie's name was mentioned it was disapproving. This did not really mean she disliked Connie, and actually Connie thought that her mother preferred her to June just because she was prettier, but the two of them kept up a pretense of exasperation, a sense that they were tugging and struggling over something of little value to either of them. Sometimes, over coffee, they were almost friends, but something would come up—some vexation that was like a fly buzzing suddenly around their heads—and their faces went hard with contempt.

One Sunday Connie got up at eleven—none of them bothered with church —and washed her hair so that it could dry all day long in the sun. Her parents and sister were going to a barbecue at an aunt's house and Connie said no, she wasn't interested, rolling her eyes to let her mother know just what she thought of it. "Stay home alone then," her mother said sharply. Connie sat out back in a lawn chair and watched them drive away, her father quiet and bald, hunched around so that he could back the car out, her mother with a look that was still angry and not at all softened through the windshield, and in the back seat poor old June, all dressed up as if she didn't know what a barbecue was, with all the running yelling kids and the flies. Connie sat with her eyes closed in the sun, dreaming and dazed with the warmth about her as if this were a kind of love, the caresses of love, and her mind slipped over onto thoughts of the boy she had been with the night before and how nice he had been, how sweet it always was, not the way someone like June would suppose but sweet, gentle, the way it was in the movies and promised in songs; and when she opened her eyes she hardly knew where she was, the back yard ran off into weeds and fence-like line of trees and behind it the sky was perfectly blue and still. The asbestos "ranch house" that was now three years old startled her—it looked small. She shook her head as if to get awake.

It was too hot. She went inside the house and turned on the radio to drown out the quiet. She sat on the edge of her bed, barefoot, and listened for an hour and a half, to a program called XYZ Sunday Jamboree, record after record of hard, fast, shrieking songs she sang along with, interspersed by exclamations from "Bobby King"; "An' look here, you girls at Napoleon's— Son and Charley want you to pay real close attention to this song coming up!"

And Connie paid close attention herself, bathed in a glow of slow-pulsed joy that seemed to rise mysteriously out of the music itself and lay languidly about the airless little room, breathed in and breathed out with each gentle rise and fall of her chest.

After a while she heard a car coming up the drive. She sat up at once, startled, because it couldn't be her father so soon. The gravel kept crunching all the way in from the road—the driveway was long—and Connie ran to the window. It was a car she didn't know. It was an open jalopy, painted a bright gold that caught the sunlight opaquely. Her heart began to pound and her fingers snatched at her hair, checking it, and she whispered, "Christ, Christ," wondering how she looked. The car came to a stop at the side door and the horn sounded four short taps, as if this were a signal Connie knew.

She went into the kitchen and approached the door slowly, then hung out the screen door, her bare toes curling down off the step. There were two boys in the car and now she recognized the driver: he had shaggy, shabby black hair that looked crazy as a wig and he was grinning at her.

"I ain't late, am I?" he said.

"Who the hell do you think you are?" Connie said.

"Toldja I'd be out, didn't I?"

"I don't even know who you are."

She spoke sullenly, careful to show no interest or pleasure, and he spoke in a fast, bright monotone. Connie looked past him to the other boy, taking her time. He had fair brown hair, with a lock that fell onto his forehead. His sideburns gave him a fierce, embarrassed look, but so far he hadn't even bothered to glance at her. Both boys wore sunglasses. The driver's glasses were metallic and mirrored everything in miniature.

"You wanta come for a ride?" he said.

Connie smirked and let her hair fall loose over one shoulder.

"Don'tcha like my car? New paint job," he said. "Hey."

"What?"

"You're cute."

She pretended to fidget, chasing flies away from the door.

"Dont'cha believe me, or what?" he said.

"Look, I don't even know who you are," Connie said in disgust.

"Hey, Ellie's got a radio, see. Mine broke down." He lifted his friend's arm and showed her the little transistor radio the boy was holding, and now Connie began to hear the music. It was the same program that was playing inside the house.

"Bobby King?" she said.

"I listen to him all the time. I think he's great."

"Listen, that guy's great. He knows where the action is."

Connie blushed a little, because the glasses made it impossible for her to see just what this boy was looking at. She couldn't decide if she liked him or if he was a jerk, and so she dawdled in the doorway and wouldn't come down or go back inside. She said, "What's all that stuff painted on your car?"

"Can'tcha read it?" He opened the door very carefully, as if he were afraid it might fall off. He slid out just as carefully, planting his feet firmly on the ground, the tiny metallic world in his glasses slowing down like gelatine hardening, and in the midst of it Connie's bright green blouse. "This here is my name, to begin with," he said. Arnold Friend was written in tarlike black letters on the side, with a drawing of a round, grinning face that reminded Connie of a pumpkin, except it wore sunglasses. "I wanta introduce myself. I'm Arnold Friend and that's my real name and I'm gonna be your friend, honey, and inside the car's Ellie Oscar, he's kinda shy." Ellie brought his transistor radio up to his shoulder and balanced it there. "Now, these numbers are a secret code, honey," Arnold Friend explained. He read off the numbers 33, 19, 17 and raised his eyebrows at her to see what she thought of that, but she didn't think much of it. The left rear fender had been smashed and around it was written, on the gleaming gold background: DONE BY CRAZY WOMAN DRIVER. Connie had to laugh at that. Arnold Friend was pleased at her laughter and looked up at her. "Around the other side's a lot more—you wanta come and see them?"

"No."

"Why not?"

"Why should I?"

"Don'tcha wanta see what's on the car? Don'tcha wanta go for a ride?"

"I don't know."

"Why not?"

"I got things to do."

"Like what?"

"Things."

He laughed as if she had said something funny. He slapped his thighs. He was standing in a strange way, leaning back against the car is if he were balancing himself. He wasn't tall, only an inch or so taller than she would be if she came down to him. Connie liked the way he was dressed, which was the way all of them dressed: tight faded jeans stuffed into black, scuffed boots, a belt that pulled his waist in and showed how lean he was, and a white pull-over shirt that was a little soiled and showed the hard small muscles of his arms and shoulders. He looked as if he probably did hard work, lifting and carrying things. Even his neck looked muscular. And his face was a familiar face, somehow; the jaw and chin and cheeks slightly darkened because he hadn't shaved for a day or two, and the nose long and hawklike, sniffing as if she were a treat he was going to gobble up and it was all a joke.

"Connie, you aint telling the truth. This is your day set aside for a ride with me and you know it," he said, still laughing. The way he straightened and recovered from his fit of laughing showed that it had been all fake.

"How do you know what my name is?" she said suspiciously.

"It's Connie."

"Maybe and maybe not."

"I know my Connie," he said, wagging his finger. Now she remembered him even better, back at the restaurant, and her cheeks warmed at the thought of how she had sucked in her breath just at the moment she passed him—how she must have looked to him. And he had remembered her. "Ellie and I come out here especially for you," he said, "Ellie can sit in back. How about it?"

"Where?"

"Where what?"

"Where're we going?"

He looked at her. He took off the sunglasses and she saw how pale the skin around his eyes was, like holes that were not in shadow but instead in light. His eyes were like chips of broken glass that catch the light in an amiable way. He smiled. It was as if the idea of going for a ride somewhere, to someplace, was a new idea to him.

"Just for a ride, Connie, sweetheart."

"I never said my name was Connie," she said.

"But I know what it is. I know your name and all about you, lots of thing," Arnold Friend said. He had not moved yet but stood still leaning back against the side of his jalopy. "I took a special interest in you, such a pretty girl, and found out all about you—like I know your parents and sister are gone somewheres and I know where and how long they're going to be gone, and I know who you were with last night, and your best girl friend's name is Betty. Right?"

He spoke in a simple lilting voice exactly as if he were reciting the words to a song. His smile assured her that everything was fine. In the car Ellie turned up the volume on his radio and did not bother to look around at them.

"Ellie can sit in the back seat," Arnold Friend said. He indicated his friend with a casual jerk of his chin, as if Ellie did not count and she should not bother with him.

"How'd you find out all that stuff?" Connie said.

"Listen: Betty Schultz and Tony Fitch and Jimmy Pettinger and Nancy Pettinger," he said in a chant. "Raymond Stanley and Bob Hutter—"

"Do you know all those kids?"

"I know everybody."

"Look, you're kidding. You're not from around here."

"Sure."

"But—how come we never saw you before?"

"Sure you saw me before," he said. He looked down at his boots, as if he were a little offended. "You just don't remember."

"I guess I'd remember you," Connie said.

"Yeah?" He looked up at this, beaming. He was pleased. He began to mark time with the music from Ellie's radio, tapping his fists lightly together. Connie looked away from his smile to the car, which was painted so bright it almost hurt her eyes to look at it. She looked at that name, ARNOLD FRIEND. And up at the front fender was an expression that was familiar— MAN THE FLYING SAUCERS. It was an expression kids had used the year before but didn't use this year. She looked at it for a while as if the words meant something to her that she did not yet know.

"What're you thinking about? Huh?" Arnold Friend demanded, "Not worried about your hair blowing around in the car, are you?"

"No."

"Think I maybe can't drive good?"

"How do I know?"

"You're a hard girl to handle. How come?" he said. "Don't you know I'm your friend? Didn't you see me put my sign in the air when you walked by?"

"What sign?"

"My sign." And he drew an X in the air, leaning out toward her. They were maybe ten feet apart. After his hand fell back to his side the X was still in the air, almost visible. Connie let the screen door close and stood perfectly still inside it, listening to the music from her radio and the boy's blend together. She stared at Arnold Friend. He stood there so stiffly relaxed, pretending to be relaxed, with one hand idly on the door handle as if he were keeping himself up that way and had no intention of ever moving again. She recognized most things about him, the tight jeans that showed his thighs and buttocks and the greasy leather boots and the tight shirt, and even that slippery friendly smile of his, that sleepy dreamy smile that all the boys used to get across ideas they didn't want to put into words. She recognized all this and also the sing-song way he talked, slightly mocking, kidding, but serious and a little melancholy, and she recognized the way he tapped one fist against the other in homage to the perpetual music behind him. But all these things did not come together.

She said suddenly, "Hey, how old are you?"

His smile faded. She could see then that he wasn't a kid, he was much older—thirty, maybe more. At this knowledge her heart began to pound faster.

"That's a crazy thing to ask. Cant'cha see I'm your own age?"

"Like hell you are."

"Or maybe a coupla years older. I'm eighteen."

"Eighteen?" she said doubtfully.

He grinned to reassure her and lines appeared at the corners of his mouth. His teeth were big and white. He grinned so broadly his eyes became slits and she saw how thick the lashes were, thick and black as if painted with a black tarlike material. Then abruptly, he seemed to become embarrassed and looked over his shoulder at Ellie. "Him, he's crazy," he said. "Ain't he a riot? He's a nut, a real character." Ellie was still listening to the music. His sunglasses told nothing about what he was thinking. He wore a bright orange shirt unbuttoned halfway to show his chest, which was a pale, bluish chest and not muscular like Arnold Friend's. His shirt collar was turned up all around and the very tips of the collar pointed out past his chin as if they were protecting him. He was pressing the transistor radio up against his ear and sat there in a kind of daze, right in the sun.

"He's kinda strange," Connie said.

"Hey, she says you're kinda strange! Kinda strange!" Arnold Friend cried. He pounded on the car to get Ellie's attention. Ellie turned for the first time and Connie saw with shock that he wasn't a kid either—he had a fair, hairless face, cheeks reddened slightly as if the veins grew too close to the surface of his skin, the face of a forty-year-old baby. Connie felt a wave of dizziness rise in her at this sight and she stared at him as if waiting for something to change the shock of the moment, make it all right again. Ellie's lips kept shaping words, mumbling along with the words blasting in his ear.

"Maybe you two better go away," Connie said faintly.

"What? How come?" Arnold Friend cried. "We come out here to take you for a ride. It's Sunday." He had the voice of the man on the radio now. It was the same voice, Connie thought. "Don'tcha know it's Sunday all day? And honey, no matter who you were with last night, today you're with Arnold Friend and don't you forget it! Maybe you better step out here," he said, and this last was in a different voice. It was a little flatter, as if the heat was finally getting to him.

"No. I got things to do."

"Hey."

"You two better leave."

"We ain't leaving until you come with us."

"Like hell I am—"

"Connie, don't fool around with me. I mean—I mean, don't fool around," he said, shaking his head. He laughed incredulously. He placed his sunglasses on top of his head, carefully, as if he were indeed wearing a wig, and brought the stems down behind his ears. Connie stared at him, another wave of dizziness and fear rising in her so that for a moment he wasn't even in focus but was just a blur standing there against his gold car, and she had the idea that he had driven up the driveway all right but had come from nowhere before that and belonged nowhere and that everything about him and even about the music that was so familiar to her was only half real.

"If my father comes and sees you—"

"He ain't coming. He's at a barbecue."

"How do you know that?"

"Aunt Tillie's. Right now they're—uh—they're drinking. Sitting around," he said vaguely, squinting as if he were staring all the way to town and over to Aunt Tillie's back yard. Then the vision seemed to get clear and he nodded energetically. "Yeah. Sitting around. There's your sister in a blue dress, huh?" And high heels, the poor sad bitch—nothing like you, sweetheart! And your mother's helping some fat woman with the corn, they're cleaning the corn—husking the corn—"

"What fat woman?" Connie cried.

"How do I know what fat woman. I don't know every goddamn fat woman in the world!" Arnold Friend laughed.

"Oh, that's Mrs. Hornsby…Who invited her?" Connie said. She felt a little lightheaded. Her breath was coming quickly.

"She's too fat I don't like them fat. I like them the way you are, honey." he said, smiling sleepily at her. They stared at each other for a while through the screen door. He said softly, "Now, what you're going to do is this: you're going to come out that door. You're going to sit up front with me and Ellie's going to sit in the back, the hell with Ellie, right? This isn't Ellie's date. You're my date. I'm your lover, honey."

"What? You're crazy—"

"Yes, I'm your lover. You don't know what that is but you will," he said. "I know that too. I know all about you. But look: it's real nice and you couldn't ask for nobody better than me or more polite. I always keep my word. I'll tell you how it is, I'm always nice at first, the first time. I'll hold you so tight you won't think you have to try to get away or pretend anything because you'll know you can't. And I'll come inside you where it's all secret and you'll give in to me and you'll love me—"

"Shut up! You're crazy!" Connie said. She backed away from the door. She put her hands up against her ears as if she'd heard something terrible, something not meant for her. "People don't talk like that, you're crazy," she muttered. Her heart was almost too big now for her chest and its pumping made sweat break out all over her. She looked out to see Arnold Friend pause and then take a step toward the porch, lurching. He almost fell. But, like a clever drunken man, he managed to catch his balance. He wobbled in his high boots and grabbed hold of one of the porch posts.

"Honey?" he said. "You still listening?"

"Get the hell out of here!"

"Be nice, honey. Listen."

"I'm going to call the police—"

He wobbled again and out of the side of his mouth came a fast spat curse, an aside not meant for her to hear. But even this "Christ!" sounded forced. Then he began to smile again. She watched this smile come, awkward as if he were smiling from inside a mask. His whole face was a mask, she thought wildly, tanned down to his throat but then running out as if he had plastered makeup on his face, but had forgotten about his throat.

"Honey—? Listen, here's how it is. I always tell the truth and I promise you this: I ain't coming in that house after you."

"You better not! I'm going to call the police if you—if you don't—"

"Honey," he said, talking right through her voice, "honey. I'm not coming in there but you are coming out here. You know why?"

She was panting. The kitchen looked like a place she had never seen before, some room she had run inside but that wasn't good enough, wasn't going to help her. The kitchen window had never had a curtain, after three years, and there were dishes in the sink for her to do—probably—and if you ran your hand across the table you'd probably feel something sticky there.

"You listening, honey? Hey?"

"—going to call the police—"

"Soon as you touch the phone I don't need to keep my promise and can come inside. You won't want that."

She rushed forward and tried to lock the door. Her fingers were shaking. "But why lock it," Arnold Friend said gently, talking right into her face. "It's just a screen door. It's just nothing." One of his boots was at a strange angle, as if his foot wasn't in it. It pointed out to the left, bent at the ankle. "I mean, anybody can break through a screen door and glass and wood and iron or anything else if he need to, anybody at all, and specially Arnold Friend. If the place got lit up with a fire, honey, you'd come runnin' out into my arms, right into my arms an' safe at home—like you knew I was your lover and'd stopped fooling around. I don't mind a nice shy girl but I don't like no fooling around." Part of those words were spoken with a slight rhythmic lilt, and Connie somehow recognized them—the echo of a song from last year, about a girl rushing into her boy friend's arms and coming home again—

Connie stood barefoot on the linoleum floor, staring at him. "What do you want?" she whispered.

"I want you," he said.

"Seen you that night and thought, that's the one, yes sir. I never needed to look anymore."

"But my father's coming back. He's coming to get me. I had to wash my hair first—" She spoke in a dry, rapid voice, hardly raising it for him to hear.

"No, your daddy is not coming and yes, you had to wash your hair and you washed it for me. It's nice and shining and all for me. I thank you sweetheart," he said with a mock bow, but again he almost lost his balance. He had to bend and adjust his boots. Evidently his feet did not go all the way down; the boots must have been stuffed with something so that he would seem taller. Connie stared out at him and behind him at Ellie in the car, who seemed to be looking off toward Connie's right, into nothing. Then Ellie said, pulling the words out of the air one after another as if he were just discovering them, "You want me to pull out the phone?"

"Shut your mouth and keep it shut," Arnold Friend said, his face red from bending over or maybe from embarrassment because Connie had seen his boots. "This ain't none of your business."

"What—what are you doing? What do you want?" Connie said. "If I call the police they'll get you, they'll arrest you—"

"Promise was not to come in unless you touch that phone, and I'll keep that promise," he said. He resumed his erect position and tried to force his shoulders back. He sounded like a hero in a movie declaring something important. But he spoke too loudly and it was as if he were speaking to someone behind Connie. "I ain't made plans for coming in that house where I don't belong but just for you to come out to me, the way you should. Don't you know who I am?"

"You're crazy," she whispered. She backed away from the door but did not want to go into another part of the house, as if this would give him permission to come through the door. "What do you ...you're crazy, you ...."

"Huh? What're you saying honey?"

Her eyes darted everywhere in the kitchen. She could not remember what it was, this room.

"This is how it is, honey: you come out and we'll drive away, have a nice ride. But if you don't come out we're gonna wait till your people come home and then they're all going to get it."

"You want that telephone pulled out?" Ellie said. He held the radio away from his ear and grimaced, as if without the radio the air was too much for him.

"I tolja shut up, Ellie," Arnold Friend said, "you're deaf, get a hearing aid, right! Fix yourself up. This little girl's no trouble and's gonna be nice to me, so Ellie keep to yourself, this ain't your date—right? Don't hem in on me, don't hog, don't crush, don't bird dog, don't trail me," he said in a rapid, meaningless voice, as if he were running through all the expressions he'd learned but was no longer sure which of them was in style, then rushing on to new ones, making them up with his eyes closed. "Don't crawl under my fence, don't squeeze in my chipmunk hole, don't sniff my glue, suck my popsicle, keep your own greasy fingers on yourself!" He shaded his eyes and peered in at Connie, who was backed against the kitchen table. "Don't mind him, honey, he's just a creep. He's a dope. Right? I'm the boy for you and like I said, you come out here nice like a lady and give me your hand, and nobody else gets hurt, I mean, your nice old bald-headed daddy and your mummy and your sister in her high heels. Because listen: why bring them in this?"

"Leave me alone," Connie whispered.

"Hey, you know that old woman down the road, the one with the chickens and stuff—you know her?"

"She's dead—"

"Don't you like her?"

"She's dead—she's—she isn't here any more—"

"But don't you like her, I mean, you got something against her? Some grudge or something?" Then his voice dipped as if he were conscious of a rudeness. He touched the sunglasses perched up on top of his head as if to make sure they were still there. "Now, you be a good girl."

"What are you going to do?"

"Just two things, or maybe three," Arnold Friend said. "But I promise it won't last long and you'll like me the way you get to like people you're close to. You will. It's all over for you here, so come on out. You don't want your people in any trouble, do you?"

She turned and bumped against a chair or something, hurting her leg, but she ran into the back room and picked up the telephone. Something roared in her ear, a tiny roaring, and she was so sick with fear that she could do nothing but listen to it—the telephone was clammy and very heavy and her fingers groped down to the dial but were too weak to touch it. She began to scream into the phone, into the roaring. She cried out, she cried for her mother, she felt her breath start jerking back and forth in her lungs as if it were something Arnold Friend was stabbing her with again and again with no tenderness. A noisy sorrowful wailing rose all about her and she was locked inside it the way she was locked inside this house.

After a while she could hear again. She was sitting on the floor with her wet back against the wall.

Arnold Friend was saying from the door, "That's a good girl. Put the phone back."

She kicked the phone away from her.

"No, honey. Pick it up. Put it back right."

She picked it up and put it back. The dial tone stopped.

"That's a good girl. Now, you come outside."

She was hollow with what had been fear but what was now just an emptiness. All that screaming had blasted it out of her. She sat, one leg cramped under her, and deep inside her brain was something like a pinpoint of light that kept going and would not let her relax. She thought, I'm not going to sleep in my bed again. Her bright green blouse was all wet.

Arnold Friend said, in a gentle-loud voice that was like a stage voice, "The place where you came from ain't there any more, and where you had in mind to go is cancelled out. This place you are now—inside your daddy's house—is nothing but a cardboard box I can knock down any time. You know that and always did know it. You hear me?"

She thought, I have got to think. I have got to know what to do.

"We'll go out to a nice field, out in the country, here where it smells so nice and it's sunny," Arnold Friend said. "I'll have my arms tight around you so you won't need to try to get away and I'll show you what love is like, what it does. The hell with this house! It looks solid all right," he said. He ran his fingernail down the screen and the noise did not make Connie shiver, as it would have the day before. "Now, put your hand on your heart, honey. Feel that? That feels solid too but we know better. Be nice to me, be sweet like you can because what else is there for a girl like you but to be sweet and pretty and give in?—and get away before her people get back?"

She felt her pounding heart. Her hand seemed to enclose it. She thought for the first time in her life that it was nothing that was hers, that belonged to her, but just a pounding, living thing inside this body that wasn't really hers either.

"You don't want them to get hurt," Arnold Friend went on. "Now, get up, honey. Get up all by yourself."

She stood.

"Now, turn this way. That's right. Come over here to me.—Ellie, put that away, didn't I tell you? You dope. You miserable creepy dope," Arnold Friend said. His words were not angry but only part of an incantation. The incantation was kindly. "Now come out through the kitchen to me, honey, and let's see a smile, try it, you're a brave, sweet little girl and now they're eating corn and hot dogs cooked to bursting over an outdoor fire, and they don't know one thing about you and never did and honey, you're better than them because not a one of them would have done this for you."

Connie felt the linoleum under her feet; it was cool. She brushed her hair back out of her eyes. Arnold Friend let go of the post tentatively and opened his arms for her, his elbows pointing in toward each other and his wrists limp, to show that this was an embarrassed embrace and a little mocking, he didn't want to make her self-conscious.

She put out her hand against the screen. She watched herself push the door slowly open, as if she were back safe somewhere in the other doorway, watching this body and this head of long hair moving out into the sunlight where Arnold Friend waited.

"My sweet little blue-eyed girl," he said in a half-sung sigh that had nothing to do with her brown eyes but was taken up just the same by the vast sunlit reaches of the land behind him and on all side of him—so much land that Connie had never seen before and did not recognize except to know that she was going to it.

Exercise:

Make a list of the implied values of Connie's parents. Which ones do you think she rejects?

Does Connie seem to have values independently of her parents? What are these and from where do you think she derives them?

What values do you think Arnold Friend represents to Connie? Do you think she chooses them?

What motives do you think lie behind the value choices that Connie seems to make?

Arnold Friend becomes increasingly surrealistic as the story progresses, it becomes difficult to know what he is and what he represents. Is this important in understanding Connie's dillema?

Where Are You Going?

It is not clear at the end of the last selection, just how far Connie is willing to go in her rejection of the universe of her childhood. In the following poem the imagined consequences are clearly laid out.

Gwendolyn Brooks,
A Song in the Front Yard

I've stayed in the front yard all my life.
I want a peek at the back
Where it's rough and untended and hungry weed grows.
A girl gets sick of a rose.

I want to go in the back yard now
And maybe down the alley
To where the charity children play.
I want a good time today.

They do some wonderful things.
They have some wonderful fun.
My mother sneers, but I say it's fine
How they don't have to go in at quarter to nine.

My mother, she tells me that Johnnie Mae
Will grow up to be a bad woman.
That George'll be taken to Jail soon or late
(ON account of last winter he sold our back gate.)

But I say it's fine. Honest I do.
And I'd like to be a bad woman, too.
And wear the brave stockings of night-black lace
And strut down the street with paint on my face.

Research Project:

Many adolescents end up by leaving their parents' homes for good. Do a survey of newspaper and magazine articles discussing the problem of teenage runaways. Present your results in a three page paper. Organize your material so that you can develop a thesis as to the causes and cures of the problem.

SECTION 4: SOCIAL CONTROL—SCHOOL

As the child grows older and she ventures further into the world, she encounters new people and becomes involved in increasingly complex relationships. These new relationships define the world within which the child grows and help to redefine her self-image, what she sees as her strengths and what she sees as her weaknesses. Most of the individuals that the growing child encounters will have relatively little effect on her perceptions, especially as compared with the effect that her family has had on her. But some will have a profound effect.

In the last section we explored some of the people that are significant in helping the child to form his perceptions of himself and of the values he will hold and act upon. In this section we look at an institution whose social role is to influence the growing child. This institution is the school.

For the maturing individual school is often the first place where his accomplishments are judged in terms of objective and public standards. This is especially true for the child whose home environment is supportive and where he and his works are uniformly cherished. For in the school environment his efforts are judged exactly as are any other child's. A school is expected to maintain accepted community standards by judging all children impartially. No matter how unfair and irrelevant the evaluation of the school seems to the child or her family, unless the child has been treated differently from others, the judgment of the school is considered appropriate.

Most importantly, the school's evaluation plays the central role in the social judgment of the child, determining to a considerable extent, how people will value her accomplishments and how much people will pay for having her skills at their disposal.

Confronting Demands

At school, what we do becomes a matter of public scrutiny. We are asked to read aloud, do math problems on the board, and find our spelling papers put on display. This public appraisal of achievements can be the source of pride as well as embarrassment, but it becomes especially crucial where the accomplishments expose the individual in a way that she would prefer to stay secret. We begin our exploration of these issues by exploring them within the family, and then we move outward.

Shirley Jackson, Afternoon in Linen

It was a long, cool room, comfortably furnished and happily placed, with hydrangea bushes outside the large windows and their pleasant shadows on the floor. Everyone in it was wearing linen—the little girl in the pink linen dress with a wide blue belt. Mrs. Kator in a brown linen suit and a big yellow linen hat. Mrs. Lennon, who was the little girl's grandmother, in a white linen dress, and Mrs. Kator's little boy, Howard, in a blue linen shirt and shorts. Like in *Alice Through the Looking-Glass*, the little girl thought, looking at her grandmother; like the gentleman all dressed in white paper. I'm a gentleman all dressed in pink paper, she thought. Although Mrs. Lennon and Mrs. Kator lived on the same block and saw each other every day, this was a formal call, and so they were drinking tea.

Howard was sitting at the piano at one end of the long room, in front of the biggest window. He was playing "Humoresque" in careful, unhurried tempo. I played that last year, the little girl thought; it's in G. Mrs. Lennon and Mrs. Kator were still holding their teacups, listening to Howard and looking at him, and now and then looking at each other and smiling. I could still play that if I wanted to, the little girl thought.

When Howard had finished playing "Humoresque," he slid off the piano bench and came over and gravely sat down beside the little girl, waiting for his mother to tell him whether to play again or not. He's bigger than I am, she thought, but I'm older. I'm ten. If they ask me to play the piano for them now, I'll say no.

"I think you play very nicely, Howard," the little girl's grandmother said. There were a few moments of leaden silence. Then Mrs. Kator said, "Howard, Mrs. Lennon spoke to you." Howard murmured and looked at his hands on his knees.

"I think he's coming along very well," Mrs. Kator said to Mrs. Lennon. "He doesn't like to practise, but I think he's coming along well."

"Harriet loves to practise," the little girl's grandmother said. "She sits at the piano for hours, making up little tunes and singing."

"She probably has a real talent for music," Mrs. Kator said. "I often wonder whether Howard is getting as much out of his music as he should."

"Harriet," Mrs. Lennon said to the little girl, "won't you play for Mrs. Kator? Play one of your own little tunes."

"I don't know any," the little girl said.

"Of course you do, dear," her grandmother said.

"I'd like very much to hear a little tune you made up yourself, Harriet," Mrs. Kator said.

"I don't know any," the little girl said.

Mrs. Lennon looked at Mrs. Kator and shrugged. Mrs. Kator nodded, mouthing "Shy," and turned to look proudly at Howard.

The little girl's grandmother set her lips firmly in a tight, sweet smile. "Harriet dear," she said, "even if we don't want to play our little tunes, I think we ought to tell Mrs. Kator that music is not our forte. I think we ought to show her our really fine achievements in another line. Harriet," she continued, turning to Mrs. Kator, "has written some poems. I'm going to ask her to recite them to you, because I feel, even though I may be prejudiced"—she laughed modestly—"even though I probably am prejudiced, that they show real merit."

"Well, for heaven's sake!" Mrs. Kator said. She looked at Harriet, pleased. "Why, dear, I didn't know you could do anything like that! I'd really love to hear them."

"Recite one of your poems for Mrs. Kator, Harriet."

The little girl looked at her grandmother, at the sweet smile, and at Mrs. Kator, leaning forward, and at Howard, sitting with his mouth open and a great delight growing in his eyes. "Don't know any," she said.

"Harriet," her grandmother said, "even if you don't remember any of your poems, you have some written down. I'm sure Mrs. Kator won't mind if you read them to her."

The huge merriment that had been gradually taking hold of Howard suddenly overwhelmed him. "Poems," he said, doubling up with laughter on the couch. "Harriet writes poems." He'll tell all the kids on the block, the little girl thought.

"I do believe Howard's jealous," Mrs. Kator said.

"Aw," Howard said, "I wouldn't write a poem. Bet you couldn't make me write a poem if you tried."

"You couldn't make me, either," the little girl said. "That's all a lie about the poems."

There was a long silence. Then "Why, Harrriet!" the little girl's grandmother said in a sad voice. "What a thing to say about your grandmother!" Mrs. Kator said, "I think you'd better apologize, Harriet," the little girl's grandmother said. Mrs. Kator said, "Why, you certainly had better."

"I didn't do anything," the little girl muttered. "I'm sorry."

The grandmother's voice was stern. "Now bring your poems out and read them to Mrs. Kator."

"I don't have any, honestly, Grandma," the little girl said desperately. "Honestly, I don't have any of those poems."

"Well, I have," the grandmother said. "Bring them to me from the top desk drawer."

The little girl hesitated a minute, watching her grandmother's straight mouth and frowning eyes.

"Howard will get them for you, Mrs. Lennon," Mrs. Kator said.

"Sure," Howard said. He jumped up and ran over to the desk, pulling open the drawer. "What do they look like?" he shouted.

"In an envelope," the grandmother said tightly. "In a brown envelope with 'Harriet's poetry' written on the front."

"Here it is," Howard said. He pulled some papers out of the envelope and studied them a moment. "Look," he said. "Harriet's poems—about stars." He ran to his mother, giggling and holding out the papers. "Look, Mother, Harriet's poetry's about stars!"

"Give them to Mrs. Lennon, dear," Howard's mother said. "It was very rude to open the envelope first."

Mrs. Lennon took the envelope and the papers and held them out to Harriet. "Will you read them or shall I?" she asked kindly. Harriet shook her head. The grandmother sighed at Mrs. Kator and took up the first sheet of paper. Mrs. Kator leaned forward eagerly and Howard settled down at her feet, hugging his knees and putting his face against his leg to keep from laughing. The grandmother cleared her throat, smiled at Harriet, and began to read.

"'The Evening Star,'" she announced.

"When evening shadows are falling,
And dark gathers closely around,
And all the night creatures are calling,
And the wind makes a lonesome sound,

I wait for the first star to come out,
And look for its silvery beams,
When the blue and green twilight is all about,
And grandly a lone star gleams."

Howard could contain himself no longer. "Harriet writes poems about stars!"

"Why, it's lovely, Harriet dear!" Mrs. Kator said. "I think it's really lovely, honestly. I don't see what you're so shy about it for."

"There, you see, Harriet?" Mrs. Lennon said. "Mrs. Kator thinks your poetry is very nice. Now aren't you sorry you made such a fuss about such a little thing?"

He'll tell all the kids on the block, Harriet thought. "I didn't write it," she said.

"Why, Harriet!" Her grandmother laughed. "You don't need to be so modest, child. You write very nice poems."

"I copied it out of a book," Harriet said. "I found it in a book and I copied it and gave it to my old grandmother and said I wrote it."

"I don't believe you'd do anything like that, Harriet," Mrs. Kator said, puzzled.

"I did so," Harriet maintained stubbornly. "I copied it right out of a book."

"Harriet, I don't believe you," her grandmother said.

Harriet looked at Howard, who was staring at her in admiration. "I copied it out of a book," she said to him. "I found the book in the library one day."

"I can't imagine her saying she did such a thing," Mrs. Lennon said to Mrs. Kator. Mrs. Kator shook her head.

"It was a book called"—Harriet thought a moment—"called *The Home Book of Verse*," she said. "That's what it was. And I copied every single word. I didn't make up one."

"Harriet, is this true?" her grandmother said. She turned to Mrs. Kator. "I'm afraid I must apologize for Harriet and for reading you the poem under false pretenses. I never dreamed she'd deceive me."

"Oh, they do," Mrs. Kator said deprecatingly. "They want attention and praise and sometimes they'll do almost anything. I'm sure Harriet didn't mean to be—well dishonest."

"I did so," Harriet said. "I wanted everyone to think I wrote it. I said I wrote it on purpose." She went over and took the papers out of her grandmother's unresisting hand. "And you can't look at them any more, either," she said, and held them in back of her, away from everyone.

Discussion Plan:

The right to privacy:

In the following situations discuss whether or not the individuals involved have the right to privacy.
1. John doesn't want to show his parents his report card.
2. Mary keeps a secret diary of her personal fantasies.
3. Susan has a diary describing what she does on dates.
4. Paul has a list of his drug transactions.
5. Mary won't show any one her paintings.
6. Paul refuses to play his guitar at his sister's wedding.
7. John refuses to participate in family "problem solving" sessions.
8. Sal won't talk to his father about his school problems.
9. Mary refuses counseling for a drug problem.
10. Sara never tells her parents about the boys she dates.

Does school alter the situation?
1. John refuses to participate in discussions in health education.
2. Paul has been writing poetry all his life and refuses to use any of his work for the school magazine.
3. Mary doesn't want to play for assembly even though she is the best pianist in the school.
4. Sue, a perfectionist, refuses to submit her notes or outline for a school assignment.
5. Joe, a perfectionist, refuses to show his art teacher preliminary sketches.
6. Jane quits the chess team the week before the finals because she feels participating in the student match might interfere with her preparation for a professional tournament.
7. Mary whose modeling career is starting to take off, refuses to participate in the school fund raising musical.
8. Joe won't take art because he feels that the art teacher is old fashioned and narrow.
9. Jane, a math wiz, cuts math all the time because it is too elementary.
10. Instead of doing the required science homework, Jill reads physics books and performs experiments at home or at her sister's college.

Responding to Expectations

It is clear that people can influence our values, determine how we think of the world including ourselves. What is less clear is how pervasive this influence is. Because teachers are authority figures and role models their influence can be crucial. In the next selection we look at a classic study which shows how the teacher's beliefs and hidden perceptions can be transmitted to the child. The structure of the school and the social role of the teacher seem to amplify the effect of the teacher's judgments until it can reproduce a mirror of the teacher in the child.

Robert Rosenthal and Lenore F. Jacobson, Teacher Expectations for the Disadvantaged

One of the central problems of American society lies in the fact that certain children suffer a handicap in their education which then persists throughout life. The "disadvantaged" child is a Negro American, a Mexican American, a Puerto Rican or any other child who lives in conditions of poverty. He is a lower-class child who performs poorly in an educational system that is staffed almost entirely by middle-class teachers.

The reason usually given for the poor performance of the disadvantaged child is simply that the child is a member of a disadvantaged group. There may well be another reason. It is that the child does poorly in school because that is what is expected of him. In other words, his shortcomings may originate not in his different ethnic, cultural and economic background but in his teachers' response to that background.

If there is any substance to this hypothesis, educators are confronted with some major questions. Have these children, who account for most of the academic failures in the U.S., shaped the expectations that their teachers have for them? Have the schools failed the children by anticipating their poor performance and thus in effect teaching them to fail? Are the massive public programs of educational assistance to such children reinforcing the assumption that they are likely to fail? Would the children do appreciably better if their teachers could be induced to expect more of them?

We have explored the effect of teacher expectations with experiments in which teachers were led to believe at the beginning of a school year that certain of their pupils could be expected to show considerable academic improvements during the year. The teachers thought the predictions were based on tests that had been administered to the student body toward the end of the preceding school year. In actuality the children designated as potential "spurters" had been chosen at random and not on the basis of testing. Nonetheless, intelligence tests given after the experiment had been in progress for several months indicated that on the whole the randomly chosen children had improved more than the rest.

The central concept behind our investigation was that of the "self-fulfilling prophecy." The essence of this concept is that one person's prediction of another person's behavior somehow comes to be realized. The prediction may, of course, be realized only in the perception of the predictor. It is also possible, however, that the predictor's expectation is communicated to the other person, perhaps in quite subtle and unintended ways, and so has an influence on his actual behavior.

An experimenter cannot be sure that he is dealing with a self-fulfilling prophecy until he has taken steps to make certain that a prediction is not based on behavior that has already been observed. If schoolchildren who perform poorly are those expected by their teachers to perform poorly, one cannot say in the normal school situation whether the teacher's expectation was the cause of the performance or whether she simply made an accurate prognosis based on her knowledge of past performance by the particular children involved. To test for the existence of self-fulfilling prophecy the experimenter must establish conditions in which an expectation is uncontaminated by the past behavior of the subject whose performance is being predicted.

It is easy to establish such conditions in the psychological laboratory by presenting an experimenter with a group of laboratory animals and telling him what kind of behavior he can expect from them. One of us (Rosenthal) has carried out a number of experiments along this line using rats that were said to be either bright or dull. In one experiment 12 students in psychology were each given five laboratory rats of the same strain. Six of the students were told that their rats had been bred for brightness in running a maze; the other six students were told that their rats could be expected for genetic reasons to be poor at running a maze. The assignment given the students was to teach the rats to run the maze.

From the outset the rats believe to have the higher potential proved to be the better performers. The rats thought to be dull made poor progress and sometimes would not even budge from the starting position in the maze. A questionnaire given after the experiment showed that the students with the allegedly brighter rats ranked their subjects as brighter, more pleasant and more likable than did the students who had the allegedly duller rats. Asked about their methods of dealing with the rats, the students with the "bright" group turned out to have been friendlier, more enthusiastic and less talkative with the animals than the students with the "dull" group had been. The students with the "bright" rats also said they handled their animals more, as well as more gently, than the students expecting poor performances did.

Our task was to establish similar conditions in a classroom situation. We wanted to create expectations that were based only on what teachers had been told, so that we could preclude the possibility of judgments based on previous observations of the children involved. It was with this objective that we set up our experiment in what we shall call Oak School, an elementary school in the South San Francisco Unified School District. To avoid the dangers of letting it be thought that some children could be expected to perform poorly we established only the expectation that certain pupils might show superior performance. Our experiments had the financial support of the National Science Foundation and the cooperation of Paul Nielsen, the superintendent of the school district.

Oak School is in an established and somewhat run-down section of a middle-sized city. The school draws some students from middle-class families but more from lower-class families. Included in the latter category are children from families receiving welfare payments, from low-income families and from Mexican-American families. The school has six grades, each organized into three classes—one for children performing at above-average levels of scholastic achievement, one for average children and one for those who are below average. There is also a kindergarten.

At the beginning of the experiment in 1964 we told the teachers that further validation was needed for a new kind of test designed to predict academic blooming or intellectual gain in children. In actuality we used the Flanagan tests of General Ability, a standard intelligence test that was fairly new and therefore unfamiliar to the teachers. It consists of two relatively independent subtests, one focusing more on verbal ability and the other more on reasoning ability. An example of a verbal item in the version of the test designed for children in kindergarten and first grade presents drawings of an article of clothing, a flower, an envelope, an apple and a glass of water; the children are asked to mark with a crayon "the thing that you can eat." In the reasoning subtest a typical item consists of drawings of five abstractions, such as four squares and a circle; the pupils are asked to cross out the one that differs from the others.

We had special covers printed for the test; they bore the high-sounding title "Test of Inflected Acquisition." The teachers were told that the testing was part of an undertaking being carried out by investigators from Harvard University and that the test would be given several times in the future. The tests were to be sent to Harvard for scoring and for addition to the data being compiled for validation. In May, 1964, the teachers administered the test to all the children then in kindergarten and grades one through five. The children in sixth grade were not tested because they would be in junior high school the next year.

Before Oak School opened the following September about 20 percent of the children were designated as potential academic spurters. There were about five such children in each classroom. The manner of conveying their names to the teachers was deliberately made rather casual: the subject was brought up at the end of the first staff meeting with the remark, "By the way, in case you're interested in who did what in those tests we're doing for Harvard ..."

The names of the "spurters" had been chosen by means of a table of random numbers. The experimental treatment of the children involved nothing more than giving their names to their new teachers as children who could be expected to show unusual intellectual gains in the year ahead. The difference, then, between these children and the undesignated children who constituted a control group was entirely in the minds of the teachers.

All the children were given the same test again four months after school had started, at the end of that school year and finally in May of the following year. As the children progressed through the grades they were given tests of the appropriate level. The tests were designed for three grade levels: kindergarten and first grade, second and third grades and fourth through sixth grades.

The results indicated strongly that children from whom teachers expected greater intellectual gains showed such gains. The gains, however, were not uniform across the grades. The tests given at the end of the first year showed the largest gains among children in the first and second grades. In the second year the greatest gains were among the children who had been in the fifth grade when the "spurters" were designated and who by the time of the final test were completing sixth grade.

At the end of the academic year 1964-1965, the teachers were asked to describe the classroom behavior of their pupils. The children from whom intellectual growth was expected were described as having a better chance of being successful in later life and as being happier, more curious and more interesting than the other children. There was also a tendency for the designated children to be seen as more appealing, better adjusted and more affectionate, and as less in need of social approval. In short, the children for whom intellectual growth was expected became more alive and autonomous intellectually, or at least were so perceived by their teachers. These findings were particularly striking among the children in the first grade.

An interesting contrast became apparent when teachers were asked to rate the undesignated children. Many of these children had also gained in I.Q. during the year. The more they gained, the less favorably they were rated.

From these results it seems evident that when children who are expected to gain intellectually do gain, they may be benefited in other ways. As "personalities" they go up in the estimation of their teachers. The opposite is true of children who gain intellectually when improvement is not expected of them. They are looked on as showing undesirable behavior. It would seem that there are hazards in unpredicted intellectual growth.

A closer examination revealed that the most unfavorable ratings were given to the children in low-ability classrooms who gained the most intellectually. When these "slow track" children were in the control group, where little intellectual gain was expected of them, they were rated more unfavorably by their teachers if they did show gains in I.Q. The more they gained, the more unfavorably they were rated. Even when the slow-track children were in the experimental group, where greater intellectual gains were expected of them, they were not rated as favorably with respect to their control-group peers as were the children of the high track and the medium track. Evidently it is likely to be difficult for a slow-track child, even if his I.Q. is rising, to be seen by his teacher as well adjusted and as potentially successful student.

How is one to account for the fact that the children who were expected to gain did gain? The first answer that comes to mind is that the teachers must have spent more time with them than with the children of whom nothing was said. This hypothesis seems to be wrong, judging not only from some questions we asked the teachers about the time they spent with their pupils, but also from the fact that in a given classroom the more the "spurters" gained in I.Q., the more the other children gained.

Another bit of evidence that the hypothesis is wrong appears in the pattern of the test results. If teachers had talked to the designated children more, which would be the most likely way of investing more time in work with them, one might expect to see the largest gains in verbal intelligence. In actuality the largest gains were in reasoning intelligence.

It would seem that the explanation we are seeking lies in a subtler feature of the interaction of the teacher and her pupils. Her tone of voice, facial expression, touch and posture may be the means by which—probably quite unwittingly—she communicates her expectations to the pupils. Such communications might help the child by changing his conception of himself, his anticipation of his own behavior, his motivation or his cognitive skills. This is an area in which further research is clearly needed.

Why was the effect of teacher expectations most pronounced in the lower grades? It is difficult to be sure, but several hypotheses can be advanced. Younger children may be easier to change than older ones are. They are likely to have less well-established reputations in the school. It may be that they are more sensitive to the processes by which teachers communicate their expectations to pupils.

It is also difficult to be certain why the older children showed the best performance in the follow-up year. Perhaps the younger children, who by then had different teachers, needed continued contact with the teachers who had influenced them in order to maintain their improved performance. The older children, who were harder to influence at first, may have been better able to maintain an improved performance autonomously once they had achieved it.

In considering our results, particularly the substantial gains shown by the children in the control group, one must take into account the possibility that what is called the Hawthorne effect might have been involved. The name comes from the Western Electric company's Hawthorne Works in Chicago. In the 1920's the plant was the scene of an intensive series of experiments designed to determine what effect various changes in working conditions would have on the performance of female workers. Some of the experiments, for example, involved changes in lighting. It soon became evident that the significant thing was not whether the worker had more or less light but merely that she was the subject of attention. Any changes that involved her, and even actions that she only thought were changes, were likely to improve her performance.

In the Oak School experiment the fact that university researchers, supported by Federal funds, were interested in the school may have led to a general improvement of morale and effort on the part of the teachers. In any case, the possibility of a Hawthorne effect cannot be ruled out either in this experiment or in other studies of educational practices. Whenever a new educational practice is undertaken in a school, it cannot be demonstrated to have an intrinsic effect unless it shows some excess of gain over what Hawthorne effects alone would yield. In our case a Hawthorne effect might account for the gains shown by the children in the control group, but it would not account for the greater gains made by the children in the experimental group.

Our results suggest that yet another base line must be introduced when the intrinsic value of an educational innovation is being assessed. The question will be whether the venture is more effective (and cheaper) than the simple expedient of trying to change the expectations of the teacher. Most educational innovations will be found to cost more in both time and money than inducing teachers to expect more of "disadvantaged" children.

For almost three years the nation's schools have had access to substantial Federal funds under the Elementary and Secondary Education Act, which President Johnson signed in April 1965. Title I of the act is particularly directed at disadvantaged children. Most of the programs devised for using Title I funds focus on overcoming educational handicaps by acting on the child—through remedial instruction, cultural enrichment and the like. The premise seems to be that the deficiencies are all in the child and in the environment from which he comes.

Our experiment rested on the premise that at least some of the deficiencies—and therefore at least some of the remedies—might be in the schools, and particularly in the attitudes of teachers toward disadvantaged children. In our experiment nothing was done directly for the child. There was no crash program to improve his reading ability, no extra time for tutoring, no program of trips to museums and art galleries. The only people affected directly were the teachers, the effect on the children was indirect.

It is interesting to note that one "total push" program of the kind devised under Title I led in three years to a 10-point gain in I.Q. by 38 percent of the children and a 20-point gain by 12 percent. The gains were dramatic, but they did not even match the ones achieved by the control-group children in the first and second grades of Oak School. They were far smaller than the gains made by the children in our experimental group.

Perhaps, then, more attention in educational research should be focused on the teacher. If it could be learned how she is able to bring about dramatic improvement in the performance of her pupils without formal changes in her methods of teaching, other teachers could be taught to do the same. If further research showed that it is possible to find teachers whose untrained educational style does for their pupils what our teachers did for the special children, the prospect would arise that a combination of sophisticated selection of teachers and suitable training of teachers would give all children a boost toward getting as much as they possibly can out of their schooling.

Exercise:

Prepare the following analysis of the article at home and come to class ready to present your views.

Describe the experimental setup upon which the article is based.

What does the term "disadvantaged" mean? At the beginning of the experiment? At the end?

Do you think the experiment should have been performed? Who was helped by the experiment? Who was injured by it?

Why do you think the teachers had the effect they had on the students?

Do you think there is a similar effect that students have on teachers?

Pressure

How we perform in school determines how people judge us. If we fail we are considered "losers." Those who pass with high achievement are considered "most likely to succeed." Sometimes the pressures are so great that the individual is damaged—sometimes killed.

Time, The Test Must Go On

Japanese students are driven by *shiken jigoku*

Most Western nations, including the U.S. envy Japan the benefits of its rigorous educational system. More than 90% of Japanese students graduate from twelfth grade (in contrast to 75% in the U.S.) despite a demanding academic agenda. By the end of third grade, children must master 881 of 2,000 essential Japanese ideograms: by sixth grade they should know 1,000 more. During high school, the Japanese must cover far more math and science than their American counterparts. By the time they take their college entrance exams, students are prepared to handle questions in English grammar, as well as Japanese, and in subject matter not generally approached until college in the U.S. such as calculus, probability and statistics.

The system has served Japan well. Since World War II it has produced a highly literate and mathematically capable population. It also prepares students for smooth entry into an overcrowded and competitive society that sets a high value on the virtues of discipline and cooperation. In a carefully ordered culture like Japan's, high educational achievement is virtually the only guarantee of a successful career. More than 65% of high school students stick with college entrance courses. Says one: "When you go into a technical course, it's very bad. Everyone knows you couldn't make it." Notes Shogo Ichikawa of the National Institute for Educational Research: "We keep long-term relationships, so we must select group members very carefully. The Japanese industrial and occupational structure requires the Japanese education and selection systems."

Industry begins early. From the time children first set foot in school, at age six, they are faced with seven hours of classes a day, 240 days a year—and twelve years of unremitting pressure. Twice a year they must take exams—to get into the next grade, to get into a respected high school or, ultimately, to gain entry into one of the very few prestigious public universities. Students devote almost all their waking hours to studies. In addition to regular classes and half-days on Saturdays, they often spend up to five additional hours at special cram schools called *juku* (private academies). This cramming is not just for high school students. A recent survey of Tokyo-area youths found that 75% of fourth-, fifth- and sixth-graders were enrolled in some sort of *juku* in order to pass early exam hurdles and get a head start on becoming one of the 96,000 students accepted each year by public universities. The last years are the hardest, says Jin Watanabe, a tenth-grader. "On the first day of tenth grade the teachers will tell you how many days you have left till the final university exams begin."

Japanese students have a name for that annual examination rite: *shiken jigoku*—"examination hell." Each year some 700,000 students (32% of Japanese high school graduates) go on to college but a candidate may apply to only one top university. Because government ministries and top firms all recruit from a handful of universities, having to settle for a low-ranking institution is an almost irreversible disaster. The thousands of students who do not get accepted at the one university of their choice spend a year, sometimes even two, in cram schools preparing to try again. These crammers are called *ronin*, a word used to describe the masterless, wandering samurai of the 17th and 18th centuries. The ultimate measure of success: acceptance by the 14,000-student Tokyo University (Todai), for which final qualifying exams took place last week. Since all the national universities have a single standard exam, academic security is taken very seriously. Says Todai Physics Professor Steve Yamamoto, who has served as an exam proctor: "I asked the higher-ups what to do in case of bomb threat. 'Use your head,' they told me. 'The test must go on.'"

Preoccupation with exams leads the Japanese to emphasize memorization rather than analytical thinking. The pedagogy is simple: the teacher talks, the students listen. Says Taeko Yamato, an English instructor at a private school outside Tokyo: "The school system doesn't let teachers teach well." Admits twelfth-grader Ayutaro Kogure: "For the tests you only memorize, which you forget as soon as the exams are over." Some students are beginning to take an uncharacteristically disrespectful course: open rebellion. Youthful crime has jumped 12.4% in the past year, with juveniles accounting for almost half of all criminal offenders in Japan. Violence on school grounds has increased 42% since 1980, and most of the crimes are committed against teachers. In January at Yoshikawa High School near Tokyo, a gang of 20 students surrounded a group of teachers in the school courtyard, accused them of inflicting pain on one of their number and began to beat them up. It took 20 patrolmen to subdue the boys, but not before ten teachers had been injured.

Most students agree that surviving years of "exam hell" provides one common experience, a bond that lasts through life. But there are those who do not survive. The pressure to do well can become so intense that some students commit suicide, even before attempting college entrance exams. The teen-age suicide rate in Japan is 17.6 per 100,000 (in the U.S. it is 10.9), and almost all of it is thought to be related to academic stress. This January one *ronin* electrocuted himself because he was afraid to take the college entrance exam a second time. Indeed, the universities do not offer much consolation. One sent this message to a rejected candidate: "You cannot go on living unless you are tough."

Discussion Plan:

How much should we push a child?

1. Should a child be trained for a career or for self-fulfillment?
2. At what age should children compete?
3. Should children be given grades for their work in elementary school?
4. Is it more important to learn job related or socially useful skills?
5. Should children engage in competitive sports at an early age?
6. In a school play should everyone be given a chance to perform?
7. Can a child understand struggling now for future benefits?
8. Is play more important than learning?
9. Is it fair to treat every one equally?
10. Should better students be rewarded?

Writing Assignment:

Write a one page essay on the role of competition in school. Try to include a discussion of some of the following:
1. What is good or bad about competition in school.
2. What alternatives to competition are there?
3. Is a non-competitive school preparing the students for "real life"?
4. Could some schools be non-competitive if most are competitive?

236

Self Motivation

*Schools promote the image of an educated person and this image reflects
some of the deepest values in our society. We equate education with intelligence, culture and potential. The individual who excels in school and school
related areas is viewed as better, as having more capabilities that will enable
him to live a more meaningful life. This creates problems for those for whom
school and school related accomplishments are especially difficult.*

Bernard Malamud, A Summer's Reading

George Stoyonovich was a neighborhood boy who had quit high school on
an impulse when he was sixteen, run out of patience, and though he was
asked everytime he went looking for a job, when people asked him if he had
finished and he had to say no, he never went back to school. This summer
was a hard time for jobs and he had none. Having so much time on his hands,
George thought of going to summer school, but the kids in his classes would
be too young. He also considered registering in a night high school, only he
didn't like the idea of the teachers always telling him what to do. He felt they
had not respected him. The result was he stayed off the streets and in his
room most of the day. He had no money to spend, and he couldn't get more
than an occasional few cents becuse his father was poor, and his sister
Sophie, a tall bony girl of twenty-three who resembled George, earned very
little and what she had she kept for herself. Their mother was dead, and
Sophie had to take care of the house.

Very early in the morning George's father got up to go to work in a fish
market. Sophie left about eight for her long ride in the subway to a cafeteria
in the Bronx. George had his coffee by himself, then hung around in the
house. When the house, a five-room railroad flat above a butcher store, got
on his nerves he cleaned it up—mopped the floors with a wet mop and put
things away. But most of the time he sat in his room. In the afternoons he
listened to the ball game. Otherwise he had a couple of old copies of the
World Almanac he had bought long ago, and he liked to read in them, and
also the magazines and newspapers that Sophie brought home, that had
been left on the tables in the cafeteria. They were mostly picture magazines
about movie stars and sports figures, also usually the *News* and *Mirror.*
Sophie herself read whatever fell into her hands, although she sometimes
read good books.

She once asked George what he did in his room all day and he said he read
a lot too.

"Of what besides what I bring home? Do you ever read any worthwhile
books?"

"Some," George answered, although he really didn't. He had tried to read a book or two that Sophie had in the house but found he was in no mood for them. Lately he couldn't stand made-up stories; they got on his nerves. He wished he had some hobby to work at—as a kid he was good in carpentry, but where could he work at it? Sometimes during the day we went for walks, but mostly he did his walking after the hot sun had gone down and it was cooler in the streets.

In the evening after supper George left the house and wandered in the neighborhood. During the sultry days some of the storekeepers and their wives sat in chairs on the thick, broken sidewalks in front of their shops, fanning themselves, and George walked past them and the guys hanging out on the candy store corner. A couple of them he had known his whole life, but nobody recognized each other. He had no place special to go, but generally, saving it till the last, he left the neighborhood and walked for blocks till he came to a darkly lit little park with benches and trees and an iron railing, giving it a feeling of privacy. He sat on a bench here, watching the leafy trees and the flowers blooming on the inside of the railing, thinking of a better life for himself. He thought of the jobs he had had since he had quit shcool—delivery boy, stock clerk, runner, lately working in a factory—and he was dissatisfied with all of them. He felt he would someday like to have a good job and live in a private house with a porch, on a street with trees. He wanted to have some dough in his pocket to buy things with, and a girl to go with, so as not to be so lonely especially on Saturday nights. He wanted people to like and respect him. He thought about these things often but mostly when he was alone at night. Around midnight he got up and drifted back to his hot and stony neighborhood.

One time while on his walk George met Mr. Cattanzara coming home very late form work. He wondered if he was drunk but then could tell he wasn't. Mr. Cattanzara, a stocky, bald-headed man who worked in a change booth on an IRT station, lived on the next block after George's, above a shoe repair store. Nights, during the hot weather, he sat on his stoop in an undershirt, reading *The New York Times* in the light of the shoemaker's window. He read it from the first page to the last, then went up to sleep. And all the time he was reading the paper, his wife, a fat woman with a white face, leaned out of the window, gazing into the street, her thick white arms folded on the window ledge.

Once in a while Mr. Cattanzara came home drunk, but it was a quiet drunk. He never made any trouble, only walked stiffly up the street and slowly climbed the stairs into the hall. Though drunk, he looked the same as always, except for his tight walk, the quietness, and the fact that his eyes were wet. George liked Mr. Cattanzara because he remembered him giving him nickels to buy lemon ice with when he was a squirt. Mr. Cattanzara was a different type from those in the neighborhood. He asked different questions than the others when he met you, and he seemed to know what went on in all the newspapers. He read them, as his fat sick wife watched from the window.

"What are you doing with yourself this summer, George?" Mr. Cattanzara asked. "I see you walkin' around at nights."

George felt embarrassed. "I like to walk."

"What are you doing in the day now?"

"Nothing much just right now. I'm waiting for a job." Since it shamed him to admit he wasn't working, George said, "I'm staying home—but I'm reading a lot to pick up my education."

Mr. Cattanzara looked interested. He mopped his hot face with a red handkerchief.

"What are you reading'?"

George hesitated, then said, "I got a list of books in the library once, and now I'm gonna read them this summer." He felt strange and a little unhappy saying this, but he wanted Mr. Cattanzara to respect him.

"How many books are there on it?"

"I never counted them. Maybe around a hundred."

Mr. Cattanzara whistled through his teeth.

"I figure if I did that," George went on earnestly, "it would help me in my education. I want to know different things than they learn there, if you know what I mean."

The change maker nodded. "Still and all, one hundred books is a pretty big load for one summer."

"It might take longer."

"After you're finished with some, maybe you and I can shoot the breeze about them?" said Mr. Cattanzara.

"When I'm finished," George answered.

Mr. Cattanzara went home and George continued on his walk. After that, though he had the urge to, George did nothing different from usual. He still took his walks at night, ending up in the little park. But one evening the shoemaker on the next block stopped George to say he was a good boy, and George figured that Mr. Cattanzara had told him all about the books he was reading. From the shoemaker it must have gone down the street, becuse George saw a couple of people smiling kindly at himn, though nobody spoke to him personally. He felt a little better around the neighborhood and liked it more, though not so much he would want to live in it forever. He had never exactly disliked the people in it, yet he had never liked them very much either. It was the fault of the neighborhood. To his surprise, George found out that his father and Sophie knew about his reading too. His father was too shy to say anything about it—he was never much of a talker in his whole life—but

Sophie was softer to George, and she showed him in other ways she was proud of him.

As the summer went on George felt in a good mood about things. He cleaned the house every day, as a favor to Sophie, and he enjoyed the ball games more. Sophie now gave him a buck-a-week allowance, and though it still wasn't enough and he had to use it carefully, it was a lot better than just having two bits now and then. What he bought with the money—cigarettes mostly, an occasional beer or movie ticket—he got a big kick out of. Life wasn't so bad if you knew how to appreciate it. Occasionally he bought a paperback book from the newsstand, but he never got around to reading it, though he was glad to have a couple of books in his room. But he read thoroughly Sophie's magazines and newspapers. And night was the most enjoyable time, because when he passed the storekeepers sitting outside their stores, he could tell they regarded him highly. He walked erect, and though he did not say much to them, or they to him, he could feel approval on all sides. A couple of nights he felt so good that he skipped the park at the end of the evening. He just wandered in the neighborhood, where people had known him from the time he was a kid playing punchball whenever there was a game of it going; he wandered there, then came home and got undressed for bed, feeling fine.

A few weeks he had talked only once with Mr. Cattanzara, and though the change maker had said nothing more about the books, asked no questions, his silence made George a little uneasy. For a while George didn't pass in front of Mr. Cattanzara's house any more, until one night, forgetting himself, he approached it from a different direction than he usually did when he did. It was already past midnight. The street, except for one or two people, was deserted, and George was surprised when he saw Mr. Cattanzara still reading his newspaper by the light of the street lamp overhead. His impulse was to stop at the stoop and talk to him. He wasn't sure what he wanted to say, though he felt the words would come when he began to talk; but the more he thought about it, the more the idea scared him, and he decided he'd better not. He even considered beating it home by another street, but he was too near Mr. Cattanzara, and the change maker might see him as he ran, and get annoyed. So George unobtrusively crossed the street, trying to make it seem as if he had to look in a store window on the other side, which he did, and then went on, uncomfortable at what he was doing. He feared Mr. Cattanzara would glance up from his paper and call him a dirty rat for walking on the other side of the street, but all he did was sit there, sweating through his undershirt, his bald head shining in the dim light as he read his *Times*, and upstairs his fat wife leaned out of the window, seeming to read the paper along with him. George thought she would spy him and yell out to Mr. Cattanzara, but she never moved her eyes off her husband.

George made up his mind to stay away from the change maker until he had got some of his softback books read, but when he started them and saw they were mostly story books, he lost his interest and didn't bother to finish them. He lost his interest in reading other things too. Sophie's magazines and newspapers went unread. She saw them piling up on a chair in his room and asked why he was no longer looking at them, and George told her it was because of all the other reading he had to do. Sophie said she had guessed that was it. So for most of the day, George had the radio on, turning to music when he was sick of the human voice. He kept the house fairly neat, and Sophie said nothing on the days when he neglected it. She was still kind and gave him his extra buck, though things weren't so good for him as they had been before.

But they were good enough, considering. Also his night walks invariably picked him up, no matter how bad the day was. Then one night George saw Mr. Cattanzara coming down the street toward him. George was about to turn and run but he recognized from Mr. Cattanzara's walk that he was drunk, and if so, probably he would not even bother to notice him. So George kept on walking straight ahead until he came abreast of Mr. Catanzara and though he felt wound up enough to pop into the sky, he was not surprised when Mr. Cattanzara passed him without a word, walking slowly, his face and body stiff. George drew a breath in relief at his narrow escape, when he heard his name called, and there stood Mr. Cattanzara at his elbow, smelling like the inside of a beer barrel. His eyes were sad as he gazed at George, and George felt so intensely uncomfortable he was tempted to shove the drunk aside and continue on his walk. But he couldn't act that way to him, and, besides, Mr. Cattanzara took a nickel out of his pants pocket and handed it to him.

"Go buy yourself a lemon ice, Georgie."

"It's not that time any more, Mr. Cattanzara," George said. "I am a big guy now."

"No, you ain't, said Mr. Cattanzara, to which George could think of no reply.

"How are all your books comin' along now?" Mr. Cattanzara asked. Though he tried to stand steady, he swayed a little.

"Fine, I guess," said George, feeling the red crawling up his face.

"You ain't sure?" The change maker smiled slyly, a way George had never seen him smile.

"Sure I'm sure. They're fine."

Though his head swayed in little arcs, Mr. Cattanzara's eyes which could hurt if you looked at them too long.

"George," he said, "name me one book on that list that you read this summer, and I will drink to your health."

"I don't want anybody drinking to me."

"Name me one so I can ask you a question on it. Who can tell, if it's a good book, maybe I might wanna read it myself."

George knew he looked passable on the outside, but inside he was crumbling apart.

Unable to reply, he shut his eyes, but when—years later—he opened them, he saw that Mr. Cattanzara had, out of pity, gone away. But in his ears he still heard the words he had said when he left: "George, don't do what I did."

The next night he was afraid to leave his room, and though Sophie argued with him, he wouldn't open the door.

"What are you doing in there?" she asked.

"Nothing."

"Aren't you reading?"

"No."

She was silent a minute, then asked, "Where do you keep the books you read? I never seen any in your room outside of a few cheap, trashy ones."

He wouldn't tell her.

"In that case you're not worth a buck of my hard-earned money. Why should I break my back for you? Go on out, you bum, and get a job."

He stayed in his room for almost a week, except to sneak into the kitchen when nobody was home. Sophie railed at him, then begged him to come out, and his old father wept, but George wouldn't budge, though the weather was terrible and his small room stifling. He found it very hard to breathe; each breath was like drawing a flame into his lungs.

One night, unable to stand the heat any more, he burst into the street at 1 A.M. a shadow of himself. He hoped to sneak into the park without being seen, but there were people all over the block, wilted and listless, waiting for a breeze. George lowered his eyes and walked, in disgrace, away from them, but before long he discovered they were still friendly to him. He figured Mr. Cattanzara hadn't told on him. Maybe when he woke up out of his drunk the next morning, he had forgotten all about meeting George. George felt his confidence slowly come back to him.

That same night a man on a street corner asked him if it was true that he had finished reading so many books, and George admitted he had. The man said it was a wonderful thing for a boy his age to read so much.

"Yeah," George said, but he felt relieved. He hoped nobody would mention the books any more, and when, after a couple of days, he accidentally met Mr. Cattanzara again, he didn't, though George had the idea he was the one who had started the rumor that he had finished all the books.

One evening in the fall, George ran out of his house to the library, where he hadn't been in years. There were books all over the place, wherever he looked, and though he was struggling to control an inward trembling, he easily counted off a hundred, then sat down at a table to read.

Exercise:

Write a short paragraph defining the following phrases:
1. a well read person
2. an educated person
3. a school drop out
4. an ignoramous
5. a book worm (nerd)
6. a cultured person
7. a person educated in the "school of life"
8. a successful person
9. an intellectual
10. a regular guy.

Discuss the positive and negative aspects of these phrases. Explore the social and personal reasons for accepting these terms as defining valuable characteristics of persons.

Choosing Goals

School is many things: the place where we learn, the place where we are judged, the place where we meet new friends, and the place where we strike out on our own. Going to college is the "big break" from family and neighborhood values especially for those for whom college means a move from home. The complex role of school reflects many different values. These values not only come into conflict but they tend to obscure each other. It is not unusual for a certain cynicism to result. School is seen as a big game, learning as a tool for social approval. How do we sort all of this out? Sometimes a little humor helps.

Lisa Birnbach,
The Official Preppy Handbook

The Four-Year Plan
Collegiate Life

College, for most Preppies, is their closest brush with democracy. Since they've taken pains to go to the right college, they feel secure enough to indulge in most of that college's activities, even with the non-Preps (who must be tenable if they were admitted). Thus, the Preppy is eager to behave just as moronically as the graduate from Abraham Lincoln High during Homecoming parades, the Christmas party, mid-winter bashes, Greek Week, and finals.

In terms of daily existence, college life is like Prep school life, except you don't have to adhere to any schedule or set of rules and a shower of demerits is no longer a threat. These may be the best years of the Prep life—no job, no family, no responsibilities other than to store a wealth of fond memories to last a lifetime. The collegiate years are a final opportunity to sow wild oats, a chance to live the carefree life to the hilt, a license to be Prep with a vengeance.

When the four years are over, you will be expected to assume the duties of Prep Adulthood, so remind yourself while you're waiting for your fraternity brothers to open that fifth keg of beer that college is a once-in-a-lifetime experience.

The first and most essential factor you should consider in planning your campus *modus vivendi* is the academic schedule. Morning and evening classes are out of the question for the obvious reason that the latter prohibit you from enjoying happy hours and the former prevent you from recovering from them. A couple of hours in the library on week nights are mandatory:

Apart from the necessary social scene, the library furnishes you with a quiet spell to shore up resources for the next drinking engagement while you scan *Othello* for choice references to be flaunted in class the next day. (Preppies love to contribute to class discussion.) But, as important as the library is during the week, there's no excuse for being stuck there on the weekend when everyone else has gone skiing.

Residence is very important to your collegiate well-being. First and foremost, you want to be always near campus in case an impromptu party pops up. There are those who would stray to off-off-campus apartments, but they are not Prep and never will be. Secondly, the dorm room assigned to you by the housing office should quickly become a Prep Palace. If the Greek life appeals to you (and it certainly should), you may move into the frat house sophomore year, and then junior year move into the best room in the house; senior year may find you moving into your own off-(as opposed to off-off) campus apartment. But no matter where you're living, the authorized Prep interior-decorating scheme will make you feel you're only one small remove from secondary school.

Preppies with a serious athletic bent may choose to participate in varsity sports like squash or lacrosse, but most won't because of the unreasonable training demands. (They had enough of those in Prep school.) More gentlemanly intramural sports are favored—they allow you to prove your athletic prowess, drink your beer afterward and provide entertainment for the Prep women who spectate when they're not flinging a ball themselves.

Although shunning any efforts of their Prep schools to expose them to culture, Preppies are quick to show off their superior breeding in college by partaking in clubs like the glee club, choral society, and philanthropic organizations. They may also attend art openings, classical concerts, and film festivals, not out of any real passion, but just to see each other—a sort of warm-up for the Junior League and the Racquet Club. Any highly specialized club is desirable for added social security.

Generally, college is an occasion to be with other Preppies, whether they are from your Prep school, from your rival schools, or simply passing for Prep. Except for the minimal forays into scholarship, you enjoy an uninterrupted stream of parties, rather like a four-year debutante season. But then again, as any self-respecting Preppy will tell you, college is just another Prep club itself.

The Gentleman's "C" or How to Choose a Major

Preppies, like everyone else, must choose a major from among the college's established list of courses of study (Beer Drinking is not one of these). Preppies know, however, that whether they go into banking, law, or business (preferably Daddy's) the specifics of the undergraduate career couldn't matter less.

This knowledge leads to three basic concerns when choosing a major—concerns that have established English, History, Economics or Classics (for the hard-core fringe), and Architecture (for the aesthetically interested) as the perennial favorites.

Not too taxing, but still respectable. A Preppy cannot choose a laughably easy or "gut" major—Geology, Anthropology, Psychology. These are considered a tacky waste of Prep school cultivation. It's fine to be concerned about taking on too much work—no one wants undue distraction from social commitments—but there's no need to get obvious about it. Your major must have the ring of serious academic pursuit—and a "C" in History sounds a lot better than a "C" in Sociology. It is, of course, perfectly acceptable to satisfy distribution requirements with a "gut" course.

Not too esoteric, but still respectable. Out-of-the-ordinary concentrations —Comparative Literature, Philosophy, Linguistics—may not require any more work than English or History, but they smack of an equally undesirable effort: thought. These majors imply all sorts of unattractive qualities like intellectualism and curiosity about the universe that a self-respecting Prep wouldn't touch with a ten-foot length of ticker tape.

Not too obviously career-oriented, but still respectable. Professional majors —Engineering, Chemistry, Mathematics—all reek of practicality. They intimate concern for the future, worry about the post-collegiate life—concepts foreign to the Prep mentality, as they should be to anyone who would associate with Preps. Classmates in these fields of endeavor are also the most academically competitive on campus (the sort who booby-trap each other's lab experiments), so it is often necessary to swear off social activity altogether just to appear somewhere on the bell curve—and there's no such thing as a Gentleman's "F."

Exercise:

Make a chart listing four basic values, *fulfillment, fun, happiness, success* across the top of a sheet of paper. List the reasons for going to college listed below, down the side of the page. Using a scale of 1 to 5, rank the reasons in so far as they tend to satisfy the four basic values.

Reasons to go to college include:

to learn to think for yourself

to get a good job

to meet boys (girls)

to become independent

to learn a skill

to broaden yourself

to get away from home

to learn about the world

to study the great minds

to become a professional

to have one last blast

to develop your mind

to express your potential

to stay stoned

Feel free to add items to the list.

The Value of Education

Why be educated? For status? To get a good job? To prove yourself to others? To prove yourself to yourself? Many of the greatest thinkers have pondered questions like these, only to come up with an answer that reflects the view of Plato: "All education is for the soul." John Dewey, one of the most important theorists of education in modern times, offers a view that sees education at the heart of what it means to be a human in the fullest sense.

John Dewey, Education and Morality

If a few words are added upon the topic of education, it is only for the sake of suggesting that the educative process is all one with the moral process, since the latter is a continuous passage of experience from worse to better. Education has been traditionally thought of as preparation: as learning, acquiring certain things because they will later be useful. The end is remote, and education is getting ready, is a preliminary to something more important to happen later on. Childhood is only a preparation for adult life, and adult life for another life. Always the future, not the present, has been the significant thing in education: Acquisition of knowledge and skill for future use and enjoyment; formation of habits required later in life in business, good citizenship and pursuit of science. Education is thought of also as something needed by some human beings merely because of their dependence upon others. We are born ignorant, unversed, unskilled, immature, and consequently in a state of social dependence. Instruction, training, moral discipline are processes by which the mature, the adult, gradually raise the helpless to the point where they can look out for themselves. The business of childhood is to grow into the independence of adulthood by means of the guidance of those who have already attained it. Thus the process of education as the main business of life ends when the young have arrived at emancipation from social dependence.

These two ideas, generally assumed but rarely explicitly reasoned out, contravene the conceptiuon that growing, or the continuous reconstruction of experience, is the only end. If at whatever period we choose to take a person, he is still in process of growth, then education is not, save as a by-product, a preparation for something coming later. Getting from the present the degree and kind of growth there is in it is education. This is a constant function, independent of age. The best thing that can be said of any special process of education, like that of the formal school period, is that it renders the subject capable of further education: more sensitive to conditions of growth and more able to take advantage of them. Acquisition of skill, possession of knowledge, attainment of culture are not ends: they are marks of growth and means to is continuing ...

Discussion Plan:

1. What is the theory of education that Dewey rejects?
2. What reasons do you think Dewey has for rejecting it?
3. To what extent does your outlook on education reflect the view he rejects?
4. What reasons can be given for the rejected viewpoint?

Exercise:

Dewey offers the following definition of education, "Getting from the present the degree and kind of growth there is in it is education." Write a two part essay of between one and two pages. The first part should be your analysis of this phrase. The second part should be a sketch of what schools would be like if Dewey's definition were taken seriously.

SECTION 5: SOCIAL CONTROL—WORK

School is a preparation for the "real world." For most of us this "real world" is the world of work. The working world, like the world of school, is a social institution: that is, a system that imposes its values on the people who enter into it. But the values in the world of work have a special character, for working gives the individual the resources upon which life depends. It is no accident that we call working "making a living." And so the values of the working world form the "bottom line": the objective world of profits and losses that, supposedly, everyone must respond to.

Facing the prospect of financial independence is a big part of growing up. Entering into the process of working is a major challenge, for the demands of the working place are, even if, compelling, frequently opposed to the values that the individual has constructed for herself. The realities of self, the realities of society and now the reality of the bottom line. How are we to reconcile them when they conflict?

The Social Context

In some traditions children are expected to work for a living. Their families depend on their earnings or their families abandon them, forcing them to support themselves. This seems cruel since the responsibilities of work conflict with the simple joys that we associate with childhood. Moreover, the child as worker is especially defenseless. Physically and emotionally weak, ignorant of the ways of the world, the child has no choice and no way out.

Anton Chekhov, Vanka

Vanka Zhukov, a nine-year old boy, who had been apprenticed to Alyahin the shoemaker these three months, did not go to bed on Christmas Eve. After his master and mistress and the journeymen had gone to midnight Mass, he got an inkpot and a penholder with a rusty nib out of the master's cupboard and having spread out a crumpled sheet of paper, began writing. Before he formed the first letter he looked fearfully at the doors and windows several times, shot a glance at the dark icon, at either side of which stretched shelves filled with lasts, and heaved a broken sigh. He was kneeling before a bench on which his paper lay.

"Dear Grandaddy, Konstantin Makarych," he wrote. "And I am writing you a letter. I wish you a merry Christmas and everything good from the Lord god. I have neither father nor mother, you alone are left me."

Vanka shifted his glance to the dark window on which flickered the reflection of his candle and vividly pictured his grandfather to himself. Employed as a watchman by the Zhivaryovs, he was a short, thin, but extraordinarily lively and nimble old man of about sixty-five whose face was always crinkled with laughter and who had a toper's eyes. By day he slept in the servants' kitchen or cracked jokes with the cook, at night, wrapped in an ample sheepskin coat, he made the rounds of the estate, shaking his clapper. The old bitch, Brownie, and the dog called Wriggles, who had a black coat and a long body like a weasel's, followed him with hanging heads. This Wriggles was extraordinarily deferential and demonstrative, looked with equally friendly eyes both at his masters and at strangers, but did not enjoy a good reputation. His deference and meekness concealed the most Jesuitical spite. No one knew better than he how to creep up behind you and suddenly snap at your leg, how to slip into the icehouse, or how to steal a hen from a peasant. More than once his hind legs had been all but broken, twice he had been hanged, every week he was whipped till he was half dead, but he always managed to revive.

At the moment Grandfather was sure to be standing at the gates, screwing up his eyes at the bright-red windows of the church, stamping his felt boots, and cracking jokes with the servants. His clapper was tied to his belt. He was clapping his hands, shrugging with the cold, and, with a senile titter, pinching now the housemaid, now the cook.

"Shall we have a pinch of snuff" he was saying, offering the women his snuffbox.

They each took a pinch and sneezed. Grandfather, undescribably delighted, went off into merry peals of laughter and shouted:

"Peel it off, it has frozen on!"

The dogs too are given a pinch of snuff. Brownie sneezes, wags her head, and walks away offended. Wriggles is too polite to sneeze and only wags his tail. And the weather is glorious. The air is still, clear, and fresh. The night is dark, but one can see the whole village with its white roofs and smoke streaming out of the chimneys, the trees silvery with hoarfrost, the snowdrifts. The entire sky is studded with gaily twinkling stars and the Milky Way is as distinctly visible as though it had been washed and rubbed with snow for the holiday...

Vanka sighed, dipped his pen into the ink and went on writing:

"And yesterday I got it hot. The master pulled me out into the courtyard by the hair and gave me a hiding with a knee-strap because I was rocking the baby in its cradle and happened to fall asleep. And last week the mistress ordered me to clean a herring and I began with the tail, and she took the herring and jabbed me in the mug with it. The helpers make fun of me, send me to the pothouse for vodka and tell me to steal pickles for them from the master, and the master hits me with anything that comes handy. And there is nothing to eat. In the morning they give me bread, for dinner porridge, and in the evening bread again. As for tea or cabbage soup, the master and mistress bolt it all themselves. And they tell me to sleep in the entry, and when the baby cries I don't sleep at all, but rock the cradle. Dear Grandaddy, for God's sake have pity on me, take me away from here, take me home to the village, it's more than I can bear. I bow down at your feet and I will pray to God for you forever, take me away from here or I'll die."

Vanka puckered his mouth, rubbed his eyes with his black fist, and gave a sob.

"I will grind your snuff for you," he continued, "I will pray to God for you, and if anything happens, you may thrash me all you like. And if you think there's no situation for me, I will beg the manager for Christ's sake to let me clean boots, or I will take Fedka's place as a shepherd boy. Dear Granddaddy, it's more than I can bear, it will simply be the death of me. I thought of running away to the village, but I have no boots and I am afraid of the frost. And in return for this when I grow big, I will feed you and won't let anybody do you any harm, and when you die I will pray for the repose of your soul, just as for my Mom's.

"Moscow is a big city. The houses are all the kind the gentry live in, and there are lots of horses, but no sheep, and the dogs are not fierce. The boys here don't go caroling, carrying the star at Christmas, and they don't let anyone sing in the choir, and once in a shop window I saw fishing-hooks for sale all fitted up with a line, for every kind of fish, very fine ones, there was even one hook that will hold a forty-pound sheatfish. And I saw shops where there are all sorts of guns, like the master's at home, so maybe each one of them is a hundred rubles. And in butchers' shops there are woodcocks and partridge and hares, but where they shoot them the clerks won't tell.

"Dear Granddaddy, when they have a Christmas tree with presents at the master's, do get a gilt walnut and put it away in the little green chest. Ask the young lady, Olga Ignatyevna, for it, say it's for Vanka."

Vanka heaved a broken sigh and again stared at the window. He recalled that it was his grandfather who always went to the forest to get the Christmas tree for the master's family and that he would take his grandson with him. It was a jolly time! Grandfather grunted, the frost crackled, and, not to be outdone, Vanka too made a cheerful noise in this throat. Before chopping down the Christmas tree, Grandfather would smoke a pipe, slowly take a pinch of snuff, and poke fun at Vanka who looked chilled to the bone. The young firs draped in hoarfrost stood still, waiting to see which of them was to die. Suddenly, coming out of nowhere, a hare would dart across the snow-drifts like an arrow. Grandfather could not keep from shouting: "Hold him, hold him, hold him! Ah, the bob-tailed devil!"

When he had cut down the fir tree, Grandfather would drag it to the master's house, and there they would set to work decorating it. The young lady, Olga Ignatyevna, Vanka's favorite, was the busiest of all. When Vanka's mother, Pelageya, was alive and a chambermaid in the master's house, the young lady used to give him goodies, and, having nothing with which to occupy herself, taught him to read and write, to count up to a hundred, and even to dance the quadrille. When Pelageya died, Vanka had been relegated to the servant's kitchen to stay with his grandfather, and from the kitchen to the shoemaker's.

"Do come, dear Granddaddy," Vanka went on. "For Christ's sake, I beg you, take me away from here. Have pity on me, an unhappy orphan, here everyone beats me, and I am terribly hungry, and I am so blue, I can't tell you how, I keep crying. And the other day the master hit me on the head with a last, so that I fell down and it was a long time before I came to. My life is miserable, worse than a dog's—I also send greetings to Alyona, one-eyed Yegorka and the coachman, and don't give my harmonica to anyone. I remain, your grandson, Ivan Zhukov, dear Granddaddy, do come."

Vanka twice folded the sheet covered with writing and put it into an envelope he had bought for a kopeck the previous day. He reflected a while, then dipped the pen into the ink and wrote the address:

To Grandfather in the village

Then he scratched himself, thought a little, and added: Konstantin Makar-ych. Glad that no one had interrupted him at his writing, he put on his cap and, without slipping on his coat, ran out into the street with nothing over his shirt.

The clerks at the butchers' whom he had questioned the day before had told him that letters were dropped into letter boxes and from the boxes they were carried all over the world in troikas with ringing bells and drunken drivers. Vanka ran to the nearest letter box and thrust the precious letter into the slit.

An hour later, lulled by sweet hopes, he was fast asleep. In his dream he saw the stove. On the stove sat grandfather, his bare legs hanging down, and read the letter to the cooks. Near the stove was Wriggles, wagging his tail.

Discussion Plan:

Vanka seems hopelessly trapped by his youth, his ignorance and the people around him. In the following cases define the personal and social pressures that control the individuals.

1. Joe is a member of a youth gang.
2. Mary is the captain of the chess club.
3. Paul has been doing drugs since he was eleven.
4. Sara writes papers three times as long as any one else in class.
5. Joe is twenty two, drives a taxi and has three kids.

6. Mary's husband is a doctor, she has two children ages five and three.
7. Susan is a first year intern in a city hospital.
8. Tom has just been elected to Congress for his first term.
9. Paula is blind.
10. Jane wants only to be a jazz saxaphonist.
11. Jim, at fifteen, is becoming increasingly certain that he is gay.
12. Ralph has been raised in a fundamentalist religion.
13. Cynthia is upper middle class, the only daughter of loving parents; she is quite beautiful.
14. Sam is captain of the football team.

The Person Responds

Working takes place within a context that defines what's available. For all too many of the human beings that have lived and now live on the globe, the context includes, poverty, oppression and the disregard of basic human rights. In the United States the most serious victims of systematic poverty and exploitation were the descendants of slaves that were brought here, mainly, from Africa. Surviving within such a context requires enormous strength.

Richard Wright, Blackboy

Hunger stole upon me so slowly that at first I was not aware of what hunger really meant. Hunger had always been more or less at my elbow when I played, but now I began to wake up at night to find hunger standing at my bedside, staring at me gauntly. The hunger I had known before this had been no grim, hostile stranger; it had been a normal hunger that had made me beg constantly for bread, and when I ate a crust or two I was satisfied. But this new hunger baffled me, scared me, made me angry and insistent. Whenever I begged for food now my mother would pour me a cup of tea which would still the clamor in my stomach for a moment or two; but a little later I would feel hunger nudging my ribs, twisting my empty guts until they ached. I would grow dizzy and my vision would dim. I became less active in my play, and for the first time in my life I had to pause and think of what was happening to me.

"Mama, I'm hungry," I complained one afternoon.

"Jump up and catch a kungry," she said, trying to make me laugh and forget.

"What's a kungry?"

"It's what little boys eat when they get hungry," she said.

"What does it taste like?"

"I don't know."

"Then why do you tell me to catch one?"

"Because you said that you were hungry," she said smiling.

I sensed that she was teasing me and it made me angry.

"But I'm hungry. I want to eat."

"You'll have to wait."

"But I want to eat now."

"But there's nothing to eat," she told me.

"Why?"

"Just because there's none," she explained.

"But I want to eat," I said, beginning to cry.

"You'll just have to wait," she said again.

"But why?"

"For God to send some food."

"When is He going to send it?"

"I don't know."

"But I'm hungry!"

She was ironing and she paused and looked at me with tears in her eyes.

"Where's your father?" she asked me.

I stared in bewilderment. Yes, it was true that my father had not come home to sleep for many days now and I could make as much noise as I wanted. Though I had not known why he was absent, I had been glad that he was not there to shout his restrictions at me. But it had never occurred to me that his absence would mean that there would be no food.

"I don't know," I said.

"Who brings food into the house?" my mother asked me.

"Papa," I said. "He always brought food."

"Well, your father isn't here now," she said.

"Where is he?"

"I don't know," she said.

"But I'm hungry," I whimpered, stomping my feet.

"You'll have to wait unti I get a job and buy food," she said.

As the days slid past the image of my father became associated with my pangs of hunger, and whenever I felt hungry I thought of him with a deep biological bitterness.

My mother finally went to work as a cook and left me and my brother alone in the flat each day with a loaf of bread and a pot of tea. When she returned at evening she would be tired and disspirited and would cry a lot. Sometimes, when she was in despair, she would call us to her and talk to us for hours, telling us that we now had no father, that our lives would be different from those of other children, that we must learn as soon as possible to take care of ourselves, to dress ourselves, to prepare our own food; that we must take upon ourselves the responsibility of the flat while she worked. Half frightened, we would promise solemnly. We did not understand what had happened between our father and our mother and the most that these long talks did to us was to make us feel a vague dread. Whenever we asked why father had left, she would tell us that we were too young to know.

One evening my mother told me that thereafter I would have to do the shopping for food. She took me to the corner store to show me the way. I was proud; I felt like a grownup. The next afternoon I looped the basket over my arm and went down the pavement toward the store. When I reached the corner, a gang of boys grabbed me, knocked me down, snatched the basket, took the money, and sent me running home in panic. That evening I told my mother what had happened, but she made no comment; she sat down at once, wrote another note, gave me more money, and sent me out to the grocery again. I crept down the steps and saw the same gang of boys playing down the street. I ran back into the house.

"What's the matter?" my mother asked.

"It's those same boys," I said. "They'll beat me."

"You've got to get over that," she said. "Now, go on."

"I'm scared," I said.

"Go on and don't pay any attention to them," she said.

I went out of the door and walked briskly down the sidewalk, praying that the gang would not molest me. But when I came abreast of them someone shouted.

"There he is!"

They came toward me and I broke into a wild run toward home. They overtook me and flung me to the pavement. I yelled, pleaded, kicked, but they wrenched the money out of my hand. They yanked me to my feet, gave me a few slaps, and sent me home sobbing. My mother met me at the door.

"They b-beat m-me," I gasped. "They t-took the m-money."

I started up the steps, seeking the shelter of the house.

"Don't you come in here," my mother warned me.

I froze in my tracks and stared at her.

"But they're coming after me," I said.

"You just stay right where you are," she said in a deadly tone. "I'm going to teach you this night to stand up and fight for yourself."

She went into the house and I waited, terrified, wondering what she was about. Presently she returned with more money and another note; she also had a long heavy stick.

"Take this money, this note, and this stick," she said. "Go to the store and buy those groceries. If those boys bother you, then fight."

I was baffled. My mother was telling me to fight, a thing that she had never done before.

"But I'm scared," I said.

"Don't you come into this house until you've gotten those groceries," she said.

"They'll beat me; they'll beat me," I said.

"Then stay in the streets; don't come back here!"

I ran up the steps and tried to force my way past her into the house. A stinging slap came on my jaw. I stood on the sidewalk, crying.

"Please, let me wait until tomorrow," I begged.

"No," she said. " Go now! If you come back into this house without those groceries, I'll whip you!"

She slammed the door and I heard the key turn in the lock. I shook with fright. I was alone upon the dark, hostile streets and gangs were after me. I had the choice of being beaten at home or away from home. I clutched the stick, crying, trying to reason. If I were beaten at home, there was absolutely nothing that I could do about it; but if I were beaten in the streets, I had a chance to fight and defend myself. I walked slowly down the sidewalk, coming closer to the gang of boys, holding the stick tightly. I was so full of fear that I could scarecely breathe. I was almost upon them now.

"There he is again!" the cry went up.

They surrounded me quickly and began to grab for my hand.

"I'll kill you!" I threatened.

They closed in. In blind fear I let the stick fly, feeling it crack against a boy's skull. I swung again, lamming another skull, then another. Realizing that they would retaliate if I let up for but a second, I fought to lay them low, to knock them cold, to kill them so that they could not strike back at me. I flayed with tears in my eyes, teeth clenched, stark fear making me throw every ounce of my strength behind each blow. I hit again and again, dropping the money and the grocery list. The boys scattered, yelling, nursing their heads, staring at me in utter disbelief. They had never seen such frenzy. I stood panting, egging them on, taunting them to come on and fight. When they refused, I ran after them and they tore out for their homes, screaming. The parents of the boys rushed into the streets and threatened me, and for the first time in my life I shouted at grownups, telling them that I would give them the same if they bothered me. I finally found my grocery list and the money and went to the store. On my way back I kept my stick poised for instant use, but there was not a single boy in sight. That night I won the right to the streets of Memphis.

Research Project:

Research the economic status of black people in the United States since 1900. Write a three page report summarizing your findings.

Striking Back

The response of Black people in the United States, like the response of oppressed people everywhere has been to find life styles that permit some freedom and self actualization within a limiting and destructive environment. These lifestyles, frequently anti-social, become popularized and become self-fulfilling characterizations to which young people are all too vulnerable. These stereotypes, when acted out, are often destructive, both to the individual and to those he encounters.

Time, In Brooklyn: A Wolf in $45 Sneakers

Baby Love sits on the stoop, rolling the largest, fattest joint in the world. He wastes little: in go twigs, seeds, everything, until it seems as big as a torpedo. Other joints are tucked over each ear, and more are secreted in plastic bags under his hat. It is Friday night, the night to get high, get drunk and strut. Baby Love's entire wrecking crew is here, sprawled over cars, squatting on the sidewalk, jiving. There is Shistang, ("He be cool with dice"), Little Spank, Gugu, Snake Eyes, Shilo, Spider Man, Daddy Rich, Little June, Snatch Pocket Earl and Snootchy Fingers.

"We be in the streets hangin' out an' gettin' high," says Baby Love. He is a very skinny, very small, very lethal 14-year-old. His eyes are slate gray, flashing to blue, when he laughs. Mischief is etched across his face as a bittersweet smile. Like his crew, he is dressed in mugger's uniform: designer jeans, T shirt and $45 Pumas, the starched laces neatly untied. A wolf in expensive sneakers, Baby Love is a school dropout, one of more than 800,000 between the ages of 14 and 17 in the U.S.

Baby Love inhabits a world few white folks ever see, a Dickensian hell of cheap thrills, senseless deaths and almost unrelieved hopelessness. He lives in Brooklyn's Bedford Stuyvesant section, one of the oldest black settlements in the U.S. Unlike the burned and ravaged South Bronx, ten miles to the north, Bedford Stuyvesant does not resemble a war zone; most of its owner-occupied row houses, brownstones and churches are more or less intact. But high unemployment and a 60% dropout rate among black high school students makes it a very dangerous place. One Bed-Stuy precinct, the 77th, has the highest murder rate in the city: 86 killings last year.

Baby Love is trapped. He can barely read or write, even though he would have been in the seventh grade this year. Because he is nearly illiterate he could never hold even the meanest job for long. He has been running wild so long now that he may be beyond redemption. Ghetto children today are seduced much earlier by drugs and the street, some of them as young as eight or nine. That is the time they need help. Sinbad Lockwood, a Bed-Stuy street

artist who tries to wean boys like Baby Love away from the streets to painting, says, "It be the parents' fault, they get rid of the kids by sending them to
the candy store where they be buying reefer and beer. These kids ain't no
monsters—they be raising themselves, that's all."

Baby Love is almost always stoned. He rises late, plays basketball in the
park or galactic-warfare games at the pinball arcade all day. If there is any
money left over, he and Daddy Rich go to karate movies. He juggles four
chicks with Casanova skill, and he makes enough from gambling and stealing to be a real "sportin' man."

For Baby Love, stealing means survival. He is the best gold-chain snatcher
on the block. "I pretends to be making a phone call when the bus be comin'
along," he explains, "so the driver won't warn the passengers. Then when it
be by, I's leapin' in the air with my hand through the window and gone befo'
anyone sees." He breaks into laughter, slapping skin all round. He has been
caught five times this summer for pickpocketing. At Macy's he was caught
boosting eight blue Izod Lacoste shirts in his Adidas bag. He has just finished 60 days' probation.

Baby Love lives on the fourth floor of a crumbling, turn-of-the century
tenement with his aunt and legal guardian, Cora Lee. He sleeps on a stained
mattress in a small room he often shares with his cousins, Butter and
Buckeye, and with an army of roaches that waddle fatly across the floor. His
two younger sisters, Shantia, 11, and Sarah, 8, are also in Cora Lee's charge.
Baby Love's mother, Rose, stays there too. They are all receiving welfare
payments.

There have been three bad fires in Baby Love's building in the past couple
of years. The fifth floor is gutted. He and his crew now use it as their
clubhouse. Baby Love uses the roof as an escape route from police. He jumps
across a yawning chasm to the next building, then he is down the stairs and
away. "We be doin' this when we drunk," says Baby Love with an impish
smile. A born hustler, he is slick at pool and dice. He gambles Friday nights in
front of BeeGee's candy store with men who feed him chiba chiba, a Puerto
Rican expression for an especially potent kind of marijuana, the reefer that
zoots you out.

He thinks Bruce Lee is a cool dude, but "Richard Pryor is the Man," says
Baby Love. "He got power." The violence Baby Love sees on the screen is not
much different from what he faces on the street. He was 13 when he first saw
a man blown away—with a shotgun. He has faced down a few gunslingers
himself. He sometimes carries a .25 automatic. "All my friends got guns," he
says. "We go and try and shoot birds in the park." Trees are beaten to death in
ghetto parks. Youngsters, too, get killed on summer evenings when there is
disco music in the air. Tough, mean young men shoot it out like Western
heroes of old. The dead are dumped in trashed buildings. Some of Baby
Love's friends did not live through the summer. A cheeky dude like him risks

death or injury every time he steps outside. Being small does not help. He was always getting beaten up until he learned to steal. Now he can bribe would-be assailants with reefer. He sometimes spends $20 a day on the stuff.

On Friday nights the crowds along Fulton and Nostrand Avenues ebb and flow like a tide. Dudes are gambling up and down the streets. The sweet smell of reefer is everywhere, and wine bottles are passed around. Up the block, twelve-year old hookers teeter on high heels, flouncing their boyish hips. There are drunken brawls, skin-and-bone addicts overdosing, police sirens screaming and the rattle of the el in the distance.

A procession of dudes pauses to talk to Baby Love. Most have done hard time. Some push dope, many are boozers. All have bitter wisdomn. Croco-dile comes by waving a bottle of vodka, his eyes gleaming yellow. He tells Baby Love, "Wait till you do hard time, boy. They'll pat your butt, they'll feel you. You'll come home, swishing like a girl." A huge dude, his muscles rippling, speaks in a cool bass: "I got a pair of $600 lizard shoes and I got silk shirts. I'm the Man, boy. I changes my clothes 15 times a day. Learn to hustle girls, and you can wear dark shades and sharkskin suits and ride a big white Caddy." Riff the horn player sniffs in disgust. "You've got to have dignity, boy, you be nothing without dignity. The only way to beat the Man is be going to school. Go back to school, boy."

Baby Love sneers. He stands up, "I'm gonna get all I wants," he says, "and I don' care if I gotta steal to get it. I'm not afraid of doin' time so long as I kin do it fast." Then he goes up the clubhouse with Daddy Rich. He lies on a mattress puffing on an El Producto cigar hollowed out and filled with chiba chiba. There is a bottle of 150-proof Bacardi rum by his side. The cassette player throbs and, for a moment, Baby Love is warm and secure, at peace and flying high.

Baby Love's real name is Curtis Anthony Devlin. This is the one he uses in family court. "He ain't bad, you understand," says his Aunt Cora. "He just don't like school. And there is no one here he minds." Cora is trying to get Baby Love into a Roman Catholic residential school in upstate New York that specializes in problem children. "But I don't know if he'll stay there. One thing I do know—if he keeps on stealing gold chains he's going to be in a heap of trouble, and that's for sure."

Where did Baby Love go wrong? His mother, Rose, 31, does not deny that she was a drug addict. "I'm an alcoholic too," she adds. She gave up legal custody of her children to Aunt Cora last year. According to Rose, Baby Love's father is an alcoholic, a drug addict and a bisexual. He was doing time at Attica during the prison's 1971 riots, shrugs Rose, and "he flipped his brains. That's why I divorced him." His father beat Baby Love up often with his fists, says Rose, and once he did so with an extension cord. When Baby Love retaliated with a piece of heavy steel pipe, she recalls, his father took him to the police and demanded, futilely, that he be locked up.

Baby Love rebelled against his mother when she started sleeping with other men. He was only five. She says, "My Curtis steals anything he can get. It is my fault. He saw me steal a woman's pocketbook. It had a lot of money in it. Curtis, he gets high on money now. It's all he wants, that an' reefer."

Despite all the stealing, the drugs, the barely suppressed rage, Baby Love can be polite, almost genteel. He is gracious at table; he learned manners from his grandmother. He can keep house, wash dishes, do the marketing and look after his sisters and baby cousin. He is the only one who can get his mother off the streets when she is drugged and nodding. Once, when she nearly overdosed, he dragged her from the kitchen, poured hot and cold water on her feet and burned her arms with a lighted cigarette to revive her.

Baby Love walks with a slight limp. His mother explains that he had a serious accident while playing ball in the streets when he was four. He was run over by a car and his left leg, right arm and most of his ribs were broken. Rose then did one of the few constructive things she has done in her sad life: she sued the driver and got a settlement of $3,000, which is now in trust. Baby Love will get the money when he turns 21. If he lives that long.

Discussion Plan:

Extenuating circumstances:

Discuss the justification of the following actions in terms of the situation that the person is in.

1. Mary is very unhappy at home, so she shoplifts.
2. Sam is traveling for the summer, he is hungry and broke; he takes food from a knapsack that has been left unattended.
3. Joe is seventy three and living on a fixed income, he shoplifts.
4. Sam is an alcoholic living on the street, he is always broke, and frequently hungry; he steals from stores whenever he can.
5. Ralph is a car mechanic, he charges a little extra if customers have expensive cars.
6. Mary owns a gourmet catering service, she calls meatloaf "beef estouffe" and charges three times what it costs in the deli.
7. Paul is a drug addict, he is in agony if he can't get drugs; Paul steals welfare checks from the mail.
8. Paul, from number seven above, sells drugs to others.
9. Sara multiplies all of her business expenses by two when filing her income tax.
10. Mr. Smith is a banker. By investing wisely his bank makes ten times more money than they pay out in interest. He earns close to $100,000 per year.

Personal Goals

Society paints an image of us that is difficult to ignore, but we also draw images of ourselves. Often the self constructed personal ideal of who we are is more compelling and more demanding than any other. The artist is one for whom the self constructed reality becomes all consuming—demanding choices that redefine the struggle of life and the place of work within it.

Willa Cather, When I Knew Stephen Crane

It was, I think, in the spring of '94 that a slender, narrow-chested fellow in a shabby gray suit, with a soft felt hat pulled low over his eyes, sauntered into the office of the managing editor of the *Nebraska State Journal* and introduced himself as Stephen Crane. He stated that he was going to Mexico to do some work for the Bacheller Syndicate and get rid of his cough, and that he would be stopping in Lincoln for a few days. Later he explained that he was out of money and would be compelled to wait until he got a check from the East before he went further. I was a junior at the Nebraska State University at the time, and was doing some work for the *State Journal* in my leisure time, and I happened to be in the managing editor's room when Mr. Crane introduced himself. I was just off the range; I knew a little Greek and something about cattle and a good horse when I saw one, and beyond horses and cattle I considered nothing of vital importance except good stories and the people who wrote them. This was the first man of letters I had ever met in the flesh, and when the young man announced who he was, I dropped into a chair behind the editor's desk where I could stare at him without being too much in evidence.

Only a very youthful enthusiasm and a large propensity for hero worship could have found anything impressive in the young man who stood before the managing editor's desk. He was thin to emaciation, his face was gaunt and unshaven, a thin dark mustache straggled on his upper lip, his black hair grew low on his forehead and was shaggy and unkept. His gray clothes were much the worse for wear and fitted him so badly it seemed unlikely he had ever been measured for them. He wore a flannel shirt and a slovenly apology for a necktie, and his shoes were dusty and worn gray about the toes and were badly run over at the heel. I had seen many a tramp printer come up the *Journal* stairs to hunt a job, but never one who presented such a disreputable appearance as this storymaker man. He wore gloves, which seemed rather a contradiction to the general slovenliness of his attire, but when he took them off to search his pockets for his credentials, I noticed that his hands were singularly fine; long, white, and delicately shaped, with thin, nervous fingers. I have seen pictures of Aubrey Beardsley's hands that recalled Crane's very vividly.

At that time Crane was but twenty-four, and almost an unknown man. Hamlin Garland had seen some of his work and believed in him, and had introduced him to Mr. Howells, who recommended him to the Bacheller Syndicate. *The Red Badge of Courage* had been published in the *State Journal* that winter along with a lot of other syndicate matter, and the grammatical construction of the story was so faulty that the managing editor had several times called on me to edit the copy. In this way I had read it very carefully, and through the careless sentence structure I saw the wonder of that remarkable performance. But the grammar certainly was bad. I remember one of the reporters who had corrected the phrase "it don't" for the tenth time remarked savagely, "If I couldn't write better English than this, I'd quit."

Crane spent several days in the town, living from hand to mouth and waiting for his money. I think he borrowed a small amount from the managing editor. He lounged aobut the office most of the time, and I frequently encountered him going in and out of the cheap restaurants on Tenth Street. When he was at the office he talked a good deal in a wandering, absent-minded fashion, and his conversation was uniformly frivolous. If he could not evade a serious question by a joke, he bolted. I cut my classes to lie in wait for him, confident that in some unwary moment I could trap him into serious conversation, that if one burned incense long enough and ardently enough, the oracle would not be dumb. I was Maupassant-mad at the time, a malady particularly unattractive in a junior, and I made a frantic effort to get an expression of opinion from him on "Le Bonheur." "O, you're Moping, are you?" he remarked with a sarcastic grin, and went on reading a little volume of Poe that he carried in his pocket. At another time I cornered him in the Funny Man's room and succeeded in getting a little out of him. We were taught literature by an exceedingly analytical method at the university, and we probably distorted the method, and I was busy trying to find the least common multiple of *Hamlet* and the greatest common divisor of *Macbeth*, and I began asking him whether stories were constructed by cabalistic formulae. At length he sighed wearily and shook his drooping shoulders, remarking: "Where did you get all that rot? Yarns aren't done by mathematics. You can't do it by rule any more than you can dance by rule. You have to have the itch of the thing in your fingers, and if you haven't—well, you're damned lucky, and you'll live long and prosper, that's all." And with that he yawned and went down the hall.

Crane was moody most of the time, his health was bad, and he seemed profoundly discouraged. Even his jokes were exceedingly drastic. He went about with the tense, preoccupied, self-centered air of a man who is brooding over some impending disaster, and I conjectured vainly as to what it might be. Though he was seemingly entirely idle during the few days I knew him, his manner indicated that he was in the throes of work that told terribly on his nerves. His eyes I remember as the finest I have ever seen, large and dark and full of luster and changing lights, but with a profound melancholy always lurking deep in them. They were eyes that seemed to be burning themselves out.

As he sat at the desk with his shoulders drooping forward his head low, and his long, white fingers drumming on the sheets of copy paper, he was as nervous as a race horse, fretting to be on the track. Always, as he came and went about the halls, he seemed like a man preparing for a sudden departure. Now that he is dead it occurs to me that all his life was a preparation for sudden departure. I remember once when he was writing a letter he stopped and asked me about the spelling of a word, saying carelessly, "I haven't time to learn to spell."

Then, glancing down at his attire, he added with an absent-minded smile, "I haven't time to dress either; it takes an awful slice out of a fellow's life."

He said he was poor, and he certainly looked it, but four years later when he was in Cuba, drawing the largest salary ever paid a newspaper correspondent, he clung to this same untidy manner of dress, and his ragged overalls and buttonless shirt were eyesores to the immaculate Mr. Davis, in his spotless linen and neat khaki uniform, with his Gibson chin always freshly shaven. When I first heard of his serious illness, his old throat trouble aggravated into consumption by his reckless exposure in Cuba, I recalled a passage from Maeterlinck's essay, "The Pre-Destined," on those doomed to early death: "As children, life seems nearer to them than to other children. They appear to know nothing, and yet there is in their eyes so profound a certainty that we feel they must know all. In all haste, but wisely and with minute care do they prepare themselves to live, and this very haste is a sign upon which mothers can scarce bring themselves to look." I remembered, too, the young man's melancholy and his tenseness, his burning eyes, and his way of slurring over the less important things, as one whose time is short.

I have heard other people say how difficult it was to induce Crane to talk seriously about his work, and I suspect that he was particularly averse to discussions with literary men of wider education and better equipment than himself, yet he seemed to feel that this fuller culture was not for him. Perhaps the unreasoning instinct which lies deep in the roots of our lives, and which guides us all, told him that he had not time enough to acquire it.

Men will sometimes reveal themselves to children, or to people whom they think never to see again, more completely than they ever do to their *confreres*. From the wise we hold back alike our folly and our wisdom, and for the recipients of our deeper confidences we seldom select our equals. The soul has no message for the friends with whom we dine every week. It is silenced by custom and convention, and we play only in the shadows. It selects its listeners willfully, and seemingly delights to waste its best upon the chance wayfarer who meets us in the highway at a fated hour. There are moments too, when the tides run high or very low, when self-revelation is necessary to every man, if it be only to his valet or his gardener. At such a moment, I was with Mr. Crane.

The hoped-for revelation came unexpectedly enough. It was on the last night he spent in Lincoln. I had come back from the theater and was in the *Journal* office writing a notice of the play. It was eleven o'clock when Crane came in. He had expected his money to arrive on the night mail and it had not done so, and he was out of sorts and deeply despondent. He sat down on the ledge of the open window that faced on the street, and when I had finished my notice I went over and took a chair beside him. Quite without invitation on my part, Crane began to talk, began to curse his trade from the first throb of creative desire in a boy to the finished work of the master. The night was oppressively warm; one of those dry winds that are the curse of that country was blowing up from Kansas. The white, western moon-lightthrew sharp, blue shadows below us. The streets were silent at that hour, and we could hear the gurgle of the fountain in the Post Office square across the street, and the twang of banjos from the lower verandah of the Hotel Lincoln, where the colored waiters were serenading the guests. The drop lights in the office were dull under their green shades, and the telegraph sounder clicked faintly in the next room. In all his long tirade, Crane never raised his voice; he spoke slowly and monotonously and even calmly, but I have never known so bitter a heart in any man as he revealed to me that night. It was an arraignment of the wages of life, an invocation to the ministers of hate.

Incidentally he told me the sum he had received for *The Red Badge of Courage*, which I think was something like ninety dollars, and he repeated some lines from *The Black Riders*, which was then in preparation. He gave me to understand that he led a double literary life, writing in the first place the matter that pleased himself, and doing it very slowly; in the second place, any sort of stuff that would sell, And he remarked that his poor was just as bad as it could possibly be. He realized, he said, that his limitations were absolutely impassable. "What I can't do, I can't do at all, and I can't acquire it. I only hold one trump."

He had not settled plans at all. He was going to Mexico wholly uncertain of being able to do any successful work there, and he seemed to feel very insecure about the financial end of his venture. The thing that most inter-ested me was what he said about his slow method of composition. He declared that there was little money in storywriting at best, and practically none in it for him, because of the time it took him to work up his detail. Other men, he said, could sit down and write up an experience while the physical effect of it, so to speak, was still upon them, and yesterday's impressions made today's "copy." But when he came in from the streets to write up what he had seen there, his faculties wre benumbed, and he sat twirling his pencil and hunting for words like a schoolboy.

I mentioned *The Red Badge of Courage*, which was written in nine days, and he replied that, though the writing took very little time, he had been unconsciously working the detail of the story out through most of his boyhood. His ancestors had been soldiers, and he had been imagining war stories ever since he was out of knickerbockers, and in writing his first war story he had simply gone over his imaginary campaigns and selected his favorite imaginary experinces. He declared that his imagination was hidebound; it was there, but it pulled hard. After he got a notion for a story, months passed before he could get any sort of personal contact with it, or feel any potency to handle it. "The detail of a thing has to filter through my blood, and then it comes out like a native product, but it takes forever," he remarked. I distinctly remember the illustration, for it rather took hold of me.

I have often been astonished since to hear Crane spoken of as "the reporter in fiction," for the reportorial faculty of superficial reception and quick transference was what he conspicuously lacked. His first newspaper account of his shipwreck on the filibuster *Commodore* off the Florida coast was as lifeless as the "copy" of a police court reporter. It was many months afterwards that the literary products of his terrible experience appeared in that marvellous sea story "The Open Boat," unsurpassed in its vividness and constructive perfection.

At the close of our long conversation that night, when the copy boy came in to take me home, I suggested to Crane that in ten years he would probably laugh at all his temporary discomfort. Again his body took on that strenuous tension and he clenched his hands, saying "I can't wait ten years. I haven't time."

The ten years are not up yet, and he has done his work and gathered his reward and gone. Was ever so much experience and achievement crowded into so short a space of time? A great man dead at twenty-nine! That would have puzzled the ancients. Edward Garnett wrote of him in the *Academy* of December 17, 1899: "I cannot remember a parallel in the literary history of fiction. Maupassant, Meredith, Henry James, Mr. Howells and Tolstoy, were all learning their expression at an age where Crane had achieved his and achieved it triumphantly." He had the precocity of those doomed to die in youth. I am convinced that when I met him he had a vague premonition of the shortness of his working day, and in the heart of the man there was that which said, "That thou doest, do quickly."

At twenty-one this son of an obscure New Jersey rector, with but a scant reading knowledge of French and no training, had rivaled in technique the foremost craftsmen of the Latin races. In the six years since I met him, a stranded reporter, he stood in the firing line during two wars, knew hair-breadth 'scapes on land and sea, and established himself as the first writer of his time in the picturing of episodic, fragmentary life. His friends have charged him with fickleness, but he was a man who was in the preoccupation of haste. He went from country to country, from man to man, absorbing all that was in them for him. He had no time to look backward. He had no leisure for camaraderie. He drank life to the lees, but at the banquet table where other men took their ease and jested over their wine, he stood a dark and silent figure, somber as Poe himself, not wishing to be understood, and he took his portion in haste, with his loins girded, and his shoes on his feet, and his staff in his hand, like one who must depart quickly.

Discussion Plan:

Stephen Crane is a famous author. He chose a life of poverty and struggle that eventually led to success. He died at 29.

1. Is what an artist does work?
2. What makes a person become an artist?
3. How do you tell who the artists are?
4. What makes art different than other forms of work?
5. Should an artist expect financial success?
6. Should artists be given special privileges?
7. Does being an artist mean that you can disregard the conventions of ordinary society?

The System

For most of us our choices are neither as restricted as those of a poverty stricken victim of oppression nor are they as challenging as the options available to a young writer of genius. What is required of most people is that they find a place within the system, and then fit into the mold required to do the job. No one wants to be just another cog in the wheel, but wheels need cogs to run.

Shirley Jackson, My Life With R.H. Macy

And the first thing they did was segregate me. They segregated me from the only person in the place I had even a speaking acquaintance with; that was a girl I had met going down the hall who said to me: "Are you as scared as I am?" And when I said, "Yes," she said, "I'm in lingerie, what are you in?" and I thought for a while and then said, "Spun glass," which was as good an answer as I could think of, and she said, "Oh. Well, I'll meet you here in a sec." And she went away and was segregated and I never saw her again.

Then they kept calling my name and I kept trotting over to wherever they called it and they would say ("They" all this time being startlingly beautiful young women in tailored suits and with short-clipped hair), "Go with Miss Cooper, here. She'll tell you what to do." All the women I met my first day were named Miss Cooper. And Miss Cooper would say to me: "What are you in?" and I had learned by that time to say, "Books," and she would say, "Oh, well, then, you belong with Miss Cooper here," and then she would call "Miss Cooper?" and another young woman would come and the first one would say, "13-3138 here belongs with you," and Miss Cooper would say, "What is she in?" and Miss Cooper would answer, "Books," and I would go away and be segregated again.

Then they taught me. They finally got me segregated into a classroom, and I sat there for a while all by myself (that's how far segregated I was) and then a few other girls came in, all wearing tailored suits (I was wearing a red velvet afternoon frock) and we sat down and they taught us. They gave us each a big book with R.H. Macy written on it, and inside this book were pads of little sheets saying (from left to right): "Comp. keep for ret. cust. d.a. no. or c.t. no. salesbook no. salescheck no. clerk no. dept. date M." After M there was a long line for Mr. or Mrs. and the name, and then it began again with "No. item. class. at price. total." And down at the bottom was written ORIGINAL and then again, "Comp. keep for ref." and "Paste yellow gift stamp here." I read all this very carefully. Pretty soon a Miss Cooper came, who talked for a little while on the advantages we had in working at Macy's, and she talked about the salesbooks, which it seems came apart into a sort of road map and carbons and things. I listened for a while, and when Miss

Cooper wanted us to write on the little pieces of paper, I copied from the girl next to me. That was training.

Finally someone said we were going on the floor, and we descended from the sixteenth floor to the first. We were in groups of six by then, all following Miss Cooper doggedly and wearing little tags saying BOOK INFORMA-TION. I never did find out what that meant. Miss Cooper said I had to work on the special sale counter, and showed me a little book called *The Stage-Struck Seal*, which it seemed I would be selling. I had gotten about halfway through it before she came back to tell me I had to stay with my unit.

I enjoyed meeting the time clock, and spent a pleasant half-hour punching various cards standing around, and then someone came in and said I couldn't punch the clock with my hat on. So I had to leave, bowing timidly at the time clock and its prophet, and I went and found out my locker number, which was 1773, and my time-clock number, was was 712, and my cash-box number, which was 1336, and my cash-register number, which was 253, and my cash-register-drawer number, which was K, and my cash-register-drawer-key number, which was 872, and my department number, which was 13. I wrote all these numbers down. And that was my first day.

My second day was better. I was officially on the floor. I stood in a corner of a counter, with one hand possessively on *The Stage-Struck Seal*, waiting for customers. The counter head was named 13-2246, and she was very kind to me. She sent me to lunch three times, because she got me confused with 13-6454 and 13-3141. It was after lunch that a customer came. She came over and took one of my stage-struck seals, and said "How much is this?" I opened my mouth and the customer said "I have a D.A. and I will have this sent to my aunt in Ohio. Part of that D.A. I will pay for with a book dividend of 32 cents, and the rest of course will be on my account. Is this book price-fixed?" That's as near as I can remember what she said. I smiled confidently, and said "Certainly; will you wait just one moment?" I found a little piece of paper in a drawer under the counter: it had "Duplicate Tripli-cate" printed across the front in big letters. I took down the customer's name and address, her aunt's name and address, and wrote carefully across the front of the duplicate triplicate "1 Stg. Strk.Sl" Then I smiled at the customer again and said carelessly "That will be seventy-five cents." She said "but I have a D.A." I told her that all D.A.'s were suspended for the Christmas rush, and she gave me seventy-five cents, which I kept. Then I rang up a "No Sale" on the cash register and I tore up the duplicate triplicate because I didn't know what else to do with it.

Later on another customer came and said "Where would I find a copy of Ann Rutherford Gwynn's *He Came Like Thunder?* and I said "In medical books, right across the way," but 13-2246 came and said "That's philosophy, isn't it?" and the customer said it was, and 13-2246 said "Right down this aisle, in dictionaries." The customer went away, and I said to 13-2246 that her guess was as good as mine, anyway, and she stared at me and explained that philosophy, social sciences and Bertrand Russell were all kept in dictionaries.

So far I haven't been back to Macy's for my third day, because that night when I started to leave the store, I fell down the stairs and tore my stockings and the doorman said that if I went to my department head Macy's would give me a new pair of stockings and I went back and I found Miss Cooper and she said, "Go to the adjuster on the seventh floor and give him this," and she handed me a little slip of pink paper and on the bottom of it was printed "Comp. keep for ref. cust. d.a. no. or c.t. no. salesbook no. salescheck no. clerk no. dept. date M." And after M, instead of a name, she had written 13-3138. I took the little pink slip and threw it away and went up to the fourth floor and bought myself a pair of stockings for $.69 and then I came down and went out the customer's entrance.

I wrote Macy's a long letter, and I signed it with all my numbers added together and divided by 11,700, which is the number of employees in Macy's. I wonder if they miss me.

Discussion Plan:

1. Make a list of the things that bother the heroine about working for Macy.
2. What are the reasons that her complaints are justified?
3. How could Macy justify the practices that she complains about?
4. Construct alternatives that would satisfy them both as much as possible?
5. Are there any complaints reasonable from the heroine's perspective that Macy could not possibly be expected to address? How should she respond?
6. Do you feel that the heroine's letter was a thoughtful response; what would you have done in the same situation?

Success and Consequences

Few of us get to attempt anything really extraordinary in our lives. For many of us a steady job, a nice home and a generally comfortable life is what we expect and what we achieve. But what if this life fails to satisfy? How do the needs of the person get reconciled with the responsibilities of being a home-maker and a breadwinner.

Thomas J. Cottle, The Mechanical Man

No one trained in psychology; as I am, can be entirely free of preconceived notions about human personality. Nevertheless, those of us whose work is devoted to life studies (Robert Coles being a pioneer of the technique) consciously strive to avoid the categories of our training.

What we try to do, simply, is listen. During the past 12 years, I have befriended people of all kinds, and their families. I have tried to record their stories in their own words, selecting for publication material that seems to provide some insight into the interior lives of modern Americans.

Almost to my embarrassment, I sometimes find that what these inter-views reveal conforms closely to textbook cases and analyses I have read. Most often, however, they illustrate smaller, more elusive truths about each person's unique view of the world and about the circumstances of life in general.

Often, the people I interview have no special problems. Ted Landis, a 46-year-old lumber supplier, is such a man. Married, the father of two teenage girls, Ted lives well, but he works hard for everything he gets, and he knows that a few slips would put him in a difficult position: he owes money on a car and a house. He doesn't worry openly about his situation, but he reflects on it more than occasionally. He reflects, too, on how little his family seems to know about what goes on inside him. His wife, daughters, and even his sister seem not to try to understand what he might be feeling, tensions he might be concealing.

"You want to summarize my life? I'm a machine. I'm the guy you wind up and he goes to breakfast, and he drinks the coffee, and he makes nice to his family. He drives the car, and he hits the traffic, and he makes it to the office, and he drinks more coffee, and he does his business, which means juggling 2,000 aggravations at one time, and goes to lunch, and does more aggrava-tion-juggling, and hits the car, and hits the traffic. He goes home and makes nice to people, and he tells them not one aggravation, because they're sick and tired of hearing his aggravations, because once or twice, 15 years ago, he mentioned some aggravations he was having and nobody seemed to care. Since they were living in a nice home with a nice yard and they had a little winter vacation and a longer summer vacation, they figured, "How big could his aggravations be?" So he doesn't complain when he does the dishes and watches the TV, and goes to sleep and gets up the next day, and does it all again.

"That's me, the machine, the nice, clean, quiet machine. Only they don't wind you up every day like some people think. They wind you up every day when you're a kid so when you become a man, and grow to be responsible, they don't have to wind you up anymore, because the fact is once you grow up, there isn't anybody around to wind you. You're either wound up for life by then, or you leave the scene entirely. You get my meaning?

"Tired? Oh, you don't get tired from this. The machine doesn't know from tired. Relaxation? Sure, you get a little of that, a little quiet now and then. But how's it going to last? Your kid goes down to the kitchen for a little sandwich, and you call, "Beedie, bring me up an apple." But you're lying there thinking: without me, there's no peanut butter, no jelly, no white bread, no shelf, no refrigerator, no knife, no apple, no staircase—maybe no kid. Do I say something? How can I! These people love me, and I love them. I'm doing it for us, for them, for me. Okay, that's fine. But I ask you, if the machine grinds to a halt, or starts making a lot of clackety-clack sounds so the whole house can hear it, what do these people do? They cannot in a million years love me, or themselves, like they do now.

"I'm supplying the base, the foundation, the quiet, invisible groundwork. You don't think about what a person has to do every day of his life in order for your bedroom to be there, and the stairs to be there, and the bacon and the eggs, and the cereal and the milk, and the walls and the floor, and everything. You don't think that. It's all just there. You expect it to be there. You expect Daddy to be hitting the traffic, and hitting the office, and drinking the coffee, and juggling the aggravations la, la, la, la ...You see it? I'm the expectation. Happiness, fulfillment, satisfaction, for now, for 10-30 years from now? No sir. Thirty years from now means the end of mortgages, means life-insurance policies, means savings accounts, means still-unpaid college tuition bills, means the machine better-the-hell keep going and the machine better-the-hell be quiet.

"I don't know me as a person any more; how can I expect anybody to know me as a person? And I'm one of the lucky ones with a good life. Believe me, I consider myself a very fortunate man. You don't think I can see worse situations? Don't get me started. Every day I tell myself, 'Is this bad?' Take a peek at the alternative: Unemployed? No money coming in? Divorced, with the routine of the wife wanting everything, and, out of the goodness of her heart, she lets you see your own flesh and blood every other Sunday, and the kids oblige you and have a hamburger and are looking at you like to say, 'What the hell did you do to our mother?'

"Oh, yes, it could be so far worse I don't even want to know about it. So you tell yourself, 'Stoke the machine; hope it's wound up nice and tight. Keep it greased with aggravation, promises, lies. Smile nicely at the people you're supposed to smile nicely to; keep everything to yourself.' Say, 'Yes, ma'am, you're absolutely right,' every time they hit you with how easy men have it and how women are tortured and denied and discriminated against. Then hit the traffic and the office and the coffee, and go into your juggling routine all over again.

"When the machine quits, it quits. In the meantime, you keep what they call the old 'low profile,' which means try to stay invisible, not only to the people you live with and work with, but to yourself as well. Eat the right foods; take care of your car, your home, your wife, your kids, your driveway, your storm windows, your attic, your garage, your tools, your yard, your compost heap, your television set, your washer, your dryer, your dishwasher, and hope the machine loves coffee. Ah, for the good life: the role of the American husband.

"I think back on the things I told you, like that machine business. It's not a wind-up machine, like I was telling you. It's the heart. It's the human heart. It's your own heart, a human heart!"

Exercise:

1. Make a list of the social roles you now play.
2. Which are related to economic success and security?
3. Which are satisfying; which are not?
4. Do you feel it practically necessary that you continue playing these roles?
5. What role do practical necessities play in deciding what you do?
6. How do you contrast practical necessity with personal satisfaction?

Success and Choices

The working world measures by its own standards. Success is often counted in terms of how much money is made and how high on the corporate ladder we climb. For the individual the path to success often requires tough decisions. Moral dilemmas in business frequently include conflicts between individual goals, corporate values and group loyalties. How we choose says a great deal about who we are and who we want to be: choice defines the self.

Charlie Russell, Quietus

No two ways about it. Randolph, Besso Oil's first Negro salesman, knew better. Now, he can offer himself no excuse, really. You simply don't go around acting on impulses, even good ones, not if you want to keep your job. Twenty-seven. He is tall, dark and thin: gray Brooks Brothers; with a thick moustache of which he is excessively proud. Randolph sits down and slaps a fist into his open palm: I blew, baby, I blew! If I don't ever blow another one, I blew that one. Though a college man, he still thinks in the language of the streets. In a less turbulent time he would tell you he is bilingual.

"I blew, I blew!" Though released unconsciously the expression feels good as it leaves the rim of his mouth. But, this only paves the way for an added agitation: Has Evelyn heard? He fingers his heavy moustache, turns, and brings into focus Evelyn Manning, the receptionist, Headquarters, Eastern Division. Her head is bent. Engrossed in typing, apparently she has not heard. Yet he stares. Thin face. Natural blond hair. While he is looking at her the hair on the left side of her face unfurls itself mischievously. In one motion there is a toss of her head and a flick of her hand, as she artfully pushes the renegade hair back into place.

Class. Randolph decides that Evelyn has almost as much class as his wife. He likes that, women with class. And he likes being the company's first and only Negro salesman, too. He has just finished a four months' training course, in which he finished first in a class of twenty, and until a few minutes ago he looked forward to a long and profitable career with Besso Oil.

"Damn," he curses himself. What had he been thinking about? He has an urge to break something. Like that night when he was fifteen, and had broken all the windows in the front of the store with rocks. Afterwards he had spent an hour ducking and dodging around corners, setting up a false trail, just in case he was hustled. But no one had followed and later in bed he was overcome with a tingling sensation that had given him a feeling of inner peace engulfing him entirely. He had had that feeling only a few times since: once or twice hearing Charlie Parker, and when he had first entered his virginal wife, Stacey.

For one moment he almost loses control by giving way to anger, as it swells then sweeps swiftly through his body.

"Be cool. Nerves! Be cool." Prayer-like, he repeats the phrase several times and soon he is calm. Randolph lights a cigarette, then quickly loses interest in it. Would you believe it, just ten minutes ago my world was neat as a six-pack, and now it is all gone because of some jive nigger I don't even know.

"Tch," Randolph's tongue feels heavy as it makes the sound against the roof of his mouth. Suddenly he stands and walks towards the far wall where there are pictures hanging. The room is elongated. Black wall-to-wall carpeting. The furniture, done in dull orange leather, has a contemporary motif. Heavy copper ashtrays shaped like boomerangs. The pictures are abstract originals, too. He stares.

He and Teddy discovered Charlie Parker at a party one Friday night. Hip sixteen. The party was in a dimly lit basement and they were drinking wine from paper cups, when somebody put on " Birds of Paradise." Their heads were light from the tokay, and Teddy demanded that the record be played again and again. The music was so good that even he had danced. Finally Teddy had stolen the record, and they spent the rest of the summer listening to "the Bird" weaving in and out of notes.

Stacey. Randolph has a sudden desire to talk to his wife. He walks over towards Evelyn's desk. Evelyn, the receptionist for both J.B. Nash and Larry Weeks, looks up as he approaches. "Say look!" he hesitates. "I'm going down the hall to my office to make a phone call. If Larry should call for me, tell him I've gone to make a phone call. Tell him I'm just down the hall in my office and I'll be right back." Now that he is finished he feels drained.

"OK," Evelyn says, returning to her typing.

Her simple dismissal adds to his anxiety. Why is she so busy all of a sudden? Most of the time, every time I look up there she is in my face. Had he missed a signal between her and Larry, and was she typing up his final papers? He almost asks her, but then decides his name is Sam, and he doesn't give a damn. He turns and walks towards the door. Where however:

It is not "Sam" but Randolph William V he sees reflected in the glass door. Old Randy of the drooping shoulders, scared, going to call his wife to tell her she must return to work because he has just made his last stand.

Randolph stands over his desk, dials his number; and wonders what Stacey will say. Beautiful Stacey who is so proper and knows what fork to use when; who comes, whispering hot obscenities into his ear. It seems only natural that he dials the wrong number. He dials again. FIVE. SIX. SEVEN. He throws the phone on the cradle, and thinks: She is either out shopping, or playing bridge, or at the beauty parlor, but wherever she is, she is doing what she does best—spending my money. He has a second thought: Maybe it is best after all, give the girl a few hours before she gets the news.

Randolph returns to the waiting room. Evelyn looks up from the typewriter, thin lips stretched into a smile, and before he can ask, she glances furtively at Larry's door, then at him and shakes her head, "No."

Randolph answers by making a silent, "Oh," with his mouth. He turns away. It seems forever he's been waiting. There is movement behind him, but even knowing it is Evelyn he jumps, anyway.

He turns. Watches her approach. Evelyn is tall, willowy and promiscuous. Head tilted slightly upwards. Simply attired: black one-piece dress. Just a dab of rouge. Nothing flashy. She is willing to try anything, but she will remain all her life below pain or joy.

Sweetly: "How is it going, Randy?"

It takes some effort, but he shrugs his shoulders. Smiles. "Fine, just fine." Such control gives him joy. He asks, "Why so busy?" indicating the typewriter.

"Oh, that," Evelyn answers matter-of-factly, "my monthly letter to the folks."

Randolph sighs deeply; he should have known. He looks into her eyes and finds in them something mysterious and hard. How could you explain a girl like her? Comes from big money, went to Wellesley, but works as a receptionist? In a real way he feels sorry for her; if he had money, he would do all his work on the French Riviera!

"You were simply wonderful in there," she says, holding his arm. A week ago she had asked him if he was weird and exotic. He had laughed and said no. She has a thing for him, he knows, but since taking this job he has been faithful and has decided that playing the role of the noble savage, or the big black buck for empty white women is no longer an adventure.

He pulls away. Gently. The smile does not leave Evelyn's lips. She is game. Discovering this about her makes him love her a second. However, when Evelyn says, "But I hadn't realized you cared so deeply about things," Randolph regrets even that second.

"Well, sometimes you have to make a stand," he explains. Softly. "You can only let them push you so far." He sees her smile broaden.

"What would you have done?" Randolph asks.

Evelyn turns from his gaze. "Frankly, I would have taken it. What does it matter, really? They can always find someone to do their dirt; but I am rather proud that you didn't." There are tears. Evelyn turns her head quickly and returns to her desk.

Randolph, resuming his pacing, returns to the picture and remembers. It had all begun two months ago and had happened because every Wednesday night he ate "soul" food at the Red Rooster, a bar/restaurant in Harlem. Larry, after taking him on a tour of the company's service stations in Harlem, had offered to drop him off at the Rooster. Passing through his old neighborhood, he had noticed an independent station run by an elderly

Negro, and observed to Larry that this man had no competitors. And did a large volume of business. "Why don't we open a station across the street?" he had suggested playfully.

This afternoon they had suddenly sprung it on him. Anyway you looked at it, it had been a tough lay and a jive scene. It had taken J.B. just twenty minutes to turn years' worth of hustling into cinders.

At lunch, Larry had casually mentioned to him that J.B., the first vice-president, wanted to see him. Routine business. Just to congratulate him for completing his training course. But Randolph had not finished top man by sleeping. From the nuance in Larry's voice he could tell there was more to it than that.

"Well, here he is," bright-eyes Larry, everybody's fat man, had bellowed. Larry, the fourth vice-president, a handshaker and a backslapper, always won at poker. He presented Randolph to J.B. as if he was a prize.

J.B., a short, slight, graying man, had shaken his hand firmly. Randolph decided that the mantle of inherited power rested easily upon J.B.'s shoulders. J.B. made a slight motion, and they had sat down.

"Well, how are things?" J.B. had begun.

Small talk.

God, these guys are cool. Power with capital P. Sometimes he hardly remembered that they were the rulers of the world. But he knew their game: "Wonderful, sir. I envision unlimited opportunities with Besso." J.B. supposed that now that he was part of the team he and his wife should be thinking about raising a family soon. "Oh, yes sir, we were just talking about that very subject last week. Children are so wonderful." Oh, yes, he had been hip to their game.

Then, just like that it was over and J.B. had buzzed Evelyn, inviting her in for a drink.

More small talk.

And while Randolph was plotting a graceful exit, J.B. had said confidentially, "Larry here tells me you have suggested a location for a new station. Good idea. I see why Larry speaks so highly of you. How would you like to be the manager?" Before J.B. finished, the others had stopped talking.

Larry had a conspiratorial expression.

"Ah ... ,sir... ," Randolph had faltered, as J.B. continued.

"Twelve pumps, twenty by thirty garage. The whole works. Leave it open twenty-four hours a day. But I'm sure you and Larry can work out the details."

By this time Randolph's wits had returned: So that was their game. He was not only to be their Negro on display, they also meant to use him to put other Negroes out of business. Why, with him running the place, and by staying open twenty-four hours a day, the poor guy across the street wouldn't last two months. The jive mothers!

"But, why me, what about all my training?" he had asked calmly.

"Be good for you, really. Learn the business inside and out." J.B. had turned to Larry. "How long you think it'll take to set it up?"

Without giving Larry time to answer, without realizing that he was going to do it, Randolph had said:

"If I have a choice, I'd just as soon not." Though he had not meant it, his voice sounded stringent. Evelyn lifted an eyebrow, smiled; Larry, shocked, trembled; only J.B. had remained unperturbed.

"Ah, yes," J.B. seemed tired. "You take that up with Larry."

Randolph, who had not meant to venture so far, was relieved to feel Larry tugging at his sleeve.

"I think you've taken our young friend here by surprise, J.B. Let me talk to him. Ha, ha," Larry had interrupted nervously. "Ha, you didn't mention the extra thousand dollars in it for him."

"Yes, yes," J.B.'s voice sounded distant. Randolph had suddenly realized that the old man was almost asleep on his feet. He had heeded the tug and followed Larry out of the office. When they entered the waiting room, Larry had said curtly: "I'll talk to you in a minute," and had slammed his door, leaving Randolph standing alone in the waiting room. Terror had momentarily set in Randolph's eyes, leaving him with a sense of dread.

Randolph, still deep in thought, turns from the picture, walks to the window and looks down into the streets below: mid-February. Cold. Dark, dull, dank. Too cold even for love.

Randolph stands stroking his moustache thoughtfully. There is in his eyes a trace of sadness. He feels alone. No more Teddy. No more "Bird." Nothing. Teddy, over ten years ago, died in Korea in a riot with "cracker" soldiers. And in the circle in which he now travels, Charlie Parker was never in style. Once he and Stacey had some friends over, and he had put on a "Bird" record. For some reason it had been no good, and he finally made everyone happy by putting on Dave Brubeck.

"Stacey!" Unconsciously. He wants to talk to her in the worst sort of way. Why not try the number again? No. Wait. He decides to think further about his situation:

So. They want to use me to keep other Negroes down, you hip to that? Do they think I'm some kinda nut? I can get another job. I don't have to stand for this mess. Ha, ha, his laughter is profane and deep. Randolph knows the game. Why, he can even predict the line Larry will take with him:

Larry will talk to me like we're all green, as if they are not using me against another colored man. White people are good at that, boy can they talk. Always trying to hide the real issues behind some abstract or unrelated principle. And when old Larry starts talking about free enterprise, I'll tell him to shove it!

Randolph again feels the urge to smash something. To run amuck. His heart cries out that it is so unfair. You spend most of your life just fighting to get on their side. You give up Charlie Parker for them, you even cut down on chasing women, and all for what? Only to be used. What right did they have to decide things among themselves and then tell him he must make a choice? Some choice! Either him, or another black man.

The yen for his wife's voice returns and Randolph finds himself standing in front of Evelyn's desk. "Look, I'm going to ... ," he begins, but the buzz of the intercom interrupts him. Evelyn, her smile erased, speaks:

"Yes, Larry." Pause. Then, tiredly: "Yes, he's standing right here, I'll send him right in." She hangs up the phone, and Randolph has no time to protest that he must call his wife. In a way he is relieved.

"Randy... ," Evelyn begins earnestly, "you were sweet in there before. But don't do or say anything you'll be sorry for afterwards."

Gee thanks. Her attitude bugs him. Next she'd be telling him she knew just how he felt ... She. They had some nerve. Telling him how to fight his battle. A battle that they themselves had once been involved in, but had never completed. But out loud, Randolph says, not unkindly, "Thanks, Evelyn, I really want to thank you for that little bit of advice."

She is a sweet kid, really, and he does not resent her always. And because he feels guilty, he asks: "How do elephants make love in tall grass?" She does not know. "Successfully," he calls over his shoulder and knocks on Larry's door.

Randolph enters, and silently closes the door behind him. Larry is busy with papers. Randolph approaches his desk. Larry, he notices, is wearing his "con-artist" expression. It is a mixture of smugness and cunning; which he tries to hide behind an inoffensive smile. Randolph hesitates, then sits down. He feels giddy and tries several matches before finally lighting his cigarette.

If only I'd had time to call Stacey.

"Randy, baby, relax, relax," Larry urges in a jovial manner. "I know how you're feeling, Randy. You're probably thinking it's all some kind of conspiracy between me and J.B. But let me assure you, I was just as surprised at J.B. as you were." Larry pauses as if weighing his words, and Randolph notices a certain detachment about his manner as he adds, "I guess old J.B. caught you by surprise, eh, fellow?"

I got your "eh, fellow" hanging, baby. Randolph checks this impulsive response; he had had enough of that today. Out loud he says: "Yes, he did sort of catch me off guard. I know what J.B. said, but still the idea of putting an old man out of business ..."

"Come on, Randy," Larry urges. "You're a bright fellow. You know what way the wind is blowing. Everything is big now, from the government on up. Somebody has to do it. If we didn't Standard would do it," he snaps a finger, "just like that. Free Enterprise! It's the law of supply and demand, fellow, the law that our system is based on," Larry finished, obviously pleased with himself.

Now, he knows, is the time to tell Larry to go to hell. That the real issue is his being used. That he does not mind being the "quota-Negro," but does mind very much indeed being used against other Negroes. However, Randolph finds himself unable to speak. Stacey, Stacey! Suddenly he realizes that he has known all along what Stacey would say; just as he knows that he will follow the voice that even now cries out inside him:

They got you in a cross, baby. And they can beat you in so many ways. From your first breath the odds are against you. And they get to you early, they start you out with Mickey Mouse, and you are hooked by the time you are three. Yea, baby, everybody's got a number, and you have to play the game whether you want to or not. When you think about it you don't really have a choice. You just got to go for yourself.

Randolph stirs uncomfortably in his chair.

"Randy, baby, why the long face?" Larry asks, lightly, yet firmly. "I know that this is all sort of sudden. You want some time to think it over? Maybe J.B. wouldn't mind. He probably likes a man who takes his time. You wanna talk it over with your wife?"

"No, no, that's all right," Randolph raises his head with a jerk. "Ha, my wife goes along with anything I say. Yeah. It just doesn't seem right, that's all." He sounds unreasonable he knows.

But Larry cries out in genuine surprise, "Why, Randy, you old shokster, you amaze me, really. Holding out for more money. Amazing. All right, you got yourself a deal. I'll tell J.B. to make it fifteen hundred. Randy, fellow, I can see you are going far with Besso, you're gonna make a lot of money."

"Yes, I'll make a lot of money," Randolph agrees, not caring whether Larry has deliberately misunderstood him or not. But even as he agrees with Larry, even as he thinks of the two cars and the split-level, he feels something in him die: that part of him that had always been free. He feels the loss already. It was vital. As long as he had it, he felt somehow better and different from them.

"So, what you say, kid?" There is a certain urgency in Larry's voice.

"Yea, sure. OK, Larry, we'll get started on it right away," Randolph says, and Larry relaxes, transformed before his eyes.

Then Larry is on his feet, congratulating him warmly, and proudly. Patting his shoulders and repeating that he will go far and make tons of money. He knows this. Yet, he feels unclean, and there is a grimy taste in his mouth.

After several minutes the ritual of the backslapping and handshaking is done. Then Randolph's hand is on the doorknob. He can hardly believe it is over. But as his hand turns the shining knob he hears Larry call, in a friendly manner:

"There is one thing, though, that J.B. did notice, Randy, fellow, you're the only one in the outfit who has a moustache."

Discussion Plan:

1. Identify the values that Randolph should take into consideration in making his choices.
2. Which of these values focus on himself (and his family); which are predominantly concerned with others?
3. How do the values associated with his being a Black person qualify the values that are concerned with himself or his family?
4. How do his racial values compare with abstract principles of social justice?
5. What values are implicit in Besso's decision?
6. How do these corporate values relate to personal values?
7. Do the corporate values have any particular relationship to the values associated with Black people?
8. How do the corporate values compare with abstract principles of social justice?

Autonomy

Earlier in the *Reader* we examined the view that causes acting on human beings freed them from responsibility for what they do. This view seems to rob us of the ability to act in a morally significant sense. There is a radically opposite view that says that the essence of human action is in the act of choice and that whatever causes are reflected in the choosing are irrelevant to morality. The ultimate meaning of human life is in decision—judging a course of action in terms of your sense of self and your values.

Jean Paul Sartre, Existentialism as Humanism

... Dostoevesky once wrote "If God did not exist everything would be permitted"; and that, for existentialism, is the starting point. Everything is indeed permitted if God does not exist, and man is in consequence forlorn, for he cannot find anything to depend upon either within or outside of himself. He discovers forthwith, that he is without excuse. For if indeed existence preceeds essence, one will never be able to explain one's action by reference to a specific human nature; or in other words, there is no determinism—man is free, man *is* freedom. Nor, on the other hand, if God does exist, are we provided with any values or commands that could legitimize our behaviour. Thus we have neither behind us, nor before us in a luminous realm of values, any means of justification or excuse. We are left alone, without excuse. That is what I mean when I say that man is condemned to be free. Condemned, because he did not create himself, yet is nevertheless at liberty, and from the moment that he is thrown into this world he is responsible for everything he does. The existentialist does not believe in the power of passion. He will never regard a grand passion as a destructive torrent upon which a man is swept into certain actions by fate, and which, therefore is an excuse for them. He thinks that man is responsible for his passion, Neither will an existentialist think that a man can find help through some sign being vouchsaved upon earth for his orientation: for he thinks that the man himself interprets the sign as he chooses. He thinks that every man, without support or help whatever, is condemned at every instant to invent man ...

As an example by which you may the better understand ... I will refer to the case of a pupil of mine, who sought me out in the following circumstances. His father was quarrelling with his mother and was also inclined to be a "collaborator"; his elder brother had been killed in the German offensive of 1940 and this young man, with a sentiment somewhat primitive but generous, burned to avenge him. His mother was living alone with him, deeply afflicted by the semi-treason of his father and by the death of her eldest son, and her one consolation was in this young man. But he, at this moment, had the choice between going to England to join the Free French Forces or of staying near his mother and helping her to live. He fully realized that this woman lived only for him and that his disappearance—or perhaps his death—would plunge her into despair. He also realized that, concretely and in fact, every action he performed on his mother's behalf would be sure of effect in the sense of aiding her to live, whereas anything he did in order to go and fight would be an ambiguous action which might vanish like water into sand and serve no purpose. For instance, to set out for England he would have to wait indefinitely, in a Spanish camp on the way through Spain; or, on arriving in England or in Algiers he might be put into an office to fill up forms. Consequently, he found himself confronted by two very different modes of action; the one concrete, immediate, but directed towards only one individual; and the other an action addressed to an end infinitely greater, a national collectivity, but for that very reason ambiguous—and it might be frustrated on the way. At the same time, he was hesitating between two kinds of morality; on the one side the morality of sympathy, or personal devotion and, on the other side, a morality of wider scope but of more debatable validity. He had to choose between those two. What could help him to choose? Could the Christian doctrine? No. Christian doctrine says: Act with charity, love your neighbour, deny yourself for others, choose the way which is hardest, and so forth. But which is the harder road? To whom does one owe the more brotherly love, the patriot or the mother? Which is the more useful aim, the general one of fighting in and for the whole community, or the precise aim of helping one particular person to live? Who can give an answer to that *a priori*? No one. Nor is it given in any ethical scripture. The Kantian ethic says, Never regard another as a means, but always as an end. Very well; if I remain with my mother, I shall be regarding her as the end and not as a means: but by the same token I am in danger of treating as a means those who are fighting on my behalf; and the converse is true, that if I go to the aid of the combatants I shall be treating them as the end at the risk of treating my mother as a means.

If values are uncertain, if they are still too abstract to determine the particular, concrete case under consideration, nothing remains but to trust in our instincts. That is what this young man tried to do; and when I saw him he said, "In the end, it is feeling that counts; the direction in which it is really pushing me is the one I ought to choose. If I feel that I love my mother enough to sacrifice everything else for her—my will to be avenged, all my longings for action and adventure—then I stay with her. If, on the contrary, I feel that my love for her is not enough, I go." But how does one estimate the strength of a feeling? The value of his feeling for his mother was determined precisely by the fact that he was standing by her. I may say that I love a certain friend enough to sacrifice such or such a sum of money for him, but I cannot prove

284

that unless I have done it. I may say, "I love my mother enough to remain with her," if actually I have remained with her. I can only estimate the strength of this affection if I have performed an action by which it is defined and ratified. But if I then appeal to this affection to justify my action, I find myself drawn into a vicious circle.

Discussion Plan:

Sartre claims that the human being is always free to decide her destiny. Discuss the following in terms of the person's probable responses. How is the individual constrained by the situation, how is she still free?
1. John's mother remarries and his new father wants him to change his religion.
2. Ralph discovers that his dead father was an alcoholic.
3. Sharon finds out that her real mother died in a mental institution.
5. Your family becomes destitute.
6. You won a lottery ticket worth five million dollars.
7. You find out that you are a 'test tube baby', and you can never know who your biological father is.
8. You are a test tube baby and your father had a genius level I.Q.
9. Robert is the son of the unknown rapist who raped his mother.
10. Roberta is the daughter of the unknown rapist who raped her mother.
11. Your family was very wealthy in Asia but was forced to immigrate—you now have to work long hours in the family store.
12. You move to a country where you become a minority.
13. You move to a country where you have twenty servants that you are not allowed to treat as equals.
14. You are drafted into the army.
15. You are sentenced to fifteen years in prison for smuggling cocain
16. Your country is occupied by a totalitarian regime.

Essay Assignment:

Sartre claims that the human being is always free, that at each moment we are free to decide for the rest of our lives. Write a two page essay attacking or defending Sartre's position.

SECTION 6: CONCEPTS THAT CONTROL: SEXISM

In previous sections we explored factors that control individuals. We looked at the physical and psychological controls that families have over growing children and then at the controlling institutions of school and work. But control is not limited to individuals, groups and social institutions; ideas control as well.

Among the ideas that control us most are the basic categories that we apply to human beings. Social class, race and sex have been the basis for unequal treatment throughout human history. Ideas used to categorize people are so deeply rooted in societies that even as astute a thinker as Aristotle could convincingly argue within the Greek world view that some individuals were "natural slaves"—people so unequal that they were capable of only a limited existence. Deeply rooted ideas about differences between kinds of people were at the basis of social controls that severely limited both what was expected of individuals and what is permitted. Ideas of inequality, however, are frequently examined in light of even more profound conceptions that conflict with discriminatory prejudice: concepts of justice and fairness.

As our ideas of equality and fairness expand to include larger and larger groups of people from all different cultural and ethnic backgrounds it becomes increasingly difficult to hold on to our beliefs that entire groups of people are to be treated differently. The most recent group to be free from the shackles of discriminatory ideas and the associated limits on life choices have been women.

Sex Roles

Sex stereotyping begins in infancy when fathers and mothers react differently to their new born sons and daughters. It is to be expected that parents' reactions reflect the cultural traditions and norms of the societies within which they were raised. Girl children have been traditionally perceived as dependent, first on the father and then on the husband. This creates problems for the new father who sees the future in terms of the males that will be his rivals for his daughter's affections.

Ogden Nash, Song to be Sung by the Father of Infant Female Children

My heart leaps up when I behold
A rainbow in the sky;
Contrariwise, my blood runs cold
When little boys go by.
For little boys as little boys,
No special hate I carry,
But now and then they grow to men,
And when they do, they marry.
No matter how they tarry,
Eventually they marry.
And, swine among the pearls,
They marry little girls.

Oh, somewhere, somewhere, an infant plays
With parents who feed and clothes him,
Their lips are sticky with pride and praise,
But I have begun to loathe him.
Yes, I loathe with a loathing shameless
This child who to me is nameless,
This bachelor child in his carriage
Gives never a thought to marriage,
But a person can hardly say knife
Before he will hunt him a wife.

I never see an infant (male),
Asleeping in the sun,
Without I turn a trifle pale
And think, is he the one?
Oh, first he'll want to crop his curls,
And then he'll want a pony,
And then he'll think of pretty girls

And holy matrimony.
He'll put away his pony,
And sigh for matrimony.
A cat without a mouse
Is he without a spouse.

Oh, somewhere he bubbles, bubbles of milk,
And quietly sucks his thumbs;
His cheeks are roses painted on silk,
And his teeth are tucked in his gums.
But alas, the teeth will begin to grow,
And the bubbles will cease to bubble;
Given a score of years or so,
The roses will turn to stubble.
He'll sell a bond, or he'll write a book,
And his eyes will get that acquisitive look.
And raging and ravenous for the kill,
He'll boldly ask for the hand of Jill.
This infant whose middle
Is diapered still
Will want to marry
My daughter Jill.

Oh sweet be his slumbers and moist his middle!
My dreams, I fear, are infanticiddle.
A fig for embryo Lohengrin!
I'll open all of his safety pins.
I'll pepper his powder and salt his bottle,
And give him readings from Aristotle,
Sand for his spinach I'll gladly bring,
And tabasco sauce for his teething ring,
And an elegant, elegant alligator
To play with in his perambulator.
Then perhaps he'll struggle through fire and water
To marry somebody else's daughter!

Exercise:

1. List all of the sexist language you can find in the poem.
2. How much of that language was intended to be offensive?
3. How much of it would have been considered offensive forty years ago?
4. How much would be considered offensive now?
5. Is the poem as a whole offensive?
6. Did Nash attempt to be offensive?

Tradition

Girls are supposed to be sexy, pretty and nice. These are three of the traits that define feminity in our culture. Women that have these traits are highly valued and frequently find these sufficient for social success. This creates problems since early success can lead to long term problems.

Jerome Weidman, Slipping Beauty

He was a little man with an untidy beard and a prominent paunch that seemed startlingly out of place because of his emaciated appearance. Winter and summer he wore a battered cap, a leather vest, and a look of indifferent resignation, well seasoned with disgust, that gave no hint of the almost violent loquacity he could attain without even a moment of preparation. In a world of trucks and automobiles he drove a flat, open wagon behind a huge, drooping horse. And although his seltzer bottles came in neatly cased boxes of ten, he preferred to carry them by their spouts, five in each hand, like clusters of grapes, and take his chances on opening doors with shoulder shoves and kicks. His service was erratic, but adequate, and when, by his strange method of rotation, your name came up again to the top of his list, you could no more prevent him from making his delivery than you could convince him that his prices were exorbitant. He has come on Sundays and holidays, during parties and illness, and once, when a severe snowstorm had tied the city's traffic into a knot, he rang the bell after midnight and carried in his ten bottles of seltzer without a word of apology or explanation.

"Look here, Mr. Yavner," I said irritably, "you can't make deliveries as late as this. You can't come ringing bells at this—"

"I can't?" he asked and his eyes widened in a look of surprise that should have warned me.

I knew from experience that it wouldn't do any good. But when you're aroused after midnight from a sleep that you have attained with difficulty and need very much to admit a middle-aged man with his hands full of seltzer bottles that, considering the temperature and the season, you don't need at all, you are apt to forget the things that experience has taught you.

"I mean," I said stubbornly, "you'll just have to learn, Mr. Yavner, that when—"

"Learn?" he said, and the surprise was now in his voice. "I gotta learn?"

I could tell by the glint in his eyes that, from the standpoint of my much-needed sleep, I could have chosen a far more opportune time to bring order into Mr. Yavner's chaotic delivery system. I made a hasty, desperate attempt to head him off.

"Not that I mean anything, Mr. Yavner," I began conciliatingly.

But it was too late.

"In America," Mr. Yavner was saying, shaking his head like a tolerant master with a slow pupil, "in America there's no such thing as learn. In America nobody learns. In America they only teach."

He set down his clusters of empty seltzer bottles and faced me squarely.

"A minute you could listen," he said bluntly, "In the old country, my father, he should rest in peace, he told me I shouldn't play with the knife, I'll cut myself, so if I didn't listen to him, and I played with the knife, so what happened, so I cut myself! He told me, maybe, I shouldn't go in the street without the coat, I'll catch a cold, so I went in the street without a coat, so like he said, I caught a cold! But in America?

He shrugged for emphasis and the habitual look of disgust on his face deepened a shade or two.

"Go try teach children something in America, go," he said. "Listen what I got. I got two daughters, the Above One should take care of them, they're beauties. Sucha two girls like I got, it could be—I don't care—even a governor, he would still be happy to have sucha two daughters, the way mine look. The oldest, my Nettie, is already ten years she's bringing money in the house, steady, every week. She went to business school, she studied hard, she got a good job, she makes steady wage, she puts in the bank, she brings home; is good, no? Comes at night, she comes home, she eats, she helps maybe the mother a little, she reads a book, she listens a little the radio, she goes to sleep like a regular person. Is bad, maybe? In Europe, a girl like that, a girl like my Yettie, she knows to cook, to sew, to bake, to clean, she knows what a dollar is; a girl like that in Europe she could find a dozen—a dozen? A hundred!— she could find a hundred fellahs they should kiss their fingers to the sky seven days a week if she would only look on them a little the right way! But in America? Go be smart in America!

"Then my other daughter, my Jennie, the baby. To look at?—a doll! But lazy—the Above One should save us from such a lazy ones. Came in the middle high school, all of a sudden she got tired! By her, it's no more school. By me, she says no school, so all right, is no school. But instead she should get a job like her older sister. Like Yettie, instead that, so a whole day she lays in bed with magazines and the tsigarettes, and the whole night she's running around with the boys those little roters, they'n got even a job, not one of them in the whole bunch! A whole night long you don't see her, and comes by day, the whole day it's the megazines and the tsigarettes. A whole day long it's smook, smook, smook, smook, smook, smook, smook! No job, no work, no nothing! Only like a king's daughter she lays in the bed the whole day, and you gotta bring her eat, yet, too, and the whole night she's running around the Above One alone knows where!

"But I'm a father, by me is the same thing my Yettie, she works and brings money in house, or my Jennie, she lays in bed there a whole day. So I talk to her, I tell her she should make something from herself; she should get a job and go sleep early like a regular person and get up early and put money in bank and stop so much with the tsigarettes and the boys! Like her sister, Yettie, I tell her she should be. She should learn to cook and sew and keep a house clean and put a little money in bank, so'll come a nice fellah some day, with a good steady job, he'll see what a nice girl she is, she knows what's in a house to do, so he'll marry her, like some day'll happen with her sister Yettie, I tell her, and she'll make for him a good wife. So you think she listens to me? Like I should talk to the wall!

"In Europe, a father talks to a child, so it happens she should know the father was right. But in America?"

He leaned toward me and tapped my shoulder with his finger as he spoke.

"In America is different," he said. "One day, she's laying there in the bed with the megazines and the tsigarettes and the smook, all of a sudden the blankets they catch on fire, in a minute more it's the whole bed, then the curtains, and in one, two, three is there the fire engines and the policemen and the firemen and there's excitement!—Above One in heaven, don't ask! And from the firemen there comes running in one, a nice young fellah, and he picks her up and carries her down from house, and before you can turn yourself around he falls in love with her and two weeks later, they're in a big hurry, they run get married! And he's got yet such a steady job by the city, there, a whole year regular he gets wages."

Mr. Yavner paused, and the disgust in his face gave way to a look of meditative resignation.

"How you think it makes a father feel, he sees his oldest daughter sitting and sitting and the youngest she gets married? Is nice, maybe? So my Yettie, she's older, she went to business school, she's got a job, she knows to cook, and to sew, and to everything, so she's still sitting, waiting! And my Jennie, she's younger, from schools she got right away tired, a job she never had, a whole day she laid in bed smooking tsigarettes and a whole nights she ran around; so my Jennie, she's the one she's got now a fine husband with a steady job!"

He reached down for his clusters of bottles, swung the door open with his foot, and held it wide for a moment with his shoulder as he looked in at me.

"That's your America," he said with the faintest hint of derision in his voice. "That's where you want I should learn things," he said, as he stepped away from the door, and it shut behind him with a crash that echoed throughout the midnight stillness of the house.

Exercise:

1. Describe Mr. Yavnor's ideal of what a woman should be?
2. What is the ideal that he sees represented by Jennie?
3. Do you think Yetta shares either ideal?
4. Is either ideal at least partially applicable today? If so, in what ways?
5. Are there arguments from a contemporary point that support or weaken the ideals implicit in Yavnor's point of view?
6. Are these contemporary arguments only appropriate today or do they apply to the 1940's?
7. Do the contemporary arguments apply to other societies as well?

Beauty

Beauty is said to be in the eye of the beholder, but nevertheless, how we stack up in the popularity sweepstakes reflects commonly shared judgments. How objective are people's estimates of physical attractiveness, and how much do such judgments affect those who are judged?

Psychology Today, Beauty

Plain Girls' High Blood Pressure

Warning: a psychologist has determined that being ugly is dangerous to your health if you are a teenage girl.

Stephen Hansell and his colleagues at Johns Hopkins University conducted four studies of 283 women and 369 men, aged 14 to 76, to determine the relationship, if any, between physical attractiveness and blood pressure. The researchers took an average of three to ten blood pressure readings and had graduate students and other adults rate the subjects, or their photographs, for attractiveness on a scale from one to nine.

Female high school and college students who were rated in the top 50 percent for attractiveness had significantly lower blood pressure than girls rated in the bottom 50 percent. In one study, for example, the pressure averages were 119/75 for the pretty women and 125/80 for the ugly ones. The difference did not turn up among boys and did not appear for grown women or men. The strain of being judged by one's looks, the researchers infer, is particularly savage for teenage girls.

Women's Beauty Fades by Male Convention, Not Conviction

It is easier for a man to age gracefully than it is for a woman: the crow's feet that middle-aged men accept as marks of distinction send middle-aged women to the cosmetic counter. But when male judgments underlie the double standard, they may be more a matter of convention than conviction.

A recent study found that male college students rated middle-aged women as less attractive than middle-aged men only when they had to give their opinion publicly to other men. Those who filled out rating forms in private said just the reverse: they considered middle-aged women more attractive than men who were the same age.

The study involved 320 undergraduates at Florida State University. They rated the attractiveness of 20 pictures of men and women 35 to 55 years old that a panel had preselected for "average" attractiveness. Eighty men and 80 women gave their ratings privately. The remaining subjects were divided into groups of eight (either all men, all women, or mixed) and held up a card with their rating while a researcher read off the number in full view of the group.

Only the men in all-male groups judged the middle-aged women to be less attractive than the middle-aged men. Men in mixed-sex groups did not reveal substantial biases either way; neither did any of the women.

The researchers conclude that "it is clear that beauty is not only in the eye of the beholder but also in the social situation in which the beholder happens to be."

Exercise:

1. Make a list of all of the characteristics that make a man beautiful (handsome).
2. Do the same standards apply to various races; to various cultures?
3. What purposes are served by physical beauty?
4. Are any of the characteristics that make a man beautiful valuable for reasons other than personal approval?
5. What does beauty have to do with social status?
6. Is physical beauty an appropriate standard to use in judging people; in which ways?

Discrimination

Sexism, like racism, places people into categories. People are seen not in terms of what they can do, but in terms of what "people like that" can do. Expectations based on sexist or racist stereotypes place the individual at a disadvantage. Even simple aspects of their lives become more difficult due to limits placed on their achievement by the attitudes of others.

Angelica Gibbs, The Test

On the afternoon Marian took her second driver's test, Mrs. Ericson went with her. "It's probably better to have someone a little older with you." Mrs. Ericson said as Marian slipped into the driver's seat beside her. "Perhaps the last time your Cousin Bill made you nervous, talking too much on the way."

"Yes, Ma'am," Marian said in her soft unaccented voice. "They probably do like it better if a white person shows up with you."

"Oh, I don't think it's that," Mrs. Ericson began, and subsided after a glance at the girl's set profile. Marian drove the car slowly through the shady suburban streets. It was one of the first hot days in June, and when they reached the boulevard they found it crowded with cars headed for the beaches.

"Do you want me to drive?" Mrs. Ericson asked. "I'll be glad to if you're feeling jumpy." Marian shook her head. Mrs. Ericson watched her dark, competent hands and wondered for the thousandth time how the house had ever managed to get along without her, or how she had lived through those earlier years when her household had been presided over by a series of slatternly white girls who had considered housework demeaning and the care of children an added insult. "You drive beautifully, Marian," she said. "Now, don't think of the last time. Anybody would slide on a steep hill on a wet day like that."

"It takes four mistakes to flunk you," Marian said. "I don't remember doing all the things the inspector marked down on my blank."

"People say that they only want you to slip them a little something," Mrs. Ericson said doubtfully.

"No," Marian said. "That would only make it worse, Mrs. Ericson, I know."

The car turned right at a traffic signal, into a side road and slid up to the curb at the rear of a short line of parked cars. The inspectors had not arrived yet.

"You have the paper," Mrs. Ericson asked. Marian took them out of her bag: her learner's permit, the car registration, and her birth certificate. They settled down to the dreary business of waiting.

"It will be marvellous to have someone dependable to drive the children to school every day," Mrs. Ericson said.

Marian looked up from the list of driving requirements she had been studying. "It'll make things simpler at the house, won't it?" she said.

"Oh, Marian," Mrs. Ericson exclaimed. If I could only pay you half of what you're worth!"

"Now, Mrs. Ericson," Marian said firmly. They looked at each other and smiled with affection.

Two cars with official insignia on their doors stopped across the street. The inspectors leaped out, very brisk and military in their neat uniforms. Marian's hands tightened on the wheel. "There's the one who flunked me last time," she whispered, pointing to a stocky, self-important man who had begun to shout directions at the driver at the head of the line. "Oh, Mrs. Ericson."

"Now, Marian," Mrs. Ericson said. They smiled at each other again, rather weakly.

The inspector who finally reached their car was not the stocky one but a genial, middle-aged man who grinned broadly as he thumbed over their papers. Mrs. Ericson started to get out of the car. "Don't you want to come along?" the inspector asked. "Mandy and I don't mind company."

Mrs. Ericson was bewildered for a moment. "No," she said, and stepped to the curb. "I might make Marian self-conscious. She's a fine driver, Inspector."

"Sure thing," the inspector said, winking at Mrs. Ericson. He slid into the seat beside Marian. "Turn right at the corner, Mandy-Lou."

From the curb, Mrs. Ericson watched the car move smoothly up the street.

The inspector made notations in a small black book. "Age?" he inquired presently, as they drove along.

"Twenty-seven."

He looked at Marian out of the corner of his eye. "Old enough to have quite a flock of pickaninnies, eh?"

Marian did not answer.

"Left at this corner," the inspector said, "and park between that truck and the green Buick."

The two cars were very close together, but Marian squeezed in between them without too much maneuvering. "Driven before, Mandy-Lou?" the inspector asked.

"Yes, sir. I had a license for three years in Pennsylvania."

"My employer needs me to take her children to and from school."

"Sure you don't really want to sneak out nights to meet some young blood?" the inspector asked. He laughed as Marian shook her head.

"Let's see you take a left at the corner and then turn around in the middle of the next block," the inspector said. He began to whistle "Swanee River." "Make you homesick?" he asked.

Marian put out her hand, swung around neatly in the street, and headed back in the direction from which they had come. "No," she said. "I was born in Scranton, Pennsylvania."

The inspector feigned astonishment. "You-all ain't Southern?" he said. "Well, dog my cats if I didn't think you-all came from down yondah."

"No, sir," Marian said.

"Turn onto Main Street and let's see how you-all does in heavier traffic."

They followed a line of cars along Main Street for several blocks until they came in sight of a concrete bridge which arched high over the railroad tracks.

"Read that sign at the end of the bridge," the inspector said.

"Proceed with caution. Dangerous in slippery weather," Marian said.

"You-all sho can read fine," the inspector exclaimed. "Where d'you learn to do that, Mandy?"

"I got my college degree last year," Marian said. Her voice was not quite steady.

As the car crept up the slope of the bridge the inspector burst out laughing. He laughed so hard he could scarcely give his next direction. "Stop here," he said, wiping his eyes, "then start 'er up again. Mandy got her degree, did she? Dog my cats!"

Marian pulled up beside the curb. She put the car in neutral, pulled on the emergency, waited a moment, and then put the car into gear again. Her face was set. As she released the brake her foot slipped off the clutch pedal and the engine stalled.

"Now, Mistress Mandy," the inspector said, "remember your degree."

"Damn you!" Marian cried. She started the car with a jerk.

The inspector lost his joviality in an instant. "Return to the starting place, please," he said, and made four very black crosses at random in the squares on Marian's application blank.

Mrs. Ericson was waiting at the curb where they had left her. As Marian stopped the car, the inspector jumped out and brushed past her, his face purple. "What happened?" Mrs. Ericson asked, looked after him with alarm.

Marian stared down at the wheel and her lip trembled.

"Oh, Marian, again?" Mrs. Ericson said.

Marian nodded. "In a sort of different way," she said and slid over to the right-hand side of the car.

Exercise:

Make a list of the racial and sex stereotypes that apply to the list below. Choose stereotypes that you think are standard (even if no longer acceptable) in modern America.

1. Gorgeous sixteen year old cheerleader.
2. Gorgeous sixteen year old female cheerleader.
3. A hippie looking forty year old male teacher.
4. Successful female executive.
5. A Chinese male math student.
6. A Jewish landlord.
7. A male WASP executive.
8. A Polish janitor.
9. A black high school student on the basketball team.
10. A Catholic grandmother.
11. An oriental storekeeper.
12. A pretty female high school teacher.
13. A male elementary school teacher.
14. A woman truck driver.
15. A male dancer
16. A group of Hispanic junior high school age girls.
17. A white high school student who dresses hippie style.
18. An inter-racial group of students dressed punk style.
19. A married couple: black male, white female.
20. A married couple: white male, Asian female.

Stereotypes and Change

No matter who you are, no matter how intelligent or capable you are, the fact that you are female points you to certain kinds of jobs rather than others. Jobs that are stereotyped as "female" frequently involve responsibilities that reflect attitudes towards what women are supposed to be.

Karen Kenyon, A Pink-Collar Worker's Blues

More and more women every day are going out to work. A myth has grown around them: the myth of the "new woman." It celebrates the women executive. It defines her look (a suit), and her drink (Dewar's or perhaps a fine white wine). It puts her "in charge." But it neglects to say whom she is in charge of—probably some other women.

The world still needs helpers, secretaries and waitresses, and the sad truth is that mostly women fill these serving roles. Today more women hold clerical jobs than ever before (4 million in 1950 and 20 million in 1981). Wherever we look, we see the image of the successful woman executive but, in fact, most women are going out to become secretaries. The current totals: 3 million women in management and 20 million clerical employees. So for the majority of working women—the so-called "pink-collar workers"—liberation from home is no liberation at all.

Recently I took a job as a part-time secretary in a department office of a university. I thought the financial security would be nice (writers never have this) and I needed the sense of community a job can bring. I found there is indeed a sense of community among secretaries. It is, in fact, essential to their emotional survival.

Human Beings: I felt a bit like the author of "Black Like Me," a Caucasian who had his skin darkened by dye and went into the South, where he experienced what it was like to be black. Here I was, "a person," disguised as "a secretary." This move from being a newly published author to being a secretary made it very clear to me that the same people who are regarded as creative human beings in one role will be demeaned and ignored in another.

I was asked one day to make some Xerox invitations to a party, then told I could keep one (not exactly a cordial invitation, I thought). The next day I was asked, "Are you coming to the party?" I brightened and said, "Well, maybe I will." I was then told, "Well, then, would you pick up the pizza and we'll reimburse you."

A friend of mine who is an "administrative assistant" told me about a campus party she attended. She was engaged in a lively, interesting conversation with a faculty wife. The wife then asked my friend, "Are you teaching here?" When my friend replied, "Well, no, actually I'm a secretary," the other woman's jaw dropped. She then said, "Don't worry. Nobody will ever guess."

I heard secretaries making "grateful" remarks like, "They really treat us like human beings here." To be grateful for bottom-line treatment was, I felt, a sorry comment.

We think we have freed our slaves, but we have not. We just call them by a different name. Every time people reach a certain status in life they seem to take pride in the fact that they now have a secretary.

It is a fact that it has to be written very carefully into a job description just what a secretary's duties are, or she will be told to clean off the desk, pick up cleaning and the like. Women in these jobs are often seen as surrogate wives, mothers and servants—even to other women.

Many times, when a secretary makes creative contributions she is not given her due. The work is changed slightly by the person in charge, who takes the credit. Most secretaries live in an area between being too assertive and being too passive. Often a secretary feels she has to think twice before stepping in and correcting the grammar, even when she knows her "superior" can't frame a good sentence.

Envy: When after three months I announced to my co-workers that I was quitting, I was met with kind goodbyes. In some I caught a glimpse of perhaps a gentle envy, not filled with vindictiveness at all, but tinged with some remorse. "I'm just a little jealous, that someone is getting out of prison," admitted one woman. "I wish I'd done that years ago," said another.

Their faces remain in my heart. They stand for all the people locked into jobs because they need the money, because they don't know where else to go, afraid there's no place else, because they don't have the confidence or feel they have the chance to do anything else.

I was lucky. I escaped before lethargy or repressed anger or extreme eagerness to please took over. Before I was drawn over the line, seduced by the daily rewards of talk over coffee, exchanged recipes, the photos of family members thumbtacked to the wall near the desk, the occasional lunches to mark birthdays and departures.

I am free now, but so many others are trapped in their carpeted, respectable prisons. The new-woman myth notwithstanding, the true tale of the woman on her own most often ends that way.

As I see it, the slave mentality is alive and well. It manicures its nails. It walks in little pumps on tiny cat feet. It's there every time a secretary says, "Yes, I'll do that. I don't mind" or finds ashtrays for the people who come to talk to someone else. The secretary has often forgotten her own dream. She is too busy helping others to realize theirs.

Research Project:

Explore, using reliable statistics, the change in women's place in the marketplace in the last fifteen years. Limit your research to the United States.

Present your results in the form of a projection as to how you think women are doing and will do.

Do you think the projection shows equality of opportunity and if not now, when.

Social Policy

One of the few persuasive arguments for treating women and men differently involves those occupations that require extraordinary abilities traditionally associated with men: mainly strength and bravery. Recently, in many societies including our own, women have been moving into such occupations.

Time, Women Cops on the Beat

Can they do the job as well as men?

On routine night patrol last August, two policewomen came upon a bizarre scene in downtown Detroit: a naked man, standing the middle of the road with a Doberman pinscher, burning dollar bills. The officers, Katherine Perkins, 35, and Glenda Rudolph, 26, radioed for help and tried to persuade the man to come along quietly. Before they could make the arrest, Sergeant Paul Janness, 31, arrived. The naked man went berserk, flailing away at the policeman. Janness was badly beaten, and claimed that the two policewomen failed to come to his aid. When witnesses agreed, Perkins and Rudolph were charged with cowardice.

Last month a police trial board found both women guilty and recommended dismissal. Then the case was reopened when a last-minute witness showed up and testified that one of the policewomen had "grabbed and kicked" the man during the scuffle with Janness. Though the trial board has met again to evaluate the new testimony, the incident has undermined the reputation of women in operation units. Some women on the force are bitter because their two colleagues were not given the chance to resign quietly. Even if Perkins and Rudolph are cleared, they say the case will leave the lingering impression that female cops are not up to the job. Admits Executive Deputy Chief James Bannon: "If a woman officer went out tomorrow and saved six male officers' lives, the men would call her a superwoman, but it wouldn't change many attitudes."

Are women cops doing the job? The most negative answer came last fall in a study by Sociologist Patricia Weiser Remington. After a year of riding five shifts a week on police patrols in Atlanta, Remington concluded that males cope with the presence of females on the force by dealing with them as natural subordinates—and the females accept the situation. A policeman talks to a policewoman in a teasing kind of banter, as if the female cop were a tomboyish kid sister. Because women cops were not trained in the martial arts or encouraged to handle tough assignments, they often showed a lack of confidence, and sometimes deliberately drove slowly to a potentially violent call. Says Remington: "Either the view of females as weaker or the view and self-image of American police as symbols of physical power will have to change."

Most police departments give a more positive view of women cops than Remington does, but the men in the ranks have their doubts. A 1977 study of the Detroit police found that the men consider women cops liabilities in dangerous situations because of "their physical size." A Philadelphia study concluded that men can handle violent situations better than women can. Not so in Washington, D.C. which has 329 female cops, more than half of them assigned to patrol duties. A sociological study done for the Police Foundation in 1974 found that males and females seem to perform equally well in handling violent citizens, but that a valid comparison is impossible because violence is so rare. TV cops may be embroiled hourly in perilous adventures, but in real life a patrolman's lot is mostly routine and paperwork. The report showed that women cops are less likely to engage in serious misconduct, but noted that they make fewer arrests.

Many supervisors worry about small women going up against large and dangerous men. "When you're dealing with a 250-pound gorilla, I'd prefer to have some beef on my side," says Rochester, N.Y. Police Sergeant Dennis Cole. "Most women are not beefy." Still, Cole admits that women do well and that "police work is getting away from brawn anyway."

An argument in favor of women cops is that they are better than men in talking people out of violence. Says Oakland, Calif., Police Sergeant Earl Sargent: "Just as you don't have to teach a man how to fight—they grow up playing war and cowboys—in the same way, you don't have to teach a woman how to talk." That statement, like many issued by male cops these days, accepts the fact that policewomen are here to stay. Indeed, women routinely face the same dangers as men. Last fall in Oakland a drunk attacked a female cop, and authorities there described it as one of the most savage beatings in recent memory. Says Sargent: "We've had quite a number of females get decked and come up spitting blood."

Time, Dick and Jane in Basic Training

Trials, and errors, of an integrated Army.

One cold April dawn in 1979, the new integrated Army arrived at Fort McClellan, Ala. The jittery recruits of Alpha Company, 87 men and 76 women mostly between the ages of 18 and 22, stepped off the ramshackle buses and began basic training together. They shared barracks (on alternate floors), mess halls and bivouacs, and few occasionally made clandestine love in the laundry room or the latrines. When the six weeks of marching, spitting, polishing, obstacle coursing and weapons training were over, and the tears, exhaustion, pride and exhileration forgotten, writer Helen Rogan asked their commanding officer, a woman, what differences she had noted between the men and women. Said she: "The men overloaded the washing machines because they didn't know how to use them."

As Rogan points out in her groundbreaking new book *Mixed Company: Women in the Modern Army* the answer was not entirely accurate. The women's physical standard was slightly different, mainly because men are generally larger and possess greater upper-body strength. Some women with small hands had trouble negotiating the handguards of the M-16 rifle, others with short legs could not keep up with the standard 30-in. marching step. The women were required to do fewer push-ups and sit-ups than the men (16 push-ups and 27 sit-ups for the women, 40 each for the men), and were allowed a little over 22 minutes, instead of just under 18, for running two miles. According to Rogan, who watched the full cycle of basic: "Some men and women couldn't run; some men cried and were scared. The most important differences were between people when it came to training soldiers." For the most part, she concludes the success of either sex depended on how well the drill sergeant dealt with those individual differences.

The U.S. has more than 67,000 women in its active Army, 8.9% of the total. The women were recruited as a result of national policy, partly in the belief that they might upgrade the declining quality of the all-volunteer force. At enlisted level many of them are, in fact, better educated and motivated than their male counterparts. But they march on the quaking ground of social change, resisted, harassed, endlessly studied with the concentration scientists might devote to a baffling new virus.

The very subject of women in the military stirs deep emotions and prejudices. Wherever women soldiers are involved, they tend to be seen as "the problem," and rarely are they asked for their own solutions. Rogan above all listens—to the veterans of the now disbanded Women's Army Corps to the officers and raw recruits, to the new West Point cadets. She is the first person to report on the experiences of women in the Army, and her book is a touching, though often dispiriting account of personal changes and dashed hopes as men and women are processed into soldiers.

"You have to laugh, or else you'd cry," says a recruit named Elizabeth on the first day of training. The women are issued boots cut so badly that many get stress fractures and muscle spasms. One week they are ordered to tuck in their blouses to look like the males. The next week they are ordered not to, to avoid attracting male attention. Blamed as a group for the failure of any one of them, most still show a stubborn patriotic pride.

Women often do better at riflery than men because they listen to instruction while men tend to think they know it all. A veteran male drill sergeant, proud of his work with female recruits, tells Rogan: "Today's women won't find anything that hard to adjust to in the military. It's the males—you're talking about reconditioning the human male to accept a woman as a wife and mother and at the same time as a fighting partner."

Most of the current arguments, says Rogan, center on physical strength and its importance in soldiering. But, she points out, women are growing up stronger because of school sports programs under Title IX. Even if most women cannot do as many chin-ups or run as far as fast as most men, can't they still make capable modern soldiers? Rogan's answer, which the book mainly bears out, is yes.

Mixed Company suggests that much of the harassment women get in the Army, especially the women cadets at West Point, is due to the Army's own confusion about changing ideas of male identity. Women officer candidates are poor at push-ups, but they prove outstanding on human flexibility, concern for the well-being of their troops and the teamwork essential to an all-volunteer Army. "In the Army, attitudes are fact," Rogan writes. If the attitude is that women are a hindrance to standards, then they tend to be treated accordingly. But one female officer snaps: "Discrimination is unprofessional." Whether or not women are discriminated against she adds, depends on the caliber of leadership at any particular base. In integrating the sexes militarily, the crucial factor seems to be numbers. Rogan concludes, "Wherever there are women, there must be enough women."

Keeping the women the Army already has is a problem. Many leave because of pregnancy (about 8% a year get pregnant). The solutions, Rogan believes, are child care and better provisions for pregnancy leave. Furthermore, Rogan says, the high attrition rate for all women could be sharply reduced if they were taken seriously, properly used and not harassed so much. As she notes of female West Point cadets, "Occasionally people would say scornfully to them, 'If you can't stand up to this, what will you do in combat?' The difference was that in combat they would not have expected to be tortured by their own side."

At the moment, the Administration has put a "pause" on increasing the number of women in the Army, while yet another review board is preparing yet another assessment of the women's role. The idea of females in uniform was new even to Rogan, 35, who was born in Edinburgh and educated at Cambridge University before coming to the U.S. "My idea of a soldier was always a man. It was startling to see women, especially in command over men. And startling to see how quickly it seemed natural." Rogan believes that arguments about women's participation in the Army are now academic. "Women want to serve, and the Army needs the women's contribution if it is to become truly representative of the country it must defend." But the issue may very well depend on whether the volunteer force continues, or the country goes back to the draft.

Discussion Plan:

1. Are there any biological factors that make women incapable of performing satisfactorily in certain occupations?
2. Are these biological factors true of women in all societies or do they have a cultural component?
3. Answer 1. and 2. substituting "men" for "women."

Another Perspective

Women in the USA and elsewhere are achieving increasing visibility as wielders of power: economic, political and intellectual. Frequently we think of this as a purely modern state of affairs. The next selection shows that women, especially older women, have had a vital place in some traditional non-western societies. This contrasts with the way we think of middle-aged women as useless because they are no longer playing the roles of sex object and mother.

Newsweek, The Myths of Middle Age

For a bride in a traditional village of northern India the honeymoon is over almost as soon as the wedding begins. Once married, she becomes a domestic drudge. She is almost completely confined to her home and requires her in-laws' permission to accompany her husband on outings. The main thing she has to look forward to is middle age. In the West, that stage of life is rarely regarded as a beacon of hope. But in India, middle age brings women greater status, authority and freedom, and anthropologists are beginning to wonder whether this isn't a universal phenomenon. "Women's lives appear to improve with the onset of middle age," says anthropologist Judith Brown of Oakland University in Rochester, Mich. "The '40-year-old jitters' and the 'empty-nest syndrome' ascribed to middle-aged women in Western society simply do not apply cross-culturally."

Middle-aged women have received less attention from sociologists than teen-agers or octogenarians. But as interest grows in both women and older people. scientists are beginning to take more notice. As they chart the passages of a woman's life that carry her from a low early in marriage to the pinnacle of prestige in middle age, they are puncturing a myth which has become as pervasive as it is pernicious: that society honors a woman for her ability to bear children and then scorns her when she reaches menopause. "Women with an empty nest are supposed to feel terrible and look worse," explains Brown. "But it just isn't like that."

In societies from the Kung bushmen in Africa to Alaskan Eskimos, there are nearly as many reasons why a woman's lot improves with age as there are reasons for relegating her in her youth to *Kinder und Kuche*. For one thing, a woman with grown children has more time for pursuits outside the family. In addition, maturity brings a flowering of the personality. With motherhood behind her, and with it the expectation that she be nurturing and nonaggressive, a woman exhibits a more "masculine" side to her personality. She often feels self-assured, assertive and independent. A middle-aged man, on the other hand, tends to become less competitive and more passive. Another explanation is the so-called "grandmother hypothesis." According to this view, a woman survives long past her childbearing years so that, once freed from nursing and diaper duty, she can care for her children's children and also keep the lights of culture burning; societies appreciate these functions and honor middle-aged women accordingly. Finally, a middle-aged woman enjoys greater freedom because, once into menopause, she no longer threatens her husband's lineage.

Political Arena: In many cultures, middle age transforms women from indentured servants to chief executive officers of the home and makes them a force in the marketplace and political arena. In India, the middle-aged woman holds the keys to the kitchen. She also pairs up the next generation, seeking daughters-in-law in nearby villages. She commonly attends temple, bhajanas formerly prohibited her and devotes herself to a local guru—sometimes despite her husband's disapproval. She owes this elevation in status not only to her loss of fertility, says Sylvia Vatuk of the University of Illinois, but also to the honor due her for bearing sons and the relief of having her own daughters-in-law assume the maid chores.

In Kelantan on the Malay Peninsula, a woman's prestige derives from her active role in the village economy. Kelantan women, once freed of most child-rearing duties, raise cash crops for the village market and sell handicrafts that they and their husbands make. Trading sometimes takes them far from the village—and from traditional passive roles. "Middle-aged women are among the most active small-scale smugglers engaged in moving long-grained rice from Thailand to Kelantan," says Douglas Raybeck of Hamilton College.

Women of any age are less active than men in village political life, but even this sex barrier tends to break down in middle age. In Botswana, older women in Bakgalagadi society assign household chores to younger ones and are free to dabble in village politics, representing their family in court, for instance. Among the warlike Yanomamo in the Amazon region, older women serve as go-betweens during wars, retrieving the bodies of slain villagers.

As with other kinds of behavior, researchers can see the evolutionary advantages of middle age much more clearly in animals than in people. Among macaque monkeys, older females provide the ties that bind the troop. They care for the youngsters whose mothers have turned their closest attention to newborns, and the middle-aged become fiercely protective in ways that young mothers, who must remain deferential to receive male protection and sexual attention, cannot. This may have been why the human female (as well as the female of several other primates) evolved a life span that is much longer than her fertile years. "A long-lived female is able to defend the genetic endowment she shares with her grandchildren," says David Gutmann of Northwestern University Medical School.

Is it possible, then, that menopause, which marks the start of middle age in women, is actually advantageous to the species? Women suffering from hot flashes and depression may find that hard to believe, but a new theory suggests that these symptoms did not always accompany menopause. Early hominid women, speculates Jane Lancaster of the University of Oklahoma, nursed their last child well into their 40s, by which time menopause was beginning. Since nursing suppresses the distressful side effects of menopause caused by wild swings in estrogen levels, these early women entered middle age without discomfort. "The unpleasant symptoms of menopause are a modern artifact," says Lancaster. "The empty-nest syndrome may derive from a hormonal situation new in human history," and is certainly not a sign that women's useful days are behind them.

Managerial Roles: Despite evidence from macaques to Malays on the value of middle age, Western societies don't exactly glorify it. One reason may be that, unlike Indian women, Western women are not able to build a power base in the home; their families are less dependent on them for food. "Here, if you don't get on with mum, you just go to McDonald's," says Judith Brown. "A woman's real power in administering food is undercut by specialists." In non-Western societies, another source of prestige is the achievement of raising children into adults. But that doesn't count for so much in societies where infant mortality is low.

Even in the West, though, women tend to assume a new role in middle age, as both men and women take over some of each other's traditional functions. Women take jobs outside the home at a time when their husbands are looking forward to retirement. They assume managerial roles abandoned by their spouses, who are becoming less competitive. Gutmann calls this a "return of the repressed," in which men accept their feminine side and women their masculine traits. Usually this is all to the good. Men enjoy a new range of emotional expression and women revel in their assertiveness. In fact, many women in their late 40s who are diagnosed as depressed are not so at all, Gutmann reports. Rather, their stress comes from a fear that their newfound energy and autonomy will provide opportunities that they might not be able to seize. Middle-aged women in America can perhaps take heart from the success of their sisters in traditional societies.

Exercise:

1. Describe the role of middle aged women portrayed in the article.
2. Does the role described differ from the role of middle aged women in American society; from the stereotype of middle aged women in America?
3. From what you know of the societies described, try to account for the status of middle aged women in them.
4. Are the roles described in the article appropriate for middle aged women in American society?
5. Are there analogues to these roles in American society that women do fill?

Society and Relativism

In the last few sections we have explored how societies, through their institu-tions and through their beliefs, influence the people in them. Throughout our explorations of the issues we saw implicit values, judgments as to what the natural and proper way to live is. As human beings have broadened their awareness of other times and different cultures, it has become apparent that what is considered normal and appropriate in one culture may be thought of differently in another. This comparison of cultures has brought into question the objectivity of cultural norms and standards. Among the most influential factors in this reevaluation of the nature of cultural traditions has been the work of anthropologists.

Ruth Benedict, Anthropology and the Abnormal

Modern social anthropology has become more and more a study of the varieties and common elements of cultural environment and the conse-quences of these in human behavior... In the higher cultures the standard-ization of custom and belief over a couple of continents has given a false sense of the inevitability of the particular forms that have gained currency, and we need to turn to a wider survey in order to check the conclusions we hastily base upon this near-universality of familiar customs. Most of the simpler cultures did not gain the wide currency of the one which, out of our experience, we identify with human nature...

As a matter of fact, one of the most striking facts that emerge from a study of widely varying cultures is the ease with which our abnormals function in other cultures. It does not matter what kind of "abnormality" we choose for illustration... there are well-described cultures in which these abnormals function at ease and with honor, and apparently without danger or difficulty to the society.

The most notorious of these is trance and catalepsy. Even a very mild mystic is aberrant in our culture. But most peoples have regarded even extreme psychic manifestations not only as normal and desirable, but even as characteristic of highly valued and gifted individuals. This was true even in our own cultural background in that period when Catholicism made the ecstatic experience the mark of sainthood. It is hard for us, born and brought up in a culture that makes no use of the experience, to realize how important a role it may play and how many individuals are capable of it, once it has been given an honorable place in any society.

... Homosexuality is an excellent example ... Homosexuals in many societies are not incompetent....Wherever homosexuality has been given an honorable place in any society, those to whom it is congenial have filled adequately the honorable roles society assigns to them. Plato's **Republic** is, of course, the most convincing statement of such a reading of homosexuality. It is presented as one of the major means to the good life, and it was generally so regarded in Greece at that time ...

The most spectacular illustrations of the extent to which normality may be culturally defined are those cultures where an abnormality of our culture is the cornerstone of their social structure. It is not possible to do justice to these possibilities in a short discussion. A recent study of an island of northwest Melanesia by Fortune describes a society built upon traits which we regards as beyond the border of paranoia. In this tribe the exogamic groups look upon each other as prime manipulators of black magic, so that one marries always into an enemy group which remains for life one's deadly and unappeasable foes. They look upon a good garden crop as a confession of theft, for everyone is engaged in making magic to induce into his garden the productiveness of his neighbors'; therefore no secrecy in the island is so rigidly insisted upon as the secrecy of a man's harvesting of his yams. Their polite phrase at the acceptance of a gift is, "And if you now poison me, how shall I repay you this present?" Their preoccupation with poisoning is constant; no woman ever leaves her cooking pot for a moment untended. Even the great affinal economic exchanges that are characteristic of this Melanesian culture area are quite altered in Dobu since they are incompatible with this fear and distrust that pervades the culture. They go farther and people the whole world outside their own quarters with such malignant spirits that all-night feasts and ceremonials simply do not occur here. They have even rigorous religiously enforced customs that forbid the sharing of seed even in one family group. Anyone else's food is deadly poison to you, so that communality of stores is out of the question. For some months before harvest the whole society is on the verge of starvation, but if one falls to the temptation and eats up one's seed yams, one is an outcast and a beachcomber for life. There is no coming back. It involves, as a matter of course, divorce and the breaking of all social ties ...

An even more extreme example, because it is of a culture that has built itself upon a more complex abnormality, is that of the North Pacific Coast of North America. The civilization of the Kwakiutl, at the time when it was first recorded in the last decades of the nineteenth century, was one of the most vigorous in North America. It was built up on an ample economic supply of goods, the fish which furnished their food staple being practically inexhaustible and obtainable with comparatively small labor, and the wood which furnished the material for their houses, their furnishings, and their arts being, with however much labor, always procurable. They lived in coastal villages that compared favorably in size with those of any other American Indians and they kept up constant communication by means of sea-going dug-out canoes.

It was one of the most vigorous and zestful of the aboriginal cultures of North America, with complex crafts and ceremonials, and elaborate and striking arts. It certainly had none of the earmarks of a sick civilization. The tribes of the Northwest Coast had wealth, and exactly in our terms. That is, they had not only a surplus of economic goods, but they made a game of the manipulation of wealth. It was by no means a mere direct transcription of economic needs and the filling of those needs. It involved the idea of capital, of interest, and of conspicuous waste. It was a game with all the binding rules of a game, and a person entered it as a child. His father distributed wealth for him, according to his ability, at a small feast or potlatch, and each gift the receiver was obliged to accept and to return after a short interval with interest that ran to about 100 percent a year. By the time the child was grown, therefore, he was well launched, a larger potlatch had been given for him on various occasions of exploit or initiation, and he had wealth either out at usury or in his own possession. Nothing in the civilization could be enjoyed without validating it by the distribution of this wealth. Everything that was valued, names and songs as well as material objects, were passed down in family lines, but they were always publicly assumed with accompanying sufficient distributions of property. It was the game of validating and exercising all the privileges one could accumulate from one's various forbears, or by gift, or by marriage, that made the chief interest of the culture. In its highest form it was played out between rival chiefs representing not only themselves and their family lines but their communities, and the object of the contest was to glorify oneself and to humiliate one's opponent. On this level of greatness the property involved was no longer represented by blankets, so many thousand of them to a potlatch, but by higher units of value. These higher units were like our bank notes. They were incised copper tablets, each of them named, and having a value that depended upon their illustrious history. This was as high as ten thousand blankets, and to possess one of them, still more to enhance its value at a great potlatch, was one of the greatest glories within the compass of the chiefs of the Northwest Coast ...

In their behavior at great bereavements this set of the culture comes out most strongly. Among the Kwakiutl it did not matter whether a relative had died in bed of disease, or by the hand of an enemy, in either case death was an affront to be wiped out by the death of another person ...

This head-hunting that takes place on the Northwest Coast after a death is no matter of blood revenge or of organized vengeance. There is no effort to tie up the subsequent killing with any responsibility on the part of the victim for the death of the person who is being mourned. A chief whose son has died goes visiting wherever his fancy dictates, and he says to his host, "My prince has died today, and you go with him." Then he kills him. In this, according to their interpretation, he acts nobly because he has not been downed. He has thrust back in return ...

These illustrations, which it has been possible to indicate only in the briefest manner, force upon us the fact that normality is culturally defined. An adult shaped to the drives and standards of either of these cultures, if he were transported into our civilization, would fall into our categories of abnormality...

No one civilization can possibly utilize in its mores the whole potential range of human behavior. Just as there are great numbers of possible phonetic articulations, and the possibility of language depends on a selection and standardization of a few of these in order that speech communication may be possible at all, so the possibility of organized behavior of every sort, from the fashions of local dress and houses to the dicta of a people's ethics and region, depends upon a similar selection among the possible behavior traits. In the field of recognized economic obligations of sex tabus this selection is as nonrational and subconscious a process as it is in the field of phonetics. It is a process which goes on in the group for long periods of time and is historically conditioned by innumerable accidents of isolation or of contact of peoples. In any comprehensive study of psychology, the selection that different cultures have made in the course of history within the great circumference of potential behavior is of great significance.

Every society, beginning with some slight inclination in one direction or another, carries its preference farther and farther, integrating itself more and more completely upon its chosen basis, and discarding those types of behavior that are uncongenial. Most of those organizations of personality that seem to us most uncontrovertibly abnormal have been used by different civilizations in the very foundations of their institutional life. Conversely the most valued traits of our normal individuals have been looked on in differently organized cultures as aberrant. Normality, in short, within a very wide range, is culturally defined. It is primarily a term for the socially elaborated segment of human behavior in any culture; and abnormality, a term for the segment that that particular civilization does not use. The very eyes with which we see the problem are conditioned by the long traditional habits of our own society.

It is a point that has been made more often in relation to ethics than in relation to psychiatry. We do not any longer make the mistake of deriving the morality of our locality and decade directly form the inevitable constitution of human nature. We do not elevate it to the dignity of a first principle. We recognize that morality differs in every society, and is a convenient term for socially approved habits. Mankind has always preferred to say, "It is a morally good," rather than "It is habitual," and the fact of this preference is matter enough for a critical science of ethics. But historically the two phrases are synonymous.

The concept of the normal is properly a variant of the concept of the good. It is that which society has approved. A normal action is one which falls well within the limits of expected behavior for a particular society. Its variability among different peoples is essentially a function of the variability of the behavior patterns that different societies have created for themselves, and can never be wholly divorced from a consideration of culturally institutionalized types of behavior.

Each culture is a more or less elaborate working-out of the potentialities of the segment it has chosen. In so far as a civilization is well integrated and consistent within itself, it will tend to carry farther and farther, according to its nature, its initial impulse toward a particular type of action, and from the point of view of any other culture those elaborations will include more and more extreme and aberrant traits.

Each of these traits, in proportion as it reinforces the chosen behavior patterns of that culture, is for that culture normal. Those individuals to whom it is congenial either congenitally, or as the result of childhood sets, are accorded prestige in that culture, and are not visited with the social contempt or disapproval which their traits would call down upon them in a society that was differently organized. On the other hand, those individuals whose characteristics are not congenial to the selected type of human behavior in that community are the deviants, no matter how valued their personality traits may be in a contrasted civilization.

The Dobuan who is not easily susceptible to fear of treachery, who enjoys work and likes to be helpful, is their neurotic and regarded as silly. On the Northwest Coast the person who finds it difficult to read life in terms of an insult contest will be the person upon whom fall all the difficulties of the culturally unprovided for. The person who does not find it easy to humiliate a neighbor, nor to see humiliation in his own experience, who is genial and loving, may, of course, find some unstandardized way of achieving satisfactions in his society, but not in the major patterned responses that his culture requires of him. If he is born to play an important role in a family with many hereditary privileges, he can succeed only by doing violence to his whole personality. If he does not succeed, he has betrayed his culture; that is, he is abnormal.

...The vast majority of the individuals in any group are shaped to the fashion of that culture. In other words, most individual are plastic to the moulding force of the society into which they are born. In a society that values trance, as in India, they will have supernormal experience. In a society that institutionalizes homosexuality, they will be homosexual. In a society that sets the gathering of possessions as the chief human objective, they will amass property...The small proportion of the number of deviants in any culture is not a function of the sure instinct with which that society has built itself upon the fundamental sanities, but of the universal fact that, happily, the majority of mankind quite readily take any shape that is presented to them ...

Exercise:

1. What are the main conclusions Benedict tries to argue for in her article.
2. Construct an outline of the major points Benedict makes in support of these conclusions.
3. Criticize the argument by finding weaknesses in the premises. Are her terms clear and well defined? Are the claims she makes plausible? Are there factors she omits that may weaken her conclusion?
4. If you accept her premises, must you agree with her conclusions?
5. What do actual social practices have to do with judging actions to be morally right or wrong?

PART III: WHERE AM I GOING?

From where you stand now in your life, how can you tell in which direction you ought to go? The choices you must make are not the relatively simple ones of whether to go to the movies or to the rock concert, whether to wear jeans or fancy duds. Instead you must choose a career, someone to love, a life style. How do you decide such important issues?

We all make choices, great and small, based on our past experience and our values. Experience tells us that rock concerts are exciting. But other factors must be taken into consideration. One set of values, economic, weighs the relative cost of a movie tickets and tickets for the concert. Often that is the value which decides the issue. Another value is more psychological, concerts make you feel great. Perhaps it is worth the price. Or social values might prevail—everyone is going! The same kind of process works in deciding on a career or a life style. But even in trivial cases past experience is, at best, an unreliable guide to the future, both in matters of fact and in values.

How can you be sure that the future will look like the past? It usually does. The sun has risen today just as it has day after day throughout the history of the world. But can we be sure, absolutely positively sure, that the sun will rise again tomorrow, or the next day, or the next year? We tend to ignore such questions, because we have so much evidence from our experience and that of others, and from scientific findings on the nature of the universe. If only decisions about what we should do in life could be based on such evidence!

The problem is making judgements based on experience is especially acute when we are young because our experience is relatively limited. Of course, we can get advise based on the experience of others: friends, parents, teachers. We can read books and consult experts. But how can we be sure what they say applies to us, to our future? Perhaps our future will not resemble their past. After all things are always changing and to complicate matters people change too, perhaps most of all.

Our value systems, as well as our world undergo periodic changes. The invention and popularization of the automobile, for example, changed America's family structure by giving individuals increased mobility. This in conjunction with industrialization and urbanization allowed people to travel, breaking family ties and patterns of interdependence. The result, values that held families together were altered.

Sometimes our perception of the world is responsible for the change of values. When we were little we accepted our parents values. But as we got older, we began questioning the legitimacy of these values. Our parents didn't seem like absolute authorities any more. Soon teachers followed as their authority seemed limited in the light of our expanded awareness of alternatives. Then political and even religious leadership was brought into question.

All of the changes actual and anticipated make a right decision, one that will be good in the near and distant future, seem impossible. It makes you want to push the button on the cosmic VCR and freeze the action. How can we be sure what aspects of the future will look enough like the past, to make our decisions work?

The urge to stabilize things takes many forms. Some people maintain that the although the things we experience changes, the invisible structure of the universe is always the same, If you are a scientist, you might maintain that the laws of nature are always true no matter how different things seem to be. If you are a clergyman, you might insist that God's laws always remain the same. We already know how deceptive appearances can be. Appearances might change but reality might not. It would be foolish to build a future on mere appearances, on a delusion. It is, of course, very difficulty to figure out what reality is all about. So we have not progressed very far in solving the problem of how to make critical decisions.

Oddly enough certain things about people do not seem to change that radically or that quickly. There are certain expectations for our lives, already recorded by ancient people, that seem unchanged today. Perennially people want happiness. Usually happiness involves loving and being loved. Gratification of these basics, mental, physical and sexual desires along with the self satisfaction of a life lived well are things that despite apparent changes show continuity with the traditions of countless societies for thousands of years. Love, romance and sex lead to marriage, and marriage leads to family. To live without these is to break with deeply ingrained patterns in human history and, seemingly, in human evolution.

We can also anticipate that at some point in a person's life the patterns will be clear enough to do some summing up. Part of being a self conscious individual, being a person who take responsibililty for the moral side of life, is being willing to stop at the junctures that show the meaning of past experience, and ask for an evaluation: Given the life I have led so far, where do I stand? How can I view what my life has been—both to see where I am heading and to see the meaning of where I have been.

This is not a common question to ask young people or for young people to ask. Traditionally, such questioning occurs at the end of life. But life is always in the process of ending., Each stage of life is both a beginning and a culmination. We end the *Reader* with a section which mimics the story by Joyce Carol Oates: Where am I going? Where have I been?

SECTION 1: LOVE AND SEX

Poets write about it. Singers sing about it and everybody yearns for it—love. Each culture erects its idols to love. The idols are arrayed in the luminous garments that each tradition dictates. Each appears different and unfamiliar to those in another culture. But disrobed the images are all the same, shaped to the human need for intimate emotional and physical relationships. The most popular image of love in our culture is dressed in romantic garments with lace and flowers, in soft tones of pink and mauve. Reality often belies the beauty of the image. The desire for love is no idol. It is real and powerful. The longing for, the possessing and the losing of love are often full of pain and pleasure, To love is in many ways to put yourself at risk.

You may love in vain and suffer the pain of rejection, You may love and be abused emotionally or physically by your loved one, You may find love only to be prevented by some one or something, from keeping it. In spite of all these possibilities we are persistant in our search for love. Human beings can be perverse. They often feel if a game isn't dangerous, it is not worth playing. But loss of love is only one of the pitfalls.

Love is not merely a spiritual union of two kindred souls. It has a physical side to it. Love and sex are clearly not identical. We frequently want (have) one without the other. The traditional image offers both in one glorious and delicious confection. Reality falls short of the image. Sexual union may be an expression of love or lust. In either case the conception that results may be physical as well as emotional.

The desire to have children is, for many the motive for finding love and having sex—part of the biological and psychological imperative to mate, to breed and insure the continuance of the human species and the genes. There may be personal imperatives involved as well: the need to pass on the family name, to live through another whose life you can shape, to create an individual who will love you uncritically. In some cases, there is no imperative. Conception is an unanticipated and undesired accident, possibly a threat to life, love or self esteem.

There are times when it seems we are inhabited by several beings within ourselves. When our sexual urges are the strongest, they seem to take on an individuality all there own. These sexual beings in us have their own single minded interest that does not coincide with our best interests. They want one thing and they want it badly. Values, logic, reason—they act as if nothing should stand in their way. Learning to live with and control these powerful beings in our life is one of life's great challenges. They must be taught to listen to us and follow our will, either because we decide that to follow these urges is contrary to our concept of duty or because we decide that the consequences of our action will be harmful to ourselves or to others. In either case the decision we are making is a moral one, the first from an ethic of principle and the second from an ethic of results.

Due to lack of experience and the strength of urges, young people do not see or do not want to see the problems inherent in forming close physical and emotional relationships. Unfortunately modern society does not make matters any easier. Traditionally, we were told to shun sex with all but our marriage partner. Purity, chastity and virginity were highly valued—clearly more for women than for men—but nonetheless these virtues are held as models of pre and extra-marital behavior. Sex we are told, must not be valued for the pleasure it gives. Pleasure is merely a side-effect that encourages us to use sex for the purpose of procreation. The picture is clear. Personal choices were pre-determined by an accepted conventional morality. Nothing seems that clear any more. Media fill our lives with sexually provocative images. Society offers us the advantage of technology in contraception and gives us a legal remedy for accidental conception. But this does not alter the principles upon which the traditional view is based. What are we to do? The moral problems are as real as our needs.

The problems multiply when we begin to see that not only are love and sex conjoined in our society but so are sex and power. The politics of domination is filled with sexual imagery. Because of their sexual characteristics, it is maintained, women must be passive and obediant and men are the masters. Masters must control and punish wayward servants and slaves so that order will be preserved. Lift the robe of our romantic image of love and you will find sexual violence, The feeling of powerlessness that prevades modern society serves to exaggerate an individuals frustrations. Sexual relationships are still acceptable outlets through which to vent these frustrations. Thinking about love and sex inevitably leads to facing violence.

There is another side of love, which, luckily and happily, makes it worth the effort. We leave it to you to experience that for yourself.

The Romantic Image: traditional

Literature and film have created an idealized image of love—a romantic image uncolored by pain and mundane reality. Love and sex appear in the most glowing colors, attracting our attention and stimulating the deep needs that seem part of peoples' natural responses. The poets have guaranteed that love seems the most desirable of all states.

William Shakespeare, Sonnet 18

Shall I compare thee to a summer's day?
Thou art more lovely and more temperate:
Rough winds do shake the darling buds of May,
And summer's lease hath all too short a date:
Sometime too hot the eye of heaven shines,
And often is his gold complexion dimm'd;
And every fair from fair sometime declines,
By chance, or nature's changing course untrimm'd;
But thy eternal summer shall not fade,
Nor lose possession of that fair thou ow'st;
Nor shall Death brag thou wander'st in his shade,
When in eternal lines to time thou grow'st.
   So long as men can breathe or eyes can see,
   So long lives this, and this gives life to thee.

Discussion Plan:

Shakespeare's metaphor, comparing ones beloved to a summer's days has become one of the best known in English literature. Spell out the metaphor by showing how the rest of the poem develops the theme. Using your analysis, describe the specific attributes Shakespeare claims his lover has.

Does the careful analysis weaken or strengthen your understanding of the sonnet? Your enjoyment of the sonnet?

Writing Assignment:

Chose a metaphor around which you will write a short poem extolling the virtues of a real or imagined lover. Make sure to develop the metaphor through the use of relevant images.

Discussion Plan:

Contrast your poetic metaphors with Shakespeares and with the poems of your classmates. What attitudes towards love are implicit in the various metaphors? How do the various metaphors express the attitudes they do?

The Romantic Image: modern

Expressing feelings of romantic love seems naturally linked to sexuality. There is a tintillating sexual tension between the two young people in the next story as they, with mutual consent, put themselves in a situation where sex can happen. There is an excitement, an innocence and a naive perfection that expresses much of the modern tradition of healthy sexual love.

Judy Blume, Forever

Sharon and Ike live in a garden apartment in Springfield. All the outside doors are painted green. "I hope nobody thinks we're trying to break in," I said, as Michael put the key in the lock, "because there's an old lady watching us." I pointed to a window.

"Don't worry about her." Michael pushed the door open. "That's Mrs. Cornick ... she lives downstairs ... she's always in the window." He waves at her and she dropped her shade. "Come on ... their place is upstairs."

The stairs led into the living room. "It's nice," I said, looking around. There wasn't much furniture but they had a fantastic Persian rug and three posters of chimpanzees riding bicycles. I walked over to a plant and held up a leaf. "Too much water ... that's why the edges are turning brown."

"I'll tell Sharon you said so."

"No, don't ... then she'll know I've been here."

"So?"

"So, I just don't want her to know ... okay?"

"I don't see why ... but okay. You want something to eat?"

"Maybe ..." We went to the kitchen which was small and narrow with no outside window.

Michael opened the refrigerator. "How about an apple ... or a grapefruit? That's about all I see."

"I'll have an apple."

He polished it off on his shirt, then tossed it to me. "I'll show you around the place," he said.

Since I'd already seen the living room and the kitchen we started with the bathroom. "Notice the indoor plumbing." Michael demonstrated how to flush the toilet.

"Very interesting," I told him.

"And hot and cold running water." He turned on both faucets.

"Luxurious."

"Also, a genuine bathtub." He stepped into it and I pulled the curtain around him. While he was in there I wrapped the apple core in some toilet paper and hid it in my pocketbook. Michael jumped out of the tub, grabbed my hand and said, "Onward ..."

We both knew there was just one room left to see. "Presenting ..." Michael said, and he bowed, "the bedroom."

There was a brass bed, covered with a patchwork quilt and a LOVE poster hanging on the wall, above it. There were also two small chests, piled high with books.

Michael jumped up and down on the bed while I watched from the doorway. "Good mattress ..." he said, "nice and firm ... in case you're interested."

"For jumping, you mean?"

"For whatever ..." He lay down and looked at the ceiling. "Kath ..."

"Hmmm ..."

"Come here ..."

"I thought we were just going to talk."

"We are ... but you're so far away ... I don't want to shout."

"I can hear you fine."

"Cut it out ... will you?"

I went to the bed and sat on the edge. "There's one thing I'd really like to know ..."

"What's that?"

"Have you brought any other girls up here?"

"Your jealous streak is showing."

"I admit it ... but I still want to know."

"Never," he said. "I've never brought a girl up here."

"Good."

"Because I just got my own key."

"You rat!" I yelled, grabbing a pillow and swatting him with it.

"Hey ..." He knocked the pillow out of my hands and pinned me down on the bed. Then he kissed me.

"Let me go, Michael ... please."

"I can't ... you're too dangerous."

"I'll be good ... I promise."

He let go of my arms and I wrapped them around him and we kissed again.

"You're beautiful," he said, looking down at me.

"Don't say things like that ..."

"Why, do they embarrass you?"

"Yes."

"Okay...you're ugly! You're so ugly you make me want to puke." He turned away and leaned over the side of the bed making this terrible retching noise.

"Michael...you're crazy...stop it...I can't stand that!"

"Okay."

We lay next to each other kissing, and soon Michael unbuttoned my sweater and I sat up and unhooked my bra for him. While I slipped out of both, Michael pulled his sweater over his head. Then he held me. "You feel so good," he said, kissing me everywhere. "I love to feel you next to me. You're as soft as Tasha."

I started to laugh.

"What?" Michael asked.

"Nothing..."

"I love you, Kath."

"And I love you," I said, "even though you're an outsy."

"What's an outsy?"

"Your belly button sticks out," I said, tracing it with my fingers.

"That's not the only thing that sticks out."

"Michael...we're talking about belly buttons."

"You are..."

"I was explaining that you're an outsy and I'm an insy...you see how mine goes in?"

"umm..." he said, kissing it.

"Do belly buttons have a taste?" I asked.

"Yours does...it's delicious...like the rest of you." He unbuckled my jeans, then his own.

"Michael...I'm not sure...please..."

"Shush...don't say anything."

"But Michael..."

"Like always, Kath...that's all..."

We both left on our underpants but after a minute Michael was easing mine down and then his fingers began exploring me. I let my hands wander across his stomach and down his legs and finally I began to stroke Ralph.

"Oh, yes...yes..." I said, as Michael made me come. And he came too.

We covered up with the patchwork quilt and rested. Michael fell asleep for a while and I watched him, thinking the better you know a person the more you can love him. Do two people ever reach the point where they know absolutely everything there is to know about each other? I leaned over and touched his hair. He didn't move.

Discussion Plan:

The scenario in *Forever* presents a model of an adolescent sexual experience:

What are the background conditions that make the experience seem so perfect?

How do the feelings and attitudes expressed by the lovers add to the sense of perfection?

How does what the lovers do make the experience ideal?

Go over your responses to the questions; which of the background conditions, attitudes and actions described seem realistic?

Does your destimations of the plausibility of the scenario presented affect your attitude towards the scenario?

Given that the situation is exactly as described, would you say the young lovers are justified in making love?

Apparently, the lovers do not "go all the way." There are obvious advantages to limiting sexual exploration. Can even limited sexual activity be harmful?

Love and Consequences

The eagerness to explore love is a characteristic of young people. A ponderous metaphor reminds us that caution might be more appropriate.

D.H. Lawrence,
The elephant is slow to mate

The elephant, the huge old beast,
is slow to mate;
he finds a female, they show no haste,
they wait.

for the sympathy in their vast shy hearts
slowly, slowly to rouse
as they loiter along the river-beds
and drink and browse

and dash in panic through the brake
of forest with the herd,
and sleep in massive silence, and wake
together, without a word.

So slowly the great old elephant hearts
grow full of desire,
and the great beasts mate in secret at last,
hiding their fire.

Oldest they are and the wisest of beasts
so they know at last
how to wait for the loneliest of feasts,
for the full repast.

They do not snatch, they do not tear;
their massive blood
moves as the moon-tides, near, more near,
till they touch in flood.

Writing Assignment:

Use any one of the following animals: rat, sheep, dog, butterfly, snake, lion or lioness as a substitute for the elephant in Lawrence's poem. Rewrite the poem by directly placing your choice of animal and its characteristics in place of Lawrence's to generate new metaphors for love.

Exercise:

Make a list on the blackboard of the images and metaphors as related to the various animals chosen by the students in the class.
Using a scale of 1 to 5, evaluate the resulting items from positive to negative in terms of a sexual relationship.
Use this ranking to make a composite of a perfect sexual love relationship.

In Love and Out of Love

A "perfect love." What power that has. The image of love sets us panting. Our bodies and our minds crave love. We can not wait. We want it all. We will pay any price. The rational cautious side of our nature is overwhelmed by the passionate, adventurous side. Rather than elephants we are tigers. But what if love ends?

John Collier, The Chaser

Alan Austen, as nervous as a kitten, went up certain dark and creaky stairs in the neighborhood of Pell Street, and peered about for a long time on the dim landing before he found the name he wanted written obscurely on one of the doors.

He pushed open this door, as he had been told to do, and found himself in a tiny room, which contained no furniture but a plain kitchen table, a rocking chair, and an ordinary chair. On one of the dirty buff-colored walls were a couple of shelves, containing in all perhaps a dozen bottles and jars.

An old man sat in the rocking-chair, reading a newspaper. Alan, without a word, handed him the card he had been given. "Sit down, Mr. Austen," said the old man very politely. "I am glad to make your acquaintance."

"Is it true," asked Alan, "that you have a certain mixture that has-er-quite extraordinary effects?"

"My dear sir," replied the old man," my stock in trade is not very large—I don't deal in laxatives and teething mixtures—but such as it is, it is varied. I think nothing I sell has effects which could be precisely described as ordinary."

"Well, the fact is—" began Alan.

"Here, for example," interrupted the old man, reaching for a bottle from the shelf. "Here is a liquid as colorless as water, almost tasteless, quite imperceptible in coffee, milk, wine, or any other beverage. It is also quite imperceptible to any known method of autopsy."

"Do you mean it is a poison?" cried Alan, very much horrified.

"Call it a glove-cleaner if you like," said the old man indifferently. "Maybe it will clean gloves. I have never tried. One might call it a life-cleaner. Lives need cleaning sometimes."

"I want nothing of that sort," said Alan.

"Probably it is just as well," said the old man. "Do you know the price of this? For one teaspoonful, which is sufficient, I ask five thousand dollars. Never less. Not a penny less."

"I hope all your mixtures are not so expensive," said Alan apprehensively.

"Oh dear, no," said the old man. "It would be no good charging that sort of price for a love potion, for example. Young people who need a love potion very seldom have five thousand dollars. Otherwise they would not need a love potion."

"I am glad to hear that," said Alan.

"I look at it like this," said the old man. "Please a customer with one article, and he will come back when he needs another. Even if it is more costly. He will save up for it, if necessary."

"So," said Alan, "you really do sell love potions?"

"If I did not sell love potions," said the old man reaching for another bottle, "I should not have mentioned the other matter to you. It is only when one is in a position to oblige that one can afford to be so confidential."

"And these potions," said Alan. "They are not just—just—er—"

"Oh, no," said the old man. "Their effects are permanent, and extend far beyond casual impulse. But they include it. Bountifully, insistently. Everlastingly."

"Dear me!" said Alan, attempting a look of scientific detachment. "How very interesting!"

"But consider the spiritual side," said the old man.

"I do, indeed," said Alan.

"For indifference," said the old man, "they substitute devotion. For scorn, adoration. Give one tiny measure of this to the young lady—its flavor is imperceptible in orange juice, soup, or cocktails—and however gay and giddy she is, she will change altogether. She will want nothing but solitude, and you."

"I can hardly believe it," said Alan. "She is so fond of parties."

"She will not like them any more," said the old man. "She will be afraid of the pretty girls you may meet."

"She will actually be jealous?" cried Alan in a rapture. "Of me?"

"Yes, she will want to be everything to you."

"She is, already. Only she doesn't care about it."

"She will, when she has taken this. She will care intensely. You will be her sole interest in life."

"Wonderful!" cried Alan.

"She will want to know all you do," said the old man. "All that has happened to you during the day. Every word of it. She will want to know what you are thinking about, why you smile suddenly, why you are looking sad."

"That is love!" cried Alan.

"Yes," said the old man. "How carefully she will look after you! She will never allow you to be tired, to sit in a draught, to neglect your food. If you are an hour late, she will be terrified. She will think you are killed, or that some siren has caught you."

"I can hardly imagine Diana like that!" cried Alan, overwhelmed with joy.

"You will not have to use your imagination," said the old man. "And, by the way, since there are always sirens, if by any chance you should, later on, slip a little, you need not worry. She will forgive you, in the end. She will be terribly hurt, of course, but she will forgive you—in the end."

"That will not happen," said Alan fervently.

"Of course not," said the old man. "But, if it did, you need not worry. She would never divorce you. Oh no! And, of course, she herself will never give you the least, the very least, grounds for—uneasiness."

"And how much," said Alan, "is this wonderful mixture?"

"It is not as dear," said the old man, "as the glove-cleaner, or life-cleaner, as I sometimes call it. No. That is five thousand dollars, never a penny less. One has to be older than you are, to indulge in that sort of thing. One has to save up for it."

"But the love potion?" said Alan.

"Oh, that," said the old man, opening the drawer in the kitchen table, and taking out a tiny, rather dirty-looking phial. "That is just a dollar."

"I can't tell you how grateful I am," said Alan, watching him fill it.

"I like to oblige," said the old man. "Then customers come back, later in life, when they are rather better off, and want more expensive things. Here you are. You will find it very effective."

"Thank you again," said Alan. "Goodbye."

"Au revoir," said the old man.

Discussion Plan:

1. What are the fears and expectations that govern Alan's concern?
2. What expectations govern the old man's attitudes?
3. Are Alan's fears and desires realistic?
4. What of the old man's?
5. Is the difference in their perspective based on different experiences?
6. Do you think the old man has the right to assume Alan's generation will share the same attitudes as his previous customers?
7. The old man thinks he understands certain facts about human nature. Given your understanding of human nature, attack or defend his views.

Love and Loss

The romantic image is of eternal love. When you are in love it is difficult to imagine that love may ever end.

Anonymous, Western Wind

Western wind, when will thou blow?
The small rain down can rain,-
Christ, if my love were in my arms
And I in my bed again!

Writing Assignment:

The above is my all time favorite sad love poem. The saddest poem I ever wrote is:

So strange to taste
the first of spring
and yet forlorn
at having lost you.

Now you try to write one.

Love and Despair

The issues of love are deep and complex. A simple love between a boy and a girl twists and turns around the other relationships that have developed between the lovers and others. Parental love, sexual love, romantic love, filial love, all work in different ways, creating obligations and mutually irreconcilable circumstances. Each love relationship commits us, and such commitment can prove dangerous. The consequences of love can be tragic.

Alphonse Daudet, The Girl in Arles

The road leading down from my mill to the village passes near a farmhouse at the other end of a big courtyard planted with hackberry trees. It is a typical Provencal farmer's house, with its red tiles, great brown irregular front, and, at the very top, the weathervane, the pulley for hoisting the hay, and some brown tufts of hay sticking out of the loft.

Why had this house arrested my attention? Why did its shut gate make my heart ache? Though I could not have explained why, the place gave me a chill. It was too quiet…When you passed by, the dogs did not bark and the guinea-fowl ran away without a sound. On the inside not a word was spoken. No sound at all, not even the tinkle of a mule's bell. Had there not been white curtains at the windows and smoke rising above the roof, you would have thought the place deserted.

Yesterday, just at noon, I was returning from the village, and to get out of the sunlight I walked beside the wall of the farm in the shade of the hackberry trees. On the road in front of the house some farm hands were silently finishing the loading of a haywagon. The gate had been left open, I glanced in as I passed and saw, at the other end of the courtyard, with his elbows on a big stone table, and his head in his hands, a tall, white-haired old man, wearing a vest that was too short and a pair of tattered breeches. I stopped. One of the men said to me in a low voice, "Shh. It's the master. He's been that way ever since his son's tragedy."

At this moment a woman and a little boy, dressed in black and carrying huge gilt prayerbooks, passed by us and went into the farmhouse.

"…the mistress and the younger son coming home from mass," the man added. "They go every day, ever since the boy killed himself. Oh, sir, what an affliction! The father is still wearing his funeral clothes; we can't get him to take them off…Get up, horse!"

The wagon began to move away. Wishing to hear more, I asked the driver if I might get up beside him, and there, atop the load of hay, I learned the whole heart-breaking story…

His name was Jan. He was a fine peasant lad, twenty years old, discreet as a girl, steady and of an open countenance. As he was very good-looking, women would stare at him; but he had no thought for any of them but one—a little girl in Arles, dressed always in velvet and lace, whom he had once met in the stadium there. At first nobody at the farm approved of this love affair. The girl was considered a flirt, and her family were not country people. But Jan wanted his Arlesienne, no matter what. He would say, "I'll die if they don't let me have her."

They had to give in. It was decided that the wedding should take place after the harvest.

One Sunday evening, in the courtyard of the farmhouse, the family were finishing dinner. It was almost a wedding feast. Jan's fiancee was not present but they had drunk her health many times ... A man came to the gate and in a shaky voice asked to speak to Master Esteve, to him only. Esteve got up and went out to the road.

"Master," said the man, "you are about to marry your boy to a deceiver, who for two years has been my mistress. I will prove what I say: here are her letters! ... Her parents know all about it and had promised her to me; but since your son has been courting her, neither they nor that fine girl want any more of me ... It would seem to me, though, that after that she couldn't be anyone else's wife."

"Very well," said Master Esteve after looking at the letters. "Come in and drink a glass of muscatel."

The man answered: "No thanks! I am too unhappy to drink." And he went away.

The father came back in, his face expressionless, and resumed his place at the table. The feast ended cheerfully.

That evening Master Esteve and his son went out together into the fields. They stayed out a long while; when they came back, the mother was waiting up for them.

"Wife," said the farmer, taking her son to her, "give him a kiss. He is unhappy..."

Jan spoke no more of the girl in Arles. He still loved her, however, all the more that he had been made to see her in someone else's arms. Only he was too proud to say anything; that is what killed him, poor fellow. Sometimes he would spend whole days alone in a corner, without moving. Other days he would rush out into the fields and by himself do the work of ten laborers. When evening came, he would set out toward Arles and walk straight ahead till he saw the slender spires of the town rising in the sunset. Then he would come back. He never went any farther.

Seeing him like this, always sad and lonely, the people at the farm did not know what to do. They were afraid something frightful would happen. At the table one day his mother, looking at him with her eyes full of tears, said to him:

"All right. Listen, Jan, if you want her in spite of everything, we'll let you have her..."

His father, red-faced with shame, lowered his head. Jan made a gesture that meant "no," and went out.

From that day on he changed his manner, pretending to be gay all the time, so as to reassure his parents. Once more he was to be seen at dances, in the tavern, and at the fair. On election day at Fonvieille, he was the one who led the dancing of the farandole.

His father said, "He is cured." His mother, though, was still worried, and kept an eye on her child more carefully than ever. Jan slept with his younger brother, very near the silkworm nursery; the poor old woman made a bed for herself near their room—she said that the silkworms might need her during the night.

The feast of Eloi, patron saint of farmers, came around. There was a great celebration at the farm: *chateau neuf* for everybody, and the mulled wine flowed like water. Fireworks of all sorts, the hackberry trees full of colored lanterns...hurrah for Saint Eloi! They almost farandoled themselves to death. The young brother burned a hole in his new blouse. Even Jan seemed to be happy; he tried to make his mother dance, and the poor woman cried for joy.

At midnight everybody went to bed. They needed sleep. Jan did not go to sleep, though. His brother said afterwards that he sobbed all night. Oh, he had it bad, let me tell you.

At dawn the next day his mother heard someone running across his room. She seemed to have a presentiment: "Jan, is that you?"

Jan did not reply, he was already on the ladder.

Instantly his mother got out of bed: "Jan, where are you going?"

He climbed up to the hayloft, she climbing after him.

"Son, in the name of heaven!"

He shut the door and bolted it.

"Jan, my little Jan, answer me. What are you going to do?"

She groped for the latch with her old, shaking hands ... A window opening the thud of a body on the flagstones of the courtyard, and that was all.

The poor fellow had said to himself, "I love her too much; I am going away..." Ah, wretched souls that we are! It is a pretty hard thing that contempt cannot extinguish love.

That morning the village people were asking each other who could be screaming that way, down at the Esteve farm.

In the front of the stone table in the courtyard, covered with dew and blood, the mother, quite naked, was wailing with her dead child in her arms.

Exercise:

The tragedy in the story involves a conflict of values. Identify the values of the participants of the drama by distinguishing between:

a) the social values, the values held in common by most of the members of the community

b) the personal values of Master Esteve, the man at the gate and the girl

c) the personal values of Jan

Given these values, look for overlaps, that is, social values that are held by particular individuals and individuals that share specific values with each other.

Identify those values that conflict in the situation of the story. How do shared and conflicted values account for the motivation of the main characters: Jan, his father, the man at the gate, and the girl.

Could the tragedy have been avoided? Attempt to define positions of reconciliation, first from the point of view of the communities shared values and then from the points of view of the key characters. Make sure to take into account values that would have to be changed in order to resolve the conflict.

Theory of Value

In exploring the tragedy of *The Girl in Arles* we were forced to compare conflicting values. This is difficult since it is hard to know how to judge among values like love and honor. In Part II we looked at the theory that claims all values are basically the same, that they all reduced to the happiness or pleasure of the individuals involved. If we had a common denominator for values, conflicts might be resolved by simple calculations. Are things really that easy?

John Stuart Mill, Utilitarianism

The creed which accepts as the foundation of morals "utility" or the "greatest happiness principle" holds that actions are right in proportion as they tend to promote happiness; wrong as they tend to produce the reverse of happiness. By happiness is intended pleasure and the absence of pain; by unhappiness, pain and privation of pleasure. To give a clear view of the moral standard set up by the theory, much more requires to be said; in particular, what things it includes in the ideas of pleasure and pain, and to what extent this is left an open question. But these supplementary explanations do not affect the theory of life on which this theory of morality is grounded—namely, that pleasure and freedom from pain are the only things desirable as ends; and that all desirable things (which are as numerous in the utilitarian as in any other scheme) are desirable either for pleasure inherent in themselves or as means to the promotion of pleasure and the prevention of pain.

Now such a theory of life excites in many minds, and among them in some of the most estimable in feeling and purpose, inveterate dislike. To suppose that life has (as they express it) no higher end than pleasure—no better and nobler object of desire and pursuit—they designate as utterly mean and groveling, as a doctrine worthy only of swine, to whom the followers of Epicurus were, at a very early period, contemptuously likened; and modern holders of the doctrine are occasionally made the subject of equally polite comparisons by its German, French and English assailants.

When thus attacked, the Epicureans have always answered that it is not they, but their accusers, who represent human nature in a degrading light, since the accusation supposes human beings to be capable of no pleasures except those of which swine are capable. If this supposition were true, the charge could not be gainsaid, but would no longer be an imputation; for if the sources of pleasure were precisely the same to human beings and to swine, the rule of life which is good enough for the one would be good enough for the other. The comparison of the Epicurean life to that of beasts is felt as degrading, precisely because a beast's pleasures do not satisfy a human's conception of happiness. Human beings have faculties more elevated than the animal appetites and, when once made conscious of them, do not regard anything as happiness which does not include their gratification. I do not, indeed, consider the Epicureans to have been by any means faultless in drawing out their scheme of consequences from the utilitarian principle. To do this in any sufficient manner, many Stoic, as well as Christian elements require to be included. But there is no known Epicurean theory of life which does not assign to the pleasures of the intellect, of the feelings and imagination, and of the moral sentiments a much higher value as pleasures than to those of mere sensation. It must be admitted, however, that utilitarian writers in general have placed the superiority of mental over bodily pleasures chiefly in the greater permanency, safety, uncostliness, etc., of the former—that is, in their circumstantial advantages rather than in their intrinsic nature. And on all these points utilitarians have proved their case; but they might have taken the other and, as it might be called, higher ground with entire consistency. It is quite compatible with the principle of utility to recognize the fact that some kinds of pleasure are more desirable and more valuable than others. It would be absurd that, while in estimating all other things quality is considered as well as quantity, the estimation of pleasure could depend on quantity alone.

If I am asked what I mean by the difference of quality of pleasures, or what makes one pleasure more valuable than another, merely as a pleasure, except it being greater in amount, there is but one possible answer. Of two pleasures, if there be one to which all or almost all who have experiences of both give a decided preference, irrespective of any feeling of moral obligation to prefer it, that is the more desirable pleasure. If one of the two is, by those who are competently acquainted with both, placed so far above the other that they prefer it, even though knowing it to be attended with a greater amount of discontent, and would not resign it for any quantity of the other pleasure which their nature is capable of, we are justified in ascribing to the preferred enjoyment a superiority of quality as far outweighing quantity as to render it, in comparison, of small account.

Now it is an unquestionable fact that those who are equally acquainted with and equally capable of appreciating and enjoying both do give a most marked preference to the manner of existence which employs the higher faculties. Few human creatures would consent to be changed into one of the lower animals for a promise of the fullest allowance of a beast's pleasures; no intelligent human being would consent to being a fool, no instructed person would be an ignoramus, no person of feeling and conscience would be selfish and base, even though they should be persuaded that the fool, the dunce, or the rascal is better satisfied with his lot than they are with theirs. They would not resign what they possess more than he for the most complete satisfaction of all the desires which they have in common with him. If they ever fancy they would, it is only in cases of unhappiness so extreme that to escape from it would exchange their lot for almost any other, however undesirable in their eyes. A being of higher faculties requires more to make him happy, is capable probably of more acute suffering, and certainly accessible to it at more points, than an inferior type; but in spite of these liabilities, he can never really wish to sink into what he feels is to be a lower grade of existence. We may give what explanation we please of this unwillingness; we may attribute it to pride, a name which is given indiscriminately to some of the most and to some of the least estimable feelings of which mankind is capable; we may refer it to love of liberty and personal independence, an appeal to which was with the Stoics one of the most effective means for the inculcation of it; to the love of power or to the love of excitement, both of which do really enter into it and contribute to it; but its most appropriate appellation is a sense of dignity, which all human beings possess in one form or other, and in some, though by no means in exact, proportion to their higher faculties, and which is so essential a part of the happiness of those in whom it is strong that nothing which conflicts with it could be otherwise than momentarily an object of desire to them. Whoever supposes that this preference takes place at a sacrifice of happiness—that the superior being, in anything like equal circumstances, is not happier than the inferior—confounds the two very different ideas of happiness and content. It is indisputable that the being whose capacities for enjoyment are low has the greatest chance of having them satisfied; and a highly endowed being will alway feel that any happiness which he can look for, as the world is constituted, is imperfect. But he can learn to bear its imperfections, if they are at all bearable; and they will not make him envy the being who is indeed unconscious of the imperfections, but only because he feels not at all the good which these imperfections qualify. It is better to be a human being dissatisfied than a pig satisfied; better to be Socrates dissatisfied than a fool satisfied. And if the fool, or the pig, are of a different opinion, it is because they only know their side of the question. The other party to the comparison knows both sides.

Exercise:

1. What is the main issue that Mill's argument is trying to clarify?
2. What is the major distinction he is trying to make?
3. What criteria does Mill propose to distinguish between qualitatively distinct pleasure?

Discussion Plan:

Do you think that Mill holds happiness as the only value? What other values does Mill allude to? Are these reducible to happiness?

What does Mill mean by "higher faculties"? How does this relate to happiness?

What is the role of "imperfection" at the end of the piece? How does this qualify the "happiness principle"?

Mill asks us to imagine ourselves as an animal or a "fool" to see whether we would accept happiness in its terms. Can we do this?

Is Mill right that the higher being "knows both sides"?

Exercise:

Mill claims that values are to be compared by looking at choices that people make. Try to develop a hierarchy of values to account for these life styles:

1. college professor
2. rock star
3. drug addict
4. nun
5. high school football player

Explore the values in terms of their relation to pleasure. Is pleasure sufficient to account for the life style choices?

Sex Roles

Love and sexuality are as dangerous as they are desirable. So each society has set up safeguards to protect the individuals who inevitably get involved in these relationships. Because love and sex expose a person and make them vulnerable, socially acceptable sexual stereotypes are constructed, giving the uninitiated the mask of expected behavior. Up until recently, it was expected that a young man would be sexually aggressive, competing for status with other young men by winning the most desirable young females. Such behavior was considered both normal and desirable. When such behavior is looked at from a distance its value might be less obvious.

Walter Bernstein, Houseparty

The small room was crowded, but the boy managed to get through without spilling the drink he held in his hand.

"Hello," he said to the girl on the window seat. "You're late," she said. "Last time you were faster."

"I couldn't help it," the boy said. "The place is filling up."

The girl accepted the glass and took a long drink. She looked up at the boy and took another drink. Then she set the glass down. "What do they put this Scotch in with—an eye-dropper?" she asked.

"I'll get you some more."

"No, never mind." She turned to look out of the window.

"That's the library," the boy said.

"Your friend told me. I guess he wanted me to get the idea. He told me five times. Look," she said, "There's a clock on the other side of that tower, too, isn't there?"

"Sure," said the boy. "Four of them."

"Does it keep the same time as this one?"

"Sure."

The girl looked triumphant. "How do you know?" she asked.

"Well—" the boy said. He was a trifle uneasy. "Well, I guess it does."

"You ought to find out," the girl insisted. "You really ought to find out. That clock on the other side might be slow. If you can see only one clock at a time, how do you know it isn't slow?"

"I guess you don't know," said the boy. "You have to take their word for it."

"I'd find out if I were you," said the girl, shaking her head slowly. She took another drink. "You really ought to know." She looked out of the window, then turned back to the boy. "What do they call this place again?"

"Dartmouth," said the boy.

"That's a silly name," said the girl. She finished her drink. "Do you think you could get me another one of these with some Scotch in it?"

"Sure," said the boy. He took the glass and started through the crowd. The girl put her nose against the pane and looked out of the window.

After a while the boy came back, holding the drink above his head so it wouldn't be spilled. He tapped the girl on the shoulder. "Hello," he said. "I'm back."

The girl looked at him. "Go away," she said, "I never heard of you."

"I'm your date," said the boy. "I'm bringing you another drink."

The girl peered at him. "So you are," she said. She took the drink and returned to the window.

"I got a little more Scotch this time," the boy said.

The girl turned around. "You're cute," she said.

The boy blushed. "Look," he said, "are you having a good time?"

"I'm having a wonderful time," the girl said. "I am having a simply wonderful time." Her eyes were very large and bright.

"I'm glad," said the boy. He sat down and took hold of her hand. The girl looked at his hand holding hers and then up at his face. She looked at his hand again and took another drink. The boy held on to her hand and leaned forward. "Do you really dance in a chorus?" he said.

"When I'm working," the girl said. "they call us chorus girls." She put her head next to his. "Who squealed?"

"Oh, no one." The boy was emphatic. "My sister told me. Remember? You know my sister. She introduced us in New York."

The girl nodded. "I know your sister." She hiccuped gently. "Little bitch."

The boy released her hand and sat up straight. Seeing his startled expression, the girl put her fingers to her mouth. "There I go again, always belching in public," she said. She leaned toward the boy, "Pardon me."

"Sure," said the boy. "Sure." He sat up very straight.

The girl was beating out a rhythm on the glass with her fingernails, watching the crowd. "How long do you have to stay in this place?" she asked.

"No special time," said the boy. "We can leave now if you want."

"Not here," said the girl. "I mean in college."

"Oh. Four years. I have one to go."

"That's a long run." She drained her glass and looked at the boy. "You're cute," she said. She put down the glass and took up his hands. "You have nice hands."

The boy gave her hands a slight squeeze. "So have you," he said, but the girl had turned away.

"You touch that glass," she was saying to a girl about to sit down, "and I'll lay you out like a rug." She retrieved the glass and held it out to the boy. "How about another drink?"

"Sure," said the boy. He took the glass and moved into the crowd. As he was pouring the liquor, another boy came over and put an arm around his shoulders.

"How're you doing?" he asked.

The boy spilled a little soda into the glass and started back toward the window.

"Fine," he called back. "Fine." He dodged someone carrying a tray. "She's a cinch." he said.

Discussion Plan:

What motives do the two characters have for acting the way they do? Why is the boy at the party? Why is the girl there?

How do you account for the differences in the things they say? The things they do?

Construct the social stereotypes that the two characters are using as the basis for their interactions with each other. What assumptions is each making about the other? Are these the most plausible assumptions given the way the characters are acting.?

Are either of the characters acting honestly in the situation? What would constitute an honest interaction given those circumstances?

Are either of the characters acting naturally? Is naturally the same as honestly?

Given your sense of their motives and their assumptions, is it possible for them to be either natural or honest and get what they want?

Some Contemporary Views

The culture role of the aggressive young man is complemented by the passive and virtuous young woman. The aggressor needs his prey. The two stereotypes reinforce each other. How do we view woman who do not accept the passive role; how do we perceive sexually aggressive woman?

Abigail Van Buren, Dear Abby

DEAR ABBY:

I wrote to you about a year ago, telling you how depressed I was because I was dumped by a boy I thought I loved. I wanted to show him I could be "popular," so I threw away my self-respect and went all the way with three different guys on the first date. None of them ever called me back, and I felt so cheap I wanted to die. Then I wrote to you and you told me I would never get a decent boy friend by going all the way with him. You encouraged me to try to rebuild my self-esteem and to keep my morals high from then on, and it would pay off.

That's exactly what I did, and you were right. I am now going with this really great guy who respects me. We have a lot of fun together, and I am all through worrying and praying and feeling cheap.

If this letter convinces only one girl that premarital sex doesn't pay, it will be worth printing. I am no kid. I'm 22, and I've never been happier in my life. You wished me good luck, Abby, and it finally came my way. Thanks for saving my life.

HAPPY IN HARTFORD

DEAR HAPPY:

No thanks due me. I only threw you a rope. You caught it.

Psychology Today, Do Sexually Active Women Have Less Character?

Coming to college has given me a chance to get out from under my parents' wing and experience life. Before, my parents kept a tight rein and watched whoever I went out with. Now I can spend the night with any man I please ... I don't have to sneak around to satisfy my desires—I can be out in front with them.

How stands the "revolution" in campus sexual values? Among university and community college students in Norfolk, Virginia, a woman who talks this way about sex still tends to be thought of as having less character and maturity than a woman who says that she is saving herself for the man she intends to marry.

In a recent study, a cross-section of undergraduates at Old Dominion University and a nearby community college read autobiographic descriptions of women whose attitudes toward sex were either permissive (as in the sketch above), conservative ("I might be willing to have sex eventually, but only with someone I plan to marry"), and neutral ("I have more friends now than I've ever had before"). Sixty men and 60 women rated each type on 25 pairs of adjectives, such as good-bad, mature-immature, and friendly-unfriendly.

While the students' opinions may be more typical of the South than of other regions, both men and women rated the permissive women as more irresponsible, immoral, immature, and insecure than the neutral or sexually conservative women. On overall character, an attribute that the researchers measured by combining the ratings on "good," "responsible," and "moral," the permissive women received a rating close to minus 10 on a scale ranging from minus 15 to plus 15 while the other two types received character ratings of about plus 5.

The students did think that the permissive women would be more friendly than the sexual conservatives. Even so, answers to another question showed that both men and women were most likely to want the conservative women as friends.

Exercise:

In the following list, identify those elements that are central to the sex roles of the group to which you belong. Using a scale of 1 to 5 rank them as to importance.

1. Girls do not ask boys out on the first date.
2. Girls can invite boys to parties.
3. A boy can ask a girl to come home with him after school.
4. Boys always "make the first move."
5. Boys want sex more than girls.
6. Girls need an excuse to have sex.
7. Girls tell their friends what happens on a date.
8. Boys who "kiss and tell" are out to ruin a girl's reputation.
9. If your going steady you owe the boy sex.
10. The girl decides "how far to go."
11. No boy refuses sex with a girl he likes.
12. A girl who has sex with many boys is a "slut."
13. A boy who is not going steady can have sex with as many girls as he is able to.

14. A girl can have sex with a boy she is not going with if he is exceptionally popular and good looking.
15. Boys can go to prostitutes.
16. Any girl can find sex if she wants it.
17. If you experiment with people of the same sex you are "gay."
18. Girls can go out with experienced older men.
19. No boy would ever want to date an older women, except perhaps for easy sex.
20. Boys like pornography and think of sex as dirty.

Discussion Plan:

The two short pieces reflect the cultural stereotype in response to sexually available women. How do your answers to the preceding exercise compare to these attitudes.?

If your answers are different from the prevailing stereotypes, how can you account for the differences in attitude? Outline those value elements that your groups sexual attitudes are based on.

What are the sources of these values; are they based on:
a) your peer groups attitudes
b) the society in which we live
b) parental authority
c) religious authority
d) the media
e) based on biological differences between males and females
f) based on psychological difference—"human nature"
g) other?

Pregnancy: traditional view

Many of the rules restricting sexuality come from the real human complications of unwanted pregnany. These complications are both personal and social, reflecting boundaries within which pregnancies can be "wanted." The social context for a wanted pregnancy is marriage, the personal context, love and desire to be together. When a child is to be born unwanted, the society makes demands on the individuals involved that frequently out-weigh the personal.

James Joyce, The Boarding House

Mrs. Mooney was a butcher's daughter. She was a woman who was quite able to keep things to herself: a determined woman. She had married her father's foreman and opened a butcher's shop near Spring Gardens. But as soon as his father-in-law was dead Mr. Mooney began to go to the devil. He drank, plundered the till, ran head-long into debt. It was no use making him take the pledge: he was sure to break out again a few days after. By fighting his wife in the presence of customers and by buying bad meat he ruined his business. One night he went for his wife with the cleaver and she had to sleep in a neighbour's house.

After that they lived apart. She went to the priest and got a separation from him with care of the children. She would give him neither money nor food nor house-room; and so he was obliged to enlist himself as a sheriff's man. He was a shabby stooped little drunkard with a white face and a white moustache and white eyebrows, pencilled above his little eyes, which were pink-veined and raw; and all day long he sat in the bailiff's room, waiting to be put on a job. Mrs. Mooney, who had taken what remained of her money out of the butcher business and set up a boarding house in Hardwicke Street, was a big imposing woman. Her house had a floating population made up of tourists from Liverpool and the Isle of Man and, occasionally, artistes from the music halls. Its resident population was made up of clerks from the city. She governed the house cunningly and firmly, knew when to give credit, when to be stern and when to let thing pass. All the resident young men spoke of her as The Madam.

Mrs. Mooney's young men paid fifteen shillings a week for board and lodgings (beer or stout at dinner excluded). They shared in common tastes and occupations and for this reason they were very chummy with one another. They discussed with one another the chances of favourites and outsiders. Jack Mooney, the Madam's son, who was clerk to a commission agent in Fleet Street, had the reputation of being a hard case. He was fond of using soldiers' obscenities: usually he came home in the small hours. When he met his friends he had always a good one to tell them and he was always sure to be on to a good thing—that is to say, a likely horse or a likely artiste. He was also handy with the mits and sang comic songs. On Sunday nights there would often be a reunion in Mrs. Mooney's front drawing-room. The music-hall artiste would oblige; and Sheridan played waltzes and polkas and vamped accompaniments. Polly Mooney, the Madam's daughter, would also sing. She sang:

"I'm a naughty girl.
You needn't sham:
You know I am."

Polly was a slim girl of nineteen; she had light soft hair and a small full mouth. Her eyes, which were grey with a shade of green through them, had a habit of glancing upwards when she spoke with anyone, which made her look like a little perverse madonna. Mrs. Mooney had first sent her daughter to be a typist in a corn-factor's office but, as a disreputable sheriff's man used to come every other day to the office, asking to be allowed to say a word to his daughter, she had taken her daughter home again and set her to do housework. As Polly was very lively the intention was to give her the run of the young men. Besides, young men like to feel that there is a young woman not very far away. Polly, of course, flirted with the young men but Mrs. Mooney, who was a shrewd judge, knew that the young men were only passing the time away: none of them meant business. Things went on so for a long time and Mrs. Mooney began to think of sending Polly back to type-writing when she noticed that something was going on between Polly and one of the young men. She watched the pair and kept her own counsel.

Polly knew that she was being watched, but still her mother's persistent silence could not be misunderstood. There had been no open complicity between mother and daughter, no open understanding but, though people in the house began to talk of the affair, still Mrs. Mooney did not intervene. Polly began to grow a little strange in her manner and the young man was evidently perturbed. At last, when she judged it to be the right moment, Mrs. Mooney intervened. She dealt with moral problems as a cleaver deals with meat: and in this case she had made up her mind.

It was a bright Sunday morning of early summer, promising heat, but with a fresh breeze blowing. All the windows of the boarding house were open and the lace curtains ballooned gently towards the street beneath the raised sashes. The belfry of George's Church sent out constant peals and worshippers, singly or in groups, traversed the little circus before the church, revealing their purpose by their self-contained demeanour no less than by the little volumes in their gloved hands. Breakfast was over in the boarding house and the table of the breakfast-room was covered with plates on which lay yellow streaks of eggs with morsels of bacon-fat and bacon-rind. Mrs. Mooney sat in the straw arm-chair and watched the servant Mary remove the breakfast things. She made Mary collect the crusts and pieces of broken bread to help to make Tuesday's bread-pudding. When the table was cleared, the broken bread collected, the sugar and butter safe under lock and key, she began to reconstruct the interview which she had had the night before with Polly. Things were as she had suspected: she had been frank in her questions and Polly had been frank in her answers. Both had been somewhat awkward, of course. She had been made awkward by her not wishing to receive the news in too cavalier a fashion or to seem to have connived and Polly had been made awkward not merely because allusions of that kind always made her awkward but also because she did not wish it to be thought that in her wise innocence she had divined the intention behind her mother's tolerance.

Mrs. Mooney glanced instinctively at the little gilt clock on the mantel-piece as soon as she had become aware through her revery that the bells of George's Church had stopped ringing. It was seventeen minutes past eleven: she would have lots of time to have the matter out with Mr. Doran and then catch short twelve at Marlborough Street. She was sure she would win. To begin with she had all the weight of social opinion on her side: she was an outraged mother. She had allowed him to live beneath her roof, assuming that he was a man of honour, and he had simply abused her hospitality. He was thirty-four or thirty-five years of age, so that youth could not be pleaded as his excuse; nor could ignorance be his excuse since he was a man who had seen something of the world. He had simply taken advantage of Polly's youth and inexperience: that was evident. The question was: What reparation would he make?

There must be reparation made in such case. It is all very well for the man: he can go his ways as if nothing had happened, having had his moment of pleasure, but the girl has to bear the brunt. Some mothers would be content to patch up such an affair for a sum of money; she had known cases of it. But she would not do so. For her only one reparation could make up for the loss of her daughter's honour: marriage.

She counted all her cards again before sending Mary up to Mr. Doran's room to say that she wished to speak with him. She felt sure she would win. He was a serious young man, not rakish or loud-voiced like the others. If it had been Mr. Sheridan or Mr. Meade or Banta Lyons her task would have been much harder. She did not think he would face publicity. All the lodgers in the house knew something of the affair, details had been invented by some. Besides, he had been employed for thirteen years in a great Catholic wine-merchant's office and publicity would mean for him, perhaps, the loss of his job. Whereas if he agreed all might be well. She knew he had a good screw for one thing and she suspected he had a bit of stuff put by.

Nearly the half-hour! She stood up and surveyed herself in the pier-glass. The decisive expression of her great florid face satisfied her and she thought of some mothers she knew who could not get their daughters off their hands.

Mr. Doran was very anxious indeed this Sunday morning. He had made two attempts to shave but his hand had been so unsteady that he had been obliged to desist. Three days' reddish beard fringed his jaws and every two or three minutes a mist gathered on his glasses so that he had to take them off and polish them with his pocket-handkerchief. The recollection of his confession of the night before was a cause of acute pain to him, the priest had drawn out every ridiculous detail of the affair and in the end had so magnified his sin that he was almost thankful at being afforded a loophole of reparation. The harm was done. What could he do now but marry her or run away? He could not brazen it out. The affair would be sure to be talked of and his employer would be certain to hear of it. Dublin is such a small city: everyone knows everyone else's business. He felt his heart leap warmly in his throat as he heard in his excited imagination old Mr. Leonard calling out in his rasping voice: "Send Mr. Doran here, please."

All his long years of service gone for nothing! All his industry and diligence thrown away! As a young men he had sown his wild oats, of course; he had boasted of his free-thinking and denied the existence of God to his companions in public-houses. But that was all passed and done with... nearly. He still bought a copy of *Reynolds's Newspaper* every week but he attended to his religious duties and for nine-tenths of the year lived a regular life. He had money enough to settle down on; it was not that. But the family would look down on her. First of all there was her disreputable father and then her mother's boarding house was beginning to get a certain fame. He had a notion that he was being had. He could imagine his friends talking of the affair and laughing. She was a little vulgar; sometimes she said "I seen" and "If I had've known." But what would grammar matter if he really loved her? He could not make up his mind whether to like her or despise her for what she had done. Of course he had done it too. His instinct urged him to remain free, not to marry. Once you are married you are done for, it said.

While he was sitting helplessly on the side of the bed in shirt and trousers she tapped lightly at his door and entered. She told him all, that she had made a clean breast of it to her mother and that her mother would speak with him that morning. She cried and threw her arms around his neck, saying:

"O Bob! Bob! What am I to do? What am I to do at all?"

She would put an end to herself, she said.

He comforted her feebly, telling her not to cry, that it would be all right, never fear. He felt against his shirt the agitation of her bosom.

It was not altogether his fault that it had happened. He remembered well, with the curious patient memory of the celibate, the first casual caresses her dress, her breath, her fingers had given him. Then late one night as he was undressing for bed she had tapped at his door, timidly. She wanted to relight her candle at his for hers had been blown out by a gust. It was her bathnight. She wore a loose open combing jacket of printed flannel. Her white instep shone in the opening of her furry slippers and the blood flowed warmly behind her perfumed skin. From her hands and wrists too as she lit and steadied her candle a faint perfume arose.

On nights when he came in very late it was she who warmed up his dinner. He scarcely knew what he was eating feeling her beside him alone, at night, in the sleeping house. And her thoughtfulness! If the night was anyway cold or wet or windy there was sure to be a little tumbler of punch ready for him. Perhaps they could be happy together...

They used to go upstairs together on tiptoe, each with a candle, and on the third landing exchange reluctant good-nights. They used to kiss. He remembered well her eyes, the touch of her hand and his delirium ...

But delirium passes. He echoed her phrase, applying it to himself: "What sin am I to do?" The instinct of the celibate warned him to hold back. But the sin was there, even his sense of honour told him that reparation must be made for such a sin.

While he was sitting with her on the side of the bed Mary came to the door and said that the missus wanted to see him in the parlour. He stood up to put on his coat and waistcoat, more helpless than ever. When he was dressed he went over to her to comfort her. It would be all right, never fear. He left her crying on the bed and moaning softly: "O my God!"

Going down the stairs his glasses became so dimmed with moisture that he had to take them off and polish them. He longed to ascend through the roof and fly away to another country where he would never hear again of his trouble, and yet a force pushed him downstairs step by step. The implacable faces of his employer and of the Madam stared upon his discomfiture. On the last flight of stairs he passed Jack Mooney who was coming up from the pantry nursing two bottles of Bass. They saluted coldly; and the lover's eyes rested for a second or two on a thick bulldog face and a pair of thick short arms. When he reached the foot of the staircase he glanced up and saw Jack regarding him from the door of the return-room.

Suddenly he remembered the nights when one of the music-hall artistes, a little blond Londoner, had made a rather free allusion to Polly. The reunion had been almost broken up on account of Jack's violence., Everyone tried to quiet him. The music-hall artiste, a little paler than usual, kept smiling and saying that there was no harm meant: but Jack kept shouting at him that if any fellow tried that sort of a game on with his sister he'd bloody well put his teeth down his throat, so he would.

Polly sat a little time on the side of the bed, crying. Then she dried her eyes and went over to the looking-glass. She dipped the end of the towel in the water-jug and refreshed her eyes with the cool water. She looked at herself in profile and readjusted a hairpin above her ear. Then she went back to the bed again and sat at the foot. She regarded the pillows for a long time and the sight of them awakened in her mind secret, amiable memories. She rested the nape of her nack against the cool iron bed-rail and fell into a revery. There was no longer any perturbation visible on her face.

She waited on patiently, almost cheerfully, without alarm, her memories gradually giving place to hopes and visions of the future. Her hopes and visions were so intricate that she no longer saw the white pillows on which her gaze was fixed or remembered that she was waiting for anything.

At last she heard her mother calling. She started to her feet and ran to the banisters.

"Polly! Polly!"

"Yes, mamma?"

"Come down, dear. Mr. Doran wants to speak to you."

Then she remembered what she had been waiting for.

Discussion Plan:

1. What are the choices of the three main characters?
2. What are their motives?
3. How are the choices related to the motives?
4. Given that the story takes place at least sixty years ago, are any of the motives justified?
5. Do the characters have options beyond the choices determined by the social context?
6. What values are implicit in the situation as you have analyzed it?
7. Can the values you have outlined be expressed in terms of the Utilitarian model of Bentham or Mill?

A Contemporary View

Our society, traditionally opposed to pre-marital sex, seems to send messages to its members via mass media that reinforce natural desires. Sex is applauded as among the most desirable of activities and involving the most precious of human emotions, abilities and characteristics. We live in an era where sexual success is often seen as an indicator of personal success, and where sexual behavior is often expected, if not demanded of us. Yet the consequences of sexual activity, unwanted pregnancy, is still unacceptable.

George F. Will, Teen-agers and Birth Control

Victoria Will is two years old and perfect. That is, she is perfectly like a two-year-old, which means she has the executive disposition of Lady Macbeth:

Me: "What is your name?"

She: "No!"

That word will stand her in good stead in about 15 years. Until then I live in blissful ignorance of the special tribulations of a parent of an adolescent daughter. But as a citizen as well as a father, I favor the Department of Health and Human Services' rule requiring federally funded birth control clinics to notify parents whose daughters 17 or under are receiving prescription contraceptive drugs or devices.

Opponents call this the "squeal rule," implying that it is dishonorable for the government to codify the fact that parents have an interest in knowing of a minor daughter's receipt of prescription materials related to sexual activity. Notice, the rule does not require parental permission. A child may need parental consent even to take a school trip to the zoo, but the HHS rule requires only parental notification, and only after prescriptions have been filled.

Civil Liberty: A civil liberty, correctly understood, is a liberty central to the functioning of democracy. The American Civil Liberties Union evidently thinks it is a civil liberty for children to be given federally subsidized contraceptive measures and counsel, in secret. In response to an ACLU suit, a judge has blocked implementation of the rule, arguing that it would lead to an increase in teen-age pregnancy and thus constitute "blatant disregard" for Congress's intent in supporting family-planning clinics. Arguing against the rule in another court, a lawyer said it would cause 33,000 such pregnancies annually. Amazing how folks can know these things.

It is devilishly difficult to prove cause-and-effect relationships between social policies and social changes, but this is clear: the problem of teen-age pregnancy has grown as contraceptives and sex education have become increasingly available. I am not saying the availability caused the growth. But it would be rash to say the availability is irrelevant. And many of those who today are predicting with such certitude awful results from the HHS rule predicted that teen-age pregnancies would decline as contraception and sex education became more available.

Supporters of the rule note that prescription birth-control measures can have serious side effects. Opponents reply that pregnancy is more dangerous than contraception, especially to adolescents. That is true, but hardly an answer to this argument: in a society where most schools will not give a child an aspirin without parental consent, parents have the minimal right to be notified after a minor daughter has received a drug related to sexual activity. Besides, adolescents have a third choice between contraception and pregnancy. It is continence.

Opponents of the rule say it constitutes governmental intrusion into family relationships. But surely the government subverts family relationships when it subsidizes 5,000 clinics that purvey to children medical treatment and counsel on morally important matters, and do so without informing those who have legal, financial and moral responsibility for children—parents.

Opponents say that if parents are told that their minor daughters are on the Pill, some daughters will be deterred from seeking contraceptives, but will be no less sexually active. This is true. But the law that the HHS rule implements does not say that all values shall be sacrificed to the single aim of reducing pregnancy. Indeed, the law stipulates that subsidized clinics must "encourage" to the extent practical, "family participation." Again, the HHS rule does not require parental participation. It does not, for example, require that parents accompany the child to the clinic. It does not even require that contraceptive drugs or devices be withheld until parents are notified. It requires only that parents receive after-the-fact information that parents can act on as they please. It is hard to imagine a more minimal compliance with Congress's mandate to "encourage" parental participation. The rule is just an executive-branch attempt to balance the various values Congress affirmed.

It has provoked a disproportionate response. The *New York Times* has editorialized against the rule at least six times, denouncing it as "cruel." The *Times* says the rule would increase bureaucracy, which in this case the *Times* is against. The *Times* says the rule is an example of intrusive government, which in this case the *Times* is against. (Force busing? Fine. Parental notification of drugs prescribed for unemancipated minors? Too intrusive.) Why such uproar over a halfhearted rule that barely constitutes compliance with Congress's unexceptionable affirmation of parental involvement? Perhaps the decay of liberalism into a doctrine of "liberation" has led to this idea:

even children must be "liberated," even from parental knowledge of even their sexual activities. Perhaps the extreme individualism of today's liberalism finds "repressive" even restraints associated with a collectivity as basic as the family.

The Rule: Many opponents of the rule seem to think that realism consists of accepting as irreversible the recent increase in teen-age promiscuity. (Be honest, readers: how many of you think the value-laden word "promiscuous" is illiberal?) Granted, governments can do nothing to make teen-agers less sexually ardent. And when traditional mores are dissolving as fast as ours are, trying to arrest the dissolution with a law is like trying to lasso a locomotive with a thread. However, policy need not passively reflect and accommodate itself to every change, however destructive. It need not regard social change as a process that is or ought to be entirely autonomous, utterly immune to the influence of judicious interventions. The HHS rule is such an intervention.

Law should express society's core values, such as parental responsibility. If HHS's mild rule is declared incompatible with public policy, what, for goodness' sake, is that policy? What values does it affirm, or subvert by neglect? HHS's rule at least does not express complacent acceptance of the inevitability of today's rate of teen-age sexual activity. Obviously the trend is against sexual restraint. But as has been said, a trend is not a destiny.

Exercise:

Earlier, in Part II, we discussed the teenagers right to sexual privacy. George Will argues forcefully that there are overriding considerations based upon societies "core values."

Reconstruct Will's argument making his value premises clear. Try to identify each individual value and state them in separate sentences.

Then try to order the sentences so that the most basic come first.

Does the argument as stated seem logical? Are there any missing premisses that are needed to tie the argument together? If you add the missing premisses does the argument seem more or less plausible?

Explore the most basic premisses, are they justified on Utilitarian grounds? If not, are there any basic premisses that need justification? What reasons could you give for his basic value assumptions?

Do you think all basic value assumptions need further justification? If not, then are the most basic assumptions self-evident, or are they arbitrary?

Psychology

The traditional view that counsels restraint in the face of sexual pressures, whether social or personal, may persuade some. Others choose to become sexually active and frequently pregnancy results. With contraceptives and sex education available, it seems puzzling that the number of teenage pregnancies is increasing. The motives seem to be more than just carelessness or laziness.

William A. Fisher, Why Teenagers Get Pregnant

Each year, 10 percent of American teenage girls (mostly unmarried) get pregnant—alarming proof that use of contraceptives by teenagers has not kept pace with their increased sexual activity. Even well-informed young people who have easy access to contraceptive devices often fail to use them.

Some time ago, social psychologist Don Byrne hypothesized that one major psychological barrier to teenage contraception was erotophobia, or fear of sex. Over the past six years, several studies that my colleagues and I have done have confirmed that hypothesis.

Erotophobia can be measured by analyzing reactions to 21 statements on a test called the Sexual Opinion Survey, developed in 1977 by Leonard White, Don Byrne, and me. For instance, a person who strongly agrees that "almost all pornographic material is nauseating" is likely to be anxious about sex, or erotophobic. Someone who strongly agrees that "masturbation can be an exciting experience" tends to be fairly free of anxiety about sex; he or she is erotophilic.

In one study, 40 students in a course on sexuality filled out the Sexual Opinion Survey. Their scores were then compared with their marks on an exam that included material on contraception. The average mark of erotophobic students was 71, significantly lower than that of erotophilic students, whose average grade was 79.

The difference suggests that erotophobic adolescents have trouble learning about contraception.

In another study, I asked 148 male undergraduates to fill out the Sexual Opinion Survey and to indicate whether or not they expected to have sexual intercourse during the coming month. Four weeks later, 96 of these students reported on whether they had actually done so. Erotophobic men, it turned out, underestimated the likelihood that they would have sex—more of them had intercourse than had intended to. That kind of underestimation may lead to contraceptive neglect; if teenagers do not expect to have intercourse, it is not likely that they will prepare for it.

Even if teenagers can admit to themselves that they will soon be having intercourse, they may be too embarrassed to buy condoms, or to ask a physician for a prescription for a diaphragm or birth control pills. To discover the link between erotophobia and going public to acquire contraceptives, my colleagues and I studied a group of female undergraduates who were inconsistent users of contraceptives. Some of them, however, had made an initial visit to the campus contraception clinic and seemed to be trying to end their on-again, off-again habits. These women, we found, were relatively erotophilic, while those who did not go to the clinic were relatively erotophobic.

To test the hypothesis that erotophobia makes it difficult for people to discuss contraception with a partner, my colleagues and I created a laboratory analogue of sexual communication. We asked 101 male and 89 female students to sit in front of a video recorder and read a speech that described foreplay, intercourse, and orgasms. Then the students indicated their reactions to communicating about sex, and filled out the Sexual Opinion Survey. The erotophobic undergraduates said that when they delivered the sexual message, they experienced embarrassment and fright; they were unwilling to allow unrestricted use of their taped speech. To the extent that we can generalize from this study, it can be assumed that erotophobic teens will avoid pre-sex discussion of contraception.

In yet another study, done in 1979, my colleagues and I administered the Sexual Opinion Survey to three groups of undergraduate women: sexually active women who were consistent users of contraception, sexually active women who were inconsistent users of contraception, and a group of virgins. The virgins were the most erotophobic, while the consistent users were the least so. The inconsistent users ranked somewhere in the middle. Thus, it seems likely that the teenagers who get pregnant without planning to are the relatively erotophobic ones: young people whose fear of sex is too great to allow them to plan for intercourse but not great enough to keep them from having it.

One technique that might be used in sex-education classes is to have teenagers "walk through," in their imaginations, each step in the contraception process, including learning about birth control, anticipating intercourse, and obtaining contraceptives. Once students feel comfortable with these procedures in fantasy, it would be useful for them to walk through them in reality, telephoning for an appointment at a birth-control clinic, for example, or role-playing a pre-sex discussion of contraception with a partner.

Students might also be encouraged to associate contraception with other preparations for a date. Get the car for the evening, decide on a movie, and pick up a three-pack of condoms. And the actual use of contraceptives might be eroticized by presenting it as a kind of foreplay. Such educational programs could turn contraception into a source of pleasure and titillation, and, in the process, lead to more reliable birth-control practices.

Discussion Plan:

The article makes two claims, first that a main reason for teenage pregnancy is the failure of teenagers to squarely face their own sexuality, second, that teenagers should be conditioned to be more comfortable with the pragmatic side of pregnancy related sex issues.

First, what are the author's reasons for holding the first view? Do you agree with his analysis? How does his survey strengthen his argument? If you disagree, can you see any weaknesses in his procedure?

Second, what value assumptions does he make in his suggested solution? Do you agree with his solutions? From what value standpoint could you disagree?

If you can find any value standpoints from which a person might disagree, how could these rival points of view be argued?

Could you use a Utilitarian basis to decide between rival value perspectives?

Exercise:

Emotions and Values:

The author of the study claims that fear of embarrassment is at the heart of teenagers unwillingness to deal rationally with contraception. Even if you disagree with the specifics of his claim, he may still have a point.

Invent situations in which negative emotions interfere with your doing, what seems to you to be the right thing. Use the following contexts as a guide. Using the emotion of:
anger
stubbornness
embarrassment,
give examples of wrong behavior:
in school
at home
with friends.

In all cases choose behavior that you would rationally consider inappropriate but where your emotions cause you to do it anyway. Try to be realistic. Feel free to add to the list of emotions and contexts.

Sociology

Each individual privately making a choice about her sexual life is part of a larger pattern. Individuals make trends that are captured in statistics. Statistics tell us that our society includes large numbers of non-traditional mothers. Some of these include the rich and famous, individuals choosing to replace the traditional image of mothering with that of the independent single mother. But not all unmarried mothers are rich and famous.

Time, Black and White, Unwed All Over

The news was not startling. The statistics were. According to federal figures, illegitimate births increased so rapidly in the 1970s that 17% of U.S. babies—one out of every six—are now born out of wedlock. In 1979, the last year for which statistics are available, an estimated 597,000 illegitimate babies were born, up 50% since 1970. Nationwide nearly a third of the babies born to white teen-agers and 83% born to black teens were illegitimate.

Blacks account for more than half of all illegitimate births, but the overall black illegitimacy rate has, in fact, dropped fairly sharply over the decade. It was down 10.7% from 95.5 births per thousand unmarried women in 1970 to 85.3 in 1979, while the white rate rose 8.6% from 13.9 per thousand to 15.1 per thousand. Though the number of abortions had increased dramatically among unmarried teens there are still three live births for every five abortions. Today about 1.3 million children live with teen-age mothers, about half of whom are unmarried.

One obvious reason that so many women are giving birth out of wedlock is the steady decline of the social stigma against it. Girls are no longer thrown out of most high schools for getting pregnant or packed off to a home for unwed mothers. Now whites, like blacks, are more likely to bear the child and refuse to put it up for adoption. In the late '60s and early '70s, about 71% of unwed white pregnant teen-agers and 26% of blacks married in haste before the birth of a child. By the late '70s, the number had fallen to 58% of white and only 8% of blacks. Says Major Helen Warnock, director of a Salvation Army maternity home outside Tulsa: "Just a short time ago, getting pregnant when you weren't married was the worst mistake a 'nice' girls could make. Now having a baby is a kind of status symbol."

A major cause of illegitimacy is more sex among younger people in a pleasure-oriented society. Says Jane Murray of the Alan Guttmacher Institute, which specializes in family planning, "We live in a world of tight jeans." Specialists in the field also stress the inability of teen-agers to understand the use of contraceptives or the consequences of non-use. Says one Chicago girl: "Birth control pills—I'd heard of them. People tell me they make your hair fall out." Captain Carol Bryant, who runs the Salvation Army's Booth Memorial home for unwed mothers in Chicago, talks of the paradoxical sophistication of the 13- or 14-year-old girl who tries to "act older, just like Brooke Shields," but does not "connect intercourse with pregnancy in any meaningful way."

A recent study done at Johns Hopkins University showed that only 14% of teen-agers seek birth control advice before their first sexual encounter. For some girls, having an illegitimate baby is a sought-after sign of maturity. Says James Whitten, director of Harlem's Reality House, "They would prefer marriage, but if it doesn't happen, O.K., they want to show they accept responsibility." Others simply want a cuddly plaything. One pregnant 14-year-old said of course she knew how to care for her baby, "I'm going to dress it up real warm in little clothes, stuff like that. You know, be a mother." Says Jeannette Alejandro of Brooklyn, who dropped out of school after the eighth grade to have a baby out of wedlock "I guess everybody wants a baby. Probably to fill in their life. They feel so bored. They got nothing to do with this life."

During the '70s, the rate of unwed births ran well ahead of the increase in the number of women of child-bearing age. The most recent statistics are among the worst illegitimate births for 1979 were up almost 10% over 1978.

Nobody knows when, or if, the number of illegitimate births will level off. However, one thing is certain. The cost to taxpayers for illegitimate child rearing will be high. This year alone, the federal program for Aid to Families with Dependent Children is expected to exceed $7 billion.

Class Project:

Go over the piece carefully and list all of the reasons the author gives as an explanation of the rise of unwanted pregnancies.

In a systematic way, attempt to devise plausible solutions for the problems as he understands them.

Are any of these solutions pertinent to your own school environment?

If they are do you think the problem is real enough within your school community to require action? If so, use your understanding of the issues to develop a program to inform others in your school of the issues of unwanted teenage pregnancies.

Before you make your work public, explore the value assumptions you are making in your analysis, would these assumptions be inconsistent with the values of others in your school community.

Pay careful attention to the values of Administrators and parents. Is there a way to alter your proposal so as to make it acceptable to people working from another value base?

Also, do not forget that emotions like anger and embarrassment get in the way of rational thinking. Your work, to be effective, must not induce negative emotions that result in irrational responses.

Abortion

One way to handle unwanted pregnancies is through abortion. Abortion is, and has been, an emotionally charged issue. In the following we offer a fair sample of the positions expressed during the period of the classic Supreme Court decision on abortion. These early positions raised most of the basic issues and defined the framework within which later debate was held—and part of the framework was the rhetoric through which the emotion was expressed.

Is Abortion Murder?

A mother stepped into the doctor's office carrying a birth and beautiful baby a year old. Seating herself near her family physician, she said, "Doctor, I want you to help me out of trouble. My baby is only one year old, and I have conceived again, and I do not want to have children so close together." "What do you expect me to do?" asked the physician.

"Oh, anything to get rid of it for me," she replied.

After thinking seriously for a moment the doctor said, "I think I can suggest a better method of helping you out. If you object to having two children so near together, the best way would be to kill the one on your lap, and let the other one come on. It is easy to get at the one on your lap, and it makes no difference to me which one I kill for you. Besides, it might be dangerous for you if I undertook to kill the younger one."

As the doctor finished speaking he reached for a knife, and continued by asking the mother to lay the baby out on her lap, and turn her head the other way.

The woman almost fainted away as she jumped from her chair and uttered one word, "Murderer!"

A few words of explanation from the doctor soon convinced the mother that his offer to commit murder was no worse than her request for the destruction of the unborn child. In either case it would be murder. The only difference would be in the age of the victim.

What the Supreme Court Ruled on Abortion Laws

When the U.S. Supreme Court struck down abortion laws in Texas and Georgia on January 22, 1973 (*Roe v. Wade*), it limited any State's right to prohibit abortion.

In effect, the Court's 7-2 ruling said that a State can prohibit an abortion only in the last three months of pregnancy and then not if the abortion is necessary to protect the health of the mother.

Basis for this decision: the right to privacy as protected by the Fourteenth Amendment.

Specifically, the Court said:

During the first three months of pregnancy, the decision to abort rests solely with the woman and her doctor.

During the second three months, the State can regulate the abortion procedure to protect maternal health.

During the third three months, when the fetus is viable, the State can regulate or even prohibit abortion except when it's necessary for the mother's mental or physical health.

Thus the Court said a State had the right to pass an anti-abortion law to protect its "interest in the potentiality of human life"—but only in the last three months of pregnancy.

The Court stated that the due-process clause "does not include the unborn."

Strong Vatican Stand Forbids All Abortion

The Vatican said today that abortion can never be justified, even when the mother's life is in danger, or the child could be abnormal. In its most strongly worded pronouncement on the subject to date, it declared:

"Never, under any pretext, may abortion be resorted to either by a family or by a political authority, as a legitimate means of regulating birth."

The 5,000-word document was issued by the Congregation for the Propagation of the Faith, which stressed that Pope Paul VI had seen and approved it.

"It may be a serious question of health, sometimes of life or death, for the mother; it may be the burden represented by an additional child, especially if there are good reasons to fear that the child will be abnormal or retarded ...We proclaim only that none of these reasons can ever objectively confer the right to dispose of another person's life, even when that life is only beginning," the Vatican said.

Acknowledging that "modern technology makes abortion more and more easy," the document insisted however, that "moral evaluation is in no way modified because of this."

Pointing out women's responsibilities on the question, the document said, "The movement for the emancipation of women, in so far as it seeks essentially to free them from all unjust discrimination, is on perfectly sound ground ... But one cannot change nature, nor can one exempt women, any more than men, from what nature demands of them."

The document said all freedoms, including sexual freedom, have a natural limitation in the rights of other people. "And must always be careful not to violate justice."

"If one tries to say that men and women are free to seek sexual pleasure, to the point of satiety, without taking into account any law or the essential orientation of sexual life to its fruits of fertility, then this idea has nothing Christian in it," the document said.

At another point, it declared, "One cannot but be astonished to see a simultaneous increase of unqualified protests against the death penalty and every form of war and the vindication of the liberalization of abortion...."

William B. Ober, M.D., We Should Legalize Abortion

The question posed by such cases is to what extent society should subordinate individual values to the codes it has inherited from generations with somewhat different values, different goals, and certainly a different role assigned to women. State and church use "moral" objections and yet permit some abortions. I submit that there is no moral difference among abortions, whether the fetus is the result of rape, incest or conjugal love. By what right does state and church claim a jurisdiction superior to that of the woman involved in pregnancy? I believe that every woman should be able to have an unwanted pregnancy aborted at her own request, subject only to the consent of her husband and the advise of her physician.

Abortion Decision: A Year Later

It is now a full year since the Supreme Court in *Roe v. Wade* effectively struck down the traditional abortion statutes of all 50 states. Not surprisingly, that decision has met with every kind of response, from outcries that it represents nothing less than legalized slaughter to claims that it will stand as the social milestone of the century. But critics and supporters have done far more than issue statements. Legislative and court battles continue in an effort to define the implications of the Court's ruling, whether in the interests of constricting its application or broadening it still further. In addition, of course, there has been a nationwide campaign to sponsor a constitutional amendment to overturn the decision.

Support for such a radical approach to the problem continues to grow, but procedural problems in the House Judiciary Committee—in particular, impeachment hearings, will probably block that road for some months. More significantly, the writing of such an amendment... would be extremely difficult if an attempt were made to include the various exceptions to an absolute ban on abortion held by different religious and ethical groups. And no amendment could promise greater protection to the fetus than is already accorded citizens by other provisions of the Constitution... If drafting an amendment will be controversial, getting it passed by both houses of Congress and three quarters of the states may be impossible. In short, a constitutional amendment, while the most direct legal route, may prove to be an enormous detour on the road to a sane abortion policy in the United States.

Attempts to change the law, of course, whether by constitutional amendment or further litigation through the courts, are perfectly appropriate, in our system of government and entirely laudable, but they should not consume all of our energy or be allowed to distract us from a pressing educational dilemma. As long as the law supported the moral position of those who opposed ready abortions, the need to consider the complicated ethical questions involved was minimal. Abortions were wrong and illegal. The fact that they have been rendered licit by Court fiat in no way changes their moral status.

At the very least, a potential human life is at stake in every determination to abort. To say that a fetus is merely a part of a woman's body runs contrary to all the biological evidence that clearly demonstrates the presence of a new and separate organism in the embryo. But it is an organism entirely dependent on the life of the mother for existence and sustenance during the first six to seven months—a fact that makes the fetus a special case. The moral question is what value shall we place on this unique form of human life? The current trend of American opinion, insofar as it is represented by the *Roe v. Wade* decision, displays a shocking callousness to the presence of life in the womb. Before the law, it is denied the protection afforded every human person, citizen or not. In the eyes of many, its rights—and most particularly, its right to exist—are secondary to the convenience of another individual. Simply to overlook or consciously ignore the inchoate humanity of the fetus threatens the very basis of our lives together in society, for it strikes at the common dignity we all claim as human beings. Because it treats human life cheaply and encourages a disregard for the value of all that is vulnerable, abortion-on-demand is an anti-human policy. That point must be made over and over again if we are not to be lulled into an uncritical acceptance of what has become legally permissible. If the decision to have an abortion has become a personal one, then the ethical burden of that decision has been increased, not diminished.

Abortions, however, are seldom purely private actions. They require assistance—doctors, nurses, a clinic or hospital. In each case, the consciences of other persons are intimately involved. If the state has decided, through its highest Court, that it has no right to force a woman to bear a child to term against her will, then by the same logic, it should have no right to compel an individual against his conscience, to aid in the termination of that life. The inviolability of one conscience demands the inviolability of the other. Some 17 states have already enacted conscience clauses to cover just such cases. They should be extended as soon as possible to all states and the federal government.

Albert E. Gunn, M.D., Letter to the Editor

In the recent Supreme Court abortion decision, Justice Blackmun has argued that since there is doubt as to when life begins we may abort the unborn. One wonders if the Court will next argue that when an accused murderer's guilt or innocence is in doubt he may legitimately be put to death.

So much has been written and said about the "presumption of innocence" in our legal system as the protection of individual rights against unjust accusations. How much more important would it have been if the Court had created a "presumption of life" in those cases where legal existence is in doubt.

The Court has made a serious mistake in taking these issues away from the people and attempting to substitute its will for the people's will as expressed in legislatures and referendums.

Surely, the Unborn Have Rights

Following the complete text of President Richard Nixon's statement against abortion which he issued on April 3rd to reverse an earlier decision by Defense Department officials approving permissive abortion in military hospitals.

Historically, laws regulating abortion in the United States have been the province of States, not the Federal Government. That remains the situation today, as one State after another takes up this question, debates it and decides it. That is where the decisions should be made.

Partly, for that reason, I have directed that the policy on abortions at American military bases in the United States be made to correspond with the laws of the State where those bases are located. If the laws in a particular State restrict abortions, the rule at the military base hospitals are to correspond to that law.

The effect of this directive is to reverse service regulations issued last Summer, which had liberalized the rules on abortions at military hospitals. The new ruling supersedes this—and has been put into effect by the Secretary of Defense.

But while this matter is being debated in State capitals, and weighed by various courts, the Country has a right to know my personal views.

From personal and religious beliefs, I consider abortions an unacceptable form of population control. Further, unrestricted abortion policies, or abortion on demand, I cannot square with my personal belief in the sanctity of human life—including the life of the yet unborn. For, surely, the unborn have rights also, recognized in law, recognized even in principles expounded by the United Nations.

Ours is a nation with a Judeo-Christian heritage. It is also a nation with serious social problems—problems of malnutrition, of broken homes, of poverty and of delinquency. But none of these problems justifies such a solution.

A good and generous people will not opt, in my view, for this kind of alternative to its social dilemmas. Rather, it will open its hearts and homes to the unwanted children of its own, as it has done for the unwanted millions of other lands.

Text of Abortion-Bill Veto

Following is the text of Governor Rockefeller's message to the Legislature vetoing repeal of the state's liberalized abortion law:

The same strong reasons that led me to recommend abortion-law reform in my annual message...for 1968—69 and 1970 and to sign into law the reform that was ultimately adopted in 1970, now compel me to disapprove the bill just passed that would repeal that reform.

The abortion-law reform of 1970 grew out of the recommendations of an outstanding select citizens committee, representative of all affected parties, that I appointed in 1968.

Under the distinguished leadership of retired Court of Appeals Judge Charles W. Froessel, the select committee found that the then-existing 19th century, near-total prohibition against abortion was fostering hundreds of thousands of illegal and dangerous abortions. It was discriminating against women of modest means who could not afford an abortion haven and the often frightened unwed, confused young women. It was promoting hypocrisy and ultimately, human tragedy.

Connecticut Case Cited

I supported the majority recommendations of the Froessel committee throughout the public debate of this issue, extending over three years, until the Legislature acted to reform the state's archaic abortion law. I can see no justification now for repealing this reform and thus condemning hundreds of thousands of women to the dark age once again.

There is, further, the recent Federal court decision invalidating the Connecticut abortion law, which is substantially the same as the pre-reform New York law. The law of that case, if upheld, would clearly invalidate the old New York law, as well, were the repeal of abortion reform allowed to stand. In such a circumstance, this state would be left with no law on the subject at all.

I fully respect the moral convictions of both sides in this painfully sensitive controversy. But the extremes of personal vilification and political coercion brought to bear on members of the legislature raise serious doubts that the votes to repeal the reform has represented the will of a majority of the people of New York State.

Risk to Life Seen

The very intensity of this debate has generated an emotional climate in which the truth about abortions and about the present state abortion law have become distorted almost beyond recognition.

The truth is that this repeal of the 1970 reform would not end abortions. It would only end abortions under safe and supervised medical conditions.

The truth is that a safe abortion would remain the optional choice of the well-to-do woman, while the poor would again be seeking abortions at a grave risk to life in back-room abortion mills.

The truth is that, under the present law, no woman is compelled to undergo an abortion. Those whose personal and religious principles forbid abortion are in no way compelled against their convictions under the present law. Every woman has the right to make her own choice.

I do not believe it right for one group to impose its vision of morality on an entire society. Neither is it just or practical for the state to attempt to dictate the innermost personal beliefs and conduct of its citizens.

The bill is disapproved.

Class Project:

Go over the various positions and rewrite them in argument form, clearly stating premises and conclusion. Put in brackets any parts of arguments that serve a purely emotional function. Then, on separate sheets of paper, list the arguments for and the arguments against.

Either randomly or according to preference choose two five person teams representing the pro and con positions as clarified. The role of the remainder of the class is to keep track of the discussion, being especially conscious of areas that require additional information or argument.

As a class project, research those areas of the abortion debate that seem unclear after the discussion.

Bring into class relevant articles that clarify the issues further. Extend your position sheets adding whatever new point have been discovered.

Hold another discussion in light of the new issues.

Sex and Violence

The sexual stereotype of the aggressive man and the passive women force a connection between sex and violence. Strong men, wealthy men, heads of state, are more attractive than their opposites. These men are desirable because they are powerful. Power can ensure security, but it also permits control. The man has and uses power on the women who seems compliant, a willing victim. The images that are found in pornography reflect this, frequently showing men in positions of power and control.

Stereotypes of power can backfire. Instead of providing a channel for security, or even fantasy, power becomes a means to express frustration. And frustration expressed with power leads to violence. Consistent with the social stereotypes, the victims of sexual violence are, most often, women.

Time, Socko Performances on Campus

College lovers, it seems beat each other up quite often.

When Sociologist James Makepeace, 35, surveyed undergraduates at Bemidji State University in Minnesota during the spring of 1979, he came on a finding that surprised him: one of every five students reported being punched, slapped or shoved by their dates or lovers. Says Makepeace, an expert on premarital family violence, "It used to be said that a marriage license was a hitting license, but now we've discovered that on college campuses there's an awful lot of hitting without the license."

After a similar poll at Oregon State University, Family Life Professor June Henton and Assistant Professor Rodney Cate estimated the number of violent lovers at about 25%. At sunny Arizona State, Sociology Associate Professor Mary Riege Laner found, in a study that may put to rest American illusions about carefree campus romance, that more than 60% of the nonmarried upper-class students had encountered "some kind of violence" while dating.

Most incidents are relatively minor. But some of the students reported being regularly beaten, kicked, bitten and pelted with objects. A few even spoke of threats with guns and knives. The case of Valerie, 20, and Steve, 23, two students at a large Western University, is in some ways typical. The couple had only been dating for three months when Steve slapped Valerie because he thought she was flirting with another man. Like most campus couples who later come to blows, they moved in together. After they began living together, his objections to imagined infidelities snowballed into furious furniture-tossing tantrums. He sometimes hurled Valerie to the floor, dragging her around by her hair, and she says, "literally beat the hell out of my face." Several black eyes later, Valerie walked out.

In their fear and confusion, few college women—and even fewer men—are willing to admit having been the victims of violence. As one woman student at Arizona State said of her regularly bruised and beaten, but steadfastly silent girlfriends: "Before they'd consider it abuse, they'd have to have broken bones."

Jealousy over a third person was cited in nearly half the violent blowups. Most of the rest grew out of arguments over sex or drinking. Yet experts wonder why college students seem so unable to settle these disagreements without black eyes and broken noses. Married couples fight but it is thought they often do so partly because they cannot escape each other, living in an unbreakable tangle of loyalties, commitments, and angers. College students, however, are free to walk out. Many of them have also disavowed traditional sex roles. They advocate sexual freedom and claim they can handle its consequences. The macho man and helpless victimized woman are supposed to be on their way to extinction. Sheila Korman, 28, a counselor at the University of Florida, wrote her master's thesis on sexual aggression in dating. "I think it comes from a number of sources," she says, "including economic frustrations and tensions and the feeling that you have no power in the world. So you show your power against someone who can't retaliate." Psychologist Paul Schauble, another counselor at the university, says there has been "perhaps a 10% increase in violent squabbles among couples seeking counseling over the past two years. Not all the women, he says, are blameless victims of brutes; some are needlers who figure that the man cannot retaliate, and others provoke violence as a way of breaking through male indifference.

Sociologist Laner blames cruelty at coeducational institutions in large part on a "violence-loving society" that has nurtured this college generation on murder movies and newspaper stories detailing crimes of passion. Other experts speculate that lack of parental rules has put too much sexual and emotional strain on the young. College students have always had a hard time deciding what comes first—school work or a loved one. On today's openly sexual, highly competitive campuses, even the most solid balancing act can come unbalanced. In such a zero-sum scenario, each hour spent with one's partner is an hour away from the books, and resentment builds. According to Princeton's Karen Tilbor, assistant dean of student affairs, "ambivalence" about priorities is at the root of violence among college couples.

But students often find separation harder to live with than abuse. Reason: fear of loneliness or of losing the status that comes from having a steady date. Tom, a 24-year-old student at a large Southwestern university, continued to date a hot-tempered classmate who, like a caricature of a wronged wife, regularly tossed plates at him and twice pushed him downstairs. Tom put up with such attacks for 22 months. "It was the first 'heavy' relationship I ever was involved in," he later explained. "You get so caught up in it you can't step out of it even though you know you're getting slugged every other week."

Some experts also note that many of these students have a tendency to see aggression as a kind of affection. They cite Oregon State students' response to questions about the "meaning of violence." Nearly 30% of the couples had at some time taken abuse as a sign of "love." And a number considered violence a "normal," even healthy part of a love affairs. Three-quarters of those who had been involved in an assault said it did not do their relationship any harm. More than one-third felt that hitting, or being hit, actually improved their relationship.

A few experts, like Sociologist Dr. Kersti Yllo of Wheaton College, Norton, Mass., speculate that "loving" violence may partly be a byproduct of women's push for equality. Uncertainty about once traditional roles, she reasons, makes men more anxious to assert themselves and women more anxious to fight back. Still, many experts see the same old patterns in the new college violence. After all, says Makepeace: "Women are still the primary victims."

Exercise:

In the following examples does the reason given *explain* why what happened (show why what happened could have been expected) or does it *justify* what happened (show why what happened is acceptable or excusable) or both or neither.

1. I don't have my homework because I didn't copy the assignment.
2. I missed the exam because I stayed home on my doctor's orders.
3. Johnny must have caught the measles when he visited Fred who came down with the measles also.
4. Johnny stutters because of a neuromuscular defect
5. Johnny stuttered during the speech because he was terribly nervous.
6. When I get angry I can't help using curse words.
7. Since Jill's parents curse so much, it is understandable that Jill does.
8. I didn't mean to hit him so hard, but I was furious.
9. I didn't mean to hit him so hard, I guess I don't know my own strength.
10. When I realized he had a knife I hit him as hard as I could.
11. Sure I hit people when I'm angry, that's the way I was raised.
12. Mothers with many young children spank more often, because it's the only way to keep them in line.
13. There is nothing wrong with hitting someone, it's a good way to show you really care about them.
14. People who are violent, have been subjected to violence as children.
15. Spare the rod and spoil the child.

Discussion Plan:

The author attempts to explain violence among college lovers. What are the various sorts of explanations he gives?
Can you categorize the explanations given, e.g. emotional, social, cultural.

Which of the explanations presuppose values? What values are presupposed.

Do any of the explanations given justify the use of violence? Which, if any, would justify the violence in the victim's mind. Which could be used as justification by the violent lover?

If both lovers accept violence as justified, is it justified; is being violent a "personal" affair?

Rape

Sexual violence is most often associated with rape: the violent forcing of sexual acts. When the violence predominates our attitude towards rape is relatively clear-cut. When the sexual aspect is more apparent, when force is used in situations that resemble the stereotypical image of aggressive man and passive woman, the issue becomes more confusing.

Elizabeth Mehren, A Case of Attempted Rape

On a cold, rainy Friday night, I opened my door to a dear and trusted friend. Not so very long before, this man had been a lover, kind and, most of all, gentle. He was a writer. A soul mate, I thought.

When he called that night he sounded troubled. "I need to talk to you," he said. "Please, it's important."

Four inches of rain fell on Los Angeles that night. With the same fury, this mild man turned violent. His rage exploded. Indulged as a child, blessed with relative tranquility as an adult, I had never been struck by a man. Suddenly the blows came at me, and verbal onslaughts, loud and harsh, like reports from a gun. At once he was pinning me to the floor. Then, in a second, dragging me, by my hair, toward my bedroom. There were sexual demands, ugly, brutal, demeaning demands. Rape, I realized as I struggled and resisted, somehow successfully. This is what they mean by rape.

Sixty percent of American couples report that domestic violence is part of their marriages, and among divorcing couples in this country, violence at home is often cited as a cause of the breakup. A vast majority of the victims of domestic violence requiring treatment are women. I knew these facts because, not one week before, I had covered a conference on domestic violence at the University of California at Los Angeles. There in my living room that Friday night, life was imitating journalism.

I will never quite know how I got this man out of my house. When I awoke the next morning I felt drugged and dopey, but functioned smoothly, if mutely. Shock, they told me later. It's typical. One day later I began to scream. The immensely sensitive policewoman who took my report assured me that this kind of delayed reaction was common.

Abused: In sum, my reactions were confused and cacophonous. I felt responsible, I had, after all, admitted this man to my house. I felt stupid: how could I have misread his character so badly. I felt abused, ripped off, violated and betrayed. I felt, in my bleakest moments, silly for stewing. I was alive, in one piece and, at least physically, not as damaged as I might have been.

But in very short order what began to fascinate me vastly more were the reactions of my friends—how these responses broke down, almost dead in the center, 50-50, along sex lines. In one camp, dead set on vengeance, were the men. From my women friends came an almost universal chorus: turn your back, carry on, forget him.

A male lawyer friend railed at me. Why, he demanded, was this man not in jail? My brother offered to fly out and kill him. A male college classmate, now a TV executive in New York, volunteered to surgically remove his masculinity. A former editor, also male, grimly warned that if I "let this pass," I'd be "a patsy for this maniac forever."

Now my female friends are for the most part paradigms of the modern woman, whatever that is. They have successful, responsible positions of respect and authority. They are strong. They attend aerobics classes, jog, meditate, play tennis and do yoga. They read and write books. Some are manless, some practice serial monogamy; others are (as we learned to say in the '70s) partnered. Mostly they are survivors, shell-shocked veterans of the sexual revolution. They have learned (as we also learned to put it in that dreadful decade) to cope.

To a one, they were horrified. But he was so nice, they said. Some, confiding similar experiences, told me stories about themselves I could never have imagined. One woman recounted how she was raped at knife point by a fellow religious pilgrim in India. Another told me her ex-husband had knocked her flat out cold in their impeccably decorated Benedict Canyon abode.

Two close friends sent flowers. A colleague took me to dinner; we ordered the most expensive champagne. Another slipped me an envelope filled with robin's-blue 10-milligram Valium tablets.

What they advised, over and over, reduced to this: take care of yourself. Get a manicure, they said. Escape to the nearest tropical isle. Florence Nightingales of the emotions, bless them, they advocated healing.

Curiously (I thought at first), these strong soldiers of the revolution counseled against legal action. He'd say he'd been drinking, a woman lawyer predicted, and get off on diminished capacity. What possible retribution could I gain from a protracted, probably futile legal battle?

My mind went back to a truism I had heard at UCLA: men who do this kind of thing have probably done it before and will almost certainly do it again. Many friends reinforced my own horrible fear that taking legal steps might make him madder still. Was I ready for a repeat performance? A wise and sensible woman gently admonished: don't be a martyr for principle.

All this seemed quite odd. Not 10 years ago we were screaming for blood-justice rectification of all cosmic and sexual injustices. Now, suddenly, it was a male photographer friend who was telling me, "Doing nothing is a form of condoning this behavior. Let it go, and you are letting it go on."

Guilt: Had the world turned inside out? Had we women won our economic liberation, only to return to the passivity of the past? Were we parroting our mothers' lessons to be polite, stand up straight and for God's sake don't make a scene? Had men swiped our rhetoric, using it to absolve themselves of any possible guilt-by-gender association? Just as my women friends were shuddering, "Ye gods, this could happen to us," were the men asking to be saved from their own potentially violent streaks?

Who can say? What I do know is that what happened that rainy Friday night probably had very little to do with me: this man and I had not known each other well enough to hate—or love—to that extreme. It was a case of anger from outer space, or perhaps inner space would be more accurate. I merely happened to be in the target path of that furious, exploding asteroid.

I've changed my phone number. I drive around the block before I park my car at night. I am cautious and I look at men more fearfully now. It rained again one recent Friday night. My phone did not ring. I was happy to be home.

Discussion Plan:

Ms. Mehren presents her male and female friends as acting within social stereotypes. What values do these stereotyped responses reflect? List the value assumptions that make the responses most likely?

Ms. Mehren herself offers an account, "I merely happened to be in the target path of that furious, exploding asteroid," how does this comment fit in with the analysis of the value bases of her male as opposed to female friends?

What is the role of the emotions in determining the appropriate response to the rape? Does rage at the loss of love justify sexual violence; does it explain sexual violence? Does rage over sexual violence justify further violence? Does it explain further violence?

If the violence is personal, are there reasons of social value that should determine the response?

If her ex-lover had merely forced his attentions on her, rather than used violence, would that have changed things? Is forced sexuality violence in and of itself?

If her lover had used emotional coercion to persuade her to have sex with him one last time, would that have been a form of violence?

Is Mehren in part responsible since she freely admitted her lover into her home? If he forced her to do only acts that she had freely performed with him in the past, is she in part responsible, since she had permitted those acts?

Rape

For those of us who see rape as an act of violence the sexual side is of little importance. Besides for the added insult of sexual abuse, rape is first and foremost abuse, violence against a person. But the sexual connotations of rape are part of our consciousness, and judgements are frequently made accordingly.

Tom Pecoraro, Jurors Go Easy on Handsome Rapists with Homely Victims

Jurors in rape cases may go easy on attractive defendants and think unattractive victims deserve their fate. The same prejudice in favor of good looks seems to make jurors most likely to convict unattractive defendants and those whose victims are attractive.

The mock jurors who thought that way in a recent study were 60 male and 60 female undergraduates at the University of Dayton. Marsha B. Jacobson, a psychologist, asked them to read this account (paraphrased here) of a rape case:

"It is 10:00 P.M. at a large midwestern university, and Judy W. is getting out of a night class. She walks across the campus toward her car, parked two blocks away. A man walking in the same direction begins to follow her. He accosts her, and she is subdued, stripped, and raped. A passerby who hears her screams but does not witness the attack calls the police. Police arrest student Charles E. in the vicinity. Although Judy positively identifies Charles E., as her assailant, he maintains his innocence. He tells police he was out for a walk at the time of the attack, but only to take a study break. He says it was a coincidence that he was in the vicinity, and a further coincidence that he resembles Judy's description of her attacker."

Every student in the study read the same account of the crime, but each was also shown one of four different pairs of photographs: an attractive defendant with an attractive victim, an attractive defendant with an unattractive victim, an unattractive defendant with an attractive victim, or an unattractive defendant with an unattractive victim. The photos had been picked as the most attractive or homely among 40 yearbook-style photographs of college-aged men and women by a panel of six male and six female graduate students in psychology.

Jacobson asked the mock jurors if they believed the defendant's alibi and how much sympathy they had for defendant and victim. Women were less likely to believe any defendant's testimony than men were, but both men and women showed greater confidence in it when it came from an attractive man. The students reported more sympathy for the handsome suspect than for the homely suspect, less sympathy for the unattractive victim than for the more attractive one.

Asked to mete out justice, 82 percent of the students who encountered an unattractive suspect found him guilty, compared with 57 percent who found an attractive suspect guilty: When they convicted the attractive suspect, they handed him an average jail term of 10 years versus nearly 14 years for the homely suspect. Both defendants were more likely to be found guilty when paired with the prettier victim.

Class Project:

It is shocking to realize that a majority of people consider physical attractiveness relevant in determining guilt or innocence in rape. But attitudes about rape are frequently shocking when responses are given honestly.

The following questionaire should be duplicated and distibuted to your class or to other. All responses are to be anonymous. Tabulate the results; see if they are different from what you expected.

Rape Questionaire

Respond to the following statement be writing 'yes' if you agree or "no" if you disagree. Pick what you think is the *best* answer.
1. Rapists are people who can't get sex any other way.
2. No sexually attractive man would rape anyone.
3. Unattractive women who get raped must have asked for it.
4. Women who can't get lovers don't really mind getting raped.
5. If rape is imminent, lay back and enjoy it.
6. Rape is a woman's problem.
7. Women who tease men get raped more frequently.
8. No woman can be raped if she fights hard enough.
9. The only excuse for letting yourself get raped is threat of death.
10. Women who get raped ask for it in some way.

Exercise:

Do you think any of the following would be viewed as extenuating circumstances in a rape case? Do you think they should be viewed as extenuating circumstances?

1. The rapist was drunk.
2. The rape victim was a woman dressed very provocatively.
3. The rape victim was a man who frequented gay bars.
4. The rape victim was a female hitchhiker.
5. The rape victim was an a date, and was raped when she refused to go further than heavy petting.
6. The rape victim was alone in an apartment with three men, they were all drinking and smoking marijuana.
7. The rape victim was a prostitute.
8. The rape victim was in jail for sexual child abuse.
9. The rape victim was married to an abusive husband who had a history of physical abuse against the victim.
10. The rapist had spent seven years of his life in jail, where he was frequently raped, he was 21 years old.

Murder

Sex and violence are linked in many ways. Both in cultural images and the psyches of individuals, there is a pairing of desire and fear, hatred and lust. This is nowhere more evident than in the minds of those individuals for whom normal boundaries have been obliterated.

Stephen King, The Man Who Loved Flowers

On an early evening in May of 1963, a young man with his hand in his pocket walked briskly up New York's Third Avenue. The air was soft and beautiful, the sky was darkening by slow degrees from blue to the calm and lovely violet of dusk. There are people who love the city, and this was one of the nights that made them love it. Everyone standing in the doorways of the delicatessens and dry-cleaning shops and restaurants seemed to be smiling. An old lady pushing two bags of groceries in an old baby pram grinned at the young man and hailed him: "Hey beautiful!" The young man gave her a half-smile and raised his hand in a wave.

She passed on her way, thinking: He's in love.

He had that look about him. He was dressed in a light gray suit, the narrow tie pulled down a little, his top collar button undone. His hair was dark and cut short. His complexion was fair, his eyes a light blue. Not an extraordinary face, but on this soft spring evening, on this avenue, in May of 1963, he was beautiful, and the old woman found herself thinking with a moment's sweet nostalgia that in spring anyone can be beautiful ... if they're hurrying to meet the one of their dreams for dinner and maybe dancing after. Spring is the only season when nostalgia never seems to turn bitter, and she went on her way glad that she had spoken to him and glad he had returned the compliment by raising his hand in half-salute.

The young man crossed Sixty-third Street, walking with a bounce in his step and that same half-smile on his lips. Partway up the block, an old man stood beside a chipped green handcart filled with flowers—the predominant color was yellow; a yellow fever of jonquils and late crocuses. The old man also had carnations and a few hothouse tea roses mostly yellow and white. He was eating a pretzel and listening to a bulky transistor radio that was sitting kitty-corner on his handcart.

The radio poured out bad news that no one listened to: a hammer murderer was still on the loose; JFK had declared that the situation in a little Asian country called Vietnam ("Vite-num" the guy reading the news called it) would bear watching; an unidentified woman had been pulled from the East River; a grand jury had failed to indict a crime overlord in the current city administration's war on heroin; the Russians had exploded a nuclear device. None of it seemed real, none of its seemed to matter. The air was soft and sweet. Two men with beer bellies stood outside a bakery, pitching nickels and ribbing each other. Spring trembled on the edge of summer, and in the city, summer is the season of dreams.

The young man passed the flower stand and the sound of the bad news faded. He hesitated, looked over his shoulder, and thought it over. He reached into his coat pocket and touched the something in there again. For a moment his face seemed puzzled, lonely, almost haunted, and then, as his hand left the pocket, it regained its former expression of eager expectation.

He turned back to the flower stand, smiling. He would bring her some flowers, that would please her. He loved to see her eyes light up with surprise and joy when he brought her a surprise—little things, because he was far from rich. A box of candy. A bracelet. Once only a bag of Valencia oranges, because he knew they were Norma's favorite.

"My young friend," the flower vendor said, as the man in the gray suit came back, running his eyes over the stock in the handcart. The vendor was maybe sixty-eight, wearing a torn gray knitted sweater and a soft cap in spite of the warmth of the evening. His face was a map of wrinkles, his eyes were deep in pouches, and a cigarette jittered between his fingers. But he also remembered how it was to be young in the spring—young and so much in love that you practically zoomed everywhere. The vendor's face was normally sour, but now he smiled a little, just as the old woman pushing the groceries had, because this guy was such an obvious case. He brushed pretzel crumbs from the front of his baggy sweater and thought: If this kid were sick, they'd have him in intensive care right now.

"How much are your flowers?" the young man asked.

"I'll make you up a nice bouquet for a dollar. Those tea roses, they're hothouse. Cost a little more, seventy cents apiece. I sell you half a dozen for three dollars and fifty-cents."

"Expensive," the young man said.

"Nothing good comes cheap, my young friend. Didn't your mother ever teach you that?"

The young man grinned, "She might have mentioned it at that."

"Sure. Sure she did. I give you half a dozen, two red, two yellow, two white. Can't do no better than that, can I? Put in some baby's breath—they love that—and fill it out with some fern. Nice. Or you can have the bouquet for a dollar."

"They?" the young man asked, still smiling.

"My young friend," the flower vendor said, flicking his cigarette butt into the gutter and returning the smile, "no one buys flowers for themselves in May. It's like a national law you understand what I mean?"

The young man thought of Norma, her happy, surprised eyes and her gentle smile, and he ducked his head a little. "I guess I do at that," he said.

"Sure you do. What do you say?"

"Well, what do you think?"

"I'm gonna tell you what I think. Hey! Advice is still free, isn't it?"

The young man smiled and said, "I guess it's the only thing left that is."

"You're damn tooting it is," the flower vendor said. "Okay, my young friend. If the flowers are for your mother, you get her the bouquet. A few jonquils, a few crocuses, some lily of the valley. She don't spoil it by saying, 'Oh, Junior, I love them how much did they cost or that's too much don't you know enough not to throw your money around?'"

The young man threw his head back and laughed.

The vendor said, "But if it's your girl, that's different thing, my son, and you know it. You bring her the tea roses and she don't turn into an accountant, you take my meaning? Hey! She's gonna throw her arms around your neck—"

"I'll take the tea roses," the young man said, and this time it was the flower vendor's turn to laugh. The two men pitching nickels glanced over, smiling.

"Hey, kid!" one of them called. "You wanna buy a weddin' ring cheap? I'll sell you mine ... I don't want it no more."

The young man grinned and blushed to the roots of his dark hair.

The flower vendor picked out six tea roses, snipped the stems a little, spritzed them with water, and wrapped them in a large conical spill.

"Tonight's weather looks just the way you'd want it," the radio said. "Fair and mild, temps in the mid to upper sixties, perfect for a little rooftop stargazing, if you're the romantic type. Enjoy. Greater New York, enjoy!"

The flower vendor Scotch-taped the seam of the paper spill and advised the young man to tell his lady that a little sugar added to the water she put them in would preserve them longer.

"I'll tell her," the young man said. He held out a five-dollar bill. "Thank you."

"Just doing the job, my young friend," the vendor said, giving him a dollar and two quarters. His smile grew a bit sad, "Give her a kiss for me."

On the radio, the Four Seasons began singing "Sherry." The young man pocketed his change and went on up the street, eyes wide and alert and eager, looking not so much around him at the life ebbing and flowing up and down Third Avenue as inward and ahead, anticipating. But certain things did impinge: a mother pulling a baby in a wagon, the baby's face comically smeared with ice cream; a little girl jumping rope and singsonging out her rhyme: "Betty and Henry up in a tree, K-I-S-S-I-N-G! First comes love, then comes marriage, here comes Henry with a baby carriage!" Two women stood outside a washateria, smoking and comparing pregnancies. A group of men were looking in a hardware store window at a gigantic color TV with a four-figure price tag—a baseball game was on, and all the players' faces looked green. The playing field was a vague strawberry color, and the New York Mets were leading the Phillies by a score of six to one in the top of the ninth.

He walked on, carrying the flowers, unaware that the two women outside the washateria had stopped talking for a moment and had watched him wistfully as he walked by with his paper of tea roses; their days of receiving flowers were long over. He was unaware of a young traffic cop who stopped the cars at the intersection of Third and Sixty-ninth with a blast on his whistle to let him cross; the cop was engaged himself and recognized the dreamy expression on the young man's face from his own shaving mirror, where he had often seen it lately. He was unaware of the two teen-aged girls who passed him going the other way and then clutched themselves and giggled.

At Seventy-third Street he stopped and turned right. This street was a little darker, lined with brownstones and walk-down restaurants with Italian names. Three blocks down, a stickball game was going on in the fading light. The young man did not go that far; half a block down he turned into a narrow lane.

Now the stars were out, gleaming softly, and the lane was dark and shadowy, lined with vague shapes of garbage cans. The young man was alone now—no, not quite. A wavering yowl rose in the purple gloom, and the young man frowned. It was some tomcat's love song, and there was nothing pretty about that.

He walked more slowly, and glanced at his watch. It was quarter of eight and Norma should be just—

Then he saw her, coming toward him from the courtyard, wearing dark blue slacks and a sailor blouse that made his heart ache. It was always a surprise seeing her for the first time, it was always a sweet shock—she looked so young.

Now his smile shone out—radiated out, and he walked faster.

"Norma!" he said.

She looked up and smiled ... but as they drew together the smile faded.

His own smile trembled a little, and he felt a moment's disquiet. Her face over the sailor blouse suddenly seemed blurred. It was getting dark now... could he have been mistaken? Surely not. It was Norma.

"I brought you flowers," he said in a happy relief, and handed the paper spill to her.

She looked at them for a moment, smiled—and handed them back.

"Thank you, but you're mistaken," she said. "My name is—"

"Norma," he whispered, and pulled the short-handled hammer out of his coat pocket where it had been all along. "They're for you, Norma ... it was always for you ... all for you."

She backed away, her face a round white blur, her mouth an opening black O of terror, and she wasn't Norma, Norma was dead, she had been dead for ten years, and it didn't matter because she was going to scream and he swung the hammer to stop the scream to kill the scream and as he swung the hammer the spill of flowers fell out of his hand, the spill spilled and broke open, spilling red, white, and yellow tea roses beside the dented trash cans where cats made alien love in the dark, screaming in love, screaming, screaming.

He swung the hammer and she didn't scream, but she might scream because she wasn't Norma, none of them were Norma, and he swung the hammer, swung the hammer, swung the hammer. She wasn't Norma and so he swung the hammer, as he had done five other times.

Some unknown time later he slipped the hammer back into his inner coat pocket and backed away from the dark shadow sprawled on the cobblestones, away from the litter of tea roses by the garbage cans. He turned and left the narrow lane. It was full dark now. The stickball players had gone in. If there were bloodstains on his suit, they wouldn't show, not in the dark, not in the soft late spring dark, and her name had not been Norma but he knew what his name was. It was ... was ...

Love.

His name was love, and he walked these dark streets because Norma was waiting for him. And he would find her. Someday soon.

He began to smile. A bounce came into his step as he walked on down Seventy-third Street. A middle-aged married couple sitting on the steps of their building watched him go by, head cocked, eyes far away, a half-smile on his lips. When he had passed by the woman said, "How come you never look that way anymore?"

"Huh?"

"Nothing," she said, but she watched the young man in the gray suit disappear into the gloom of the encroaching night and thought that if there was anything more beautiful than springtime, it was young love.

Discussion Plan:

Stephen King increases the horror of the violence by couching the story in language that reflects the cultural attitude towards romance. What are the cultural values that King expresses through the characters and images in the story?

Does the strength of the values described explain the young man's conduct? Does this explanation justify the young man in any way?

Most people would think that the young man is insane, yet he acts perfectly normally in all ways except for his murderous violence. If everything else he did seems perfectly sane, would you consider him insane just because he murders?

If his murder is the act of an insane man is he responsible? If anyone who commits a hideous enough crime is judged insane, does that mean that no one can be held responsible for crimes as long as they are hideous enough?

SECTION 2: MARRIAGE

Do you expect to marry? Most people do. Our traditions are very strong and marriage seems to fulfill our need for intimacy. Contemplate one of those little figures of a bride and groom on top of a wedding cake and consider the sources for our idea of what marriage is or should be. We look at our parents' marriage and realise how much a product of our society we are when we think of marriage. The traditional images shape our marriages, fictional and real. They are the major source of our expectations.

Traditions are like habits developed over years by groups of people. These habits help people cope with the exigencies of their lives, determining both how we see and how we do things. And social habits like personal habits are hard to break. In the case of marriage society has painted a vivid picture of how it should be. Influenced by this image we form our relationships. If we perceive the image as an ideal we measure our success by how close we approximate it.

The reality of marriage invariably falls short of the ideal. Partners perceive each other through the veil of their own self-interest and expectations. The veil interferes with the clear recognition of who and what the other partner really is. Often our personal needs are so powerful that we do not see our mates as individuals with needs of their own. Since a true partnership requires considerable work by both parties, it is often easiest to suppress the ideals goals and priorities of the less aggressive partner and call it a "marriage made in heaven." For those who wish to be cared for and protected, to be secure and untroubled by decisions, domination by another is a relief not a problem. For many others, it is the source of profound frustration and anger leading to resentment and even hostility toward spouses, marriage and even the family.

Some compromise is inevitable. Two people living in a one bathroom house requires sensitivity and cooperation. Life is full of such trivialites. Learning to give in to the demands of daily life is good practice for coming to terms with larger responsibilities. This is especially true in a society like ours which emphasizes the right of the individual to choose for himself. How can the demand for freedom be reconciled with the need to form close personal relationships with other human beings? Relationships come ready made with sets of responsibilities. Entering into a marriage means accepting limitations on choices and actions, especially when children become involved. Recognition of the limitations as well as the benefits is essential any evaluation of marriage as an institution.

In some case the loss of freedom outweighs the advantage of being in a relationship. Although the traditional formula in a marriage ceremony declares "until death do us part," few persons entering into a marriage in the modern world can make that vow without reservation. The reality is that marriages dissolve for many reasons. The dissolution of a marriage forces the re-evaluation of personal goals and the re-assessment of values. The newly single must reconsider what independence means. It is interesting to reflect on the image of marriage interacting with the way we see divorce.

The Traditional View

Marriage, seen as the natural outcome of love, is cloaked in romantic garments. It is the culmination of love, a blissful state of togetherness in which we live happily ever after. Much has happened in recent decades to bring this image into question, but yet it has a hold on us.

Washington Irving, The Wife

The treasures of the deep are not so precious
As are the conceal'd comforts of a man
Locked up in woman's love. I scent the air
Of blessings, when I come but near the house.
What a delicious breath marriage sends forth ...
The violet bed's not sweeter.   —*Middleton*

I have often had the occasion to remark the fortitude with which women sustain the most overwhelming reverses of fortune. Those disasters which break down the spirit of a man, and prostrate him in the dust, seem to call forth all energies of the softer sex, and give such intrepidity and elevation to their character, that at times it approaches to sublimity. Nothing can be more touching than to behold a soft and tender female, who had been all weakness and dependence, and alive to every trivial roughness, while treading the prosperous paths of life, suddenly rising in mental force to be the comforter and support of her husband under misfortune, and abiding, with unshrinking firmness, the bitterest blasts of adversity.

As the vine, which has long twined its graceful foliage about the oak, and been lifted by it into sunshine, will, when the hardy plant is rifted by the thunderbold, cling round it with its caressing tendrils and bind up its shattered boughs, so is it beautifully ordered by Providence, that woman, who is the mere dependent and ornament of man in his happier hours, should be his stay and solace when smitten with sudden calamity; winding herself into the rugged recesses of his nature, tenderly supporting the drooping head, and binding up the broken heart.

I was once congratulating a friend, who had around him a blooming family, knit together in the strongest affection. "I can wish you no better lot," said he with enthusiasm, "than to have a wife and children. If you are prosperous, there they are to share your prosperity; if otherwise, there they are to comfort you." And indeed, I have observed that a married man falling into misfortune is more apt to retrieve his situation in the world than a single one; partly because he is more stimulated to exertion by the necessities of the helpless and beloved beings who depend upon him for subsistence; but chiefly because his spirits are soothed and relieved by domestic endearments, and his self-respect kept alive by finding that, though all abroad is darkness and humiliation, yet there is still a little world of love at home, of which he is the monarch. Whereas a single man is apt to run to waste and self-neglect; to fancy himself lonely and abandoned, and his heart to fall to ruin like some deserted mansion, for want of an inhabitant.

These observations call to mind a little domestic story, of which I was once a witness. My intimate friend, Leslie, had married a beautiful and accomplished girl, who had been brought up in the midst of fashionable life. She had, it is true, no fortune, but that of my friend was ample; and he delighted in the anticipation of indulging her in every elegant pursuit, and administering to those delicate tastes and fancies that spread a kind of witchery about the sex.—"Her life," said he, "shall be like a fairy tale."

The very difference in their characters produced a harmonious combination: he was of a romantic and somewhat serious cast; she was all life and gladness. I have often noticed the mute rapture with which he would gaze upon her in company, of which her sprightly powers made her the delight; and how, in the midst of applause, her eyes would still turn to him, as if there alone she sought favor and acceptance. When leaning on his arm, her slender form contrasted finely with his tall manly person. The fond confiding air with which she looked up at him seemed to call forth a flush of triumphant pride and cherishing tenderness, as if he doted on his lovely burden for its very helplessness. Never did a couple set forward on the flowery path of early and well-suited marriage with a fairer prospect of felicity.

It was the misfortune of my friend, however, to have embarked his property in large speculations; and he had not been married many months when, by a succession of sudden disasters, it was swept from him, and he found himself reduced almost to penury. For a time he kept his situation to himself, and went about with a haggard countenance and a breaking heart. His life was but a protracted agony; and what rendered it more insupportable was the necessity of keeping up a smile in the presence of his wife; for he could not bring himself to overwhelm her with the news. She saw, however, with the quick eye of affection, that all was not well with him. She marked his altered looks and stifled sighs, and was not to be deceived by his sickly and vapid attempts at cheerfulness. She tasked all her sprightly powers and tender blandishments to win him back to happiness; but she only drove the arrow deeper into his soul. The more he saw cause to love her, the more torturing was the thought that he was soon to make her wretched. A little while, thought he, and the smile will vanish from that cheek—the song will die away from those lips—the lustre of those eyes will be quenched with sorrow; and the happy heart, which now beats lightly in that bosom, will be weighed down like mine by the cares and miseries of the world.

At length he came to me one day, and related his whole situation in a tone of the deepest despair. When I heard him through I inquired, "Does your wife know all this?"—At the question he burst into an agony of tears. "For God's sake!" cried he, "if you have any pity on me, don't mention my wife; it is the thought of her that drives me almost to madness!"

"And why not?" said I. "She must know it sooner or later; you cannot keep it long from her, and the intelligence may break upon her in a more startling manner, than if imparted by yourself; for the accents of those we love soften the harshest tidings. Besides, you are depriving yourself of the comforts of her sympathy; and not merely that, but also endangering the only bond that can keep hearts together—an unreserved community of thought and feeling. She will soon perceive that something is secretly preying upon your mind; and true love will not brook reserve; it feels under-valued and outraged, when even the sorrows of those it loves are concealed form it."

"Oh, but my friend! to think what a blow I am to give to all her future prospects—how I am to strike her very soul to the earth by telling her that her husband is a beggar; that she is to forego all the elegancies of life—all the pleasures of society—to shrink with me into indigence and obscurity! To tell her that I have dragged her down from the sphere in which she might have continued to move in constant brightness—the light of every eye—the admiration of every heart—How can she bear poverty? she has been brought up in all the refinements of opulence. How can she bear neglect? she has been the idol of society. Oh! it will break her heart—it will break her heart!—"

I saw his grief was eloquent, and I let it have its flow; for sorrow relieves itself by words. When his paroxysm had subsided, and he had relapsed into moody silence, I resumed the subject gently, and urged him to break his situation at once to his wife. He shook his head mournfully, but positively.

"But how are you going to keep it from her? It is necessary she should know it, that you may take the steps proper to the alteration of your circumstances. You must change your style of living—nay," observing a pang to pass across his countenance, "don't let that afflict you. I am sure you have never placed your happiness in outward show—you have yet friends, warm friends, who will not think the worse of you for being less splendidly lodged; and surely it does not require a place to be happy with Mary—"

"I could be happy with her," cried he, convulsively, "in a hovel!—I could go down with her into poverty and the dust!—I could—I could—God bless her!—God bless her!" cried he, bursting into a transport of grief and tenderness.

"And believe me, my friend," I said, stepping up and grasping him warmly by the hand, "believe me she can be the same with you. Ay, more; it will be a source of pride and triumph to her—it will call forth all the latent energies and fervent sympathies of her nature; for she will rejoice to prove that she loves you for yourself. There is in every true woman's heart a spark of heavenly fire, which lies dormant in the broad daylight of prosperity; but which kindles up and beams and blazes in the dark hour of adversity. No man knows what the wife of his bosom is—no man knows what a ministering angel she is—unless he has gone with her through the fiery trials of this world."

There was something in the earnestness of my manner, and the figurative style of my language, that caught the excited imagination of Leslie. I knew the auditor I had to deal with; and following up the impression I had made, I finished by persuading him to go home and unburden his sad heart to his wife.

I must confess, notwithstanding all I had said, I felt some little solicitude for the result. Who can calculate on the fortitude of one whose life has been a round of pleasure? Her gay spirits might revolt at the dark downward path of low humility suddenly pointed out before her, and might cling to the sunny regions in which they had hitherto revelled. Besides, ruin in fashionable life is accompanied by so many galling mortifications, to which in other ranks it is a stranger.—In short, I could not meet Leslie the next morning without trepidation. He had made the disclosure.

"And how did she bear it?"

"Like an angel! It seemed rather to be a relief to her mind, for she threw her arms around my neck, and asked if this was all that had lately made me unhappy.—But, poor girl," added he, "she cannot realize the change we must undergo. She has no idea of poverty but in the abstract; she has only read of it in poetry, where it is allied to love. She feels as yet no privation, she suffers no loss of accustomed conveniences nor elegancies. When we come practically to experience its sordid cares, its paltry wants, its petty humiliations—then will be the real trial."

"But," said I, "now that you have got over the severest task, that of breaking it to her, the sooner you let the world into the secret the better. The disclosure may be mortifying; but then it is a single misery and soon over; whereas you otherwise suffer it in anticipation, every hour of the day. It is not poverty so much as pretence, that harasses a ruined man—the struggle between a proud mind and an empty purse—the keeping up a hollow show that must soon come to an end. Have the courage to appear poor and you disarm poverty of its sharpest sting." On this point I found Leslie perfectly prepared. He had no false pride himself, and as to his wife, she was only anxious to conform to their altered fortunes.

Some days afterwards he called upon me in the evening. He had disposed of his dwelling house and taken a small cottage in the country, a few miles from town. He had been busied all day in sending out furniture. The new establishment required few articles, and those of the simplest kind. All the splendid furniture of his late residence had been sold, excepting his wife's harp. That, he said, was too closely associated with the idea of herself; it belonged to the little story of their loves; for some of the sweetest moments of their courtship were those when he had leaned over that instrument and listened to the melting tones of her voice. I could not but smile at this instance of romantic gallantry in a doting husband.

He was now going out to the cottage, where his wife had been all day superintending its arrangements. My feelings had become strongly interested in the progress of this family story, and, as it was a fine evening, I offered to accompany him.

He was wearied with the fatigues of the day, and as he walked out, fell into a fit of gloomy musing.

"Poor Mary!" at length broke, with a heavy sigh, from his lips.

"And what of her?" asked I: "has anything happened to her?"

"What," said he, darting an impatient glance, "is it nothing to be reduced to this paltry situation—to be caged in a miserable cottage—to be obliged to toil almost in the menial concerns of her wretched habitation?"

"Has she then repined at the change?"

"Repined! she has been nothing but sweetness and good humor. Indeed, she seems in better spirits than I have ever known her; she has been to me all love, and tenderness, and comfort!"

"Admirable girl!" exclaimed I. "You call yourself poor, my friend; you never were so rich—you never knew the boundless treasures of excellence you possess in that woman."

"Oh! but, my friend, if this first meeting at the cottage were over, I think I could then be comfortable. But this is her first day of real experience; she has been introduced into a humble dwelling—she has been employed all day in arranging its miserable equipments—she has, for the first time, known the fatigues of domestic employment—she has, for the first time, looked around her on a home destitute of everything elegant,—almost of everything convenient; and may now be sitting down, exhausted and spiritless, brooding over a prospect of future poverty."

There was a degree of probability in this picture that I could not gainsay, so we walked on in silence.

After turning from the main road up a narrow lane, so thickly shaded with forest trees as to give it a complete air of seclusion, we came in sight of the cottage. It was humble enough in its appearance, for the most pastoral poet; and yet it had a pleasing rural look. A wild vine had overrun one end in a profusion of foliage; a few trees threw their branches gracefully over it; and I observed several pots of flowers tastefully disposed about the door and on the grassplot in front. A small wicket gate opened upon a footpath that wound through some shrubbery to the door. Just as we approached, we heard the sound of music—Leslie grasped my arm; we paused and listened. It was Mary's voice singing. In a style of the most touching simplicity, a little air of which her husband was peculiarly fond.

I felt Leslie's hand tremble on my arm. He stepped forward to hear more distinctly. His step made a noise on the gravel walk. A bright, beautiful face glanced out at the window and vanished—a light footstep was heard—and Mary came tripping forth to meet us; she was in a pretty rural dress of white; a few wild flowers were twisted in her fine hair; a fresh bloom was on her cheek; her whole countenance beamed with smiles—I had never seen her look so lovely.

"My dear George," cried she, "I am glad you are come! I have been watching and watching for you; and running down the lane, and looking out for you. I've set out a table under a beautiful tree behind the cottage; and I've been gathering some of the most delicious strawberries for I know you are fond of them—and we have such excellent cream—and everything is so sweet and still here—Oh!" said she, putting her arm within his, and looking up brightly in his face. "Oh, we shall be so happy!"

Poor Leslie was overcome. He caught her to his bosom—he folded his arms round her—he kissed her again and again—he could not speak, but the tears gushed into his eyes; and he has often assured me, that though the world has since gone prosperously with him, and his life has indeed, been a happy one, yet never has he experienced a moment of more exquisite felicity.

Exercise:

Washington Irving's story is a textbook of traditional values, so first let's get them organized. Make two lists, one from the husband's point of view and one from the wife's. On each, list the aspects of the traditional marriage that result in benefits or disadvantages. Tag each with either a "B" or "D" depending on how you categorize it.

Try to organize the lists so as to make them comparable. Which partner gets the advantage, that is, who has more benefits and fewer obligations?

Are the benefits and obligations interrelated. Do some benefits depend on the other partner fulfilling obligations?

Try to do a risk analysis. If one partner does not perform is the other in greater jeopardy of losing benefits than the other? Which one?

Discussion Plan:

For the marriage to work so that each partner gets benefits the other partner must have certain *virtues*, that is, certain strengths of character that make them reliable, that make it likely that they will be willing and able to perform their obligations. Using the list of values that you have developed, describe the virtues of the ideal husband and of the ideal wife.

Another Perspective

Romantic love and marriage were not always bedfellows. Some societies have an ideal of marriage in which love does not have a prominent place. Such societies see marriage to be too important to be left up to individual choice—choice that is often based on the romantic ideal.

Harry Golden, Marriages Were Made In Heaven

The *shadkhan* was an important member of the first-generation society which I knew as a boy.

The "outside" people whom the young immigrant met immediately after settling himself with his relatives were first, the fellow who sold him a gold watch and chain "so you'll become a real American," and then the Tammany Hall worker who advised him about night study classes "so you can become a citizen and vote"; and, finally the *shadkhan*—the marriage broker.

Usually the *shadkhan* entered into the preliminary negotiations with the parent of the boy and girl, and in cases of a "single" boy, an orphan, or whose parents were still in Europe, the *shadkhan* dealt with an aunt or other relatives. After these initial discussions the parents of the girl told her of the negotiations and a formal meeting was arranged. The immediate reaction of the girl was based on an old East Side *shadkhan* joke: At the age of eighteen she asks, "What does he look like?" At the age of twenty five, she asks, "What does he do for a living?" And at the age of thirty, she asks "Where is he?"

The *shadkhan's* biggest headache was the amateur competition. Everybody was a part-time *shadkhan*. The average housewife with a million things to do for a family of a half-dozen children, always had a few irons in the fire with at least one *shidduch* (match) on tap for a niece, a nephew, or even boarder.

But the professionals, too, started out on a part-time basis. This was not a business which offered an immediate return. The remuneration was based on a small fee in the early days of the negotiations, followed by a percentage of the dowry involved, payable on the evening of the wedding. The *shadkhan* could not depend upon this profession for a livelihood. Often it was a rabbi or cantor who embarked on this career as a side line, as well as for its purely religious value: a *mitzvah* (a good deed added to the final reckoning). A part-time *shadkhan* I knew on my block operated a small cleaning-and-dyeing establishment. Eventually his many successful matches gave him a good reputation and he branched out a full-time *shadkhan*.

Eventually the *shadkhan* adopted certain symbols of his office: namely, a beard, a derby hat, and an umbrella. No one ever saw a *shadkhan* without an umbrella.

The umbrella was of tremendous importance to the immigrant people of the East Side. Folks bought an umbrella even before they bought a pair of eyeglasses, for the umbrella was the symbol of urban middle-class life.

The *shadkhan* had no sense of humor at all. The milieu which practices humor on a grand scale this fellow never cracked a smile. There were many jokes about the *shadkhan* and he was determined to do nothing that would add to the hilarity. "This is no laughing matter." No matter how two people are brought together, they will have the usual stormy courtship: quarrels, breaking off the engagement, making up, saying "good-bye forever," etc.

The great anxiety in a Jewish household was concerned with marrying off the daughter, and the anxiety increased a hundredfold for each additional daughter. And they had to be married off in proper sequence according to their age, the eldest first, and so on. The greatest fear of the family was that the eldest would be "left"—spinsterhood. The idea that a younger sister's marrying out of turn was bad luck for the older girl was based on fact rather than superstition. The word got around that the younger sister could no longer wait; this meant the family had abandoned hope for the older girl; therefore, there must be something wrong with her.

The whole operation required great tact. The first meeting of the couple was usually a Friday evening Sabbath dinner at the girl's home. Often the *shadkhan* came along, casual-like, just an old friend of the family bringing along a young stranger to a Sabbath meal. No one gave the slightest indication of what it was all about.

The younger children of school age were urged and bribed to be on their good behavior. But now for the problem. The younger sister who was PRETTY. The young man could very well come to see the older sister but fall in love with the younger one. The mother used tact. She began planning this the previous Wednesday; "Rachel, this Friday night go to spend the evening with your friend Naomi. I'll tell her mother when I see her in the market tomorrow." The younger sister had raised all kinds of hell for this very privilege many times, but now she is hesitant; she wants to know why. She knows why, of course, but before she is through, her mother will have to spell it out to her, every detail. The younger sister goes off to "hide" from her sister's fellow, and she is very happy about the whole thing. She is very happy about it because she's a woman who has been told she is pretty.

At the inception of the *shadkhan's* activities, the mother went into the details of her daughter's qualifications. She can cook, sew, take care of children, and play the piano.

There are other virtues. *"Mein Sarah is alle drei"* (My Sarah is all three). This meant that the girl had completed a course in business school and was now—*"ah stenographerinn, ah bookkeeperinn, und a typewriterka."* These Yiddish words need no translation. It was a big thing on the East Side for the girls to become "all three," and it makes me feel a little sad when I think of the drive behind it; the saving, the scrimping, the intensity, and the anxiety. Of course, when a mother extolled her daughter with all these qualifications, it meant one thing; that the girl was not what you would call pretty. But the *shadkhan* listened politely—all the time waiting for *takhlis*, a wonderful word which means "goal," "purpose," "essence"—the dowry.

The dowry (*nadan*) was not a "gift." These are two separate words in Hebrew. Neither should this *nadan*, in cash or real estate, be confused with the centuries-old custom in Eastern lands of the purchase price in money or goods for a wife. The *nadan* may or may not have been brought into Europe by the Jews, but it has long been part of the culture of the West. In fact, the *nadan* was a mark of status; and a girl in France, Ireland, Spain, and Italy would tease her friends if her parents had a larger dowry set aside for her. Often the dowry was part of the marriage contract, even when the bridegroom had not requested or expected it, or if he had independent means of his own. The situation added another English word to the Yiddish language. The word was "*millionaire*," and was used indiscriminately for any boy or man who made more than sixty dollars a week. "My Yetta is marrying a regular millionaire," said the mother to all her friends and neighbors. The use of this word became so widespread that it was modified eventually to "Jewish millionaire," which meant anyone worth $2,500 and up.

Basically the dowry was for the son-in-law so that he could continue to read or study the Torah—the Law—as free from financial care as possible. With the expansion of the commercial world, however, the purpose was extended to help the son-in-law get a start in some business. There is many a vast business enterprise in our country today which was started with a bride's dowry.

Since the negotiations involved many people—the two principals, the four parents, a few aunts, and the *shadkhan*—there were many areas of misunderstanding, perhaps even a bit of chicanery once in a while. A middle-aged widower calls on a widow. During the six or seven weeks of the courtship he has been her guest at the Friday evening Sabbath supper. On each of these Friday evenings, the widower sees the widow's little boy, a cute, curly-haired, eight-year-old child, and the widower grows very fond of the boy. Now could he suddenly break the spell of a pleasant evening and, out of a clear sky, ask, "Do you happen to have other children?" What kind of a stupid question is that? They are married and the day following, the widow's married sister brings over the other children, three little girls, probably. The widow smiles and says to her new husband, "Can you imagine such a thing, every Friday the three girls yell and holler that they want to visit their aunt, so what could I do?" The new-husband-widower listens to this tale as he watches the charming little boy joined by his three little sisters. If the guy has imagination and a sense of humor, he goes along and makes the best of it like a gentleman. But if he's a *grubbe yung* (ignoramus), he'll sue.

The philanthropists had set up a Jewish court on the East Side, still doing great work, which has saved the State of New York millions of dollars in court costs over a half century.

A groom may have misunderstood the terms of the dowry. The bride's parents may have promised to pay it in installments; the groom may have expected it all in one sum. There were all sorts of problems before the court. I examined the minutes of one such case tried in 1921.

The wedding guests were all assembled and the bride looked lovely. The rabbi was there and so were the musicians and the caterers, but no groom. Finally a message came from the groom. It was addressed to the bride's father and later was read into the court records: "You'll not see me there tonight, you faker. You promised a dowry of two thousand dollars cash and I haven't received it." The poor man was staggered and had to make an embarrassing excuse to his two hundred guests. The proprietor of the hall demanded payment for his outlay for one hundred couples. The jeweler was there. He had sold the ring to the bridegroom on credit. He immediately changes his status from guest to jeweler and wanted to know where he stood in the matter. During the hearing before the Jewish court, the bride's father testified that he had never promised a dowry of two thousand dollars. "My daughter," he said, "is known as the belle of Washington Heights, and the bridegroom is a window cleaner. It is reasonable that I, the father of the belle of Washington Heights, would offer a window cleaner a dowry of two thousand dollars? For two thousand dollars I could get a doctor, a lawyer, or a whatnot." The bride's father was suing the family of the groom for one thousand dollars' damages for the wedding arrangements. The court tried a reconciliation between the two young people and when that failed, it decided against the bride's father, stating that "dowry was ordained by rabbis, and each man must give part of his property to his marriageable daughter." The court also ordered the bride to return the ring to the jeweler, because the man was an innocent bystander. The court further publicly reprimanded the *shadkhan* as incompetent.

Most of the litigation before that court today involves business disputes or domestic relations complaints by litigants who want a quick decision or who cannot afford the legal expenses to see their matter through the State courts. There are not many dowry arguments today. The kids born in America have acquired great resourcefulness. They eased themselves into the American milieu with dances, proms, parties, socials, clubs, introductions, blind dates; and they bring home their own fellows.

Exercise:

Golden gives a enormous amounts of information, much of it representing values. These values are not disconnected, they form a *world view*, a way of life. To analyze a complex way of life we first identify elements and kinds of elements. Then we connect them in order to construct a hierarchy, showing which attitudes and practices reflect and influence which.

First, list as many beliefs and values held the people Golden describes.

The, classify the beliefs into three categories:

a) general beliefs about human nature

b) beliefs about what is desired and desirable

c) specific and general causal claims; what causes what to happen.

Don't be afraid to add and subtract from your lists as you develop the last part of the project.

Finally, order the items you have enumerated into a structure. Draw arrows showing which beliefs are supported by which others. Show patterns that reflect ways of justifying and ways of explaining. Construct little substructures that show characteristic arguments or patterns of justification.

Distinguish arrows that reflect inferences based on factual evidence or claims from those that are derived from ethical principles

Realism

After the initial excitement of setting up housekeeping wears off, the married couple settles into the routine of daily life. Sometimes the routine becomes so overpowering that it prevents the couple from seeing each other clearly. Image and reality, romance and practicality, and then sometimes the shock of recognition.

Sally Benson, The Overcoat

It had been noisy and crowded at the Milligans and Mrs. Bishop had eaten too many little sandwiches and too many iced cakes, so that now, out in the street, the air felt good to her, even if it was damp and cold. At the entrance of the apartment house, she took out her change purse and looked through it and found that by counting the pennies, too, she had just eighty-seven cents, which wasn't enough for a taxi from Tenth Street to Seventy-third. It was horrid never having enough money in your purse, she thought. Playing bridge, when she lost, she often had to give I.O.U.'s and it was faintly embarrassing, although she always managed to make them good. She resented Lila Hardy who could say, "Can anyone change a ten?" and who could take ten dollars from her small smart bag while the other women scurried about for change.

She decided it was too late to take a bus and that she might as well walk over to the subway, although the air down there would probably make her head ache. It was drizzling a little and the sidewalks were wet. And, as she stood on the corner waiting for the traffic lights to change, she felt horribly sorry for herself. She remembered as a young girl, she had always assumed she would have lots of money when she was older. She had planned what to do with it—what clothes to buy and what upholstery she would have in her car.

Of course, everybody nowadays talked poor and that was some comfort. But it was one thing to have lost your money and quite another never to have had any. It was absurd, though, to go around with less than a dollar in your purse. Suppose something happened? She was a little vague as to what might happen, but the idea fed her resentment.

Everything for the house, like food and things, she charged. Years ago, Robert had worked out some sort of budget for her but it had been impossible to keep their expenses under the right heading, so they had long ago abandoned it. And yet Robert always seemed to have money. That is, when she came to him for five or ten dollars, he managed to give it to her. Men were like that, she thought. They managed to keep money in their pockets but they had no idea you ever needed any. Well, one thing was sure: she would insist on having an allowance. Then she would at least know where she stood. When she decided this, she began to walk more briskly and everything seemed simpler.

The air in the subway was worse than usual and she stood on the local side waiting for a train. People who took the expresses seemed to push so and she felt tired and wanted to sit down. When the train came, she took a seat near the door and, although inwardly she was seething with rebellion, her face took on the vacuous look of other faces in the subway. At Eighteenth Street, a great many people got on and she found her vision blocked by a man who had come in and was hanging to the strap in front of her. He was tall and thin and his overcoat, which hung loosely on him and swayed with the motion of the train, smelled unpleasantly of damp wool. The buttons of the overcoat were of imitation leather and the button directly in front of Mrs. Bishop's eyes evidently had come off and been sewed back on again with black thread, which didn't match the coat at all.

It was what is known as a swagger coat but there was nothing very swagger about it now. The sleeve that she could see was almost threadbare around the cuff and a small shred from the lining hung down over the man's hand. She found herself looking intently at his hand. It was long and pallid and not too clean. The nails were very short as though they had been bitten and there was a discolored callus on his second finger where he probably held his pencil. Mrs. Bishop, who prided herself on her powers of observation, put him in the white collar class. He most likely, she thought, was the father of a large family and had a hard time sending them all through school. He undoubtedly never spent money on himself. That would account for the shabbiness of his overcoat. And he was probably horribly afraid of losing his job. His house was always noisy and smelled of cooking. Mrs. Bishop couldn't decide whether to make his wife a fat slattern or to have her an invalid. Either would be quite consistent.

She grew warm with sympathy for the man. Every now and then he gave a slight cough, and that increased her interest and her sadness. It was a soft, pleasant sadness and made her feel resigned to life. She decided that she would smile at him when she got off. It would be the sort of smile that couldn't help but make him feel better, as it would be very obvious that she understood and was sorry.

By the time the train reached Seventy-second Street, the smell of wet wool, the closeness of the air, and the confusion of her own worries had made her feelings less poignant, so that her smile, when she gave it, lacked something. The man looked away embarrassed.

Her apartment was too hot and the smell of broiling chops sickened her after the enormous tea she had eaten. She could see Maude, her maid, setting the table in the dining-room for dinner. Mrs. Bishop had bought smart little uniforms for her, but there was nothing smart about Maude and the uniforms never looked right.

Robert was lying on the living-room couch, the evening newspaper over his face to shield his eyes. He had changed his shoes, and the gray felt slippers he wore were too short for him and showed the imprint of his toes, and looked depressing. Years ago, when they were first married, he used to dress for dinner sometimes. He would shake up a cocktail for her and things were quite gay and almost the way she had imagined they would be. Mrs. Bishop didn't believe in letting yourself go and it seemed to her that Robert let himself go out of sheer perversity. She hated him as he lay there, resignation in every line of his body. She envied Lila Hardy her husband who drank but who, at least, was somebody. And she felt like tearing the newspaper from his face because her anger and disgust were more than she could bear.

For a minute she stood in the doorway trying to control herself and then she walked over to a window and opened it roughly. "Goodness," she said. "Can't we ever have any air in here?"

Robert gave a slight start and sat up. "Hello, Mollie," he said. "You home?"

"Yes, I'm home," she answered. "I came home in the subway."

Her voice was reproachful. She sat down in the chair facing him and spoke more quietly so that Maude couldn't hear what she was saying. "Really, Robert," she said, "it was dreadful. I came out from the tea in all that drizzle and couldn't even take a taxi home. I had just exactly eighty-seven cents. Just eighty-seven cents!"

"Say," he said. "That's a shame. Here." He reached in his pocket and took out a small roll of crumpled bills. "Here," he repeated. And handed her one. She saw that it was five dollars.

Mrs. Bishop shook her head. "No, Robert," she told him. "That isn't the point. The point is that I've really got to have some sort of allowance. It isn't fair to me. I never have any money! Never! It's got so it's positively embarrassing!"

Mr. Bishop fingered the five dollar bill thoughtfully. "I see," he said. "You want an allowance. What's the matter? Don't I give you money every time you ask for it?"

"Well, yes," Mrs. Bishop admitted. "But it isn't like my own. An allowance would be more like my own."

"Now, Mollie," he reasoned. "If you had an allowance, it would probably be gone by the tenth of the month."

"Don't treat me like a child," she said. "I just won't be humiliated any more."

Mr. Bishop sat turning the five dollar bill over and over in his hand. "And how much do you think you should have?" he asked.

"Fifty dollars a month," she told him. And her voice was harsh and strained. "That's the very least I can get along on. Why, Lila Hardy would laugh at fifty dollars a month."

"Fifty dollars a month," Mr. Bishop repeated. He coughed a little, nervously, and ran his fingers through his hair. "I've had a lot of things to attend to this month. But, well, maybe if you would be willing to wait until the first of next month, I might manage."

"Oh, next month will be perfectly all right," she said, feeling it wiser not to press her victory. " But don't forget all about it. Because I shan't."

As she walked toward the closet to put away her wraps, she caught sight of Robert's overcoat on the chair near the door. He had tossed it carelessly across the back of the chair as he came in. One sleeve was hanging down and the vibration of her feet on the floor had made it swing gently back and forth. She saw that the cuff was badly worn and a bit of the lining showed. It looked dreadfully like the sleeve of the overcoat she had seen in the subway. And, suddenly, looking at it, she had a horrible sinking feeling, as though she were falling in a dream.

Discussion Plan:

Love, commitment and respect are certainly among the most central of the virtues in a marriage.

Which attitudes and behaviors reflect the absence or the presence of love, in the Bishop's life together, which reflect commitment and which respect?

What in the lives of the Bishops makes love, commitment and respect more difficult?

What aspects of their live is love, commitment and respect necessary for?

Desire

Marriage is supposed to solve the problem of sexuality. The sexual urges of the partners are to be directed at each other. All thought of others as sexually attractive stops and the sexual act is confined to the marriage bed. But something in this picture does not ring true. The sexual urge is not so easily contained.

Colette, The Secret Woman

He had been looking for a long time at the sea of masks in front of him, suffering vaguely from their mixture of colours and from the synchronization of two orchestras which were too close. His hood constricted his temples; a nervous headache was coming on between his eyes. But he relished, without impatience, a state of *malaise* and pleasure which permitted the imperceptible passing of the hours. He had wandered along all the corridors of the Opera, drunk the silvery dust of the dance-floor, recognized bored friends and placed round his neck the indifferent arms of a very plump girl who was disguised as though humorously as a sylph.

This hooded doctor was embarrassed by his fancy-dress and staggered about like a man in skirts, but he dared not remove either his costume or his hood, because of his school-boy lie:

"I'll be spending tomorrow night at Nogent," he had said to his wife the day before. "They've just telephoned me, and I'm very much afraid that my patient, you know, the poor old lady.... Just imagine, I was looking forward to this ball like any kid. Isn't it ridiculous, a man of my age who's never been to the Opera ball?"

"Utterly ridiculous, darling, utterly! If I'd known, perhaps, I wouldn't have married you...."

She laughed, and he admired her narrow face, pink, matt and long, like a delicate sugared almond.

"Don't you want to go to the green and purple ball? Even without me, if it amuses you, darling...."

She had trembled, there passed through her one of those long shudders of disgust which brought a tremble to her hair, her delicate hands and her bosom beneath her white dress, whenever she saw a slug or a filthy passer-by:

"As for me.... Can you see me in a crowd, at the mercy of all those hands.... What do you think, I'm not straitlaced, I'm.... I'm put out! There's nothing to be done about it!"

Leaning against the loggis balustrade, above the great staircase, he thought of this trembling hand, as he contemplated before him two enormous square hands, with black nails, clasped round the bare back of a sultana. Emerging from the braided sleeves of a Venetian lord they dug into the white female flesh as though it were dough.... Because he was thinking of her he jumped violently as he heard beside him a little uh-hum, a kind of cough typical of his wife.... He turned round and saw someone sitting astride the balustrade, wearing a long and impenetrable disguise, looking like Pierrot because of the smock with vast sleeves, the loose trousers, the headband and the plaster-white colour which covered the small area of skin visible below the fluffy lace of the mask. The fluid fabric of the costume and the cap, woven of dark purple and silver, shone like the conger-eels that you fish for at night with iron hooks from boats lit by lamps burning resin. Overwhelmed with astonishment he awaited the recurrence of the little uh-hum, which did not come....The eel-like Pierrot remained seated in nonchalant fashion and its heel tapped against the marble baluster, revealing only two satin slippers, while a black-gloved hand lay folded at one hip. The two oblique slits in the mask, carefully meshed over with tulle, revealed only a subdued glint of indeterminate colour.

He almost called out "Irene!" And restrained himself, remembering his own lie. Since he was clumsy at play-acting he also rejected the idea of disguising his voice. The Pierrot scratched its thigh, with a free, proletarian gesture, and the anxious husband breathed again.

" Ah! It's not her."

But the Pierrot pulled out of a pocket a flat gold box, opened it and took out a lipstick, and the anxious husband recognized an antique snuff-box fitted with a mirror inside, the last birthday gift.... He placed his left hand over the painful area of his heart with such a brusque and involuntary gesture that the eel-like Pierrot noticed him.

"Is that a declaration, purple Domino?"

He didn't reply, for he was half stifled with surprise, waiting and nightmare, and listened for a long moment at the barely disguised voice—the voice of his wife. The Eel looked at him, as it sat in cavalier fashion, its head on one side like a bird; it shrugged its shoulders, jumped to the ground and moved away. Its movement liberated the anxious husband who, restored to a state of active and normal jealousy, began to think again and rose without haste to follow his wife.

"She's here for someone, with someone. In less than an hour I'll know everything."

A hundred hoods, purple and green, guaranteed that he would be neither noticed nor recognized. Irene walked in front of him, nonchalantly; he was astonished to find that she rolled her hips softly and dragged her feet a little as though she were wearing Turkish slippers. A Byzantine figure, wearing emerald green, embroidered with gold, seized her as she went by, and her body bent in his arms; she looked thinner, as though the embrace would cut her in two. Her husband ran a few steps and reached the couple just as Irene was crying flatteringly "You big brute!"

She moved away, with the same relaxed and quiet step, stopping often, musing at the doors to the open boxes, hardly ever looking round. She hesitated at the foot of the steps, turned off to the side, came back towards the entrance of the orchestra stalls, joined a noisy, closely packed crowd with a skillful gliding movement like the blade of a knife fitting neatly into its sheath. Ten arms imprisoned her, an almost naked wrestler pinned her firmly against the edge of the ground-floor boxes and held her there. She gave way beneath the weight of the naked man, threw back her head in laughter that was drowned by other laughter, and the man in the purple hood saw her teeth gleam beneath the lace of the mask. Then she escaped easily and sat down on the steps which led to the dance-floor. Her husband, standing two paces behind her, looked at her. She readjusted her mask and her crumpled smock, then tightened the headband. She seemed as calm as if she had been alone, and moved away again after a few moments' rest. She went down the steps, placed her hand on the shoulders of a warrior who asked her, silently, to dance, and she danced, clinging to him.

"That's the man," the husband said to himself.

But she did not say a word to the dancer encased in iron whose skin was damp, and left him quietly after the dance. She went off to drink a glass of champagne at the buffet, then a second glass, paid, stood by motionless and curious as two men began to fight among screaming women. She also amused herself by placing her little satanic hands, which were entirely black, on the white bosom of a Dutch woman wearing a gold head-dress, who cried out nervously.

At last the anxious man who was following her saw her stop, as though bumping against him on the way, close to a young man who had collapsed on a bench, out of breath, and was fanning himself with his mask. She bent down, disdainfully held the savage, handsome young face, and kissed the panting, half-open mouth....

But her husband, instead of rushing forward and forcing the two mouths apart, disappeared into the crowd. In his consternation he no longer feared, no longer hoped for betrayal. He was sure now that Irene did not know the young man, drunk with dancing, whom she was kissing, nor the Hercules; he was sure that she was neither waiting nor looking for anyone, and that abandoning the lips she held beneath her own like an empty grape, she was going to leave again the next moment, wander about once more, collect some other passer-by, forget him, and simply enjoy, until she felt tired and went back home, the monstrous pleasure of being alone, free, honest in her crude, native state, of being the unknown woman, eternally solitary and shameless, restored to her irremediable solitude and immodest innocence by a little mask and a concealing costume.

Exercise:

In the following examples tell if you think the behavior described should or should not be permitted in a primary love relationship. If permitted should they be kept private or not.

1. Going out with someone other than your lover.
2. Going to a party or concert with someone other than your lover.
3. Going to a party alone and picking someone else up.
4. Flirting with someone else.
5. Necking at a party with someone else
6. Making love with someone else as a casual flirtation..
7. Fantasizing about someone other than your lover.
8. Looking at pornography.
9. Looking to someone else for sympathy or support.
10. Having a romantic but not sexual interlude.
11. Looking to another lover for fantasies that you cannot satisfy with your lover
12. Looking to another lover to achieve sexual satisfaction that you cannot get from your lover.
13. Getting warmth and personal respect that you are not getting from your lover from someone who is a possible sex partner.
14. Having a close friend that is attractive to you, and who means a great deal to you.

Exercise:

The "Secret Woman" presents an image of pleasure seeking individuals protected by their anonymity from any but the most immediate consequences of their actions. Such an attitude is frequently referred to as *hedonistic*, it assumes that pleasure, usually thought of as sensual and immediate, is the determining value. In the following outline a hedonistic argument to justify the decisions described.

1. After a grueling day at school, Jack decides to spend the afternoon watching a double feature at the movies.
2. Jill decides to spend her entire allowance on a cashmere sweater.
3. Jack, at the Thanksgiving dinner, has a piece of all three pies.
4. Jill, exhausted, postpones her homework and watches soap operas instead.

5. Jack reads a copy of *Playboy* instead of doing Geometry.

6. Jill at a rock concert ends up necking with a boy she just met.

7. Jack gets roaring drunk during a Halloween party.

8. Jill smokes pot on the way to school to get her in a good mood for the day.

9. Jack discovers his mother's Valiums and finds that they help ease the tension of classes, especially during tests.

10. After limiting their relationship to petting for almost a year, Jack and Jill go all the way.

11. Jack decides to go to Florida during spring break.

12. Jill and a friend decide to catch a ride to Mexico with a group of collegeboys.

Now go back over all of the justifications you gave and give an argument against the decisions based on Mill's discussion of pleasure in *Utilitarianism*.

Responsibility

We enthusiastically enter into marriage because it promises us something that is missing in our lives—love, security, intimacy. Seldom do we consider the things we must give up and the new limitations imposed on us by the married state. The complications that come with marriage, children, personal and financial responsibility, make us yearn for a simpler life, a freer life.

Tennessee Williams, Moony's Kid Don't Cry

MOONY	A Workingman
JANE	His Wife
MOONY'S KID	(Not a speaking part)

SCENE: Kitchen of a cheap three-room flat in the industrial section of a large American city.

Stove and sink are eloquent of slovenly housekeeping. A wash-line, stretched across one corner of the room, is hung with diapers and blue work-shirts. Above the stove is nailed a placard, KEEP SMILING. The kitchen table supports a small artificial Christmas tree.

By far the most striking and attractive article in the room is a brand-new hobby-horse that stands stage Center. There is something very gallant, almost exciting, about this new toy. It is chestnut brown, with a long flowing mane, fine golden nostrils and scarlet upcurled lips. It looks like the very spirit of unlimited freedom and fearless assault.

As the curtain opens, the stage is dark except for a faint bluish light through the widow—and door-panes. Offstage in the next room are heard smothered groans and creaking bedsprings.

> Jane. (Off-stage.) Quit that floppin' around. It keeps me awake.
>
> Moony. Think I'm gettin' any sleep, do you?! (SOUND: More rattling.)
>
> Jane. Quiet! You'll wake the kid up.
>
> Moony. The kid, the kid! What's more important, him sleeping or me? Who brings home the pay-check, me or the kid? (Pause.)
>
> Jane. I'll get up an' fix you a cup of hot milk. That'll quiet you down maybe. (MOONY grumbles incoherently. JANE pads softly on stage, into the kitchen. She is amazingly slight, like a tiny mandarin, enveloped in the ruins of a once gorgeously-flowered Japanese silk kimono. As she prepares the hot milk for MOONY, she pads about the kitchen in a pair of men's felt slippers which she has a hard time keeping on her small feet. She squeezes the kimono right about her chest, and shivers. Coughs once or twice. Glances irritably at the alarm-clock on window-sill, which says nearly four o'clock in the morning. JANE is still young, but her pretty, small-featured

face has a yellowish unhealthy look. Her temples and nostrils are greased with Vick's Vap-o-Rub and her dark hair is tousled.)

Jane. (Strident whisper.) What for? I'll bring yer milk in. (SOUND: scraping of furniture and heavy footsteps.) That's it, be sure you wake the kid up—clumsy ox! (MOONY appears in the doorway, a strongly built young workingman about twenty-five years old. He blinks his eyes and scowls irritably as he draws on his flannel shirt and stuffs it under the belt of his corduroy pants) It's that beer-drinkin'. Makes gas on yer stomach an' keeps yuh from sleepin'.

Moony. Aw, I had two glasses right after dinner.

Jane. Two a them twenty-six ounces!—Quit that trampin' around, for Christ's sake! Can't you set still a minute?

Moony. Naw, I feel like I got to be moving.

Jane. Maybe you got high blood-pressure.

Moony. Naw, I got a wild hair. This place's give me the jitters. You know it's too damn close in here. Can't take more'n six steps in any direction without coming smack up against another wall. (Half grinning.) I'd like to pick up my axe and swing into this wall—Bet I could smash clean through it in a couple of kicks!

Jane. Moony! Why didn't I marry an ape an' go live in the zoo?

Moony. I don't know. (JANE pours the steaming milk into a blue cup.)

Jane. Set down an' drink that. Know what time it is? Four o'clock in the morning!

Moony. Four o'clock, huh? (He continues to move restlessly about.) Yeah. Soon ole fact'ry whistle be blowin'. Come on, you sonovaguns! Git to work!—Old Dutchman be standin' there with his hands on his little pot-belly, watchin' em punch in their cards. "Hi, dere, Moony," he says. "Late agin, huh? Vot you tink dis iss maybe, an afdernoon tea?" That's his joke. You know a Dutchman always has one joke that he keeps pluggin' at. An' that's his. Ev'ry morning the same damn thing—

Jane. Yeah? Well—

Moony. "Ha, ha, Moony," he says, "you been out star-gazin' las' night! How many vas dere, Moony? How many stars vas dere out las' night? Ha, ha, ha!" (Strides over to the window—flings it up.)

Jane. Put that back down! I ain't got a stitch a clothes on under this.

Moony. I'll say to him, "Sure, I seen 'em las' night. But not like they was in Ontario, not by a long shot, Mister." Grease-bubbles! that's what they look most like from here. Why, up in the North Woods at night—

Jane. (Impatiently.) The North Woods! Put that thing down!

Moony. Okay. (Obeys.)

Jane. Here. Drink yer milk. You act like a crazy man, honest to Jesus you do!

Moony. Okay. Would that give the Dutchman a laugh!

Jane. What would? You better be careful.

Moony. He'll go all over the plant—tell the boys what Moony said this morning—said he'd seen the stars las' night but not like they was in Ontario when he was choppin' down the big timber.

Jane. Yes, you'll give him a swell impression with talk of that kind. I'm dog-tired. (Pours herself some of the steaming milk.)

Moony. Ever seen the St. Lawrence river?

Jane. Naw, I've seen wet diapers, that's all, for so long that—!

Moony. That's what I'll ask the Dutchman. I'll ask him if he's ever seen the St. Lawrence river.

Jane. (Glancing at him suspiciously.) What would you ask him that for?

Moony. She's big. See? She's nearly as big and blue as the sky is, an' the way she flows is straight north. You ever heard of that, Jane? A river that flowed straight north?

Jane. (Indifferently, as she sips her hot milk.) No.

Moony. Only river I ever known of that flowed north!

Jane. Emma says a drop of paregoric would keep his bowels from runnin' off like that. I think I'll try it next time.

Moony. We was talkin' about it one day an' Spook says it's because the earth is curved down that way toward the Arctic Circle! (Grins.)

Jane. What?

Moony. He said that's why she flows north—

Jane. Who cares?

Moony. Naw, the Dutchman don't neither. That's why I tell him. Makes it funny, see? I'll tell him she's big, damn big, an' they call her the Lake of a Thousand Islands!

Jane. He'll say you're crazy. He'll tell you to go an' jump in it!

Moony. Sure he will. That's what makes it funny. I'll tell him she's big an' blue as the sky is, with firs an' pines an' tamaracks on both sides of her fillin' the whole God-beautiful air with—the smell of—Hot milk, huh? Wouldn't that give the Dutchman a laugh!—Hot milk at four o'clock in the morning!— He'd go all over the plant an' tell the boys that Moony must have his liddle hot milk at night when he goes bye-bye with the Sandman.

Jane. Louise Krause's husband commenced sayin' such things an' they called out the ambulance squad. Right now he's in a straitjacket in the psychopathic ward an' when Louise went up to see him he didn't remember who she was even! Demen-shuh pre-cox they called it! (MOONY seizes cup and dashes milk on the floor!

Moony. Hot milk, huh?

Jane. Oh, dear Christ! You an' your kid, what a mess you both are! No wonder they all make fun of you down at the plant. The way that you act there's only one word for it—crazy! (MOONY snorts indignantly.) Yes, crazy! Crazy is the only word for your actions!

Jane. Original, yeah, you're so stinkin' original it ain't even funny! Believe me if I'd a-known—

Moony. I look at things diff'runt—(Struggling for self-justification.)—that's all. Other guys—you know how it is—they don't care. They eat, they drink, they sleep with their women. What the hell do they care? The sun keeps rising and Saturday night they get paid!—Okay, okay, okay! Some day they kick off. What of it? they got kids to grow up an' take their places. Work in the plant. Eat, drink, sleep with their women—an' get paid Saturday night!—But me—(He laughs bitterly.) My God, Jane, I want something more than just that!

Jane. What more do you want, you poor fool? There ain't nothing more than just that—Of course if you was rich and could afford a big house and a couple of limoozines—

Moony. (Disgustedly.) Aw, you—you don't even get what I'm aimin' at, Jane! (He sinks wearily down on checkered linoleum and winds arms about his knees.) You never could get it. It's something that ain't contagious.

Jane. Well, I'm glad for that. I'd rather have small-pox.

Moony. I found a guy once that did. An old duck up on the river. He got his back hurt, couldn't work, was waiting to be shipped home—We got drunk one night an' I spilled how I felt about things. He said, "Sure. You ain't satisfied. Me neither. We want something more than what life ever gives to us, kid."

Jane. It gives you what you can get.

Moony. Oh, I dunno. I look at my hands sometimes, I look an' I look at 'em. God, but they look so damn funny!

Jane. You look at your hands! Such crap!

Moony. They're so kind of empty an' useless! You get what I mean? I feel like I oughta be doin' something with these two han's of mine besides what I'm doin' now—runnin' bolts through an everlastin' chain!

Jane. Here's something. (Flings him a dish rag.) Try holdin' this for a change in them wonderful hands—Mop that milk up off the floor!

Moony. (Idly twisting the cloth.) An' then sometimes I think it ain't my han's that're empty. It's something else inside me that is.

Jane. Yeh, it's probably yer brain. Will you get that milk swabbed up?

Moony. It's already swabbed! (Rises and stretches.) Moony's a free agent. He don't give a damn what anyone thinks. Live an' die, says, Moony, that's all there is to it! (He tosses the wet rag back to the sink.)

Jane. (Straightening things in a lifeless, ineffectual way.) Believe me, if I'd a-known you was gonna turn out this way, I'd a-kept my old job. I'd a-said to Mr. O'Connor, "Sure thing! Go ahead an' get me that chinchilla coat."

Moony. Sure you would. I know it, sweetheart.

Jane. (Beginning to sniffle.) What's the good of a girl trying to keep herself straight? The way things turns out, a good proposition like Mr. O'Connor could offer would be the best thing. But no! I had such delusions about cha! You talked so swell! You made such a lovely impression that time we first met!

Moony. Lots of water's run under the bridge since then.

Jane. Yeah.

Moony. When was that, Jane? How long ago was it?

Jane. Ten months; an' it seems ten years!

Moony. Ten months. And how old's the kid? One month? Exactly one month?

Jane. (Furiously.) You've got a nerve to say that? As if it was me that insisted, that couldn't wait even until we'd—

Moony. Naw, it wasn't your fault. It was nature got hold of us both that night, Jane. Yuh remember? The Paradise dance-hall down on the water-front huh? My first night in town after six months up in the woods. You had on a red silk dress. Yuh remember? Cut down sorta low in front. Hah, you was real pretty then—your hair frizzed up in the back in a thousan' or so little curls that I could just barely poke my littlest finger through!

Jane. (Falling under a nostalgic spell.) Yeah. (Her face softens.) I useter have it done ev'ry Satiddy night. Mamie said she never seen hair that could take such a curl!

Moony. (With sly cruelty.) Yeh, that's how it was—them curls—an' the red silk dress—it was nature got hold us both that night, huh, Jane?

Jane. (Suspecting an innuendo.) What d'yuh mean by that?

Moony. The way you pressed up against me when we was dancing—that was nature, wasn't it, Jane? And when they played "Roses of Picardy" an' the lights was turned out—we was dancin' real slow—we was almost standin' still—your breath was so warm on my neck, so warm—you had on a kind of perfume—

Jane. Perfume? Oh, yes, Narcissus perfume!—Mr. O'Connor give it to me for my birthday.

Moony. Yeah, narcissus, that's it—narcissus! An' what was it, Jane you whispered in my ear?

Jane. (Indignantly.) Me whispered? It was you that whispered, not me!

Moony. Was it? Maybe it was. You didn't have to say nothin', the way you danced was enough!—Anyhow, I got hooked.

Jane. (Furiously.) Hooked! Hooked! You dare to say such a thing?!

Moony. Yes, I was hooked all right. Narcissus perfume, little curls, an' a low-cut dress. Makin' me think that holdin' you in my arms an' waltzin' around a two-bit arch-acher was better'n holdin' an axe in my two han's up in the North woods an' choppin' down big trees!

Jane. (Choking.) You—you—! (Covers her face.)

Moony. (A little less harshly.) Aw, well, I don't mean that I'm—sorry about it—exactly…

Jane. (Brokenly.) How didja mean it, I'd liketa know then?

Moony. (Pacing about the kitchen.) Oh, I dunno, I dunno! (Suddenly stops and catches Jane in his arms.) People say things happen! What does it mean? I dunno. Seems to me like a crazy man, deaf, dumb, and blind, could have put together a better kind of a world than this is! (He kisses JANE'S bare shoulder where the kimono has slipped down a little.) Let's get out of it, honey!

Jane. (Sniffling.) Out of it? What d'yuh mean?

Moony. (Violently.) Chuck it all; the whole damn thing—that's what!

Jane. You mean—(She backs away from him, frightened.) Kill ourselves?

Moony. (Laughing impatiently.) Well, no—no! I don't wanta die! I wanta live!—What I mean is, get out of this place, this lousy town—Smoke, whistles, plants, factories, buildings, buildings, buildings!—You get caught in 'em, you never can find your way out!—So break away quick while you can!—Get out where it's clean an' there's space to swing an axe in! An' some time to swing it! Oh, God, Jane, don't you see—see—see?

Jane. Yes. You mean hop a freight train! (Laughs mockingly.)

Moony. Sure that's it if you want to! Tell the Dutchman good-bye—tell him to kiss my Aunt Fanny!

Jane. (Hysterically.) Me with the baby an' my infection of the breast—you with your axe! We'll spend Christmas in a box-car, won't we, Moony?

Moony. You bet!—Me with my axe, we'll chop a way through this world!

Jane. (Laughing.) What a joke,—what a lovely scream that is!

Moony. A joke, huh? Who said a joke?

Jane. Moony, Moony, my great big wonderful man! He'll cut a way—(Chokes with laughter.)—through this world!

Moony. (Getting sore.) Make fun of me, huh?

Jane. Moony they call him! Down at the plant it's Moony this, Moony that! All of them making fun of my man, laughing at him right to his face, and he's so damn dumb he don't know it! They got your number, they have! The Dutchman's got your number. You're just a star-gazer! You oughta put up your tent an' tell fortunes! Oh, you damn fool! If it wasn't so funny I could cry, I could cry! You with your axe! We'll spend Christmas in a boxcar! You'll chop a way through the world! Ha, ha! You with your axe? What a scream!—Couldn't even chop down a kid's Christmas tree—I hadda buy one at the dime store! And that horse—(She gets breathless and hoarse from laughter.) That's the best one! Bring home a five-dollar hobby-horse when we ain't even got money enough to pay the hospital bill!

Moony. I lied to you, Jane, I paid ten-fifty for that little horse.

Jane. (Aghast.) Ten-fifty? You—you—No, it's impossible—even you couldn't—

Moony. It was worth more than that!

Jane. Worth more? More?! Worth—! (She is breathless.)

Moony. Sure it was!

Jane. Buys a ten-fifty hobby-horse for a month-old-baby—They lock people up for doing less than that!

Moony. Aw, he'll grow up to it, Jane. (He is a little abashed.) I had one o' these things when I was a kid.

Jane. You musta got thrown off it an' landed on your head!

Moony. Naw, Dad got drunk on Saturday night, an' bought me one at a junk-shop. Mother, she felt like you did, when he come home with it. But me, I was nuts about it. Him an' me, both, we got on the horse—him in back, me in front—an' sang "Ride a Cock-horse to Danbury Cross."

Jane. Oh, my God! Now I know where you got it. He was a lunatic, too!

Moony. Naw, he was smart. He run out on us.

Jane. Run out on your mother, he did? Well, it's not surprising!

Moony. I never heard of him since.

Jane. Well—he probably got what was coming to him.

Moony. (With quick rage.) Better than what I got!

Jane. What you got?

Moony. A skinny yellow cat—that's what I got!

Jane. (Gasping.) Oh—! God oughta strike you down dead for saying a thing like that!

Moony. Yeah? I say it again—a yellow cat,—a skinny yellow cat! (JANE strikes him across the face, MOONY becomes like a mad animal. Roars and lunges forward—clutches JANE by the throat. They grapple fiercely for several moments. Than JANE collapses in his arms)

Jane. (Weakly.) Lemme go—please—for God's sake!

Moony. (Disgustedly.) Ahhh—yer too soft! (He flings her away from him. She falls against interior door, and hangs onto knob and edge of sink for support. MOONY hitches his belt undecidedly. He can't look at JANE'S dazed face. He is ashamed, but still defiant.) I'm leaving you now—get that? I'm checking out. You can tell the Dutchman to give you my pay—owes me three days—Time an' a ha'f for Saturday—(Gives his belt final hitch, and moves over to peg where his lumberman's jacket is hanging. He gives JANE a swift furtive glance as he puts on the jacket; says: "H'mmm!" Stoops down to pick up his axe. Feels the blade with a gingerly pride. Takes awkward practice swing. Eyes glow triumphantly to life. He looks again at JANE like an escaped animal at a cage. She does not move. She stares at him with hurt animal eyes. MOONY spits on his fingers, runs them along the axe blade again. Hoarsely) Pretty sharp, still. Good ole axe-h'mmm! (He starts toward the outer door.) Maybe I'll—see you sometime—Jane. (Fumbles with latch.) So long. (He jerks door open. Stands on threshold.) H'mmm. Feel that wind. Good an' clear tonight. A touch a frost in the air. An' them stars. Millions of 'em, huh? Quantity production, everything on a big scale,—that's God! Millions of stars—millions of people. Only He knew what to do with the stars.

Stuck 'em up there in the sky to look pretty. But people—down here in the mud. Ugh, too many of 'em, God! They must have run away with you, I guess. Crawling over each other, snatching and tearing, living an' dying till the earth's just a big soup of dead bodies!—How did that happen? Gosh, it's sure funny!—Oh, well what's the use? A man's gotta live his own life. Cut his own ways through the woods somehow—(The cold air sweeping into the room brings JANE our of her stupefaction. She slides to the floor and crawls toward MOONY like a half-crushed animal.)

Jane. Moony!—(Hoarsely.)—You wouldn't walk out on me, honey? Me with the baby and my infection of the breast, and no money or nothing? (MOONY turns toward her a tortured face. Snatches at his pockets and flings a few coins on the floor.)

Moony. Four bits! Tobacco money! Now you got the whole works—so good-bye!

Jane. Wait! (She clutches his arm and her fury makes her inescapable.) There's something you got to take with you! Your property, Moony—you might as well take it along!

Moony. I got all I want.

Jane. No, you ain't. There's something else that goes with you. You just wait here for a second, I'll wrap it up for you—(Crosses quickly to door upstage.)

Moony. What the hell are you—! (He hesitates at the door. JANE quickly reappears with the baby in her arms.)

Jane. Here! Here's the kid, Moony! Take him with you. Sure.—Go along, now, the two of you! (Shoves baby into MOONY'S unwilling arms.) Me, I can't be bothered with no brats. I got to go back to work. O'Connor will give me my old job back. Sure he will. You two can go an' hop a freight an' spend Christmas in a box-car. Maybe you'll find your old man—You'll have a swell time singing "Ride a Cock-horse" together! (She laughs wildly and runs out of the room. MOONY gingerly holds the baby. Looks helplessly down at its face. Frowns. Swears under his breath. Finally slams the door shut.)

Moony. Another one of her lousy tricks! (Baby starts crying.) SHUT UP! (The more softly.) Moony's kid don't cry! Grows up an' swings a big axe like his Daddy. Cuts his own way through the woods. (He walks away from the door, completely absorbed now in the baby, and apparently forgetting that he ever had any intention of going away.) Lookit the hobby-horse! (Stands above the new toy.) Santie Claus bought it for Moony's Kid. Ten-fifty it cost! See? How shiny it is! Nice, huh? Nice! What are you crying for? Daddy ain't going nowhere. Naw!—Daddy was only—fooling ...

Discussion Plan:

Decisions in life are built upon expectations, and moral choices frequently are the result of taking into account expected consequences. But if we do not know what to expect, how can we choose the right course of action?

1. What expectations seemed to govern Moony's choice of wife?
2. What situations in the play show Moony to have been wrong?
3. Where Moony's expectations reasonable?
4. What would you say were Jane's expectations for life with Moony?
5. Have her expectations been realized?
6. Given that things have turned out as they have, do you think Moony is still obligated to his family?
7. What does Moony expect from a life without his wife and child?
8. Are these expectations reasonable?
9. Explain the symbol of the rocking horse as a metaphor for the characters' way of looking at life? Does this help us to understand their expectations and the values behind their choices?
10. What expectations are behind Jane's wanting Moony to take the baby? What obligations?
11. How does the title of the play relate to the various characters and the way they see their lives?

Duty

What makes an act moral? The complexities of life make the results of our actions hard to predict, and their consequences difficult to evaluate. Immanuel Kant has taken the most rigorous view; morality requires no more and no less than the intention to do good—the good will. What we do is right independently of the consequences of our acts and even independently of our desires and wishes for happiness. To be moral is to act in order to be moral!

Immanuel Kant, The Categorical Imperative

The Good Will

Nothing can possibly be conceived in the world, or even out of it, which can be called good without qualification, except a *good will*. Intelligence, wit, judgment, and the other *talents* of the mind, however they may be named, or courage, resolution, perseverance, as qualities of temperament, are undoubtedly good and desirable in many respects; but these gifts of nature may also become extremely bad and mischievous if the will which is to make use of them, and which, therefore, constitutes what is called *character*, is not good. It is the same with *gifts of fortune*. Power, riches, honor, even health, and the general well-being and contentment with one's condition which is called *happiness*, inspire pride, and often presumption, if there is not a good will to correct the influence of these on the mind, and with this also to rectify the whole principle of acting, and adapt it to its end. The sight of a being who is not adorned with a single feature of a pure and good will, enjoying unbroken prosperity can never give pleasure to an impartial rational spectator. Thus a good will appears to constitute the indispensable condition even of being worthy of happiness.

There are even some qualities which are of service to this good will itself, and may facilitate its action, yet which have no intrinsic or unconditional value, but always presuppose a good will, and this qualifies the esteem that we justly have for them, and does not permit us to regard them as absolutely good. Moderation in the affections and passions, self-control, and calm deliberation are not only good in many respects, but even seem to constitute part of the intrinsic worth of the person; but they are far from deserving to be called good without qualification, although they have been so unconditionally praised by the ancients. For without the principle of the good will, they may become extremely bad; and the coolness of the villain not only makes him far more dangerous, but also directly makes him more abominable in our eyes than he would have been without it.

A good will is good not because of what it performs or effects, not by its aptness for the attainment of some proposed end, but simply by virtue of the volition—that is, it is good in itself, and considered by itself is to be esteemed higher than all that can be brought about by it in favor of any inclination, nay, even of the sum-total of all inclinations. Even if it should happen that, owing to special disfavor of fortune, or even the niggardly provision of a step-motherly nature, this will should wholly lack power to accomplish its purpose, if with its greatest efforts it should achieve nothing, and there should remain only the good will (not, to be sure, a mere wish, but the summoning of all means in our power), then, like a jewel, it would shine by its own light, as a thing which has its whole value in itself. Its usefulness or fruitlessness can neither add to nor take away anything from its value...

Why Reason Was Made to Guide the Will

... reason is imparted to us as a practical faculty that is, as one which is to have influence on the *will*, therefore, admitting that nature generally in the distribution of her capacities has adapted the means to the end, its true destination must be to produce a *will*, not merely as a *means* to something else, but *good in itself,* for which reason it is absolutely necessary. This will then, though not indeed the sole and complete good, must be the supreme good and the condition of every other, even of the desire of happiness. Under these circumstances, there is nothing inconsistent with the wisdom of nature in the fact that the cultivation of reason, which is requisite for the first and unconditional purpose, does in many ways interfere, at least in this life, with the attainment of the second, which is always conditional—namely happiness. Nay, it may even reduce it to nothing, without nature thereby failing of her purpose. For reason recognizes the establishment of the the good will as it highest practical destination, and in attaining this purpose is capable only of a satisfaction of its own proper kind, namely, that from the attaining of an end, which end again is determined by reason only, notwithstanding that this may involve many a disappointment to the ends of inclination.

The First Proposition of Morality

We have then to develop a notion of a will which deserves to be highly esteemed for itself, and is good without a view to anything further... and which in estimating the value of our actions always takes the first place and constitutes the condition of all the rest. In order to do this, we will take the notion of duty, which includes that of the good will ...

I omit here all actions which are already inconsistent with duty... It is much harder to make this distinction when the action accords with duty, and the subject has besides a *direct* inclination to it. For example, it is always a matter of duty that a dealer should not overcharge an inexperienced purchaser; and wherever there is much commerce the prudent trademan does not overcharge, but keeps a fixed price for every one, so that a child buys of him as well as any other. Men are thus *honestly* served; but this is not enough to make us believe that the trademan has so acted from duty and from the principle of honesty; his own advantage required it ... Accordingly the action was done ... merely with a selfish view.

On the other hand it is a duty to maintain ones's life; and, in addition, everyone has a direct inclination to do so. But on this account the often anxious care which men take for it has no intrinsic worth, and their maxim has no moral import. They preserve their life *as duty requires*, no doubt, but not *because duty requires*. On the other hand, if adversity and hopeless sorrow have completely taken away the relish of life, if the unfortunate one, strong in mind, indignant at his fate rather than desponding or dejected, wishes for death, and yet preserves his live without loving it—not from inclination or fear, but from duty—then his maxim has moral worth.

To be beneficent when we can is a duty; and besides this, there are many minds so sympathetically constituted that, without any other motive of vanity or self interest, they find a pleasure in spreading joy around them, and can take delight in the satisfaction of others so far as it is their own work. But I maintain that in such a case an action of this kind, however proper, however amiable it may be, has nevertheless no moral worth ... For the maxim lacks the moral import, namely that such actions be done *from duty*, not from inclination ...

It is in this manner, undoubtedly, which we are to understand those passages of Scripture also in which we are commanded to love our neighbor, even our enemy. For love, as an affection, cannot be commanded, but beneficence for duty's sake may, even though we are not impelled to it by any inclination—nay, even repelled by a natural and unconquerable aversion. This is ... a love which is seated in the will, and not in the propensions of sense—in principles of action and not of tender sympathy; and it is this love alone which can be commanded.

The Second Proposition of Morality

...That an action done from duty derives its moral worth, *not from the purpose* which is attained by it, but from the maxim by which it is determined, and therefore does not depend on the realization of the object of the action, but merely on the *principle of volition* by which the action has taken place, without regard to any object of desire. It is clear from what precedes that the purposes which we have in view in our actions, or their effects regarded as ends and springs of will, cannot give to actions any unconditional moral worth. In what, then, can their worth lie if it is not to consist in the will and in reference to its expected effect? It cannot lie anywhere but in the *principle of the will* without regard to the ends which can be attained by the action ...

The Third Proposition of Morality

The third proposition, which is a consequence of the two preceeding, I would express thus: *Duty is the necessity of acting from respect for the law...* Now an action done from duty must wholly exclude the influence of inclination, and with it every object of the will, so that nothing remains which can determine the will except objectively the *law* and subjectively *pure respect* for this practical law, and consequently the maxim that I should follow this law even to the thwarting of all my inclinations.

Thus the moral worth of an action does not lie in the effect expected from it, nor in any principle of action which requires to borrow its motive from this expected effect ...The pre-eminent good which we call moral can therefore consist in nothing else than the *conception of law* in itself...

The Supreme Principle of Morality: The Categorical Imperative

But what sort of law can that be the conception of which must determine the will, without paying any regard to the effect expected from it, in order that this will may be called good absolutely and without qualification? As I have deprived the will of every impulse which could arise to it from obedience to any law, there remains nothing but the universal conformity of its action to law in general, which alone serves the will as a principle, that is, I am never to act otherwise than so *that I could also will that my maxim could become a universal law*... Let the question be, for example: May I when in distress make a promise with the intention not to keep it?...The shortest way, however, and an unerring one, to discover the answer to this question whether a lying promise is consistent with duty, is to ask myself, Should I be content that my maxim (to extricate myself from difficulty with a false promise) should hold good as a universal law, for myself as well as for others; and should I be able to say to myself "Every one may make a deceitful promise when he finds himself in a difficulty from which he cannot otherwise extricate himself"? Then I presently become aware that, while I can will the lie, I can by no means will that lying should be a universal law. For with such a law there would be no promises at all, since it would be vain to allege my intention in regard of my future actions to those who would not believe this allegation, or if they over-hastily did so, would pay me back in my own coin. Hence my maxim, as soon as it should be made universal law would necessarily destroy itself.

I do not, therefore, need any far-reaching penetration to discern what I have to do in order that my will be morally good, Inexperienced in the course of the world, incapable of being prepared for all its contingencies, I only ask myself: Canst thou also will that thy maxim should be a universal law? If not, then it must be rejected ...

Exercise:

1. Develop, as a brief argument, the steps Kant takes to establish the Categorical Imperative.
2. Kant envisions certain problems of clarification. What are they?
3. He takes great pains to distinguish actions in accordance with duty from action in response to duty? Why is this?
4. Why is he so concerned with distinguishing duty from inclination?
5. Kant's principle tells us what not to do, does it also tell us what to do?
6. Kant's views have often been analyzed as placing *Justice* at the heart of morality. Can you explain this?
7. Kant and Mill are often opposed. How would Mill argue against Kant? Which of Kant's arguments are especially crucial as contrary to Mill?
8. Give a Kantian argument to warrent Moony staying with his family?
9. Give a Utilitarian argument for Moony staying with his family?
10. Which do you think is a better argument, taking into consideration your depth analysis of the play and of Kant's position?

Freedom

The traditional wife is dependent on her husband for her emotional and financial well being. Dependency can be comforting; it permits the dependent individual to be disengaged or even irresponsible. Such dependency is often seen as desirable. But having someone to look after you can seem like a trap. The individual, with limited choices in a constraining marriage may find the need to express self overpowering.

Kate Chopin, The Story of an Hour

Knowing that Mrs. Mallard was afflicted with a heart trouble, great care was taken to break to her as gently as possible the news of her husband's death.

It was her sister Josephine who told her, in broken sentences, veiled hints that revealed in half concealing. Her husband's friend Richards was there, too, near her. It was he who had been in the newspaper office when intelligence of the railroad disaster was received, with Brently Mallard's name leading the list of "killed." He had only taken the time to assure himself of its truth by a second telegram, and had hastened to forestall any less careful, less tender friend in bearing the sad message.

She did not hear the story as many women have heard the same, with a paralyzed inability to accept its significance. She wept at once, with sudden, wild abandonment, in her sister's arms. When the storm of grief had spent itself she went away to her room alone. She would have no one follow her.

There stood, facing the open window, a comfortable, roomy armchair. Into this she sank, pressed down by a physical exhaustion that haunted her body and seemed to reach into her soul.

She could see in the open square before her house the tops of trees that were all aquiver with the new spring life. The delicious breath of rain was in the air. In the street below a peddler was crying his wares. The notes of a distant song which some one was singing reached her faintly, and countless sparrows were twittering in the eaves.

There were patches of blue sky showing here and there through the clouds that had met and piled above the other in the west facing her window.

She sat with her head thrown back upon the cushion of the chair quite motionless, except when a sob came up into her throat and shook her, as a child who has cried itself to sleep continues to sob in its dreams.

She was young, with a fair, calm face, whose lines bespoke repression and even a certain strength. But now there was a dull stare in her eyes, whose gaze was fixed away off yonder on one of those patches of blue sky. It was not a glance of reflection, but rather indicated a suspension of intelligent thought.

There was something coming to her and she was waiting for it, fearfully. What was it? She did not know; it was too subtle and elusive to name. But she felt it, creeping out of the sky, reaching toward her through the sounds, the scents, the color that filled the air.

Now her bosom rose and fell tumultuously. She was beginning to recognize this thing that was approaching to possess her, and she was striving to beat it back with her will—as powerless as her two white slender hands would have been.

When she abandoned herself a little whispered word escaped her slightly parted lips. She said it over and over under her breath: "Free, free, free!" The vacant stare and the look of terror that had followed it went from her eyes. They stayed keen and bright. Her pulses beat fast, and the coursing blood warmed and relaxed every inch of her body.

She did not stop to ask if it were not a monstrous joy that held her. A clear and exalted perception enabled her to dismiss the suggestion as trivial.

She knew that she would weep again when she saw the kind, tender hands folded in death; the face that had never looked save with love upon her, fixed and gray and dead. But she saw beyond that bitter moment a long procession of years to come that would belong to her absolutely. And she opened and spread her arms out to them in welcome.

There would be no one to live for during those coming years; she would live for herself. There would be no powerful will bending her in that blind persistence with which men and women believe they have a right to impose a private will upon a fellow-creature. A kind intention or a cruel intention made the act seem no less a crime as she looked upon it in that brief moment of illumination.

And yet she had loved him—sometimes. Often she had not. What did it matter! What could love, the unsolved mystery, count for in face of this possession of self-assertion, which she suddenly recognized as the strongest impulse of her being!

"Free! Body and soul free!" she kept whispering.

Josephine was kneeling before the closed door with her eye to the keyhole, imploring for admission. "Louise, open the door! I beg, open the door—you will make yourself ill. What are you doing, Louise? For heaven's sake open the door."

"Go away, I am not making myself ill." No, she was thinking on a very elixir of life through that open window.

Her fancy was running riot along those days ahead of her. Spring days, and summer days, and all sorts of days that would be her own. She breathed a quick prayer that life might be long. It was only yesterday she had thought with a shudder that life might be long.

She arose at length and opened the door to her sister's importunities. There was a feverish triumph in her eyes and she carried herself unwittingly like a goddess of Victory. She clasped her sister's waist, and together they descended the stairs. Richards stood waiting for them at the bottom.

Some one was opening the front door with a latchkey. It was Brently Mallard who entered, a little travel-stained, composedly carrying his grip-sack and umbrella. He had been far from the scene of accident, and did not even know there had been one. He stood amazed at Josephine's piercing cry; at Richards' quick motion to screen him from the view of his wife.

But Richards was too late.

When the doctors came they said she had died of heart disease—of joy that kills.

Discussion Plan:

The Story of an Hour was written by an 19th century author and takes place before 1900. This may account for Mrs. Mallard's extreme reaction.

1. Can you come up with a plausible story of Mrs. Mallard's married life to justify her feelings?
2. Do you think Mr. Mallard would have to have been a cruel husband for her to feel the way she does?
3. What sort of social pressures would have kept Mrs. Mallard in a marriage?
4. Do you believe that a women in her place could have had options that she did not see?
5. We are led to have sympathy for Mrs. Mallard, how do you think the marriage looked from Mr. Mallard's perspective?
6. Are there any relevant differences between her situation and Moony's?
7. If Moony did not have a child would there still be differences?
8. Is there any way to justify a social system that would keep Mrs. Mallard in her place?
10. How about a social system that would keep Moony in his place?

420

Divorce

Once marriage is perceived as a denial of personal freedom, the decision to dissolve the bonds follows soon after. Separation and divorce are seen as solutions to problems, but they create a whole new range of difficulties—often unanticipated. The freedom and independence of the newly unmarried presents a variety of choices that extend beyond their past experience. To make matters even more difficult many of the responsibilities of the marriage persist.

Thomas J. Cottle, Pregnant With What?

Mary Ellis Krause's divorce became official on the eve of her daughter Caroline's ninth birthday. A final trip to court on Friday afternoon, a night spent mostly on the telephone, a birthday party the next afternoon, dinner with friends that night, a movie with her daughter and 11-year-old son Sunday afternoon, a late-afternoon snack at a fast-food restaurant, a blind date arranged by a woman who, like Mary Ellis, works for the state; then a one o'clock in the morning phone call from her former (by 48 hours) husband, regarding still another unsettled detail of the divorce settlement, and another weekend had come to an end. And she smiled about it. She smiled about it at two o'clock in the morning when she got off the phone convinced she had heard penitence in Howard's voice, and once again the next morning as the kids and she stumbled about the house trying to get yet another dreaded Monday morning underway without too much noise and despair.

Mary Ellis was 23 when she married. Howard Krause was in his last year of law school. He had advised her not to quit college, but she preferred to work, eventually finding a "perfect" job in one of the legal departments in the State House. She was 25 when Hoyt was born, 27 when Caroline was born, 29 when she realized her marriage was destined to end. When Caroline was three, Mary Ellis returned to the State House, to a new job; she had been home raising children for almost five years. Howard was doing exceptionally well in his law firm; Mary Ellis was doing exceptionally badly at home, not that anyone noticed her unhappiness. Well, that wasn't totally true. Howard had noticed a change; he simply could not seem to help her. For that matter, she admitted to not letting anyone get close enough to her to help, not that she could have defined what "help" meant.

A temporary separation gave way to a reconciliation. Howard seemed amenable to all of her suggestions and wishes; she never denied his willingness to make accommodations. He was a good father, probably a good husband, too. It was all unclear, vague indefinable. But their marriage was dead; there wasn't a spark of anything left in the house. Once again they separated, each hoping it might work out. But they had become invisible to each other. For a while, Mary Ellis went about the routines of her life as if the air were thick and time moved in no particular direction. In her words:

"There are moments, you know, and they can be ever so long, when you're not aware of living or dying. The days come and go, and you're aware, at the same time, of all the things you've always been aware of and nothing at all. You seem to be able to remember things, and yet forget them almost at the same time. You know people are recognizing you to be a different person, and you feel they're right, and wrong. You are the same, different, differently the same. I would talk with my husband as though we were still married, not married, never married, about to be married.

"I might be counting the amount of money needed for the children's laundry bills, and suddenly I would remember our first dates, first touches, and I'd be aroused, utterly aroused. "Well, let's see: laundry, then there's the lunch money; which is going up, pediatrician and dentist bills, which you can't accurately predict. Hoyt's hockey equipment, and someone will grow too big for their bike, or their skates, and the back stairs still haven't been fixed. Is that my responsibility or yours? Who pays for home insurance? No, I don't expect you to pay for clothes or shoes or luggage for me, or trips." My voice was cold and distant and mechanical, and I felt aroused. I felt aroused by the touch of nightgown, and there would be no one. I couldn't have stood anyone. Robert Redford at the door? Caroline, could you ask him if maybe he could come back in two months. I'll need two months. Does he need two months? Is he alone, Caroline, or does he come equipped with a little slimy lawyer who tells me, "Mrs. Krause, understand, I'm not interested in prying, but I'll need a list from you of every man you have been out with during the period of your settlement, and the men you've entertained in your home will have to be mentioned as well, and we may question your son and daughter about these matters as well."

"You don't know whether to laugh or cry when you hear this sort of thing. I think I do both. I pass mirrors and look, very quickly, so I'm not actually studying myself, and I see a face that looks as though it's about to laugh or cry. I go months when I feel that the real divorce is not from this man, whatever he means to me, wherever he is, but of the top half of my body from the lower half. Weeks will pass and I will miss, or avoid, or not think of anything sexual or erotic. A man makes the slightest pass at me, and I want to order a policeman to arrest him. And then, other weeks, weeks that suddenly are there without warning or any preparation on my part, I want men. I want them all. No matter how ugly they might act, or how they might mistreat me or offend me, I want them; one at a time, all of them together, with the light on, the light off, the lights blinking 'til I'm drunk on it.

"One lives with resentments in and out of marriage. You resent what others have done and not done, what you've done and not done. There's a different sort of silence around here now; at work, too. People detest or resent and still feel attached to the divorced person. They pity me, they resent me, they envy me, they worry, wonder; God only knows what they feel. Nobody looks at you when you're married. Now they look at me, men and women both for little signs. It's like my eyes will reveal to them whether or not I'm pregnant! But pregnant with what! A new guy? A new emptiness? A new life? What are they looking for? My life is partly a mirror to them, and partly it is opaque. Believe me, they cannot possibly see it all—because I can't. I can't tell distances between people anymore. I can't tell closeness. I can't be sure that what I see in other people's relationships with one another is true or not because I know that I am wishing and envying and despising and loving all sorts of things in these people.

"I don't want to give the impression, you know, that I'm shattered by the divorce. I don't think I am. I even initiated it. We're friends. No, we aren't friends. There isn't a word for what we are. We're litigants, ex's, former friends, nonfriends, but not friends like we were friends. The two of us are mere acquaintances who spent over a decade together. Howard is the mere acquaintance who fathered the only two children I shall ever bear.

"I suppose the problem is that I have to figure out for myself what lies below the surface of a good friendship, any friendship—even one with my children. I find it hard now to know exactly what I can expect in a friendship, or what I can give. Ideally, I'd like to be giving and receiving all the time, and at the same time. It isn't possible, of course. Right now, too many people seem to be on the take.

"So often I feel owned by someone when literally there is no one in my life. Maybe I'm being owned by my liberation. Maybe I want to be imprisoned by someone. Maybe my ex-husband offered me too much choice. I can't tell. I'm filled with secrets, secrets I often think I'd just as soon not even know about myself. I know I must concentrate on my mind for a while along with feeling out these ties one makes to friends or mere acquaintances. I think it's the ties to people and the feeling that maybe I could begin to start anew and selfishly just pick the parts of me, and of the world I'd like to keep. Maybe that's it, the selfishness that from time to time I feel I'm entitled to. What a frightening feeling.

"Can selfishness ever be good. I wonder? I think my children see me as selfish. I know I want to be selfish or have someone take care of me. No one's really hurt me. I hunt for reasons for feeling the way I do, but no one's really hurt me. Yet I feel hurt. It's so strange. Maybe you hurt when you've never known real pleasure, although I thought I had.

"And now we're not husband and wife, we're acquaintances, and I must start again, or anew. You go on, I suppose, that's what people tell me is the delicious challenge. Well, it may be, although I, for one, have yet to taste it. The fact is I don't know how too much of life tastes these days. I wonder what my mere acquaintance would say about that. I wonder how long it takes for regrets to burn out completely. I suppose it's time for time to heal all this."

Exercise:

Mary Ellis presents a confusing picture of seemingly incompatible desires and values.

Begin by listing all the the things that seem important to Mary.

Distinguish between positive and negative aspects of her life. Make sure to notice things that are both positive and negative.

Which of the things that are important are basically Mary's immediate emotions?

Which are more subtle states of being?

Are any of them directed towards others, for example, obligations?

Which of these create conflict in Mary's life?

Try to place her values in an order of importance. Which values win out when in conflict with which others?

Time, Split Decisions

Divorce and Consequences

With the spread of marital breakups, divorce American-style is cracking open a widening set of legal problems. Divorce is now a simple enough procedure in almost every state. But as three quite different recent cases show, the consequences of the split can challenge the creativity of the courts.

Take the question of who should get what after Mark and Janet Sullivan parted. During most of their ten-year marriage, Janet, now 35, worked while Mark trained to be a doctor. Then in 1978, just before Mark set up his urology practice, Janet moved out, and divorce followed. As the couple divided up property, Janet sought standard items like furniture and one of the two cars. But one thing on her list stopped Mark cold: a partial interest in his medical degree. For her support, Janet reasoned, she should receive a percentage of the $660,000 that she says is the added money he will earn as a urologist. A state appeals court in San Bernardino ruled that she has a point, and professionals up and down California are wondering if the case could affect them some day.

In its decision, the three-judge panel noted that Mark is paying $250 a month to help support the couple's daughter, who divides her time between parents. But there was no question of alimony because Janet's salary enables her to maintain the standard of living she had while married. So the value of her support of Mark's studies could be measured only in the property settlement. The court refused to rule that the degree was "community property," which in California is split equally, but it did reason that Janet's sizable investment in Mark's education entitled her to at least part of its value. A trial judge will determine the amount.

Mark, who plans to appeal, took to the Op-Ed page of the *Los Angeles Times* to argue that he had contributed his share of support by working while at school. Queried Mark: "What if I am lucky enough to win a Nobel Prize? Would she be entitled to part of the prize money?"

Though the decision broke new ground in California, Janet is not the first supporting spouse to win compensation. A number of courts, using various theories, have rewarded similar efforts with a larger share of the couple's property or more alimony. In most cases, however, the courts have reimbursed the wife only for what she contributed to help her husband get his degree. That is inadequate, insists New York Attorney Doris Jonas Freed, an expert on matrimonial law. Says she, "It is unfair to limit the compensation to just what the wife has spent without considering the enhancement of the husband's earning power." The California court took that extra step, and if the ruling withstands appeal, that state's precedent should prompt others to follow.

Questions of property are hard fought, but quarrels over who keeps the children can be even rougher. A solution that has been gaining acceptance is joint custody, now available in some 20 states. Perhaps the ultimate in sharing was put together last month by Circuit Judge Charles Forster in Traverse City, Mich. Cheryl and Allan Church may go their separate ways, he said, but their three teen-age boys in a sense will get custody of the house. Under the plan, the ex-mates will move in and out each month. For the Churches, at least, the arrangement is perfect. Says Cheryl: "Nobody's a loser."

Children sometimes have other rights that can come into play during a divorce. When her parents broke up in 1979, Adrienne Zimmerman, now 23, sided with her mother. She says that her choice angered her father, Theodore, a New York attorney, and that he consequently reneged on a promise to pay her college tuition. Dismissed from Adelphi University after her junior year because she owed $6,700, Adrienne sued her dad, claiming she had been harmed by his failure to honor his pledge. Last month a state appeals court ordered him to pay up. Though pleased by the decision, Adrienne, now a bookkeeper, concedes that money isn't everything. Says she: "I want a father." Unfortunately, that problem—and the deep pain that causes most of these lawsuits—is beyond the power of even the most creative judge.

Discussion Plan:

Take the cases one at a time and answer the following questions.
1. What are the issues at controversy?
2. What is the basis for the plaintiffs claim?
3. What for the defendant?
4. What principles of equity would you use in making the judgement?
5. Are these principles sex neutral, i.e. would you use the same standards if the sex of the contending parties were reversed?
6. If these cases occurred in a truly sex egalitarian society, should the cases be decided differently?

SECTION 3: SUMMING UP A LIFE

All human beings search for something that makes life worth living. Some find it in activity, some in achieving a goal, some through interpersonal relationships. Socrates, an ancient Greek Philosopher, is often held up as a model of someone who found true meaning and satisfaction in life.

Socrates, faced with a jury ready to condemn him to death if he did not cease his endless questioning of Athenian values, replied simply, "An unexamined life is not worth living." It was not just life he prized but the quality of life. He did not view his life in terms of his own happiness and physical well-being. The search for true value, transcended all personal happiness. He suffered hardship and persecution because of his relentless search for truth and he was ready to face death. Death held no terror for he had done his duty throughout his life. To have extended the length of his life would not have made it any better. He could feel confident that having followed his principles, he had lived well.

The ancient Stoics maintained that the goal of life is to achieve peace of mind, an attitude. Living in a time of political and social turmoil it became clear to them that we are not masters of our own lives. Depression, fear and anger haunt those who feel that they are victims of of the endless and pointless forces that surround them. The Stoics pointed out that, although events are beyond our control, our ideas and attitudes are not. It is impossible, for example, for someone to insult you unless *you* accept the remark as an insult. Events are not tragedies unless we think they are. A full understanding of nature and of each individuals essential being gives tranquility of mind that is sufficient to calmly accept whatever happens. Looking back over life a Stoic should have no regrets.

Such equanimity is hard to achieve and not everyone is content with passive acceptance of what will be. Some, like Aristotle, saw the value of life bound to the achievement of a goal, this goal men call happiness. We all want to be happy; but happiness is an elusive goal. Even if we could actually know what would make us happy, we would still have to discover how to achieve our goal. Aristotle, in contradiction to modern popular opinion, said that young people could not possibly be happy. Why not? Because happiness is a matter of fulfilling your potential and the young have not yet developed to the point where their potential is defined, much less fulfilled. Can we tell that we are happy only at the end of our lives, looking back, summing up? Or is there a sense of happiness as a goal or end of life which will allow us to be truly happy at this moment?

Modern existentialist philosophers face the problem of value in modern life in a unique way. What makes life worth living is *arbitrarily* decided by each individual for himself alone. It matters little what we do as long as we *choose* to so it. Our freedom to choose becomes the source of all value in our own lives. Freedom, in this sense, can be a crushing burden since, if we are truly free to choose any alternative, we are also fully responsible for all the consequences of our actions or inactions.

But there are two events in our lives for which we are not responsible, because we do not choose them: our birth and our death. These are inevitable. By the time we are aware of it our birth is given. Death is somewhat different, for although inevitable, death seems to allow for some choice. We cannot choose not to die when death overtakes us but we can choose to die. Death, whether chosen or given, is the end of life. Now "end" can mean "finish" or "goal," which leads to the question: Is the purpose of life death? Existentialist have focused on this crucial ambiguity. For them death becomes the central issue of the meaning of life.

For Albert Camus, a 20th century French philosopher, suicide was the most important philosophical problem because suicide makes death a choice and all values comes from choosing. For Camus, values do not exist in the world of things or even in human beings. This is the Existentialist position that there is nothing in the world to make life worth living. And so, death might appear as a welcome solution to the absurd situation that life is. But this is not what Camus concluded. He maintains that the whole point of life is centered on the existential *relationship* of a person in the world. In other words, the world exists, a person exists, and the person, being conscious and self-conscious, is aware that both exist. This awareness of existence is the whole point of life.

Unlike other philosophers Camus does not think there is any special activity or goal other than awareness that makes life worth living. Camus is sure that you can never have too much life, too much awareness. It does not even matter what the quality of life is. Suffering, anguish, joy and pleasure are all the same in his view. They are all part of the awareness of life. Quantity is more important than quality and suicide is never justifiable. The whole situation *is* absurd. So what?

Each of the philosophical positions alluded to gives us a different set of standards by which to measure our lives. Which position is correct? Which perspective should we choose? Does the choice matter? It seems to, for the choice of the standard against which we measure of our lives has profound implications for how we are to live.

Self and Others

Some things we were given and some things we choose. The combination defines our life-style. And our life style reflects its component parts, our strengths and weaknesses and the standards and patterns expressed by those around us—by the jobs we do, the people we involve ourselves and the place in space and time we find ourselves in. And when we look around sometimes we are shocked.

Carson McCullers, The Jockey

The Jockey came to the doorway of the dining room, then after a moment stepped to one side and stood motionless, with his back to the wall. The room was crowded, as this was the third day of the season and all the hotels in the town were full. In the dining room bouquets of August roses scattered their petals on the white table linen and from the adjoining bar came a warm, drunken wash of voices. The jockey waited with his back to the wall and scrutinized the room with pinched, creepy eyes. He examined the room until at last his eyes reached a table in a corner diagonally across from him, at which three men were sitting. As he watched, the jockey raised his chin and tilted his head back to one side, his dwarfed body grew rigid, and his hands stiffened so that the fingers curled inward like gray claws. Tense against the wall of the dining room, he watched and waited in this way.

He was wearing a suit of green Chinese silk that evening, tailored precisely and the size of a costume outfit for a child. The shirt was yellow, the tie striped with pastel colors. He had no hat with him and wore his hair brushed down in a stiff, wet bang on his forehead. His face was drawn, ageless, and gray. There were shadowed hollows at his temples and his mouth was set in a wiry smile. After a time he was aware that he had been seen by one of the three men he had been watching But the jockey did not nod; he only raised his chin still higher and hooked the thumb of his tense hand in the pocket of his coat.

The three men at the corner table were a trainer, a bookie, and a rich man. The trainer was Sylvester—a large, loosely built fellow with a flushed nose and slow blue eyes. The bookie was Simmons. The rich man was the owner of a horse named Seltzer, which the jockey had ridden that afternoon. The three of them drank whiskey with soda, and a white-coated waiter had just brought on the main course of the dinner.

It was Sylvester who first saw the jockey. He looked away quickly, put down his whiskey glass, and nervously mashed the tip of his red nose with his thumb. 'It's Bitsy Barlow,' he said. 'Standing over there across the room. Just watching us.'

'Oh, the jockey,' said the rich man. He was facing the wall and he half turned his head to look behind him. 'Ask him over.'

'God, no,' Sylvester said.

'He's crazy,' Simmons said. The bookie's voice was flat and without inflection. He had the face of a born gambler, carefully adjusted, the expression a permanent deadlock between fear and greed.

'Well, I wouldn't call him that exactly,' said Sylvester. 'I've known him a long time. He was O.K. until about six months ago. But if he goes on like this, I can't see him lasting another year. I just can't.'

'It was what happened in Miami,' said Simmons.

'What?' asked the rich man.

Sylvester glanced across the room at the jockey and wet the corner of his mouth with his red, fleshy tongue. 'Accident. A kid got hurt on the track. Broke a leg and a hip. He was a particular pal of Bitsy's. A Irish kid. Not a bad rider, either.'

'That's a pity,' said the rich man.

'Yeah. They were particular friends,' Sylvester said. 'You would always find him up in Bitsy's hotel room. They would be playing rummy or else lying on the floor reading the sports page together.'

'Well, those things happen,' said the rich man.

Simmons cut into his beefsteak. He held his fork prongs downward on the plate and carefully piled on mushrooms with the blade of his knife. 'He's crazy,' he repeated. 'He gives me the creeps.'

All the tables in the dining room were occupied. There was a party at the banquet table in the center, and green-white August moths had found their way in from the night and fluttered about the clear candle flames. Two girls wearing flannel slacks and blazers walked arm in arm across the room into the bar. From the main street outside came the echoes of holiday hysteria.

'They claim that in August Saratoga is the wealthiest town per capita in the world.' Sylvester turned to the rich man. 'What do you think?'

'I wouldn't know,' said the rich man. 'It may very well be so.'

Daintily, Simmons wiped his greasy mouth with the tip of his forefinger. 'How about Hollywood? And Wall Street—'

'Wait,' said Sylvester. 'He's decided to come over here.'

The jockey had left the wall and was approaching the table in the corner. He walked with a prim strut, swinging out his legs in a half-circle with each step, his heels biting smartly into the red velvet carpet on the floor. On the way over he brushed against the elbow of a fat woman in white satin at the banquet table; he stepped back and bowed with dandified courtesy, his eyes quite closed. When he had crossed the room he drew up a chair and sat at a corner of the table, between Sylvester and the rich man, without a nod of greeting or a change in his set, gray face.

'Had dinner?' Sylvester asked.

'Some people might call it that.' The jockey's voice was high, bitter, clear.

Sylvester put his knife and fork down carefully on his plate. The rich man shifted his position, turning sidewise in his chair and crossing his legs. He was dressed in twill riding pants, unpolished boots, and a shabby brown jacket—this was his outfit day and night in the racing season, although he was never seen on a horse. Simmons went on with his dinner.

'Like a spot of seltzer water?' asked Sylvester. 'Or something like that?'

The jockey didn't answer. He drew a gold cigarette case from his pocket and snapped it open. Inside were a few cigarettes and a tiny gold penknife. He used the knife to cut a cigarette in half. When he had lighted his smoke, he held up his hand to a waiter passing by the table. 'Kentucky bourbon, please.'

'Now, listen, Kid,' said Sylvester.

'Don't Kid me.'

'Be reasonable. You know you got to behave reasonable.'

The jockey drew up the left corner of his mouth in a stiff jeer. His eyes lowered to the food spread out on the table, but instantly he looked up again.

Before the rich man was a fish casserole, baked in a cream sauce and garnished with parsley. Sylvester had ordered eggs Benedict. There was asparagus, fresh buttered corn, and a side dish of wet black olives. A plate of French-fried potatoes was in the corner of the table before the jockey. He didn't look at the food again, but kept his pinched eyes on the center piece of full-blown lavender roses. 'I don't suppose you remember a certain person by the name of McGuire,' he said.

'Now, listen,' said Sylvester.

The waiter brought the whiskey, and the jockey sat fondling the glass with his small, strong, calloused hands. On his wrist was a gold link bracelet that clinked against the table edge. After turning the glass between his palms, the jockey suddenly drank the whiskey neat in two hard swallows. He set down the glass sharply. 'No, I don't suppose your memory is that long and extensive,' he said.

'Sure enough, Bitsy,' said Sylvester. 'What makes you act like this? You hear from the kid today?'

'I received a letter,' the jockey said. 'The certain person we were speaking about was taken out from the cast on Wednesday. One leg is two inches shorter than the other one. That's all.'

Sylvester clucked his tongue and shook his head. 'I realize how you feel.'

'Do you?' The jockey was looking at the dishes on the table. His gaze passed from the fish casserole to the corn, and finally fixed on the plate of fried potatoes. His face tightened and quickly he looked up again. A rose shattered and he picked up one of the petals, bruised it between his thumb and forefinger, and put it in his mouth.

'Well, those things happen,' said the rich man.

The trainer and the bookie had finished eating, but there was food left on the serving dishes before their plates. The rich man dipped his buttery fingers in his water glass and wiped them with his napkin.

'Well,' said the jockey. 'Doesn't somebody want me to pass them something? Or maybe perhaps you desire to re-order. Another hunk of beefsteak, gentlemen, or—'

'Please,' said Sylvester. 'Be reasonable. Why don't you go on upstairs?'

'Yes, why don't I' the jockey said.

His prim voice had risen higher and there was about it the sharp whine of hysteria.

'Why don't I go up to my god-damn room and walk around and write some letters and go to bed like a good boy? Why don't I just—' He pushed his chair back and got up. 'Oh, foo,' he said. 'Foo to you. I want a drink.'

'All I can say is it's your funeral,' said Sylvester. 'You know what it does to you. You know well enough.'

The jockey crossed the dining room and went into the bar. He ordered a Manhattan, and Sylvester watched him stand with his heels pressed tight together, his body hard as a lead soldier's, holding his little finger out from the cocktail glass and sipping the drink slowly.

'He's crazy,' said Simmons. 'Like I said.'

Sylvester turned to the rich man. 'If he eats a lamb chop, you can see the shape of it in his stomach a hour afterward. He can't sweat things out of him any more. He's a hundred and twelve and a half. He's gained three pounds since we left Miami.'

'A jockey shouldn't drink,' said the rich man.

'The food don't satisfy him like it used to and he can't sweat it out. If he eats a lamb chop, you can watch it tooching out in his stomach and it don't go down.'

The jockey finished his Manhattan. He swallowed, crushed the cherry in the bottom of the glass with his thumb, then pushed the glass away from him. The two girls in blazers were standing at his left, their faces turned toward each other, and at the other end of the bar two touts had started an argument about which was the highest mountain in the world. Everyone was with somebody else; there was no other person drinking alone that night. The jockey paid with a brand-new fifty-dollar bill and didn't count the change.

He walked back to the dining room and to the table at which the three men were sitting, but he did not sit down. 'No, I wouldn't presume to think your memory is that extensive,' he said. He was so small that the edge of the table top reached almost to his belt, and when he gripped the corner with his wiry hands he didn't have to stoop. 'No, you're too busy gobbling up dinners in dining rooms. You're too—'

'Honestly,' begged Sylvester. 'You got to behave reasonable.'

'Reasonable! Reasonable!' The jockey's gray face quivered, then set in a mean, frozen grin. He shook the table so that the plates rattled, and for a moment it seemed that he would push it over. But suddenly he stopped. His hand reached out toward the plate nearest to him and deliberately he put a few of the French-fried potatoes in his mouth. He chewed slowly, his upper lip raised, then he turned and spat out the pulpy mouthful on the smooth red carpet which covered the floor. 'Libertines,' he said, and his voice was thin and broken. He rolled the word in his mouth, as though it had a flavor and a substance that gratified him. 'You libertines,' he said again, and turned and walked with his rigid swagger out of the dining room.

Sylvester shrugged one of his loose, heavy shoulders. The rich man sopped up some water that had been spilled on the tablecloth, and they didn't speak until the waiter came to clear away.

Discussion Plan:

1. What in the Jockey's life was outside of his control?
2. What was chosen by him?
3. Did he see his limitations as strengths or weaknesses?
4. How did his attitude towards himself and others reflect his personal values?
5. Given his limitations could he have chosen a better life?
6. Was he free to make judgements other than the ones he seemed to make?
7. What realizations does he seem to come to about himself by the end of the story?
8. What realizations about others?

Writing Assignment:

In the story the events leading up to the confrontation in the dining room and the confrontation itself seems to alter the jockey's perspective on the world that he inhabits. Write a short story that portrays an "existential moment," a moment when the meaning of our life changes as a response to a new awareness.

Self and Family

Other people play a crucial role in determining the value we place on our accomplishments. Among the people who have a significant effect on our judgements of personal achievement are those whose lives we have influenced the most. For a parent, looking back at the trials and rewards of life, self evaluation is often a reflection of the success or failure of the children they raised.

Tillie Olsen, I Stand Here Ironing

I stand here ironing, and what you asked me moves tormented back and forth with the iron.

"I wish you would manage the time to come in and talk with me about your daughter. I'm sure you can help me understand her. She's a youngster who needs help and whom I'm deeply interested in helping."

"Who needs help."... Even if I came, what good would it do? You think because I am her mother I have a key, or that in some way you could use me as a key? She has lived for nineteen years. There is all that life that has happened outside of me, beyond me.

And when is there time to remember, to sift, to weigh, to estimate, to total? I will start and there will be an interruption and I will have to gather it all together again. Or I will become engulfed with all I did or did not do, with what should have been and what cannot be helped.

She was a beautiful baby. The first and only one of our five that was beautiful at birth. You do not guess how new and uneasy her tenancy in her now-loveliness. You did not know her all those years she was thought homely, or see her poring over her baby pictures, making me tell her over and over how beautiful she had been—and would be, I would tell her—and was now, to the seeing eye. But the seeing eyes were few or non-existent. Including mine.

I nursed her. They feel that's important nowadays. I nursed all the children, but with her, with all the fierce rigidity of first motherhood, I did like the books then said. Though her cries battered me to trembling and my breasts ached with swollenness, I waited till the clock decreed.

Why do I put that first? I do not even know if it matters, or if it explains anything.

She was a beautiful baby. She blew shining bubbles of sound. She loved motion, loved light, loved color and music and textures. She would lie on the floor in her blue overalls patting the surface so hard in ecstasy her hands and feet would blur. She was a miracle to me, but when she was eight months old I had to leave her daytimes with the woman downstairs to whom she was no miracle at all, for I worked or looked for work and for Emily's father, who "could no longer endure" (he wrote in his good-bye note) "sharing want with us."

I was nineteen. I was the pre-relief, pre-WPA world of the depression. I would start running as soon as I got off the streetcar, running up the stairs, the place smelling sour, and awake or asleep to startle awake, when she saw me would break into a clogged weeping that could not be comforted, a weeping I can hear yet.

After a while I found a job hashing at night so I could be with her days, and it was better. But it came to where I had to bring her to his family and leave her.

It took a long time to raise the money for her fare back. Then she got chicken pox and I had to wait longer. When she finally came, I hardly knew her, walking quick and nervous like her father, looking like her father, thin, and dressed in a shoddy red that yellowed her skin and glared at the pock-marks. All the baby loveliness gone.

She was two. Old enough for nursery school they said, and I did not know then what I know now—the fatigue of the long day, and the lacerations of group life in the kinds of nurseries that are only parking places for children.

Except that it would have made no difference if I had known. It was the only place there was. It was the only way we could be together, the only way I could hold a job.

And even without knowing, I knew, I knew the teacher that was evil because all these years it has curdled into my memory, the little boy hunched in the corner, her rasp, "why aren't you outside, because Alvin hits you? that's no reason, go out, scaredy." I knew Emily hated it even if she did not clutch and implore "don't go Mommy" like the other children, mornings.

She always had a reason why we should stay home. Momma, you look sick, Momma. I feel sick. Momma, the teachers aren't there today, they're sick. Momma, we can't go, there was a fire there last night. Momma, it's a holiday today, no school, they told me.

But never a direct protest, never rebellion. I think of our others in their three-, four-year-oldness—the explosions, the tempers, the denunciations, the demands—and I feel suddenly ill. I put the iron down. What in me demanded that goodness in her? And what was the cost, the cost to her of such goodness?

The old man living in the back once said in his gentle way: "You should smile at Emily more when you look at her." What was in my face when I looked at her? I loved her. There were all the acts of love.

It was only with the others I remembered what he said, and it was the face of joy, and not of care or tightness or worry I turned to them—too late for Emily. She does not smile easily, let alone almost always as her brothers and sisters do. Her face is closed and sombre, but when she wants, how fluid. You must have seen it in her pantomimes, you spoke of her rare gift for comedy on the stage that rouses a laughter out of the audience so dear they applaud and applaud and do not want to let her go.

Where does it come from, that comedy? There was none of it in her when she came back to me that second time, after I had had to send her away again. She had a new daddy now to learn to love, and I think perhaps it was a better time.

Except when we left her alone nights, telling ourselves she was old enough.

"Can't you go some other time, Mommy, like tomorrow?" she would ask. "Will it be just a little while you'll be gone? Do you promise?"

The time we came back, the front door open, the clock on the floor in the hall. She rigid awake. "It wasn't just a little while, I didn't cry. Three times I called you, just three times, and then I ran downstairs to open the door so you could come faster. The clock talked loud. I threw it away, it scared me what it talked."

She said the clock talked loud again that night I went to the hospital to have Susan. She was delirious with the fever that comes before red measles, but she was fully conscious all the week I was gone and the week after we were home when she could not come near the new baby or me.

She did not get well. She stayed skeleton thin, not wanting to eat, and night after night she had nightmares. She would call for me, and I would rouse from exhaustion to sleepily call back: "You're all right, darling, go to sleep, it's just a dream," and if she still called, in a sterner voice "now go to sleep, Emily, there's nothing to hurt you." Twice, only twice, when I had to get up for Susan anyhow, I went in to sit with her.

Now when it is too late (as if she would let me hold and comfort her like I do the others) I get up and go to her at once at her moan or restless stirring. "Are you awake, Emily? Can I get you something?" And the answer is always the same: "No, I'm all right, go back to sleep, Mother."

They persuaded me at the clinic to send her away to a convalescent home in the country where "she can have the kind of food and care you can't manage for her, and you'll be free to concentrate on the new baby." They still send children to that place. I see pictures on the society page of sleek young women planning affairs to raise money for it, or dancing at the affairs, or decorating Easter eggs or filling Christmas stockings for the children.

They never have a picture of the children so I do not know if the girls still wear those gigantic red bows and the ravaged looks on the every other Sunday when parents can come to visit "unless otherwise notified"—as we were notified the first six weeks.

Oh it is a handsome place, green lawns and tall trees and fluted flower beds. High up on the balconies of each cottage the children stand, the girls in their red bows and white dresses, the boys in white suits and giant red ties. The parents stand below shrieking up to be heard and the children shriek down to be heard, and between them the invisible wall "Not To Be Contaminated by Parental Germs or Physical Affection."

There was a tiny girl who always stood hand in hand with Emily. Her parents never came. One visit she was gone. "They moved her to Rose Cottage" Emily shouted in explanation. "They don't like you to love anybody here."

She wrote once a week, the labored writing of a seven-year-old. "I am fine. How is the baby. If I write my letter nicely I will have a star. Love." There never was a star. We wrote every other day, letters she could never hold or keep but only hear read—once. "We simply do not have room for children to keep any personal possessions," they patiently explained when we pieced one Sunday's shrieking together to plead how much it would mean to Emily, who loved to keep things, to be allowed to keep her letters and cards.

Each visit she looked frailer. "She isn't eating," they told us.

(They had runny eggs for breakfast or mush with lumps, Emily said later, I'd hold it in my mouth and not swallow. Nothing ever tasted good, just when they had chicken.)

It took us eight months to get her released home, and only the fact that she gained back to little of her seven lost pounds convinced the social worker.

I used to try to hold and love her after she came back, but her body would stay stiff, and after a while she'd push away. She ate little. Food sickened her, and I think much of life too. Oh she had physical lightness and brightness, twinkling by on skates, bouncing like a ball up and down up and down over the jump rope, skimming over the hill; but these were momentary.

She fretted about her appearance, thin and dark and foreign-looking at a time when every little girl was supposed to look or thought she should look a chubby blonde replica of Shirley Temple. The doorbell sometimes rang for her, but no one seemed to come and play in the house or be a best friend. Maybe because we moved so much.

There was a boy she loved painfully through two school semesters. Months later she told me how she had taken pennies from my purse to buy him candy. "Licorice was his favorite and I brought him some every day, but he still liked Jennifer better'n me. Why, Mommy?" The kind of question for which there is no answer.

School was a worry to her. She was not glib or quick in a world where glibness and quickness were easily confused with ability to learn. To her overworked and exasperated teachers she was an over conscientious "slow learner" who kept trying to catch up and was absent entirely too often.

I let her be absent, though sometimes the illness was imaginary. How different from my now-strictness about attendance with the others. I wasn't working. We had a new baby, I was home anyhow. Sometimes, after Susan grew old enough, I would keep her home from school, too, to have them all together.

Mostly Emily had asthma, and her breathing, hard and labored, would fill the house with a curiously tranquil sound. I would bring the two old dresser mirrors and her boxes of collections to her bed. She would select beads and single earrings, bottle tops and shells, dried flowers and pebbles, old post-cards and scraps, all sorts of oddments; then she and Susan would play Kingdom, setting up landscapes and furniture, peopling them with action.

Those were the only times of peaceful companionship between her and Susan, no, Emily toward Susan that poisonous feeling between them, that terrible balancing of hurts and needs I had to do between the two, and did so badly, those earlier years.

Oh there are conflicts between the others too, each one human, needing, demanding, hurting, taking—but only between Emily and Susan. I have edged away from it, that no, Emily toward Susan that corroding resentment. It seems so obvious on the surface, yet it is not obvious. Susan, the second child, Susan, golden- and curly-haired and chubby, quick and articulate and assured, everything in appearance and manner Emily was not; Susan, not able to resist Emily's precious things, losing or sometimes clumsily breaking them; Susan telling jokes and riddles to company for applause while Emily sat silent (to say to me later: that was my riddle, Mother, I told it to Susan); Susan, who for all the five years' difference in age was just a year behind Emily in developing physically.

I am glad for that slow physical development that widened the difference between her and her contemporaries, though she suffered over it. She was too vulnerable for that terrible world of youthful competition, of preening and parading, of constant measuring of yourself against every other, of envy, "If I had that copper hair," "If I had that skin ..." She tormented herself enough about not looking like the others, there was enough of the unsure-ness, the having to be conscious of words before you speak, the constant caring—what are they thinking of me? without having it all magnified by the merciless physical drives.

Ronnie is calling. He is wet and I change him. It is rare there is such a cry now. That time of motherhood is almost behind me when the ear is not one's own but must always be racked and listening for the child cry, the child call. We sit for a while and I hold him, looking out over the city spread in charcoal with its soft aisles of light. "Shoogily," he breathes and curls closer. I carry him back to bed asleep. Shoogily. A funny word, a family word, inherited from Emily, invented by her to say: comfort.

In this and other ways she leaves her seal, I say aloud. And startle at my saying it. What do I mean? What did I start to gather together, to try and make coherent? I was at the terrible, growing years. War years. I do not remember them well. I was working, there were four smaller ones now, there was not time for her. She had to help be a mother, and housekeeper, and shopper. She had to set her seal. Mornings of crisis and near hysteria trying to get lunches packed, hair combed, coats and shoes found, everyone to school or Child Care on time, the baby ready for transportation. And always the paper scribbled on by a smaller one, the book looked at by Susan then mislaid, the homework not done. Running out to that huge school where she was one, she was lost, she was a drop; suffering over the unpreparedness, stammering and unsure in her classes.

There was so little time left at night after the kids were bedded down. She would struggle over books, always eating (it was in those years she developed her enormous appetite that is legendary in our family) and I would be ironing, or preparing food for the next day, or writing V-mail to Bill, or tending the baby. Sometimes, to make me laugh, or out of her despair, she would imitate happenings or types at school.

I think I said once: "Why don't you do something like this in the school amateur show?" One morning she phoned me at work, hardly understandable through the weeping: "Mother, I did it. I won. I won; they gave me first prize; they clapped and clapped and wouldn't let me go."

Now suddenly she was Somebody, and as imprisoned in her difference as she had been in anonymity.

She began to be asked to perform at other high schools, even in colleges, then at city and statewide affairs. The first one we went to, I only recognized her that first moment when thin, shy, she almost drowned herself into the curtains. Then: Was this Emily? The control, the command, the convulsing and deadly clowning, the spell, then the roaring, stamping audience, unwilling to let this rare and precious laughter out of their lives.

Afterwards: You ought to do something about her with a gift like that—but without money or knowing how, what does one do? We have left it all to her, and the gift has as often eddied inside, clogged and clotted, has been used and growing.

She is coming. She runs up the stairs two at a time with her light graceful step, and I know she is happy tonight. Whatever it was that occasioned your call did not happen today.

"Aren't you ever going to finish the ironing, Mother? Whistler painted his mother in a rocker. I'd have to paint mine standing over an ironing board." This is one of her communicative nights and she tells me everything and nothing as she fixes herself a plate of food out of the icebox.

She is so lovely. Why did you want me to come in at all? Why were you concerned? She will find her way.

She starts up the stairs to bed. "Don't get me up with the rest in the morning." "But I thought you were having midterms." "Oh, those," she comes back in, kisses me, and says quite lightly, "in a couple of years when we'll all be atom-dead they won't matter a bit."

She has said it before. She believes it. But because I have been dredging the past, and all that compounds a human being is so heavy and meaningful in me, I cannot endure it tonight.

I will never total it all. I will never come in to say: She was a child seldom smiled at. Her father left me before she was a year old. I had to work her first

438

six years when there was work, or I sent her home and to his relatives. There were years she had care she hated. She was dark and thin and foreign-looking in a world where the prestige went to blondeness and curly hair and dimples, she was slow where glibness was prized. She was a child of anxious, not proud, love. We were poor and could not afford for her the soil of easy growth. I was a young mother. I was a distracted mother. There were the other children pushing up, demanding. Her younger sister seemed all that she was not. There were years she did not want me to touch her. She kept too much in herself, her life was such she had to keep too much in herself. My wisdom came too late. She has much to her and probably little will come of it. She is a child of her age, of depression, of war, of fear.

Let her be. So all that is in her will not bloom—but in how many does it? There is still enough left to live by. Only help her know—help make it so there is cause for her to know—that she is more than this dress on the ironing board, helpless before the iron.

Discussion Plan:

1. What are the events in Emily's live that are most significant in her mother's recollection?
2. Are these events generally considered important or do they show a special perspective or values?
3. Would these events be as likely in modern society as they would have been fifty years ago.
4. Are the issues faced common to all people or more representative of some social or economic situations?
5. Which of the events in Emily's life does the mother use for self-evaluation?
6. Which of these events are the responsibility of the mother?
7. Of which events is the mother a victim of circumstance?
8. Does the mother make the distinction brought out in questions 6. and 7. when evaluating her life?
9. Does the distinction in 6. and 7. make a difference to Emily?
10. Discuss the same issues from the perspective of Emily making a self-evaluation at age twenty one.
11. What is the meaning of the last sentence of the story?

Self and Luck

We are told that the best approach to life is to set goals, to plan, to prepare. Thoughtfulness is the way that we can achieve something meaningful in our life. Somehow, no matter how hard we try to control the direction of our lives something interferes, altering our course. Careful planning and good intentions cannot take into account the factor of "luck." Luck plays an important part of our lives, cancelling plans or granting unearned rewards. How can we judge ourselves by our accomplishments if life is capricious?"

Somerset Maugham, The Ant and the Grasshopper

When I was a very small boy, I was made to learn by heart certain of the fables of La Fontaine, and the moral of each was carefully explained to me. Among those learned was *The Ant and the Grasshopper,* which is devised to bring home to the young the useful lesson that in an imperfect world industry is rewarded and giddiness punished. In this admirable fable (I apologize for telling something which everyone is politely, but inexactly, supposed to know) the ant spends a laborious summer gathering its winter store, while the grasshopper sits on a blade of grass singing to the sun. Winter comes and the ant is comfortably provided for, but the grasshopper has an empty larder: he goes to the ant and begs for a little food. Then the ant gives him her classic answer:

"What were you doing in the summer time?"

"Saving your presence, I sang, I sang all day, all night."

"You sang. Why, then go and dance."

I do not ascribe it to perversity on my part, but rather to the inconsequence of childhood, which is deficient in moral sense, that I could never quite reconcile myself to the lesson. My sympathies were with the grasshopper and for some time I never saw an ant without putting my foot on it. In this summary (and as I have discovered since, entirely human) fashion I sought to express my disapproval of prudence and common-sense.

I could not help thinking of this fable when the other day I saw George Ramsay lunching by himself in a restaurant. I never saw anyone wear an expression of such deep gloom. He was staring into space. He looked as though the burden of the whole world sat upon his shoulders. I was sorry for him: I suspected at once that his unfortunate brother had been causing trouble again. I went up to him and held out my hand.

"How are you?" I asked.

"I'm not in hilarious spirits," he answered.

"Is it Tom again?"

He sighed.

"Yes, it's Tom again."

"Why don't you chuck him? You've done everything in the world for him. You must know by now that he's quite hopeless."

I suppose every family has a black sheep. Tom had been a sore trial to his for twenty years. He had begun life decently enough: he went into business, married and had two children. The Ramsays were perfectly respectable people and there was every reason to suppose that Tom Ramsay would have a useful and honourable career. But one day, without warning, he announced that he didn't like work and that he wasn't suited for marriage. He wanted to enjoy himself. He would listen to no expostulations. He left his wife and his office. He had a little money and he spent two happy years in various capitals of Europe. Rumours of his doings reached his relations from time to time and they were profoundly shocked. He certainly had a very good time. They shook their heads and asked what would happen when his money was spent. They soon found out: he borrowed. He was charming and unscrupulous. I have never met anyone to whom it was more difficult to refuse a loan. He made a steady income from his friends and he made friends easily. But he always said that the money you spent on necessities was boring; the money that was amusing to spend was the money you spent on luxuries. For this he depended on his brother George. He did not waste his charm on him. George was respectable. Once or twice he fell to Tom's promises of amendment and gave him considerable sums in order that he might make a fresh start. On these Tom bought a motorcar and some very nice jewelry. But when circumstances forced George to realise that his brother would never settle down and he washed his hands of him, Tom, without a qualm, began to blackmail him. It was not very nice for a respectable lawyer to find his brother shaking cocktails behind the bar of his favourite restaurant or to see him waiting on the box-seat of a taxi outside his club. Tom said that to serve in a bar or to drive a taxi was a perfectly decent occupation, but if George could oblige him with a couple of hundred pounds he didn't mind for the honour of the family giving it up. George paid.

Once Tom nearly went to prison. George was terribly upset. He went into the whole discreditable affair. Really Tom had gone too far. He had been wild, thoughtless and selfish, but he had never before done anything dishonest, by which George meant illegal, and if he were prosecuted he would assuredly be convicted. But you cannot allow your only brother to go to gaol. The man Tom had cheated, a man called Cronshaw, was vindictive. He was determined to take the matter into court; he said Tom was a scoundrel and should be punished. It cost George an infinite deal of trouble and five hundred pounds to settle the affair. I have never seen him in such a rage as when he heard that Tom and Cronshaw had gone off together to Monte

Carlo the moment they cashed the cheque. They spent a happy month there.

For twenty years Tom raced and gabled, philandered with the prettiest girls, danced, ate in the most expensive restaurants, and dressed beautifully. He always looked as if he had just stepped out of a bandbox. Though he was forty-six you would never have taken him for more than thirty-five. He was a most amusing companion and though you knew he was perfectly worthless you could not but enjoy his society. He had high spirits, an unfailing gaiety and incredible charm. I never grudged the contributions he regularly levied on me for the necessities of his existence. I never lent him fifty pounds without feeling that I was in his debt. Tom Ramsay knew everyone and everyone knew Tom Ramsay. You could not approve of him, but you could not help liking him.

Poor George, only a year older than his scapegrace brother, looked sixty. He had never taken more than a fortnight's holiday in the year for a quarter of a century. He was in his office every morning at nine-thirty, and never left it till six. He was honest, industrious and worthy. He had a good wife, to whom he had never been unfaithful even in thought, and four daughters to whom he was the best of fathers. He made a point of saving a third of his income and his plan was to retire at fifty-five to a little house in the country, where he proposed to cultivate his garden and play golf. His life was blameless. He was glad that he was growing old because Tom was growing old too. He rubbed his hands and said:

"It was all very well when Tom was young and good-looking, but he's only a year younger than I am. In four years he'll be fifty. He won't find life too easy then. I shall have thirty thousand pounds by the time I'm fifty. For twenty-five years I've said that Tom would end in the gutter. And we shall see how he likes that. We shall see if it really pays best to work or be idle."

Poor George! I sympathised with him. I wondered now as I sat down beside him what infamous thing Tom had done. George was evidently very much upset.

"Do you know what's happened now?" he asked me.

I was prepared for the worst. I wondered if Tom had got into the hands of the police at last. George could hardly bring himself to speak.

"You're not going to deny that all my life I've been hard working, decent, respectable and straightforward. After a life of industry and thrift I can look forward to retiring on a small income in gilt-edged securities. I've always done my duty in that state of life in which it has pleased Providence to place me."

"True."

"And you can't deny that Tom has been an idle, worthless dissolute and dishonourable rogue. If there were any justice he'd be in the workhouse."

"True."

George grew red in the face.

"A few weeks ago he became engaged to a woman old enough to be his mother. And now she's died and left him everything she had. Half a million pounds, a yacht, a house in London and a house in the country."

George Ramsay beat his clenched fist on the table.

"It's not fair, I tell you, it's not fair. Damn it, it's not fair."

I could not help it. I burst into a shout of laughter as I looked at George's wrathful face. I rolled in my chair, I very nearly fell on the floor. George never forgave me. But Tom often asks me to excellent dinners in his charming house in Mayfair, and if he occasionally borrows a trifle from me, that is merely from force of habit. It is never more than a sovereign.

Exercise:

Which of the following situations is *unfair* because of good luck or bad luck? Support your answer.

1. John has played the lottery every day for this last two years and never wins, Ralph wins the first time he ever plays.
2. Jill is so talented that she invariably gets the lead in the school musical.
3. Fred is very good looking and is well liked by almost everyone, so he never has trouble getting dates.
4. Jim works very hard on a school project and gets a 'B'.
5. Frank practices the violin daily but never gets much better.
6. Mary has loved football all of her life and always played with the boys on the block, but is not allowed to try out for the school team, she is 5'6" and weighs 115 pounds.
7. Jane, whose family is quite wealthy, wins an art scholarship to a fine college and therefore pays no tuition.
8. Harry is all ready to start college when his father's business fails postponing college indefinitely.
9. Joan's grades are lower than Hal's but she is accepted to a college that Hal is rejected for; Joan is non-white; Hal is white.
10. Because of federal budget cuts, Tom cannot afford the college of his choice.

Self in the World

*Things used to move a great deal more slowly, or so it seems to those of us
who have lived long enough. We grow up expecting to live one way and
technology pulls the rug out from under us. We must learn to live a new life in
keeping with the times. Some of us have a difficult time coping with the
alterations in our conception of reality that change demands. When reality is
no longer familiar either the world or ourselves appear deranged.*

Shirley Jackson, Colloquy

The doctor was competent-looking and respectable. Mrs. Arnold felt
vaguely comforted by his appearance, and her agitation lessened a little. She
knew that he noticed her hand shaking when she leaned forward for him to
light her cigarette, and she smiled apologetically, but he looked back at her
seriously.

"You seem to be upset," he said gravely.

"I'm very much upset," Mrs. Arnold said. She tried to talk slowly and
intelligently. "That's one reason I came to you instead of going to Doctor
Murphy—our regular doctor, that is."

The doctor frowned slightly. "My husband," Mrs. Arnold went on, "I don't
want him to know that I'm worried and Doctor Murphy would probably feel
it was necessary to tell him." The doctor nodded, not committing himself,
Mrs. Arnold noted.

"What seems to be the trouble?"

Mrs. Arnold took in a death breath. "Doctor," she said, "how do people
tell if they're going crazy?"

The doctor looked up.

"Isn't that silly," Mrs. Arnold said. "I hadn't meant to say it like that. It's
hard enough to explain anyway, without making it so dramatic."

"Insanity is more complicated than you think," the doctor said.

"I know it's complicated," Mrs. Arnold said. "That's the only thing I'm
really sure of. Insanity is one of the things I mean."

"I beg your pardon?"

"That's the trouble, Doctor." Mrs. Arnold sat back and took her gloves out
from under her pocketbook and put them carefully on top. Then she took
them and put them underneath the pocketbook again.

"Suppose you just tell me all about it," the doctor said.

Mrs. Arnold sighed. "Everyone else seems to understand," she said, "and
I don't. Look." She leaned forward and gestured with one hand while she
spoke. "I don't understand the way people live. It all used to be so simple.
When I was a little girl I used to live in a world where a lot of other people

lived too and they all lived together and things went along like that with no fuss." She looked at the doctor. He was frowning again, and Mrs. Arnold went on, her voice rising slightly. "Look. Yesterday morning my husband stopped on his way to his office to buy a paper. He always buys the *Times* and he always buys it from the same dealer, and yesterday the dealer didn't have a *Times* for my husband and last night when he came home for dinner he said the fish was burned and the desert was too sweet and he sat around all evening talking to himself."

"He could have tried to get it at another dealer," the doctor said. "Very often dealers downtown have papers later than local dealers."

"No," Mrs. Arnold said, slowly and distinctly, "I guess I'd better start over. When I was a little girl—" she said. Then she stopped. "Look," she said, "did there use to be words like psychosomatic medicine? Or international cartels? Or bureaucratic centralization?"

"Well," the doctor began.

"What do they mean?" Mrs. Arnold insisted.

"In a period of international crisis," the doctor said gently, "when you find, for instance, cultural patterns rapidly disintegrating ... "

"International crisis," Mrs. Arnold said. "Patterns." She began to cry quietly. "He said the man had no right not to save him a *Times*," she said, hysterically, fumbling in her pocket for a handkerchief, "and he started talking about social planning on the local level and surtax net income and geopolitical concepts and deflationary inflation." Mrs. Arnold's voice rose to a wail. "He really said deflationary inflation."

"Mrs. Arnold," the doctor said, coming around the desk, "we're not going to help things any this way."

"What is going to help?" Mrs. Arnold said. "Is everyone really crazy but me?"

"Mrs. Arnold," the doctor said severely, "I want you to get hold of yourself. In a disoriented world like ours today, alienation from reality frequently—"

"Disoriented," Mrs. Arnold said. She stood up. "Alienation," she said. "Reality." Before the doctor could stop her she walked to the door and opened it. "Reality," she said, and went out.

Exercise:

1. Make a list of the words that Mrs. Arnold sees as the basis of her husband's problems.
2. Try to define these words.
3. What aspects of the world do these words refer to?
4. Are the aspects of the world referred to by these terms special aspects of today's world?
5. How do these aspects affect peoples' lives.

Discussion Plan:

1. How much of the world does a person have to understand in order to be sane?
2. Does a person have to accept what is happening to them, in order to be sane?
3. Does a person have to see reality as making sense in order to be sane.
4. Does a person have to be able to cope with reality in order to be sane?

Introspection

Our lives are full of activity. The standard of fulfillment seems to be: the more activity the better. It is difficult for us to assess those people for whom inactivity is a necessity. What can be the point of sitting quietly and doing nothing? What is accomplished?

Jerome Weidman, My Father Sits in the Dark

My father has a peculiar habit. He is fond of sitting in the dark, alone. Sometimes I come home very late. The house is dark. I let myself in quietly because I do not want to disturb my mother. She is a light sleeper. I tiptoe into my room and undress in the dark. I go to the kitchen for a drink of water. My bare feet make no noise. I step into the room and almost trip over my father. He is sitting in a kitchen chair, in his pajamas, smoking his pipe.

'Hello, Pop,' I say.

'Hello, son.'

'Why don't you go to bed, Pa?'

'I will,' he says.

But he remains there. Long after I am asleep I feel sure that he is still sitting there, smoking.

Many times I am reading in my room. I hear my mother get the house ready for the night. I hear my kid brother go to bed. I hear my sister come in. I hear her do things with jars and combs until she, too, is quiet. I know she has gone to sleep. In a little while I hear my mother say good night to my father. I continue to read. Soon I become thirsty, (I drink a lot of water.) I go to the kitchen for a drink. Again I almost stumble across my father. Many times it startles me. I forget about him. And there he is—smoking, sitting, thinking.

'Why don't you go to bed, Pop?'

"I will, son.'

But he doesn't. He just sits there and smokes and thinks. It worries me. I can't understand it. What can he be thinking about? Once I asked him.

'What are you thinking about, Pa?'

'Nothing.' he said.

Once I left him there and went to bed. I awoke several hours later. I was thirsty. I went to the kitchen. There he was. His pipe was out. But he sat there, staring into a corner of the kitchen. After a moment I became accustomed to the darkness. I took my drink. He still sat and stared. His eyes did not blink. I thought he was not even aware of me. I was afraid.

'Why don't you go to bed, Pop?'

'I will, son,' he said. 'Don't wait up for me.'

'But,' I said, 'you've been sitting here for hours. What's wrong? What are you thinking about?'

'Nothing, son,' he said. 'Nothing. It's just restful. That's all.'

The way he said it was convincing. He did not seem worried. His voice was even and pleasant. It always is. But I could not understand it. How could it be restful to sit alone in an uncomfortable chair far into the night, in darkness?

What can it be?

I review all the possibilities. It can't be money. I know that. We haven't much, but when he is worried about money he makes no secret of it. It can't be his health. He is not reticent about that either. It can't be the health of anyone in the family. We are a bit short on money, but we are long on health. (Knock wood, my mother would say.) What can it be? I am afraid I do not know. But that does not stop me from worrying.

Maybe he is thinking of his brothers in the old country. Or of his mother and two step-mothers. Or of his father. But they are all dead. And he would not brood about them like that. I say brood, but it is not really true. He does not brood. He does not even seem to be thinking. He looks too peaceful, too, well not contented, just too peaceful, to be brooding. Perhaps it is as he says. Perhaps it is restful. But it does not seem possible. It worries me.

If I only knew what he thinks about. If I only knew that he thinks at all. I might not be able to help him. He might not even need help. It may be as he says. It may be restful. But at least I would not worry about it.

Why does he just sit there, in the dark? Is his mind failing? No, it can't be. He is only fifty-three. And he is just as keen-witted as ever. In fact, he is the same in every respect. He still likes beet soup. He still reads the second section of the *Times* first. He still wears wing collars. He still believes that Debs could have saved the country and that T.R. was a tool of the moneyed interests. He is the same in every way. He does not even look older than he did five years ago. Everybody remarks about that. Well-preserved, they say. But he sits in the dark, alone, smoking, staring straight ahead of him, unblinking, into the small hours of the night.

If it is as he says, if it is restful, I will let it go at that. But suppose it is not. Suppose it is something I cannot fathom. Perhaps he needs help. Why doesn't he speak? Why doesn't he frown or laugh or cry? Why doesn't he do something? Why does he just sit there?

Finally I become angry. Maybe it is just my unsatisfied curiosity. Maybe I am a bit worried. Anyway, I become angry.

'Is something wrong, Pop?'

'Nothing, son. Nothing at all.'

But this time I am determined not to be put off. I am angry.

'Then why do you sit here all alone, thinking, till late?'

'It's restful, son. I like it.'

I am getting nowhere. Tomorrow he will be sitting there again. I will be puzzled. I will be worried. I will not stop now. I am angry.

'Well, what do you think about, Pa? Why do you just sit here? What's worrying you? What do you think about?'

'Nothing's worrying me, son. I'm all right. It's just restful. That's all. Go to bed, son.'

My anger has left me. But the feeling of worry is still there. I must get an answer. It seems so silly. Why doesn't he tell me? I have a funny feeling that unless I get an answer I will go crazy. I am insistent.

'But what do you think about, Pa? What is it?'

'Nothing, son. Just things in general. Nothing special. Just things.'

I can get no answer.

It is very late. The street is quiet and the house is dark. I climb the steps softly, skipping the ones that creak. I let myself in with my key and tiptoe into my room. I remove my clothes and remember that I am thirsty. In my bare feet I walk to the kitchen. Before I reach it I know he is there.

I can see the deeper darkness of his hunched shape. He is sitting in the same chair, his elbows on his knees, his cold pipe in his teeth, his unblinking eyes staring straight ahead. He does not seem to know I am there. He did not hear me come in. I stand quietly in the doorway and watch him.

Everything is quiet, but the night is full of little sounds. As I stand there motionless I begin to notice them. The ticking of the alarm clock on the icebox. The low hum of an automobile passing many blocks away. The swish of papers moved along the street by the breeze. A whispering rise and fall of sound, like low breathing. It is strangely pleasant.

The dryness in my throat reminds me. I step briskly into the kitchen.

'Hello, Pop,' I say.

'Hello, son,' he says. His voice is low and dreamlike. He does not change his position or shift his gaze.

I cannot find the faucet. The dim shadow of light that comes through the window from the street lamp only makes the room seem darker. I reach for the short chain in the center of the room. I snap on the light.

He straightens up with a jerk, as though he has been struck. 'What's the matter, Pop?' I ask.

'Nothing,' he says. 'I don't like the light.'

'What's the matter with the light?' I say. 'What's wrong?'

'Nothing,' he says. 'I don't like the light.'

I snap the lift off. I drink my water slowly. I must take it easy, I say to myself. I must get to the bottom of this.

'Why don't you go to bed? Why do you sit here so late in the dark?'

'It's nice,' he says. 'I can't get used to lights. We didn't have lights when I was a boy in Europe.'

My heart skips a beat and I catch my breath happily. I begin to think I understand. I remember the stories of his boyhood in Austria. I see the wide-beamed kretchma, with my grandfather behind the bar. It is late, the customers are gone, and he is dozing. I see the bed of glowing coal, the last of the roaring fire. The room is already dark, and growing darker. I see a small boy, crouched on a pile of twigs at one side of the huge fireplace, his starry gaze fixed on the dull remains of the dead flames. The boy is my father.

I remember the pleasure of those few moments while I stood quietly in the doorway watching him.

'You mean there's nothing wrong? You just sit in the dark because you like it, Pop?' I find it hard to keep my voice from rising in a happy shout.

'Sure,' he says. 'I can't think with the light on.'

I set my glass down and turn to go back to my room. 'Good night, Pop,' I say.

'Good night,' he says.

Then I remember. I turn back. 'What do you think about, Pop?' I ask.

His voice seems to come from far away. It is quiet and even again, 'Nothing,' he says softly. 'Nothing special.'

Discussion Plan:

1. What is father doing?
2. Is it appropriate to do?
3. Would it be appropriate behavior in a fifteen year old?
4. What is the difference between what the father is doing and procrastinating?
5. Is the father wasting time?
6. Is the father escaping from reality?
7. Does productive thinking have to be future oriented?
8. Is it wrong to dwell on the past?
9. If the father's recollections were full of anger and resentment, would it be wrong to do?
10. Can we learn from the past without applying our lessons to the future

Old Age

Old age comes to all of us, if we just live long enough. We cannot argue with this if we consider old age to be a chronological phenomenon. But age may be a psychological phenomenon too, a matter of self perception—a view of ourselves reinforced by social attitudes. If this is so, the reality of aging may be controllable, not with pills and potions but with will and a positive attitude.

Guy De Maupassant, An Old Man

All the newspapers had carried this advertisement:

The new spa at Rondelis offers all the advantages desirable for a lengthy stay or even for permanent residence. Its ferruginous waters, recognized as the best in the world for countering all impurities of the blood, also seem to possess special qualities calculated to prolong human life. This remarkable circumstance may be due in part to the exceptional situation of the little town, which lies in a mountainous region, in the middle of a forest of firs. The fact remains that for several centuries it has been noted for cases of extraordinary longevity.

And the public came along in droves.

One morning the doctor in charge of the springs was asked to call on a newcomer, Monsieur Daron, who had arrived a few days before and had rented a charming villa on the edge of the forest. He was a little old man of eighty-six, still quite sprightly, wiry, healthy and active, who went to infinite pains to conceal his age.

He offered the doctor a seat and started questioning him, straight away.

"Doctor," he said, "if I am in good health, it is thanks to careful living. Though not very old, I have already attained a respectable age, yet I keep free of all illnesses and indispositions, even the slightest malaise, by means of careful living. It is said that the climate here is very good for the health. I am perfectly prepared to believe it, but before settling down here I want proof. I am therefore going to ask you to come and see me once a week to give me the following information in detail."

"First of all I wish to have a complete, absolutely complete, list of all the inhabitants of the town and the surrounding area who are over eighty years old. I also need a few physical and physiological details regarding each of them. I wish to know their professions, their way of life, their habits. Every time one of those people dies you will be good enough to inform me, giving me the precise cause of death and describing the circumstances."

Then he added graciously "I hope, Doctor, that we shall become good friends," and held out his wrinkled little hand. The doctor shook it, promising him his devoted co-operation.

Monsieur Daron had always had an obsessive fear of death. He had deprived himself of nearly all the pleasures of this world because they were dangerous, and whenever anyone expressed surprise that he should not drink wine—wine, that purveyor of dreams and gaiety—he would reply in a voice in which a note of fear could be detected: "I value my life." And he stressed the word "my," as if that life, his life, possessed some special distinction. He put into that my such a difference between his life and other people's lives that any rejoinder was out of the question.

For that matter he had a very special way of stressing the possessive pronouns designating parts of his person and even things which belonged to him. When he said "my eyes, my legs, my arms, my hands," it was quite obvious that there must be no mistake about this: those organs were not at all like other people's. But where this distinction was particularly noticeable was in his references to his doctor. When he said "my doctor," one would have thought that that doctor belonged to him and nobody else, destined for him alone, to attend to his illnesses and to nothing else, and that he was superior to all the other doctors in the world, without exception.

He had never regarded other men as anything but puppets of a sort, created to fill up an empty world. He divided them into two classes: those he greeted because some chance had put him in contact with them, and those he did not greet. But both these categories of individuals were equally insignificant in his eyes.

However, beginning with the day when the Rondelis doctor brought him the list of the seventeen inhabitants of the town who were over eighty, he felt a new interest awaken in his heart, an unfamiliar solicitude for these old people whom he was going to see fall by the wayside one by one. He had no desire to make their acquaintance, but he formed a very clear idea of their persons, and when the doctor dined with him, every Thursday, he spoke only of them. "Well, doctor," he would say, "and how is Joseph Poincot today? We left him feeling a little ill last week." And when the doctor had given him the patient's bill of health, Monsieur Daron would suggest changes in his diet, experiments, methods of treatment which he might later apply to himself if they had succeeded with the others. Those seventeen old people provided him with an experimental field from which he learnt many a lesson.

One evening the doctor announced as he came in : "Rosalie Tournel has died."

Monsieur Daron gave a start and immediately asked, "What of?"

"Of a chill."

The little old man gave a sigh of relief. Then he said, "She was too fat, too heavy, she must have eaten too much. When I get to her age I'll be more careful about my weight." (He was two years older than Rosalie Tournel, but he claimed to be only seventy.)

A few months later it was the turn of Henri Brissot. Monsieur Daron was very upset. This time it was a man, and a thin man at that, within three months of his own age, and careful about his health. He did not dare to ask any questions, but waited anxiously for the doctor to give him some details.

"Oh, so he died just like that, all of a sudden," he said. "But he was perfectly all right last week. He must have done something silly, I suppose, Doctor?"

The doctor, who was enjoying himself, replied: "I don't think so. His children told me he had been very careful."

Then, unable to contain himself any longer, and filled with fear, Monsieur Daron asked: "But ... but ...what did he die of, then?"

"Of pleurisy."

The little old man clapped his dry hands in sheer joy.

"I told you so! I told you he had done something silly. You don't get pleurisy for nothing. He must have gone out for a breath of air after his dinner and the cold must have gone to his chest. Pleurisy! Why, that's an accident, not an illness. Only fools die of pleurisy."

And he ate his dinner in high spirits, talking about those who were left.

"There are only fifteen of them now, but they are all hale and hearty, aren't they? The whole of life is like that: the weakest go first; people who live beyond thirty have a good chance of reaching sixty; those who pass sixty often get to eighty, and those who pass eighty nearly always live to be a hundred, because they are the fittest, toughest and most sensible of all."

Another two disappeared during the year, one of dysentery and the other of a choking fit. Monsieur Daron was highly amused by the death of the former and concluded that he must have eaten something stimulating the day before.

"Dysentery is the disease of careless people. Dammit all, Doctor, you ought to have watched over his diet."

As for the man who had been carried off by a choking fit, his death could only be due to a heart condition which had hitherto gone unnoticed.

But one evening the doctor announced the decease of Paul Timonet, a sort of mummy of whom it had been hoped to make a centenarian and an advertisement for the spa.

When Monsieur Daron asked, as usual: "What did he die of?" the doctor replied, "Bless me, I really don't know."

"What do you mean, you don't know. A doctor always knows. Hadn't he some organic lesion?"

The doctor shook his head.

"No, none."

"Possibly some infection of the liver or the kidneys?"

"No, they were quite sound."

"Did you check whether the stomach was functioning properly? A stroke is often caused by poor digestion."

"There was no stroke."

Monsieur Daron, very perplexed, said excitedly: "Look, he must have died of something! What do you think it was?"

The doctor threw up his hands.

"I've no idea, no idea at all. He died because he died, that's all."

Then Monsieur Daron, in a voice full of emotion, asked: "Exactly how old was that one? I can't remember."

"Eighty-nine."

And the little old man, at once incredulous and reassured, exclaimed:

"Eighty-nine! So whatever it was, it wasn't old age ..."

Exercise:

How old is old?

Make a list of those qualities that would make a person seem old at the following ages:

15
20
25
30
40
50
65
70
80

Distinguish between physical attributes, attitudes and activities.

Death

Life usually needs no apology. It has value or makes value attainable. It offers fulfillment or hope. It is open to possibilities, good and bad. Life is full of risks, but if you risk nothing, you gain nothing. What if there is nothing left to gain? Death is always inevitable, but it remains, for most of us, a vague threat because we do not know the time and agency of our deaths. How would you react if you knew when and how you would die? In the next selection death publicly seeks its victim. All who meet the agent of death are effected by it.

Ernest Hemingway, The Killers

The door of Henry's lunchroom opened and two men came in. They sat down at the counter.

"What's yours?" George asked them.

"I don't know," one of the men said. " What do you want to eat, Al?"

Outside it was getting dark. The street-light came on outside the window. The two men at the counter read the menu. From the other end of the counter Nick Adams watched them. He had been talking to George when they came in.

"I'll have a roast pork tenderloin with apple sauce and mashed potatoes," the first man said.

"It isn't ready yet."

"What the hell do you put it on the card for?"

"That's the dinner," George explained. "You can get that at six o'clock," George looked at the clock on the wall behind the counter.

"It's five o'clock."

"The clock says twenty minutes past five," the second man said.

"It's twenty minutes fast."

"Oh, to hell with the clock," the first man said. "What have you got to eat?"

"I can give you any kind of sandwiches," George said. "You can have ham and eggs, bacon and eggs, liver and bacon, or a steak."

"Give me the chicken croquettes with green peas and cream sauce and mashed potatoes."

"That's the dinner."

"Everything we want's the dinner, eh? That's the way you work it."

"I can give you ham and eggs, bacon and eggs, liver—"

"I'll take ham and eggs," the man called Al said. He wore a derby hat and a black overcoat buttoned across the chest. His face was small and white and he had tight lips. He wore a silk muffler and gloves.

"Give me bacon and eggs," said the other man. He was about the same size as Al. Their faces were different, but they were dressed like twins. Both wore overcoats too tight for them. They sat leaning forward, their elbows on the counter.

"Got anything to drink?" Al asked.

"Silver beer, bevo, ginger-ale," George said.

"I mean you got anything to drink?"

"Just those I said."

"This is a hot town," said the other. "What do they call it?"

"Summit."

"Ever hear of it?" Al asked his friend.

"No," said the friend.

"What do they do here nights?" Al asked.

"They eat the dinner," his friend said. "They all come here and eat the big dinner."

"That's right," George said.

"So you think that's right?" Al asked George.

"Sure."

"You're a pretty bright boy, aren't you?"

"Sure," said George.

"Well, you're not," said the other little man. "Is he, Al?"

"He's dumb," said Al. He turned to Nick. "What's your name?"

"Adams."

"Another bright boy," Al said. "Ain't he a bright boy, Max?"

"The town's full of bright boys," Max said.

George put the two platters, one of ham and eggs, the other of bacon and eggs, on the counter. He set down two side-dishes of fried potatoes and closed the wicket into the kitchen.

"Which is yours?" he asked Al.

"Don't you remember?"

"Ham and eggs."

"Just a bright boy," Max said. He leaned forward and took the ham and eggs. Both men ate with their gloves on. George watched them eat.

"What are you looking at?" Max looked at George.

"Nothing."

"The hell you were. You were looking at me."

"Maybe the boy meant it for a joke, Max," Al said.

George laughed.

"You don't have to laugh," Max said to him. "You don't have to laugh at all, see?"

"All right," said George.

"So he thinks it's all right." Max turned to Al. "He thinks it's all right. That's a good one."

"Oh, he's a thinker," Al said. They went on eating.

"What's the bright boy's name down the counter?" Al asked Max.

"Hey, bright boy," Max said to Nick. "You go around on the other side of the counter with your boy friend."

"What's the idea?" Nick asked.

"There isn't any idea."

"You better go around, bright boy," Al said. Nick went around behind the counter.

"What's the idea?" George asked.

"None of your damned business," Al said. "Who's out in the kitchen?"

"The nigger."

"What do you mean the nigger?"

"The nigger that cooks."

"Tell him to come in."

"What's the idea?"

"Tell him to come in."

"Where do you think you are?"

"We know damn well where we are," the man called Max said. "Do we look silly?"

"You talk silly," Al said to him. "What the hell do you argue with this kid for? Listen," he said to George, "tell the nigger to come out here."

"What are you going to do to him?"

"Nothing. Use your head, bright boy. What would we do to a nigger?"

George opened the slit that opened back into the kitchen. "Sam," he called. "Come in here a minute."

The door to the kitchen opened and the nigger came in. "What was it?" he asked. The two men at the counter took a look at him.

"All right, nigger. You stand right there," Al said.

Sam, the nigger, standing in his apron, looked at the two men sitting at the counter. "Yes, sir," he said. Al got down from his stool.

"I'm going back to the kitchen with the nigger and bright boy," he said. "Go on back to the kitchen nigger. You go with him, bright boy." The little man walked after Nick and Sam, the cook, back into the kitchen. The door shut after them. The man called Max sat at the counter opposite George. He didn't look at George but looked in the mirror that ran along back of the counter. Henry's had been made over from a saloon into a lunch counter.

"Well, bright boy," Max said, looking into the mirror, "why don't you say something?"

"What is it all about?"

"Hey, Al," Max called, "bright boy wants to know what it's all about."

"Why don't you tell him?" Al's voice came from the kitchen.

"What do you think it's all about?"

"I don't know."

"What do you think?"

Max looked into the mirror all the time he was talking.

"I wouldn't say."

"Hey, Al, bright boy says he wouldn't say what he thinks it's all about."

"I can hear you, all right," Al said from the kitchen. He had propped open the slit that dishes passed through into the kitchen with a catsup bottle. "Listen, bright boy," he said from the kitchen to George. "Stand a little further along the bar. You move a little to the left, Max." He was like a photographer arranging for a group picture.

"Talk to me, bright boy," Max said. "What do you think's going to happen?"

George did not say anything.

"I'll tell you," Max said. "We're going to kill a Swede. Do you know a big Swede named Ole Andreson?"

"Yes."

"He comes here to eat every night, don't he?"

"Sometimes he comes here."

"He comes here at six o'clock, don't he?"

"If he comes."

"We know all that, bright boy," Max said. "Talk about something else. Ever go to the movies?"

"Once in a while."

"You ought to go to the movies more. The movies are fine for a bright boy like you."

"What are you going to kill Ole Andreson for? What did he ever do to you?"

"He never had a chance to do anything to us. He never even seen us."

"And he's only going to see us once," Al said from the kitchen.

"What are you going to kill him for, then?" George asked.

"We're killing him for a friend. Just to oblige a friend, bright boy."

"Shut up," said Al from the kitchen. "You talk too goddam much."

"Well, I got to keep bright boy amused. Don't I, bright boy?"

"You talk too damn much," Al said. "The nigger and my bright boy are amused by themselves. I got them tied up like a couple of girl friends in the convent."

"I suppose you were in a convent."

"You never know."

"You were in a kosher convent. That's where you were."

George looked up at the clock.

"If anybody comes in you tell them the cook is off, and if they keep after it, you tell them you'll go back and cook yourself. Do you get that, bright boy?"

"All right," George said. "What you going to do with us afterward?"

"That'll depend," Max said. "That's one of those things you never know at the time."

George looked up at the clock. It was quarter past six. The door from the street opened. A street-car motorman came in.

"Hello, George," he said. "Can I get supper?"

"Sam's gone out," George said. "He'll be back in about half an hour."

"I'd better go up the street," the motorman said. George looked at the clock. It was twenty minutes past six.

"That was nice, bright boy," Max said. "You're a regular little gentleman."

"He knew I'd blow his head off," Al said from the kitchen.

"No," said Max. "It ain't that. Bright boy is nice. He's a nice boy. I like him."

At six-fifty-five George said: "He's not coming."

Two other people had been in the lunch room. Once George had gone out to the kitchen and made a ham-and-egg sandwich "to go" that a man wanted to take with him. Inside the kitchen he saw Al, his derby hat tipped back, sitting on a stool beside the wicket with the muzzle of a sawed-off shotgun resting on the ledge. Nick and the cook were back to back in the corner, a towel tied in each of their mouths. George had cooked the sandwich, wrapped it up in oiled paper, put it in a bag, brought it in, and the man had paid for it and gone out.

"Bright boy can do everything," Max said. "He can cook and everything. You'd make some girl a nice wife, bright boy."

"Yes?" George said. "Your friend, Ole Andreson, isn't going to come."

"We'll give him ten minutes," Max said.

Max watched the mirror and the clock. The hands of the clock marked seven o'clock and then five minutes past seven.

"Come on, Al," said Max. "We better go. He's not coming."

"Better give him five minutes," Al said from the kitchen.

In the five minutes a man came in, and George explained that the cook was sick.

"Why the hell don't you get another cook?" the man asked. "Aren't you running a lunch-counter?" He went out.

"Come on, Al," Max said.

"What about the two bright boys and the nigger?"

"They're all right."

"You think so?"

"Sure. We're through with it."

"I don't like it," said Al. "It's sloppy. You talk too much."

"Oh, what the hell," said Max. "We got to keep amused, haven't we?"

"You talk too much all the same," Al said. He came out from the kitchen. The cut-off barrels of the shotgun made a slight bulge under the waist of his too tight-fitting overcoat. He straightened his coat with his gloved hands.

"So long, bright boy," he said to George. "You got a lot of luck."

"That's the truth," Max said. "You ought to play the races, bright boy."

The two of them went out the door. George watched them, through the window, pass under the arc-light and across the street. In their tight over-coats and derby hats they looked like a vaudeville team. George went back through the swinging door into the kitchen and untied Nick and the cook.

"I don't want any more of that," said Sam, the cook. "I don't want any more of that."

Nick stood up. He had never had a towel in his mouth before. "Say," he said. "What the hell?" He was trying to swagger it off.

"They were going to kill Ole Andreson," George said. "They were going to shoot him when he came in to eat."

"Ole Andreson?"

"Sure."

The cook felt the corners of his mouth with his thumbs.

"They all gone?" he asked.

"Yeah," said George. "They're gone now."

"I don't like it," said the cook. "I don't like any of it at all."

"Listen," George said to Nick. "You better go see Ole Andreson."

"All right."

"You better not have anything to do with it at all," Sam, the cook, said. "You better stay way out of it."

"Don't go if you don't want to," George said.

"Mixing up in this ain't going to get you anywhere," the cook said. "You stay out of it."

"I'll go see him," Nick said to George. "Where does he live?" The cook turned away.

"Little boys always know what they want to do," he said.

"He lives up at Hirsch's rooming-house," George said to Nick.

"I'll go up there."

Outside the arc-light shone through the bare branches of a tree. Nick walked up the street beside the car-tracks and turned at the next arc-light down a side street. Three houses up the street was Hirsch's rooming-house. Nick walked up the two steps and pushed the bell. A woman came to the door.

"Is Ole Andreson here?"

"Do you want to see him?"

"Yes, if he's in."

Nick followed the woman up a flight of stairs and back to the end of a corridor. She knocked on the door.

"Who is it?"

"It's somebody to see you, Mr. Andreson," the woman said.

"It's Nick Adams."

"Come in."

Nick opened the door and went into the room. Ole Andreson was lying on the bed with all his clothes on. He had been a heavyweight prizefighter and he was too long for the bed. He lay with his head on two pillows. He did not look at Nick.

"What was it?" he asked.

"I was up at Henry's" Nick said, "and two fellows came in and tied up me and the cook and they said they were going to kill you."

It sounded silly when he said it. Ole Andreson said nothing.

"They put us out in the kitchen," Nick went on. "They were going to shoot you when you came in to supper."

Ole Andreson looked at the wall and did not say anything.

"George thought I better come and tell you about it."

"There isn't anything I can do about it," Ole Andreson said.

"I'll tell you what they were like."

"I don't want to know what they were like," Ole Andreson said. He looked at the wall. "Thanks for coming to tell me about it."

"That's all right."

Nick looked at the big man lying on the bed.

"Don't you want me to go and see the police?"

"No," Ole Andreson said. "That wouldn't do any good."

"Isn't there something I could do?"

"No. There ain't anything to do."

"Maybe it was just a bluff."

"No. It ain't just a bluff."

Ole Andreson rolled over toward the wall.

"The only thing is," he said, talking toward the wall, "I just can't make up my mind to go out. I been here all day."

"Couldn't you get out of town?"

"No," Ole Andreson said. "I'm through with all that running around."

He looked at the wall.

"There ain't anything to do now."

"Couldn't you fix it up some way?"

"No, I got in wrong." He talked in the same flat voice. "There ain't anything to do. After a while I'll make up my mind to go out."

"I better go back and see George," Nick said.

"So long," said Ole Andreson. He did not look toward Nick. "Thanks for coming around."

Nick went out. As he shut the door he saw Ole Andreson with all his clothes on, lying on the bed looking at the wall.

"He's been in his room all day," the landlady said downstairs. "I guess he don't feel well. I said to him: 'Mr. Andreson, you ought to go out and take a walk on a nice fall day like this,' but he didn't feel like it."

"He doesn't want to go out."

"I'm sorry he don't feel well," the woman said. "He's an awfully nice man. He was in the ring, you know."

"I know it."

"You'd never know it except from the way his face is," the woman said. They stood talking just inside the street door. "He's just as gentle."

"Well, good night, Mrs. Hirsch," Nick said.

"I'm not Mrs. Hirsch," the woman said. "She owns the place. I just look after it for her. I'm Mrs. Bell."

"Well, good night, Mrs. Bell," Nick said.

"Good night," the woman said.

Nick walked up the dark street to the corner under the arc-light, and then along the car-tracks to Henry's eating-house. George was inside, back of the counter, "Did you see Ole?"

"Yes," said Nick. "He's in his room and he won't go out."

The cook opened the door from the kitchen when he heard Nick's voice.

"I don't even listen to it," he said and shut the door.

"Did you tell him about it?" George asked.

"Sure, I told him but he knows what it's all about."

"What's he going to do?"

"Nothing."

"They'll kill him."

"I guess they will."

"He must have got mixed up in something in Chicago."

"I guess so," said Nick.

"It's a hell of a thing."

"It's an awful thing," Nick said.

They did not say anything. George reached down for a towel and wiped the counter.

"I wonder what he did?" Nick said.

"Double-crossed somebody. That's what they kill them for."

"I'm going to get out of this town," Nick said.

"Yes," said George. "That's a good thing to do."

"I can't stand to think about him waiting in the room and knowing he's going to get it. It's too damned awful."

"Well," said George, "you better not think about it."

462

Discussion Plan

A. There are three main groups of characters in the story, the killers, the onlookers and the victim. Answer the following questions from the point of view of each. You may divide any of the groups into sub-groups if you think their attitudes need to be distinguished.

1. Is Ole Andreson's death certain?
2. Does he deserve to die?
3. Do the killers have the right to kill him?
4. Should he struggle to escape his death?
5. Has he done everything he could to escape death?
6. Is his death his personal concern or does it involve others?
7. Does anyone else bear responsibility for his death?
8. Does his imminent death affect how the other people look at death.

B. Discuss the following:
1. Would Ole Andreson's situation be different if he was told he had incurable cancer?
2. If he was caught in a flood and drowning seemed certain?
3. If we was in his bed at ninety five years old after a severe heart attack, waiting to die?

C. Hemingway uses many techniques to offer us an in-depth perspective of the characters in the story. One of these is the casual use of racist language.

How does this affect our attitudes towards the people involved?

Do you think the language would have had the same effect on readers in the 1930's?

Morality

The killers seem confident that they have the power of might and the sanction of whoever it is that decided that Ole Andreson's crime required death. The idea that groups with power have the authority to sanction and condemn is as old as the history of mankind. All governments assume the right to punish, even to kill, and many thinkers have gone no further than self assertion as the basis for morality.

Friedrich Nietzsche, Beyond Good and Evil

Wandering through many fine and coarse moralities which have hitherto ruled on earth, as well as those which still rule, I found certain features regularly occurring together and bound up with one another. Finally they revealed two basic types to me, and a basic difference leaped to my eye. There is *master-morality* and *slave-morality*. I add immediately that in all mixed cultures there are also attempts at a mediation between these two, and even more frequently a mix-up of them and a mutual misunderstanding; at times in fact a relentless juxtaposition even within the psyche of a single individual. The moral value-differentiation arose either among a ruling type which was pleasantly conscious of its difference from the ruled—or else among the ruled, the slaves and dependents of all kinds. In the first case, when the rulers determine the concept "good" it is the elevated and proud conditions of the psyche which are felt to be what excels and determines the order of rank. The distinguished human being divorces himself from the being in whom the opposite of such elevated and proud conditions is expressed. He despises them. One may note immediately that in the first type of morality the antithesis "good vs. bad" means "distinguished vs. despicable"; the antithesis "good vs. evil" has a different origin. What is despised is the coward, the timid man, and the petty man, he who thinks in terms of narrow utility; likewise the suspicious man with his cowed look, the one who humiliates himself, the dog-type who lets himself be mistreated, the begging flatterer, and above all the liars. "We truthful ones" the nobles called themselves in ancient Greece...The distinguished type of human being feels *himself* as value determining; he does not need to be ratified; he judges that "which is harmful to me is harmful as such"; he knows that *he* is the something which gives honor to objects; he *creates values*. This type honors everything he knows about himself; his morality is self glorification. In the foreground is the feeling of fullness, of power that would flow forth, the bliss of high tension, the consciousness of riches which would like to give and lavish. The distinguished man, too, helps the unhappy, but not—at least not mainly—from compassion, but more from an internal pressure that has built up an excess of power. The distinguished man honors himself in the mighty, including those who have power over themselves; those who know when to talk and when to keep silent; those who take delight in being rigorous and hard with themselves and who have respect for anything rigorous and hard. "Wotan placed a hard heart in my breast," says an old Scandinavian saga: this is the proper poetic expression for the soul of a proud Viking. Such a type of man is proud *not* to have been made for compassion; hence the hero of the saga adds a warning: "Whoever has not a hard heart when young will never get it at all."...The ability and the duty to sustain enduring gratitude and enduring vengefulness—both only towards ones equals; subtlety in requital and retaliation; a subtly refined concept of friendship; a certain need to have enemies (as outlet for the passions: envy, quarrelsomeness and wantonness—basically, in order to be capable of being a good friend): all these are typical marks of the distinguished type of morality which, as I have indicated, is not the morality of "modern ideas" and hence is difficult today to empathize with and equally difficult to dig out and uncover.—The situation is different with the second type of morality, the slave-morality. Assuming that the violated ones, the oppressed, the suffering, the unfree, those who are uncertain, and tired of themselves—assuming that they moralize: What will they have in common in their moral evaluations? Probably a pessimistic suspiciousness against the whole situation of mankind will appear; perhaps a judgment against mankind together with its position. The eye of the slave looks unfavorably upon the virtues of the powerful; he *subtly* mistrusts all the "good" that the others honor—he would like to persuade himself that even their happiness is not real. Conversely, those qualities are emphasized and illuminated which serve to make existence easier for the sufferers: here compassion, the complaisant helping hand, the warm heart, patience, diligence, humility and friendliness are honored, for these are the useful qualities and almost the only means for enduring the pressure of existence. Slave-morality is essentially a utility-morality. Here is the cornerstone for the origin of the famous antithesis "good vs. evil." Power and dangerousness, a certain frightfulness, subtlety and strength which does not permit of despisal, are felt to belong to evil. Hence according to the slave morality the "evil" man inspires fear; according to the master morality, the "good" man does and wants to, whereas the "bad" man is felt to be despicable. The antithesis reaches its sharpest point when ultimately the "good" man within a slave morality becomes the logical target of a breath of disdain—however slight and well-meaning, because he is the *undangerous* element in his morality: a good natured, easily deceived, perhaps a little stupid, *un bonhomme*. Wherever slave morality preponderates, language shows a tendency to reconcile the meanings of "good" and "dumb."

Discussion Plan:

Nietzche distinguishes between two sorts of moral codes.

1. Characterize the virtues and attitudes associated with each.
2. Which of these virtues and attitudes would you consider to be generally positive?
3. Which, on the whole, negative?
4. On what grounds could either kind of morality be justified?
5. Develop a justification of either one or both.
6. On the basis of the principles or consequences of one or the other, argue for its inadequacy as a basis for morality.
7. Do you find traces of either morality in the moral principles current in American society?
8. What aspects of other social systems seem in conformity with either of the two kinds of morality?
9. If you were in a position of social power which morality would you prefer overall?
10. What if you were not in a position of power?

Suicide

What happens when life is full of more pain, physical or psychological, than pleasure? Lives are worth living, we think, when they either promise or actually deliver the things that we value. If disease, old age of mental illness destroy the value of the moment by eliminating hope for the future, is it natural, normal or rational to want to eliminate the vehicle of hopelessness and pain—life? The finality of suicide, a choice that precludes all others, makes it imperative to consider the issue carefully.

Anne-Grace Scheinin, The Burden of Suicide

My mother died seven years ago by her own hand. My father found her when her returned home from work that Friday, her body already cold where it lay huddled in the back of the little red Corvair Monza. A hose led from the exhaust pipe through the rear window of the car.

I can't imagine what he must have felt when he found her. I can imagine how my mother must have felt as she descended the stairs to the garage for the last time. There was a numbness, a sense of suspended disbelief; her body already seemed not to belong to her. In her anesthetized mind was a single spark of clarity, the knowledge, vivid and unfrightening, that the peace she had longed for was now, really and truly, to be hers. Maybe she left in anger, maybe that was why. But the only reality for her in those last moments was the desperate hunger for a final, eternal end to pain. She never fought against the blackness that swallowed her.

I know. I've been there. I tried suicide several times in my life when I was in my early 20s and was quite serious at least twice. I bitterly resented having my life saved. I despised and raged against the doctors and nurses who prevented my death, against the psychiatrists who locked me up until I was cajoled into wanting to live again, or was at least willing to give it a try. All I really wanted was the kind of peace of mind everyone in the whole world seemed blessed with except me. Was that asking too much?

Nightmare: Apparently so. A manic-depressive like my mother, I have a physiology that never seemed to give me an even break. Just when my internal seas began to calm and I began to think living might be palatable after all, minute chemicals in my brain would either recede or reassert themselves and I'd be off on another nightmare rollercoaster ride, out of control, a stranger to myself and to everyone who thought they knew me. Some manic-depressives are greatly helped by medication, notably lithium carbonate. Nothing seemed to help me. Suicide often seemed the most sane resolution to the insanity my body forced on me. Besides actually attempting suicide, I've wanted, wished and even prayed to die more times than I can count.

Well, I'm 32 now and I'm still alive. I'm even married and have moved from a secretarial position into entry-level management in a Fortune 500 company. I keep house and look after my husband and our three cats, Lila, Blackberry and little Snailbait. I have bills to pay, a bus to catch every weekday morning, laundry that never seems quite white or bright enough, a body that refuses to conform to Cheryl Tieg's configuration. I'm a lousy cook. But I'm alive because of my mother's death. She taught me that in spite of my illness I had to live. Suicide just isn't worth it.

I saw the torment my mother's death caused others: my father, my brother, her neighbors and friends. When I saw their overwhelming grief, I knew I could never do the same thing she had done—force other people to take on the burden of pain I'd leave behind if I died by my own hand.

Suicide is not a normal death. It is tragic beyond the most shattering experiences, and the ultimate form of abandonment. There is no fate on which to place the blame. It rests squarely on the shoulders of the victim and the people left behind, many of whom spend the rest of their lives wondering, never knowing, if there was anything they could have done to prevent such a tragedy.

There is something about suicide that, even when done as an escape from an agonizing terminal illness, signals complete and utter defeat. It is without any semblance of nobility or pride. Life can become too heavy a burden to bear, but the release that suicide offers is not a triumph of life, the ultimate mastery of self over fate, but a grim renunciation of hope and a failure of the human spirit. There may be legitimate rationalizations for committing suicide. But my experiences have taught me that suicide, by and large, is a decision made by a desolate soul. The many suicidal patients I met in my hospital stays had no philosophy of death; their desire to die was not a condemnation of current socioeconomic or political realities. They were in profound emotional pain, and all they wanted was an end to that suffering.

For years I was no different. My illness was a source of immeasurable pain to my family and friends, and seeing my irrationality and despair mirrored in their eyes was often unendurable. I still have seizures of profound depression, and I can still see that ugly self reflected in the faces of the people I love. Then, too, there is the stigma of being a mental patient, a victim of a major psychotic disorder, which is as humiliating as it has always been.

However, I will not, cannot, end my life as my mother did. Suicide no longer can offer me any peace.

Wasteland: She was 55 when she died. She looked behind her and saw a wasteland, never willing to accept that she was loved by many and had richly contributed to the lives of friends, family and strangers. She perished because she allowed herself to be deceived by her own mind into believing she was worthless. She refused professional help because, like many of her

468

generation, she felt it was shameful to seek psychiatric aid. What would the neighbors and relatives think? She was consumed at the end by unbearable depression. The best thing she could do for those who cared about her was to remove herself from their presence—permanently. She could not have been more wrong.

She taught me the most valuable lesson of my life: no matter how bad the pain is, it's never so bad that the only escape is a false one. Suicide doesn't end pain. It only lays it on the broken shoulders of the survivors.

Ironically, my mother's final gift to me was not death, but life, a determination to live as she chose not to.

By the way: to all the doctors, nurses and psychiatrists who forced me to live when I didn't want to—thank you for keeping breath in my lungs and my heart bearing and encouraging hope in me when I didn't have any hope.

I'm glad I'm alive to say that.

Discussion Plan:

1. Ms. Scheinin bases her argument on personal experience, does her argument apply to other people in similar situations?
2. Is the main argument against suicide the pain it will cause others?
3. Is such an argument fair to the suicide?
4. Can suicide be justified if it causes pleasure for others?
5. How do we measure the pain of the suicide against the pain of his loved ones?
6. Can the suicide justify his act in terms of his future?
8. Is it possible to be sure that the future will remain without hope?
9. Is it absurd to want to not exist?
10. Are there any reasonable grounds for not wanting to exist?

Suicide and Society

Your answers to the questions following the last selection may or may not have tended to justify suicide as a possibly rational course of action for an individual, but suicide is more than a personal issue. It is also a social issue that has increasingly generated a social response. In recent years many people have felt that the right to suicide is part of the right to live as one chooses. Others have felt that this right must be limited by the larger considerations underlying societies response to deviant behavior.

Herbert Hendin, A Saner Policy on Suicide

Suicide seems such an individual and personal act with tragic consequences for a relatively small group consisting of family, colleagues, and friends, that it is easy to lose sight of its social dimension. Yet the subject was of concern in most societies long before Emile Durkheim made the modern world aware of the degree to which suicide is a barometer of social stress. We tend to be mildly amused at the attitude of the classical Greeks, who required the would-be suicide to first secure permission from the senate: but that attitude certainly reflected an awareness that suicide has social, or antisocial, implications.

Our own social policy—and our laws—reflects some confusion on the issue. The recent deaths by suicide of several students in succession in a New Jersey school, and of nearly 1,000 people in Guyana, call attention both to the "contagious" element in suicide and to the policy questions.

A sense of controlling exactly when they die appeals to the omnipotent wishes of some who are suicidal; a willingness to die in order to be noticed is the mark of others. Suicidal individuals often set conditions on life, death, and other people in a grandiose and controlling manner, as if to say: "If you love me, you will do what I want: if you don't do what I want, I'll kill myself." "If you love me, you will be willing to die with me" is the test often put to the reluctant partner in a suicide pact. On a larger scale, the coercive grandiosity of Reverend James Jones suggests the social relations of many who are suicidal.

Suicidal persons often find one another. A few years ago, I interviewed the sole survivor of a group of five young men who had discussed suicide together. One young man had said he would drive his motorcycle off a bridge; he left the group and did just that. He was seen as a sadly heroic figure by the others, and described as such by the press. A second shot himself two months later; two others died in motorcycle accidents. The vulnerability of the survivor was great.

A sense of sharing in the suicide of someone famous, or of identifying one's suicide with a cause, enables some to feel their death has a meaning it would otherwise lack. Just after Marilyn Monroe's death, a number of people left suicide notes linking their own deaths to her presumed suicide.

Until relatively recently, Western cultures have tried to prevent suicide by attaching social shame to the memory of the deceased, threatening punishment in an afterlife, denying proper burial to the corpse, and imposing fines and imprisonment on anyone who survives a suicide attempt. A more compassionate contemporary approach is currently reflected in various organizations composed primarily of lay volunteers that encourage suicidal people to contact them and seek to persuade them to deal with their problems in some other way. In England, those volunteers, the Samaritans, have been credited with a decline in the country's suicide rate.

In the United States, a network of suicide-prevention centers based on that approach grew up, with the public expectation that they would reduce the incidence of suicide. Those centers have had no demonstrable effect on the suicide rate in their communities. In the opinion of many counselors, the overwhelming number of calls and contacts they receive are coming not from the seriously suicidal segment of the population, but from troubled individuals who need to talk to someone. Recently, a carefully controlled study in England demonstrated that there is no difference in the suicide rate in otherwise comparable communities that have or do not have Samaritan groups.

Yet those findings should not lead us, or the English, to abandon such efforts as enthusiastically as we once embraced them. Both the Samaritans and our suicide-prevention centers have given aid and comfort to a great number of people. They have also helped to make us aware of the need for walk-in and call-in facilities for people in all sorts of emotional crises. That is worth doing for its own sake, without the illusion that we are reducing the suicide rate.

That there are estimated to be several hundred thousand suicide attempts in this country each year, and an accumulated total of several million individuals who have attempted suicide, provides some sense of the magnitude of the problem. Follow-up studies have shown that about 10 percent of the attempted suicide population go on to kill themselves within a 10-year period. Other retrospective studies have shown that two-thirds of those who kill themselves have a history of prior attempts. Those findings indicate that the attempted-suicide population contains the eventual-suicide population, plus an even larger number of people who will not go on to kill themselves.

Clearly, it is inefficient to try to stem suicide by finding and referring all cases to treatment. But it is possible, on the basis of current clinical knowledge, to identify the high-risk cases among those who attempt suicide. Once they are identified, we could determine what treatment should be offered, and what, if any, government support would be appropriate. That identification and treatment might involve as many as 10,000 new cases a year throughout the country, but such a program would be far more manageable —and probably more fruitful—than attempting to identify and somehow treat the millions who call in to suicide-prevention centers. The advantage of such an approach is that its efficacy could first be tried and tested in a limited way to avoid the sequence of enthusiasm and disillusion that has characterized the suicide-prevention centers.

For, as it became evident that the centers were not preventing suicide, an inevitable reaction set in. Not only was the federal Center for the Study of Suicide Prevention eliminated and the regional centers left to founder, but there was also a retreat from any national effort to deal with the problem. If we could not prevent suicide as easily as had been claimed, we would just forget about it, it seemed.

The neglectful attitude has been reinforced by those who maintain that suicide is a fundamental human right and who deplore all attempts to prevent it as an interference with that right. Friedrich Nietzsche said: "There is a certain right by which we may deprive a man of life, but none by which we may deprive him of death: this is mere cruelty." Supporters of that position are not put off by the fact that many people who try to kill themselves are later glad they failed.

The laissez-faire position toward suicide has been urged most strongly by those who advocate a similar attitude toward drug use and abuse. Thomas Szasz is one who objects to all interference with the sale and use of drugs as an infringement of civil liberties; Szasz feels we rationalize such an oppressive policy by calling any deviation "illness" and thereby encourage psychiatrists and psychologists to become enforcers of the policy. While not advocating drug use, Szasz believes that "dangerous drugs, addicts and pushers are the scapegoats of our modern secular therapeutically inbred societies," and that "the ritual persecution of these pharmacological and human agents must be seen against the historical backdrop of the ritual persecution of other scapegoats, such as witches, Jews, and madmen." Of suicide prevention, Szasz writes, "He who does not accept and respect those who want to reject life does not truly accept and respect life itself." Causing one's own death, he says, "should be called 'suicide' only by those who disapprove of it; and should be called 'death control' by those who approve of it."

Those who do not trust hospitalization as a routine way of dealing with the risk of suicide do have a point, and not only because of the possible infringement of civil liberties. Often suicidal patients are hospitalized not because hospitalization will improve their condition or prevent their suicide, but because it shifts worry and responsibility onto an institution and away from a family or an individual therapist who may feel uncomfortable with it.

Most suicidal patients who come to hospitals do so as a consequence of injuries sustained in their suicide attempts. Are we to refuse treatment for such injuries out of respect for the patient's suicidal intent? Most of those patients have not asked for help; when it is offered, some will accept it and others will reject it. Should we not even offer it unless the patient explicitly requests it? Would those who argue for the "right to die" make the same argument with regard to a suicidal child or adolescent?

Szasz, who is passionately eloquent in defense of the right to commit suicide and the right to use or sell drugs, seems to show little appreciation of the desperately wretched lives of drug abusers and of those who would kill themselves. His position would be more understandable if his legitimate concerns about social and medical coercion were accompanied by a corresponding concern for the plight of those whose lives are self-destructively out of control—many of whom want help. As it is, Szasz invites a policy of indifference to them. His argument that social help undermines individual autonomy has been used in the past to justify opposition to every kind of social reform. Ultimately, his view is as socially narrow as the view of those he criticizes.

The mass deaths in Guyana dramatized another aspect of the right to die that, on a smaller scale, is a common occurrence with suicide. The line between respect for another's right to die and murder can be a thin one. The problem of distinguishing between the two arises whenever individuals aid or encourage others in their suicides. I am not talking of so-called mercy killings, involving terminally ill people who are suffering intolerable pain; I am thinking, to take two examples, of a woman who did not call an ambulance for eight hours after finding her husband comatose following a suicide attempt; and of a young man who sold a depressed "friend" a lethal dose of sleeping pills and watched her take them.

The young man who sold the pills did so in a state that has no law making it a crime to encourage or help anyone to kill himself. Some thought needs to be given to the kind of law that can best protect people, individually and collectively, in such situations. If suicidal people were to organize to recruit others to their point of view—not quite so unbelievable a fantasy now as it was when Robert Louis Stevenson wrote his story, "The Suicide Club"—society should be able to intervene. Whenever pathology is psychosocial—whenever the community has a stake in it—personal rights are not without limits.

Exercise:

1. Identify the main considerations that the author develops in the course of his discussion.
2. Organize these considerations into arguments, each one of which will come to a specific conclusion on the basis of one or more claims.
3. Distinguish between arguments that deal with social policies and those that are based on individual rights.

Research Project:

The saddest of suicides are those that are seemingly unnecessary, based on a limited understanding of what life is and what it has to offer. Suicides among teenagers are frequently seen within that category. Using newspapers and magazine reports develop an account of teenage suicides. Who are the teenagers that commit suicide? Do they tend to be successful, apparently happy etc.? What sorts of reasons are given by the suicide? What are the consequences to family and friends? Be sure to explore "copy cat" suicides, that is, suicides prompted by media suicides or by other teenage suicides.

Suicide and Choice

The complexities of suicide as a social phenomena can make us a forget the compelling personal perspective that suicide reflects, especially for those convinced of the appropriateness of their desire to control the time of their dying.

Psychology Today, Death By Design: A Case in Point

Last August, Wallace Proctor committed suicide at the home of his old friend Morgan Sibbett. Proctor did not face imminent death, nor was he suffering unbearable pain. He simply felt his life was no longer worth living, and, with Sibbett's help, carefully arranged to end it. Because Proctor's death presents a good example of what Doris Portwood calls "balance-sheet suicide," and because I was curious to learn how a man can kill himself in such a seemingly cold and rational way, I went to see Sibbett to reconstruct the story of Proctor's suicide.

Proctor and Sibbett had been friends for nearly 40 years. Proctor, 75, had been a successful dermatologist in California. Sibbett, 65, is a retired engineer-economist who lives in Swarthmore, Pennsylvania, a suburb of Philadelphia. Both men were married, and the two couples had exchanged visits and letters over the years.

In 1966, Dr. Proctor developed Parkinson's disease, a nonfatal but progressively degenerating illness for which no cure exists. Despite increasing doses of medication, his condition continued to deteriorate. He moved to Idaho in 1971, hoping to open a less demanding practice, but within a year, he was forced to abandon it.

By 1975, Wallace Proctor began to contemplate suicide. A switch to a new drug brought temporary relief from the pain, and long talks with his wife and Sibbett convinced him he still had pleasures and obligations worth living for.

Still, he often worried about becoming a physical, emotional, and financial burden to his family. In may 1976, to allay these fears, Sibbett and Proctor signed a formal "mutual assistance agreement" in which each promised to help the other terminate his life in the event of "any incurable or hopelessly incapacitating physical or mental condition which deprives life of significant purpose, and unreasonably burdens relatives, friends or society."

During the following year, increasing doses of medication were unable to slow Proctor's deterioration and the growing pain of arthritis. After a heart attack in April 1977, he could no longer go hiking, drive the car, or garden. Never a husky man, his weight had dropped to 106 pounds.

Proctor now felt the time had come to exercise his agreement with Sibbett. He could not bear to ask his wife to help him, nor did he want his suicide to bring her painful publicity. He decided to make one last visit to Swarthmore.

A meticulous man, Proctor put his legal and financial affairs in order, and packed his clothing and a lethal stockpile of Seconal. He said good-bye to his dog, his teenage son, and his wife, who did not know that this time he would not return.

When Morgan Sibbett picked up his friend at the Philadelphia airport, he could sense his friend had made up his mind. They spent Proctor's last few days doing the few things he could still enjoy. They took drives in the country, bought some plants, watched the backyard birds feeding, read, and talked.

On Sunday, when they drove into Philadelphia for dinner at a restaurant, Proctor joked to the hostess, "This is the first and last time you'll ever see me." When they returned home, he told Sibbett not to make any plans for Tuesday evening. The two men paid visits to the coroner and district attorney to inform them discreetly of Proctor's intentions, to prevent later legal problems.

Tuesday evening they ate dinner together as usual by the living-room picture window. "He was definitely not depressed," Sibbett recalls. "After dinner, he said, very simply, 'This is our last meal together.'"

Proctor finished a last affectionate letter to his wife and edited his final suicide note. The two friends parted without any melodrama. Proctor simply said good-bye, and went to his bedroom. He called his wife one last time, and then took about 40 Seconals. Soon he was dead.

In his final letter to his family and relatives, Proctor wrote, "Each day seems to be a little less worth living ... my heart rebels at any more physical activity ... I am tired all the time ... Much as I would object to being an inmate of an institution for the aged ... I am gravitating toward that possibility; that, and the burden upon my family of my disability, with its uncertain duration, is something which they, and the world too, do not deserve ... I have no will nor desire to live any longer, and should not do so ..."

When news of Proctor's suicide got out, it caused a minor stir in Swarthmore, and made the national news media. Sibbett received letters from several people who were "touched" or "moved" by his compassion for his friend. One woman, however, accused Proctor of "arrogance."

Proctor's wife, though sad, was not surprised by her husband's suicide. "We had talked about this openly many times," she says. "I knew it would happen someday, but I didn't know when. I understand why he did it, but I can't accept it. Mentally, he was still very alert, and there were many things he could do around the house. And we still loved each other very much. But I'm not ashamed, and I have no regrets, because I know that now he's at peace."

"It's hard to know where to draw the line," Sibbett admits, "and each person must decide for himself. You may have to take matters into your own hands if nature doesn't do it for you." Looking back on his friend's death, he says, "Coming to me under these circumstances was the natural thing, and the only thing—the only way he could do it with dignity, and without the sordidness and the furtiveness of being alone. This way there was no sense of desperation, no pall of gloom. He wanted those last days to be peaceful, and they were, in a measure that is difficult to imagine. It was a good death."

Suicide and Religion

The personal and the social are not the only perspectives from which suicide can be viewed. The very mystery of death requires that our perspective on suicide encompass the possibilities that lie behind the limits of our knowledge of life.

Knights of Columbus, The Sanctity of Life

Suicide as we mentioned signifies any act whereby a man deliberately chooses to end his life on his own authority. According to Catholic teaching suicide is a grave sin whose malice consists in an invasion of the supreme and total dominion of God over human life. Suicide is essentially immoral. We have heard many times where a man may expose himself to certain death in order to save the life of another person, but this is not suicide, it does not mean killing oneself, but accepting death for another. Suicide is the deliberate taking away of one's own life, and no matter what the motive, this is never allowed.

Man is but a steward of his corporeal life and of all his faculties, he is not the owner of his life in the sense that he owns a car, a boat or a summer home. When he deliberately takes his own life he exercises a sort of ownership which does not belong to him. "The intrinsic evil of suicide is clear also from a consideration of the truth that, since God is the Maker and Last End of man, man belongs totally and essentially to God, he is the property and servant of God." T. Higgins, S.J. *Man as Man.*

Man was created to love, honor, serve and obey God here on earth and to be happy with Him forever in Heaven. By suicide man is rejecting his status of servitude, he is invading God's exclusive right and by taking his life, he assumes the role of God. The suicide puts an end to the potentiality of further service to society and of his own moral growth and perfection. It is a deliberate challenge to the moral law and an act of rebellion against God.

The first and foremost inalienable right is that of life and physical existence. This primary right flows from the concept of person and the nature of man. Since all human persons have this right, the right is possessed from the moment of conception. The right to life and especially to bodily integrity is possessed regardless of physical or mental condition (See Pius XI, Encyclical on *Christian Marriage*). The only exception to the right of life is the case of one who is being deprived of his life in just punishment for crime. The criminal can forfeit his right of life, as the common good takes precedence over individual good, and it may become necessary that certain crimes be punished by deprivation of life in order that the rights of one's fellowmen are safe and secure.

Debate:

Having explored a number of aspects of the problem of suicide and reconstructed a variety of arguments we leave it up to the class to attempt to formulate a reasonable policy on suicide.

Choose sides according to your attitude on suicide and debate the following:

The well being of its citizens is a legitimate concern of social institutions, both secular and religious. Since death is the ultimate harm a person can experience the society has an obligation to prevent the suicides of its members.

Meaning

Does life have a point? Where is its meaning to be found? We live accepting the world as it is given to us. Our very imaginations are mere reflections of the possibilities that our life has shown us. By good fortune we may be born into an environment rich enough to hide the essential limitedness of our existence. But what if in a sudden flash of insight we see all that we could never be?

George Blond, An Odyssey of Birds

The man was bracing himself against a wall of rock which rose vertically more than six hundred feet above him. His crushing load, whose weight was at least as great as his own, was jammed against the wall. He could just manage to maintain this position by the wide spread of his spindly legs, which were already trembling in a pair of blue cotton trousers, and indeed were visibly on the point of giving way. He wore tattered, ropesoled canvas shoes, which had held out only by a miracle this far, and his torn trousers flapped like a flag in the freezing wind that blew over the whole width of the mountain pass. It was only August and the wind came from the south, but for all that it was icy. The caravan, with its bearers and horses, was making its way slowly and painfully over the mountains, battling against the wind, and the man leaning his back against the wall of rock surveyed it with an impenetrable expression.

He might have been thirty-five years old, or else sixty—how is one to guess at the age of a Chinaman? This human machine, worn down to the thread, had no age whatsoever. His skinny forearms emerged from the amputated sleeves of an American army jacket, which had incredibly bargained and bartered its way to the heart of Asia. The caravan was traveling from Qulja to Aqsu, on the edge of the desert, three hundred miles as the crow flies, and the horses seemed as near the point of collapse as the men. From Qulja to the Muzart Pass, they had covered two hundred miles, most of it through the mountains.

The man leaning against the rock, whose knees were now slightly bent so that he was even less erect than before, had covered the two hundred miles in the following manner: first he took fifty short, quick steps, with his back bent under his load at a forty-five degree angle; then he stopped, stuck his stick into the ground or ice, spread his two hands over the top and let his stomach rest upon them, while he breathed heavily, making a noise like that of a pair of defective bellows. Two to five seconds later, he began the cycle again with fifty more steps. For at least two hundred years, as every traveler's account tells us, the technique has been exactly the same, and caravan bearers have carried as much as two hundred and fifty pounds of tea on their backs. Naturally, they do not live to a ripe old age, but then, in most of Asia, the care and feeding of a man is less expensive than that of a horse.

The Muzart Pass is in the middle of the high central range of the Tien Shan Mountains: a vast agglomeration in Turkestan, whose area is greater than that of France. These mountains are never in the newspapers; they hold no interest for famous climbers, because their highest peak is only about twenty-four thousand feet above sea level. Indeed, the topography of the central range is in many places uncertainly defined, for few geographers are tempted to haul their instruments to this far-away and chaotic region. And any pilot who flies over it watches his dials and listens to his motors with particular attention, knowing that a landing is impossible and a parachute jump would unquestionably be the prelude to slow death from exposure. The Muzart Pass crosses this range at an altitude of twelve thousand feet, rimmed by glaciers which sweep down from the surrounding mountains, every one of them higher than the Mont Blanc. For three quarters of the year, violent winds raise tempests of snow. The whole length of the pass and some distance to either side are littered with bones, but snow conceals them most of the time from view.

The man leaning against the rock watched as the caravan passed slowly before him. Every now and then a bearer, with his back bent at a forty-five degree angle, stopped to rest on his stick. The furious blast of the wind and the chatter of a mountain stream smothered the bearers' groaning sighs and the tread of the horses, which other men, bending their bodies to meet the wind's impact, were leading by the bridles. The men moved like so many pale ghosts, and indeed their whole existence had something unreal and ghostlike about it.

For convenience, let us give the man leaning against the rock a name. Let us call him Chuan. It is more than likely that neither this name or any other which the reader may choose was ever entered in the birth records of a village or town. A peasant family from the borderland of Chinese Turkestan has little legal existence, and for years no one had had occasion to call Chuan anything at all. A caravan bearer doesn't wait to be called; he is there, with fifty ghostly companions, and if he is not there no one is going to miss him. He may be dead, or he may be curled up in a corner, smoking remnants of opium; it doesn't really matter.

Chuan felt himself slipping and closed his eyes. His legs had crumpled, and finally he sat on his haunches, with his load resting partially on the ground although the straps still dug into his shoulders. From this sloping position he could no longer see the stooping men of the caravan pass before him. His head was turned slightly to the right, and beyond the pass, to the southeast, between two snow-clad mountains, he saw a slope, slightly lower than the rest, covered with pines. The dark green trees, with a ray of sunlight upon them, stood in closed ranks, like the soldiers of a motionless army.

Neither poverty nor wind had bent them over; they carried no load and stood marvelously straight, just as they had grown, pointing toward the sky. The picture they made was one of dignity and freedom and power.

Chuan relaxed his legs and stretched them out in front of him. Still feeling the straps cut into the area between his chest and his shoulders, he threw back the upper part of his body and at once obtained relief. The pine forest was now lower in his line of vision, and without moving his head he could see a large part of the snowy mountain summits. Twenty times or more he had crossed the Tien Shan Mountains, and his eyes had been blinded by the dazzling whiteness of the plateaus, but never for more than a fleeting second had he been able to lift them to see the jagged, white peaks stand out against the sky. For a bearer marches bent over at an angle of forty-five degrees.

Chuan looked, then, upon the jagged, white peaks. The mountains ceased to form the infernally hostile world to which a bearer must return over and over again in order to make his wretched living; they seemed now like the immobile waves of a majestic white ocean, tinged here and there with rose and blue lights. Chuan no longer saw the caravan pass by or wondered whether one of the ghostly figures had gone out of his mind. The cold had dangerously invaded his thin, ill-protected body, but he did not feel either the cold or the bite of the wind on his parchment-like skin. Only the great snowy waves rolled over and penetrated him. By now he was lying alongside his load, flat on the ground. For a long moment he closed his eyes, and when he opened them he saw the sky filled with birds.

The infinite depth of the sky was pale blue and absolutely cloudless, and the wild geese, flying at a single level, cut it horizontally in two. There were dozens and dozens of groups of birds, all of them in chevron or V formation, flying straight from north to south. As far as Chuan could see, the birds filled the sky, flying in the rarefied air high above the mountain pass. The air was so clear that Chuan could make out every bird, every neck outstretched parallel to the one next to it and every pair of wings making the same regular, powerful rowing motion. Although the wind was blowing from the south and the geese were flying against it, their pace was faultlessly even. Each chevron was like a compass, with unequally long legs; the compasses were all open at exactly the same angle, but without rigidity. They might be compared, also, to large, light-weight, flexible kites, pulled by invisible strings in the same direction.

The rays of the setting sun lit up the ranks of wild geese from below, and those on the western side seemed to be of a lighter color than the rest, a pale gray very close to white. Chuan knew their exact shading, for as a child he had watched them go by, once in spring and once at the end of summer. At dawn he had seen them fly low over the plains, and occasionally his father had got him out of bed at night and led him into the dark and silent fields in order that he might hear the strange whirring noise produced by the beat of thousands of wings. Sometimes, he remembered, the noise had continued for hours on end, and long after he had gone back to bed the geese were still flying over.

How many years had gone by since these dawn and midnight vigils? How long had it been since the stooped caravan bearer had looked up to see the great migration of the graylag geese, high in the sky? All this time the birds had continued, at the same seasons, to fly over. The bearer's body had become more and more bent, and turned into a rag more miserable than the rags which covered it; the insectlike steps he took under his killing load were increasingly jerky, and his hoarse breathing was very painful to the ear. And yet the movement of the birds was just what it had been before. Now the intermediate period of time, was contracted and wiped out, and the birds' motion seemed to Chuan like a part of himself which had been preserved from age and poverty and degradation. A great peace came over him. Probably none of the bearers or the men who were leading the horses through the windswept pass had noticed that the flight of the geese had begun. Only Chuan, to all appearances a still, parchment-skinned mummy, discolored by the icy cold but delivered forever of the crushing load it had been his lot to carry, was aware of what was going on. As long as he liked he would gaze upon this unparalleled sight, yes, just as long as the child Chuan, for whom the passage of time had no meaning.

The graylag geese were flying over the Tien Shan Mountains; soon they would cross the Desert of Takla Makan, the wild Altyn Tagh, the stifling Tibetan plateau, and finally, at an altitude of twenty-six thousand feet, the Himalayas, which no other migrant birds are known to pass. Just now their first line was passing over the Muzart Pass, above the only human face turned in their direction, the face of a miserable caravan bearer, whose stare was gradually congealing. Chuan's eyes no longer moved, but he could still see the passage of the great flexible kites overhead. The sky was beginning to darken, but still the wild geese flew over. Their great flight across the high heaven was the last movement registered by the retinas of the poor bearer, who had for so long bent nearly double over the ground.

Discussion Plan:

1. The author gives the man a name "for convenience." In what sense is a name more meaningful than just a convenient label?

2. Is Chuan's life meaningless because of its circumstances? In what way is the life of a more favorable placed individual more meaningful?

3. As a child Chuan thought the passage of time was meaningless. As a bearer what is the meaning of the passage of time? What meaning does the passage of time have for you?

4. Does mind killing labor make life meaningless? Does endless labor make life meaningless?

5. How is Chuan's life less meaningful than the stereotypical commuter who follows the same daily round for his entire working life?

6. If Chuan filled his non-working life with the unspeakable delights of the opium pipe, would that make his life more meaningful?

7. If Chuan had children would that make his life meaningful? If they were bearers like he is? If they escaped to a better life?

8. What is the meaning of the geese? What do they mean to Chuan?

9. Is there any sense in which the birds' odyssey is meaningful? Is it meaningful to the geese? To God?

Justice

Is it possible to understand life from a moral point of view? Life frequently presents events that are obviously unfair—evils and rewards fall to people independently of their actions and choices. How can we understand right and wrong in a world that seems uninterested in justice and fairness? For many the obvious injustices of the world can only be understood in terms of a larger universe in which good is eventually rewarded. In such a world virtue will be rewarded and evil punished; if not now, later, for "God sees the Truth."

Leo Tolstoy, God Sees the Truth, But Waits

In the town of Vladimir lived a young merchant named Ivan Dmitrich Aksionov. He had two shops and a house of his own.

Aksionov was a handsome, fair-haired, curly-headed fellow, full of fun, and very fond of singing. When quite a young man he had been given to drink, and was riotous when he had had too much; but after he married he gave up drinking, except now and then.

One summer Aksionov was going to the Nizhny Fair, and as he bade good-bye to his family, his wife said to him, "Ivan Dmitrich, do not start to-day; I have had a bad dream about you."

Aksionov laughed, and said, "You are afraid that when I get to the fair I shall go on a spree."

His wife replied: "I do not know what I am afraid of; all I know is that I had a bad dream. I dreamt you returned from the town, and when you took off your cap I saw that your hair was quite grey."

Aksionov laughed. "That's a lucky sign," said he. "See if I don't sell out all my goods, and bring you some presents from the fair."

So he said good-bye to his family, and drove away.

When he had travelled half-way, he met a merchant whom he knew, and they put up at the same inn for the night. They had some tea together, and then went to bed in adjoining rooms.

It was not Aksionov's habit to sleep late, and, wishing to travel while it was still cool, he aroused his driver before dawn, and told him to put in the horses.

Then he made his way across to the landlord of the inn (who lived in a cottage at the back), paid his bill, and continued his journey.

When he had gone about twenty-five miles, he stopped for the horses to be fed. Aksionov rested awhile in the passage of the inn, then he stepped out into the porch, and, ordering a samovar to be heated, got out his guitar and began to play.

Suddenly a troika drove up with tinkling bells and an official alighted, followed by two soldiers. He came to Aksionov and began to question him, asking him who he was and whence he came. Aksionov answered him fully, and said, "Won't you have some tea with me?" But the official went on cross-questioning him and asking him, "Where did you spend last night? Were you alone, or with a fellow-merchant? Did you see the other merchant this morning? Why did you leave the inn before dawn?"

Aksionov wondered why he was asked all these questions, but he described all that had happened, and then added, "Why do you cross-question me as if I were a thief or a robber? I am travelling on business of my own, and there is no need to question me"

Then the official, calling the soldiers, said, "I am the police-officer of this district, and I question you because the merchant with whom you spent last night has been found with his throat cut. We must search your things."

They entered the house. The soldiers and the police-officer unstrapped Aksionov's luggage and searched it. Suddenly the officer drew a knife out of a bag, crying "Whose knife is this?"

Aksionov looked, and seeing a blood-stained knife taken from his bag, he was frightened.

"How is it here is blood on this knife?"

Aksionov tried to answer, but could hardly utter a word, and only stammered: "I—don't know—not mine."

Then the police-officer said: "This morning the merchant was found in bed with his throat cut. You are the only person who could have done it. The house was locked from inside, and no one else was there. Here is this blood-stained knife in your bag, and your face and manner betray you! Tell me how you killed him, and how much money you stole?"

Aksionov swore he had not done it; that he had not seen the merchant after they had had tea together; that he had no money except eight thousand rubles of his own, and that the knife was not his. But his voice was broken, his face pale, and he trembled with fear as though he were guilty.

The police-officer ordered the soldiers to bind Aksionov and to put him in the cart. As they tied his feet together and flung him into the cart, Aksionov crossed himself and wept. His money and goods were taken from him, and he was sent to the nearest town and imprisoned there. Enquiries as to his character were made in Vladimir. The merchants and other inhabitants of that town said that in former days he used to drink and waste his time, but that he was a good man. Then the trial came on; he was charged with murdering a merchant from Ryazan, and robbing him of twenty thousand rubles.

His wife was in despair, and did not know what to believe. Her children were all quite small; one was a baby at her breast. Taking them all with her, she went to the town where her husband was in jail. At first she was not allowed to see him; but after much begging, she obtained permission from the officials, and was taken to him. When she saw her husband in prison-dress and in chains, shut up with thieves and criminals, she fell down, and did not come to her senses for a long time. Then she drew her children to her, and sat down near him. She told him of things at home, and asked about what had happened to him. He told her all, and she asked, "What can we do now?"

"We must petition the Czar not to let an innocent man perish."

His wife told him that she had sent a petition to the Czar, but it had not been accepted.

Aksionov did not reply, but only looked downcast.

Then his wife said, "It was not for nothing I dreamt your hair had turned grey. You remember? You should not have started that day." And passing her fingers through his hair, she said: "Vanya dearest, tell your wife the truth; was it not you who did it?"

"So you, too, suspect me!" said Aksionov, and, hiding his face in his hands, he began to weep. Then a soldier came to say that the wife and children must go away; and Aksionov said good-bye to his family for the last time.

When they were gone, Aksionov recalled what had been said and when he remembered that his wife also had suspected him, he said to himself, "It seems that only God can know the truth; it is to Him alone we must appeal, and from Him alone expect mercy."

And Aksionov wrote no more petitions; gave up all hope, and only prayed to God.

Aksionov was condemned to be flogged and sent to the mines. So he was flogged with a knot, and when the wounds made by the knot were healed, he was driven to Siberia with other convicts.

For twenty-six years Aksionov lived as a convict in Siberia. His hair turned white as snow, and his beard grew long, thin, and grey. All his mirth went; he stooped; he walked slowly, spoke little and never laughed, but often prayed.

In prison Aksionov learnt to make boots, and earned a little money, with which he bought *The Lives of the Saints*. He read this book when there was light enough in the prison; and on Sundays in the prison-church he read the lessons and sang in the choir; for his voice was still good.

The prison authorities liked Aksionov for his meekness, and his fellow-prisoners respected him: they called him "Grandfather," and "The Saint." When they wanted to petition the prison authorities about anything, they always made Aksionov their spokesman, and when there were quarrels among the prisoners they came to him to put things right, and to judge the matter.

No news reached Aksionov from his home, and he did not even know if his wife and children were still alive.

One day a fresh gang of convicts came to the prison. In the evening the old prisoners collected round the new ones and asked them what towns or villages they came from, and what they were sentenced for. Among the rest Aksionov sat down near the newcomers, and listened with downcast air to what was said.

One of the new convicts, a tall, strong man of sixty, with a closely-cropped grey beard, was telling the others what he had been arrested for.

"Well, friends," he said, "I only took a horse that was tied to a sledge, and I was arrested and accused of stealing. I said I had only taken it to get home quicker, and had then let it go; besides, the driver was a personal friend of mine. So I said, 'It's all right.' 'No,' said they, 'you stole it.' But how or where I stole it they could not say. I once really did something wrong, and ought by rights to have come here long ago, but that time I was not found out. Now I have been sent here for nothing at all ... Eh, but it's lies I'm telling you; I've been to Siberia before, but I did not stay long."

"Where are you from?" asked someone.

"From Vladimir. My family are of that town. My name is Makar, and they also call me Semyonich."

Aksionov raised his head and said: "Tell me, Semyonich, do you know anything of the merchants Aksionov of Vladimir? Are they still alive?"

"Know them? Of course I do. The Aksionovs are rich, though their father is in Siberia: a sinner like ourselves, it seems! As for you, Granddad, how did you come here?"

Aksionov did not like to speak of his misfortune. He only sighed, and said, "For my sins I have been in prison twenty-six years."

"What sins?" asked Makar Semyonich.

But Aksionov only said, "Well, well-I must have deserved it!" He would have said no more, but his companions told the newcomers how Aksionov came to be in Siberia; how some one had killed a merchant, and had put the knife among Aksionov's things, and Aksionov had been unjustly condemned.

When Makar Semyonich heard this, he looked at Aksionov, slapped his own knee, and exclaimed, "Well, this is wonderful! Really wonderful! But how old you've grown, Gran'dad!"

The others asked him why he was so surprised, and where he had seen Aksionov before; but Makar Semyonich did not reply. He only said: "It's wonderful that we should meet here, lads!"

These words made Aksionov wonder whether this man knew who had killed the merchant; so he said, "Perhaps, Semyonich, you have heard of that affair, or maybe you've seen me before?"

"How could I help hearing? The world's full of rumours. But it's a long time ago, and I've forgotten what I heard."

"Perhaps you heard who killed the merchant?" asked Aksionov.

Makar Semyonich laughed, and replied: "It must have been him in whose bag the knife was found! If some one else hid the knife there, 'He's not a thief till he's caught,' as the saying is. How could any one put a knife into your bag while it was under your head? It would surely have woke you up."

When Aksionov heard these words, he felt sure this was the man who had killed the merchant. He rose and went away. All that night Aksionov lay awake. He felt terribly unhappy, and all sorts of images rose in his mind. There was the image of his wife as she was when he parted from her to go to the fair. He saw her as if she were present; her face and her eyes rose before him, he heard her speak and laugh. Then he saw his children, quite little, as they were at that time; one with a little cloak on, another at his mother's breast. And then he remembered himself as he used to be—young and merry. He remembered how he sat playing the guitar in the porch of the inn, where he was arrested, and how free from care he had been. He saw, in his mind, the place where he was flogged, the executioner, and the people standing around; the chains, the convicts, all the twenty-six years of his prison life, and his premature old age. The thought of it all made him so wretched and he was ready to kill himself.

"And it's all that villain's doing!" thought Aksionov. And his anger was so great against Makar Semyonich that he longed for vengeance, even if he himself should perish for it. He kept repeating prayers all night, but could get no peace. During the day he did not go near Makar Semyonich, nor even look at him.

A fortnight passed in this way. Aksionov could not sleep at night, and was so miserable that he did not know what to do.

One night as he was walking about the prison he noticed some earth that came rolling out from under one of the shelves on which the prisoners slept. He stopped to see what it was. Suddenly Makar Semyonich crept out from under the shelf, and looked up at Aksionov with frightened face. Aksionov tried to pass without looking at him, but Makar seized his hand and told him that he had dug a hole under the wall, getting rid of the earth by putting it into his high-boots, and emptying it out every day on the road when the prisoners were driven to their work.

"Just you keep quiet, old man, and you shall get out too. If you blab, they'll flog the life out of me, but I will kill you first."

Aksionov trembled with anger as he looked at his enemy. He drew his hand away, saying, "I have no wish to escape, and you have no need to kill me; you killed me along ago! As to telling of you—I may do so or not, as God shall direct."

Next day, when the convicts were led out to work, the convoy soldiers noticed that one or other of the prisoners emptied some earth out of his boots. The prison was searched and the tunnel found. The Governor came and questioned all the prisoners to find out who had dug the hole. They all denied any knowledge of it. Those who knew would not betray Makar Semyonich, knowing he would be flogged almost to death. At last the Governor turned to Aksionov whom he knew to be a just man, and said:

"You are a truthful old man; tell me, before God, who dug the hole?"

Makar Semyonich stood as if he were quite unconcerned, looking at the Governor and not so much as glancing at Aksionov. Aksionov's lips and hands trembled, and for a long time he could not utter a word. He thought, "Why should I screen him who ruined my life? Let him pay for what I have suffered. But if I tell, they will probably flog the life out of him, and maybe I suspect him wrongly. And, after all, what good would it be to me?"

"Well, old man," repeated the Governor, "tell me the truth; who has been digging under the wall?"

Aksionov glanced at Makar Semyonich, and said, "I cannot say, your honour. It is not God's will that I should tell! Do what you like with me; I am in your hands."

However much the Governor tried, Aksionov would say no more, and so the matter had to be left.

That night, when Aksionov was lying on his bed and just beginning to doze, some one came quietly and sat down on his bed. He peered through the darkness and recognized Makar.

"What more do you want of me?" asked Aksionov. "Why have you come here?"

Makar Semyonich was silent. So Aksionov sat up and said, "What do you want? Go away, or I will call the guard!"

Makar Semyonich bent close over Aksionov, and whispered, "Ivan Dmitrich, forgive me!"

"What for?" asked Aksionov.

"It was I who killed the merchant and hid the knife among your things. I meant to kill you too, but I heard a noise outside, so I hid the knife in your bag and escaped out of the window."

Aksionov was silent, and did not know what to say. Makar Semyonich slid off the bed-shelf and knelt upon the ground. "Ivan Dmitrich," said he, "forgive me! For the love of God, forgive me! I will confess that it was I who killed the merchant, and you will be released and can go to your home."

"It is easy for you to talk," said Aksionov, "but I have suffered for you these twenty-six years. Where could I go to now?...My wife is dead, and my children have forgotten me. I have nowhere to go...."

Makar Semyonich did not rise, but beat his head on the floor. "Ivan Dmitrich, forgive me!" he cried. "When they flogged me with the knot it was not so hard to bear as it is to see you now…yet you had pity on me, and did not tell. For Christ's sake forgive me, wretch that I am !" And he began to sob.

When Aksionov heard him sobbing he, too, began to weep.

"God will forgive you!" said he. "Maybe I am a hundred times worse than you." And at these words his heart grew light, and the longing for home left him. He no longer had any desire to leave the prison, but only hoped for his last hour to come.

In spite of what Aksionov had said, Makar Semyonich confessed his guilt. But when the order for his release came, Aksionov was already dead.

Discussion Plan:

1. Given what we know of Aksionov's life before his arrest, what would you say the rest of his life should have been like?
2. Was his arrest just from the point of view of the Russian authorities?
3. If he had been proved guilty would his punishment have been just to his wife and family?
4. Aksionov accepts his punishment, does he consider it just?
5. Does his attitude towards his punishment mitigate the injustice of his case?
6. Does his relationship to the other prisoners alter the injustice of his treatment?
7. What is Aksionov's notion of justice? What is the relationship of God to his views?
8. Does Makar Semyonich have a concept of justice?
9. Does the incident of the tunnel change Makar's concept of justice?
10. Can Aksionov's life be justified in terms of its special qualities?
11. Why does Tolstoy have him die before he can be released?

Truth

Justice and injustice, rewards and punishment are all judged from a human perspective. We can only give meaning to our choices and our goals through the world view that we construct on the basis of our lives: our experiences and the experiences of others that we come in contact with. But no matter how rich our experience our how vast our learning we only can see through the windows that are there; we can only go through the doors that are opened. If Truth is the reality behind appearances is it even possible to imagine that we could know Truth?

Franz Kafka, Three Parables

1. An Imperial Message

The Emperor, so it runs, has sent a message to you, the humble subject, the insignificant shadow cowering in the remotest distance before the imperial sun; the Emperor from his deathbed has sent a message to you alone. He has commanded the messenger to kneel down by the bed, and has whispered the message to him; so much store did he lay on it that he ordered the messenger to whisper it back into his ear again. Then by a nod of the head he has confirmed that it is right. Yes, before the assembled spectators of his death—all the obstructing walls have been broken down, and on the spacious and loftily-mounting open staircases stand in a ring the great princes of the Empire—before all these he has delivered his message. The messenger immediately sets out on his journey; a powerful, an indefatigable man; now pushing with his right arm, now with his left, he cleaves a way for himself through the throng; if he encounters resistance he points to his breast, where the symbol of the sun glitters; the way, too, is made easier for him than it would be for any other man. But the multitudes are so vast; their numbers have no end. If he could reach the open fields how fast he would fly, and soon doubtless you would hear the welcome hammering of his fists on your door. But instead how vainly does he wear out his strength; still he is only making his way through the chambers of the innermost palace; never will he get to the end of them; and if he succeeded in that nothing would be gained; he must fight his way next down the stairs; and if he succeeded in that nothing would be gained; the courts would still have to be crossed; and after the courts the second outer palace; and once more stairs and courts; and once more another palace; and so on for thousands of years; and if at last he should burst through the outermost gate—but never, never can that happen—the imperial capital would lie before him, the center of the world, crammed to bursting with its own refuse. Nobody could fight his way through here, least of all one with a message from a dead man.—But you sit at your window when evening falls and dream it to yourself.

2. Before the Law

"Before the Law stands a doorkeeper on guard. To this doorkeeper there comes a man from the country who begs for admittance to the Law. But the doorkeeper says that he cannot admit the man at the moment. The man, on reflection, asks if he will be allowed, then, to enter later. 'It is possible,' answers the doorkeeper, 'but not at this moment.' Since the door leading into the Law stands open as usual and the doorkeeper steps to one side, the man bends down to peer through the entrance. When the doorkeeper sees that, he laughs and says: 'If you are strongly tempted, try to get in without my permission. But note that I am powerful. And I am only the lowest doorkeeper. From hall to hall keepers stand at every door, one more powerful than the other. Even the third of these has an aspect that even I cannot bear to look at.' These are difficulties which the man from the country has not expected to meet; the Law, he thinks, should be accessible to every man and at all times, but when he looks more closely at the doorkeeper in his furred robe, with his huge pointed nose and long, thin, Tartar beard, he decides that he had better wait until he gets permission to enter. The doorkeeper gives him a stool and lets him sit down at the side of the door. There he sits waiting for days and years. He makes many attempts to be allowed in and wearies the doorkeeper with his importunity. The doorkeeper often engages him in brief conversation, asking him about his home and about other matters, but the questions are put quite impersonally, as great men put questions, and always conclude with the statement that the man cannot be allowed to enter yet. The man, who has equipped himself with many things for his journey, parts with all he has, however valuable, in the hope of bribing the doorkeeper. The doorkeeper accepts it all, saying, however, as he takes each gift: 'I take this only to keep you from feeling that you have left something undone.' During all these long years the man watches the door-keeper almost incessantly. He forgets about the other doorkeepers, and this one seems to him the only barrier between himself and the Law. In the first years he curses his evil fate aloud; later, as he grows old, he only mutters to himself. He grows childish, and since in his prolonged watch he has learned to know even the fleas in the doorkeeper's fur collar, he begs the very fleas to help him and to persuade the doorkeeper to change his mind. Finally his eyes grow dim and he does not know whether the world is really darkening around him or whether his eyes are only deceiving him. But in the darkness he can now perceive a radiance that stems immortally from the door of the Law. Now his life is drawing to a close. Before he dies, all that he has experienced during the whole time of his sojourn condenses in his mind into one question, which he has never yet put to the doorkeeper. He beckons the doorkeeper, since he can no longer raise his stiffening body. The doorkeeper has to bend far down to hear him, for the difference in size between them has increased very much to the man's disadvantage. 'What do you want to know now?' asks the doorkeeper, 'you are insatiable.' 'Everyone strives to attain the Law,' answers the man, 'how does it come about, then, that in all these years no one has come seeking admittance but me?' The doorkeeper perceives that the man is at the end of his strength and that his hearing is failing, so he bellows in his ear: 'No one but you could gain admittance through this door, since this door was intended only for you. I am now going to shut it.'"

"So the doorkeeper deluded the man," said K. immediately, strongly attracted by the story.

"Don't be too hasty," said the priest, "don't take over an opinion without testing it. I have told you the story in the very words of the scriptures. There's no mention of delusion in it."

"But it's clear enough," said K. "And your first interpretation of it was quite right. The doorkeeper gave the message of salvation to the man only when it could no longer help him."

"He was not asked the question any earlier," said the priest, "and you must consider, too, that he was only a doorkeeper, and as such he fulfilled his duty."

"What makes you think he fulfilled his duty?" asked K. "He didn't fulfill it. His duty might have been to keep all strangers away, but this man, for whom the door was intended, should have been let in."

"You have not enough respect for the written word and you are altering the story," said the priest. "The story contains two important statements made by the doorkeeper about admission to the Law, one at the beginning, the other at the end. The first statement is: that he cannot admit the man at the moment, and the other is: that this door was intended only for the man. If there were a contradiction between the two, you would be right and the doorkeeper would have deluded the man. But there is no contradiction. The first statement, on the contrary, even implies the second. One could almost say that in suggesting to the man the possibility of future admittance the doorkeeper is exceeding his duty. At that moment his apparent duty is only to refuse admittance, and indeed many commentators are surprised that the suggestion should be made at all, since the doorkeeper appears to be a precisian with a stern regard for duty. He does not once leave his post during these many years, and he does not shut the door until the very last minute; he is conscious of the importance of his office, for he says: 'I am powerful'; he is respectful to his superiors, for he says, 'I am only the lowest doorkeeper'; he is not garrulous, for during all these years he puts only what are called 'impersonal questions'; he is not to be bribed, for he says in accepting a gift: 'I take this only to keep you from feeling that you have left something undone'; where his duty is concerned he is to be moved neither by pity nor rage, for we are told that the man 'wearied the doorkeeper with his importunity'; and finally even his external appearance hints at a pedantic character, the large, pointed nose and the long, think, black Tartar beard. Could one imagine a more faithful doorkeeper? Yet the doorkeeper has other elements in his character which are likely to advantage anyone seeking admittance and which make it comprehensible enough that he should somewhat exceed his duty in suggesting the possibility of future admittance. For it cannot be denied that he is a little simple-minded and consequently a little conceited. Take the statements he makes about his power and the power of the other doorkeepers and their dreadful aspect which even he cannot bear to see—I hold that these statements may be true enough, but that the way in which he brings them out shows that his perceptions are confused by simpleness of mind and conceit. The commentators note in this connection: 'The right perception of any matter and a misunderstanding of the same matter do not wholly exclude each other.' One must at any rate assume that such simpleness and conceit, however sparingly indicated, are likely to weaken his defense of the door; they are breaches in the character of the doorkeeper. To this must be added the fact that the doorkeeper seems to be a friendly creature by nature, he is by no means always on his official dignity. In the very first moments he allows himself the jest of inviting the man to enter in spite of the strictly maintained veto against entry; then he does not, for instance, send the man away, but gives him, as we are told, a stool and lets him sit down beside the door. The patience with which he endures the man's appeals during so many years, the brief conversations, the acceptance of the gifts, the politeness with which he allows the man to curse loudly in his presence the fate for which he himself is responsible—all this lets us deduce certain motions of sympathy. Not every doorkeeper would have acted thus. And finally, in answer to a gesture of the man's he stoops low down to give him the chance of putting a last question. Nothing but mild impatience —the doorkeeper knows that this is the end of it all—is discernible in the words: 'You are insatiable.' Some push this mode of interpretation even further and hold that these words express a kind of friendly admiration, though not without a hint of condescension. At any rate the figure of the doorkeeper can be said to come out very differently from what you fancied."

"You have studied the story more exactly and for a longer time than I have," said K. They were both silent for a little while. Then K. said: "So you think the man was not deluded?"

"Don't misunderstand me," said the priest., "I am only showing you the various opinions concerning that point. You must not pay too much attention to them. The scriptures are unalterable and the comments often enough merely express the commentator's bewilderment. In this case there even exists an interpretation which claims that the deluded person is really the doorkeeper."

"That's a far-fetched interpretation," said K. "On what is it based?"

"It is based," answered the priest, "on the simple-mindedness of the door-keeper. The argument is that he does not know the Law from inside, but he knows only the way that leads to it, where he patrols up and down. His ideas of the interior are assumed to be childish, and it is supposed that he himself is afraid of the other guardians whom he holds up as bogies before the man. Indeed, he fears them more than the man does, since the man is determined to enter after hearing about the dreadful guardians of the interior, while the doorkeeper has no desire to enter, at least not so far as we are told. Others again say that he must have been in the interior already, since he is after all engaged in the service of the Law and can only have been appointed from inside. This is countered by arguing that he may have been appointed by a voice calling from the interior, and that anyhow he cannot have been far inside, since the aspect of the third doorkeeper is more than he can endure. Moreover, no indication is given that during all these years he ever made any remarks showing a knowledge of the interior except for the one remark about the doorkeepers. He may have been forbidden to do so, but there is no mention of that either. On these grounds the conclusion is reached that he knows nothing about the aspect and significance of the interior, so that he is in a state of delusion. But he is deceived also about his relation to the man from the country. For he is subject to the man and does not know it. He treats the man instead as his own subordinate, as can be recognized from many details that must still be fresh in your mind. But, according to this view of the story, it is just as clearly indicated that he is really subordinated to the man. In the first place, a bondsman is always subject to a free man. Now the man from the country is really free, he can go where he likes, it is only the Law that is closed to him, and access to the Law is forbidden him only by one individual, the doorkeeper. When he sits down on the stool by the side of the door and stays there for the rest of his life, he does it of his own free will; in the story there is no mention of any compulsion. But the doorkeeper is bound to his post by his very office, he does not dare strike out into the country, nor apparently may he go into the interior of the Law, even should he wish to. Besides, although he is in the service of the Law, his service is confined to this one entrance; that is to say, he serves only this man for whom alone the entrance is intended. On that ground too he is subject to the man. One must assume that for many years, for as long as it takes a man to grow up to the prime of life, his service was in a sense empty formality, since he had to wait for a man to come, that is to say, someone in the prime of life, and so had to wait a long time before the purpose of his service could be fulfilled, and, moreover, had to wait on the man's pleasure, for the man came of his own free will. But the termination of his service also depends on the man's term of life, so that to the very end he is subject to the man. And it is emphasized throughout that the doorkeeper apparently realizes nothing of all this. That is not in itself remarkable, since according to this interpretation the doorkeeper is deceived in a much more important issue, affecting his very office. At the end, for example, he says regarding the entrance to the Law: 'I am now going to shut it,' but at the beginning of the story we are told that the door leading into the Law stands always open, and if it stands open always, that is to say, at all times, without reference to the life or death of the man, then the doorkeeper is incapable of closing it. There is some difference of opinions about the motive behind the doorkeeper's statement, whether he said he was going to close the door merely for the sake of giving an answer, or to emphasize his devotion to duty, or to bring the man into a state of grief and regret in his last moments. But there is no lack of agreement that the doorkeeper will not be able to shut the door. Many indeed profess to find that he is subordinate to the man even in wisdom, towards the end, at least, for the man sees the radiance that issues from the door of the Law while the doorkeeper in his official position must stand with his back to the door, nor does he say anything to show that he has perceived the change."

"That is well argued," said K., after repeating to himself in a low voice several passages form the priest's exposition. "It is well argued, and I am inclined to agree that the doorkeeper is deluded. But that has not made me abandon my former opinion, since both conclusions are to some extent compatible. Whether the doorkeeper is clear-sighted or deluded does not dispose of the matter. I said the man is deluded. If the doorkeeper is clear-sighted, one might have doubts about that, but if the doorkeeper himself is deluded, then his delusion must of necessity be communicated to the man. That makes the doorkeeper not, indeed, a swindler, but a creature so simple-minded that he ought to be dismissed at once from his office. You mustn't forget that the doorkeeper's delusions do himself no harm but do infinite harm to the man."

"There are objections to that," said the priest. "Many aver that the story confers no right on anyone to pass judgment on the doorkeeper. Whatever he may seem to us, he is yet a servant of the Law; that is, he belongs to the Law and as such is set beyond human judgment. In that case one dare not believe that the doorkeeper is subordinate to the man. Bound as he is by his service, even at the door of the Law, he is incomparably freer than anyone at large in the world. The man is only seeking the Law, the doorkeeper is already attached to it. It is the Law that has placed him at his post; to doubt his integrity is to doubt the Law itself."

"I don't agree with that point of view," said K. shaking his head, "for if one accepts it, one must accept as true everything the doorkeeper says. But you yourself have sufficiently proved how impossible it is to do that."

"No," said the priest, "it is not necessary to accept everything as true, one must only accept it as necessary."

"A melancholy conclusion," said K. "It turns lying into a universal principle."

3. Couriers

They were offered the choice between becoming kings or the couriers of kings. The way children would, they all wanted to be couriers. Therefore there are only couriers who hurry about the world, shouting to each other—since there are no kings—messages that have become meaningless. They would like to put an end to this miserable life of theirs but they dare not because of their oaths of service.

Exercise:

Kafka is a notoriously deep and difficult thinker. We end the *Reader* by giving you the same exercise that we began Part I with. Do it carefully and systematically, separate analyses for each of the parables. Don't be fooled by the different lengths of the Parables, in many respects the third is the most important.

1. Go over the selection and carefully explain each of the elements in the parable. What does each one mean? What makes the choice of metaphor an effective vehicle to present the idea it represents?
2. What large points are made by the parable?
3. Does the parable offer insights into the problem it attempts to describe?
4. Do you agree with Kafka's point of view?
5. Construct realistic analogues to the points Kafka makes.
6. Present realistic analogues that support your point of view if it is different from Kafka's.